D0379911

GUIDE TO
National Parks
OF THE
United States

NATIONAL
GEOGRAPHIC

GUIDE TO
National Parks
OF THE
United States

NATIONAL GEOGRAPHIC
WASHINGTON, D.C.

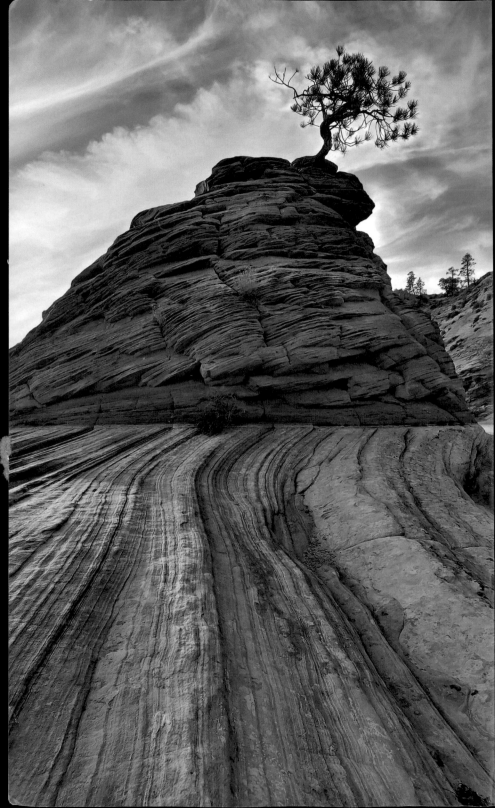

CONTENTS

Cover: El Capitan, Yosemite NP
pp. 2-3: Mountain goats, Glacier NP
Opposite: A lone tree atop a rocky outcrop, Zion NP

Snowy landscape along stream, Great Smoky Mountains National Park

SEE WHAT'S OUT THERE

Even I wasn't prepared for such a tremendous success. National Geographic had been working with the National Park Service on a program of annual "BioBlitzes," two-day marathons in which hundreds of volunteer naturalists fanned out across selected national parks to undertake species counts, and we had been reaping unexpected harvests.

Held in 2007 in Washington, D.C.'s Rock Creek Park, one of the oldest properties in the National Park System, the first BioBlitz netted some 650 species. But subsequent programs, in parks ranging from California to Florida, had been pulling in truly astonishing numbers, well over a thousand species in some cases, many new to those areas and some even new to science! How well I

remember urging those first eager participants in 2007 to just go and "see how many organisms are out there." That's exactly what they had done.

It was going and seeing for himself that convinced National Geographic's legendary editor, Gilbert H. Grosvenor, that the national parks were a cause the Society should be supporting in the first place.

In 1916 Grosvenor had joined industrialist Stephen Mather and companions on a pack trip into California's Sierra Nevada. By day he saw with his own eyes the magnificent old-growth forests in Sequoia and King's Canyon National Parks. By night, gathered around the campfire, he listened to Mather explain how everything they had seen around them was at stake unless a National

Park Service was established to guard and protect such lands, which at that time had been set aside in name only.

Grosvenor swung into line. For one thing, he ensured that a copy of the April 1916 *National Geographic* magazine, devoted entirely to America's scenic wonders and featuring superb color photographs, soon found its way into every congressman's hand. Shortly afterward the National Park Service was voted into law, with Mather its first chief.

Our two organizations have marched in tandem ever since. Yet hardly had the battle to establish a Park Service been won before new challenges loomed. Anyone who has marveled at the Giant Forest in Sequoia National Park can understand why National Geographic, that same year of 1916, moved so quickly to purchase vulnerable privately owned stands and deed them over to

Mather's new Park Service for safekeeping. Visitors can appreciate why our Society fought so long and so hard to see them preserved, though it wasn't until 1968 that President Lyndon B. Johnson signed Redwood National Park into law.

Should you be fortunate enough to visit Katmai National Park in Alaska, I urge you to take the 23-mile tour from park headquarters to the Valley of Ten Thousand Smokes. You'll see no "smokes" today on that spectacular, almost lunar landscape; but in 1916, when explorer Robert F. Griggs first arrived, it was a seething cauldron, from the eruption of nearby Mount Katmai. The National Geographic expeditions he subsequently led into that inferno so captured the public imagination that the valley became the reason that park was established in 1918.

Or should Mesa Verde National Park in Colorado be your destination, be sure, after that first heart-stopping view of Cliff Palace, to undertake the 12-mile drive to Wetherill Mesa. There a ranger will show you Long House, which was filled with rubble before 1958, when the Society and the Park Service undertook an archaeological project that led to its being opened for public viewing.

After reviewing National Geographic's long history of close association with the Park Service—not to mention the longer list of magazine articles, books, maps, and television documentaries that over the years we have devoted to the subject—one thing strikes me as certain: You too may want to go out there and see our national parks.

John M. Fahey, Jr.
Chairman of the Board &
Chief Executive Officer,
National Geographic Society
Commissioner, National Parks
Second Century Commission

Diving amid giant kelp forest, Channel Islands National Park

USING THE GUIDE

Each of the 58 scenic parks offers you fun, adventure, and—usually—enthralling splendor. What you experience will depend on where you go and what you do. But exploring an unknown land is best done with a guide, a companion who has tested the trail and learned the lore.

Our coverage of each park begins with a portrait of its natural wonders, ecological setting, history, and, often, its struggles against man and alien species. You'll see why a single step off a trail can harm fragile plants, and why visitors are detoured from certain areas that shelter wildlife. The parks are not just for people; they conserve ecosystems. Thirteen parks have been designated United Nations World Heritage sites for their outstanding scenic and cultural wonders; 22 have international biosphere reserve status, signaling the distinctive natural qualities.

Before starting off on your park exploration, use this *Guide* to preview the parks you may want to visit. You'll notice that each park introduction is followed by the following three how-and-when sections:

How to Get There

You may be able to include more than one park in your trip. The regional chapter maps show the connecting highways. Base your itinerary not so much on mileage as on time, remembering that parks do not lie alongside interstates; park roads are usually rugged—and, in summer, crowded.

When to Go

Instead of going to a popular park in midsummer, avoid peak crowds by scheduling the trip for June or late August and timing your arrival early on a weekday. In many parks, fall is glorious, and autumn vistas coincide with a relative scarcity of visitors. Spring brings wildflowers to many parks and with winter comes snow-swept beauty, summoning cross-country skiers, snowshoe hikers, and ice skaters. Although parks are generally open year-round, off-season visitor facilities may be limited. Consult this heading for each park.

How to Visit

Don't rush through a park. Give yourself time to savor the beauty. Incredibly, the average time the typical visitor spends in a park is half a day. Often, that blur of time flashes past a windshield. No matter how long you decide to stay, spend at least part of that time outdoors, not in your car. Each park's **How to Visit** section recommends a plan for visits of one-half, one, two, or more days. *Guide* writers devised the plans and trekked every tour, but don't be afraid to explore on your own. And don't neglect the **Excursions** at the end of many park entries; they take you to other natural areas nearby.

Other features of the *Guide:*

Maps

The park maps and regional maps were prepared as an aid in planning your trip. For more detail on trails and other facilities inside a park, contact the Park Service, call the park, or visit www.nps.gov. Always use a road map or GPS when traveling.

The maps note specially designated areas within park borders: *Wilderness Areas* are managed to retain their primeval quality. Roads, buildings, and vehicles are not allowed in them. *National Preserves* may allow hunting. For a list of abbreviations see p. 479.

Information & Activities

This section, which follows each park entry, offers detailed visitor information. Call or write the park, or visit the Park Service's website (www.nps.gov) for further details. Brochures are usually available free of charge from the parks. You can download a copy of the "National Park System Map and Guide" by visiting www.pueblo.gsa.gov.

Entrance Fees. The entrance fees listed in this book reflect fees at press time. In addition to daily or weekly fees, most parks also offer a yearly fee, with unlimited entries.

For $80 you can buy an America the Beautiful Pass, which is good for a year and admits up to four occupants of a private vehicle to all national parks, as well as unlimited admission to U.S. Fish and Wildlife Service, U.S. Forest Service, Bureau of Land Management, and Bureau of Reclamation sites. The pass does not cover parking fees where applicable.

Citizens 62 and older can obtain a lifetime America the Beautiful Senior Pass for $10, and blind and disabled people are entitled to a lifetime America the Beautiful access pass for free, both of which admit all occupants of a private vehicle to all national parks and other federal sites and a discount on usage fees. These are available from any federal area that charges entrance fees. For further information on buying park passes, call (888) 275-8747 or visit www.recreation.gov.

Pets. Generally they're not allowed on trails, in buildings, or in the backcountry. Elsewhere, they must be leashed. Specific rules are noted.

Accessible Services. This section of the *Guide* explains which parts of each park, including visitor centers and trails, are accessible to visitors with disabilities.

Special Advisories.

• Do not take chances. People are killed or badly injured every year in the parks. Most casualties are caused by recklessness or failure to heed warnings.

• Stay away from wild animals. Do not feed them or try to touch them—not even raccoons or chipmunks (which can transmit diseases). Try not to surprise a bear and do not let one approach. If one does, scare it off by yelling, clapping your hands, or banging pots. Store all your food in bear-proof containers (often available at parks); keep food out of sight in your vehicle, with windows closed and doors locked. Or suspend it at

least 15 feet above ground, and 10 feet out from a post or tree trunk.
• Guard your health. Know your limitations; don't overtax yourself. Boil water that doesn't come from a park's drinking-water tap. Chemical treatment of water will not kill *Giardia,* a protozoan that causes severe diarrhea; it lurks even in crystal clear streams. Heed park warnings about hypothermia and Lyme disease. In western parks,

take precautions to prevent hantavirus pulmonary syndrome, caused by a potentially fatal airborne virus transmitted by deer mice.
• Expect RV detours. Check road regulations as you enter a park. Along some stretches of road you will not be able to maneuver large vehicles.
Campgrounds. The National Recreation Reservation Service (NRRS) (877-444-6777, www.recreation.gov) handles reservations for almost 300 of the

750 Park Service campgrounds at the following parks: Acadia, Arches, Big Bend, Black Canyon of the Gunnison, Bryce Canyon, Channel Islands, Death Valley, Everglades, Grand Canyon, Great Smoky Mountains, Joshua Tree, Katmai, Lassen Volcanic, Mount Rainier, Mammoth Cave, North Cascades, Olympic, Rocky Mountain, Sequoia & Kings Canyon, Shenandoah, Voyageurs, Waterton-Glacier, Yosemite, and Zion. Check early for the reservation schedules.

Hotels, Motels, & Inns. The *Guide* lists accommodations as a service to its readers. The lists are by no means comprehensive, and listing does not imply endorsement by the National Geographic Society. The information can change without notice. Many parks keep lists of lodgings in their areas, which they will provide on request. You might also contact local chambers of commerce and tourist offices for suggestions.

THE EAST

THE EAST

Not until well into the 20th century, long after the idea of preserving the West's grand vistas had taken hold, did park planners turn their attention to the more subtle beauties of eastern scenery. The threats to nature from expanding cities and, after World War I, the surge in automobile travel and highway building boosted the movement to create eastern parks. Between 1919 and 1926, Congress authorized the first three in

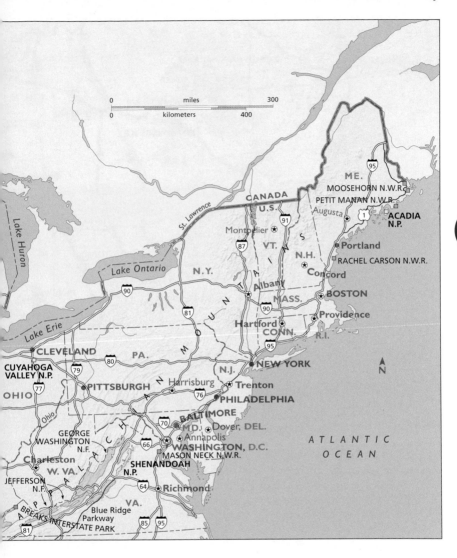

the crumpled belt of the Appalachian Mountains. Today these parks—Acadia, Great Smoky Mountains, and Shenandoah—rank among the most visited in the nation.

Acadia protects the plants and animals that inhabit the mountains, islands, sea, and tide pools along a stretch of wild New England coast. The hardwood forests and flowering meadows of Shenandoah, on land that had been logged, farmed, and

Americans' love for the automobile led to the demand for highways to drive and helped spur the creation of national parks in the East. In 1935 the Blue Ridge Parkway was begun as a public works project. It became part of the Park Service the following year. The parkway receiving the most recreational use, the Blue Ridge links Shenandoah's Skyline Drive to Great Smoky Mountains National Park. Together, the drives create a spectacular 574-mile stretch of ridgetop road punctuated by wayside exhibits and trails.

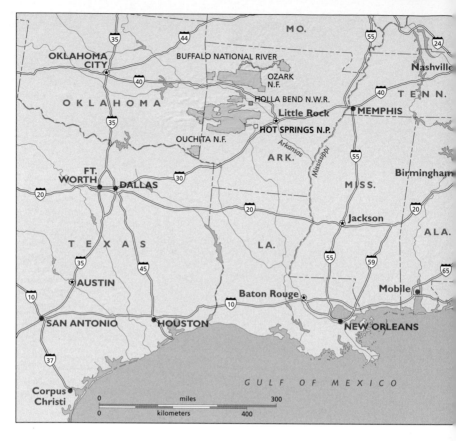

grazed for 250 years, are studies in nature's power of recuperation. Great Smoky preserves large stands of virgin forest on 6,000-foot slopes and shelters more than a hundred species of trees.

Since the 1920s, Congress has moved to safeguard other distinctive eastern biomes. Inside Mammoth Cave lies the world's longest known cave network, with more than 350 miles of mapped passages. Isle Royale on the U.S.-Canada border encompasses an entire island ecosystem. In and around its lakes, thick forest, and fjordlike coast live wolves and their prey, moose.

Not far away, scores of lakes and streams lace the forests of Voyageurs National Park, named for the late 18th-century French-Canadian fur traders who for 100 years paddled these waters.

Other kinds of waters inspired the creation of diminutive Hot Springs National Park. Most of the 47 thermal springs lead into the plumbing of this former resort town's bathhouses.

Underwater wilderness awaits visitors to Florida's Biscayne National Park, home of the northernmost living coral reef in the continental United States. West of Biscayne lies Everglades National Park, established in 1947 less to preserve scenery than to safeguard the unique ecosystem created by a slow-moving river, inches deep and some 50 miles wide. Itself

MAMMOTH CAVE N.P.
81 Blue Ridge VA.
K.Y. Parkway
65 75
CUMBERLAND GAP N.H.P. 85
G SOUTH FORK
NAT. RIVER &
RECREATION
AREA
Knoxville PISGAH 95
N.F.
40 Raleigh
GREAT SMOKY
MOUNTAINS N.P. 77 N.C.
Asheville CHARLOTTE
CHEROKEE 40
N.F. 1
NANTAHALA N.F. CAROLINA SANDHILLS
N.W.R.
85 26
75 CHATTAHOOCHEE Columbia
N.F. CONGAREE N.P.
59 ATLANTA 20 S.C.
SANTEE
N.W.R. ATLANTIC
OCEAN
85 95
Montgomery 16
GA.
75

ATLANTIC OCEAN
Saint John
Charlotte Tortola
Amalie
Saint
Thomas U.S. U.K.
VIRGIN
ISLANDS
N.P. 0 miles 20
0 kilometers 30
Caribbean Sea
BUCK ISLAND REEF
NAT. MON.
Saint Croix
N

10
Tallahassee JACKSONVILLE
10
95
75
N
FLORIDA
Lake
Okeechobee
Cape Coral BAHAMAS
J.N. "DING" DARLING N.W.R. BIG CYPRESS NAT. PRES.
Naples BISCAYNE N.P.
CORKSCREW SWAMP SANCTUARY Miami
EVERGLADES N.P.
JOHN PENNEKAMP CORAL REEF S.P. 1
GREAT WHITE HERON N.W.R.
DRY TORTUGAS N.P. Key West NAT. KEY DEER
REFUGE

In the 1960s the National Park Service set a goal to create a park as a "vignette of primitive America" in every major natural community in the country. The newer parks of the East—Cuyahoga Valley, Biscayne, Voyageurs, Congaree, and Dry Tortugas—have expanded the diversity of the region's parks.

endangered by the diversion of water to the towns and agribusinesses of South Florida, Everglades provides habitat for an enormous variety of wildlife.

About 70 nautical miles west of Key West, on a 7-mile-long archipelago rich with birds and marine creatures, Dry Tortugas National Park maintains an abandoned 19th-century brick fortress, the largest

from that century in America. And far to the southeast, Virgin Islands National Park protects much of St. John, where hillsides thick with bay, mango, and trumpet trees slope to crescent beaches rimmed by coral reefs.

Otter Cliff, one of the highest Atlantic coastal headlands north of Rio de Janeiro

▶ACADIA

MAINE
ESTABLISHED FEBRUARY 26, 1919
49,600 acres

Sea and mountain meet at Acadia, where, as one presumably ambidextrous visitor wrote, "you can fish with one hand and sample blueberries from a wind-stunted bush with the other." Most of the park is on Mount Desert Island, a patchwork of parkland, private property, and seaside villages that seasonally fill with what residents call "the summer people." Other bits are scattered on smaller islands and a peninsula.

Mount Desert Island once was continental mainland, a mountainous granite ridge on the edge of the ocean. Some 20,000 years ago, towering glacial ice sheets—sometimes more than a mile thick—flowed over the mountains, rounding their tops, cutting passes, gouging out lake beds, and widening valleys. As the glaciers melted, the sea rose, flooding valleys and drowning the coast. The pre-glacier ridge was transformed into today's lake-studded, mountainous

island, which thrusts from the Atlantic like a lobster's claw.

Samuel de Champlain, who explored the coast in 1604, named the island L'Isle des Monts Déserts, sometimes translated as "the island of barren mountains," because the summits are mostly bare of trees. The summer people rediscovered Mount Desert in the mid-19th century, built mansions they called "cottages," anchored their yachts in rock-girt harbors, and cherished the wild. To preserve it, they donated the nucleus land for the park, the first east of the Mississippi. The original name, Lafayette National Park, was changed in 1929.

Dependent on donated land since its inception, the park took what it could get, skirting around private property and growing piece by piece. Acadia's real estate was so patchy that not until 1986 did Congress set its official boundaries.

Although one of the smaller national parks, Acadia is one of the most visited—by almost two and one-half million people a year. Heavy traffic can produce a phenomenon unknown to Mount Desert's first summer people: gridlock. The Island Explorer shuttle bus has helped alleviate the problem.

How to Get There

From Ellsworth, 28 miles southeast of Bangor, follow Me. 3 south for 9.5 miles to Mount Desert Island, where most of the park is located; the visitor center is 3 miles north of Bar Harbor. Another section lies east of Ellsworth, on the Schoodic Peninsula, a 1-hour drive from Bar Harbor. To get to the park's islands, see The Islands p. 24. Airports: Bangor and Bar Harbor.

When to Go

Year-round, but the main visitor center is open only from mid-April through October. Expect heavy traffic in July and August. Spectacular foliage also attracts crowds around mid-September to mid-October. Snow and ice close most park roads from early December through mid-April, but parts of the park are open for cross-country skiing.

How to Visit

Allow at least a day for Mount Desert Island, with a drive on the 20-mile Park Loop Road and the road to the

summit of Cadillac Mountain. If fog comes, enjoy its gift: a softening of sights and sounds. On a second day, enjoy an uncrowded view of the rocky coast of Maine by visiting the Schoodic Peninsula. If you have more time, take your pick of one of the trails or smaller islands.

MOUNT DESERT ISLAND

60 miles; at least a full day

To get the most from a tour of Mount Desert Island on the Park Loop Road in summer, get up very early. (On clear days, traffic is heaviest between 10 a.m. and 3 p.m.) The day before, check the time of sunrise in a local newspaper or at the visitor center. About 30 minutes before dawn, take coffee and a blanket and drive from the visitor center to 1,530-foot Cadillac Mountain. The 3.5-mile mountain road switchbacks up to a parking area.

From there walk to the Summit Trail, find an east-facing niche in the rocks, and settle in on the highest east coast mountain north of Brazil. Here is one of the places where dawn first touches the continental United States. After enjoying the sunrise, hunt for blueberries along the trails radiating from the summit. The blueberry season runs from late July through August.

On the way back down the mountain, stop at one of the eastern overlooks for a view of Frenchman Bay, a vast, island-dotted seascape; its name takes note of the role of the French in the area's history. (Another way to see the bay is on a 2-hour cruise; check schedules at the Municipal Pier in Bar Harbor or in the park's publication, "Beaver Log.")

Return to the loop road and turn right. Less than a half mile

ACADIA

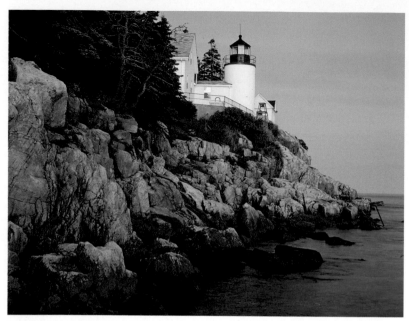

Bass Harbor Head lighthouse at dusk

farther, bear right again (here the road becomes one-way), and continue south toward the ocean. Two worthwhile stops you'll soon approach are the **Sieur de Monts Spring Nature Center** (June–mid-Oct.) and the **Wild Gardens of Acadia,** both of which showcase the habitats of Mount Desert Island.

Farther along the road, pass up **Sand Beach** for now. You may want to return to the beach later for sunbathing or a very brisk swim (the summer water temperature remains between 50°F and 55°F).

Not quite a mile farther, a sign marks **Thunder Hole.** Park on the right side and walk down the concrete steps to the cleft in the rocks, named for the roars produced when air, trapped and squeezed by incoming surf, explodes out of a cavern. A stop here may disappoint you, for you'll probably hear the thunder only at half tide with a rising sea, or during a storm. Other times, you may hear only gurgles and sloshes.

Continue to the 110-foot **Otter Cliff.** Park, cross the road, and walk the Ocean Path to **Otter Point.** Numerous brightly colored lobster buoys bob offshore. Linger here to savor the essence of the Maine coast: rocks, gulls, the tang of salt air. At **Hunters Head** the loop road turns away from the sea and soon becomes two-way as you head back to where you started. You'll pass **Jordan Pond,** one of many glacier-carved ponds on the island.

Your drive has taken you around the eastern side of the island. To explore the western side, you must drive out of park property and back in again. Continue north on the loop road, cross the bridge, and bear right to get on Me. 233. Head west to Me. 198, then head south on Me. 102 toward Southwest Harbor. Continue south. On your left, though obscured, is **Somes Sound,** the only fjord on the U.S. Atlantic coast. On your right is

Echo Lake, a swimming spot with a small beach.

Me. 102 passes through Southwest Harbor. Beyond, near Manset, bear left on Me. 102A, which leads into a large patch of park property. You can picnic at **Seawall,** then stretch your legs on the nearby 1.25-mile **Ship Harbor Trail,** which gives a lesson in how a forest shore is knit to the tidal sea.

A short detour off Me. 102A takes you to **Bass Harbor Head,** site of a 19th-century lighthouse. Take Me. 102A through **Bass Harbor** and bear left on Me. 102 toward Tremont. Continue north for 7 miles to a tract of park called **Pretty Marsh,** a beautiful picnic spot. A short, worn path leads to the rock-strewn shore. Continue on Me. 102 and retrace your route from Somesville to the visitor center.

CARRIAGE ROADS & HIKES

In 1917 John D. Rockefeller, Jr., a summer resident of Mount Desert Island, launched the building of a 57-mile network of broken stone roads for horse-drawn carriages. Convinced that the newfangled automobile would destroy the tranquillity of the island, he banned it from the carriage roads. The roads were graced by 17 hand-built granite bridges, each a unique work of art. Rockefeller later donated most of the road network, along with 11,000 acres

ACADIA

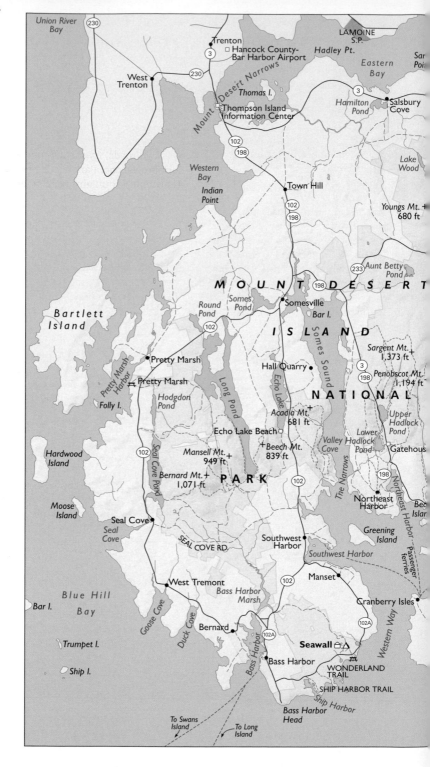

Union River Bay

230

Trenton

3

□ Hancock County-
Bar Harbor Airport

LAMOINE S.P.

Hadley Pt.

Eastern Bay

Sar Poi

West Trenton

230

Mount Desert Narrows

Thomas I.

Thompson Island Information Center

3

Salsbury Cove

Hamilton Pond

102

198

Western Bay

Indian Point

Town Hill

102

198

Lake Wood

Youngs Mt. +
680 ft

233

Aunt Betty Pond

M O U N T   D E S E R T

198

Round Pond

Somes Pond

Somesville

Bar I.

Bartlett Island

I S L A N D

Somes Sound

Sargent Mt. +
1,373 ft

3

198

Pretty Marsh

Hall Quarry

Echo Lake

Penobscot Mt. +
1,194 ft

Pretty Marsh Harbor

Pretty Marsh

N A T I O N A L

Folly I.

Hodgdon Pond

Long Pond

Acadia Mt. +
681 ft

Upper Hadlock Pond

Hardwood Island

Echo Lake Beach □

Beech Mt. +
839 ft

Valley Cove

Lower Hadlock Pond

Gatehous

102

Seal Cove Pond

Mansell Mt. +
949 ft

The Narrows

198

Moose Island

Bernard Mt. +
1,071 ft

P A R K

102

Northeast Harbor

Bec Islar

Seal Cove

Greening Island

Seal Cove

SEAL COVE RD.

Southwest Harbor

Southwest Harbor

Passenger ferries

Northeast Harbor Rd.

Bar I.

Blue Hill Bay

West Tremont

Bass Harbor Marsh

102

Manset

Cranberry Isles

Trumpet I.

Goose Cove

Duck Cove

Bernard

102A

102A

Western Way

Ship I.

Bass Harbor

Seawall □ △

WONDERLAND TRAIL

Bass Harbor

Bass Harbor

SHIP HARBOR TRAIL

To Swans Island

To Long Island

Bass Harbor Head

Ship Harbor

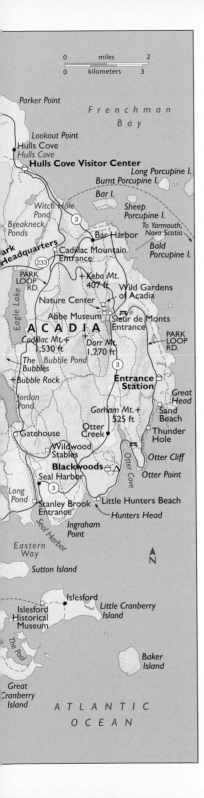

of his land, to the park. The carriage roads, still not open to cars, are a treasure prized by hikers, bikers, horseback riders, cross-country skiers, and anyone seeking a respite from the incessant hum of the internal combustion engine.

To introduce yourself to the carriage roads, try the 4.5-mile **Hadlock Brook Loop.** Park at the Me. 198 (Parkman Mountain) parking area just north of **Upper Hadlock Pond** and walk to the trailhead. Take the left fork east toward **Hemlock Bridge,** a gem of hand-hewn stone. Follow the rising road to another handsome span, **Waterfall Bridge,** site of a 40-foot cascade. (You can turn around here, cutting your hike to about 2 miles round-trip.) Cross the bridge and walk south for 1.8 miles to one of the network's well-marked intersections. Turn right at intersection 19 and right again at intersection 18 and continue along the pond. Watch for loons—and listen for their haunting call. The road crosses **Hadlock Brook Bridge** and loops back to the trailhead.

The park has more than 120 miles of hiking trails, which range from easy strolls along the ocean or around ponds to steep climbs up Cadillac and other mountains. For a jaunt into history try the **Gorge Path,** which, like several other trails, has stone steps to ease your way up slopes. The steps, flat stones imbedded in rising ground, were built by turn-of-the-20th-century summer people who wanted to rough it, but not too much. The path begins at a parking spot on the Park Loop Road, near 407-foot **Kebo Mountain,** and leads to a wooded trail. Cairns mark the trail when it follows a rocky, brook-washed ravine. About a mile into the woods is an intersection. Depending upon your time and stamina, you can turn and retrace

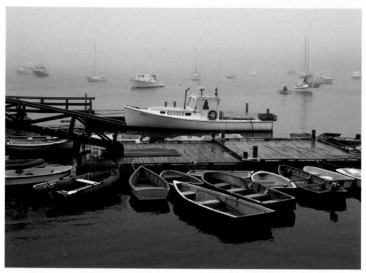

Morning fog over rowboats and fishing boats in Seal Harbor

your steps or push on to Cadillac or **Dorr Mountain,** each a steep hike of more than 1.5 miles.

SCHOODIC PENINSULA

100 miles; a half day

The 45-mile drive around French- man Bay to the park's only mainland portion, the Schoodic Peninsula, provides several scenic views of Mount Desert Island. Starting from Bar Harbor, take Me. 3 to US 1 south of Ellsworth, and head east to West Gouldsboro. Go south via Me. 186 to Winter Harbor, then follow signs to the park entrance. From there, drive or bike the 6-mile one-way road to **Schoodic Point.** The massive granite rocks here are laced by black diabase dikes, the product of magma that welled up into cracks. Schoodic's dis- plays of thundering surf usually top those of Mount Desert Island. And the audiences are much smaller; the peninsula does not draw crowds the way Mount Desert does.

A trail system explores the western section of the point, run- ning through wetland and forest with spurs to the ocean. The long- est is the **Anvil Trail,** which begins at the Blueberry Hill parking lot and climbs about 440 feet for views of Little Moose Island and Frenchman Bay. In this wilderness, watch out for white-tailed deer, rab- bits, porcupines, raccoons, and the rare moose.

THE ISLANDS

a full day each

Fragments of Acadia are on islands. Two worth visiting are Isle au Haut, about half of which is park property, and Little Cranberry Island, home to the Islesford Historical Museum. Both islands are served all year by mail boats and seasonally by tour boats. Get boat schedules from the visitor center or the boat operators.

The trip to **Isle au Haut,** or "high island," named by Samuel de Champlain, begins at Stonington, at the tip of Deer Isle, about 40 miles from Ellsworth. To make the boat on time from Mount Desert Island, allot at least 2 hours for the drive and for finding a rare legal parking place near the harbor. Bring lunch. The mail boat takes passengers on a first-come, first-served basis. The 45-minute voyage ends at the Town Landing. In summer, the boat also stops at **Duck Harbor,** a park campsite and trailhead.

For a fine hike, get off at the Town Landing and turn right. A short distance down the road is a ranger station. Here begins the 4-mile **Duck Harbor Trail,** which takes you through upland forest, along the shore, and past blueberry brambles (picking and eating allowed) to Duck Harbor. Spend the day here wandering the area's trails, enjoying woods-and-water scenery, and watching for ospreys and bald eagles. Catch the late afternoon boat back.

The 2.5-mile boat ride from Northeast Harbor to **Little Cranberry Island** takes about 20 minutes in good weather; you can also catch a boat at Southwest Harbor, on the opposite side of Somes Sound.

The tiny island, with quiet rocky shores, spruce trees, and peaceful country lanes, boasts 80 year-round residents, many of whom can trace their ancestry back to the 18th century. As your boat nears the picturesque village of **Islesford,** winding among bobbing lobster boats in the protected harbor, you'll spot two buildings of note: the gabled, wooden **Blue Duck Ships's Store** and, directly behind, the **Islesford Historical Museum,** housed in a brick Georgian Revival building. Both structures are part of Acadia National Park. The museum contains turn-of-the-20th-century ship models, navigation aids, dolls and toys, photographs, tools, and other relics that tell the story of the Cranberry Isles—a cluster of five islands—and their seafaring people.

Another option for getting out on the water is to take an **Islesford Historical Cruise** (207-276-5352; fare, reservations required), a ranger-led boat tour that stops on Little Cranberry and focuses on island history. Meet at the municipal pier in Northeast Harbor.

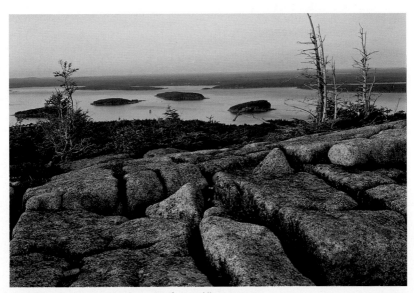

View of the Porcupines in Frenchman Bay, from Cadillac Mountain

INFORMATION & ACTIVITIES

VISITOR & INFORMATION CENTERS
Hulls Cove Visitor Center on Me. 3 just south of Hulls Cove, open daily mid-April through October. **Thompson Island Information Center** on Me. 3, just before crossing onto Mount Desert Island. Open mid-May to mid-September. Off season, information at headquarters.

SEASONS & ACCESSIBILITY
Open all year. In winter visitor facilities close and much of the Park Loop Road is unplowed. For recorded weather information call (207) 667-8910. For boats to Isle au Haut call (207) 367-5193; for mail boat ferry call (207) 244-3575.

HEADQUARTERS
P.O. Box 177, Bar Harbor, ME 04609. 2.5 miles west of Bar Harbor on Me. 233. Phone (207) 288-3338. www.nps.gov/acad

ENTRANCE FEE
Mid-June–mid-Oct.: $20 per vehicle for 7-day pass; May–mid-June & mid–end of Oct., $10 per vehicle for 7-day pass.

PETS
Permitted on leashes except on swimming beaches, in public buildings, on restricted trails, and at Isle au Haut campsite.

ACCESSIBLE SERVICES
Visitor center, some restrooms, and carriage roads are wheelchair accessible. Wildwood Stables has two carriages designed to hold wheelchairs. Free guidebook available.

THINGS TO DO
Free ranger-led activities: nature walks, hikes, talks, children's programs, boat tours, stargazing, films, slide shows. Also available, bus tours—call (207) 288-0300 for national park tours or (207) 288-9899 for Oli's Trolley—bay and island cruises, carriage rides, auto tape tour, hiking, bicycling, swimming, fishing, cross-country skiing, snowshoeing, ice-skating and ice fishing, and snowmobiling.

SPECIAL ADVISORIES
• Be careful on ledges and rocks along shore; loose gravel and algae make the rocks slippery.
• In spring and fall, watch out for strong storm waves.

OVERNIGHT BACKPACKING
Not allowed.

CAMPGROUNDS
Blackwoods open all year; reserve through NRRS (see p. 10)—suggested May–Oct.; other times first come, first served. Fee $20 per night. **Seawall** open late May–Sept.; half sites are first come, first served, and half can be reserved through www.recreation.com. Fees $14–$20 per night. Showers outside park. Tent and RV sites; no hookups. **Duck Harbor** on Isle au Haut open mid-May–mid-Oct.; reservations required (207) 288-3338. Fee $25 for a special use permit.

HOTELS, MOTELS, & INNS
(unless otherwise noted, rates are for 2 persons in a double room, high season)

In Bar Harbor, ME 04609:
Bar Harbor Inn Newport Dr. (800) 248-33511. 153 units. $89-$379. Pool, rest.
Bayview 111 Eden St. (800) 356-35851. 32 units. $175-$500. Pool. Mid-May–mid-Oct.
Cleftstone Manor 92 Eden St. (207) 288-4951. 17 units. $100-$195. Mid-April–late Oct.
Cromwell Harbor Motel 359 Main St. (207) 288-3201. 29 units. $78-$158.
In Northeast Harbor, ME 04662:
Asticou Inn Me. 3 & 198. (800) 258-3373. 48 units. $95-$360. Rest. Late May–Oct.
In Southwest Harbor, ME 04679:
Moorings Inn 133 Shore Rd., Manset. (800) 596-5523 or (207) 244-5523. 20 units, 3 with kitchenettes. $105-$165. Mid-May–mid-Oct.

For additional accommodations, call the Chambers of Commerce of Bar Harbor, (800) 345-4617, www.Barharborinfo .com; Northeast Harbor, (207) 276-5040; or Southwest Harbor (207) 244-9264, www .acadiamagic.com.

EXCURSIONS

MOOSEHORN NATIONAL WILDLIFE REFUGE
CALAIS, MAINE

At dawn and dusk in spring, the male American woodcock soars into the air to begin his mating ritual. The refuge's two units along the Atlantic flyway protect the essential habitat of the bird as well as other waterfowl and forest wildlife species. 28,887 acres. Hiking, boating, bicycling, fishing, hunting, winter sports. Open all year, dawn to dusk. Headquarters at the Baring Unit, off US 1, about 75 miles from Acadia NP. (207) 454-7161.

MAINE COASTAL ISLANDS NATIONAL WILDLIFE REFUGE
STEUBEN, MAINE

Migrating waterfowl and shorebirds take rest on Petit Manan Peninsula and more than 49 offshore islands. The peninsula's two hiking trails lead visitors through spruce-fir forests, blueberry barrens, and along the rugged rocky coastline. Petit Manan Island features one of the largest seabird nesting colonies in Maine and a 123-foot lighthouse (closed April–Aug.). 8,000 acres. Hiking trails. Peninsula open all year, dawn to dusk. Accessible from US 1 in Steuben, about 35 miles from Schoodic Unit of Acadia NP. (207) 546-2124.

RACHEL CARSON NATIONAL WILDLIFE REFUGE
WELLS, MAINE

Stretching along Maine's coast from Kittery to Cape Elizabeth, this refuge's 11 units protect the fragile and dynamic world of the tidal estuary. The unit at Wells contains the 1-mile-long self-guided Carson Trail. Breeding and migrating shorebirds, wading birds, waterfowl, and raptors also featured. More than 5,300 acres. Hiking, canoeing, hunting, scenic drives, cross-country skiing. Picnic areas, handicapped access. Open all year, dawn to dusk. Headquarters at Wells, on Me. 9, off US 1, about 160 miles from Acadia NP. (207) 646-9226.

Elkhorn coral beds attract snorkelers.

▶ BISCAYNE

FLORIDA
ESTABLISHED JUNE 28, 1980
172,924 acres

Biscayne, a seascape in watercolor, offers vistas ashore and beneath the sea. Standing on the park's narrow shore, you look out upon a bay that is tranquil on the surface and teeming with life below. Aboard a glass-bottom boat or, better yet, on a snorkeling tour, you look down and see some of that life—dazzlingly colored fish, fantastically shaped corals, gently waving fronds of sea grass.

Biscayne is an underwater wilderness. Only 5 percent of the park is land—about 40 small barrier coral reef islands and a mangrove shoreline, the longest such undeveloped shore on Florida's east coast. Park wildlife exists underwater in the form of minuscule, unusual, or rarely seen animals. The most extensive life-form is a community known as the coral reef—colonies of tiny polyps that secrete limestone and live within ever growing rocky crannies. The coral reefs at Biscayne are part of the only living ones found in the continental United States.

The park reprieved a living system condemned to die under the pressure of progress. The threat came in the 1960s, when developers were making plans to build resorts and subdivisions on Florida's northern keys, from Key Biscayne to Key Largo. Conservationists campaigned to preserve Biscayne Bay; it became a national monument in 1968. When Biscayne National Park was established, boundaries were expanded to encompass several more of the bay's keys and reefs.

Biscayne embraces a complex ecosystem that extends from the mangrove shoreline to the Gulf Stream. Besides the mangrove coast and living reef, the ecosystem includes two other biological realms found on the small islands and the shallow bay's marine nursery. The realms are interwoven, and each sustains still other webs of life.

Guarding all this are the northernmost Florida Keys, ancient exposed coral reefs that keep ocean waves from battering the bay. Thus shielded, the bay offers sanctuary to the life within it and beauty to those who come to look beneath the surface.

How to Get There

From Miami, take Florida's Turnpike (Fla. 821) south to Speedway Boulevard, and turn left (south). Continue 4 miles on Speedway Boulevard to North Canal Drive and turn left (east). Follow Canal Drive another 4 miles to the park entrance. From Homestead (about 9 miles), take s.w. 328th Street (N. Canal Dr.) to the park entrance at Convoy Point. Airport: Miami.

When to Go

Year-round. The best time to visit the park's islands is from mid-December to mid-April, subtropical Florida's dry season. In summer, you face the perils of mosquitoes and fast-moving thunderstorms, but seas are generally the calmest—making it ideal for snorkeling and diving. Hurricanes are occasional.

How to Visit

Unless you have your own boat, plan to see Biscayne on a concessioner-run cruise. You can look underwater on a **reef cruise** aboard a glass-bottom boat or swim the shallow

waters on a snorkeling cruise. There are also scuba cruises to the outer reef for qualified divers. You should make reservations in advance. Cruises may be canceled if there are too few passengers or the weather is inclement. Although this is a water park, a walk around the mangrove shore will give you a chance to examine the coastal edges of the bay's ecosystem. The Dante Fascell Visitor Center offers a museum, audiovisual programs, and ranger talks.

REEF CRUISE
a half day

Sign up for a cruise well ahead (see Information & Activities p. 34 for details). Schedules vary by season. At **Convoy Point,** the glass-bottom boat's home port and site of **Dante Fascell Visitor Center,** you can get an orientation to the bay's unique flora and fauna before setting out. A cruise for boaters or snorkelers takes about 3 hours. Cruises for scuba divers last longer and cost more.

BISCAYNE

Gorgonian coral

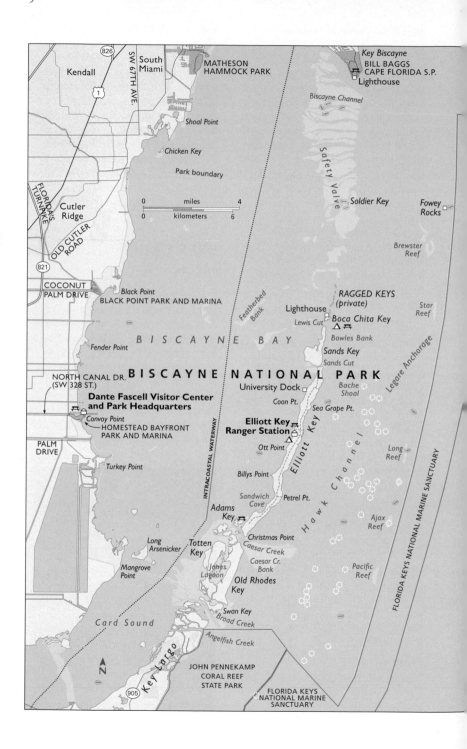

826
SW 67TH AVE.
South Miami
Kendall
MATHESON HAMMOCK PARK
1
Key Biscayne
BILL BAGGS CAPE FLORIDA S.P.
Lighthouse

Biscayne Channel

Shoal Point

Chicken Key

Park boundary

0   miles   4
0   kilometers   6

FLORIDA'S TURNPIKE
Cutler Ridge
OLD CUTLER ROAD

Safety Valve

Soldier Key

Fowey Rocks

Brewster Reef

821

COCONUT PALM DRIVE
Black Point
BLACK POINT PARK AND MARINA

Featherbed Bank

Lighthouse
Lewis Cut
RAGGED KEYS (private)
Boca Chita Key

Star Reef

Bowles Bank

B I S C A Y N E   B A Y

Fender Point

Sands Key
Sands Cut

Legare Anchorage

NORTH CANAL DR. (SW 328 ST.)
B I S C A Y N E   N A T I O N A L   P A R K

Dante Fascell Visitor Center and Park Headquarters

University Dock

Bache Shoal

Coon Pt.

Sea Grape Pt.

Elliott Key
Ranger Station

Convoy Point
HOMESTEAD BAYFRONT PARK AND MARINA

Ott Point

Elliott Key

Long Reef

PALM DRIVE

Turkey Point

Billys Point

Hawk Channel

INTRACOASTAL WATERWAY

Sandwich Cove
Petrel Pt.

Adams Key

Ajax Reef

Long Arsenicker
Totten Key

Christmas Point
Caesar Creek

Mangrove Point

Jones Lagoon

Caesar Cr. Bank

Old Rhodes Key

Pacific Reef

FLORIDA KEYS NATIONAL MARINE SANCTUARY

Swan Key
Broad Creek

Card Sound

Angelfish Creek

N

Key Largo

905

JOHN PENNEKAMP CORAL REEF STATE PARK

FLORIDA KEYS NATIONAL MARINE SANCTUARY

The light of a sunset on Florida mangroves

The center of the boat's deck is a rectangular viewing chamber. Rows of broad, angled windows make up its floor. Passengers line rails around the chamber and peer down at the constantly changing, green-tinted scene.

As the boat crosses the bay, a park ranger prepares the audience by passing out pieces of hard coral and previewing the sights that will be seen in the reefs. A ruffled seabed and waving strands of turtle grass pass under the windows. Vast beds of turtle grass and water only 4 to 10 feet deep make Biscayne Bay a nursery for a host of young marine animals, including shrimp, spiny lobsters, sponges, and crabs. You may see some of these through the windows. More than 500 types of fish swim in park waters. You may also see large, graceful sea turtles.

If you walk to the outer edge of the deck, you can watch boats skimming the bay and brown pelicans flapping by. When they spot fish,

they dive headfirst into the sea to scoop them up in their huge bills. Among the many other birds you will see are cormorants and herons.

Through the bay runs the Intracoastal Waterway, marked by posts whose signs bear numbers keyed to navigational charts. In one short, shallow stretch near the waterway natural grass beds rise near the surface and are visible at low tide. Bonefish, prized by sportfishermen for their speed and strength, inhabit the grass beds.

The boat slips through the keys toward the reefs beyond. Once it arrives at its destination, the boat lingers for the floor show: the multicolored flash of a passing parrotfish, the sinuous glide of an angelfish, the little jungles of coral. Slowly the boat moves to another vantage point, and a new seabed show begins to roll by. Giant brain coral and mountainous star coral dominate the reefs, many so high that the glass bottom of the boat seems close enough to graze

Florida manatee

north is **Boca Chita Key,** which has a boat dock, primitive campsites, and restrooms, but no drinking water. The lighthouse is only ornamental.

MANGROVE SHORE

0.25 mile; at least an hour

If you have little time, no boat, but some curiosity, walk the shore around **Convoy Point,** a fine place for a picnic. If you have more time, inquire about renting a canoe or kayak to explore mangrove tidal creeks.

The mangroves are critical to this marine environment. They stabilize the shore, trapping their own fallen leaves and other organic material in the tangles of their stiltlike roots. While the trees appeal to many birds—including, on rare occasion, mangrove cuckoos and frigatebirds— the water attracts both endangered manatees and threatened crocodiles, two of the species monitored by park scientists. Barnacles, fish, and other sea creatures cluster at the trees' half-submerged roots. The decaying mangrove leaves, rich in protein, provide food to the tiny animals at the bottom of a food chain that ends with the fisherman who eats the gray snapper he caught in the bay.

The mangroves also filter damaging pollutants from the freshwater runoff into the bay. Whether you walk or paddle a boat, watch carefully for the bay animals that find food and refuge in the mangrove waterways. On a winter's day the creatures may include the manatee, a huge, grass-chewing "cow of the sea"; they can reach over 13 feet long and weigh up to 3,000 pounds. The scene keeps changing as each outgoing tide carries its bounty of nutrients out to sea and each incoming tide brings in new inhabitants for the sheltering mangroves.

them. Sea fans and other soft corals ripple in the calm, clear water. The ranger helps viewers identify the vibrantly colored fish flitting around the massive coral formations. Before reaching the outer reefs the boat turns for home.

The cruise passes through **Caesar Creek,** named for Black Caesar, a legendary pirate said to have lurked here in the 1700s. More than 40 shipwrecks have been cataloged within park boundaries. Federal law protects them from salvagers or souvenir collectors. Visitors who have made the trip in their own boats can also dock at Adams Key for a picnic and walk on a nature trail.

Elliott Key has primitive campsites, restrooms, a nature trail, a swimming area, a ranger station, and what conservationists label a "road scar"—a bulldozer's legacy and a reminder of how close devastation came to these keys. To the

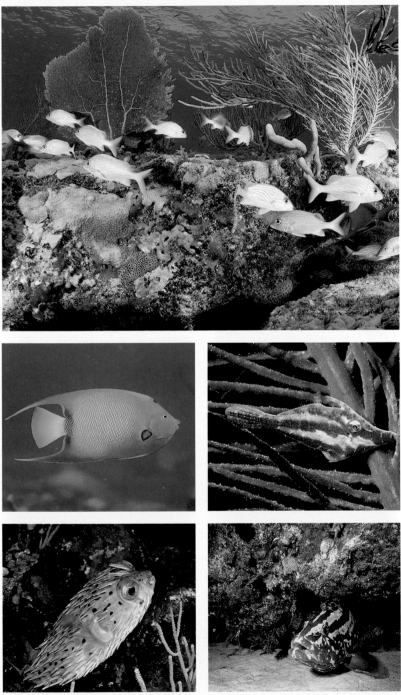

Clockwise from top: Schooling fish; filefish on soft coral; Nassau grouper; porcupine fish; queen angelfish

INFORMATION & ACTIVITIES

VISITOR & BOAT INFORMATION

Dante Fascell Visitor Center open daily all year. For park information, call (305) 230-7275.
For information and reservations for concessioner-run glass-bottom boat, snorkeling, scuba diving, and island and canoe trips, call (305) 230-1100. Rentals available. Tours leave from Convoy Point.

SEASONS & ACCESSIBILITY

Open all year. Keys (islands) can be reached by boat only. Private concessioners operate daily, though underbooked cruises may be canceled in the off-season. Private boats allowed; boat docks available on Elliott, Adams, and Boca Chita Keys ($15 overnight docking fee at Elliott and Boca Chita).

HEADQUARTERS

9700 S.W. 328th St., Homestead, FL 33033. Phone (305) 230-1144. www.nps.gov/bisc

ENTRANCE FEES

None. $15 overnight docking fee for private boats at Elliott and Boca Chita Keys (free campsite included). Fees charged by concessioner for boat trips.

PETS

Allowed on leashes (6-ft maximum length) in the developed areas of Convoy Point and Elliott Key. Not permitted on boat tours.

ACCESSIBLE SERVICES

Dante Fascell Visitor Center is fully accessible, as are restrooms at Elliott Key and Boca Chita Key. Concessioner boat tours accessible with assistance.

THINGS TO DO

Ranger-led activities: glass-bottom boat tours, canoe trips, island nature tours, interpretive exhibits. Also available: swimming, snorkeling, scuba diving, water skiing, boating, canoe rentals, fishing, lobstering, hiking, bird-watching. Special events: Family Fun Fests, lecture series. Offered seasonally; call for details.

SPECIAL ADVISORIES

• Do not touch coral or other living things on the reef. They are easily damaged; they can also inflict deep cuts and cause serious infections.
• Mosquitoes and other insects can be a problem on the islands, particularly from April to December; carry plenty of repellent.

CAMPGROUNDS

Two boat-in campgrounds, both with 14-day limit. **Elliott Key** and **Boca Chita Key** open all year, first come, first served. Water at Elliott Key only. Tent sites only. $15 fee per site per night (without boats); one campsite is free with overnight docking ($20). Group campground (30 people and 5 tents) at Elliott Key. Fees $30 per site per night. Cash only.

HOTELS, MOTELS, & INNS
(unless otherwise noted, rates are for 2 persons in a double room, high season)

In Florida City, FL 33034:
Best Western 411 S. Krome Ave. (305) 246-5100 or (880) 981-5100. 114 units. $140. AC, pool.
Comfort Inn 333 S.E. 1st Ave./US 1. (305) 248-4009. 124 units. $79-$250. AC, pool.
Coral Roc Motel 1100 N. Krome Ave. (305) 247-4010. 17 units, 5 with kitchenettes. $36-$159. AC, pool.
Ramada Inn 124 E. Palm Dr. (305) 247-8833 or (800) 272-6232. 123 units. $89-149. AC, pool, breakfast incl.

In Homestead, FL 33030:
Days Inn 51 S. Homestead Blvd. (305) 245-1260. 100 units. $109. AC, pool, bar.

For additional accommodations, write or call the Greater Homestead/Florida City Chamber of Commerce, 455 N. Flagler Ave., Homestead, FL 33030. (305) 247-2332 or (888) 352-4891, www.chamberinaction.com.

EXCURSIONS

JOHN PENNEKAMP CORAL REEF STATE PARK
KEY LARGO, FLORIDA

In the world's first undersea park, a living coral reef may be viewed through a diver's mask or a glass-bottom boat. 63,085 acres. Visitor center, 47 campsites, trails, boating, boat ramps, fishing, picnic areas, water sports, handicapped access. Open all year during daylight. Off US 1 in Key Largo, about 40 miles from Biscayne NP and 35 from Everglades NP. (305) 451-1202.

NATIONAL KEY DEER REFUGE
BIG PINE KEY, FLORIDA

The Key deer—a diminutive subspecies of the white-tailed deer—struggle to survive in this mangrove and pine-palm habitat. It's illegal to feed them. 9,150 acres. Hiking and wildlife observation. Open all year, dawn to dusk. Off US 1 on Big Pine Key, about 150 miles south of Biscayne NP. (305) 872-0774.

GREAT WHITE HERON NATIONAL WILDLIFE REFUGE
BIG PINE KEY, FLORIDA

Dedicated to the protection of the great white heron, this site partly overlaps the National Key Deer Refuge. These mangrove islands also shelter ibis, white-crowned pigeon, and the roseate spoonbill. 192,584 acres. No camping or other facilities. Access by boat only. No pets allowed. Open all year, dawn to dusk. Information at National Key Deer Refuge; see above.

BISCAYNE

Boardwalk Loop Trail

▶CONGAREE

CENTRAL SOUTH CAROLINA
ESTABLISHED NOVEMBER 10, 2003
24,180 acres

Congaree is an ancient forest with towering trees and an incredible claim to biodiversity. Originally established as Congaree Swamp National Monument in 1976, and redesignated as a national park in 2003, it protects the largest remaining tract of old-growth bottomland hardwood forest in the country.

While Congaree National Park exhibits characteristics of a swamp, technically it is not a swamp, because it does not contain standing water throughout most of the year. It is actually a floodplain forest that floods about ten times a year. Spreading northeast from the meandering Congaree River, the land is the largest contiguous tract of old-growth bottomland hardwoods in the United States.

Push back the ghostly Spanish moss that drips from the bald cypresses, and you enter a lush backcountry inhabited by bobcats, deer, and playful river otters. Yellow-bellied sapsuckers drill holes into trees one day and return the next to feast on the sap that has filled the holes. The rapid-fire series of knocks you hear is from one of the many woodpeckers found in the park, also hard at work boring holes into trees.

At night in the fall and spring, rangers lead visitors on an "owl prowl," so they can hear the eerie calls of barred owls and see the glowing fungi that grows on the cypresses. According to local legends, the cypress tree's trademark "knees"—small, knobby wood growths that rise around the trunk's base—are really wood elves who come to life at night to dance through the forest.

Congaree was named for the Native American tribe that lived here centuries ago. They were decimated in the 18th century, victims of a smallpox epidemic that came over with European settlers.

Toward the end of the next century, the country's burgeoning lumber industry moved south, with an eye on Congaree's giant hardwood trees. However, because of the remoteness of the area and the lack of navigable waterways many of the old giants were saved from the ax.

Conservationists worked hard to save this forest and thus the park has been designated as a national natural landmark, a globally important bird area, and an international biosphere reserve. Congaree National Park offers its visitors opportunities for canoeing, kayaking, fishing, hiking, picnicking, and bird-watching.

How to Get There
Twenty miles southeast of Columbia, via I-77 and Bluff Road or S.C. 48. Follow the Congaree National Park direction signs to the park.

When to Go
Year-round. Spring and fall are the most pleasant seasons. Boaters find easier paddling after a rain in late winter and early spring.

How to Visit
Allow a full or half day. From the visitor center, take the **Low** and **Elevated Boardwalk Trails** (2.4 miles total). Then do the **Weston Lake Loop Trail** (4.4 miles) around the oxbow lake. Birders like the 11.7-mile **Kingsnake Trail** into a remote part of the park.

BOARDWALK TRAIL
2.4 miles; 2 hours

In this woodland, giant loblolly pines and hardwoods rise to a canopy higher than in the Amazon rain forest. Loblolly pines rise up more than 160 feet to reach the sunlight, and some majestic old bald cypresses measure more than 25 feet in circumference, their leafy crowns shuttering the world below into a dappled landscape of brown and green shadows.

Congaree is home to some of the country's tallest trees, some state and/or national champions. The tallest water hickory is 143 feet tall, and the park's tallest loblolly pine reaches 167 feet, as high as a 17-story building.

CONGAREE

Bald cypress knees

Logging began in swamps across the Southeast in the 1880s, and soon thereafter it focused on the old-growth bald cypress. During the next two decades all the stands within easy reach were cut, and South Carolina's floodplain forests suffered a drastic reduction. However, along the Congaree a lack of accessible waterways needed to remove the timber helped save the irreplaceable tract.

Fierce winds from Hurricane Hugo in 1989 put a dent in the old-growth forest, toppling some of the national and state champion trees harbored here. The storm also opened up holes in the dense canopy, clearing the way for fresh growth. Dead trees, meanwhile, became homes for various birds, bats, reptiles, insects, and fungi.

About ten times a year, the floodplain is inundated, usually following dam releases and heavy rains from upstate. Sloughs and guts (narrow creeks) overflow, carrying nutrients that enrich the soil. Shallow-rooted hardwoods occasionally fall, but cypress trees with far-reaching roots and supportive knees as tall as 7 feet rarely topple. Animals seek higher ground, and some even find refuge on floating logs.

On a topographical map you will see very few contour lines within the park's boundaries; the elevation dips only about 20 feet from the west side to the east, so excess water can slosh all over the floodplain. Yet even that slight, seemingly insignificant change of elevation produces dramatically different biological communities: At the higher, drier levels of the park live sweet gums, cherrybark

oaks, and hollies, whereas cypresses, water tupelos, and water ashes thrive at the lower, wetter levels.

Pick up the **Boardwalk Loop Trail** at the visitor center where trail maps, information, and suggestions for other hikes are available. As you gradually enter the floodplain forest, the vegetation changes from upland pines and hardwoods to the old-growth loblolly pines and mixed hardwoods of the swamp.

During floods, the water level can rise as high as the elevated boardwalk, or even higher. Thick

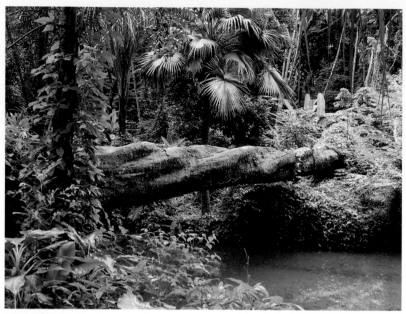

Atlantic forest

vines of muscadine grapes and climbing hydrangeas hug the trunks of ancient trees, adding to the primordial atmosphere. The hairy vines belong to poison ivy, and it's worth noting that these vines and dormant stems can irritate the skin as much as the leaves.

Farther along, tupelos and cypresses grow in standing brown water, stained by the tannin of decayed vegetation. A light rainfall is an especially evocative time for a walk through here—raindrops ping the reflective water, a gauzy mist blankets the forest making it look primeval, and the birdsong seems to come from far away in time. In these shady depths you almost expect to find creatures from another age.

Continue down the boardwalk toward picturesque **Weston Lake.** Dwarf palmettos just off the walk lend a tropical accent to the surroundings. The riddled trunks of

sweet gums and other trees bear the marks of woodpeckers. All eight varieties of woodpeckers found in the South—red-bellied, red-cockaded, red-headed, pileated, downy, hairy, yellow-bellied sapsucker, and yellow-shafted flicker—inhabit Congaree.

In summer, hummingbirds zoom for the showy orange flowers of the trumpet vine, while sparrows dart about for berries and seeds. Fallen logs lie moldering in puddles of wet vegetation. Small-scale communities are built upon the pits and mounds of overturned trees.

River otters can occasionally be seen frolicking in Weston Lake, and red-bellied turtles line up on floating logs. The small oxbow lake, measuring 25 feet deep, was once a bend in the Congaree River; thousands of years ago, the river changed course —leaving the bend as a lake—and now flows 2 miles away. Near here stand dwarf forests of gnarled cypress knees; the farther you walk around to the east, the more old-growth cypress you encounter.

The boardwalk then takes you through a forest of tupelos, hollies, loblolly pines, and, above all, cypresses. Touch the rippling bell-bottom trunks of the older cypresses; their mossy surface feels like velvet. Extend the Boardwalk Loop by taking the 4.4-mile **Weston Lake Loop Trail,** which follows a cypress-tupelo slough down to Cedar Creek. In this largest of the park's creeks, you have the best chance of spotting herons and otters.

MORE TRAILS IN THE PARK
a half to full day

For a longer outing, the **Oakridge Trail,** accessible off the Weston Lake Loop Trail, pushes farther south into the old-growth forest and makes for a 6.6-mile round-trip hike from the visitor center. If you want to walk to the river and back, plan to spend most of the day on a trek starting with the boardwalk, then taking the western sections of the Weston Lake Loop and Oakridge Trails; the 10-mile **River Trail** takes you the rest of the way.

The 11.7-mile out-and-back **Kingsnake Trail** offers further opportunities for wildlife-watching—especially birds—and secluded exploration in the park's little-visited eastern section. The trailhead is off the Cedar Creek parking area.

The **Cedar Creek canoe trail** within Congaree slips through sunless channels of brown water haunted by reclusive birds and other animals. The stillness of the place will make you feel you've entered another world. On weekends, the park staff offers a guided trip into these mysterious parts and provides canoes for participants. Otherwise, plan to rent a canoe from one of the many outfitters in nearby Columbia.

CONGAREE

North American river otter

INFORMATION & ACTIVITIES

VISITOR & INFORMATION CENTER
Open daily year-round. **Visitor center** located off S.C. 48, 1.2 miles beyond park entrance on National Park Road.

SEASONS & ACCESSIBILITY
Open all year. Call after heavy rains to see if park is flooded or for current foot trail and canoe trail conditions.

HEADQUARTERS
100 National Park Road, Hopkins, SC 29061. Phone (803) 776-4396. www.nps.gov/cong

ENTRANCE FEE
There is no fee to enter the park.

PETS
Pets must be on leashes and are not allowed on the boardwalk.

ACCESSIBLE SERVICES
Visitor center, restrooms, picnic shelter, and primitive campgrounds are wheelchair accessible. So is the 2.4-mile Boardwalk Loop Trail.

THINGS TO DO
Free naturalist-led activities: nature walks and canoe tours. Environmental education and nature study. Hiking, fishing (S.C. state license required), primitive camping, bird-watching, picnicking, canoeing, kayaking (bring your own boat, rentals are not available in the park). Canoes can be rented or trips can be arranged through Adventure Carolina Canoeing & Camping (1107 State St., Cayce, SC 29033. 803-796-4505) and River Runner Outdoor Center (905 Gervais St., Columbia, SC 29201. 803-771-0353).

SPECIAL ADVISORIES
• Carry plenty of water as there is no potable water outside developed areas. If you drink surface water, first chemically purify it.
• Check weather conditions and water levels before leaving on a canoe or kayak trip.
• Take a detailed map when kayaking or canoeing.
• Mosquitoes can be brutal, carry plenty of repellent.
• There are venomous snakes in the park; give all snakes a wide pass.

OVERNIGHT BACKPACKING
Permit required; available free from visitor center. Campsites must be at least 200 feet away from roads, trails, lakes, and flowing water.

CAMPGROUNDS
One primitive campground and back-country camping with 14-day limits year-round. Free permits required; available at the visitor center no more than one day in advance. After-hours primitive campsite can accommodate groups of 8 or less. Portable toilets, fire rings, grills, and picnic tables. The Bluff primitive campsite also can accommodate larger groups; fire rings, grills, and picnic tables in open field. No open fires permitted in backcountry camping.

HOTELS, MOTELS, & INNS
(unless otherwise noted, rates are for 2 persons in a double room, high season)

In Columbia, SC:
Comfort Inn & Suites Fort Jackson Maingate 7337 Garners Ferry Rd., 29209. (803) 695-5555. 67 units. $89-$159. AC, pool.
Fort Jackson Inn 4486 Fort Jackson Blvd., 29209. (803) 738-0510. 34 units. $50-$85. AC.
Holiday Inn Express Columbia–Fort Jackson 7329 Garner's Ferry Rd., 29209. (803) 695-1111. 100 units. $119-$209. AC, pool.
Clarion Town House Hotel 1615 Gervais St., 29201. (803) 771-8711 or (800) 277-8711. 163 units. $120-$140. AC, pool, restaurant.
Inn at Claussen's 2003 Greene St., 29205. (803) 765-0440. 28 units. $145-$160. AC.

For other accommodations, contact the Columbia Metropolitan Convention & Visitors Bureau, (800) 264-4884 or (803) 545-0000, www.columbiacvb.com.

EXCURSIONS

CAROLINA SANDHILLS NATIONAL WILDLIFE REFUGE
McBEE, SOUTH CAROLINA

Lying between the Piedmont Plateau and the Atlantic Coastal Plain, Carolina Sandhills is home to towering longleaf pines. These pines provide homes to the largest population of red-cockaded woodpeckers in the country. The refuge offers a 9-mile auto trail, 3 marked hiking trails, 20 fishing ponds, and 2 wooden 15-foot observation towers. More than 750 plant species, 190 bird species, 42 species of mammals, 41 types of reptiles, and 25 different amphibians reside within the refuge. 45,348 acres. Open all year; best months April through May and September through October. Approximately 75 miles northeast of Congaree NP off US 1 north of McBee. (843) 335-8401.

CONGAREE

SANTEE NATIONAL WILDLIFE REFUGE
SUMMERTON, SOUTH CAROLINA

Located to the north of Lake Marion, this refuge provides a haven for nesting and migratory birds. The bald eagle, peregrine falcon, and wood stork are among the 300 species recorded here. It is also a delight for fishing enthusiasts. Opportunities abound to see deer, alligator, bobcat, turkey, and coyote. No camping is permitted to protect the resident and migratory birds. Pine Island is available only to foot traffic. Wildlife drive and hiking trails. 15,095 acres. Open all year. Approximately 50 miles southeast of Congaree NP. (803) 478-2217.

White-tailed deer grazing under a giant red oak

▶CUYAHOGA VALLEY

OHIO
ESTABLISHED OCTOBER 11, 2000
33,000 acres

If there is one word that typifies Cuyahoga Valley, it might well be "surprise." To begin, many people are surprised that a national park even exists in northeastern Ohio, between Cleveland and Akron. It was established in 1974 as Cuyahoga Valley National Recreation Area, but became Cuyahoga National Park in 2000.

Visitors find more surprises: Secluded trails through rugged gorges that seem far removed from civilization; vistas of tree-covered hills where the urban world is out of sight; marshes where beaver, herons, and wood ducks thrive.

Crisscrossed by roads and freeways, encompassing towns, private attractions, and metro parks, Cuyahoga Valley is hardly comparable to the vast western wilderness parks—a circumstance that leads to

even more surprises. Visitors can ride a scenic railroad, hear a symphony concert, attend an art exhibit, play golf, or, in winter, zoom down snowy ski slopes.

The park's history is as unique as its potpourri of natural and man-made attractions. In the 1960s, local citizens and public officials became concerned that commercial and residential development was threatening the scenic Cuyahoga River Valley, with its villages, quiet byways, and forests. In 1974, Congress passed a bill creating a National Recreation Area, administered by the National Park Service. The park began acquiring private land within the designated 33,000 acres, as well as working out cooperative agreements with developments already in place, such as Cleveland and Summit County metropolitan park districts and Blossom Music Center, the summer home of the Cleveland Orchestra. Eventually, confusion about the meaning of "recreation area" led supporters to call for a change in the park's name.

Today, Cuyahoga Valley NP serves the metropolitan area in a multitude of ways. Residents jog, ride bicycles, or picnic in the park; local children ride sleds down its hills in winter; nature-lovers love its pockets of wild greenery, home to dozens of species of birds and wildflowers; fans of the arts watch professional summer theater at Kent State University's Porthouse Theatre. Cuyahoga Valley may not fit everyone's idea of a national park, but that doesn't tarnish the appeal of its many rewards.

How To Get There
From Cleveland, take I-77 15 miles south; from Akron, go 13 miles north on I-77 or Ohio 8; from the east or west, I-80 bisects the park, as does I-271. Airports: Cleveland or Akron.

When to Go
Year-round. Weekends can be crowded along the Ohio & Erie Canal Towpath Trail from spring through fall, and especially in summer. Many activities are curtailed in winter, but downhill skiing, cross-country skiing, snowshoeing, and sledding are popular. Spring wildflowers and fall foliage make these especially colorful and appealing seasons.

How To Visit
Stop at the **Canal Visitor Center** for an overview of canal and valley history

and information on park activities; ask about ranger-led hikes, programs, and special events. Walk or bike a portion of the **Towpath Trail** before driving east to take in **Tinkers Creek Gorge.** Then head south to see **Brandywine Falls,** continuing to the villages of **Boston** and **Peninsula** for museums and exhibits. Walk some of the scenic trails south of the Happy Days Lodge, especially in the area called the **Ledges.**

OHIO & ERIE CANAL TOWPATH TRAIL
2 hours to a half-day or more

A few decades ago, the notoriously polluted **Cuyahoga River** seemed an odd choice to be at the heart of a national park. The Cuyahoga (an American Indian word meaning "crooked river") is far cleaner today, after extensive rehabilitation efforts. Though park personnel still don't recommend swimming or boating, the river corridor serves as a thread of life running 22 miles through the center of the park, home to a surprising diversity of wildlife.

During the 1820s, a canal constructed parallel to the river opened up commercial boat traffic between Lake Erie and the Ohio River, fostering economic growth in the Cuyahoga Valley and the nation. Made obsolete by railroads, the Ohio & Erie Canal has long been abandoned—but the adjacent towpath, where mules once trudged towing boats, has been converted into one of the area's most popular hiking and bicycling trails. Running nearly 20 miles through the park (and extending both north into Cleveland and south into Akron), the **Ohio & Erie Canal Towpath Trail** is in many ways the heart of recreational activity in Cuyahoga Valley. Passing

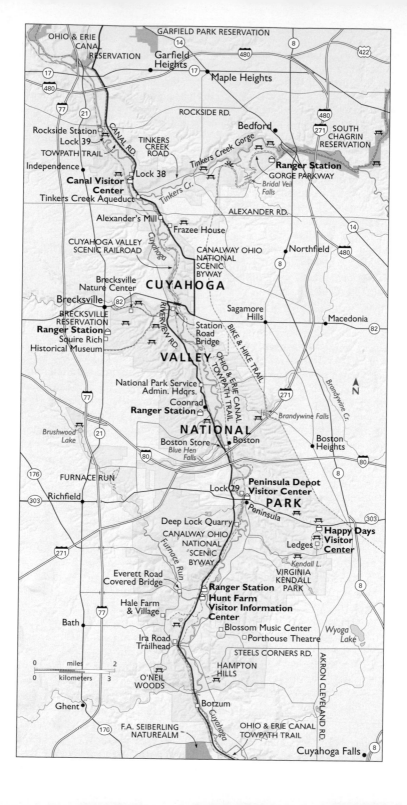

through forests, meadows, and wetlands, the fully accessible trail invites casual walking and serious fitness running or biking.

At the **Canal Visitor Center,** an 1820s canal house off Canal Road, you can watch a video and inspect historical displays. Just outside is **Lock 38,** the canal's last operational lock within the park, one of a series that allowed boats to negotiate 395 feet of elevation change as they traveled from Lake Erie to Akron, and vice versa. Costumed rangers and volunteers demonstrate the lock's function on summer and fall weekends.

As you explore the Towpath Trail (and the rest of the Cuyahoga Valley), consider taking advantage of the **Cuyahoga Valley Scenic Railroad.** It parallels the river on its route from Akron to Independence, making seven stops within the park. Regular excursions include the award-winning *Voice of the Valley* audio tour. Some trips allow hikers and bikers to follow the Towpath Trail as far as they wish, then board the train and return to their starting point. Themed rail trips are offered throughout the year.

Within the park's boundaries, but technically on land owned by Cleveland Metroparks, are several worthy excursions. Drive east along Tinkers Creek Road and Gorge Parkway into beautiful **Tinkers Creek Gorge,** a national natural landmark. An overlook offers a fine view of the wooded valley and creek 200 feet below. Farther east is the parking lot for **Bridal Veil Falls,** where a short walk into a steep-sided valley brings you to a pretty spot where a tributary of **Tinkers Creek** drops over a series of sandstone ledges—one of nearly 70 waterfalls in the gorge. Here the shaded ravine is home to hemlocks, beeches, maples, oaks, and birches, reminiscent of more northerly hardwood forests. The paths that meander

A 19th-century barn

through the gorge make up part of 186 miles of trails in the Cuyahoga Valley, allowing short strolls just off paved roads and day-long loop hikes.

BRANDYWINE FALLS & THE LEDGES

a full day or more

Perhaps the park's most-visited natural feature, **Brandywine Falls** cascades over a staircase-like series of sandstone-covered shelves in the eastern part of the park, reached by a walkway to viewing platforms, one high and another lower, at streamside. The falls' winter aspect can be striking, with flows and icicles creating a white curtain of columns and swirls. Not quite so grand, but also exquisite and always less crowded, **Blue Hen Falls** is just minutes away on the west side of the Cuyahoga River, in an intimate valley forested in maple and beech.

Be sure to stop at the 1836 **Boston Store Visitor Center,** in the nearby village of Boston. You'll enjoy a fascinating exhibit on the design and building of the boats that plied the Ohio & Erie Canal during its heyday

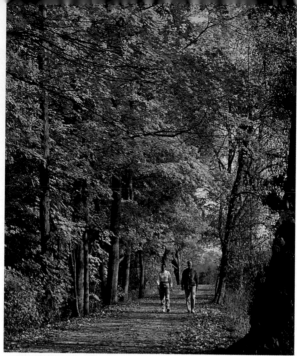

Fall hiking on the Ohio & Erie Canal Towpath Trail

as a thriving commercial corridor. Just south, the village of **Peninsula** produced boats in its workshops that were widely regarded as the best on the canal. Today, Peninsula is a charming village of shops, cafés, and art galleries, as well as of a bike-rental facility for those who'd like to ride on the adjacent Towpath Trail.

A must-see site can be found southeast of Peninsula, on Kendall Park Road. The main trail at the **Ledges** arcs around a small plateau, beneath dramatically eroded bluffs of 320-million-year-old sandstone conglomerate. The evocative setting of tall trees, ferns, and mosses makes this a hike to be taken slowly, enjoying the chattering of red squirrels and the scolding calls of chickadees. On the east side of the Ledges, venture into the tight passageways of **Ice Box Cave;** on the west, the **Ledges Overlook** is a fine spot for sunset views over wooded ridges rolling away to the horizon.

Backing up to the Ledges is **Happy Days Lodge,** located on Ohio 303 in Peninsula. This park facility hosts concerts and lectures year-round. Check the park schedule during your visit for activities.

Ask nearby residents about favorite stretches of the Towpath Trail and you'll get a different answer from nearly everyone. For nature-lovers, though, the section just north of the **Ira Road Trailhead** ranks at the top. You'll find an extensive marsh created by beaver, which returned to the Cuyahoga Valley in the late 1970s after an absence of 100 years. Great blue herons, rose-breasted grosbeaks, red-winged blackbirds, belted kingfishers, and prothonotary warblers are just a few of the wetlands' denizens, along with muskrat, otters, and white-tailed deer (best seen at dawn or dusk, as are beaver).

Moving from natural to human history: **Hale Farm & Village,** on Oak Hill Road in the southwestern part of the park, near Bath, is a living-history

INFORMATION & ACTIVITIES

VISITOR & INFORMATION CENTERS

Boston Store Visitor Center, 1550 Boston Mills Rd., Peninsula, open year-round. (330) 657-2752. **Canal Visitor Center,** 7104 Canal Rd., open year-round. (216) 524-1497. **Hunt Farm Visitor Information Center,** 2054 Bolanz Rd., along Towpath Trail. Open spring through fall, hours vary. **Peninsula Depot Visitor Center,** 1630 Mill St., serves as welcome center for park; hours coincide with train schedule. Closed mid-December to early January.

SEASONS & ACCESSIBILITY
Open all year for individual activities and scheduled events.

HEADQUARTERS
Cuyahoga Valley NP, 15610 Vaughn Rd., Brecksville, OH 44141. (330) 657-2752. www.nps.gov/cuva

ENTRANCE FEE
Free to enter park. Some concerts, events, and programs charge fees.

PETS
Permitted on 6-ft leashes.

ACCESSIBLE SERVICES
Many trails, visitor centers, historic properties, and activities accessible. Crushed limestone of the 20-mile Ohio & Erie Canal Towpath Trail is fully accessible. Contact park for detailed information.

THINGS TO DO
Park personnel and volunteers lead tours and nature walks; cultural events abound year-round at facilities such as the Blossom Music Center, (330) 920-8040; and the Porthouse Theatre, (330) 672-3884. Summer activities: picnicking, golfing, fishing, bicycling, horseback riding (no horse rentals inside the park). Winter activities: sledding, skiing, snowshoeing. For an easy way to explore the park take the **Cuyahoga Valley Scenic Railroad,** (800) 468-4070.

CAMPGROUNDS
Backcountry camping is permitted at the Stanford Trailhead Campsites, 6093 Stanford Rd., Peninsula. Contact the Conservancy for Cuyahoga Valley National Park (330-657-2909 ext. 119) for reservations or information.

HOTELS, MOTELS, & INNS
(unless otherwise noted, rates are for 2 persons in a double room, high season)

INSIDE THE PARK:
Inn at Brandywine Falls 8230 Brandywine Rd., Sagamore Hills, OH 44067. (888) 306-3381 or (330) 467-1812. 3 rooms, 3 suites. $139-$325. AC, breakfast incl. **Stanford House** 6093 Stanford Rd., Peninsula, OH 44264. (330) 657-2909. 9 rooms, 1 limited mobility room with attached bathroom; self-service kitchen, community restrooms. Entire facility available as single rental.

For additional accommodations contact Akron/Summit Convention & Visitors Bureau, (800) 245-4254, www.visitakron summit.org; or Convention & Visitors Bureau of Greater Cleveland, (800) 321-1001, www.positivelycleveland.com.

CUYAHOGA VALLEY

museum open May through October. Re-creating life in a typical mid-19th-century Cuyahoga Valley community, the centerpiece is the 1826 farm of the pioneer Hale family. Other historic buildings have been relocated here to reproduce an early village, where costumed interpreters spin thread, weave cloth, make baskets and candles, blow glass, shape iron in a blacksmith shop, and tell stories. A short drive north, the **Everett Road Covered Bridge** is a re-creation of an 1870s structure that was destroyed in a 1975 flood.

Civilization, in the form of highways, suburbs, and commercial development, is never far away in Cuyahoga Valley NP. But perhaps that is the point: A variety of natural beauty and attractions can endure in an urban setting, and can so reward those who take time to explore.

Bird's-eye view of Fort Jefferson

▶ DRY TORTUGAS

FLORIDA
ESTABLISHED OCTOBER 26, 1992
64,700 acres

In the Gulf of Mexico, about 70 nautical miles west of Key West, Florida, a 7-mile-long archipelago of seven low-lying islands forms the centerpiece of Dry Tortugas National Park. A bird and marine life sanctuary, it harbors some of the healthiest coral reefs remaining off North American shores. Towering incongruously in the midst of this subtropical Eden is Fort Jefferson, a relic of 19th-century military strategy.

Barely 93 acres of the park's 100 square miles (64,000 acres) are above water. Three easterly keys are little more than spits of white coral sand. A stone's throw from the visitor center in Fort Jefferson, Bush Key is home to a tangle of bay cedar, sea grape, mangrove, sea oats, and prickly pear cactus that reflect the original "desert island" character of the islands. The chain ends about 3 miles west with 49-acre Loggerhead Key, where a lighthouse completed in 1858 still flashes a beacon to mariners.

Spanish explorer Juan Ponce de León, the first European to describe the Florida peninsula, dropped anchor here in 1513. He found pellucid waters teeming with green, hawksbill, leatherback, and loggerhead turtles, and so named the islands Las Tortugas, which means "the turtles." For the next three centuries, mariners relied on the turtles for meat and eggs; they also raided the sandy nests of roosting sooty and noddy terns, up to 80,000 of which descend on Bush Key every year between March and September. By 1825, when the islands' first lighthouse began to alert sailors of surrounding reefs and shoals—a grave for more than 200 ships wrecked here since the 1600s—nautical charts warned that the Tortugas were "dry," because of the lack of fresh water.

In 1846, U.S. Army strategists were concerned that hostile nations could disrupt shipping lanes in the Gulf of Mexico. As a result, they decided to build a 420-gun, 1,500-man fort on Garden Key. The intimidating bulk of the 45-foot-high, three-level hexagon, whose 2,000 archways run half a mile around, spared it from ever having to fire a shot in anger. A prison for Union deserters in the Civil War, it also held four conspirators that were convicted in Abraham Lincoln's assassination. The most famous of these was the physician Dr. Samuel Mudd, who (unknowingly, he claimed) set the broken leg of fugitive assassin John Wilkes Booth. He served four years before being released.

Still unfinished after nearly 30 years of intermittent construction, the "Gibraltar of the Gulf" finally succumbed in 1874 to several factors: yellow fever, hurricane damage, and the new rifled cannon, which rendered its 8-foot-thick walls obsolete. It was revived in 1898 as a Navy coaling station—the battleship *Maine* steamed from here to its infamous destiny in Havana's harbor 90 miles south—but the fort was permanently abandoned in 1907. In 1935 President Franklin D. Roosevelt signed papers naming the site a national monument.

How to Get There
Access to Dry Tortugas is by boat or seaplane. Boat passage from Key West takes about three hours; 45 minutes by air. The *Yankee Freedom II* ferry runs from Key West to the park daily. Visit the website for more information: www.yankeefreedom.com or call (800) 634-0939 or (305) 294-7009. Private boaters should refer to NOAA Chart #11434 ("Sombrero Key To Dry Tortugas") and Chart #11438 ("Dry Tortugas"). For seaplane travel, contact Seaplane Adventures of Key West via their website (www.keywestseaplanecharters.com) or call (305) 293-9300.

When to Go
Year-round. Temperatures range from the mid-80s to the low 50s. Moderate weather prevails in April and May, when visitation is at its peak. Winter is often windy with rough seas. The tropical storm or "hurricane" season lasts from June through November, when temperatures and humidity are highest.

How to Visit
A day trip by boat or floatplane will permit you an unhurried visit to **Garden Key.** Guided tours of **Fort Jefferson** are provided by ferry and seaplane staff. A self-guided walking tour of the fort is also possible. A stroll around the fort's marine life-rich seawall, swimming, and snorkeling are also inviting excursions for visitors. If **Bush Key** is open and you can spare an hour, consider swimming the narrow channel to experience a true "desert island" environment. Or use the new land bridge.

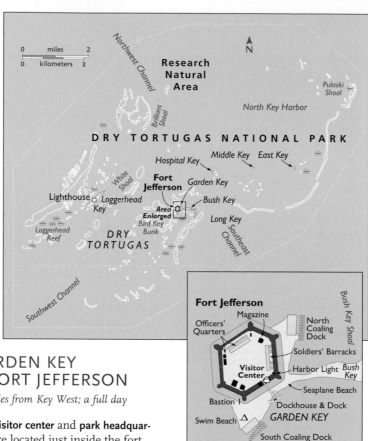

GARDEN KEY & FORT JEFFERSON

70 miles from Key West; a full day

The **visitor center** and **park headquarters** are located just inside the fort entrance. A Florida National Parks and Monuments Association bookstore is located in the visitor center with posted hours of operation. View the self-operated video orientation program, then take a self-guided tour of **Fort Jefferson's** massive architecture and parklike parade ground. Granite spiral staircases lead to open-air gun emplacements atop the fort, where visitors will find splendid 360-degree views—excellent vantage points for bird-watching. (Early on, the population of terns, cormorants, boobies, plovers, pelicans, peregrine falcons, and twin-tailed frigatebirds caught the attention of naturalists like John James Audubon, who sailed here from Key West in 1832 to study

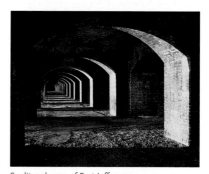

Sunlit archways of Fort Jefferson

INFORMATION & ACTIVITIES

VISITOR & INFORMATION CENTERS

Visitor Center on Garden Key open daily all year.

SEASONS & ACCESSIBILITY

Open all year. Visitation peaks in spring, when advance boat or plane reservations are advised. Only Garden Key offers overnight stays (in campground). Loggerhead and Bush Keys available for day use only. Bush Key is closed from March to Sept. during nesting season.

HEADQUARTERS

Dry Tortugas NP headquarters is located at Everglades NP, 40001 State Rd. 9336, Homestead, FL 33034. Phone (305) 242-7700. www.nps.gov/drto

ENTRANCE FEE

$5 per person.

PETS

Permitted only in the campground and must be leashed at all times.

ACCESSIBLE SERVICES

Dock, visitor center, ground level of fort, Fort Jefferson campground are accessible.

THINGS TO DO

Daily ferry and seaplane tours and occasional ranger-led activities. Walking tours of Fort Jefferson. Swimming, snorkeling, wreck diving, underwater photography, bird-watching, sportfishing, camping.

SPECIAL ADVISORIES

• Plan to bring all water, food, fuel, and supplies. There is no fresh water available for campers, and no showers for rinsing after swimming.
• Private boats must anchor offshore in designated areas. No fuel or provisions available on the island. Slips available for use for up to 2 hours. Dinghy beach available for longer stays ashore.
• No public telephone service to the Tortugas.

CAMPGROUNDS

Camping is permitted only on Garden Key, which has 10 primitive sites. First come, first served. 14-day limit. Fees are $3 per person per night. Groups of ten or more must obtain a special permit in advance from park. Call 305-242-7700 for application or visit www.nps.gov/drto.

HOTELS, MOTELS, & INNS

(unless otherwise noted, rates are for 2 persons in a double room, high season)

In Key West, FL 33040:
Best Western Key Ambassador Resort Inn 3755 S. Roosevelt Blvd. (800) 432-4315 or (305) 296-3500. 100 units. $129-$199. AC.
Duval House 815 Duval St. (800) 223-8825 or (305) 294-1666. 29 units, 2 with kitchens. $245-$395. AC.
The Marquesa Hotel 600 Fleming St. (305) 292-1919. 27 units. $190-$495. AC, pool, restaurant.
Westwinds 914 Eaton St. (800) 788-4150 or (305) 296-4440. 26 units, 7 kitchenettes. $185-$255. AC.

For other area accommodations, contact the Key West Chamber of Commerce, 510 Greene St., Key West, FL 33040. (800) 527-8539 or (305)294-2587, www.keywest chamber.org.

---

them.) Visit the **Garden Key harbor light,** and stroll the parapet, where huge coastal guns are on display.

Stroll along the fort's 0.6-mile-long **seawall** and moat, a sheltered habitat favored by queen conch, yellow stingray, gray snapper, sea stars, and other creatures. Outside the wall, a superb snorkeling area—

chest deep and decorated with sea fans, brain coral, and turtle grass—teems with many of the 442 species of fish identified in this protected marine sanctuary.

With a companion for mutual safety, try swimming from the campground's bathing beach along the wall, where fish congregate.

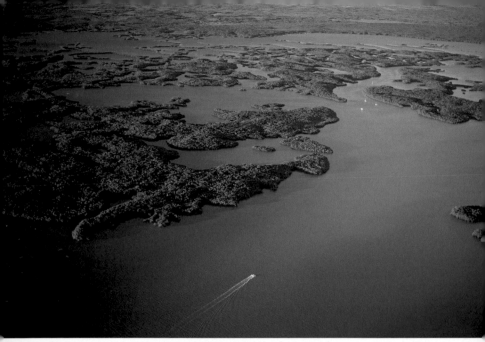

Aerial view of Everglades' Thousand Islands mangrove trees

▶EVERGLADES

FLORIDA
ESTABLISHED DECEMBER 6, 1947
1,542,526 acres

A short parade of visitors follows a ranger on an Everglades nature walk. For more than an hour she has shown them the living wonders around them—butterflies and snails, alligators and fish, and bird after bird. Near the end of the walk, she gathers the visitors around her. She points to a string of nine white ibis coursing a cloudless sky.

"Imagine seeing ibis in the 1930s," she says. "That would have been a flight of about 90 birds. We are seeing only about 10 percent of the wading birds that were here then. When you get home, write your congressmen and tell them we have to save Everglades." Though park staff may not lobby Congress, in this threatened national park, lobbying happens on nature walks and appears in official literature.

Everglades National Park is at the southern tip of Florida's Everglades, a 100-mile-long subtropical wilderness of saw-grass prairie, jungle-like hammock, and mangrove swamp, that originally ran from Lake Okeechobee to Florida Bay. Water, essential to the survival of this ecosystem, once flowed south from the lake unhindered. But as the buildup of southern Florida has intensified, canals, levees, and dikes have increasingly diverted the water to land developments and agribusinesses. Vast irrigated farmlands have spread to the park's gates. The waning of the ibis carries a warning: Watery habitats in the park are shrinking because not enough water is getting to Everglades.

The park's special mission inspires the crusade to save it. Unlike early parks established to protect scenery, Everglades was created to preserve a portion of this vast ecosystem as a wildlife habitat. The park's unique mix of tropical and temperate plants and animals—including more than 700 plant and 300 bird species, as well as the endangered manatee and Florida panther, and the threatened crocodile—has prompted UNESCO to grant it international biosphere reserve status as well as World Heritage site designation.

Everglades environmentalists and crusaders urge the purchase of privately owned wetlands east and north of the park. This would further protect the ecosystem and give the park a larger claim to the water that Everglades shares with its thirsty neighbors.

The diverse life of Everglades National Park, from algae to alligators, depends upon a rhythm of abundance and drought. In the wet season, a river inches deep and miles wide flows, almost invisibly, to the Gulf of Mexico. In the dry season, the park rests, awaiting the water's return. The plants and animals are a part of this rhythm. When humans change it, they put Everglades life at risk.

How to Get There

South from Miami, take US 1— Florida's Turnpike to Florida City, then go west on Fla. 9336 (Palm Dr.) to the Ernest F. Coe Visitor Center, about 50 miles from Miami. West from Miami, take US 41 (the Tamiami Trail) to Shark Valley Visitor Center. From Naples, head east on US 41 to Fla. 29, then south to Everglades City. Airports: Miami and Naples.

When to Go

Everglades has two seasons: dry (mid-December through mid-April) and wet (the rest of the year). The park schedules most of its activities in the dry season; hot, humid weather and clouds of mosquitoes make park visitors quite uncomfortable during the wet season.

How to Visit

If you can stay only a day for a drive-in visit, get out of your car and learn about Everglades ecology by taking self-guided walks at road turnoffs on the drive from the **Ernest F. Coe Visitor Center** to Flamingo. For a longer stay, pick either **Flamingo** or **Everglades City** as your base and time your travels to the schedules of concession boat tours. In wet or dry season, only a boat or canoe gives you access to the backcountry. Because of mosquitoes, the dry season is best for canoeing. (Near park entrances you'll see signs advertising airboat rides; airboats, which can disturb wildlife and tear up saw grass, are not licensed to operate in the park.)

ROYAL PALM TO FLAMINGO

76 miles round-trip; a full day

The main park road connects the main entrance, southwest of Florida City, with Flamingo on Florida Bay. Make the drive an exploration, not a dash. Stops at the suggested sites can be made on the way to or from

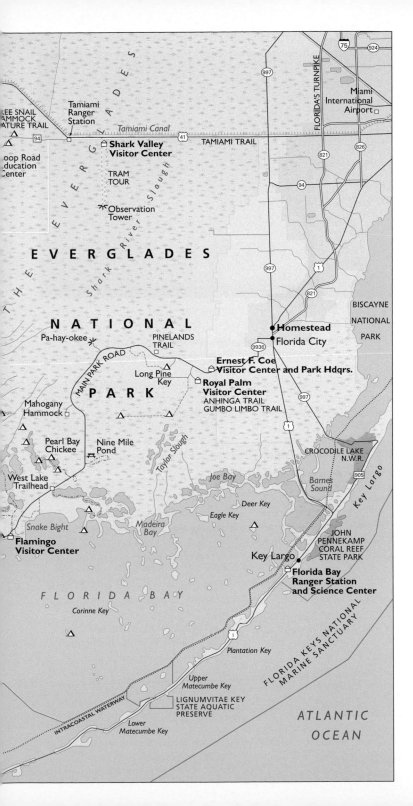

EE SNAIL
AMMOCK
ATURE TRAIL

Tamiami
Ranger
Station

oop Road
ducation
enter

94

Tamiami Canal

Shark Valley
Visitor Center

41

TAMIAMI TRAIL

TRAM
TOUR

Observation
Tower

THE EVERGLADES

Shark River Slough

E V E R G L A D E S

N A T I O N A L

Pa-hay-okee

PINELANDS
TRAIL

MAIN PARK ROAD

Long Pine
Key

P A R K

Mahogany
Hammock

Pearl Bay
Chickee

Nine Mile
Pond

West Lake
Trailhead

Taylor Slough

Snake Bight

Flamingo
Visitor Center

Madeira
Bay

F L O R I D A   B A Y

Corinne Key

997

75

924

Miami
International
Airport

826

821

94

997

1

821

Homestead

Florida City

9936

Ernest F. Coe
Visitor Center and Park Hdqrs.

Royal Palm
Visitor Center
ANHINGA TRAIL
GUMBO LIMBO TRAIL

997

1

CROCODILE LAKE
N.W.R.

Joe Bay

Deer Key

Eagle Key

Barnes
Sound

905

Key Largo

BISCAYNE

NATIONAL

PARK

JOHN
PENNEKAMP
CORAL REEF
STATE PARK

Key Largo

Florida Bay
Ranger Station
and Science Center

FLORIDA'S TURNPIKE

1

Plantation Key

Upper
Matecumbe Key

LIGNUMVITAE KEY
STATE AQUATIC
PRESERVE

Lower
Matecumbe Key

INTRACOASTAL WATERWAY

FLORIDA KEYS NATIONAL
MARINE SANCTUARY

ATLANTIC
OCEAN

Dwarf cypress trees at dusk

Flamingo, depending upon when you want to board a concession tour boat there. Check on that day's cruises by calling the concessioner (see **Things to Do** p. 62).

At the **Ernest F. Coe Visitor Center,** get oriented to this complex park. A short film stresses environmental threats to the park and alerts you to the subtle, imperiled beauty you will be seeing. Check the center's daily posted schedule for ranger-led walks and talks at the Royal Palm Visitor Center, just ahead, and for that day's cruises at Flamingo, 38 miles away. Time your road travel each way by adjusting to the day's schedules.

Egrets, herons, and other species dot the saw grass and roadside trees. On the road, use a passenger as a bird spotter; simultaneous driving and bird-watching can be dangerous. At 4 miles, turn off to the **Royal Palm Visitor Center.** There are two trails here to stroll.

You can walk the half-mile **Anhinga Trail** on your own, but if you join a ranger-led group you'll have a better chance of spotting wildlife. The boardwalk trail skirts a shallow,

freshwater slough (pronounced slew) home to many wetland plants including grasses, sedges, shrubs, and trees. You almost certainly will see alligators and some fascinating birds, including the long-necked, long-beaked fish-spearer for which the trail is named.

The ranger adds inside knowledge to what you see: Those white egg sacs on that branch will hatch apple snails, the prime food of the endangered snail kite. That slim, long-snouted fish gliding through the clear water is a gar; in the dry season it can survive in a mudhole because a primitive lung allows it to breathe air. That alligator loosens the muck in water-filled "solution holes"—limestone depressions that hold moisture and become miniature ecosystems in the dry season—and sweeps it away with its tail; in the dry season the gator-made oasis keeps fish, frogs, snails, and birds alive—as long as they are wary of the major resident. In Everglades, unusual adaptations and delicate balances sustain the park's astonishing variety of animals and plants.

The other trail here is the quarter-mile **Gumbo Limbo Trail,** named for a tree whose peeling red bark gives it another name: tourist tree. The trail takes you to a hardwood hammock, an island of tropical hardwoods—including gumbo limbos and some magnificent examples of strangler figs—surrounded by contrasting vegetation. The slight elevation keeps the ground drier, permitting the hardwoods to flourish and creating a shaded habitat for many creatures, from snakes to deer, foxes, and raccoon.

Back on the road, pull off to visit the roadside exhibits. Stop-and-walk lessons begin on the 0.25-mile **Pinelands Trail,** 7 miles along the road. Slash pines grow on high ground—5 to 7 feet above sea level—most of the pinelands were wiped out during the development of Miami and other towns. What you see here are remnants of the pines that once covered southeastern Florida. It is the most botanically diverse habitat in the Everglades, allowing the growth of flowers such as the perky tickseed and the ruellia with purple blooms.

Upon leaving the pinelands, a wayside exhibit presents Pinnacle Rock, a sample of the porous limestone that is South Florida's bedrock. At 12 miles, stop again to see dwarf cypresses, trees stunted by shallow and inorganic soil.

Half a mile farther is an overlook called **Pa-hay-okee,** or "grassy waters," the Indian name for the Everglades. A boardwalk takes you to a shaded observation stage where you can look out on a seemingly endless prairie of grassy waters. At 19.5 miles is **Mahogany Hammock,** where a boardwalk leads to the largest living, wild mahogany tree in the United States.

If you want to picnic, there are fine spots at **Long Pine Key** (at 6 miles), **Nine Mile Pond** (at 26.5 miles), and **West Lake** (at 30.5 miles).

At **Flamingo** sign up for a boat tour in the marina ticket office near the visitor center. While you are waiting, take the self-guided, half-mile walk around the waterfront to see **Florida Bay,** a marine nursery protected by the park. Roseate spoonbills, raccoons, and manatees

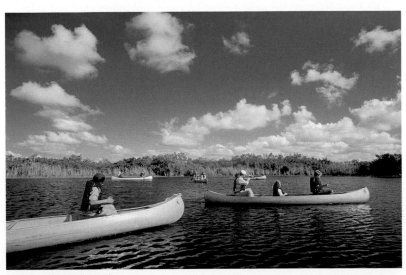

Canoeing at Nine Mile Pond

are just some of the out-of-water critters often spotted here.

The nearly 2-hour backcountry cruise begins in the marina and enters **Buttonwood Canal,** built in 1957. Among the spidery roots of the three species of mangrove you will see along the waterway, watch for shy crocodiles, which sometimes sun themselves on the banks of the canal. The cruise crosses **Coot Bay** and enters **Whitewater Bay,** where backcountry canoeists camp on chickees, tent-size platforms raised on poles. Don't expect to see flamingos; they rarely appear at their namesake town.

SHARK VALLEY TO EVERGLADES CITY
49 miles one-way; a full day

The **Tamiami Trail** (US 41) forms part of the park's northeastern border. Near the eastern park entrance, stop at the **Shark Valley Visitor Center.** Here is a 15-mile loop road accessible only on foot, on bike, or, year-round, on a 2-hour, narrated tour aboard an open-sided concessioner tram.

You will not see sharks. The valley gets its name from the **Shark River;** sharks gather at its mouth in the Gulf of Mexico. But you will see alligator trails leading to hammocks in the saw grass—and you will almost certainly see alligators and wading birds. A pathway leads to a 65-foot tower looking down on the vista that became a name: glades that seem to go on forever. It's a marvelous place to spot turtles, alligators, and wading birds. Look for red-shouldered hawks, snail kites, northern harriers, and rare short-tailed hawks over the marsh.

Return to US 41, which veers northward into the 2,400-square-mile **Big Cypress National Preserve,**

part of the Everglades ecosystem. Most of the water flowing into the park comes through four floodgates that you can see north of the highway along the park boundary.

At Fla. 29, turn south for Everglades City. Follow the highway through the town to the waterfront. Sign up for one of the regularly scheduled, round-trip, narrated concessioner boat tours (or explore by boat or kayak on your own).

The **Ten Thousand Island** trip explores mangrove islands in the Gulf of Mexico. On the way to and from the islands, protected sea mammals—sleek bottlenose dolphins and lumbering manatees—often pop up to look at the boat. You can usually see ospreys, pelicans, and cormorants. From a distance, the islands look like a solid stretch of low-lying green land. Close up, you see a labyrinth of thousands of waterways.

There are far fewer than 10,000 islands, but the exact number is unknown and constantly changing. Islands form from the buildup of leaves and other organic material among the stilt-rooted mangroves. As an island grows, storms and tidal forces may break it into fragments, and these continue to grow and spread. The islands, ranging in size from a couple of trees to several hundred acres, provide shelter, habitat, and food for many creatures in the Gulf web of life.

The boat crosses **Chokoloskee Bay,** which shares its name with an island of shells, 15 feet high and 147 acres, built by Native Americans long before the first white men appeared here. The bay is the northern end of the 99-mile Everglades City–to–Flamingo **Wilderness Waterway,** a system of backcountry canoe trails through the estuarine fringes of the park.

Clockwise from top left: Snowy egret; palmetto plants; anhinga; American alligator; wildflower

INFORMATION & ACTIVITIES

VISITOR & INFORMATION CENTERS
Ernest F. Coe Visitor Center on Fla. 9336 at park entrance. **Royal Palm Visitor Center** off main park road a few miles inside park entrance. **Flamingo Visitor Center** on main park road at Florida Bay; may have intermittent ranger presence off-season. **Shark Valley Visitor Center** at north end of park on US 41. **Gulf Coast Visitor Center** at Everglades City on Fla. 29 at northwest entrance.

SEASONS & ACCESSIBILITY
Open all year; some facilities and services limited or unavailable during off-season, May to mid-December.

HEADQUARTERS
40001 State Rd. 9336, Homestead, FL 33034. Phone (305) 242-7700. www.nps.gov/ever

ENTRANCE FEES
$10 per car per week. $5 per person biking or walking in.

PETS
Pets must be on leashes and are allowed in the campgrounds and parking lots only.

ACCESSIBLE SERVICES
Most facilities in the park are accessible. Several boardwalk trails are at least partly accessible. In the backcountry, Pearl Bay Chickee is accessible. Call park headquarters for additional information.

THINGS TO DO
Free naturalist-led activities: nature walks and talks, hikes, exhibits, seasonal evening programs. Also, tram tours; sightseeing boats; canoe, kayak, houseboat, motorboat, and bicycle rentals; fishing (need license); crabbing; shrimping (ask about regulations). Dec. to April, guided tours of a historic Nike Missile Base, relic of the Cuban Missile Crisis, are offered. In winter and on holidays, call to reserve space on guided tours and activities.
  Rentals and boat tours in Flamingo: (239) 695-3101 ext. 355. Tram tour at Shark Valley: (305) 221-8455. Boat tours and rentals at Everglades City: (239) 695-2591, or (800) 445-7724 in Florida.

SPECIAL ADVISORIES
• You'll need insect repellent year-round, but especially April to December.
• Swimming not advised; alligators and snakes live in ponds; crocodiles, sharks and barracuda, in saltwater areas.

WILDERNESS CAMPING
Permits required, $10 per permit and $2 per person; obtainable in person, no more than 24 hours before trip, at Flamingo or Everglades City. Fees collected mid-Nov. through April only. No reservations; first come, first served; limits on number of people and length of stay.

CAMPGROUNDS
Two campgrounds, 14-day limit Nov. to May; otherwise 30-day limit. $16 per site collected Nov. through May only. **Flamingo** and **Long Pine Key** open all year. Reservations available mid-Nov. to March; reserve through NRRS (see p. 10); rest of year, first come, first served. Tent and RV sites; 41 sites with electric hookups available in Flamingo. Three group campgrounds; reservations suggested.

HOTELS, MOTELS, & INNS
(unless otherwise noted, rates are for 2 persons in a double room, high season)

In Florida City, FL 33034:
Comfort Inn 333 S.E. 1st Ave./US 1. (305) 248-4009. 124 units. $59-$250. AC, pool.
Coral Roc Motel 1100 N. Krome Ave. (305) 247-4010. 16 units, 4 kitchenettes. $36-$89. AC, pool.
Knights Inn 1223 N.E. 1st Ave./US 1. (305) 247-6621. 49 units. $49-$169. AC, pool.
In Homestead, FL 33030:
Days Inn 51 S. Homestead Blvd. (305) 245-1260. 111 units. $59-$79. AC, pool, bar.
Everglades Motel 605 S. Krome Ave. (305) 247-4117. 14 units. $45-$90. AC, pool.
Redland Hotel & Historic Inn 5 S. Flagler Ave. (800) 595-1904 or (305) 246-1904. 13 units. $89-$129, breakfast incl. AC.

For other lodgings, contact the Greater Homestead/Florida City Chamber of Commerce, 455 N. Flagler Ave., Homestead FL 33030. (305) 247-2332 or (888) 352-4891, www.chamberinaction.com.

EXCURSIONS

BIG CYPRESS
NATIONAL PRESERVE
OCHOPEE, FLORIDA

Dispensing life-giving fresh water to the Everglades and coastal estuaries, this preserve contains marshes, cypress stands, prairies, hardwood hammocks, pinelands, and mangrove forests, along with wading birds and alligators. The endangered Florida panther and black bears roam the area. 729,000 acres. Hiking, birding, fishing, canoeing, off-road vehicles, scenic drives. Six campgrounds, picnic areas. On US 41 (Tamiami Trail); adjoins Everglades NP. (239) 695-1201.

CORKSCREW SWAMP
SANCTUARY
NAPLES, FLORIDA

A 2.25-mile-long boardwalk takes visitors on a self-guided tour through this Audubon Society site featuring the country's largest stand of virgin bald cypress forest and varied wildlife, including alligators. 13,000 acres. Walking and picnic areas. Open all year. Off Fla. 846, about 50 miles northwest of Everglades NP. (239) 348-9151.

J. N. "DING" DARLING
NATIONAL WILDLIFE REFUGE
SANIBEL, FLORIDA

Migratory songbirds and a large population of roseate spoonbills feature among the 230 bird species on this island refuge named for Pulitzer Prize–winning political cartoonist and refuge system pioneer Jay Norwood Darling. 6,400 acres. Hiking, canoeing, bicycling, fishing, scenic drive. Open all year, dawn to dusk (closed on Fridays). Visitor center off US 41, about 75 miles northwest of Everglades NP. (239) 472-1100.

Mist-shrouded autumn view from Clingmans Dome

▶GREAT SMOKY MOUNTAINS

NORTH CAROLINA & TENNESSEE
ESTABLISHED JUNE 15, 1934
521,896 acres

The fact invariably stated about Great Smoky is this: It is the nation's busiest park, drawing more than nine million visitors a year, twice the number of any other national park. Most of the millions see the park from a mountain-skimming scenic highway that, on a typical weekend day during the summer, draws 60,000 people, bumper-to-bumper.

Luckily, there is plenty of park, thinly laced by 384 miles of mountain roads. You can pull off the road, park the car, and stroll one of Great Smoky's many Quiet Walkways, quarter-mile paths into what the signs call a "little bit of the world as it once was." Eight hundred miles of hiking trails, from a half mile to 70 miles long, also give you that world.

The park covers 800 square miles of mountainous terrain. It preserves

the world's best examples of deciduous forest and a matchless variety of plants and animals, including the reintroduced elk that can be seen near the Oconaluftee Visitor Center. Because the park contains so many types of eastern forest vegetation—much of it old growth—the park has been designated an international biosphere reserve.

The Smoky Mountains are among the oldest on earth. Ice Age glaciers stopped their southward journey just short of these mountains, which became a junction of southern and northern flora. Rhododendron and mountain laurel thrust from the weathered rocks. Amid the woodland and craggy peaks bloom more than 1,600 species of flowering plants, some found only here. Shrubs take over in places, creating tree-free zones called heath balds, laurel slicks (because of the shiny leaves), or just plain hells (because they are so hard to get through).

The tangle of brush and trees forms a close-packed array of air-breathing leaves. The water and hydrocarbons exuded by the leaves produce the filmy "smoke" that gives the mountains their name. Air pollution in recent years has added microscopic sulfate particles to the haze, cutting visibility back about 60 percent since the 1950s. The pollution has also affected the park's red spruce stand—the southern Appalachians' largest. Insects are destroying the Fraser fir, the spruce's high-altitude companion, and sadly, the park has also experienced widespread loss of its magnificent hemlock population since the introduction of the non-native woolly adelgid pest to the area in 2002.

The park also preserves the humble churches, cabins, farmhouses, and barns of the mountain people who began settling here in the late 1700s. Most people left when the park was founded; but some chose to stay and live out their lives here.

How to Get There

From Knoxville, Tenn. (about 25 miles away), take I-40 to Tenn. 66, then US 441 to Gatlinburg entrance. From Asheville, N.C. (about 40 miles away), take I-40 west to US 19, then US 441, to park's southern entrance near Cherokee, N.C. For a scenic, low-speed approach, take the 469-mile Blue Ridge Parkway that connects Virginia's Shenandoah National Park with Great Smoky. Airports: Knoxville and Asheville.

When to Go

Year-round. In summer and in fall (when spectacular foliage draws huge crowds), time your visit to midweek, and arrive early. Visitor centers open year-round.

How to Visit

On a 1-day visit, take the **Newfound Gap Road** to **Clingmans Dome** and get the best overview of the park by seeing it from the highest point. The best second-day activity is the **Cades Cove loop road,** a chance to drive or cycle through pioneer history. For a longer stay, focus on the self-guided nature trails and drives, which get you away from the crowds and show you the flora and fauna.

NEWFOUND GAP ROAD TO CLINGMANS DOME

40 to 45 miles; a half to full day

Newfound Gap Road, which begins at 1,200 feet and ascends to 5,048 feet, connects the park's major visitor centers, **Sugarlands** (near Gatlinburg, Tenn.) and **Oconaluftee** (near Cherokee, N.C.). The road, passing from lowland hardwood timber to high-altitude spruce-fir forests, gives you a vertical trip that is ecologically equivalent to a journey from Georgia to Canada. Be prepared

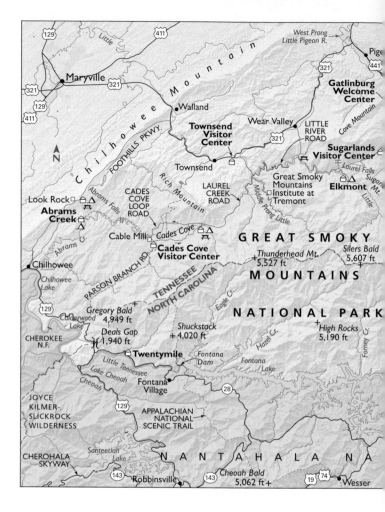

for rain on almost any day. A clear day below can be a day of mist and fog on high. From Sugarlands (for an Oconaluftee start, reverse the order below), stop after 5 miles at **Chimneys,** a fine picnic spot. Stretch your legs on the 0.75-mile self-guided **Cove Hardwood Nature Trail.** Return to the car for a short drive to the **Chimney Tops Overlooks,** which offer views of the double summits the Cherokee called Duniskwal-guni ("forked antlers").

Here you can extend your stop with a hike on the steep, 4-mile round-trip **Chimney Tops Trail** through an old-growth forest and up 1,335 feet to the sheer cliffs named the Chimneys. Depending on your time and stamina, you can also get out of the car and hike at the next overlook, where a trailhead leads to a steep climb to **Alum Cave Bluffs,** site of a 19th-century commercial alum mine and reputedly a source of saltpeter for Civil War gunpowder. The trail begins with an easy 1.3-mile trail along a tree-bordered creek to **Arch Rock,** a tunnel made by eons of erosion. The trees include towering

200-year-old eastern hemlocks. This is a magnificent spot for a spring wildflower hike serenaded by the songs of nesting warblers. You can return to your car or continue on a steep 0.9-mile ascent to the bluffs.

Back in the car, continue on to **Newfound Gap** (5,048 feet), through which runs the Tennessee–North Carolina state line and a long leg of the Appalachian Trail. From the overlook here, on a clear day, you can see **Mount LeConte** (6,593 feet) and your next stop, **Clingmans Dome.** The 7-mile Clingmans Dome Road veers

sharply off here and winds through a spruce-fir forest to a parking lot.

There begins a steep half-mile trail ending at a spiral ramp. It leads to a lookout tower at the top of the 6,643-foot dome, the highest point in the park, where you get either a panoramic view or a sense of floating on a sea of churning clouds. From here retrace the route to Sugarlands or, depending on time and destination, continue on to Oconaluftee Visitor Center. Here you should stop off to learn about the reintroduction of elk near here and in the **Cataloochee** area of the park.

The **Mountain Farm Museum,** a cluster of farm buildings gathered from their original locations within the park, stands adjacent to the visitor center. Pioneer-costumed park employees, playing farmstead roles, give demonstrations spring through October. (Between May and October, at **Mingus Mill,** a miller explains how cornmeal and flour would have been produced on an ingenious water-run turbine.)

CADES COVE LOOP ROAD

11 miles; at least a half day

Follow Little River and Laurel Creek Roads for 25 miles from Sugarlands Visitor Center to the Cades Cove loop road. **Cades Cove** traces its history to 1819, when, under a treaty with the Cherokee Indians, settlers cleared the broad, high valley. By 1850 more than 680 people were living there. They left behind structures that evolved into an open-air museum whose galleries are sites along the paved, 11-mile one-way loop road. Official sites are well marked but you may find yourself making unofficial stops to watch white-tailed deer bounding across the valley, or to see black bears feed on acorns or wild grapes.

The first stop is **John Oliver Place,** site 3. The small cabin was built with split-wood shingles and hand-hewn logs. Stand on the porch and look down the long, green-carpeted valley that drew the family to this place, the edge of the American world in 1826. **Primitive Baptist Church,** site 4, is skipped by some visitors because it lies on a two-way dirt road off the loop road. Don't miss it. The plain white-frame church, organized in 1827, guards a small graveyard; time

Mountain laurel along one of the Pigeon River prongs

has rendered many stones nameless. The church closed during the Civil War because, a letter says, "we was Union people and the Rebels was too strong here in Cades Cove." **Methodist Church,** site 5, had a door for men and another for women and children. During services, the separation was enforced in the pews by a barrier.

Just past the church is **Hyatt Lane,** an old road out of Cades Cove and today a shortcut that slices off a big piece of the tour. Stay on the loop road and continue to **Missionary Baptist Church,** site 7, formed in 1839 by expelled members of the Primitive Baptist Church. Because the congregation split between Union and Confederacy sympathizers, this church also closed during the Civil War.

Continue on the road, past **Rich Mountain Road,** site 8. Save this for another day. The gravel road, laid over an Indian trail, goes up **Rich Mountain** and provides a spectacular backward glance at Cades Cove before exiting the park. Also requiring more time is the **Cooper Road Trail,** site 9, a onetime wagon road that is now a 13-mile hiking trail ending outside the park.

Ahead on the right is a short, two-way road to the next stops, **Abrams Falls,** site 10, and **Elijah Oliver Place,** site 11. If you take this offshoot, you come to a parking lot and a choice: a 2-hour, 2.5-mile hike up to stunning Abrams Falls, or a half-mile hike to another rustic farmstead owned by early settler Elijah Oliver. The latter features a smokehouse, springhouse, and corn crib.

Continue your drive along the loop road to the next offshoot, which leads to **John Cable Mill,** site 12, where corn was ground into meal. Here, the **Cades Cove Visitor Center** offers maps and visitor information as well as books, videos, and DVDs on the

Hikers on one of Great Smoky's trails *(top)* White-tailed buck leaping over a fence *(bottom)*

park for sale. Now leave the center and wander about, reliving the life that centered on the old mill.

Other buildings—a blacksmith shop, a large cantilever barn, a smokehouse—were imported from elsewhere in the park. Check at the visitor center for schedules of farm-life demonstrations; they include the making of sorghum molasses: A horse-powered mill squeezes juice from the stalks, which is then boiled down in an open-air vat.

Just beyond the Cable Mill area is **Parson Branch Road,** which can take you out of the park—and the 21st century. The narrow winding one-way dirt road (sometimes closed by weather; check with the park) was carved out of wilderness about 1838. The 8-mile trip to US 129 can take an hour. If prudence keeps you on the loop road, your next stop will be **Tipton Place,** site 17. Built by Hamp

Black bear climbing down from a cherry tree after an all-night gorge

Tipton shortly after the Civil War, it later became the home of a blacksmith, who put up his shop nearby.

Drive on to the last stop, **Carter Shields Cabin,** site 18. Log cabins like this would be succeeded by board houses, which arrived with lumbering in the early 1900s.

HIKES & DRIVES

Self-guided nature trails begin with an honor system document rack. You drop in 50 cents and pluck out a leaflet keyed to numbered stops. **Balsam Mountain Trail** is the easiest climbing trail in the park, a 1.5-mile loop from Balsam Mountain Campground. The trail gives you a short lesson in the identification of trees and, especially in spring, wildflowers. **Laurel Falls Trail** is paved. The 2.5-mile round-trip trail, which starts on Little River Road near Elkmont, winds through thickets of mountain laurel and rhododendron to one of the park's many waterfalls.

For a longer stay in the park, try some of the more rugged trails. The most rewarding hike is to **Mount LeConte,** at 6,593 feet the park's third highest peak. The shortest (though steepest) way up is via the **Alum Cave Trail,** which starts at Newfound Gap Road (see Newfound Gap Road tour p. 65). Here begins a steep 5-mile climb to the summit of LeConte. At one point the trail skirts a cliff face so sheer that hikers must grasp a cable to make their way up.

For the motorist, there are also self-guided nature trails using roads. The **Roaring Fork Motor Nature Trail,** 4 miles from Gatlinburg off Cherokee Orchard Road, is a 5-mile curvy, one-way road with a well-warranted 10 mph speed limit. About a mile before the trail begins, you will see the **Noah "Bud" Ogle Place** on your right. A 0.75-mile path takes you around the remains of a farm—a mill, a barn, and the historic Ogle family house.

At the Roaring Fork Trail, avail yourself of the self-guiding booklet that suggests scenic stops. The road climbs a hill that provides, on clear days, a splendid view of **Sugarland** and **Cove Mountains.** Along the roadside is an old-growth hemlock forest. Here and there, moldering chestnut logs are poignant reminders of the blight that struck down the onetime forest king.

INFORMATION & ACTIVITIES

VISITOR & INFORMATION CENTERS
Sugarlands, on US 441 south of the Gatlinburg, Tenn., entrance; **Oconaluftee,** on US 441 north of Cherokee, N.C., entrance; **Cades Cove Visitor Center,** near Townsend, Tenn., entrance; enter off US 321, east of Townsend. All open daily. Call park headquarters for information.

SEASONS & ACCESSIBILITY
Open all year. The road to Clingmans Dome and some unpaved roads closed in winter.

HEADQUARTERS
107 Park Headquarters Rd., Gatlinburg, TN 37738. Phone (865) 436-1200. www .nps.gov/grsm

ACCESSIBLE SERVICES
Visitor centers and restrooms are wheelchair accessible. The Sugarlands Valley Nature Trail (a quarter mile south of the Sugarlands Visitor Center) was custom built for visitors with visual or mobility impairments. Laurel Falls Trail is paved but steep; negotiable with assistance only. Free brochure.

THINGS TO DO
Free naturalist-led activities: nature walks (day and evening), children's and campfire programs, pioneer exhibits and demonstrations, slide talks. Also, annual festivals, auto tape tour, hiking, bicycling, fishing (permit needed), horseback riding (several stables in park).

OVERNIGHT BACKPACKING
Permit required; free from visitor centers and ranger stations. Camping only permitted in designated sites. You can reserve rationed sites and shelters up to 30 days in advance; call (865) 436-1231.

CAMPGROUNDS
Ten campgrounds, most with a 7-day limit mid-May through October; other times 14-day limit. **Cades Cove** and **Smokemont** open all year; **Elkmont** open April through October. Reservations required mid-May through October; available through www .recreation.gov. Other campgrounds open mid-March through October, first come, first served. Fees $14-$23 per night. No showers. Tent and RV sites; no hookups. Seven group campgrounds; reservations required; contact park headquarters.

HOTELS, MOTELS, & INNS
(unless otherwise noted, rates are for 2 persons in a double room, high season)

INSIDE THE PARK:
LeConte Lodge (atop Mount LeConte; access by hiking trail) 250 Apple Valley Rd., Sevierville, TN 37862. (865) 429-5704. 10 cabins, no electricity, shared bathrooms. $116, includes 2 meals. Late March–late Nov.

OUTSIDE THE PARK:
In Bryson City, NC 28713:
Hemlock Inn (on Galbraith Creek Rd., off US 19) P.O. Box 2350. (828) 488-2885. 25 units, $169-$230, includes 2 meals. Restaurant.
In Cherokee, NC 28719:
Chestnut Tree Inn US 19s, P.O. Box 1929. (828) 497-9181. 154 units. $99-$130. AC, pool, restaurant.
In Fontana Dam, NC 28733:
Historic Fontana Village Resort US 28N, P.O. Box 68. (800) 849-2258 or (828) 498-2211. 90 rooms, $99-$209; 120 cottages with kitchens, $99-$289. AC, pool, rest.
In Gatlinburg, TN 37738:
Buckhorn Inn 2140 Tudor Mountain Rd. (866) 941-0460 or (865) 436-4668. 9 rooms, 7 cottages, 3 guest houses. $115-$320. AC, restaurant.
Gillette Motel 235 Historic Nature Trail, P.O. Box 231. (800) 437-0815 or (865) 436-5601. 80 units. $92. AC, pool.
Garden Plaza Hotel 520 Historic Nature Trail, P.O. Box 1130. (800) 435-9201 in Tenn. or (865) 436-9201. 190 units. $89-$140. AC, pool.
Park Vista Doubletree 705 Cherokee Orchard Rd., P.O. Box 30. (800) 421-7275 or (865) 436-9211. 300 units. $90-$170. AC, pool, restaurant.

For other accommodations in Gatlinburg, call the Chamber of Commerce, P.O. Box 527, Gatlinburg, TN 37738. (800) 588-1817 or (865) 436-4178, www.gatlinburg.com.

EXCURSIONS

PISGAH NATIONAL FOREST
ASHEVILLE, NORTH CAROLINA

The Blue Ridge Parkway traverses this mountainous forest of mixed hardwoods, azaleas, rhododendrons, rocky gorges, and delicate waterfalls. Stunning in spring and fall. Contains three wilderness areas and Mount Mitchell, the highest peak east of the Mississippi. 519,036 acres. 447 campsites, picnic areas. Hiking, fishing, horseback riding, scenic drives, swimming. Open all year; most campsites open spring to late fall. Visitor center on US 276, about 50 miles from Great Smoky Mountains NP. (828) 257-4200.

NANTAHALA NATIONAL FOREST
ASHEVILLE, NORTH CAROLINA

The hardwood-covered mountains here contain deep, narrow valleys, canyons, and waterfalls. Noted for azaleas, rhododendrons. Contains three wilderness areas. 525,507 acres. Hiking, boating, fishing, horseback riding, scenic drives. 395 campsites, boat ramps, picnic areas, handicapped access. Open all year; most campsites open spring to late fall. Adjoins Great Smoky Mountains NP on the south. (828) 257-4200.

BREAKS INTERSTATE PARK
BREAKS, VIRGINIA

Russell Fork cuts through the Pine Mountains here, creating Breaks Canyon, the "Grand Canyon of the South." Features class VI white water. Rhododendrons blooming season, mid-May through June; fall leaves peak mid-October. Gospel music festivals Memorial and Labor Day weekends. 4,600 acres. Hiking, boating, fishing, scenic drives, swimming. 138 campsites, cottages and motel units, visitor center, food service, boat ramp, picnic areas, handicapped access. Open all year; most facilities available April to mid-December. On Va. 80, about 190 miles from Great Smoky Mountains NP. (276) 865-4413.

BIG SOUTH FORK NATIONAL RIVER & RECREATION AREA
ONEIDA, TENNESSEE

The Big South Fork of the Cumberland River bisects the Cumberland Plateau, yielding white water as well as calm stretches, sandstone cliffs, waterfalls, and natural arches. 116,000 acres, part in Kentucky. Hiking, horseback riding, fishing, swimming, hunting. 235 campsites, boat ramp, picnic areas. Open all year. Off US 27, about 100 miles northwest of Great Smoky Mountains NP. (423) 286-7275.

CHEROKEE NATIONAL FOREST
CLEVELAND, TENNESSEE

This rugged mountain backcountry is densely wooded with mixed pines and hardwoods, azaleas, mountain laurels. 640,000 acres. Hiking, boating, fishing, hunting, scenic drives, swimming, mountain biking, horseback riding. 29 campgrounds, boat ramps, 30 picnic sites. Open all year; most campgrounds open May through October. Adjoins Great Smoky Mountains NP on northeast and southwest. (423) 476-9700.

CHATTAHOOCHEE NATIONAL FOREST
GAINESVILLE, GEORGIA

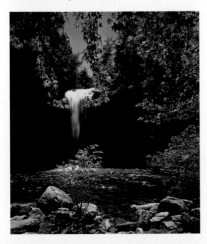

This hardwood forest encompasses a mix of terrain—lakes, streams, valleys, mountains, and piedmont plateau. Contains ten wilderness areas and a stretch of the Chattooga Wild and Scenic River with Tallulah Gorge. Also, Brasstown Bald, the state's highest mountain at 4,784 feet. 750,000 acres. Hiking, sailing, fishing, hunting, scenic drives, swimming. More than 25 campgrounds, boat ramps, picnic areas, handicapped access. Open all year; campsites open May through September. On US 129, about 95 miles from Great Smoky Mountains NP. (770) 297-3000.

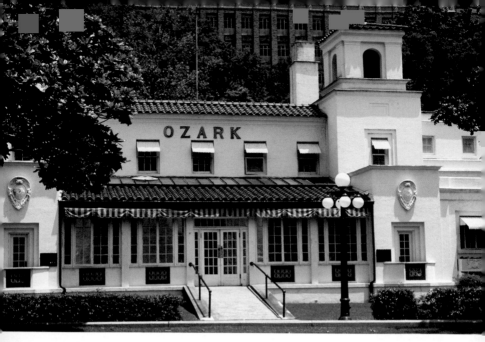

The Hotel Eastman, which opened in 1890 in Hot Springs

▶ HOT SPRINGS

ARKANSAS
ESTABLISHED MARCH 4, 1921
5,550 acres

Most national parks cover hundreds of thousands of acres, are far from city streets, and keep natural resources away from commercial users . . . but not Hot Springs. This smallest of national parks borders a city that has made an industry out of tapping and dispensing the park's major resource: mineral-rich waters of hot springs.

The heart of this peculiar park is Bathhouse Row on Central Avenue, the main street of Hot Springs, Arkansas. Rising above Central Avenue is Hot Springs Mountain, from which the waters flow. The mountain's lower western side once was coated with tufa, a milky-colored, porous rock formed of minerals deposited from the hot springs' constant cascade.

When Hot Springs prospered as a health spa from the mid-19th

through mid-20th centuries, promoters covered, piped, and diverted the springs into Central Avenue bathhouses. They also prettified the slope by covering it with tons of dirt and planting grass and shrubs. "Ever since then," a longtime Hot Springs resident says, "it's been afflicted by eastern landscape architects who can't stand the sight of rocks."

The park calls itself the "longest preserved area in the national park system" because in 1832, 40 years before Yellowstone became the first national park, Congress and President Andrew Jackson set aside the hot springs as a special reservation. The federal land became a national park in 1921. By then Hot Springs had long been famous as a spa where people "took the waters," seeking relief from bunions, rheumatism, and other afflictions.

The park preserves the mountains that surround the hot springs and act as their "recharge zone," and the "discharge zone," which contains 47 thermal springs. Each day about 700,000 gallons of water—at 143°F—flow from the springs into a complex piping and reservoir system. This supplies water to commercial baths and to free "jug fountains," where people flock daily to fill containers with the odorless, fresh-tasting, chemical-free water.

How to Get There
From Little Rock, about 55 miles west on I-30, US 70, and Ark. 7; from the south, Ark. 7; from the west, US 70 or US 270. Airport: Little Rock.

When to Go
Year-round. Summers are hot and July is crowded. Try the late fall, when mountains around Hot

Springs flowing over Tufa Terrace

Springs produce spectacular foliage. Winter is usually short and mild; four-petaled bluets, the first of many wildflowers, appear in February.

How to Visit
Walk Central Avenue's Bathhouse Row, then continue north to explore on the genteel trails of an urban hillside. To see the rugged side of the park, hike the woodland trails of Gulpha Gorge.

BATHHOUSE ROW
4 city blocks; 2 hours

In the early years of the 20th century, elegant buildings lined a stretch of **Central Avenue** dubbed Bathhouse Row. In later years, as medical science's faith in the therapeutic powers of hot springs faded, so did the bathhouses. But you can still enjoy the mystique of taking the waters. First visit the **Hot Springs National Park Visitor Center** (in the former Fordyce Bathhouse), a restored "temple of health and beauty" adorned with stained-glass windows and statuary. In rooms full of gleaming plumbing and luxurious tubs, you walk through a **museum** of the ritual, which in its full form involved three weeks of daily baths and massage. The **Buckstaff Bathhouse** offers visitors a traditional bath. The **Quapaw Bathhouse,** opened in 2008, operates as a modern-day spa with public pools and salon services. (Some hotels also have baths; ask for information at the visitor center.) The **Ozark Bathhouse** is now open with the **Museum of Contemporary Art of Hot Springs.**

THERMAL FEATURES
a half mile; 2 hours

At the corner of Central Avenue and Fountain Street look for **Tufa Rock,** the

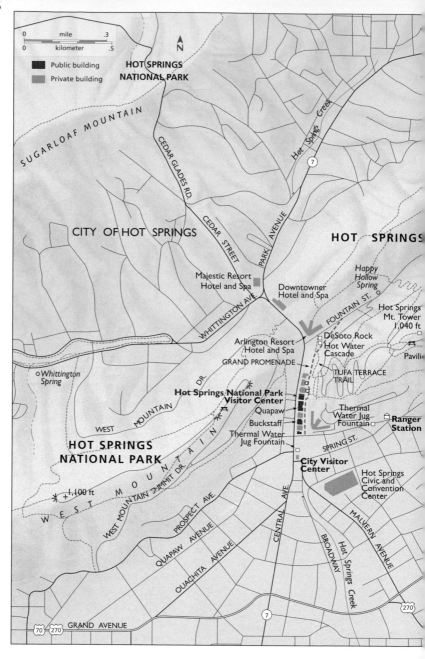

huge boulder on **Arlington Lawn.** Visit the hot springs pool where you can see and touch the water. Beware, it is hot. Head up the trail adjacent to the **Hot Water Cascade,** created in 1982. The water flowing here began its journey up to 4,000 years ago when it fell as rain and seeped through fractures. Heated deep belowground, the water returns through the faults in the rock of the mountain in a year or two, hardly enough time to cool off.

The **Tufa Terrace Trail,** near the Hot Water Cascade, takes you by many concealed springs. To get there, cross the **Grand Promenade,** a landscaped brick walkway that runs behind the bathhouses.

The springs are sealed off—and thus kept free from contamination—by locked green bunkers that jut out of the lawns carpeting the slope. Historically when some of the hillside springs were open, men and women discreetly took turns soaking their feet at one of them; at another, people cooked eggs. To see more water bubbling out of the earth, follow the trail to **Open Springs** behind the Maurice Bathhouse. Here, the two springs flow into a collecting pool, where you can safely touch the water.

Go up the stairs and finish your trek on the **Grand Promenade.** The walkway, which took 30 years to build and landscape, serves as a pleasant transition between the formal architecture of the bathhouses and the trails of the wooded hillside.

GULPHA GORGE

1.6 miles round-trip; 2 hours

To find the more traditional terrain of a national park, leave **Hot Springs** on Ark. 7 heading north and turn right onto US 70B for Gulpha Gorge Campground, about 3 miles from downtown Hot Springs. Near the amphitheater pick up the **Gulpha Gorge Trail,** which crosses **Gulpha Creek** and courses a woodland rich in dogwood and redbud; in spring and early summer wildflowers flank the trail. In less than a mile the trail intersects with another up to **Goat Rock,** a fine overlook for viewing the mountains. In nearby quarries, Indians once mined novaculite for making arrowheads and spearpoints; it is used today as a whetstone.

The tufa created by the cascade's splashing waters builds up at a rate of an eighth of an inch a year. The rare brilliant blue-green algae is one of 30 plant species that can survive in the hot waters.

INFORMATION & ACTIVITIES

VISITOR & INFORMATION CENTER
Hot Springs National Park Visitor Center, in the middle of Bathhouse Row. Open daily. For information call (501) 620-6715.

SEASONS & ACCESSIBILITY
Open all year. Bathing facilities open generally Monday through Saturday, most Sundays, all year.

HEADQUARTERS
101 Reserve Street, Hot Springs, AR 71901. Phone (501) 623-2824. www.nps.gov/hosp

ENTRANCE FEE
None, but fees for thermal baths.

PETS
Not allowed in buildings; otherwise permitted on leashes.

ACCESSIBLE SERVICES
Visitor center is fully accessible; the Hot Springs Discovery Tour and the Bathhouse Row Tours are partially accessible.

THINGS TO DO
Free ranger-led activities: hikes and bathhouse tours. Also, audiovisual and educational exhibits, hiking, horseback riding (no stables in park); bathing facilities offering thermal baths, whirlpools, steam cabinets, hot packs, massages.

SPECIAL ADVISORY
• Bathing in thermal waters not recommended for people with certain ailments; consult your doctor if in doubt.

CAMPING
One campground, **Gulpha Gorge,** with 14-day limit. Open all year on first-come, first-served basis. Fees $10 per night for tent camping, $24 per night for campsites with RV utility hookups.

HOTELS, MOTELS, & INNS
(unless otherwise noted, rates are for 2 persons in a double room, high season)
In Hot Springs, AR:
1890 Williams House Inn 420 Quapaw Ave., 71901. (800) 756-4635 or (501) 624-4275. 9 units. $129-$229, incl. breakfast. AC.
Arlington Resort Hotel & Spa 239 Central Ave., 71901. (800) 643-1502. 478 units. $99-$350. AC, 2 pools, 2 restaurants.
Austin Hotel 305 Malvern Ave., 71901. (501) 623-6600. 200 units. $110. AC, pool, restaurants.
Sun Bay Resort 4810 Central Ave., 71913. (800) 468-0055 or (501) 525-4691. 115 condos. $119-$219. AC, 3 pools, restaurants.
The Springs Hotel and Spa 135 Central Ave. 71901. (501) 624-5521; 133 units. $89; AC, pool, restaurants.

For additional accommodations, write or call the Hot Springs Convention & Visitors Bureau, 134 Convention Blvd., Hot Springs, AR 71901. (800) 772-2489 or (501) 321-2835, www.hotsprings.org.

EXCURSIONS

OUACHITA NATIONAL FOREST
HOT SPRINGS, ARKANSAS

This pine-hardwood forest has lakes, springs, waterfalls, and the Ouachita River. Six wilderness areas. 1.8 million acres, part in Oklahoma. Hiking, boating, fishing, horseback riding, hunting, water sports. 24 campgrounds, picnic areas, handicapped access. Open all year. Entrances on US 270, about 10 miles west of Hot Springs NP. (501) 321-5202.

HOLLA BEND NATIONAL WILDLIFE REFUGE
DARDANELLE, ARKANSAS

Wintering bald eagles and immense flocks of migratory waterfowl share this site along the Arkansas River. 7,055 acres. Hiking, boating, fishing, hunting, scenic drives. Boat ramp. Open all year, dawn to dusk. Off Ark. 154, about 60 miles from Hot Springs NP. (479) 229-4300.

OZARK NATIONAL FOREST
RUSSELLVILLE, ARKANSAS

Oak, hickory, and pine cover the high Ozark mountain bluffs. Many streams and lakes offer excellent fishing. Features Blanchard Springs Caverns and five wilderness areas. 1.2 million acres. Hiking, boating, fishing, hunting, horseback riding, scenic drives, water sports. 359 campsites, 9 cabins, boat ramps, picnic areas, handicapped access. Open all year, including some of the campsites. Information in Russellville on US 64, 80 miles north of Hot Springs NP. (479) 964-7200.

BUFFALO NATIONAL RIVER
HARRISON, ARKANSAS

This park preserves 135 miles of the Buffalo River and adjacent lands. White water on upper river, calmer stretches on lower. 95,700 acres. Boating, fishing, hunting, swimming. 12 campgrounds, restaurant, picnic areas. Open all year, including most campsites. Headquarters at Harrison off Ark. 65, about 170 miles from Hot Springs NP. (870) 439-2502.

HOT SPRINGS

Fog over lake at sunrise

▶ISLE ROYALE

MICHIGAN
ESTABLISHED APRIL 3, 1940
571,790 acres

Out of the vastness of Lake Superior rises an island known more for its immigrant wolves and moose than for its splendors as a park. But the people who discover Isle Royale treat this isolated realm like no other park: Isle Royale visitors typically stay there 3.5 days, while the average visit to a national park is about 4 hours.

Most people get to the 45-mile-long island aboard a commercial or Park Service boat. As soon as they touch land in this wilderness park, they are on their own. They must pack in what they need and carry out their refuse.

This is rough, untamed country. Waterways may be fogbound and trails muddy. Blackflies and mosquitoes may descend upon hikers in swarms. And, because campsites cannot be reserved, a backpacker is never certain where the day's trek may end.

"It's not like deciding to drive into Yellowstone, see Old Faithful, and drive out," a ranger says. In an entire year Isle Royale gets fewer people than Yellowstone sees in a day.

Everyone who lands on Isle Royale—even day-trippers—must stop near dockside to hear a ranger talk about low-impact hiking and camping. For example, water must be boiled for 2 minutes or filtered;

chemical purifiers will not wipe out tapeworm cysts.

Human hikers share trails with wolves and moose. They are descendants of the mainlanders that made Isle Royale an unexpected ark—moose presumably by swimming to it in the early 1900s; wolves likely by walking across the frozen lake between 1945 and 1950. Scientists have been studying the interplay of predator and prey since 1958.

On the trails, all you can expect to see are the animals' tracks and droppings, although quietly grazing moose do surprise hikers, particularly in swamps or dense forest. On beaver ponds you may spot the rippling Vs of the ponds' creators. At campsites watch for foxes looking for a hand-out. Remember: Feeding the animals is illegal. It is not healthy for them and increases the likelihood that they will scavenge for people's food and damage equipment.

How to Get There

Make reservations well in advance for passenger boats from Houghton or Copper Harbor, Michigan, or Grand Portage, Minnesota. Interpretive programs are held aboard the *Ranger III* between Houghton and Isle Royale. For information about boats and charter seaplane service, see Information & Activities p. 85. Isle Royale is 56 miles from the Michigan mainland, 18 miles from Minnesota's shore, 2 hours or 22 miles from Grand Portage. Airports: Houghton, Michigan, and Duluth, Minnesota.

When to Go

Late June to September; park closes from November to mid-April. Mosquitoes, blackflies, gnats are most pesky in June and July. Summer can be cool (40°F at night). Blueberries

and thimbleberries ripen in late July and August.

How to Visit

Although 1-day visits are feasible at **Rock Harbor** or **Windigo,** you need a longer stay to appreciate the wild beauty of Isle Royale. A 1-day visitor must sandwich a couple of hours of sightseeing between boat arrival and departure. Voyages take 2 to 6 hours, depending on the starting point. The best way to see the park is to backpack to campsites strung along the park's 165 miles of trails. Noncampers who plan well ahead can reserve lodgings at Rock Harbor and explore on tour boats and on foot.

WINDIGO

a full day

Take the *Sea Hunter,* a concessioner passenger boat that makes the trip from Grand Portage, Minnesota, in 1.5 hours—the shortest from any port serving Isle Royale. On the way into fjordlike **Washington Harbor,** watch for the buoy marking the resting place of the *America,* a 183-foot lake steamer that went down in 1928; the wreck rests at a sharp angle, its ghostly bow about 2 feet below the surface. Scuba divers, with permits, frequently prowl this and the other nine major wrecks around Isle Royale.

As soon as you land, check at the ranger station for the next **Windigo Nature Walk,** a 1-hour ramble around this western entrance to the park that explores many of the area's natural and cultural resources.

If you miss the ranger-guided walk, try the **Windigo Nature Trail,** a 1.25-mile loop that shows the power that Lake Superior exerts on an island molded by fire and ice. You'll learn how the island was born: As

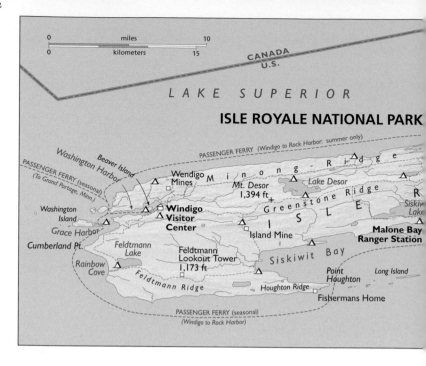

glacial ice retreated some 10,000 years ago, Isle Royale rose above what would become Lake Superior. Gouges in the barren rocks became lakes. Early migrants—lichens, mosses, bird-borne seeds—drifted into cracks and crannies, beginning the long work of building soil. Animals also found their way onto Isle Royale, and an ecosystem emerged. It still evolves, with some animals appearing, as did the wolves and moose, and some animals disappearing, as did caribou and coyotes. Be sure to take the short side trip to the fenced-in **Moose Exclosure,** which shows how differently a forest grows when moose don't munch on it. Your stay—about 2.5 hours—will depend on your boat's schedule. So you may have time to stroll westward a while along the **Feldtmann Lake Trail.** This shoreline stretch gives you a view of **Beaver Island** and the harbor's forested northern shore.

ROCK HARBOR

1 or more days

A 1-day visit to Rock Harbor, the park's eastern gateway, can be tight. The voyage aboard *Isle Royale Queen IV* from Copper Harbor takes about 3 hours. You have 3 hours to explore the Rock Harbor area.

If you can stay longer and aren't a backpacker, Rock Harbor offers many relatively easy sojourns. But make advance reservations at the Rock Harbor Lodge (see Information & Activities p. 85).

Begin with a walk along **Stoll Trail,** a 4-mile loop that starts at Rock Harbor Lodge and winds through forest and plank-pathed bog. After about half a mile, you'll come to an area where Indians once chipped away, stone on stone, at shallow mining pits to extract outcrops of copper. Unmarked, these pits are hard to detect. Mining here began around

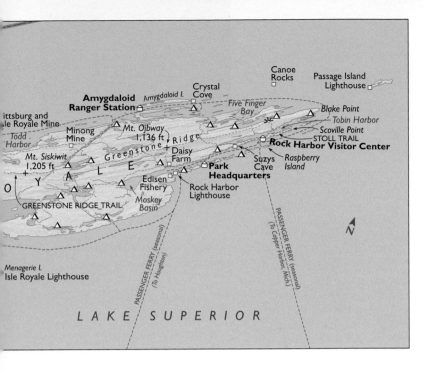

2500 B.C. and continued for at least 1,500 years. The copper, traded along the upper Mississippi Valley, was formed into fishhooks, knives, and awls. More than a thousand mining pits have been found on Isle Royale.

Continue another 1.5 miles, mostly along a rocky shore, to craggy **Scoville Point,** a fine spot for viewing some of the roughly 200 rocky islets that form the Isle Royale archipelago. On the way back you can switch to a branch trail that clings to the forested shore of **Tobin Harbor.** As the trail nears the lodge, you can see traces of **Smithwick Mine,** one of many relics of 19th-century mining ventures.

For a small round-trip fee you can take a shuttle boat from Rock Harbor across a half mile of usually calm water to **Raspberry Island,** where a 1-mile trail introduces you to a boreal forest—white spruce, balsam fir, paper birch, aspen—and a bog. You'll also see a pit dug in 1848 in a vain search for copper. Bring a picnic.

Another boat *(fee)* takes you on a half-day, guided tour into history. The first stop is **Edisen Fishery,** which belonged to the late Pete Edisen, one of the last commercial fishermen on the island. The Park Service has restored his jumble of moss-chinked log cabins and shacks made of odds and ends. Here park employees demonstrate mid-20th-century fishing techniques for visitors. A short trail leads to the **Rock Harbor Lighthouse,** which contains a maritime exhibit. Erected in 1855 to guide

Bull moose feeding on water plants

ore ships, the lighthouse closed in 1859 when the mines shut down; it reopened between 1874 and 1879 during a second mining venture.

INTO THE BACKCOUNTRY

3 to 5 days

To savor Isle Royale's isolated grandeur you must venture into the island's great beyond. Plan your 3- or 5-day stay around passenger boat arrivals and departures.

A sample 5-day itinerary: Arrive at Rock Harbor on Monday aboard the *Isle Royale Queen IV* and hike southwest along the **Rock Harbor Trail** that courses forest, bog, and slanted rocks and roots. At not quite 2 miles, look for a sign to **Suzys Cave,** about 80 yards up a side trail. The cave is an unusual, water-carved arch. At 3 miles is Three Mile Campground. Stay here and head out next morning on the 4.5-mile shore trail to **Daisy Farm;** in this spot daisies have flourished where vegetables never would.

You can camp here for 3 days and start back early Friday to meet the returning *Queen.* Or split the hike into 2 days by spending Thursday night at Three Mile Campground.

While at Daisy Farm, climb **Mount Ojibway Trail,** a moderate 1.75-mile ascent up the 1,136-foot mountain, which is topped by a lookout tower. You're welcome to climb as far as the cabin, which houses a solar-powered, air-monitoring station. The Park Service runs a network of such monitors to check on air quality in 65 national park areas. From the tower take the **Greenstone Ridge Trail,** which runs about 40 miles along the backbone of the island. About 1.5 miles west of the tower look for the wooden post

Gray wolf

marking the **Daisy Farm Trail,** which winds back to the campground.

THE WOLVES OF ISLE ROYALE

Visitors to Isle Royale probably will never see a gray wolf. Wolves live in packs as social animals, but avoid people. Only the dominant male and female—the alpha pair—mate and produce young. Others help protect and feed the pups born each spring.

Hundreds of thousands of wolves once roamed North America. But early settlers killed or drove away most of them. Today North America has as few as 66,000 gray wolves, principally in Canada and Alaska.

When the first wolves arrived on Isle Royale, between 1945 and 1950, presumably by crossing frozen Lake Superior, they found a growing moose herd with no natural predators. The wolves hunted the old, the young, and the sickly. Both species prospered, the wolves increasing to 50 in 4 packs.

By 1980 the smaller moose herd provided few easy targets, and the wolf population began to fall. As moose rose, the wolves' decline mysteriously continued. The relationship has been in sync in recent years, but remains in a fluctuating state.

INFORMATION & ACTIVITIES

VISITOR & INFORMATION CENTERS
Windigo Visitor Center at west end of island, **Rock Harbor Visitor Center** at east end. Both open daily in season. Phone park headquarters for information.

SEASONS & ACCESSIBILITY
Open mid-April through October, reached by boat or seaplane only; full services available mid-June through August. $4 per day fee. Weather and rough waters may delay departures; allow extra time. Mainland headquarters open year-round.

HEADQUARTERS
800 East Lakeshore Dr., Houghton, MI 49931. Phone (906) 482-0984. www.nps .gov/isro

BOAT & SEAPLANE INFORMATION
Reservations required 1 to 2 months in advance. Contact park for boat schedule from **Houghton** to Rock Harbor. (The Park Service's boat, *Ranger III,* will transport boats 20 feet and under between those points.)
• For boats from **Copper Harbor** to Rock Harbor, contact Royale Line, Box 24, Copper Harbor, MI 49918. (906) 289-4437. www.isleroyale.com
• For boats from **Grand Portage** to Windigo and Rock Harbor, contact Grand Portage-Isle Royale Transportation Line, P.O. Box 10529, White Bear Lake, MN 55110. (651) 653-5872.
• For seaplane information, contact Royale Air Service Inc., P.O. Box 15184, Duluth, MN 55815. (877) 359-4753 or (218) 721-0405.

PETS
Not allowed on boats or within park boundaries, which extend 4.5 miles into Lake Superior.

ACCESSIBLE SERVICES
Park headquarters at Houghton, Rock Harbor Lodge, both visitor centers, and a campsite at Daisy Farm, accessible. Boats to island require assistance.

THINGS TO DO
Free naturalist-led nature walks and evening programs. Lighthouse, copper mine, and Edisen Fishery tours. Also, boating (motorized crafts permitted on Lake Superior only), canoeing (rentals at Windigo and Rock Harbor; permit required), kayaking, hiking, scuba diving (permit required), fishing (license required for Lake Superior only), boat cruises to the outer islands.

SPECIAL ADVISORIES
• Expect sudden squalls and rough seas on Lake Superior. Do not try to take boats under 20 feet across. Have the park service transport small boats.

CAMPING
Thirty-six backcountry camping areas; 1- to 5-day limit. Camping allowed mid-April through Oct. First come, first served. No fees but permit required (from visitor centers). Group camping (reservations required) at 17 areas; contact park headquarters for information.

HOTELS, MOTELS, & INNS
(unless otherwise noted, rates are for 2 persons in a double room, high season)

INSIDE THE PARK:
Rock Harbor Lodge P.O. Box 605, Houghton, MI 49931. (906) 337-4993. From Oct. to April write c/o P.O. Box 207, Mammoth Cave, KY 42259. (270) 758-2001. 60 lodge rooms. $223-$254. 20 cabins with kitchenettes $222-$246. Restaurant. Late May–early Sept.
OUTSIDE THE PARK:
In Copper Harbor, MI 49918:
Bella Vista Motel P.O. Box 26. (906) 289-4213. 30 units. $48-$65. May–Oct.
Keweenaw Mountain Lodge US 41. (906) 289-4403. 42 units. $95-$189. Restaurant. May–mid-Oct and Dec.–March.
Lake Fanny Hooe Lodge 505 2nd St. (off US 41). (800) 426-4451. 17 units. $79-$99. Year-round. 64 campsites. $28-$40. Mid-May–mid-Oct.
In Grand Portage, MN 55605:
Grand Portage Lodge & Casino 70 Casino Dr. (800) 543-1384 or (218) 475-2401. 100 units. $95-$115. Pool, restaurant.
In Houghton, MI 49931:
Magnuson Franklin Square Inn 820 Shelden Ave. (888) 487-1700 or (906) 487-1700. 104 units. $109. AC, pool, rest.

EXCURSIONS

GRAND PORTAGE NATIONAL MONUMENT
GRAND PORTAGE, MINNESOTA

In the 18th and 19th centuries, voyageurs paddling for the North West Company converged at this central supply depot. Tour the reconstructed stockade, great hall, kitchen, and canoe warehouse. Open late May to early October. The Grand Portage Trail, open all year, follows the nearly 9-mile route used by voyageurs to avoid the rapids and falls of the Pigeon River. 710 acres. Hiking, historic exhibits, cross-country skiing, snowshoeing. Handicapped access. Off US 61, about 22 miles from Isle Royale NP by boat to Grand Portage. (218) 475-0123.

CHEQUAMEGON-NICOLET NATIONAL FOREST
PARK FALLS, WISCONSIN

Chequamegon (Sho-WAH-ma-gon) means "place of shallow water." Laced with many lakes, streams, and a river, Wisconsin's only national forest, Chequamegon-Nicolet is a lush medley of spruce, maple, aspen, and pine. 1.5 million acres. Bird-watching, boating, hunting, scenic drives, nature study, photography, cross-country skiing, snowshoeing. Campgrounds, picnic areas. Open all year. Headquarters on Wisc. 13, 220 miles from Isle Royale NP. (715) 762-2461.

HIAWATHA NATIONAL FOREST
ESCANABA, MICHIGAN

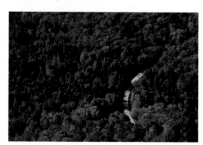

This mixed evergreen-and-hardwood forest dotted with lakes descends to the shores of Lake Superior, Lake Michigan, and Lake Huron. Six wilderness areas and parts of the North Country National Scenic Trail. 893,348 acres. Boating, fishing, horseback riding, hunting, scenic drives, winter sports. 25 campgrounds, handicapped access. Open all year; most campsites open mid-May to mid-September. Information at Rapid River, Escanaba, Munising, and other locations. More than 300 miles from Isle Royale NP (via ferry). (906) 786-4062.

APOSTLE ISLANDS
NATIONAL LAKESHORE
BAYFIELD, WISCONSIN

This national lakeshore encompasses 21 of the 22 remote, densely forested Apostle Islands and 12 miles of mainland shoreline. Access to islands by boat; commercial and charter boats, charter fishing trips available. 42,160 land acres. Hiking, boating, fishing, winter sports, sea kayaking. 65 campsites (permits required), picnic areas, handicapped access. Open all year, including campsites. Visitor center in Bayfield near Wisc. 13, about 250 miles from Isle Royale NP (via ferry). (715) 779-3397.

PICTURED ROCKS
NATIONAL LAKESHORE
MUNISING, MICHIGAN

Sandstone cliffs sculptured by nature into formations resembling castles and palisades give this first national lakeshore (1966) its name. The site also features extensive dunes and banks, sand beaches, forests, inland lakes, streams, and waterfalls. 71,400 acres. Hiking, boating, backpacking, fishing, hunting, winter sports, water sports. 66 campsites, picnic areas, handicapped access. Open all year; campsites open mid-May to October. Visitor center at Munising on Mich. 28, about 335 miles from Isle Royale NP (via ferry). (906) 387-3700 or (906) 387-2607.

OTTAWA NATIONAL FOREST
IRONWOOD, MICHIGAN

Lakes, streams, rivers, and waterfalls abound in this ski-country forest. Also features three wilderness areas, Black River Harbor Recreation Area, and the North Country National Scenic Trail. Nearly one million acres. Hiking, canoeing, kayaking, fishing, hunting, winter sports. 30 campgrounds, boat ramps, picnic areas, handicapped access. Open all year; campsites May to December. Visitor center in Watersmeet on US 2, about 140 miles from Isle Royale NP (via ferry). (906) 932-1330.

ISLE ROYALE

Drapery Room on the Frozen Niagara Tour

▶ MAMMOTH CAVE

KENTUCKY
ESTABLISHED JULY 1, 1941
52,830 acres

Under a swath of Kentucky hills and hollows is a limestone labyrinth that became the heartland of a national park. The surface of Mammoth Cave National Park encompasses about 80 square miles. No one knows how big the underside is. More than 365 miles of the five-level cave system have been mapped, and new caves are continually being discovered. Two types of stone underlie Mammoth's hilly woodlands.

A sandstone and shale cap, as thick as 50 feet in places, acts as an umbrella over limestone ridges. The umbrella leaks at places called sinkholes, from which surface water makes its way underground, eroding the limestone into a honeycomb of caverns.

Mammoth, the world's longest known cave system, a United Nations World Heritage site and the core area of an international biosphere reserve, still is as "grand, gloomy, and peculiar" as it was when Stephen Bishop, a young slave and early guide, described it. By a flickering lard-oil lamp he found and mapped some of Mammoth's passages. Bishop died in 1857. His grave, like his life, is part of Mammoth; it lies in the Old Guide's Cemetery near the entrance.

Most visitors see the eerie beauty of the caverns on some of the 10 miles of passages available for tours. Rangers dispense geological lore and tell tales about real and imagined happenings 200 or 300 feet down. The tours are hikes inside the Earth; uphill stretches can be hard going for some visitors. Few seem frightened; people terrified by darkness or tight spots naturally avoid caves. Rangers say they rarely have problems guiding the 390,000 men, women, and children who venture below yearly.

Mammoth does not glamorize the underworld with garish lighting. You never forget that you are deep in the Earth. And nowhere else can you get a better lesson in the totality of darkness and the miracle of light. Usually on a tour a ranger gathers everyone and, after a warning, switches off the lights. The darkness is sudden, absolute. Then the ranger lights a match and the tiny dot of light magically spreads, illuminating a circle of astonished faces.

How to Get There

Mammoth Cave, 9 miles northwest of I-65, is nearly equidistant (about 85 miles) between Louisville, Kentucky, and Nashville, Tennessee. From the south, take the exit at Park City and head northwest on Ky. 255 to the park; from the north, take the exit at Cave City and head northwest on Ky. 70 to the park. Airports: Nashville, Tenn., and Louisville, Ky.

When to Go

Year-round. Underground, all days are about the same; temperatures in interior passages fluctuate from the mid-50s to the low 60s. Summer brings the most people, and a greater variety of tours are offered. Though there are fewer tours the rest of the year, they are less crowded.

How to Visit

The tours vary greatly; pick ones to fit your time and stamina. All require you to purchase a ticket. Reservations are strongly advised in summer, on holidays, and on spring and fall weekends. For a half-day visit, you might take the **Historic Tour,** which combines geology with Mammoth's rich history, or the challenging **Introduction to Caving Tour.** If you plan to stay longer, consider the fairly strenuous 4-mile **Grand Avenue Tour** (there are three steep hills, each nearly 90 feet high). To enjoy the caves safely and comfortably, wear shoes with nonskid soles and take a jacket. Complete your underground trips with a river trip or a walk on the **River Styx Spring Trail.**

The least arduous cave tour (0.25 mile, 75 minutes) is the **Frozen Niagara Tour.** A modified version of the tour has only 6 steps each way (plus an optional 49) and is designed for visitors who want a short and easy trip. The toughest challenge is the 5-mile, 6-hour, belly-crawling **Wild Cave Tour,** offered daily in summer and weekends year-round. By reservation.

HISTORIC TOUR

2 miles; 2 hours

You leave daylight and walk into dimly lit gloom at the **Historic Entrance,** discovered by pioneers in the 1790s and by Indians thousands of years before. Near the entrance, at the **Rotunda,** 140 feet down, are relics of the cave's use as a nitrate mine. Slaves hauled in logs, built leaching vats, and filled them with cave dirt.

Water, poured into the vats, trickled into a trough as brine. Two pipelines of hollowed-out logs carried water in and brine out. The residue, nitrate crystals, was used to make gunpowder, a good deal of which found its way into the War of 1812.

Broadway, an underground avenue, leads to a spot called **Methodist Church,** where services may have been conducted in the 1800s. Farther on, **Booth's Amphitheater** recalls the visit of actor Edwin Booth. Here, Edwin, brother of assassin John Wilkes Booth, recited Hamlet's famous soliloquy.

The **Bottomless Pit** looked that way to early visitors; it's 105 feet deep; looking up, you see its dome 38 feet above. (The top of a shaft is a dome, the bottom a pit.) On your way back toward the entrance you pass through **Fat Man's Misery,** a passage polished smooth by generations of squirming spelunkers. You emerge into **Great Relief Hall,** a large chamber where you are able to stand upright. Then back on the trail for the final spectacles: **Mammoth Dome**—192 feet from floor to ceiling—carved by water dripping through a sinkhole, and the **Ruins of Karnak,** a cluster of gleaming limestone pillars that look like an Egyptian temple.

INTRODUCTION TO CAVING TOUR

1 mile; about 3 hours

Cave exploring, otherwise known as spelunking, can be fun and challenging. Led by park rangers, the Introduction to Caving Tour gives visitors 10 and up some firsthand

Historic Entrance

Visitor Center

Rotunda

Booth's Amphitheater

BROADWAY

Display of Indian Artifacts

Nitrate Mine Works

Methodist Church

Fat Man's Misery

Mammoth Dome

MAIN

Sidesaddle Pit

Bottomless Pit

Tuberculosis Hospital Ruins

Great Relief Hall

River Styx

Lake Lethe

Cascade Hall

Ruins of Karnak

Echo River
360 feet below surface

Eyeless, colorless cave amphipod

Cave cricket on a Mammoth ceiling

experience in underground exploration. Offered daily in summer and on weekends in spring and fall, this trip involves hands-and-knees crawling, climbing, stooping, and even canyon-walking, with feet on different ledges and nothing but air in between. Straying from traditional walking paths, you will visit the twisting, convoluted canyons and crawls of **Fox Avenue,** emerging at **Frozen Niagara.** Along the way rangers will explain the geologic processes that result in the varied subterranean spaces. You will also learn the basic rules of safe caving, including what you should do if you ever get lost.

Helmets and lights are provided. Participants should bring knee pads *(no Rollerblade type or hard plastic knee pads allowed).* Long pants

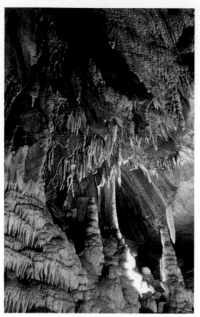

Cave formations in the Frozen Niagara area

and shoes with good traction are required; a jacket and gloves are recommended. Restrooms are not available. Youths 10 to 15 must be accompanied by an adult.

GRAND AVENUE TOUR
4 miles; 4.5 hours

The tour (likely to be very crowded in summer) begins with a 5- to 10-minute bus ride from the visitor center to the **Carmichael Entrance,** a concrete bunker and stairway that leads down to **Cleaveland Avenue,** a long tubular chamber tunneled out by a river. Its walls sparkle with flowery patches of gypsum. The white mineral crystallizes below the surface of the limestone from seeping moisture, then bursts out in blossomlike designs (it takes a thousand years for one cubic inch of gypsum to form) that are fascinating.

About a mile beyond is the **Snowball Room,** where the tour stops for lunch. (Food service here is limited to sandwiches, candy, and drinks.)

Another river canyon, **Boone Avenue,** takes you 300 feet into the Earth along a passage so narrow you can touch both walls. The tour

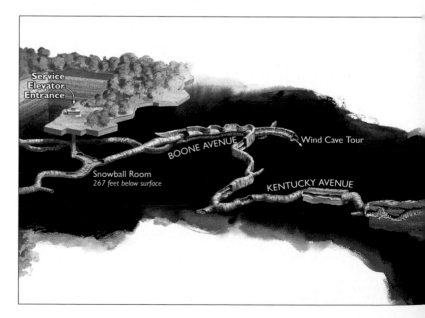

ends at **Frozen Niagara,** a massive cascade of flowstone—the legacy of mineral-laden water that seeped here, vanished, and left behind the shimmering stalactites and stalagmites. Such formations build up at the rate of about a cubic inch every 200 years.

BOAT TRIPS & HIKES

To explore the **Green River,** which winds 25 miles through the park, you can ask about canoeing at the visitor center—several canoe/kayak liveries service the park. Or you can walk the **River Styx Spring Trail,** which leads to the river. The trail, which begins near the Historic Entrance to Mammoth, shows the interplay between surface features and the cave's underworld. At **River Styx Spring** the water emerges from the cave and flows into the Green River. Farther along the shore, you see **Cave Island,** covered in logs from past flooding.

Most of the park's 85 miles of trails are in the backcountry across the Green River. Since within the

park, there are no bridges over the river, you can drive onto the Green River Ferry at a crossing southwest of the visitor center, or go to Houchins Ferry at the western edge of the park. Ferries have carried people and their vehicles across the river since the 1800s. While at the Green River ferry landing, try the short **Echo River Spring Trail** that leads past a series of pools formed when the underground river emerges from the caves.

Head north on **Green River Ferry Road** to Maple Springs group campground and trailhead. A gravel road there leads to **Good Spring Church,** founded in 1842. Nearby, you can pick up a 10-mile walking trail that meanders through forests that are slowly reclaiming land that was once cleared for farming and logging.

Before leaving the park, make one last stop at **Sloan's Crossing Pond** where a depression in the sandstone has collected enough water to create a tiny ecosystem.

MAMMOTH CAVE

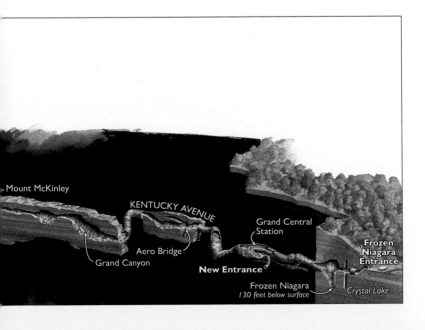

Mount McKinley

KENTUCKY AVENUE

Grand Central Station

Aero Bridge

Grand Canyon

New Entrance

Frozen Niagara
130 feet below surface

Frozen Niagara Entrance

Crystal Lake

INFORMATION & ACTIVITIES

VISITOR & INFORMATION CENTER

Visitor Center, 1 Mammoth Cave Parkway, open daily. If space is available, you can buy tickets there for all tours except the Wild Cave, which requires advance reservations. Tours sell out quickly, especially in summer and on spring and fall weekends; tickets also available in advance through the NRRS (see p. 10) or online at www.recreation.gov. For more information on ranger-led activities, call (270) 758-2180.

SEASONS & ACCESSIBILITY

Open all year. Visitors must join a guided tour to view caves.

HEADQUARTERS

P.O. Box 7, Mammoth Cave Parkway, Mammoth Cave, KY 42259. Phone (270) 758-2180. www.nps.gov/maca

ENTRANCE FEE

None. Fees required for tours, $5-$24 for adults and youths; free for children under 6. Higher fees for special tours; the Wild Cave Tour is $48 per person.

PETS

Permitted on leashes except in caves and visitor center. Kennel facilities through the Mammoth Cave Hotel (see below).

ACCESSIBLE SERVICES

Visitor center, some sites at Mammoth Cave Campground, and restrooms are accessible. The 0.5-mile Pond Walk, 0.25-mile Heritage Trail, and 0.1-mile Sand Cave Trail are fully accessible.

THINGS TO DO

Naturalist-led activities: cave tours (12 in summer, 5 the rest of the year), children's exploration (Junior Ranger) program, nature walks, evening programs. Nature trails, fishing (no license required), horseback riding, canoeing, bicycling.

SPECIAL ADVISORIES

• Cave tours are strenuous; talk with a park staff if you have difficulty walking or have trouble with your heart or lungs.
• Visitors must follow explicit park instructions intended to minimize the spread of white-nose syndrome, a fungus threatening bats in the eastern U.S.
• Wear sturdy shoes and take a jacket.

OVERNIGHT BACKPACKING

Permits required. They are free and available at the visitor center.

CAMPGROUNDS

Three campgrounds, all with a 14-day limit. Fees: $12-$30 per night. Tent and RV sites at **Mammoth Cave;** no hookups; showers and laundry nearby for a fee; open year-round. Tents only at **Maple Springs Group Campgrounds,** open March through Nov., and at **Houchins Ferry,** open all year, first come, first served. Use NRRS (see p. 10) to reserve at Mammoth Cave and Maple Springs. Food services in park.

HOTELS, MOTELS, & INNS

(unless otherwise noted, rates are for 2 persons in a double room, high season)

INSIDE THE PARK:
Mammoth Cave Hotel Mammoth Cave, KY 42259. (270) 758-2225. 92 units. $89-$117. Cottages. $60-$104. AC, restaurant.

OUTSIDE THE PARK:
In Cave City, KY 42127:
Best Western Kentucky Inn 1009 Doyle Ave. (800) 528-1234 or (270) 773-3161. 50 units. $60-$99, incl. breakfast. AC, pool.
America's Best Value Inn 822 Mammoth Cave St. (270) 773-2151. 110 units. $65. AC, pool.
Days Inn 102 Gardner Ln. (270) 773-3101. 89 units. $65-$75. AC, pool.

In Park City, KY 42160:
Park Mammoth Resort (I-65 and US 31W) P.O. Box 307. (270) 749-4101. 92 units. $99. AC, pool, restaurant.

In Bowling Green, KY 42104:
Bowling Green Bed & Breakfast 3313 Savannah Dr. (270) 781-3861. 2 rooms. $70, incl. breakfast. AC.
New's Inn 3160 Scottsville Rd. (270) 781-3460. 48 units. $50-$60. AC, pool.

For additional accommodations, call the Chamber of Commerce of Cave City, (270) 773-5159, ccchamber@scrtc.com; or the Bowling Green Area Chamber of Commerce, (270) 781-3200, www.bgchamber.com.

EXCURSIONS

DANIEL BOONE NATIONAL FOREST
WINCHESTER, KENTUCKY

Daniel Boone, impressed by vast forest and abundant wildlife, called this land Eden. The 269-mile Sheltowee Trace National Recreation Trail, linking many of the forest's recreation sites, memorializes Boone's Indian name, Sheltowee, or "big turtle." Geologic wonders include more than 100 sandstone arches and 3,400 miles of cliff, carved by 70 million years of wind and water. The forest contains two wilderness areas and five wildlife management areas. More than 700,000 acres. Hiking, boating, fishing, hunting, off-road vehicle routes, scenic drives, water sports, horseback riding. Approximately 1,000 campsites, boat ramps, marinas, picnic areas, handicapped access. Open all year; most campsites open April through November. Information at Supervisor's Office, Winchester, Kentucky, about 125 miles from Mammoth Cave NP. (859) 745-3100.

CUMBERLAND GAP NATIONAL HISTORICAL PARK
MIDDLESBORO, KENTUCKY

Indian hunters breached the great wall of the Appalachians long before westering pioneers "discovered" the gap in the mid-18th century. In 1775 Daniel Boone and his band of men forged the Wilderness Trail into Kentucky, opening the West to its first wave of expansion. More than 60 miles of hiking trails lead visitors to the Pinnacle Overlook, White Rocks, Sand Cave, and to the Hensley Settlement atop Brush Mountain—an early 20th-century effort at self-sufficient living. 22,000 acres, part in Virginia and Tennessee. Hiking, scenic drives, cave tours. 160 campsites, picnic areas, handicapped access. Open all year, including campsites. Visitor center at Middlesboro on US 25E, about 190 miles from Mammoth Cave NP. (606) 248-2817.

A babbling brook in Shenandoah National Park

▶SHENANDOAH

VIRGINIA
ESTABLISHED DECEMBER 26, 1935
197,411 acres

Skyline Drive, which runs for 105 miles along the crest of the Blue
Ridge mountains, is flanked by a rumpled panorama of forests and
mountains. To many who travel the drive, the highway itself is a
park, complete with numerous deer-sightings along the way. But
the cars are passing the real Shenandoah. More than 500 miles
of trails can be reached from Skyline Drive, and the Appalachian
Trail roughly parallels it for nearly its entire length.

The long, narrow park flows out-
ward, upward, and downward from
the highway that splits it. The drive,
following ridge trails walked by
Indians and early settlers, transports
visitors to a park built on a frontier
that lingered into modern times.

Unlike most national parks,
Shenandoah is a place where settlers
lived for over a century. To create the
park, Virginia state officials acquired

1,088 privately owned tracts and
donated the land to the nation. Never
before had a large, populated expanse
of private land been converted into a
national park. And never before had
planners made a park of land so used
by humans. In the decade before and
during the early 1930s when the park
opened, some 465 families moved or
were moved from their homes and
resettled outside the proposed park

boundaries. A few mountaineers, though, lived out their lives in the park and were buried in the secluded graveyards of Shenandoah's vanished settlements.

Much of Shenandoah consisted of farmland and second- or third-growth forests logged since the early 1700s. Today the marks of lumbering, grazing, and farming have mostly disappeared, as forests have slowly come back.

Spring arrives first in the park valleys and then moves upward. Walking up a valley trail, a visitor can follow spring's path and see, in a single day, a variety of flowers that bloom elsewhere over a span of weeks.

How to Get There

From Washington, D.C. (about 70 miles away), take I-66 west to US 340, then head south to the park's Front Royal (North) Entrance. From Charlottesville, take I-64 to the Rockfish Gap (South) Entrance. From the west, take US 211 through Luray to the Thornton Gap (Middle) Entrance or head east on US 33 to the Swift Run Gap Entrance. Airports: Dulles International, near Washington, D.C., and Charlottesville, Va.

When to Go

Of the more than 1 million people who visit the park each year, the majority go in October to see the foliage. To avoid fall traffic jams, arrive early (preferably on a weekday), park at an overlook, and walk a trail. Snowstorms sometimes close Skyline Drive, the park's north-south highway. Facilities close in winter. Campgrounds fill on summer weekends, but day-trippers still have plenty of park. Wildflowers bloom from early spring to late fall.

How to Visit

On a day's drive-in visit, whatever entrance you use, get out and walk

a trail. Even if you venture only a few hundred feet from an overlook, you will see a different Shenandoah beyond the scenic drive. For a longer stay, make a base at one place, such as **Big Meadows** or **Skyland,** and explore from there. Numbered mileposts along the west side of Skyline Drive are used to reference facilities and trails for visitors.

SKYLINE DRIVE FROM FRONT ROYAL TO BIG MEADOWS

51 miles; a full day

Not quite 5 miles south of the **Front Royal Entrance Station** is the **Dickey Ridge Visitor Center,** where exhibits introduce you to the park and its facilities along Skyline Drive.

To walk a path of mountain life, cross the drive at the visitor center and start the self-guided, 1.2-mile **Fox Hollow Trail,** named for the family that first settled this hollow, as tenant farmers, in 1837. Their houses have disappeared, but you can see relics of their toil: large, well-stacked piles of rock cleared from farmland. Other stones—rough and dimly lettered—jut from the family graveyard.

Along Skyline Drive, stop at the various overlooks for views of the **Shenandoah Valley** and the peaks looming above it. The views are magnificent (except when pollution levels or fog mar visibility). At many overlooks there are signposts for well-marked trails. Daubs of paint on trees identify the trails: white, the **Appalachian Trail;** blue, a park hiking trail; yellow, a horse trail (hiking also allowed).

At Mathews Arm Campground, 22 miles from Front Royal, the easily accessible 1.7-mile **Traces Trail** takes you through an oak forest

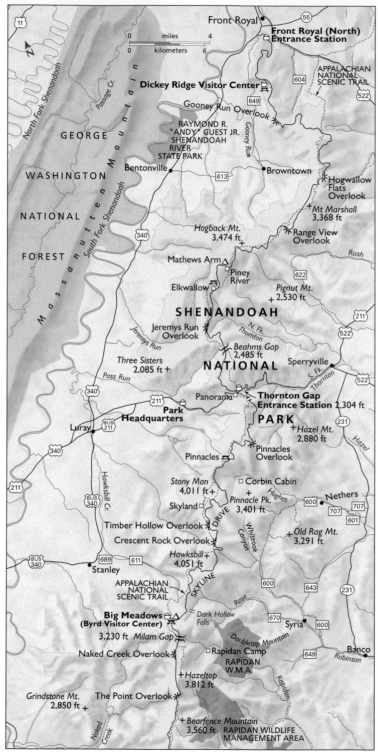

11

55

Front Royal

Front Royal (North)
Entrance Station

604

APPALACHIAN
NATIONAL
SCENIC TRAIL

522

Dickey Ridge Visitor Center

649

Gooney Run Overlook

RAYMOND R.
"ANDY" GUEST JR.
SHENANDOAH
RIVER
STATE PARK

Gooney Run

GEORGE

Bentonville

613

Browntown

Hogwallow
Flats
Overlook

WASHINGTON

Mt Marshall
3,368 ft

340

Hogback Mt.
3,474 ft

Range View
Overlook

NATIONAL

Rush

FOREST

Mathews Arm

Piney
River

622

Elkwallow

Pignut Mt.
2,530 ft

SHENANDOAH

211

Jeremys Run
Overlook

N. Fk.
Thornton

522

Three Sisters
2,085 ft

Beahms Gap
2,485 ft

NATIONAL

Sperryville

522

Pass Run

Panorama

Thornton Gap
Entrance Station 2,304 ft

231

340

211

Park
Headquarters

PARK

Hazel Mt.
2,880 ft

Luray

BUS
211

Pinnacles

Pinnacles
Overlook

340

Stony Man
4,011 ft

Corbin Cabin

211

BUS
340

Skyland

Pinnacle Pk.
3,401 ft

600

Nethers

707

707

601

Timber Hollow Overlook

Old Rag Mt.
3,291 ft

Crescent Rock Overlook

BUS
340

689

611

Hawksbill
4,051 ft

Stanley

APPALACHIAN
NATIONAL
SCENIC TRAIL

600

643

231

Big Meadows
(Byrd Visitor Center)

Dark Hollow
Falls

670

Syria

600

3,230 ft Milam Gap

Naked Creek Overlook

Rapidan Camp

RAPIDAN
W.M.A.

649

Banco

Robinson

Hazeltop
3,812 ft

Grindstone Mt.
2,850 ft

The Point Overlook

Bearfence Mountain
3,560 ft

RAPIDAN WILDLIFE
MANAGEMENT AREA

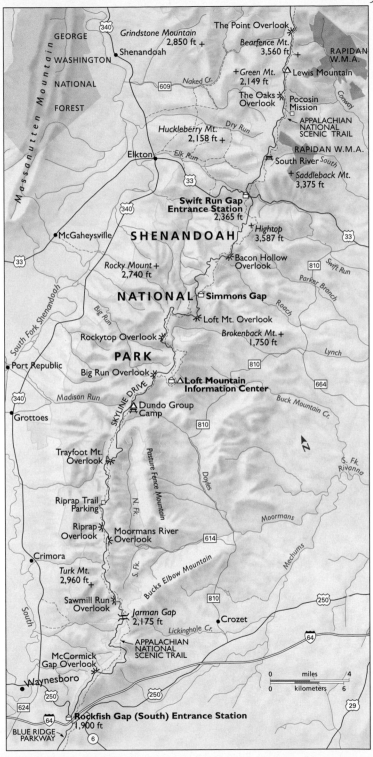

GEORGE

WASHINGTON

NATIONAL

FOREST

Massanutten Mountain

Grindstone Mountain
2,850 ft +

Shenandoah

The Point Overlook

Bearfence Mt.
3,560 ft +

RAPIDAN
W.M.A.

609

Naked Cr.

+Green Mt.
2,149 ft

△ Lewis Mountain

Conway

The Oaks
Overlook

Pocosin
Mission

APPALACHIAN
NATIONAL
SCENIC TRAIL

Huckleberry Mt.
2,158 ft +

Dry Run

RAPIDAN W.M.A.

Elkton

Elk Run

South River

South

+ Saddleback Mt.
3,375 ft

33

340

**Swift Run Gap
Entrance Station**
2,365 ft

•McGaheysville

SHENANDOAH

+Hightop
3,587 ft

33

33

Rocky Mount +
2,740 ft

Bacon Hollow
Overlook

810

Swift Run

Parker Branch

NATIONAL

Simmons Gap

Big Run

Loft Mt. Overlook

Roach

Rockytop Overlook

Brokenback Mt. +
1,750 ft

Lynch

PARK

South Fork Shenandoah

•Port Republic

Big Run Overlook

810

664

SKYLINE DRIVE

△Loft Mountain
Information Center

Madison Run

△Dundo Group
Camp

Buck Mountain Cr.

•Grottoes

340

810

N

*S. Fk.
Rivanna*

Trayfoot Mt.
Overlook

Pasture Fence Mountain

Doyles

Riprap Trail
Parking

N. Fk.

614

Moormans

Riprap
Overlook

Moormans River
Overlook

•Crimora

S. Fk.

Turk Mt.
2,960 ft +

Bucks Elbow Mountain

Mechums

Sawmill Run
Overlook

810

Jarman Gap
2,175 ft

250

South

•Crozet

Lickinghole Cr.

64

APPALACHIAN
NATIONAL
SCENIC TRAIL

64

McCormick
Gap Overlook

250

•Waynesboro

250

29

624

64

Rockfish Gap (South) Entrance Station
1,900 ft

BLUE RIDGE
PARKWAY

6

| 0 | miles | 4 |
| 0 | kilometers | 6 |

Corbin Cabin, relic of a mountaineer past

back to the time of the earliest white settlers. The traces are faint: an old road, trees, tumbling stone walls.

For a more rugged hike into the past, stop at the parking area past milepost 37 and take the **Corbin Cabin Cutoff Trail.** The steep trip (1.5 miles each way) ends at **Corbin Cabin,** a typical rural residence. In 1909 George Corbin cut and hewed logs and, with the help of neighbors, built this cabin. The Corbin family, like many others, lived mostly on what they grew or made, including brandy from peaches and apples. The Potomac Appalachian Trail Club maintains the cabin for rent to members and the public, one of six rustic cabins scattered through the park's backcountry.

Skyland (near milepost 42) dates from the 1890s. The resort, which includes guest rooms, dining room, and cabins, is open from April through November. The 1.6-mile **Stony Man Trail** begins near the parking area and, climbing about 340 feet, reaches the cliffs of **Stony Man's** summit (4,011 feet, second highest point in the park). From an outcrop on the cliffs you get a sweeping view. The trail loops back around to the start.

The **Limberlost Trail** (near milepost 43), a gently winding walkway of crushed green stone, passes through sunny areas where old-growth hemlocks once stood before crossing over Whiteoak Canyon Run on a wooden bridge. The 1.3-mile trail has a gentle grade with numerous benches located at intervals for hikers to rest and contemplate their surroundings.

Stop at **Crescent Rock Overlook** (near milepost 44) for a look at **Hawksbill Mountain,** at 4,051 feet the highest point in park. Then, 6 miles farther, stop at **Dark Hollow Falls Trail,** a 1.4-mile round-trip to a waterfall, the shortest route to any falls in the park. The steep trail takes you past clusters of ferns, mosses, and liverworts. Split-log benches offer a rest en route. **Big Meadows** (milepost 51) has trails, a campground, a lodge, facilities for visitors, and the **Byrd Visitor Center,** where exhibits tell the stories of the park.

Today the defoliated trees you see attest to the presence of a natural phenomenon—the hemlock woolly adelgid—among other pests and diseases. Since 1988 the park has lost as much as 85 percent of its hemlock stands due to this pest. Such loss could mean changes to the forest more significant than those following the blight of the chestnut tree in the early 20th century.

You can end your day at Big Meadows with a wildflower walk through the gently undulating meadowlands that give the area its name. On the way, you may startle a deer or two (or even a black bear).

RAPIDAN CAMP TO ROCKFISH GAP

54 miles; a full day

Park at the west side of Skyline Drive at **Milam Gap** (mile 52.8). Cross the drive to a trail marker to begin the 4-mile round-trip walk to Rapidan Camp. You walk a short distance on the Appalachian Trail, then turn left onto the **Mill Prong Trail,** which passes through a wooded tract, descends to a small waterfall, crosses three streams, and meets a road. Turn right and continue toward the cabins of **Rapidan Camp,** a national historic landmark.

The camp satisfied President Herbert Hoover's three requirements for a hideaway: It had to be within 100 miles of Washington, have a trout stream, and be cooler than Washington, D.C. The President and First Lady used the camp as a summer White House between 1929 and 1933. The **Brown House,** President Hoover's cabin, has been restored to its 1931 appearance and includes some furnishings. It can be visited during the summer and fall on tours from the Byrd Visitor Center. Also part of Rapidan Camp, the **Prime Minister's Cabin** with its self-guided exhibits can be explored individually.

An 0.8-mile, 1.5-hour hike to **Bearfence Mountain** starts at mile 56.4 before the Lewis Mountain Campground. It demands some scrambling over rocks but finally rewards with a spectacular 360-degree view.

The **Swift Run Gap Entrance** (near milepost 65) is an old Blue Ridge crossing now paved by US 33. In May, wildflower seekers climb the nearby **Hightop Summit Trail** (3 miles round-trip) to see wildflowers.

Loft Mountain (near milepost 79), with campground and wayside with restaurant, gas station and gift shop, is a southern base for exploring the park. Near a service complex along Skyline Drive, look for the trailhead to the **Frazier Discovery Trail,** a 1.3-mile loop that demonstrates how pasture is evolving back into forest. After the demise of the chestnut trees, other trees and shrubs began repopulating the land. You can see it happening here, and from a rocky vantage point on the trail you can also see it happening on a grand scale throughout the park. Two summit viewpoints offer views to the west, over the Shenandoah Valley to undulating peaks beyond.

At **Rockfish Gap,** near the **Rockfish Entrance Station,** a bison path evolved into a colonial road, and later a modern highway. Here, at the park's southern end, begins the **Blue Ridge Parkway,** a National Park Service highway that connects Shenandoah and Great Smoky Mountains National Parks.

Doe and fawn, Big Meadow

INFORMATION & ACTIVITIES

VISITOR & INFORMATION CENTERS

Dickey Ridge Visitor Center, near North Entrance, open daily late March through November. **Byrd Visitor Center** at Big Meadows, near center of park, open daily late March through November. Opening and closing dates vary each year.

SEASONS & ACCESSIBILITY

Open all year. For recorded information call (540) 999-3500. Skyline Drive may close temporarily during heavy snow or hazardous ice conditions. For weather and road information, call (540) 999-3500.

HEADQUARTERS

3655 US 211E, Luray, VA 22835. Phone (540) 999-3500. www.nps.gov/shen

ENTRANCE FEE

$15 March–Nov.; $10 Dec.–Feb. per car allows 7-day access.

PETS

Must be kept on leash; not allowed on posted trails or in park buildings.

ACCESSIBLE SERVICES

Visitor centers, amphitheaters, picnic grounds, and campgrounds are accessible to wheelchairs. Restrooms, lodges, and restaurants are also accessible.

THINGS TO DO

Free ranger-led activities: interpretive walks, talks, evening programs (spring through fall only). Also available, fishing, horseback riding, hiking on some 500 miles of trails.

SPECIAL ADVISORIES

• Rocks around waterfalls are very slippery and dangerous.
• Pull off the road completely when stopping for a view.
• Do not feed or chase wildlife.

OVERNIGHT BACKPACKING

Permits required and available free of charge from headquarters, visitor centers, and entrance stations.

CAMPGROUNDS

Four campgrounds with single and group sites. **Mathews Arm** and **Loft Mountain** open mid-May–Oct., available with reservations. **Big Meadows** open mid-March–Nov. **Lewis Mountain** open mid-April–Oct. Reservations recommended from late May–Oct., available through the NRRS (see p. 10). Fee $16-$20 per night. Tent and RV sites; no hookups. Camp stores and restaurants near the campground. Showers and laundry (except at Mathews Arm).

HOTELS, MOTELS, & INNS

(unless otherwise noted, rates are for 2 persons in a double room, high season)

INSIDE THE PARK:

P.O. Box 727, Luray, VA 22835. (800) 999-4714 or (540) 843-2100.
Big Meadows Lodge (mile 51.3) Lodge rooms $139-$149. Cabins $106-$109. Suites $156-$166. Restaurant. Mid-April–Oct.
Lewis Mountains Cabins (mile 57.6) Hiker's cabin $28. Ten cabins with outdoor grills. $94-$127. Mid-April–Oct.
Skyland Resort (miles 41.7 and 42.5) 177 units. Lodge units $128-$149. Suites $147-$194. Cabins $78-$259. Restaurant. Early April–Nov.

OUTSIDE THE PARK:

In Front Royal, VA 22630:
Quality Inn 10 S. Commerce Ave. (540) 635-3161. 107 units. $75-$85. AC, pool.
Woodward House on Manor Grade Bed & Breakfast 413 S. Royal Ave. (800) 635-7011 or (540) 635-7010. 7 rooms, 2 cottages. $105-$220, incl. breakfast. AC.
In Sperryville, VA 22740:
Conyers House Inn and Stable 3131 Slate Mills Rd. (540) 987-8025. www.conyers house.com. 7 rooms, 2 cottages. $150-$300, inc. breakfast. AC, restaurant.
In Waynesboro, VA 22980:
The Inn at Afton I-64 at US 250. (800) 860-8559 or (540) 942-5201. 118 units. $60-$100. AC, pool.

EXCURSIONS

GEORGE WASHINGTON NATIONAL FOREST
ROANOKE, VIRGINIA

Administratively combined with the Jefferson National Forest in 1995, the George Washington National Forest flanks the Shenandoah Valley, rich in Civil War history. Excellent fishing and fall color. Contains six wilderness areas and 62 miles of Appalachian Trail. 1,065,232 acres in three sections, part in West Virginia. Boating, fishing, hiking, horseback riding, hunting, water sports. 807 campsites, food services, boat ramp, picnic areas, handicapped access. Open all year, including many campsites. (540) 265-5100.

JEFFERSON NATIONAL FOREST
ROANOKE, VIRGINIA

Some 272 miles of the Appalachian Trail traverse mountains blanketed in hardwood, pine, and rhododendron. Streams and waterfalls abound. Contains 11 wilderness areas and Mount Rogers National Recreation Area. 723,300 acres, part in West Virginia and Kentucky. Hiking, boating, fishing, horseback riding, hunting, water sports. 670 campsites, picnic areas, boat ramp, handicapped access. Open all year, including some campsites. Information at USFS Roanoke headquarters, about 65 miles south of Shenandoah NP, via Blue Ridge Parkway. (540) 265-5100.

ELIZABETH HARTWELL MASON NECK NATIONAL WILDLIFE REFUGE
LORTON, VIRGINIA

Dedicated to the protection of the bald eagle, this refuge lies on the Potomac River, near Washington, D.C. Hardwood forest and marsh combine to form ideal habitat for the eagles and for numerous other wildlife species such as great blue herons, wood ducks, beaver, and deer. 2,277 acres. Hiking, bird-watching. Open all year. On Va. 242, about 75 miles from Shenandoah NP. (703) 490-4979.

Trunk Bay, renowned for its beauty

▶VIRGIN ISLANDS

UNITED STATES VIRGIN ISLANDS
ESTABLISHED AUGUST 2, 1956
15,135 acres

High green hills dropping down to enchanting turquoise bays, white powdery beaches, coral reefs, and ruins that evoke an era of sugar and a tragic period of slavery all find protection on St. John, one of about a hundred specks of Caribbean land known as the Virgin Islands.

Despite its small size—19 square miles—St. John's wide range of rainfall and exposure give it surprising variety. More than 800 subtropical plant species grow in areas from moist, high-elevation forests to desertlike terrain to mangrove swamps, among them mangoes, soursops, turpentine trees, wild tamarind, century plants, and sea grapes. Around the island live the fringing coral reefs—beautiful, complex, and exceedingly fragile

communities of plants and animals, which St. John's famous beaches depend upon.

In 1493 Columbus sighted the large assemblage of islands and cays and named it after St. Ursula's legendary 11,000 virgins. Since then, Spain, France, Holland, England, Denmark, and the United States have controlled various islands at different times. The Danes began colonization in the 17th century, and in 1717 planters arrived on St. John. By mid-century 88 plantations had been established there; slaves stripped the steep hillsides of virgin growth and cultivated the cane. By the time the Danes abolished slavery in 1848, the sugar industry was doomed. A fallow, century-long period known as the "subsistence era" followed.

Fearful that the Germans might capture the islands during World War I, the United States bought St. John, St. Croix, St. Thomas, and about 50 smaller islands from Denmark for $25,000,000. In 1956 conservationist Laurance S. Rockefeller donated more than 5,000 acres for a national park on St. John; in 1962 the park acquired 5,650 undersea acres off the northern and southern coasts. Today, though its boundary includes three-quarters of St. John, the national park owns only slightly more than half the island. Of increasing concern is the escalating pace of development on private inholdings inside its borders. The island unfortunately also feels pressure from the numerous cruise ships that disgorge large numbers of visitors at once, badly straining park resources. Some of the park's trails may be closed for maintenance work; check at the visitor center for more information.

When to Go
Year-round. High season is mid-December to mid-April.

How to Get There
By plane to Charlotte Amalie, St. Thomas, then taxi or bus to Red Hook, then ferry across Pillsbury Sound to Cruz Bay, a 20-minute ride. Or, try to catch one of the less frequently scheduled ferries from Charlotte Amalie—the boat takes 45 minutes, but the dock is much nearer the airport.

How to Visit
If you have only 1 day, drive the **North Shore Road** as far as the **Annaberg Sugar Mill Ruins,** taking time to stretch your legs along some seaside trails—and perhaps do a little snorkeling. Return via **Centerline Road,** stopping at the ruins of **Catherineberg Sugar Mill.** On a second day, consider hiking the **Reef Bay Trail,** explore the island's **East End,** visit **Saltpond Bay,** and walk to **Ram Head.** With more time, sign up for some of the excellent ranger-led tours and activities.

If you're driving yourself, be prepared for steep, often potholed roads with blind curves, and *stay on the left.* The speed limit is 20 mph. An alternative is to hire a taxi and guide.

NORTH SHORE ROAD–CENTERLINE ROAD LOOP
15 miles; 3 hours to a full day

Begin your visit with a stop at the park visitor center in **Cruz Bay** to pick up a map and a trail brochure, and to find out what ranger-led activities are scheduled. Head north out of town along the **North Shore Road** (Route 20). This road is in good condition but very steep in places. Near the top of the hill, pull off at the overlook for a bird's-eye view of the picturesque town and harbor, the many small adjacent islands, and the big island of **St. Thomas** across the sound. For an even better view of **St. John's West End,** climb **Caneel Hill;** the 0.8-mile, moderately strenuous trail begins a short distance ahead on the right, across the road from the Park

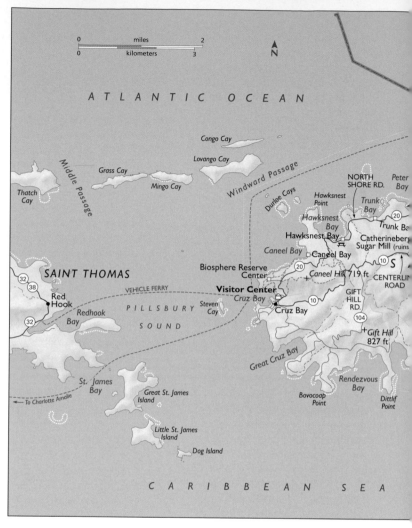

Service sign. (Or save this hike for sunset, when it's cooler and the view from the hilltop spectacular.)

Stop at the next overlook a half mile farther along the road for a view of **Caneel Bay** and, to the northeast, the big island of **Jost van Dyke,** one of the British Virgins. Since the 1930s the site of a famous resort, Caneel Bay was a sugar plantation for most of the 18th and 19th centuries. Its name, both Dutch and Danish for "cinnamon," comes from the cinnamony leaves of the bay tree, a member of the myrtle family. (From

the 1860s to the 1930s, oil from the leaves was used to make St. John Bay Rum cologne.)

The entrance to the Caneel Bay resort is down the hill on the left, past road marker 1.5. The resort, once owned by the Rockefellers, still functions as a resort on lands donated by the Rockefellers to the park. To get a look at its lovely beaches and bays—and palm-studded grounds flowered with bougainvillea and pink oleander—walk the mostly level **Turtle Point Trail** around **Hawksnest Point,** which takes about an hour.

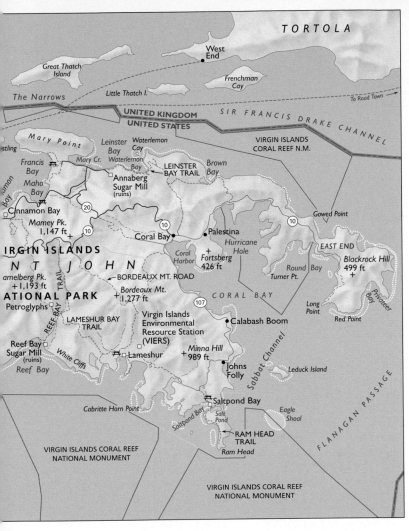

The resort management asks only that you register as a day guest at the front desk; ask there for directions to the trailhead.

From Caneel Bay the road climbs steeply and descends to **Hawksnest Beach,** where you can swim, snorkel, and picnic. Visitors tend to bypass this beach, but locals flock here on weekends. Exhibits describe the damage being done to the island's fragile reefs by pollutants, swimmers, snorkelers, and the anchors of careless boaters—and strongly urge you not to touch, stand, or sit on the coral.

One of the Caribbean's premier vistas awaits you a mile farther up the road. From the overlook, **Trunk Bay** with its lush palm-fringed crescent beach and dozens of bobbing sailboats lies before you. Off a point in the middle distance is **Whistling Cay,** where in the 19th century a customs shed stopped boats plying the passage between the Danish and British Virgins. Trunk Bay's beauty draws many visitors, especially on days when cruise ships are in. The park has set up an underwater nature trail for snorkelers here;

Snorkelers bobbing toward a coral reef off Caneel Bay resort

some 16 plaques identify the reef's plants and animals. If you're a serious snorkeler, however, you might want to skip this reef for a less traveled one farther along.

Beyond Trunk Bay's entrance, be prepared for the road to sharply steepen. Near the top of the hill is the multimillion-dollar development at **Peter Bay,** a private inholding that has been a model for preventing the sediment runoff that other developments have allowed. Park officials and environmentalists say that runoff damages the sensitive reefs and sea grass beds.

At **Cinnamon Bay** (road marker 4.5) are a campground and, across the road, the ruins of the Danish (first Dutch) Cinnamon Bay sugar factory, one of the island's oldest. Plaques along the 1-mile trail tell you its history and point out native trees such as bay, lime, teyer palm, and calabash, which produces a gourd-like fruit that's carved into bowls. If you're lucky enough to be there for a tour led by one of the Virgin Islanders on the park staff, you'll learn some colorful local lore as well.

Continue down the road a half mile to yet another stunning, sweeping view—**Maho Bay, Francis Bay,** where sea turtles come to feed,

and **Mary Point.** You'll see diving pelicans and frigate birds, which, to avoid water-logging their own enormous wings, harass other seabirds for food. The red roofs visible in the trees belong to a house built in 1952 by an American eccentric named Ethel McCully, who swam ashore from a boat and stayed. Since no paved roads or automobiles existed on St. John then, donkeys hauled the materials from Cruz Bay—a 4-hour trip.

Down the hill, the road flattens, passing a stretch of beach on the left. Continue on for a mile to the road's end and then turn right toward **Annaberg.** On the right, you'll see a thick mangrove swamp, one of many on the island. Its large, tangled roots help protect the shoreline and provide a breeding ground for fish.

On the left, about 100 yards from the turnoff, look for the marker identifying one of the toxic manchineel trees common to the Caribbean; Columbus called their green fruit "death apples." Do not stand under this tree in the rain: Runoff can raise painful blisters on your skin.

Just ahead is **Mary Creek** with a view of Mary Point. An important marine community inhabits the shallow reefs and sea-grass beds of the creek, site of a weekly naturalist-led seashore walk. If you wade out *(be sure to wear something on your feet)*, you can find brilliantly colored conchs, spiny black sea urchins, and brittle stars that regenerate their tentacles. Coral rocks host many tiny animals. Pick up and examine the rocks, but put them back as you found them.

From here consider an easy walk along the 0.8-mile **Leinster Bay Trail,** which follows the seashore east to **Waterlemon Bay** and some of the best snorkeling in the park. You can swim and snorkel off the sandy beach at the trail's end. Better yet if you have the stamina, walk out to the point and swim across the narrow channel to snorkel around little **Waterlemon Cay.**

Back at the Leinster Bay trailhead, park in the small lot and walk up the hill to the partially restored ruins of the **Annaberg Sugar Mill.** A quarter-mile self-guided walk introduces you to the slave quarters, windmill, horse mill, oven, cistern, and factory that for much of two centuries produced raw sugar, molasses, and rum for Denmark. Native stone, ballast brick, and coral went into building the thick walls.

From the overlook you can see a number of other Virgin Islands across the narrows, including **Tortola,** largest of the British Virgins, and the dinosaur shape of Britain's **Great Thatch** on the left. In winter, humpback whales sometimes cruise by. Annaberg slaves reportedly tried to swim to Great Thatch after the British freed their slaves in 1833, 15 years ahead of the Danes. Before leaving the overlook, treat yourself to the scent of a frangipani blossom from the nearby tree.

To return to Cruz Bay, drive the more level Centerline Road (Route 10), watching out for blind curves. Slow speeds should pose no hardship,

however: The views of the island's East End are truly spectacular. If you have time, look for the Catherineberg Road on the right after driving about 3 miles. A short way up this road are the ruins of the area's 18th-century Catherineberg Sugar Mill. The outer shell of the windmill has been restored, and there are 4-foot stone walls, handsome archways, a massive stone pillar, and some original beams to see.

EAST END: CORAL BAY & SALTPOND BAY

26 miles round-trip; at least a half day

Take Centerline Road (Route 10) out of Cruz Bay, stopping after nearly 3 miles at the Catherineberg Sugar Mill (see above), if you haven't already been there. About a half mile farther is the **Konge Vey Overlook,** where a wayside exhibit points out Jost van Dyke, Great Thatch, and other islands and bays to the north.

The popular **Reef Bay Trail** begins after another 1.25 miles. It descends into a steep V-shaped valley through moist, subtropical forest to dry forest to acacia scrub near the coast. Ruins of sugar estates can be seen along its 2.5 miles and nearby are some mysterious petroglyphs. Walk this trail at least partway to experience the lush forest or, even better, save it for the ranger-led trip ($21), when a boat meets you at the coast and spares you the hike back up.

Back in your car, continue on to the overlook near **Mamey Peak** for a lovely view of Coral Bay and the island's East End. The name of the bay comes not from the island's abundant coral but from an 18th-century Dutch corral *(kraal)* here. The Danes established their first plantations at this end of the island, among them the vast Estate Carolina,

INFORMATION & ACTIVITIES

VISITOR & INFORMATION CENTER
Cruz Bay Visitor Center, at west end of St. John, open daily all year. Call (340) 776-6201.

SEASONS & ACCESSIBILITY
Open all year. Access by boat. Climate does not vary much during the year, though summers can be hot. Hurricane season here runs typically from June through November.

HEADQUARTERS
1300 Cruz Bay Creek, St. John, USVI 00830. Phone (340) 776-6201. www.nps .gov/viis

ENTRANCE FEE
There is no entrance fee for the park.

However, there is a user fee to enter Trunk Bay: $4 for adults; children 16 and under admitted free. $10 annual fee.

PETS
Not allowed on public beaches, in public buildings, picnic areas, or campgrounds. Permitted elsewhere on leashes.

ACCESSIBLE SERVICES
Some ferries to St. John are accessible to wheelchairs, with assistance. The visitor center, several Cinnamon Bay campsites, and restrooms there and at Trunk Bay and Hawksnest Bay are also accessible.

THINGS TO DO
Free naturalist-led activities: interpretive talks and exhibits, nature and history walks, hikes, snorkel tours, cultural demonstrations, evening programs. Also available, self-guided nature and underwater trails, swimming, snorkeling, boating, fishing (no license needed),

once the property of the king. They built a fort—called **Fort Frederik**—on **Fortsberg** on the bay's eastern shore. In 1733 a bloody slave uprising began here, reputedly the first in the New World. It would have succeeded—1,087 of the island's 1,295 inhabitants were slaves—had the French not sailed in to quell it.

Continue on Route 10 as it winds eastward outside the park to the village of **Coral Bay,** about 2 miles away. You may well see a mongoose scuttering across the road. Introduced a century ago to kill rats, the mongoose has multiplied explosively, to the detriment of some native island fauna. At Coral Bay, stop to see the handsome pink-roofed **Emmaus Church,** built by Moravian missionaries in the 1780s. If you continued on, you'll be rewarded with magnificent views of **Hurricane Hole, Round Bay,** and the British Virgins. But for now backtrack a short distance and turn

left at the intersection of Route 107. Drive 4 miles along the coast to the trailhead for **Saltpond Bay** and a wilder part of the island.

About a fifth of a mile beyond the parking area, the horseshoe bay is fringed by a wide, sandy beach, gently lapped by transparent waters. Continue around the beach and onto the rocky 1-mile **Ram Head Trail** that winds up a promontory and down the other side. There a blue pebbly beach and an arid environment await you. Plants include several kinds of cactuses and the century plant, which takes 15 to 20 years to bloom, then dies.

Continue to the crest of the hill for a grand Caribbean view. Watch your footing and hold onto any children you've brought on this windswept point 200 feet above the sea. Here at **Ram Head** you'll be standing on rock that emerged some 108 million years ago, the oldest land on St. John.

windsurfing, bird-watching, photography workshops, archaeology digs, occasional historic bus tours.

OVERNIGHT BACKPACKING
Not allowed in park.

CAMPGROUNDS
One park campground, **Cinnamon Bay**; 14-day limit December to mid-May; other times 21-day limit. Open all year. Reservations recommended; contact Cinnamon Bay Campground, P.O. Box 720, Cruz Bay, St. John, USVI 00831. (800) 539-9998 or (340) 776-6330. Nightly for 2 persons: $27 for bare sites; $80 for tents; $110-$140 for cottages. Cold showers. Food services.
Also, **Maho Bay**; reservations, Maho Bay Camp, 17-A E. 73rd St., New York, NY 10021. (800) 392-9004 or (212) 472-9453. 114 equipped tent-cottages, central baths. $110 per night December through April; $75 per night May through

November. Reserve early for December to May.

HOTELS, MOTELS, & INNS
(unless otherwise noted, rates are for 2 persons in a double room, high season)

On St. John, USVI 00831:
Gallows Point Resort P.O. Box 58. (800) 323-7229 or (340) 776-6434. 60 units, kitchens. $465-$655. Pool, restaurant.
St. John Inn P.O. Box 37. (800) 666-7688 or (340) 693-8688. 10 units, some kitchens. $175-$275.
Westin Resort St. John P.O. Box 8310. (340) 693-8000 or (800) 937-8461. 321 units. $759-$909. AC, 3 pools, restaurant.

For additional accommodations, contact the U.S. Virgin Islands Hotel and Visitors Association, (800) 372-8784, www.visit usvi.com.

VIRGIN ISLANDS

EXCURSION

BUCK ISLAND REEF NATIONAL MONUMENT
ST. CROIX, U.S. VIRGIN ISLANDS

A coral reef nearly encircles this small island, 1 mile north of St. Croix. A marked underwater trail guides snorkelers or passengers of glass-bottom boats through the exquisite reef ecosystem. Breathtaking views of St. Croix and the reef can be had from the top of Buck Island's hiking trail. 176 land acres; 18,839 undersea acres. Trail, picnic areas, swimming, snorkling. Open all year (daytime only). Access by charter boat from Christiansted, St. Croix (charter operators supply snorkeling equipment). (340) 773-1460.

Sunset over Lake Kabetogama

▶ VOYAGEURS

MINNESOTA
ESTABLISHED APRIL 8, 1975
218,054 acres

From the air, the forest areas of Voyageurs look like green pieces of a jigsaw puzzle scattered on a huge mirror. A North Woods realm of more than 30 lakes and more than 900 islands, Voyageurs spans a watery stretch of the U.S.-Canada border.

A third of this national park's area is water, most of it in four large lakes—Rainy, Kabetogama, Namakan, and Sand Point—linked by narrow waterways. Smaller lakes gleam in the forests and bogs of Voyageurs' terra firma, which consists of small islands, a strip of mainland shore, and the Kabetogama Peninsula, a long, bay-fringed landmass.

The splendors of this 55-mile-long park can be reached primarily only by water. Motorboats *(banned*

in the adjacent Boundary Waters Canoe Area Wilderness) churn the lakes. Canoes and kayaks glide the narrow waterways. Fishermen sit at the rails of houseboats, hoping to hook walleye, smallmouth bass, and northern pike. Nearly every lake is haunted by the cry of the loon. And probably in no other national park in the lower 48 states is there a better chance to see bald eagles on the nest and on the wing or hear wolves howl at night.

The park is named for French

Canadian voyageurs who paddled birchbark canoes for fur trading companies in the late 18th and early 19th centuries. The voyageurs were famous for stamina—paddling up to 16 hours a day—and roisterous songs. Their canoe route between Canada's northwest and Montreal is cited as part of the U.S.-Canada border in the treaty that ended the American Revolution.

In a boat in the labyrinth of waterways and islands, you can unwittingly cross this border. Be sure to take along a high-quality map that includes navigational markers to tell you where you are.

How to Get There
From Duluth, drive north about 110 miles on US 53. For Crane Lake, turn east at Orr and drive 28 miles on County Roads 23 and 24. For Ash River, stay on US 53 for 25 more miles, turn right at the Ash River Trail sign, and continue for 10 miles. For Kabetogama Lake Visitor Center, stay on US 53 for 3 more miles, turn right onto County Road 122, and drive to the lakeshore. For Rainy Lake, stay on US 53 to International Falls, then head east for 12 miles on Minn. 11 to the park's entrance road, following highway information signs; turn right to go to the

visitor center. Airports: Duluth and International Falls, Minnesota; and Fort Frances, Ontario.

When to Go
Year-round, but most accessible from spring through early fall. Water travel is curtailed by freeze-up in late fall and ice breakup in early spring. Winter opens the park to cross-country skiing, snowshoeing, snowmobiling, and ice fishing. And the 7-mile ice road at Rainy Lake provides a unique entry into the park: You drive your car on the ice to places that in other seasons you can reach only by boat or floatplane.

How to Visit
The only way to access the heart of this park is by water. **Kabetogama Lake, International Falls, Crane Lake,** and **Ash River** are resort communities that, though not within the park, serve as entrances. Begin planning your trip itinerary by choosing an entrance; each of them is widely spaced and offers a different experience. You can make motel or lodge reservations at one of the area's resorts or motels listed in the park's newspaper, the *Rendezvous,* or in the Information & Activities section on p. 118. You can also stay in a car campground and use the resort as a

VOYAGEURS

A kayaker watches a rainbow arc over the lake.

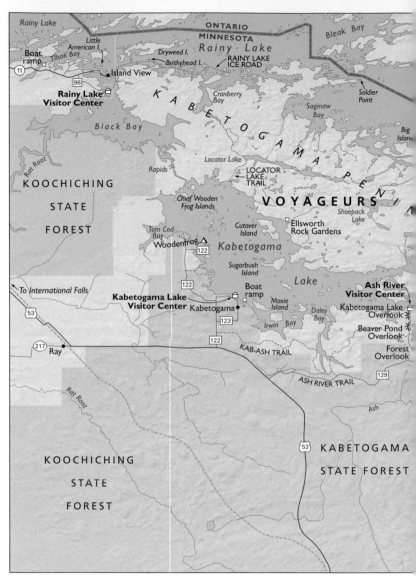

base from which to engage in park activities, including fishing and wildlife-watching, or rent a houseboat or camp out by boat. Guides, canoes, houseboats, and motorboats are available for hire. If you are sufficiently experienced, you can also tow in your own craft.

Sightseeing tour boats, with park naturalists aboard, also operate out of visitor centers. Even if you have your own boat, you may want to take a commercial cruise and rely on experienced navigators to steer the course; the lakes are broad with submerged rocks in shallow areas, and they are sometimes brushed by stiff winds, testing even the most experienced boater.

If your time is limited, Kabetogama Lake is a good place for exploring and understanding the park.

0   miles   4
0   kilometers   6

N

Rainy
Lake

Rat River Bay

CANADA
UNITED STATES

Browns Bay

Pound Net
Bay

Stokes Bay

Oakpoint
Island

Kettle Falls

Dams

Hale
Bay

Voyageur
Narrows

U L A

NATIONAL

Blackstone
Island

Williams
Island

Namakan
Island

Namakan Lake

Namakan
Narrows

Moose
Bay

Sullivan Bay

Junction Bay

PARK

Ash River

Boat ramp

Moose

Tooth
Lake

Sand
Point
Lake

Grassy Bay

Ash River
Falls

Gannon Creek

Lucille
Lake

Spring
Lake

Browns
Bay

Little
Johnson
Lake

Johnson
Lake

Staege
Bay

Mukooda
Lake

Canada
Customs

Northwest
Bay

SUPERIOR

NATIONAL

FOREST

King
Williams
Narrows

Crane
Lake

Vermilion

Crane Lake
Ranger Station

Crane Lake
US Customs

24

KABETOGAMA LAKE

at least a full day

At the **Kabetogama Lake Visitor Center,** learn about boat tours, guided canoe trips, or children's programs. Or, rent one of the park's cached canoes at Locator Lake (reserve it and pick up the key at the visitor center). If you do this, you must get to the Locator Lake

trailhead on your own, with a guide, or in a rented boat. You leave the boat at the trailhead for a 2-mile hike along a spruce bog and past a beaver pond, dam, and lodge. The trail climbs to a ridge and drops to the lakeshore. There you launch your reserved cached canoe and paddle around the lake, watching for muskrat, bald eagles, loons, and blue-winged teal.

Orange leaves in a deciduous forest

Another exciting way to explore the park is on an all-day guided cruise to **Kettle Falls.** For details see **Crane Lake & Ash River,** below. The 21-mile **Kabetogama to Ash River Trail** travels through the park and state forest lands; three trailheads, all car-accessible, offer a variety of opportunities.

RAINY LAKE
at least a full day

Although this lake is large—60 miles long, 12 miles wide—you can safely explore it in your own or a rented motorboat, houseboat, or canoe. At the **Rainy Lake Visitor Center** get weather and navigation information. About 1.5 miles northwest is **Little American Island,** where the discovery of gold set off a short-lived gold rush over a hundred years ago. A short interpretive trail on the island gives a view to the past. About 2 miles east is **Bushyhead Island,** where a mine shaft is carved into the rock.

Lacking your own boat, you can still explore. The park offers naturalist-led tour boat trips from the visitor center, as well as free trips aboard a 26-foot reproduction of a voyageurs canoe, guided trips aboard contemporary canoes, and programs for children.

Trails near Rainy Lake Visitor Center: The 2-mile **Oberholtzer Trail** travels through a variety of habitats. The short, water-accessible **Black Bay Beaver Pond Trail** takes visitors to an active beaver pond habitat.

CRANE LAKE & ASH RIVER
at least 1 to 2 days each

Near the Ash River resort area is a visitor center where you can launch your boat, get information about camping, set off on hikes (see below), and obtain charts for navigating the lakes. If you're new to the lakes, *don't fail to use charts.*

For a good exploratory voyage, go to **Kettle Falls,** a waterways hub used by Native Americans, voyageurs, loggers, fishermen, and, during Prohibition, bootleggers smuggling liquor from Canada.

From Crane Lake you travel north through **King Williams Narrows,** across **Sand Point Lake,** and through **Namakan Narrows,** then west across **Namakan Lake** along the U.S.-Canada border, which veers northward here.

From Ash River you go the length of **Sullivan Bay** to the river mouth, then weave through a string of islands into **Moose Bay.** For a scenic trip, pass through the channel on the south side of **Williams Island** (site of a primitive campsite) into **Hoist Bay,** named for the hoisting of logs that were loaded onto a train. You can see pilings that supported a train track, which ran from the middle of the bay to a white-pine sawmill on the mainland. Head north toward **Namakan Island,** site of other campsites, and go around the island's western side.

Both courses take you to the southern end of **Voyageur Narrows.** Pass through the narrows, then head east along the border to Kettle Falls. Near the dock, a dam serves a regional system regulating water flow for electric power. At the dock is a gravel road, a portage trail. Walk the road for about a quarter mile to a white clapboard building with a long front porch—the **Kettle Falls Hotel.** Built in 1910, the hotel welcomed lumberjacks and their money; it still hosts guests—those who reserve well ahead.

Another way to get to Kettle Falls is to take a cruise boat. Trips are run several times a week out of the visitor center at Kabetogama Lake. The all-day trip is timed for you to eat lunch at the hotel before the return voyage.

Trails near Ash River Visitor Center: Three short trails—the **Voyageurs Forest, Beaver Pond,** and **Kabetogama Lake Overlook**—leave from pull-offs

A beaver-chewed tree along Kabetogama Lake *(top)* Moss-covered rocks along a lakeshore *(bottom)*

VOYAGEURS

on the road to the visitor center. The 2-mile **Blind Ash Bay Trail,** from the visitor center to the mouth of Blind Ash Bay, wends along rock cliffs through pine forest.

118

INFORMATION & ACTIVITIES

VISITOR & INFORMATION CENTERS

Rainy Lake, on Minn. 11 at northwest edge of park; call (218) 286-5258.
Kabetogama Lake, on County Road 123 at southwest edge of lake, open late May through September; call (218) 875-2111.
Ash River, on southeast edge of Kabetogama Lake, open late May through September. Call (218) 374-3221. Days vary at all locations; call ahead.

SEASONS & ACCESSIBILITY

Open all year. Travel within by boat, and foot in summer; snowmobile, snowshoes, cross-country skis, and ski-plane in winter. Limited access during lake freeze-up (mid-Nov. to mid-Dec.) and breakup (April). In winter, weather permitting, an ice road on Rainy Lake connects the visitor center to Cranberry Bay, 7 miles into the park.

HEADQUARTERS

360 Highway 11 East, International Falls, MN 56649. Phone (218) 283-6600. www.nps.gov/voya

ENTRANCE FEE

None.

PETS

Permitted on leashes in developed areas and at tent, houseboat, and day-use sites on major lakes. Not allowed on park trails, in backcountry, or on interior lakes.

ACCESSIBLE SERVICES

Kabetogama Lake, Rainy Lake, and Ash River Visitor Centers are wheelchair accessible, as is the Kettle Falls Hotel, guided boat trips, and a campsite; call Kabetogama Lake for reservations. Fact sheet available.

THINGS TO DO

Free naturalist-led activities: canoe trips (reserve at visitor centers), children's programs, films, exhibits. Hiking, canoeing, rowboating (boats on Interior Lakes Program $10 a day), boat touring, fishing and ice fishing (guides available, ask park for list; license required), swimming, water-skiing, snowmobiling, cross-country skiing, snowshoeing.

SPECIAL ADVISORY

• Practice safe boating: Use navigational maps; be aware of weather conditions; well equip your boat; do not overload it.

CAMPING & HOUSEBOATING

All park sites reached by water. Over 200 lake country boat-in campsites, 14-day limit. Open all year (may be inaccessible during fall freeze-up and spring thaw); first come, first served. Free permit required for overnights, available at visitor centers and boat launches. No showers. Sites designated for tent camps or houseboats. Also, two small campgrounds. In winter, access mainly by snowmobile, cross-country skis, or snowshoes. Private campgrounds with tent and RV sites near park.

HOTELS, MOTELS, & INNS

(unless otherwise noted, rates are for 2 persons in a double room, high season)

INSIDE THE PARK:

Kettle Falls Hotel (15 miles by water from the Ash River Trail) 12977 Chippewa Trail, Kabetogama, MN 56669. (218) 240-1726. 12 hotel rooms. $70 double; lodge and suites nearby, some with kitchens, $170-$190.

OUTSIDE THE PARK:

In International Falls, MN 56649:
American Inn 1500 US 71. (800) 634-3444 or (218) 283-8000. 126 units. $80-$130. AC, pool, restaurant.
Island View Lodge (on Rainy Lake) 1817 Hwy. 11E. (800) 777-7856 or (218) 286-3511. 9 rooms, $115; 14 cabins with kitchens, $850-$2,025 per week. AC, restaurant.

In Kabetogama, MN 56669:
Voyageur Park Lodge 10436 Waltz Rd. (800) 331-5694 or (218) 875-2131). 11 cabins with kitchens (summer only). $759-$2,250 per week.

For a listing of accommodations, contact Ash River Tourism, (800) 950-2061, www.ashriver.com; Kabetogama Tourism Bureau, (800) 524-9085, www.kabetogama.com; Crane Lake Visitor & Tourism Bureau, (800) 362-7405, www.visitcranelake.com; or Rainy Lake Convention & Visitors Bureau, (800) 325-5766, www.rainylake.org.

ss

EXCURSIONS

SUPERIOR NATIONAL FOREST
DULUTH, MINNESOTA

Here the northern lights preside over stands of pine, fir, aspen, and birch, and loons bob on 1,000-plus portage-linked lakes of the Boundary Waters Canoe Area Wilderness (*permit reqd.*). Reservations suggested during summer. 2.2 million acres. Hiking, boating, fishing, winter sports, water sports, scenic drives. Campsites, food services, boat ramp, picnic areas. Open all year. La Croix Visitor Center west of Cook on US 53 about 15 miles from Orr, Minn., the southern gateway to Voyageurs NP. (218) 626-4300.

CHIPPEWA NATIONAL FOREST
CASS LAKE, MINNESOTA

This lake-country forest boasts a large breeding bald eagle population and offers a variety of water-based recreation, including the chance to explore the Mississippi's headwaters by canoe. More than 660,000 acres. Hiking, boating, fishing, mountain biking, scenic drives, historic sites with summer interpretive programs, winter sports, hunting. 23 campgrounds, picnic areas, boat ramps, handicapped access. Open all year; campsites generally open mid-May to mid-Sept. Information at Cass Lake on MN 371, about 80 miles from Voyageurs NP. (218) 335-8600.

AGASSIZ NATIONAL WILDLIFE REFUGE
MIDDLE RIVER, MINNESOTA

More than 300 species of migratory and resident birds share this wetlands refuge with about 20 moose and two resident packs of eastern gray wolves—few such packs exist outside Alaska. 61,500 acres. Hiking, hunting, scenic drives, bird-watching. Handicapped access. Open all year (Lost Bay Habitat Dr. and Maakstad Hiking Trail open May–Oct.). Headquarters on Marshall County Rd. 7, 11 miles east of Holt, 185 miles from Voyageurs NP. (218) 449-4115.

VOYAGEURS

THE
SOUTHWEST

COLORADO   KANSAS

AZTEC RUINS
NAT. MON.

64

Rio Grande

ROCKY

Sangre de Cristo Mountains

GREAT

Cimarron

Canadian

Santa Fe

25

10

Albuquerque

40

Amarillo

40

EL MALPAIS
NAT. MON.

NEW

MEXICO

BOSQUE
DEL APACHE
N.W.R.

MOUNTA

27

P

285

Pecos

LINCOLN

Lubbock

L

380

25

380

Brozos

WHITE
SANDS
NAT. MON.

NATIONAL

62 180

87

A

70

Alamogordo

FOREST

10

N

Carlsbad

20

Whites City

CARLSBAD CAVERNS N.P.

I

U.S.

EL PASO

GUADALUPE MTS.
N.P.

Midland

Colorado

MEXICO

62 180

Odessa

N

Salt Flat

54

T

E

X

CHIHUAHUAN

Van
Horn

10

Pecos

Edwards

90

Fort
Stockton

10

Plateau

Rio Grande

DESERT

Alpine

385

118

Marathon

N

Presidio

170

RIO GRANDE
NATIONAL
WILD AND
SCENIC RIVER

90

U.S.

BIG BEND N.P.

MEXICO

Nueces

0   miles   200
0   kilometers   300

35

Laredo

THE SOUTHWEST

The national parks of the Southwest, all set in the Chihuahuan Desert, offer scenery ranging from underground caves to high and rugged mountain peaks. Sparse vegetation opens the spectacular vistas up to visitors without their having to go above tree line.

Water sculptured these landscapes. A reef from an ancient sea forms the 40-mile-long Guadalupe mountain chain. The seeping of water over millions of years created the cool, dark world of Carlsbad Caverns. Rivers etched out the dramatic canyons of Big Bend, and flash floods still tumble boulders from the steep Chisos mountaintops, continuing to rearrange the scenery.

The vagaries of yearly precipitation also determine whether the visitor beholds a land of blossoms— Texas bluebonnets, brilliant red and orange cactus flowers, heavy stalks of white yucca blooms—or, more often, a parched terrain dominated by creosote bush, prickly pear, and dagger-sharp lechuguilla. Where water flows year-round, oases produce gardens that resound with birdsong.

Visitors to the Southwest parks have a chance to view wildlife as diverse as multicolored lizards and snakes, the elusive mountain lion, deer, hundreds of species of birds, and, in Big Bend, pig look-alikes called javelinas. Paleontologists have found fossils of many other creatures, including giant crocodiles and the Big Bend pterosaur, the largest animal ever to fly.

Hikers may take their own trip back in time by climbing up to the pine-fir forests that cloak the cooler, moister mountaintops in the Guadalupes and Big Bend. This type of forest probably covered the region at the end of the last ice age, when early peoples hunted camels, mammoths, and four-horned antelope.

Carlsbad Caverns and Guadalupe Mountains National Parks are linked by the Lincoln National Forest; proposals have been made to unite the three areas into one large park encompassing the Guadalupe range. Base yourself at Carlsbad or, even closer, in Whites City to visit these areas. Allow a day to drive the 250 miles from Guadalupe to Big Bend.

Mexico across the Rio Grande from Castolon Visitor Center

▶ BIG BEND

TEXAS
ESTABLISHED JUNE 12, 1944
801,163 acres

As the Rio Grande winds south along the Texas-Mexico border, it suddenly veers northward in a great horseshoe curve before continuing its journey. Inside the horseshoe lies the region of Texas known as the Big Bend; Big Bend National Park flanks the river at the southerly tip of the curve. A wild and surprising land, the park remains remote enough that only the dedicated reach it.

Chihuahuan Desert vegetation—bunchgrasses, creosote bushes, cactuses, lechuguillas, yuccas, sotols, and more—covers most of the terrain. But the Rio Grande and its lush floodplains and steep, narrow canyons form almost a park of their own. So do the Chisos Mountains; up to 20 degrees cooler than the desert floor, they harbor pine, juniper, and oak, as well as deer, mountain lions, bears, and other wildlife. A heavy rain transforms the desert: Normally dry creek beds roar with water, and seeds long dormant burst into fields of wildflowers.

The rocks of Big Bend are a complex lot. Two seas, one after another, flowed and subsided in the region hundreds of millions of years ago, leaving thick deposits of limestone and shale. The present mountains, except the Chisos, uplifted along with the Rockies, roughly 75 million years ago. Around the same time, a 40-mile-wide trough—most of the present-day park—sank along fault lines, leaving the cliffs of Santa Elena Canyon to the west and the Sierra del Carmen to the east rising 1,500 feet and more above the desert floor. In the center, volcanic activity spewed layer upon layer of ash into the air and squeezed molten rock up through the ground to form the Chisos Mountains some 35 million years ago. Molten rock also cooled and hardened underground later to be exposed by erosion.

Big Bend's topographic variety supports a remarkable diversity of life, including 1,200 plant species—some found nowhere else in the world. More species of birds—more than 450—have been counted here than in any other U.S. national park.

People have passed through this terrain for at least 10,000 years. The human pageant in historical times has included Apache, Spanish conquistadores, Comanche, U.S. soldiers, miners, ranchers and farmers, Mexican revolutionaries, and international outlaws and bandits.

How to Get There

From Marathon US 385 leads south to the north entrance to the park; Tex. 118 from Alpine leads south to the west entrance; Ranch Road 170, from Presidio, joins Tex. 118 shortly before the west entrance. Nearest airports: El Paso (325 miles) and Midland-Odessa (230 miles).

When to Go

Year-round, though fall and winter may be the best seasons. Deciduous leaves turn color in the mountains in autumn; winters are mild. Summer temperatures in the desert can exceed 110°F; the Chisos Mountains remain cooler. If enough rain falls, the desert blooms stunningly in early spring, and again in late summer. Bird-watching is good all year, but especially in March, April, and May.

How to Visit

Allow several days, especially if you plan to hike. Explore the **Chisos Mountains Basin** and the **Ross Maxwell Scenic Drive,** engineered to take you past many of the park's geological and scenic highlights. Ideally, devote the better part of a day to each area. With extra time on the second afternoon, or on a third day, drive out to **Rio Grande Village** and the **Boquillas Canyon Overlook** to experience the river environment and enjoy views of the Sierra del Carmen, particularly spectacular at sunset. On your way in or out, view the landscape and exhibits along the road between **Panther Junction** and **Persimmon Gap.** For an extended visit, try more of the many rewarding hikes, drive some dirt roads, and consider a leisurely float trip along the Rio Grande through one of the park's three major canyons.

Mexican plum

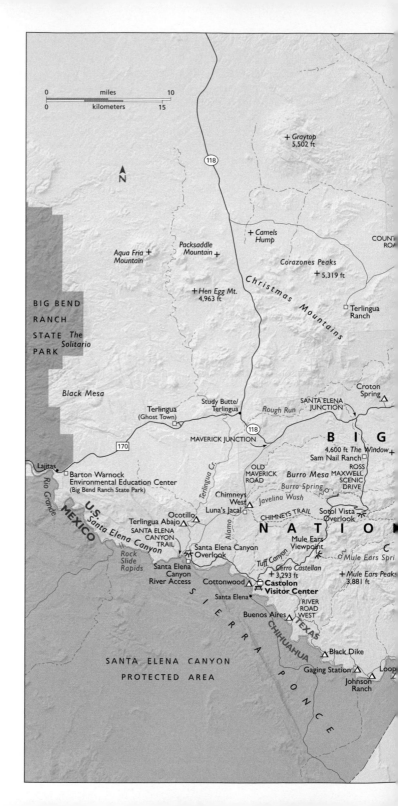

miles
0   10
kilometers
0   15

N

118

+ Graytop
5,502 ft

+ Camels
Hump

COUNT
ROA

+ Corazones Peaks
+ 5,319 ft

Aqua Fria +
Mountain

Packsaddle
Mountain +

□ Terlingua
Ranch

Christmas Mountains

+ Hen Egg Mt.
4,963 ft

BIG BEND
RANCH
STATE *The
Solitario*
PARK

Black Mesa

Croton
Spring △

Terlingua
(Ghost Town) □

Study Butte/
Terlingua

Rough Run

SANTA ELENA
JUNCTION

170

118

MAVERICK JUNCTION

B I G

4,600 ft *The Window* +

Lajitas

□ Barton Warnock
Environmental Education Center
(Big Bend Ranch State Park)

Rio Grande

MEXICO

U.S. *Santa Elena Canyon*

OLD
MAVERICK
ROAD

Terlingua C.

Sam Nail Ranch □

ROSS
MAXWELL
SCENIC
DRIVE

Burro Mesa

Burro Spring

Chimneys
West

Javelina Wash

Sotol Vista ⋇
Overlook

Ocotillo △

Luna's Jacal □

CHIMNEYS TRAIL

Terlingua Abajo △

SANTA ELENA
CANYON
TRAIL

Alamo

N   A   T   I   O

Mule Ears
Viewpoint

C

*Rock
Slide
Rapids*

Santa Elena Canyon
Overlook ⋇

Santa Elena
Canyon
River Access

Tuff Canyon

○ *Mule Ears Spri*

Cerro Castellan
+ 3,293 ft

+ *Mule Ears Peaks*
3,881 ft

Cottonwood △ □ **Castolon**
🏠 **Visitor Center**

Santa Elena •

RIVER
ROAD
WEST

Buenos Aires △ △ TEXAS

S
I
E
R
R
A

CHIHUAHUA

△ Black Dike

Gaging Station △
△ Loop

SANTA ELENA CANYON

PROTECTED AREA

P
O
N
C
E

Johnson
Ranch

Santiago Mountains

385

Persimmon Gap Visitor Center

Stillwell Store and RV Park

Dog Canyon

Nine Point Draw

2627

BLACK GAP

WILDLIFE MANAGEMENT

AREA

NORTH

ROSILLOS

S I E R R A

Dagger Flat

Sierra Larga

Rosillos

+ Rosillos Peak
5,373 ft

Mountains

ROSILLOS RANCH

DAGGER FLAT AUTO TRAIL

Tornillo Flat

Sierra del Caballo

Heath Canyon
La Linda

int Gap
Hills

Grapevine Spring

Fossil Bone Exhibit

McKinney Spring

TELEPHONE CANYON TRAIL

Adams Ranch

Paint Gap

GRAPEVINE HILLS ROAD

Grapevine Hills

Roys Peak Vista

Telephone Canyon

Telephone Canyon

RIO GRANDE WILD & SCENIC RIVER

U.S.

MEXICO

Government Spring

Hannold Draw

Roys Peak +
3,945 ft

CHISOS MTS. BASIN JUNCTION

Panther Junction Visitor Center and Park Headquarters

Willow Tank

Ernst Basin

Muerto

MADERAS DEL CARMEN PROTECTED AREA

B   E   N   D

Chisos
Basin

Lost Mine Peak
+ 7,550 ft

Dugout Wells

PINE CANYON TRAIL

Ernst Basin

STRAWHOUSE TRAIL

Boquillas Canyon

Tornillo Creek

Pine Canyon

La Noria

Ernst Tinaja

Chisos Basin Visitor Center

JUNIPER CANYON TRAIL

Rice Tank

Camp de Leon

Emory Pk.
7,825 ft

Twisted Shoe

GLENN SPRING RD.

Rio Grande Overlook

Rio Grande Village Visitor Center

Boquillas Canyon Overlook

ODSON TRAIL

Robbers Roost

Candelilla

Boquillas del Carmen

A   L   P   A   R   K

Daniels Ranch

S O S

Hot Springs

+ Elephant Tusk
5,249 ft

Talley Mt.
+ 3,765 ft

La Clocha

Gravel Pit

+ Dominguez Mt.
5,156 ft

Elephant Tusk

RIVER ROAD EAST

San Vicente

BLACK GAP RD.

Fresno

TEXAS

COAHUILA

Cerro del Veinte

DOMINGUEZ SPRING TRAIL

Mariscal Mine

Mariscal Mountain

SIERRA DE SAN VICENTE

Dominguez Trailhead

Solis

RIO GRANDE NATIONAL WILD AND SCENIC RIVER

Jewels

Woodsons

3,932 ft +

U.S.

Talley

Mariscal Canyon

MEXICO

Rio Grande

Tight Squeeze Rapids

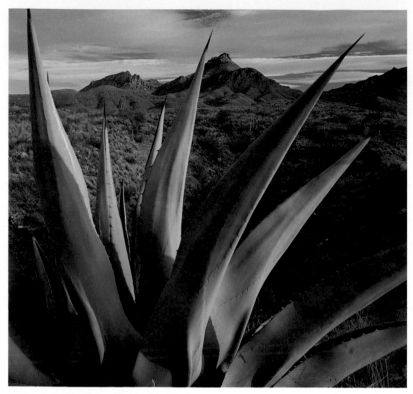

Century plant *(Agave harvardiana)* in Chicos Basin

PANTHER JUNCTION TO THE CHISOS BASIN

10 miles one way; at least a half day

Start your tour at the visitor center at Panther Junction. Collect maps, information on hiking, and safety tips on avoiding encounters with rattlesnakes, mountain lions, and flash floods. Don't miss **Panther Path**—the 50-yard nature trail near the visitor center entrance whose self-guiding pamphlet provides an excellent introduction to the plants you'll see on much of your trip. Behind the visitor center lie the **Chisos Mountains,** the southernmost range in the continental United States, and your destination. When ready, return to your car and turn left out of the visitor center, then left at **Basin Junction** in 3 miles. Ahead on the right looms **Pulliam Bluff.** Look closely and you might see in the mountain the profile of a man's face, reclining. Legend relates that the man is Alsate, an important Apache chief whose ghost lives on in the high Chisos Mountains, and whose campfire can occasionally be seen at night. At 2.5 miles, the jagged summit to your left is **Lost Mine Peak.** Spanish explorers, it is told, discovered a rich silver mine near the summit and enslaved Indians to work it. The miners rebelled, killed their overlords, and sealed the entrance to the mine so that it might remain lost forever. As you drive on, the castlelike summit of **Casa Grande**— big house—will be straight ahead, a landmark for much of the park.

The road climbs higher into the mountains through a canyon called **Green Gulch:** Watch the vegetation change from desert shrub to sotol grasslands, then to pinyon pine, juniper, and oak woodland. The Chisos form a cooler, moister island in the surrounding desert. Some 10,000 years ago, pinyon-juniper forests extended down to the desert floor, but the trees withdrew to higher altitudes as the climate gradually warmed at the end of the Ice Age. In about 5 miles the road hits its highest point at **Panther Pass** (5,770 feet), named for the mountain lions that still roam these hills. Only the lucky few ever see one. If you have time, park at the nearby trailhead for the **Lost Mine Trail,** a self-guided nature trail with an informative booklet. The panorama from the top, one of the grandest in the park, makes the moderately strenuous 4.8-mile round-trip well worth the trek. But if you're short of time, just hike the 2-mile round-trip to the **Juniper Canyon Overlook,** for good vistas of wooded **Juniper Canyon** to the south and Pulliam Bluff to the northwest.

After Panther Pass, the road descends in hairpin curves to the basin, a 3-mile-wide depression in the mountains, chiseled by wind and water. Many of the park's choice hikes start from the basin trailhead, west of the ranger station. At the least, make sure to stroll the easy 0.3-mile round-trip **Window View Trail.** Particularly photogenic at sunset, the Window is a V-shaped opening, or pour off, in the mountains, through which all rain and meltwater from the basin drains. A more challenging trail descends through desert and shady canyon to the **Window** itself, offering classic afternoon views of Casa Grande framed by oaks and pines. In summer, take this and other lower elevation hikes in early morning or late afternoon.

BIG BEND

Adobe ruins under a brooding sky

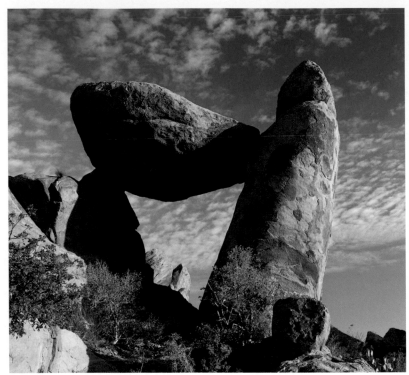

Balanced Rock found along the trail of the same name

The literal high point of many visitors' trips to the park is a hike to the **South Rim** (7,400 feet), a moderately steep 13-mile round-trip that provides unforgettable vistas of much of the park. At **Boot Canyon**, 4.5 miles up the trail to the South Rim, lives an oasis of bigtooth maple, Douglas fir, and Arizona cypress. The gray-and-yellow Colima warbler nests on the canyon floor, its only home in the United States.

Before you hike, check at the **Chisos Basin Visitor Center** for maps and hiking tips, and make sure you carry plenty of water. At the visitor center, ask also about the presence of peregrine falcons. Several of these endangered birds nest in the Chisos.

ROSS MAXWELL SCENIC DRIVE: SANTA ELENA

30 miles one way; a half to full day

Heading south from Santa Elena Junction, **Burro Mesa**—named for the burros that once grazed the top—will be to your right, and the Chisos to your left. After 2 miles, stop at the exhibit on the left for a fine view of the Window framing Casa Grande. Drive on a little over a mile, then park at the old **Sam Nail Ranch** and stroll the short path to the remains of windmills and a ranch house. The shade of the pecan and willow trees the Nails planted makes a fine resting and bird-watching spot. Walk back to your car and motor on. In about a mile, long walls of rock traverse the landscape. They are dikes, created by molten rock that squeezed up into underground cracks before hardening. The softer rock layers around them eventually eroded away, leaving the erosion-resistant dikes.

Stop next at the **Blue Creek Ranch** (Homer Wilson Ranch) **Overlook.** A century ago most of Big Bend was cloaked in grasses. But drought and ranchers grazing thousands of cattle, sheep, and goats destroyed the grass and exposed the topsoil to erosion. Creosote, mesquite, allthorn, and other spiny shrubs moved into the damaged areas. Here, and elsewhere in the park, grasses are slowly returning.

Go back to the road and take a quick left onto the **Sotol Vista** spur road, named for the ridge's rich growth of sotol, the bright green plant with sawlike teeth on the edges of the leaves. Indians roasted and ate the heart of the sotol and fermented it to yield an alcoholic drink. The parking lot at the top provides vistas of the surrounding mountains, and a plaque at the end of the loop identifies what's what.

Return to the main road; an exhibit on the left in about 6.5 miles describes how volcanism shaped this striking landscape. Take the next spur road on the left, for an excellent view of the peaks known as **Mule Ears,** a name explained at a glance. During the 1930s, Army Air Corps pilots drilled by flying planes between the twin peaks. Stop again after 4.5 miles to see **Tuff Canyon,** carved by **Blue Creek** through layers of lava flows, boulders, and compressed volcanic ash called tuff. Stroll the short trail to the right to view the canyon. The trail at the left of the parking lot provides a moderately steep hike down into the canyon, a 0.75-mile round-trip.

Back in your car, you will be approaching **Cerro Castellan,** another important landmark, rising 1,000 feet above its surroundings. Turn left into **Castolon** to stroll around the old Army post that was built after the 1914–18 border troubles with Mexico. The main building, originally the barracks, was converted to a frontier trading post around 1920. A new visitor center has exhibits and a bookstore.

After leaving Castolon, the road parallels the **Rio Grande,** passing the scattered remains of adobe houses dating back to the turn of the 20th century. The occupants once grew food crops and cotton in the Rio Grande's fertile floodplain.

Be sure to stop about 8 miles from Castolon at the parking area for the **Santa Elena Canyon Overlook.** Laden with abrasive silt and gravel, the Rio Grande sculptured the canyon 1,500 feet deep, through the cliffs that tower above the geological trough that forms the bulk of the park.

Drive on to the end of the road, put on some old shoes, and, if the water is low, wade across **Terlingua Creek** to reach the **Santa Elena Canyon Trail.** The moderate 1.7-mile round-trip trail leads the hiker with striking views.

PANTHER JUNCTION TO RIO GRANDE VILLAGE & BOQUILLAS
24 miles one way; a half to full day

Before starting this tour, check at the visitor center for the condition of Hot Springs road. The main road, heading southeast, descends nearly

BIG BEND

Northeast Rim of Chisos Mountain

left and continue another 3 miles to the paved spur road to **Boquillas Canyon Overlook.** Turn left onto the main road, then left again to visit **Rio Grande Village,** an excellent place to watch birds. Don't miss the nature trail starting across from site No. 18 in the campground. This easy 0.75-mile loop leads through jungle-like floodplain vegetation before climbing onto a ridge that provides terrific views of the river and the Sierra del Carmen.

2,000 feet through desert shrub, terminating near the willows and cottonwoods on the banks of the Rio Grande.

After about 6.5 miles, turn left onto the unpaved road to see the spring at **Dugout Wells,** formerly the site of a ranch and schoolhouse, and now a fine place to picnic and look for wildlife. Return to the main road. As you continue, the peak aptly named **Elephant Tusk** will be on your right in the distance, and **Chilicotal Mountain** closer to the road. Far ahead looms the **Sierra del Carmen** in Mexico. Its striated rock formations are the same limestone and shale as in the cliffs at **Santa Elena Canyon.**

If you're up to a somewhat rough ride, be sure to take the turnoff to **Hot Springs,** whose mineral waters were valued for centuries and continue to be usable. Look for Indian pictographs on the cliffs along the trail to the springs, just beyond the old motel.

After returning to the main road, pull over at the **Rio Grande Overlook** just past the tunnel on the right and stroll a 50-yard trail for superb views of the Sierra del Carmen, the river floodplain, and part of **Boquillas del Carmen** village in Mexico. Big Bend bluebonnets bloom profusely here during a well-watered springtime.

Back on the road, continue straight for half a mile, then turn

PANTHER JUNCTION TO PERSIMMON GAP

26 miles one way; 2 hours

This drive from park headquarters at Panther Junction to Persimmon Gap, the park's northern entrance, follows an ancient trail used by the Comanche on their annual raiding forays into Mexico, and by Army expeditions, settlers, and miners of silver and lead. The road descends gently to Tornillo Creek and Tornillo Flat, one of the park's most over-grazed and poorly recovered areas. The mountains forming the ridge to the east are the Dead Horse Mountains, the Sierra del Carmen's northernmost reach.

Highlights along the way include a view of Dog Canyon, through which camels once lumbered in a 19th-century U.S. Army experiment, and, near the north end of the Tornillo Creek bridge, an exhibit of fossil mammal bones; the fossils were found in the park in sandstone dating from 50 million years ago.

For an excellent self-guided auto tour, pick up a pamphlet at either end of the road and, if it's spring-time, ask whether the giant dagger yuccas are in bloom. (If so, be sure to take the unpaved Dagger Flat Auto Trail to see stalkfuls of white blooms weighing up to 70 pounds.)

INFORMATION & ACTIVITIES

VISITOR & INFORMATION CENTERS
Panther Junction and **Chisos Basin Visitor Centers** open daily all year. **Castolon** open November to April.

SEASONS & ACCESSIBILITY
Open all year. Check current conditions before driving dirt roads.

HEADQUARTERS
1 Panther Junction, Big Bend NP, TX 79834. Phone (432) 477-2251. www.nps .gov/bibe

ENTRANCE FEE
$20 per car per week.

ACCESSIBLE SERVICES
Visitor center and two nature trails are wheelchair accessible. Free brochure.

THINGS TO DO
Free naturalist-led activities: nature walks, workshops, evening programs, nature seminars. Also, hiking, fishing, river-running (permit required), cycling.

OVERNIGHT BACKPACKING
Backpacking and river permits required. $10 permit for all overnight backcountry use. Obtain in person at visitor centers or ranger stations within 24 hours of trip.

CAMPGROUNDS
Three campgrounds with 14-day limit. Open all year. Fees $14 per night or $7 with a Golden Access Pass. For mid-November through mid-April reservations: (877) 444-6777; www.reserveusa .com. Tent and RV sites. At **Rio Grande Village Trailer Park,** full hookups only available, $32 per night. Three group campgrounds; reservations through headquarters for groups of 10 or more.

HOTELS, MOTELS, & INNS
(unless otherwise noted, rates are for 2 persons in a double room, high season)
Big Bend Resort and Adventures 100 Main St., Terlingua, TX 79852. (800) 848-2363 or (432) 371-2218. 82 rooms, 4 duplexes, 3-bedroom cottage. $102-$299. AC, restaurant.
Chisos Mountains Lodge Basin Rural Station, Big Bend NP, TX 79834. (432) 477-2291. 72 rooms, including 6 cottages, $130-$141. AC, restaurant.
Gage Hotel US 90 and US 385, Marathon, TX 79842. (800) 884-4243 or (432) 386-4205. 39 units. $97-$242. AC, restaurant.
Lajitas Golf Resort Star Rte. 70, Lajitas, TX 79852. (877) 525-4827 or (432) 424-5000. 101 rooms. $179-$599. AC, pool, restaurant.

For a full list of accommodations contact the Alpine visitor Information Center, (800) 561-3712 or (432) 837-2326, www .alpinetexas.com.

BIG BEND

EXCURSIONS

RIO GRANDE WILD AND SCENIC RIVER
BIG BEND NATIONAL PARK, TEXAS

Don't pass up a float down the Rio Grande. Easy floats include the Mariscal and Boquillas Canyons; Santa Elena and the Lower Canyons are more difficult. 196 Wild and Scenic miles. Permits required. Main access to Lower Canyons in Mexico; most takeout points fall on private land in Texas *(permission reqd.).* Primitive camping, hiking, fishing; tubing and swimming not recommended. Information about half-day to 1-week trips at Panther Junction. (432) 477-2251.

Visitors on the lantern-lit Left Hand Tunnel Tour

▶CARLSBAD CAVERNS

NEW MEXICO
ESTABLISHED MAY 14, 1930
46,766 acres

The Chihuahuan Desert, studded with spiky plants and lizards, offers little hint that what Will Rogers called the "Grand Canyon with a roof on it" waits underground. Yet, at this desert's northern reaches, underneath the Guadalupe Mountains, lies one of the deepest, largest, and most ornate caverns ever found.

Water molded this underworld 4 to 6 million years ago. Some 250 million years ago, the region lay underneath the inland arm of an ancient sea. Near the shore grew a limestone reef. By the time the sea withdrew, the reef stood hundreds of feet high, later to be buried under thousands of feet of soil. Some 15 to 20 million years ago, the ground uplifted. Naturally occurring sulfuric acid seeped into cracks in the limestone, gradually enlarging them to form a honeycomb of chambers. Millions of years passed before the cave decoration began. Then, drop by drop, limestone-laden moisture built an extraordinary variety of glistening formations—some six stories tall; others tiny and delicate.

Cave explorers have mapped more than 30 miles of passageways of Carlsbad Cavern, the park's most famous cave, and investigation continues. Visitors may tour 2 miles of paved trail without a guide. Slaughter Canyon Cave provides the hardy an opportunity to play caver, albeit with a guide. The park has more than 117 other caves.

Some visitors think the park's most spectacular sight is the one seen at the cave's mouth. More than a quarter million Brazilian (Mexican) free-tailed bats summer in a section of the cave, and around sunset they spiral up from the entrance to hunt for insects. The nightly exodus led to the discovery of the cave in modern times. Around the turn of the 20th century, miners began to excavate bat guano—a potent fertilizer—for shipment to the citrus groves of southern California. One of the guano miners, James Larkin White, became the first to explore and publicize the caverns beyond Bat Cave.

How to Get There

The park is off US 62/180, 20 miles southwest of Carlsbad and 164 miles east of El Paso, Texas. For the visitor center, turn west at Whites City and drive 7 miles. For Slaughter Canyon, turn west on County Road 418, 5 miles south of Whites City; drive another 11 miles, some unpaved, to the parking lot. Airports: Carlsbad, New Mexico, and El Paso, Texas.

When to Go

Year-round. The weather underground remains a constant 56°F. The main cavern gets crowded, especially in summer and on major holiday weekends. Either spring or fall, when the desert's in bloom, is an excellent time to go. You'll see the bats fly from April or mid-May through October.

How to Visit

One full day allows you time to tour the main cavern and take a nature walk or a drive before watching the bats fly at sunset. For a second day's activity, reserve space on a more rugged cave tour, like **Left Hand Tunnel, Lower Cave, Slaughter Canyon Cave, Hall of the White Giant,** or **Spider Cave.**

At the visitor center, select either the **Natural Entrance Tour** or the **Big Room Tour** (both are 1.25-mile walks). Try the first unless you have walking, breathing, or heart problems. It starts at the natural entrance and is mostly downhill, except for one stretch where you climb 40 feet; an elevator whisks you back to ground level. The Natural Entrance Tour is more intimate and may be less crowded than the Big Room.

The Big Room Tour begins with an elevator ride to the Big Room, in which you can see most of the types of formations visible in areas of the cave not open to the public. If after this tour you want to see more caves, take the elevator back up to ground level and proceed with the first half of the Natural Entrance Tour.

Another option, the **Kings Palace Tour** (see **Other Trails & Sights** p. 139), visits the stunning formations in the scenic rooms.

NATURAL ENTRANCE TOUR
1 mile; about 1 hour

The visitor center rents audio guides, if you wish. Follow the path to the cavern's natural entrance. The opening formed when part of the cave's ceiling collapsed thousands of years ago. Once in the mouth of the cave, glance right to spot 1,000-year-old red and black pictographs high on the wall. Indians knew of the

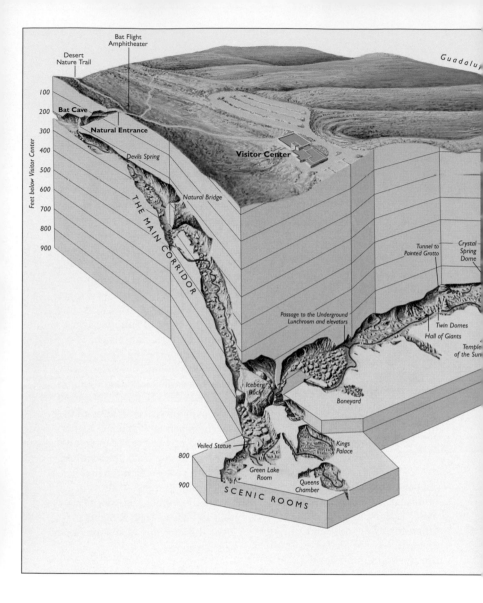

Desert Nature Trail

Bat Flight Amphitheater

Guadalup

100
200 **Bat Cave**
300 **Natural Entrance**
400 Devils Spring
500 **Visitor Center**
600
700 Natural Bridge
800
900

Feet below Visitor Center

THE MAIN CORRIDOR

Tunnel to Painted Grotto

Crystal Spring Dome

Passage to the Underground Lunchroom and elevators

Twin Domes

Hall of Giants

Temple of the Sun

Iceberg Rock

Boneyard

Veiled Statue

Kings Palace

800

Green Lake Room

900

Queens Chamber

SCENIC ROOMS

cavern and used the entrance for shelter. But without dependable lighting they could not have gone very far past the small sunlit area. You are descending the **Main Corridor,** which, if you keep looking around and up, conveys some of the cavern's enormity: The ceiling at times rises more than 200 feet above the path.

The trail soon passes **Devils Spring.** Here cave decoration continues. As water from rain and snow percolates through the ancient reef, it forms carbonic acid, which slowly dissolves the limestone. Upon reaching the cave, the water then releases calcite with each drop, splattering onto the floor as the water drips—producing a stalagmite—or leaving the calcite on the ceiling as the water discharges carbon dioxide into the cave air— creating a stalactite. (Park rangers

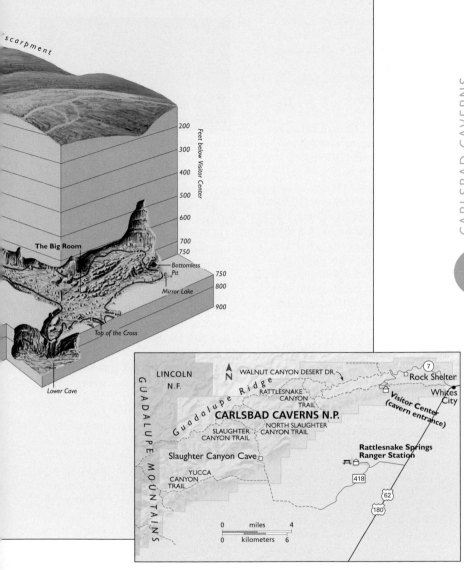

scarpment

200
300
400
500
600
700
750

Feet below Visitor Center

The Big Room

Bottomless Pit

750
800
900

Mirror Lake

Top of the Cross

Lower Cave

LINCOLN N.F.

WALNUT CANYON DESERT DR.

Rock Shelter

Whites City

Visitor Center (cavern entrance)

GUADALUPE Ridge

RATTLESNAKE CANYON TRAIL

CARLSBAD CAVERNS N.P.

NORTH SLAUGHTER CANYON TRAIL

SLAUGHTER CANYON TRAIL

Slaughter Canyon Cave

YUCCA CANYON TRAIL

Rattlesnake Springs Ranger Station

418

62

180

GUADALUPE MOUNTAINS

0   miles   4
0   kilometers   6

like to repeat the mnemonic that stalactites "hang tight" to the ceiling, while stalagmites "might touch the ceiling.") You would have heard a lot more dripping 10,000 years ago, when the climate was wetter. Now the Guadalupes receive only about 14 to 19 inches of precipitation a year, and most of the formations are no longer growing.

The trail soon skirts **Iceberg Rock,** a 200,000-ton boulder that crashed down from the ceiling thousands of years ago. After climbing **Appetite Hill,** stroll on past the **Boneyard,** which probably resembles the cavern of 4–6 million years ago, when water filled the chambers. Follow the signs to the **Underground Lunchroom** to have a meal, if you've

138

worked up an appetite. To reach
ground level, take the nearby elevator back up to the visitor center.

BIG ROOM TOUR
1 mile; 1 hour

After a minute's elevator ride, you
will be 754 feet, or about 75 stories, underground. (Compare your
entrance to that of visitors of the
early 1920s: They entered by "bucket
elevator," as a pulley lowered them
into the Bat Cave in a guano bucket.)
Follow the signs for the Big Room:
For the next hour or so, you'll be circling one gigantic chamber.

The **Big Room** is the largest single
room most cave visitors will ever see
(unless they go to Borneo, where
there is a cave with a larger, undeco-
rated chamber), 1,800 feet long at
its longest point, and 1,100 feet at its
widest. It encompasses 8.2 acres.

To best enjoy the tour, linger, look,
listen, and above all let loose your
imagination. What do the various formations look like to you? Layer cakes?
Chinese friezes? Fossilized bonsai?
Jellyfish? Draperies? The Park Service
removed labels from many of the formations, so now you can enjoy naming the fantasyscape yourself.

Near the beginning of the walk,
the **Hall of Giants** sports some of
the largest formations in the cave,
many of them about six stories
tall. Look for **Giant Dome,** a 62-foot-
high stalagmite, flanked by two
42-foot-high deputies. Appearances
are deceptive here because of the
immensity of the chamber.

The trail continues along the
periphery of the room (resist the
call of the shortcut) and leads past
a view of **Lower Cave,** accessible by
reserved tour. Farther along, at **Top
of the Cross,** you can get a panorama
of the big room. Glance up: The

Summer evening bat flight

ceiling here soars to 255 feet, its
highest point above the trail.

The footpath continues through
an area that was once a bat roost.
The so-called **Bottomless Pit** has been
measured at about 140 feet in depth;
it does not lead to other passages. As
you proceed, take a good look at sparkling **Crystal Spring Dome,** the cave's
largest active stalagmite: Each drop of
water adds crystals that make it infini-
tesimally bigger. Iron carried in the
water delicately stains the formations
of the Painted Grotto. Just a few minutes past the grotto, you will reach the
elevator and ascend to daylight.

In the visitor center, don't miss
the exhibits on cave environments
and the surrounding Chihuahuan
Desert. Be sure to take in the view
from the parking area. Standing
high above the ancient reef, you see
a striking vista of the reef's seaward
side (the slope past the parking lot)
and the ancient seabed, called the
Delaware Basin. If it's a clear day,
the panorama before you will extend
100 miles or more into Texas.

OTHER TRAILS & SIGHTS

Desert Nature Trail: This easy half-
mile loop makes an interesting
diversion before the evening bat
flight program. The trail's interpretive plaques describe how Indians
made use of virtually every plant in

Visitors gaze up at the natural entrance of a large cave room.

sight. The trail starts to the right of the cave's natural entrance.

Walnut Canyon Desert Drive: An alternative introduction to the area's natural history. A booklet available at the start guides you along this 9.5-mile gravel loop off the main park road, before the visitor center. (This road is not recommended for low-clearance vehicles.)

Kings Palace Tour: Led by park rangers, this 1.5-hour tour visits four highly decorative rooms, including the Kings Palace, which may be one of the world's most ornate cave rooms. Tour participants descend an additional 80 feet below the level of the Big Room (830 feet below ground level). This is the deepest part of the paved trail. *(Note: visitors must walk back out.)* Look for the giant draperies, formed by tricking water down the slanted ceiling. Visitors will also find soda-straw stalactites, columns, and other interesting speleothems. Tours (ages 4 and up) are offered several times a day throughout the year.

Bat Flight: Don't miss the evening cyclone of bats; at its peak, more than 5,000 bats per minute speed out of the cave on their way to consume some three tons of insects. From the visitor center, walk to the amphitheater, at the natural entrance. Check at the visitor center or call (575) 785-3012 for the program times. Cameras are not allowed, as lights and high-frequency sounds disturb the bats—this rule is strictly enforced.

Slaughter Canyon Cave: Be prepared to clamber as you explore an "unimproved" cave for 2 hours by flashlight (ages 8 and up). Accompanied by rangers, you'll see formations not found in the main cave, after a steep half-mile climb up to the cave's entrance from the parking lot in Slaughter Canyon. Open Friday, Saturday, and Sunday in summer; weekends only in winter.

Other guided tours include **Left Hand Tunnel** (ages 6 and up), **Spider Cave** (ages 12 and up), **Lower Cave** (ages 12 and up), and **Hall of the White Giant** (ages 12 and up). For reservations call (877) 444-6777 or visit www.recreation.gov.

INFORMATION & ACTIVITIES

VISITOR & INFORMATION CENTER

The **visitor center** is 7 miles from Whites City on N. Mex. 7; open daily all year. Call headquarters for information. Cave tour reservations (877) 444-6777 or www.recreation.gov.

SEASONS & ACCESSIBILITY

Open all year.

HEADQUARTERS

3225 National Parks Hwy., Carlsbad, NM 88220. Phone (575) 785-2232. www.nps .gov/cave

ENTRANCE FEES

Entrance Fee: Adults $6, children 15 and under free. Tours additional: **Kings Palace** $8 for adults, $4 for children. **Slaughter Canyon Cave,** $15 for adults, $7.50 for children. **Left Hand Tunnel** $7 for adults, $3.50 for children. **Lower Cave,** $20 for adults, $10 for children. **Hall of the White Giant,** $20 for adults, $10 for children. **Spider Cave,** $20 for adults, $10 for children. No charge for bat flight program.

PETS

Not allowed in caves or backcountry. Kennel at the visitor center ($6 per day).

ACCESSIBLE SERVICES

The visitor center and Bat Flight Amphitheater are wheelchair accessible, as is a portion of the Big Room Tour. Picnic area and restrooms accessible at Rattlesnake Springs.

THINGS TO DO

Ranger-led activities: tours of the main cavern (call park for details), cavern talks, dusk bat flight programs (for bat flight times call 575-785-3012), flashlight trip into Slaughter Canyon Cave and other adventure tours (see p. 139; reservations required). Also available, self-guided Desert Nature Trail, self-guided Walnut Canyon Desert Drive, backcountry trails.

SPECIAL ADVISORIES

• Wear low-heeled, nonskid shoes in the caverns, and take a jacket.

• Intense summer thunderstorms may cause floods in low-lying areas, lightning strikes in higher areas.
• Watch out for rattlesnakes when hiking the backcountry trails.
• Cactuses and other spiny desert plants can inflict painful injuries.
• Baby strollers are not permitted on cave trails.

OVERNIGHT BACKPACKING

Permits required. Available free at the visitor center.

CAMPGROUNDS

None; backcountry camping only. Food services in park. Note that campfires are not permitted in park.

HOTELS, MOTELS, & INNS
(unless otherwise noted, rates are for 2 persons in a double room, high season)

In Whites City, NM 88268:
Rodeway Inn 17 Carlsbad Cavern Hwy., P.O. Box 128. (800) 228-3767 or (575) 785-2291. 42 units. $110. AC, pool, restaurant.

In Carlsbad, NM 88220:
Best Western Stevens Inn 1829 S. Canal St., P.O. Box 580. (800) 730-2851 or (575) 887-2851. 220 units, 28 with kitchenettes. $110. AC, pool, restaurant.
Carlsbad Super 8 3817 National Parks Hwy. (800) 800-8000 or (575) 887-8888. 56 units. $90, includes breakfast. AC, pool.
Continental Inn 3820 National Parks Hwy. (575) 887-0341. 60 units. $60. AC, pool.
Great Western Inn & Suites 3804 National Parks Hwy. (800) 987-5535 or (575) 887-5535. 87 units, 25 with kitchenettes. $96-$65. AC, pool.
America's Best Value Inn 3706 National Parks Hwy. (575) 887-2861. 123 units. $70. AC, pool, restaurant.

Contact the Carlsbad Chamber of Commerce for a full list of accommodations: 302 South Canal St., Carlsbad, NM 88220. (575) 887-6516, www.carlsbad chamber.com.

EXCURSIONS

LINCOLN NATIONAL FOREST
ALAMOGORDO, NEW MEXICO

In 1950, a game warden here rescued a black bear cub from a forest fire and named him Smokey Bear—he became a famous symbol of fire prevention. Lincoln contains life zones from desert to subalpine forest and limestone caves. 1,103,441 acres. 370 campsites. Hiking, fishing, horseback riding, hunting, picnicking, winter sports. Open all year; most campsites open seasonally. Adjoins Carlsbad Caverns NP on west. Information at Carlsbad on US 285, about 20 miles from park. (575) 434-7200.

WHITE SANDS NATIONAL MONUMENT
ALAMOGORDO, NEW MEXICO

Waves of gypsum sand, some 50 feet high, offer an ever changing vista here in the Tularosa Basin. Weathered rock from surrounding highlands settles in Lake Lucero and adjacent alkali flats; scouring southwest winds create the dunes. Features 16-mile-long Dunes Drive. 144,420 acres. Primitive camping, food services, picnic areas. Hiking. Open daily except Christmas. Visitor center on US 70, about 190 miles from Carlsbad Caverns NP. (575) 479-6124.

BOSQUE DEL APACHE NATIONAL WILDLIFE REFUGE
SOCORRO, NEW MEXICO

The Rio Grande bisects this refuge where carefully maintained ponds and marshes shelter wintering snow geese and other waterfowl, as well as sandhill cranes and bald eagles. 57,191 acres. Hiking, fishing (in summer), biking, hunting, scenic drives. Open all year, from 1 hour before sunrise to 1 hour after sunset. Visitor center on N. Mex. 1, off I-25, about 270 miles from Carlsbad Caverns NP. (575) 835-1828.

The Guadalupe Mountains rising over Salt Basin Dunes

▶GUADALUPE MOUNTAINS

TEXAS
ESTABLISHED SEPTEMBER 30, 1972
86,416 acres

In West Texas, only about 40 miles southwest of Carlsbad Caverns, lies a gem of a park that few people outside the state have ever heard of, let alone visited. Guadalupe Mountains National Park contains the southernmost, highest part of the 40-plus-mile-long Guadalupe range. From the highway, the mountains resemble a nearly monolithic wall through the desert. But drive into one of the park entrances, take even a short stroll, and surprises crop up: dramatically contoured canyons, shady glades surrounded by desert scrub, a profusion of wildlife and birds.

Some 80 miles of trails can lead the more energetic hiker to Guadalupe Peak, the highest point in Texas (8,749 feet), and to mountaintops with scattered but thick conifer forests typical of the Rockies hundreds of miles to the north. The range's origins may be surprising too: The Guadalupe Mountains were once a reef growing beneath the waters of an ancient inland sea. That same vanished sea spawned the honeycomb of the Carlsbad Caverns.

Pottery, baskets, and spear points found in the mountains suggest that people first visited the Guadalupes about 12,000 years ago, hunting the camels, mammoths, and other animals that flourished in the wetter climate of the waning Ice Age. When the Spaniards arrived in the Southwest in the mid-16th century, Mescalero Apache periodically camped near the springs at the base of the mountains and climbed to the highlands to hunt and forage. Both the Apache and Europeans spun legends of fabulous caches of gold in these mountains.

As American prospectors, settlers, and cavalry pushed west, the Apache made the mountainous areas their bases and fought to ward off encroachers. By the late 1880s, however, virtually all the Indians had been killed or forced onto a reservation.

Donations of ranchlands eventually gave impetus to the park. In 1998 the park acquired 10,000 acres adjacent to its then western boundary, including some 2,000 acres of white gypsum sand dunes and dunes of brick red quartzose, both deposits left by the ancient sea.

How to Get There

The main visitor center and most visitor activities are located in the Pine Springs-Frijole Ranch area, off US 62/180, 55 miles southwest of Carlsbad and 110 miles east of El Paso. For McKittrick Canyon, turn off US 62/180 about 7 miles northeast of the main visitor center, then continue 4 miles to the parking lot. For Dog Canyon, either hike 12 miles from Pine Springs Campground or drive north on US 62/180, then west on Cty. Rd. 408, and south on N. Mex. 137, about 105 miles total from Pine Springs. Airports: Carlsbad, New Mexico, and El Paso, Texas.

When to Go

Year-round, but spring and fall are best. In spring, the foliage is fresh and, with enough rain, the blossoms abundant. In late October to mid-November, changing leaves provide hues of red, yellow, and burgundy.

How to Visit

On a day trip, head to the visitor center and Pine Springs; take at least a short hike. On a second day, visit McKittrick Canyon for a stroll through a hidden oasis. To visit a wilder, more isolated area, where trails take you quickly into the high country, drive about 2.5 hours to reenter the park at Dog Canyon in the north.

PINE SPRINGS-FRIJOLE RANCH AREA
a half to full day

Pick up maps and trail information at the **Headquarters Visitor Center,** where you can also enjoy audio-visual programs on the park's ecology, geology, and history. Fill your water bottles before leaving. Then stroll to **The Pinery** or drive back to the highway, turn left in about a tenth of a mile, and park. The stone walls remain from the 1858 Pinery Station of the Butterfield Overland Mail Line—forerunner of the Pony Express. Buy a self-guiding leaflet, if you wish, to learn about the colorful local history. Return to your car, and go back to the highway and turn left. Go left again in about a mile onto a dirt road. Park at the end near the **Frijole Ranch,** the 1870s ranch house that now preserves artifacts and exhibits the park's cultural history.

Be sure to walk the easy 2.3-mile loop trail to **Smith** and **Manzanita Springs,** an excellent introduction to the striking contrasts the Chihuahuan Desert presents. Bear right at the trailhead. The thorny plants may seem forbidding, but the Mescalero Apache used a great majority of the plants in sight for food or fiber. Their diet consisted largely of mescal, the

NEW MEXICO
TEXAS

Cutoff Mountain⁺
6,933 ft

BROKEOFF MOUNTAINS
Cutoff Ridge

Crow Flats

GUADALUPE

BUTTERFIELD STAGE ROUTE

Gypsum Sand Dunes

NATIONAL

Shumard Canyon △

Williams Ranch

Patterson Hills

Quail Mountain⁺
4,962 ft

Cone Peak⁺
5,017 ft

Salt Basin

LINCOLN NATIONAL FOREST

137

Dog Canyon
Ranger Station
Corral

West Dog Canyon

BUSH MT.
TRAIL

rcus

TEJAS TRAIL

Upper Dog Canyon

Lost Peak
+ 7,830 ft

McKittrick
Ridge
7,716 ft

GUADALUPE MOUNTAINS

South McKittrick Canyon

Wilderness
Ridge

Pratt Cabin

McKittrick Canyon

PERMIAN
REEF
GEOLOGY
TRAIL

Grotto
Picnic
Area

McKittrick
Canyon
Visitor
Center

Blue
Ridge

Mescalero

WILDERNESS

MOUNTAINS

Tejas

ush Mountain
,631 ft

BUSH MT. TRAIL
Pine Spring Canyon

Pine
Top

The Bowl

BOWL TR.

BEAR
CANYON
TRAIL

Smith
Spring

Frijole Ridge

ARK

DEVILS HALL
TRAIL

Hunter Pk.
8,368 ft

TEJAS TR.

G

Guadalupe Peak
(highest peak in Texas)
8,749 ft

Pine Springs

Manzanita
Spring

Frijole Ranch
History Museum

Corral

Headquarters
Visitor Center

The Pinery
Butterfield Stage
Station Ruins

Bone
Spring

El Capitan
8,085 ft

Glover Canyon

Salt Basin
Overlook

Guadalupe Pass
5,420 ft

Guadalupe Canyon

Delaware Mountains

Delaware

N

Brushy Mesa

Guadalupe Arroyo

62
180

54

0 miles 2
0 kilometers 3

62
180

heart of the agave plant, one of the succulents with spikes at the tips of the leaves—hence the culture's name. You'll soon approach **Manzanita Spring,** a place to spot wildlife.

Continue on to **Smith Spring,** a veritable garden of maidenhair ferns, Texas madrone trees (the ones shedding layers of paper-thin bark), alligator juniper (named for its distinctively textured bark), oak, and maple. As you loop back to your car, bear left at the fork.

Return to the highway and drive west-southwest about 5 miles, or at least as far as the first pullover, for a superb view of **El Capitan** (8,085 feet), the southernmost bluff of the Guadalupes. Late afternoon light shows off this imposing symbol of the region, once the beacon for conquistador, stagecoach driver, and homesteader.

McKITTRICK CANYON
a half to full day

The walls of McKittrick Canyon shelter the only year-round stream in the park; the water creates a 3-mile-long oasis of oak and juniper, madrone and maple. The canyon itself is nearly 5 miles long. Pick up a self-guiding booklet on the area's human and natural history at the **McKittrick Canyon Visitor Contact Station** near the trailheads. For an easy hike (although the trail is rocky and best negotiated in hiking boots), walk the 2.4 miles to **Pratt Cabin.** If you have time, continue another mile through the woods that border the intermittent stream to the Grotto picnic area. Because the canyon plants are fragile, be sure to stay on the trail.

McKittrick Canyon exposes millions of years of geological events. During the Permian period, about 260–270 million years ago, an inland sea covered parts of West Texas and southeast New Mexico. Along the shore of the sea grew a reef of lime-secreting algae, sponges, other marine organisms, and calcium carbonate precipitated from the water. After millions of years, the climate changed and the ocean dried up; the Capitan Reef loomed hundreds of feet high in a horseshoe 400 miles long. Sediments and mineral salts buried both basin and reef over the next eons. Later, the region began to rise, and erosion slowly reexposed the seabed with part of the fossil reef—today's Guadalupe range—towering above.

As you walk into McKittrick Canyon, you are entering the Capitan Reef from the seaward side. To best observe the reef's varied formation and fossils, try the **Permian Reef Geology Trail.** You'll see layers of the ancient reef exposed by centuries of cutting by McKittrick Creek. The trail—4.5 miles one way—climbs the 2,000-foot ridge to a ponderosa forest on the top.

DOG CANYON
a half to full day

Accessibility to the forested high country and its spectacular scenery make Dog Canyon well worth the drive. Ask a ranger to point out Apache mescal-roasting pits, still visible among the hip-high grasses, creosote bushes, and succulents. Then picnic and hike; the trails begin past the stables. Popular hikes include the **Bush Mountain Trail,** which, in about 3 miles, leads through open pinyon-juniper woodland to splendid views of the Guadalupes and the **Cornudas Mountains,** 55 miles to the west. The **Tejas Trail** offers similar views and in about 4 miles climbs into a temperate woodland of Gambel oak, Douglas fir, southwestern white pine, and ponderosa pine. This forest is a relic of the plant

INFORMATION & ACTIVITIES

VISITOR & INFORMATION CENTERS

Headquarters Visitor Center, 0.1 mile off US 62/180 near Guadalupe Pass. **McKittrick Canyon Visitor Contact Station,** off US 62/180 on eastern edge of park. **Dog Canyon Visitor Contact Station** to the north open intermittently. Call for details.

SEASONS & ACCESSIBILITY

Open all year but may be inaccessible for brief periods in winter due to snowstorms. Check with park.

HEADQUARTERS

400 Pine Canyon Drive Salt Flat, TX 79847. Phone (915) 828-3251 ext. 2124. www.nps.gov/gumo

ENTRANCE FEE

$5 per person (under 16 free), 7-day pass. Guadalupe Mountains Annual Pass, $20.

PETS

Not permitted on trails or in buildings; elsewhere must be leashed.

ACCESSIBLE SERVICES

Visitor centers, restrooms, Pine Springs Campground and amphitheater, Pinery Trail, and Smith Spring Trail to Manzanita Spring are wheelchair accessible.

THINGS TO DO

Hikes, horseback trail rides (no rentals), ranger-led hikes and talks, and evening and children's programs.

SPECIAL ADVISORIES

• Take at least one gallon of water per person, per day.
• No gas, food, or services in the park.
• No wood or charcoal fires permitted.

OVERNIGHT BACKPACKING

Designated sites only; permits required (free; from Headquarters Visitor Center). Use permits required to bring a horse into the park, available at Headquarters Visitor Center or Dog Canyon. Maximum 3 consecutive nights permitted at any backcountry campground. Horses not allowed overnight; can be stabled in Frijole Ranch (915) 828-3251 and Dog Canyon (575) 981-2418 corrals; call for reservations.

CAMPGROUNDS

Two campgrounds (Pine Spring and Dog Canyon), 14-day limit. Open all year; first come, first served. $8 per night. No showers. Tent and RV sites; no hookups. Two group campsites, call headquarters for info and reservations.

HOTELS, MOTELS, & INNS

(unless otherwise noted, rates are for 2 persons in a double room, high season)
In Whites City, NM 88268:
Cavern Inn 17 Carlsbad Cavern Hwy. (800) 228-3767 or (575) 785-2291. 42 units. $110. AC, pool, restaurant.
In Van Horn, TX 79855:
Knights Inn and Suites 1309 W. Broadway. (800) 621-2478 or (432) 283-2030. 33 units. $95. AC, pool.

See also Carlsbad Caverns NP listings p. 140

---

communities that cloaked the region in the last ice age. It still survives because of the particular, unusual combination of temperature and humidity at this high-altitude site.

OTHER HIKES

Hikers may find the following treks rewarding. They all begin from Pine Springs Campground; ask a ranger for information:

Guadalupe Peak, 8.4 miles roundtrip. Lightning storms can quickly gather on hot summer afternoons—it's best to begin your ascent by 8 a.m. and your descent by 1 p.m. If you see a storm coming, start down.

The Bowl, a lush area of relict Ice Age conifer forest. The 8.7-mile loop comprises the Tejas, Bowl, and Bear Canyon Trails.

Devils Hall, a steep, narrow canyon; 4.2 miles round-trip, mostly level.

THE COLORADO PLATEAU

IDAHO

WYO

HUMBOLDT-
TOIYABE
N.F.

95

93

84

15

80

Great
Salt
Lake

Salt Lake City

N E V A D A

80

G R E A T

Utah Lake

U T A H

Green

COLORADO
N.M.

50

93

HUMBOLDT-TOIYABE
N.F.

B A S I N

ARCHES N.P.

CANYONLANDS N.P.

MANTI-LASAL
N.F.

95

6

Henry Mountain Buffalo Herd

CAPITOL REEF N.P.

Westwater
Canyon

50

50

GREAT
BASIN
N.P.

FISHLAKE
N.F.

70

Moab

HUMBOLDT-TOIYABE
N.F.

DIXIE N.F.

BRYCE CANYON N.P.

24

95

NATURAL
BRIDGES
N.M.

6

CEDAR BREAKS N.M.

Cedar City

15

89

12

Lake
Powell

SPRING
MOUNTAIN
N.R.A.

93

DIXIE N.F.

ZION N.P.

GLEN
CANYON
N.R.A.

RAINBOW BRIDGE
N.M.

160

DEATH
VALLEY N.P.
(See The Pacific
Southwest)

DESERT
N.W.R.

9

Kanab

89

ALT
89

C O L O R A D O

MESA
VERDE
N.P.

395

95

157

Lake
Mead

LAKE MEAD
N.R.A.

67

89

160

CANYON
DE CHELLY
N.M.

C A L I F O R N I A

Las
Vegas

LAKE
MEAD
N.R.A.

93

GRAND
CANYON
N.P.

64

P L A T E A U

191

180

WUPATKI
N.M.

15

40

JOSHUA TREE N.P.
(See The Pacific Southwest)

Colorado

95

A R I Z O N A

Flagstaff

WALNUT
CANYON
N.M.

17

40

53

PETRIFIED
FOREST N.P.

EL MORR
N.

Mogollon Rim

5

15

Salton
Sea

10

Salt

PHOENIX

191

SAN
DIEGO

95

Gila

8

Gila

UNITED STATES
MEXICO

ORGAN PIPE
CACTUS N.M.

10

SAGUARO N.P.

Tucson

Sabino
Canyon

19

KARTCHNER
CAVERNS S.P.

PACIFIC
OCEAN

Gulf of California

0   miles   300

0   kilometers   400

N

THE COLORADO PLATEAU

Theodore Roosevelt called the Grand Canyon "the one great sight . . . every American should see." Although the Grand Canyon remains the most famous sight on the Colorado Plateau, this high desert drained by the Colorado River and its tributaries teems with scenic treasures. Numerous gorges slice the colorfully layered rock; stairstep terraces, buttes, and spires embellish it. The region contains the nation's largest concentration of national parks.

The striated cliffs of the canyon parks collectively encompass nearly two billion years of Earth's history, divulging tales of ancient seas and volcanoes, deserts and dinosaurs. The rush of rivers sculptured the colossal gorges and side canyons of Grand Canyon, Zion, and Canyonlands. Grit-bearing winds and the freeze and thaw of water droplets chiseled multihued rock into the hoodoos, arches, and pinnacles visible in Arches and Bryce Canyon.

Although one of the most sparsely populated regions of the United States today, the plateau features some of the country's richest remains of early Native American civilizations. Archaeological highlights range from petroglyphs in Canyonlands, Capitol Reef, and Saguaro to pueblos and solstice markers in Petrified Forest to spectacular cliff dwellings in Mesa Verde.

Thanks to abrupt changes in elevation, the canyon parks shelter a wide diversity of plants and animals. Desert or semi-desert at canyon bottom gives way to pinyon-juniper woodland and then ponderosa pine and spruce-fir forests. Lizards and deer, cottontails and bighorn sheep can coexist in the same park. The desert park Saguaro protects North America's largest cactus, as well as the many other plants and animals of the vast Sonoran Desert.

Flagstaff, Arizona, makes a convenient base for the South Rim of the Grand Canyon and for Petrified Forest. From Kanab, Utah, you can visit Grand Canyon's North Rim, Bryce Canyon, Capitol Reef, and Zion. Just west of the plateau, a 5-hour drive from Kanab, lies Great Basin. For Arches and Canyonlands, Moab, Utah, is the place to stop, and to visit Saguaro, head for Tucson, Arizona.

Star trails streak the night sky behind Delicate Arch.

▶ARCHES

UTAH
ESTABLISHED NOVEMBER 12, 1971
76,359 acres

This park contains more than 2,000 natural arches—the greatest concentration in the country. But numbers have no significance beside the grandeur of the landscape—the arches, the giant balanced rocks, spires, pinnacles, and slickrock domes against the enormous sky.

Perched high above the Colorado River, the park is part of southern Utah's extended canyon country, carved and shaped by eons of weathering and erosion. Some 300 million years ago, inland seas covered the large basin that formed this region. The seas refilled and evaporated—29 times in all—leaving behind salt beds thousands of feet thick. Later, sand and boulders carried down by streams from the uplands eventually buried the salt beds beneath thick layers of stone. Because the salt layer is less dense than the overlying blanket of rock, it rises up through it, forming it into domes and ridges, with valleys in between.

Most of the formations at Arches are made of soft red sandstone deposited 150 million years ago. Much later, groundwater began to dissolve the underlying salt deposits. The sandstone domes collapsed and weathered into a maze of vertical rock slabs called "fins." Sections of these slender walls eventually wore through, creating the spectacular rock sculptures that visitors to Arches see today.

The land has a timeless, indestructible look that is misleading.

The million visitors to the park each year threaten the fragile high desert ecosystem. One concern is a dark scale called biological soil crust composed of cyanobacteria, algae, fungi, and lichens that grow in sandy areas in the park. Footprints tracked across this living community may remain visible for years. In fact, the aridity helps preserve traces of past activity for centuries. Visitors are asked to walk only on designated trails or stay on slickrock or wash bottoms.

How to Get There

From Moab, take US 191 north 5 miles to the park entrance. From I-70, exit at Crescent Junction and follow US 191 south for 25 miles to the entrance. Airport: 15 miles north of Moab and at Grand Junction, Colorado, about 120 miles away.

When to Go

Year-round, but spring and fall are best; moderate temperatures are ideal for hiking in the high desert. Summers are hot and winters mild. Wildflowers peak in April and May.

How to Visit

Take the **Arches Scenic Drive** at least as far as the Windows Section. If possible, carry on to the historic Wolfe Ranch, Fiery Furnace, and the Devils Garden. Also allow time for hiking at least one of the park's spectacular trails, perhaps to **Delicate Arch** or even **Tower Arch,** in the park's remote Klondike Bluffs. If it's spring, summer, or fall (and you're not bothered by heights), consider joining a naturalist-led 3-hour hike through **Fiery Furnace** *(fee, reservations required for tours)*. It's strenuous, but you'll appreciate the shade in summer's heat. Go to www.recreation .gov for reservations and tickets *(walks fill quickly; reserve early)*.

ARCHES SCENIC DRIVE
18 miles one way; a half to full day

The scenic drive climbs from the floor of **Moab Canyon** to **Devils Garden,** passing through the heart of the park with spur roads leading to the **Windows Section** and **Wolfe Ranch** and to the **Delicate Arch** area. Numerous pull-offs allow leisurely viewing of the park's major features.

From the visitor center the road winds up the canyon wall. Pull off after 2 miles at the **Park Avenue Viewpoint and Trailhead** for a view down an open canyon flanked by sandstone skyscrapers. If you have a willing driver (or don't mind the 320-foot return climb), walk the easy 1-mile path to the **Courthouse Towers** parking area, where you can be picked up. Here signs describe nearby rock formations that show the birth and death of an arch.

Continue your drive to the beautiful slickrock expanse known as the **Petrified Dunes.** Here you skirt

ARCHES

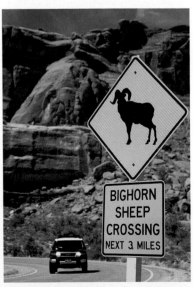

A sign alerts drivers of bighorn sheep country.

knolls—ancient dunes turned to stone—as the **La Sal Mountains** rise nearly 13,000 feet in the distance. Farther along, stop at the **Balanced Rock** pull-off where a 0.4-mile trail loops past this classic hoodoo, a strangely eroded rock spire 128 feet high. Edward Abbey wrote his classic *Desert Solitaire* after living in a trailer near here as a park ranger. Just beyond, turn onto the paved road leading to The Windows.

The road to the right passes a cluster of pinnacles and monoliths called **Garden of Eden** and ends at a parking area fronted by a sandstone wall perforated by several arches. Short trails lead to closeup views of these colossal gateways. The 0.3-mile walk to **South Window**, 105 feet wide, also gives you good views of **North Window** and **Turret Arch.** If time allows walk the half-mile trail for a dramatic closeup look at **Double Arch.**

Return to the main road. A road leaves the scenic drive and leads 1.5 miles to historic **Wolfe Ranch,** where a Civil War veteran raised cattle around the turn of the 20th century, and the **Delicate Arch Viewpoint,** 1 mile farther. The distant view of Delicate Arch is disappointing, so if you have the stamina and at least 2 extra hours consider hiking the **Delicate Arch Trail** from Wolfe Ranch (see pp. 156-157). Though it is one of the most rewarding hikes in canyon country, you may be better off saving it for a second day if you plan to take the full drive and do other walks.

Return to the main road. Skip the **Salt Valley Overlook** but pull off at **Fiery Furnace,** a dense array of red fins that appear to ignite when the sun is low in the west. Here you see a world standing on end—hoodoos, spires, and slabs 200 feet high. It's easy to get lost in the maze of deeply grooved slots and dead-end passageways.

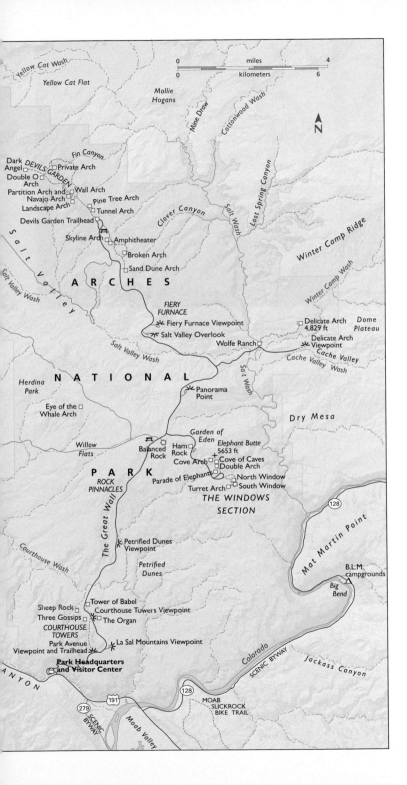

0
miles
4
kilometers
6

Yellow Cat Wash

Yellow Cat Flat

Mollie
Hogans

Mine Draw

Cottonwood Wash

N

Fin Canyon

Lost Spring Canyon

Dark DEVILS GARDEN
Angel □ □ Private Arch
Double O □ □
Arch
Partition Arch and □ □ Wall Arch
Navajo Arch □ Pine Tree Arch
Landscape Arch
□ Tunnel Arch

Devils Garden Trailhead

Clover Canyon

Salt Wash

Winter Camp Ridge

Skyline Arch □ □ Amphitheater

□ Broken Arch

Winter Camp Wash

□ Sand Dune Arch

Salt Valley

A R C H E S

Salt Valley Wash

FIERY
FURNACE
Fiery Furnace Viewpoint
Salt Valley Overlook
Wolfe Ranch □

Delicate Arch
4,829 ft
Delicate Arch
Viewpoint

Dome
Plateau

Cache Valley

Salt Valley Wash

Salt Wash

Cache Valley Wash

Herdina
Park

N A T I O N A L

Panorama
Point

Dry Mesa

Eye of the □
Whale Arch

Willow
Flats

Garden of
Eden
Balanced
Rock
Ham □
Rock
Cove Arch □
Elephant Butte
5653 ft
Cove of Caves
Double Arch

P A R K

ROCK
PINNACLES

Parade of Elephants
Turret Arch □

North Window
South Window

THE WINDOWS
SECTION

The Great Wall

Courthouse Wash

Petrified Dunes
Viewpoint

Petrified
Dunes

128

Mat Martin Point

B.L.M.
campgrounds

Big
Bend

Sheep Rock □ □ Tower of Babel
Three Gossips □ Courthouse Towers Viewpoint
□ □ The Organ
COURTHOUSE
TOWERS
Park Avenue
Viewpoint and Trailhead
La Sal Mountains Viewpoint

Park Headquarters
and Visitor Center

Colorado

SCENIC BYWAY

Jackass Canyon

CANYON

128

191

279

SCENIC
BYWAY

Moab Valley

MOAB
SLICKROCK
BIKE TRAIL

Turret Arch in the Windows area of the park

Note that visitors who are not part of a guided walk will need a permit *(fee; available only at visitor center)* to explore Fiery Furnace.

Continue your drive. Take the 0.2-mile walk to the cool shade of **Sand Dune Arch,** tucked between two fins, but save **Broken Arch** for another time. Farther down the road **Skyline Arch** comes into view. In 1940 a great rock mass broke from the arch, doubling the size of the opening to 45 by 69 feet.

The road ends at the Devils Garden campground and trailhead beyond. The **Devils Garden Trail** meanders 7.2 miles to seven major arches, each with its own character. Be sure to save enough time to walk at least as far as **Landscape Arch,** 0.8 mile down the trail. Here a narrow ribbon of stone 306 feet long appears to defy gravity as it floats in a graceful span above a dune. It's one of the world's longest freestanding natural arches.

If you walk the trail in early morning, watch for the white evening primrose. As the sunlight grows stronger, the flowers wilt, turning the petals pink. Though primitive beyond Landscape Arch, the trail continues on another mile to **Double O Arch,** a 160-foot-wide circular arch that hangs above a smaller bore. From here you can walk about half a mile to the rock spire known as the **Dark Angel.** A primitive trail curves from Double O Arch back to Landscape for those seeking a challenge.

DELICATE ARCH HIKE

3 miles round-trip; at least 2 hours

This delightful trail gains 500 feet in elevation as it traverses 1.5 miles of slickrock as smooth and cambered as the back of a whale. It tops out, suddenly and dramatically, at the foot of Delicate Arch, a must-see.

As nature writer Edward Abbey put it in *Desert Solitaire,* "If Delicate Arch has any significance it lies, I will venture, in the power of the odd and unexpected to startle the senses and surprise the mind out their ruts of habit, to compel us into a re-awakened awareness of the wonderful—that which is full of wonder."

The hike begins on the grounds of the Wolfe Ranch, which include a weathered corral and a tattered log cabin. Follow the bridge across Salt Wash to the cliff on the left, where it is believed the Ute Indians left petroglyphs. The Ute, who once roamed from the eastern slope of the Colorado Rockies to the canyonlands of southern Utah, perhaps camped here, probably trading with Wolfe for provisions.

The trail is ingeniously designed to hide Delicate Arch from view until your very last step. From the valley floor the route threads patches of cryptobiotic soil before reaching flat slabs of sandstone, where cairns mark the way. Juniper trees grow from cracks so small the trunks seem to emerge from solid rock. The final third of a mile is a teaser. As the path climbs, it hugs a sandstone fin, then edges along a steep bowl that bars all view of the famous arch. The last few steps require some nerve, but you will be rewarded with a marvelous look at Delicate Arch straddling the edge of a slickrock basin.

Standing 45 feet tall at its highest point, Delicate Arch frames the **La Sal Mountains** some 35 miles away. Over the years other names have been attached to this famous arch— Schoolmarm's Pants, Old Maid's Bloomers, and Cowboy Chaps.

The best time to photograph Delicate Arch is near sunrise or sunset. Time your evening hike for the full moon and you may have the thrill of seeing the moon rise above the arch—though the return trip in dim light can be tricky.

TOWER ARCH TRAIL

2.4 miles round-trip; 2 hours

Located in the park's remote **Klondike Bluffs** area, this 1.2-mile one-way trail to Tower Arch winds through an intricate landscape of weird sandstone formations, cresting ridge tops now and then for outstanding vistas of the Fiery Furnace, the La Sal Mountains, Book Cliffs, and clusters of towering hoodoos.

To reach the trailhead, drive 1 mile south on the main park road from the Devils Garden parking lot, then turn west on the high-clearance road just past **Skyline Arch.** *(This unpaved road may be impassable during or after storms.)* Follow the road 7.7 miles through Salt Valley to the turnoff on the left for Tower Arch Trail.

Cairns direct you from the parking lot up a steep rock ridge, and the route soon leads down through a land littered with fins and other rock outcroppings to Tower Arch, which takes its name from the pinnacle standing nearby.

ARCHES

Ute Indian petroglyphs

INFORMATION & ACTIVITIES

VISITOR & INFORMATION CENTER

Visitor center, on US 191 at park entrance, open daily all year. Call headquarters number for visitor information.

SEASONS & ACCESSIBILITY

Open year-round. Some unpaved roads may become temporarily impassable after heavy rains. Call headquarters for current weather and road information.

HEADQUARTERS

P.O. Box 907, Moab, UT 84532. Phone (435) 719-2299. www.nps.gov/arch

ENTRANCE FEE

$10 per car per week allows multiple entries. Yearly fee of $25 is also good at Canyonlands NP and Natural Bridges and Hovenweep NM.

PETS

Prohibited on all hiking trails and in the backcountry.

ACCESSIBLE SERVICES

Visitor center and its restrooms are wheelchair accessible. Restroom and one campsite accessible in Devils Garden Campground. Park Avenue and Delicate Arch Viewpoints are accessible to wheelchairs.

THINGS TO DO

Naturalist-led activities: nature hikes and talks, evening programs. Reservations must be made online at www .recreation.gov for the Fiery Furnace Walk ($10); children under 6 not permitted. Also available, geological and historical exhibits, self-guided auto tour, hiking, jeep tours, sight-seeing flights. Contact park headquarters for list of concessioners offering rental and guide services.

SPECIAL ADVISORIES

• Always carry water on hikes—at least a gallon a day per person is recommended in summer.
• Stay on trails to protect fragile desert soils and plant life.
• Sandstone slickrock crumbles easily

and can make climbing dangerous. It is often easier to go up than down.

OVERNIGHT BACKPACKING

Permits required (free from visitor center).

CAMPGROUNDS

One campground, **Devils Garden,** 18 miles from the park entrance, has a 7-day limit. Open all year. Fifty-one sites (1 wheelchair accessible), all reserved online at www.recreation.gov from March through Oct. Sites are often booked several months in advance. Nov. through Feb. all sites are first come first served. Fees $20 per night. No showers. Tent and RV sites; no hookups. Reservations also required for the **Devils Garden Group Campgrounds.** Call (435) 719-2299 or visit the website.

HOTELS, MOTELS, & INNS
(unless otherwise noted, rates are for 2 persons in a double room, high season)

In Moab, UT 84532:
Best Western Green Well Motel 105 S. Main St. (800) 528-1234 or (435) 259-6151. 72 units. $100-$189. AC, pool, restaurant.
Big Horn Lodge 550 S. Main St. (800) 325-6171 or (435) 259-6171. 58 units. $100. AC, pool, restaurant.
Pack Creek Ranch 15 miles south of Moab, off La Sal Mountain Loop Rd. (435) 259-5091. Cabins, houses, bunkhouses. $105-$300. Massages for a fee. AC, pool. Reservations at www.park creekranch.net.
Ramada Moab Downtown 182 S. Main St. (800) 272-6232 or (435) 259-7141. 81 units. $79-$182. AC, pool, restaurant.

For other accommodations in the area, contact Moab Area Travel Council, Main & Center Sts., Moab, UT 84532. (800) 635-6622 or (435) 259-8825, www.discover moab.net.

EXCURSIONS

MANTI-LA SAL NATIONAL FOREST
MOAB, UTAH

Mountains, densely wooded with aspen, pine, fir, and spruce and rugged grassland-covered plateaus, provide cool contrast here in red-rock country. Contains Dark Canyon Wilderness. 1,265,254 acres, part in Colorado. Hiking, climbing, bicycling, fishing, horseback riding, hunting, winter sports. 25 developed campgrounds, picnic areas. Open year-round; services open late May through October. Information in Moab on US 191. The Moab District of the NF is located about 5 miles southeast of Arches NP; the Monticello District borders Canyonlands NP to the south. (435) 259-7155 or (435) 637-2817.

COLORADO NATIONAL MONUMENT
FRUITA, COLORADO

The 23-mile-long Rim Rock Drive and well-maintained trails with gentle switchbacks provide easy access to this monument's small, sheer-walled canyons and sandstone monoliths. Shelters mule deer, bighorn sheep, and mountain lions. 20,533 acres. Hiking, climbing, bicycling, scenic drives, winter sports. 80 campsites, picnic areas, handicapped access. Open year-round. Located on Colo. 340, about 100 miles from Arches NP. (970) 858-3617.

ARCHES

View from Sunrise Point at dawn

▶ BRYCE CANYON

UTAH
ESTABLISHED SEPTEMBER 15, 1928
35,835 acres

Perhaps nowhere are the forces of natural erosion more tangible than at Bryce Canyon. Its wilderness of phantom-like rock spires, or hoodoos, attracts more than one million visitors a year. Many descend on trails that give hikers and horseback riders a close look at the fluted walls and sculptured pinnacles.

The park follows the edge of the Paunsaugunt Plateau. On the west are heavily forested tablelands more than 9,000 feet high; on the east are the intricately carved breaks that drop 2,000 feet to the Paria Valley. Many ephemeral streams have eaten into the plateau, forming horseshoe-shaped bowls. The largest and most striking is Bryce Amphitheater. Encompassing 6 square miles, it is the park's scenic heart.

For millions of years water has carved, as it continues to, Bryce's rugged landscape. Water may split rock as it freezes and expands in cracks—a cyclic process that occurs some 200 times a year. In summer, runoff from cloudbursts etches into the softer limestones and sluices through the deep runnels. In about 50 years the present rim will be cut back another foot. But there is more here than spectacular erosion.

In the early morning you can stand for long moments on the rim, held by the amphitheater's mysterious blend of rock and color. Warm yellows and oranges radiate from the deeply pigmented walls as scatterings of light illuminate the pale spires.

There is a sense of place here that goes beyond rocks. Some local Paiute Indians explained it with a legend. Once there lived animal-like creatures that changed themselves into people. But they were bad, so Coyote turned them into rocks of various configurations. The spell-bound creatures still huddle together here with faces painted just as they were before being turned to stone.

How to Get There

From Zion NP (83 miles west), follow Utah 9 east, turn north on Utah 89, then continue east on Utah 12 to Utah 63, which is the park entrance road. From Capitol Reef NP (about 120 miles away), follow Utah 12 southwest to Utah 63. Airports: Salt Lake City, Utah, or Las Vegas, Nevada.

When to Go

All-year park. Wildflowers peak in spring and early summer; the greatest variety of the park's 170 bird species appear between May and October. Winter lasts from November through March; snow highlights the colored cliffs and provides fine cross-country skiing and snowshoeing.

How to Visit

On a 1-day visit, tour the **Bryce Amphitheater,** beginning, if possible, with sunrise at **Bryce Point.** If limited time requires choosing between the scenic drive or a walk beneath the rim, take the walk. On a longer stay, drive to **Rainbow Point;** consider a moonlight stroll among the hoodoos.

BRYCE AMPHITHEATER

8 miles; 2 hours to a full day

Watch sunrise from **Bryce Point,** one of the highest overlooks along the rim of the amphitheater. Drive about 4 miles south of the visitor center, then walk a short distance from the parking lot to the viewpoint. Colors begin to glow just as the sun breaks over the **Aquarius Plateau,** at over 10,000 feet the highest plateau in North America. First light catches the rim of the amphitheater, then drops into the basin, igniting the crowded pillars of rock. From this vantage point you see shallow caves along the rim called the **Grottoes.** Look for the **Alligator,** a sharply incised butte that appears reptilian from above, and the **Sinking Ship,** which resembles a vanishing prow.

Drive back to **Inspiration Point,** bypassing the **Paria View** turnoff. From the parking lot walk up a short but steep trail to upper Inspiration Point. If the trail looks too ambitious, stay below at the lower viewpoint. Both look over the head of the amphitheater and place you close to the rock formations. No matter what time of day, they provide excellent all-around views.

In the valley below is the small town of **Tropic.** Scottish emigrant Ebenezer Bryce and his wife, Mary, homesteaded nearby in 1875. They grazed cattle in Bryce Canyon but

BRYCE CANYON

Hoodoos near Sunrise Point

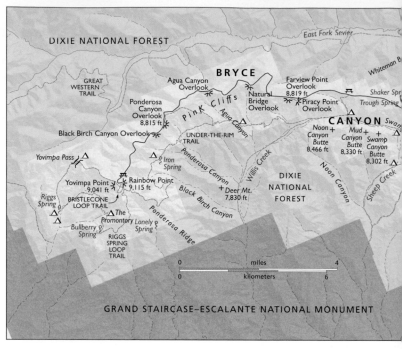

DIXIE NATIONAL FOREST

East Fork Sevier

BRYCE

GREAT
WESTERN
TRAIL

Agua Canyon
Overlook

Farview Point
Overlook
8,819 ft

Whiteman B.

Shaker Spr

Ponderosa
Canyon
Overlook
8,815 ft

Natural
Bridge
Overlook

Piracy Point
Overlook

Trough Spring

Pink Cliffs

Agua Canyon

Black Birch Canyon Overlook

UNDER-THE-RIM
TRAIL

CANYON

Swan.

Noon
Canyon
Butte
8,466 ft

Mud
Canyon
Butte
8,330 ft

Swamp
Canyon
Butte
8,302 ft

Yovimpa Pass

Iron
Spring

Ponderosa Canyon

Willis Creek

Noon Canyon

Sheep Creek

Yovimpa Point
9,041 ft

Rainbow Point
9,115 ft

Black Birch Canyon

Deer Mt.
7,830 ft

DIXIE
NATIONAL
FOREST

Riggs
Spring

BRISTLECONE
LOOP TRAIL

The
Promontory

Bullberry
Spring

Lonely
Spring

Ponderosa Ridge

RIGGS
SPRING
LOOP
TRAIL

0   miles   4

0   kilometers   6

GRAND STAIRCASE–ESCALANTE NATIONAL MONUMENT

moved away 5 years later, leaving behind little more than their name.

Continue on to **Sunset Point.** The name is misleading since the viewpoint faces east, limiting sundown views. But the mix of shadows and deep-hued colors makes this an excellent vantage point in the low-angled light of later afternoon. To the left is **Thor's Hammer;** to the right is the **Silent City**—a gridwork of deep ravines that divide turreted walls suggesting the ruins of an ancient metropolis.

Those with time and stamina can follow the **Navajo Loop Trail,** a fairly strenuous 1.3-mile loop into the canyon. The trail drops steeply in a series of switchbacks before entering a narrow, steep-walled gorge called **Wall Street.** Several Douglas firs, two of them 500 years old, grow between the towering cliffs.

Continue down the trail to the junction with **Queen's Garden Trail,** the least strenuous trail below the rim. It winds along the bottom of the amphitheater to Queen's Garden, then climbs to the rim at Sunrise Point, passing weird rock formations and occasional bristlecone pines. From Sunrise Point follow the **Rim Trail** a half mile back to your car at Sunset Point.

THE DRIVE TO RAINBOW POINT

17 miles; 3 hours to a half day

Following the edge of the gently tilted plateau, this scenic drive ascends over a thousand feet to Rainbow Point, the plateau's southernmost reach.

From the **Visitor Center,** proceed South past the Sunset Point turn-off and on beyond the Bryce Point turnoff. You will leave the ponderosa pine forest behind and quickly find yourself among the high-elevation Douglas fir and blue spruce.

Pull in at **Farview Point** for a panoramic view of **Table Cliffs** and a series of broad platforms stair-

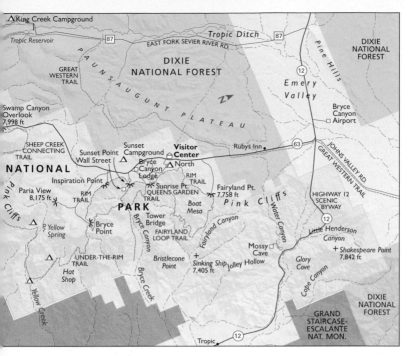

stepping southeast to the **Kaibab Plateau** at the North Rim of the **Grand Canyon.**

Continue south to **Natural Bridge** pull-off. Here you have a closeup view of a natural arch 85 feet long and 125 feet high. Its bright rusty red contrasts with the deep green of the trees below and the deep blue of the sky above.

The next pull-off is **Agua Canyon,** one of the finest vistas in the park. Massive hoodoos stand close to the rim; farther off are the vividly colored **Pink Cliffs;** and on the far horizon is the domed profile of **Navajo Mountain,** over 10,000 feet high.

Continue to the end of the road at **Rainbow Point.** You might choose to stop for a picnic among the thick stands of fir on the park's highest elevation, 9,115 feet. A pleasant mile walk follows the **Bristlecone Loop Trail** to expansive views. A spur trail leads to more views at **Yovimpa Point;** the cliffs that descend from there in stairsteps are named for

their rock colors—pink, gray, white, vermilion, and chocolate. A stand of ancient bristlecone pines grows on the exposed edge of the plateau, which you can see when hiking the Bristlecone Loop Trail.

As you backtrack through the park but just before you leave, a mile-long spur road leads to the **Fairyland Point** overlook (you bypassed this on the way in). This is one of the finest vistas in the park. In colorful array, spires and monoliths rise close at hand. Some stand isolated like chess pieces; others

Exploring Bryce Canyon on horseback

INFORMATION & ACTIVITIES

VISITOR & INFORMATION CENTER
Visitor center on main road, 1 mile inside park boundary. Open all year. Call headquarters for visitor information.

SEASONS & ACCESSIBILITY
Park open year-round. Roads may be closed for short periods due to snowstorms. Some spur roads closed in winter for cross-country skiing. Phone headquarters for information.

HEADQUARTERS
P.O. Box 640201, Bryce, UT 84764-0201. Phone (435) 834-5322. www.nps.gov/brca

ENTRANCE FEE
$25 per car per week. From May through Sept., visitors may leave their cars near the entrance. From there, a shuttle system will transport visitors to points throughout the park.

ACCESSIBLE SERVICES
Visitor center accessible to wheelchairs; all viewpoints and a half-mile stretch of trail between Sunset and Sunrise Points also accessible.

THINGS TO DO
Free naturalist-led activities (summer): nature walks, history and geology talks, evening programs, night sky programs, moonlight walks. Also, hiking, guided trail rides (inquire at Bryce Lodge or call 435-679-8665), cross-country skiing, snowshoeing.

OVERNIGHT BACKPACKING
Allowed on the **Under-the-Rim Trail** and the **Riggs Spring Loop Trail**. Purchase permits for $5-$15 at visitor center.

CAMPGROUNDS
Two campgrounds; 14-day limit. Part of **North** open all year. **Sunset** open May through Sept. Some sites reserve through NRRS (see p. 10) mid-May–Sept. $15 per night. Showers nearby. Tent and RV sites; no hookups. **Sunset Group Campground** reservations required; call (877) 444-6777 or visit www.recreation.gov to reserve group sites. Food services in park.

HOTELS, MOTELS, & INNS
(unless otherwise noted, rates are for 2 persons in a double room, high season)

INSIDE THE PARK:
Lodge of Bryce Canyon (south of Utah 12 on Utah 63) Forever Resorts, Bryce Canyon NP, UT 84717. 40 cabins, 70 rooms, 3 suites, 1 studio. $130-$179. (877) 386-4383. www.brycecanyonforever.com.

OUTSIDE THE PARK:
In Bryce, UT 84764:
Best Western Ruby's Inn 26 S. Main St. (800) 528-1234 or (435) 834-5341. 368 units. $110-$200. AC, pool, restaurant.
Bryce Canyon Pines Motel Utah 12. (435) 834-5441. 50 rooms; 4 cabins, 1 kitchenette. $110. Pool, restaurant.
Bryce Canyon Resorts 13500 E. Hwy 12. (866) 834-0043 or (435) 834-5351. 6 cabins, 3 cottages, 62 rooms. $149. AC, pool, restaurant.

In Panguitch, UT 84759:
Adobe Sands Motel 390 N. Main St. (435) 676-8874. 33 units. $59. AC. Open May through Oct.
New Western Motel 180 E. Center St., P.O. Box 73. (435) 676-8876. 55 units. $75. AC, pool.
Color Country Motel 526 N. Main St., P.O. Box 163. (435) 676-2386. 26 units. $54-$62. AC.

group together like a Greek chorus. A short hike down the trail takes you right among them—a final immersion course in the effects of erosion before you depart.

An interesting note about the park: Acoustic studies have found that the natural silence in Bryce equals the quality of a sound studio. The park boasts some of the nation's best air quality as well. But naturalists worry that this purity will be threatened by development on adjacent lands.

EXCURSIONS

DIXIE NATIONAL FOREST
CEDAR CITY, UTAH

Four sections of this canyon-country forest fan out across southwestern Utah, featuring unusual rock formations and sections of the historic Spanish Trail. 1,967,129 acres. Hiking, boating, mountain biking, fishing, horseback riding, scenic drives, winter sports, water sports. 27 campgrounds, boat ramp, picnic areas. Open year-round; most campsites open May through Oct. Information in Cedar City on I-15, about 70 miles from Bryce Canyon NP. (435) 865-3700.

CEDAR BREAKS NATIONAL MONUMENT
CEDAR CITY, UTAH

Erosion carved an immense amphitheater in a 10,000-foot southern Utah plateau; in it are extraordinary rock shapes colored by iron and manganese. 6,155 acres. Hiking, scenic drives, winter sports, daily ranger-led activities. 29 campsites, picnic areas, handicapped access. Services and roads closed late fall and winter. Visitor center on Utah 148, about 60 miles from Bryce Canyon NP. (435) 586-9451.

FISHLAKE NATIONAL FOREST
RICHFIELD, UTAH

Fish Lake, hopping with splake and trout (including 35-pound Mackinaw), is only one attraction of this region of dense forests, mountains, and plateaus. The Skyline Trail winds through its 11,000-foot peaks and a large village of the prehistoric Fremont people lies within its boundaries. Over 1.7 million acres. Hiking, boating, fishing, horseback riding, hunting, scenic drives, winter sports. 40 campsites, boat ramp, handicapped access. Open year-round; most campsites open May through October. Information at Richfield, off US 89, about 80 miles from Bryce Canyon NP. (435) 896-9233.

BRYCE CANYON

The Green River running through Canyonlands

▶CANYONLANDS

UTAH
ESTABLISHED SEPTEMBER 12, 1964
337,598 acres

From the rim you glimpse only segments of the Green River and the Colorado River, which flow together at the heart of Canyonlands. But everywhere you see the water's work: canyon mazes, unbroken scarps, sandstone pillars.

The paths of the merging rivers divide the park into three districts. The high mesa known as the Island in the Sky rises as a headland 2,000 feet above the confluence. South of the Island and east of the confluence is The Needles, where red- and white- banded pinnacles tower 400 feet over grassy parks and sheer-walled valleys. A confusion of clefts and spires across the river to the west marks The Maze, a remote region of pristine solitude. On every side the ground drops in great stairsteps.

Flat benchlands end abruptly in rock walls on one side and sheer drops on the other. It is a right-angled country of standing rock, and only a few paved roads probe the edges of the park's 527 square miles.

Sandstone layers of varying hardness make up Canyonlands' visible rock. But the character of the land is largely shaped by underlying salt deposits, which, under tremendous pressure from the rock above, push upward, forming domes that fracture the surface.

Yearly rainfall averages 8 inches but varies greatly from year to year. Trees that grow here have to be tough and resilient. In drought years, junipers survive by limiting growth to a few branches, letting the others die. Gnarled juniper and pinyon pine take root in the rim-lands wherever soil collects, includ-ing slickrock cracks and potholes.

How to Get There

Island in the Sky District: From Moab (35 miles away), take US 191 north 12 miles to Utah 313 and proceed 23 miles southwest to the visitor center.

Needles District: From Moab (75 miles away), follow US 191 south to Utah 211 and then west for 34 miles to park entrance.

Maze District: From Green River, take I-70 west to Utah 24, then south to a well-marked dirt road leading 46 miles to Hans Flat Ranger Station.

Ground shuttles are available from Salt Lake City and Grand Junction, Colo. Air shuttles fly between Canyonlands Airport and Denver and Las Vegas. The airport at Grand Junction is about 115 miles from the Island in the Sky.

When to Go

Spring and fall are ideal for exploring by foot or vehicle. Summer is hot, but humidity low. Snow and cold can make it hard to get around in winter.

How to Visit

The park's isolation and preponder-ance of backcountry make visiting a spectacular experience, but there are few visitor facilities and paved roads. A four-wheel-drive vehicle will let you explore. If you have only 1 day, visit the **Island in the Sky.** On another day, go to **The Needles** for a chance to explore classic canyon country. With more time, focus on the hiking trails and four-wheel-drive routes to **The Maze** and other remote areas.

ISLAND IN THE SKY
23 miles; a half to full day

CANYONLANDS

The road enters the park just before you cross **The Neck,** a rock span not much wider than the road that con-nects the mesa to the rimlands.

For a sweeping view of the park's narrow, interlocked canyons and its wide skies, drive right to the end of the road at **Grand View Point Overlook** (6,080 feet). Directly below in **Monument Basin,** stone col-umns rise more than 300 feet from the canyon floor.

Hidden in deep gorges to the south, the **Green River** joins the **Colorado River.** During his explora-tion of the Colorado in 1869, John Wesley Powell scaled the canyon

Flowering paintbrush

Horseshoe Canyon
Barrier Cr.
Horsethief Point

HORSESHOE CANYON UNIT
Great Gallery Pictographs

Horsethief Canyon

Fort Ruin

Upheaval Canyon
Upheaval Dome
Whale Rock
ISLAND
THE SK

WHITE

WHITE RIM RD.

Willow Flat
Me
Arc

Green River Overlook

The Spur

Millard Canyon

GLEN

Stillwater Canyon

Green

CANYON

Cleopatra's Chair 6,250 ft

Ekker Butte 6,226 ft

CANYON

Panorama Pt. Overlook

Grand View Point Overlook 6,080 ft

Junction Butte

WHITE RIM RD.

Hans Flat Ranger Station
Natural Arch

Horse Canyon

NATIO

Petes Mesa
Maze Overlook

NATIONAL

Elaterite Butte 6,552 ft

Harvest Scene Pictographs

THE MAZE

Confluenc 3,855 ft

Orange Cliffs

Chimney Rock 5,563 ft

Confluer Overloo

Land of

PAR

RECREATION

Standing

Bagpipe Butte Overlook
Bagpipe Butte 6,679 ft

Rocks

Elephant Hil

AREA

Ernies Country

Colorado

TH

Cataract Canyon

The Grabens

Ches
Park

Teapot Rock 6,221 ft

DARK CANYON PRIMITIVE AREA

Waterhole Flat

0 miles 4
0 kilometers 6

Lake Powell

CANYON R

DARK CANYON PRIMITIVE AREA

RECREATION

walls at the confluence and discovered a strangely carved landscape. "Wherever we looked," he wrote, "there was a wilderness of rocks."

Drive back the way you came, bypassing **Buck Canyon** and **Murphy Point Overlooks.** Turn left onto the road leading to Upheaval Dome, then follow the paved spur road past Willow Flat Campground to **Green River Overlook.** Here you view a wide expanse of canyon country: Below, a quiet stretch of the Green River runs through **Stillwater Canyon,** with **The Maze** beyond and the **Henry Mountains** topping the distant horizon.

Continue on to **Upheaval Dome,** where the road ends at a good picnic spot shaded by junipers and pinyon pines. Stretch your legs on the half-mile trail to the lip of this unusual geological feature. Here the surface drops into a mile-wide crater enclosed by rock strata upturned in concentric circles, with a center rock spire. Some geologists believe that

CANYONLANDS

Butte at Island in the Sky area of the park

a meteorite collided with Earth here. Retrace your path to the main road.

Be sure to pull off at the **Mesa Arch Trailhead.** An easy half-mile loop takes you through a pinyon-juniper woodland to a small natural arch carved from the rim. The curve of the arch frames a magnificent view of the **Washer Woman Arch** and the **La Sal Mountains,** snowy in winter.

Just before leaving the park, stop at the **Shafer Canyon Overlook.** The short trail leads along a promontory above canyons gouged from miles of layered stone. In late afternoon, the rocks seem to ignite in the low angle of the setting sun.

THE NEEDLES

35 miles; most of a day

Unless you have decided to camp, you'll probably be driving from Moab, 1.5 hours away, or Monticello, an hour away. The Needles area covers a lattice of canyons, flat-bottomed valleys called grabens, arches, and

Remnants of a cowboy camp along Cave Spring Trail

spectacular sandstone walls notched by rocky spires and columns. To the north, **Island in the Sky** and **Junction Butte** stand silhouetted against the horizon.

Utah 211 will take you directly to The Needles Visitor Center, where a dirt road heads north to the **Colorado River Overlook.** This road makes for rough going; don't take it unless you have a four-wheel-drive vehicle.

Continue on the paved road to the **Roadside Ruin** pull-off. Stretch your legs on a quarter-mile self-guided nature trail that leads to a small but well-preserved granary used by Indians to store corn more than 700 years ago. These ancient farmers were related to the ancestral Puebloans of Mesa Verde and Chaco Canyon. Pick up an interpretive booklet at the trailhead to learn how they used the native plants.

Your next stop will be **Pothole Point,** where a half-mile trail leads past depressions in the sandstone that fill with water after a rain. Although the water looks as still as the rock, the depressions often teem with life. Snails, fairy shrimp, and horsehair worms lay eggs that survive the heat of summer encased in dried mud. When the rains come, they hatch in days.

The road ends at **Big Spring Canyon Overlook,** where squat columns of sandstone rise from barren bedrock. Here the 5.5-mile **Confluence Overlook Trail** climbs the far side of the canyon by a ladder and ends at a point 930 feet above the junction of the rivers. This is a popular trail with most park visitors. More scenic is the 2.5-mile **Slickrock Foot Trail,** which begins just before the road ends at the overlook. If time allows, stop here on your return drive for a moderate hike across slickrock balds of Cedar Mesa sandstone.

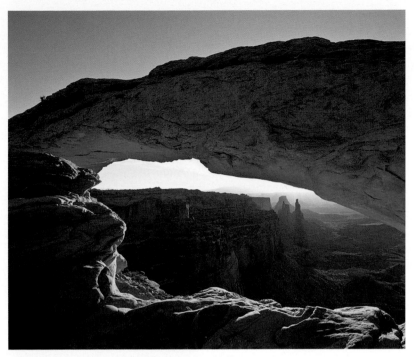

Early morning view through Mesa Arch

Turn on the **Elephant Hill** spur, a graded dirt road that leads to the base of a notorious climb for four-wheel drivers. Along the road are great views of **The Needles.** You see tall fingers of rock arrayed along the skyline, their red and white bands created by the interlayering of ancient river deposits with sand dunes. A shaded area at the end of the graded road makes a good place to picnic.

HIKES & FOUR-WHEEL-DRIVE ROUTES

To really explore Canyonlands—85 percent of which is backcountry—you must leave your car and proceed on foot, mountain bike, or by four-wheel-drive vehicle.

In The Needles District, **Chesler Park Trail** leads 2.9 miles to a grassland sunk in a wide rock pocket

rimmed by colorful spires. **Druid Arch Trail** branches off at **Elephant Canyon** and leads another 2.4 miles with a short ladder climb to the great arch that resembles a megalithic ceremonial site.

Elephant Hill Trail, a route only for rugged four-wheel-drive vehicles, runs 9 miles to the **Confluence Overlook.** It begins by climbing Elephant Hill's jaw-clenching switchbacks and 40 percent grade and ends with a half-mile walk to the overlook.

White Rim Road in Island in the Sky is one of the park's most popular jeep roads. Near the entrance, the **Shafer Trail** will take you to it. It follows a broad bench, lunar white along the edge where the red talus has been stripped to bedrock. For more than 80 miles it stays above the inner gorge, 1,200 feet below the Island, as it meanders through prime desert bighorn sheep country.

Northwest of The Maze lies a detached section of the park, the **Horseshoe Canyon Unit,** entered by way of a 3.5-mile trail from the boundary fence. You follow an old road into the canyon, then walk up **Barrier Creek** past some of the continent's finest prehistoric rock art. At the **Great Gallery,** ghostly figures painted in red ocher stare through eerie hollow eyes as the centuries pass. Archaeologists believe these life-size pictographs may be more than 3,000, perhaps as much as 6,000, years old.

The **Maze Overlook** can be reached by a 14-mile hike beginning at **North Trail Canyon,** 3.5 rough miles past **Hans Flat Ranger Station.** Reaching the trailhead can be an adventure, but the views from the rim of this isolated wedge of canyon country make it worth the effort. And the quiet is as expansive as

the vistas. The trail passes north of **Elaterite Butte** for a tantalizing view into the twists and blind alleys of The Maze.

With a high-clearance four-wheel-drive vehicle you can drive the 34 miles from **Hans Flat** to the overlook. This is one of the park's classic jeep routes. Negotiating steep switch-backs allows the driver little chance to sightsee, and with winter snows the route becomes impassable.

Rock formations in the Needles area of park

Green River

INFORMATION & ACTIVITIES

VISITOR & INFORMATION CENTERS
Moab boasts a large **multiagency visitor center** (805 N. Main St., 800-635-6622 or 435-259-8825). Visitor centers by entrances to the **Island in the Sky** and **The Needles,** and at **Hans Flat Ranger Station,** just outside park near The Maze, open all year. **Headquarters** is 3 miles south of Moab.

SEASONS & ACCESSIBILITY
Park open year-round. Flash floods from July through September can temporarily close dirt and gravel roads.

HEADQUARTERS
2282 S.W. Resource Blvd., Moab, UT 84532. Phone (435) 719-2313. www.nps.gov/cany

ENTRANCE FEE
$10 per vehicle good for 7 days, multiple entries. Annual permit $25, also good at Arches National Park and Natural Bridges and Hovenweep National Monuments.

PETS
Must be leashed at all times. Not allowed on hiking trails, in river corridors, or on backcountry roads.

ACCESSIBLE SERVICES
The visitor centers and Moab headquarters are wheelchair accessible.

THINGS TO DO
Free naturalist-led activities: nature walks, interpretive exhibits. Hiking, boating, rafting (permit needed), bicycling. Contact park for list of concessioners offering four-wheel-drive (some areas require permit), mountain biking, hiking, and river-running trips.

SPECIAL ADVISORIES
• Always carry water when hiking—at least a gallon per person per day. Water available near Squaw Flat Campground and at visitor centers.
• Use care near cliff edges and on slickrock surfaces; falls often fatal.
• Do not walk on cryptobiotic crust; it is a fragile, crunchy, black soil that is composed of living plants.

OVERNIGHT BACKPACKING
Permits and reservations (fee) required for backpacking and four-wheel-drive trips. May be obtained at visitor centers or ranger stations. For information on reservations, call (435) 259-4351. Campsites along the **White Rim Trail,** in Island in the Sky, are available to mountain bikers and campers in four-wheel-drive high-clearance vehicles.

CAMPGROUNDS
Two campgrounds, **Squaw Flat** and **Willow Flat,** both with 14-day limit. Open all year, first come, first served; March to October filled by midmorning. Fees $10-$15 per night. No showers. Tent and RV sites; no hookups. Three group campsites in **The Needles;** reservations required; contact park headquarters. No food services inside park.

HOTELS, MOTELS, & INNS
(unless otherwise noted, rates are for 2 persons in a double room, high season)
In Moab, UT 84532:
Best Western Green Well Motel 105 S. Main St. (800) 528-1234 or (435) 259-6151. 72 units. $100-$150. AC, pool, restaurant.
Big Horn Lodge 550 S. Main St. (800) 325-6171 or (435) 259-6171. 58 units. $110. AC, pool, restaurant.
Pack Creek Ranch 15 miles south of Moab, off La Sal Mountain Loop Rd. (435) 259-5091, www.packcreekranch.net. Cabins, houses, bunkhouses. $105-$300. AC, pool.
Ramada Moab Downtown 182 S. Main St. (800) 272-6232 or (435) 259-7141. 81 units. $79-$182. AC, pool, restaurant.
In Monticello, UT 84535:
Monticello Inn 164 E. Center St. on Hwy. 491. (435) 587-2274. 26 units. $55-$90. AC.

For other area accommodations, contact Moab Area Travel Council, Main & Center Sts., Moab, UT 84532. (800) 635-6622 or (435) 259-8825, www.discovermoab.com.

CANYONLANDS

EXCURSIONS

WESTWATER CANYON
MOAB, UTAH

The names of the rapids on this 17-mile section of the Colorado River tell all: Skull, Sock-it-to-Me, Last Chance. Only experienced boaters (18 and over) should attempt them; permits *(fee)* and reservations required. Sights: natural arches, mining ruins, a desperadoes' hide-out, and many bird species. Hiking, boating, fishing, picnic areas, swimming. Primitive camping (limited to 1 night), boat ramp, picnic areas. Open all year. Information at West-water, about 80 miles northeast of Canyonlands NP. (435) 259-7012.

HENRY MOUNTAINS BUFFALO HERD
HANKSVILLE, UTAH

This herd's 520 bison roam to 11,000 feet in summer. 150,000 acres. Hiking, climbing, rockhounding, hunting, picnicking, horseback riding, scenic drives (high-clearance 4x4s only). 3 campgrounds, primitive camping. Open all year. Information Mon. through Fri. at Hanksville BLM, off Utah 24, 110 miles west of Canyonlands NP. (435) 542-3461.

NATURAL BRIDGES NATIONAL MONUMENT
LAKE POWELL, UTAH

Three natural bridges here represent different states of development: youth, maturity, and old age. First discovered by white men in 1883, the three bridges bear Hopi names: Sipapu, Kachina, and Owachomo. Site also features ancestral Puebloan ruins and what was once the world's largest photovoltaic power system. 7,779 acres. 13 campsites (may fill early), primitive campsites, picnic area, scenic drive. Trails may be impassable in winter; campsites open all year. Visitor center on Utah 275, 4 miles off US 95, about 95 miles from Canyonlands NP. (435) 692-1234.

GLEN CANYON NATIONAL RECREATION AREA
PAGE, ARIZONA

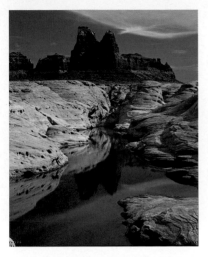

The centerpiece of Glen Canyon NRA is Lake Powell, 186 miles of the Colorado River backed up behind one of the world's highest dams. The lake and the desert and canyons around it offer memorable experiences for boaters, anglers, hikers, and campers. Fishing for bass, black crappie, catfish, walleye available; trout thrive below the dam. Free dam tours. 1,217,403 acres, most in Utah. Fishing, hiking, boating (rentals available), water sports. Tent and RV campsites, 5 marinas, lodging, food services, picnic areas, boat ramp, handicapped access. Area and campsites open all year. Adjoins Canyonlands NP and Grand Staircase-Escalante NM to the north. (928) 608-6404.

RAINBOW BRIDGE NATIONAL MONUMENT
PAGE, ARIZONA

To the Navajo this 290-foot-high pink sandstone bridge is a sacred "rainbow of stone." Rough foot or horse trails lead to it through the Navajo reservation (permits required)—a vigorous trip for the fit only. Most visitors to the world's largest natural bridge boat in from Lake Powell in Glen Canyon NRA (see above), via Halls Crossing, Bullfrog, or Wahweap. 160 acres.

CANYONLANDS

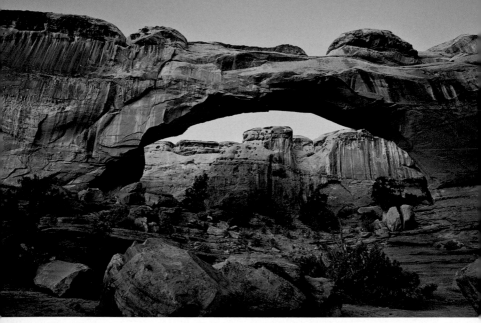

Hickman Bridge

▶ CAPITOL REEF

UTAH
ESTABLISHED DECEMBER 18, 1971
241,904 acres

The unifying geographic feature of Capitol Reef is the Waterpocket Fold. For a hundred miles its parallel ridges rise from the desert like the swell of giant waves rolling toward shore. Exposed edges of the uplift have eroded into a slickrock wilderness of massive domes, sheer cliffs, and a maze of twisting canyons.

Geologists know the fold as one of the largest and best exposed monoclines on the North American continent. Travelers know it as a place of dramatic beauty and serenity so remote that the nearest traffic light is 78 miles away. And even though its 378 square miles are off the beaten track, the park still attracts nearly 750,000 visitors each year.

Capitol Reef is named for a particularly colorful section of the fold where rounded Navajo sandstone forms capitol-like domes and sheer cliffs form a barrier to travel, often referred to as a "reef." Although a highway now crosses the "reef," travel is still challenging for those wishing to see the park's more remote regions.

The southern end of the fold offers fine wilderness backpacking in the Muley Twist Canyon and Halls Creek Narrows. Along the park's northern border lies Cathedral Valley, a repository of quiet solitude where jagged monoliths rise hundreds of feet.

The middle region is best known. Here the raw beauty of the towering cliffs contrasts with the green oasis that 19th-century Mormon pioneers created along the Fremont River, establishing the village of Fruita. Their irrigation ditches still water fruit trees in fields abandoned by Fremont Indians 700 years ago. Mule deer now graze on orchard grasses and alfalfa, and park visitors harvest the apples, peaches, and apricots.

The most striking reminder of the Fremont culture is the fine rock art it produced. Figures resembling bighorn sheep crowd many petroglyph panels. The last sighting in the park of a native desert bighorn, a subspecies, occurred in 1948. Their disappearance is attributed to overhunting and various diseases caught from domestic sheep. The Park Service reintroduced desert bighorn sheep in 1984, 1996, and 1997. These herds have survived.

How to Get There

From Green River (about 85 miles away), take I-70 to Utah 24, which leads to the east entrance. For a scenic approach, start at Bryce Canyon National Park. Follow Utah 12 over Boulder Mountain to Utah 24, just outside the park's west entrance. Airport: Salt Lake City.

When to Go

Year-round. Spring and fall are mild and ideal for hiking. Winter is cold but brief. Back roads can become impassable during spring thaw, summer rains, and winter snows at higher elevations.

How to Visit

On a 1-day visit, take Utah 24 along the **Fremont River** and then the **Scenic Drive** through the heart of the park. This section offers fine hiking on nearly 40 miles of developed trails. The best second-day activity is a drive along portions of the **Burr Trail Loop** with a walk to **Strike Valley Overlook.** For a longer stay, drive the **Cathedral Valley Loop** or hike in one of the more remote canyons of the **Waterpocket Fold.** Always check road, trail, and weather conditions.

FREMONT RIVER & SCENIC DRIVE
35 miles; a half to full day

Drive east on Utah 24 as you enter the park from the west. Ahead of you rises the eroded west face of the **Waterpocket Fold,** a massive line of cliffs running north and south. After the first few miles, the highway follows the course cut through the rock wilderness by the swift Fremont River, named for frontier explorer John C. Frémont.

Take the unpaved spur road to the **Goosenecks Overlook.** From the parking area an easy 0.1-mile trail ends above the deeply entrenched meanders of **Sulphur Creek.** Another short walk takes you to **Sunset Point** for a sweeping view of the **Capitol Reef** section of the Waterpocket Fold.

CAPITOL REEF

Section of Waterpocket Fold

Take the Chimney Rock turnoff to the 3.5-mile **Chimney Rock loop trail.** The trail provides an opportunity to get up close and personal with some of Capitol Reef's most interesting geology. The trail begins with a steep climb to the rim high above Chimney Rock, a pinnacle of red Moenkopi formation protected from erosion by a golden Shinarump cap. The trail loops back around through the gray-green and maroon Chinle formation famous for exposures of colorful petrified wood.

Stop at the visitor center on the edge of **Fruita,** the remnants of the Mormon frontier community settled in the 1880s and now part of the national park. Be sure to see the 15-minute video—the view of the red sandstone cliffs from the theater window is itself worth the stop.

Take the 25-mile round-trip **Scenic Drive** along the rugged face of Capitol Reef. This paved road follows a century-old wagonway known as the Blue Dugway. The old road was used by Indians, outlaws, gypsies, and once even the devil himself, according to an early pioneer who chased him off by brandishing the Book of Mormon. Take the short spur road into **Grand Wash.** Look high on the cliff rim for **Cassidy Arch** named for outlaw Butch Cassidy, who reportedly used the canyon as a hideout. A 2.25-mile trail from the parking area leads down Grand Wash through spectacular narrows to the Fremont River. Another trail climbs 1.75 miles to Cassidy Arch. The Scenic Drive ends with a winding 2-mile spur road into **Capitol Gorge.** This was the main road through the reef before 1962. It now ends at a parking area where an easy 1-mile trail continues down into the canyon to historic inscriptions and a series of natural waterpockets, popular among desert denizens.

Return by the same road to Fruita, then go east on Utah 24, passing well-maintained orchards. Turn in at the **Petroglyphs** pull-off. Here Fremont Indians pecked into the cliff large humanlike figures in headdresses. Since you can view this cliff art only at a distance, binoculars come in handy; spotting scopes are mounted on the main panel boardwalk.

The origin of these Indian farmers about A.D. 600 and their disappearance six centuries later are still mysteries. Early settlers found what appeared to be remnants of their irrigation ditches, granaries, and pit houses. One unusual discovery was a brick of tule sugar, grass seeds, and pulverized grasshoppers—thought to have been emergency food.

Continue down the highway a short distance to the **Hickman Bridge** parking area. Stretch your legs with a 1-mile hike up a self-guided nature trail that leads under the natural bridge, 125 feet above. For a longer and more arduous hike, take the 2.25-mile **Rim Overlook Trail** along the cliff tops. It ends at a 1,000-foot drop to the Fremont River, providing a good vantage point to view the green pocket of Fruita enclosed in a landscape of tilted rock.

Farther along the road, pull off at the **Behunin Cabin.** This one-room

Fremont Indian petroglyph

Black Mt.
+ 6,938 ft

miles 10
kilometers 15

Gypsum
Sinkhole

*Cathedral
Valley*

MIDDLE DESERT

Temple of
the Sun

Factory Butte
6,321 ft +

Upper South
Desert Overlook

Polk Cr.

Temple of
the Moon

CAINEVILLE
WASH ROAD

Deep Cr.

SOUTH DESERT

Lower South
Desert
Overlook

Caineville Wash

North
Caineville
Mesa

FISHLAKE

NATIONAL

FOREST

Chimney
Rock

CAPITOL

24

Caineville

Fremont

Twin
Rocks

24

**Visitor
Center**

Waterpocket

Petroglyphs
Hickman
Bridge

South
Caineville
Mesa

Sulphur Cr.

24

Torrey

Goosenecks
Overlook

Fruita

Behunin Cabin

Sandy Cr.

Fremont

12

Grover

SCENIC
DRIVE

Capitol Gorge

Notom

Sweetwater Cr.

CAPITOL

NOTOM-
BULLFROG
ROAD

Miners Mt.

REEF

HENRY

Singletree

Pocket

DIXIE

Larb Hollow
Overlook

Pleasant Cr.

Fold

Pleasant Creek

Oak Creek

Oak Cr.

NATIONAL

Steep Creek
Overlook

*Dry
Bench*

NOTOM-
BULLFROG
ROAD

McMillan
Springs

MOUNTAINS

Homestead
Overlook

FOREST

Cedar
Mesa

NATIONAL

*Tarantula
Mesa*

Circle Cliffs

ANASAZI
STATE PARK

BURR TRAIL RD.

Waterpocket

Strike Valley
Overlook

Boulder

Steep Cr.

Strike Valley

Burr Trail
Switchbacks

12

Fold

The Post

Muley Twist Canyon

Lower Muley
Twist Trailhead

Deer Cr.

*Wagon Box
Mesa*

Muley Cr.

Calf
Creek

GRAND STAIRCASE-ESCALANTE

PARK

Escalante

NATIONAL MONUMENT

Muley Tanks

BURR
TRAIL
ROAD

Big Thompson Mesa

Halls Creek
Overlook

Silver Falls Cr.

Circle Cliffs

Brimhall Bridge +
4,800 ft

Hall Mesa

N

Halls Cr.

Harris Wash

Escalante

GLEN CANYON
NATIONAL
RECREATION AREA

stone cabin was once home to a family of ten. The parents and the two youngest children slept inside, the girls in a wagon box outside, and the boys in a nearby rock alcove.

BURR TRAIL LOOP
125 miles; at least a full day

The drive begins at the visitor center. Go east on Utah 24 to **Notom-Bullfrog Road.** Paved for the first several miles of its southbound route, the road becomes dirt, skirting the uplift where rock has pushed skyward at 70-degree angles. It crosses several washes that turn into slot canyons where they cut into the east flank of the Waterpocket Fold.

At the junction with **Burr Trail Road,** you must decide whether to return to the visitor center (half-day trip) or take a full day to complete the loop. If you decide to continue, turn west and climb a series of spectacular switchbacks to the high rim of the fold. Views of the **Henry Mountains** to the east, and **Burr Canyon** straight below, are dramatic.

One of the finest vistas in the park is the **Strike Valley Overlook** in the **upper Muley Twist Canyon.** Many visitors walk the 2.5 miles from the hikers' parking area to the overlook trailhead through a beautiful canyon with double arches and a large rock window on the rim. High-clearance, four-wheel-drive vehicles can follow the canyon floor to a parking area near the overlook. From the parking area the trail continues up the canyon another 6.5 miles, passing several large arches.

Those looking for solitude can backpack into **upper** or **lower Muley Twist Canyon** and its miles of fine slickrock wilderness (free backcountry permits required; available at visitor center). Bends in the canyon are so tight, early teamsters said, a mule had to twist itself to get through.

Burr Trail Road becomes paved as it leaves Capitol Reef and continues west to the town of Boulder. Turn north on paved Utah 12, which winds up and over **Boulder Mountain** through a high alpine forest. Here you join Utah 24 about 10 miles west of the visitor center.

CATHEDRAL VALLEY LOOP
70 miles; a half to full day

A high-clearance, two- or four-wheel-drive vehicle is recommended for this scenic trip; check unpaved road conditions before setting out. Follow Utah 24 for 11 miles east of the visitor center. At a marked crossing, turn off Utah 24 and ford the Fremont River. If the river is too high for your vehicle, use the Caineville access to reach Cathedral Valley.

Browsing deer

Desert mallow

INFORMATION & ACTIVITIES

VISITOR & INFORMATION CENTER
The **visitor center** on Utah 24 at the north end of park is open all year. Phone headquarters for information.

SEASONS & ACCESSIBILITY
Park open year-round. Many roads are unpaved. The Scenic Drive may close briefly during rainy weather and in winter. Driving dirt roads, including Cathedral Valley Loop, may require high-clearance or four-wheel-drive vehicles. Call headquarters or ask at visitor center for latest weather and road conditions.

HEADQUARTERS
HC 70 Box 15, Torrey, UT 84775. Phone (435) 425-3791. www.nps.gov/care

ENTRANCE FEE
$5 per car per week.

ACCESSIBLE SERVICES
The visitor center, restrooms, and the Petroglyphs Trail are accessible to wheelchairs.

THINGS TO DO
Free ranger-led activities: evening programs. Also available, interpretive exhibits, auto tour, hiking, fruit picking, bird-watching. For information on horseback trips, jeep tours, and other recreational activities, contact the Wayne County Travel Council at (800) 858-7951.

SPECIAL ADVISORIES
• Always carry water: except for tap water, most water in park is not drinkable.
• Watch out for flash floods between July and September.
• Let someone know your itinerary.

OVERNIGHT BACKPACKING
Permits required. They are free and can be obtained at the visitor center or from any park ranger.

CAMPGROUNDS
Three campgrounds, all with 14-day limit. Open year-round on a first-come, first-served basis. The campground at **Fruita** has tent and RV sites, but no hookups or showers. Fees $10 per night. The primitive campgrounds at **Cathedral Valley** and **Cedar Mesa** are free but have limited sites and no water.

HOTELS, MOTELS, & INNS
(unless otherwise noted, rates are for 2 persons in a double room, high season)

In Bicknell, UT 84715:
Aquarius Inn 240 W. Main St. (435) 425-3835. 29 units, 2 with kitchenettes. $52-$56. AC, RV park.
Sunglow Motel 63 E. Main St., P.O. Box 68. (435) 425-3821. 15 units. $48. AC, restaurant.

In Torrey, UT 84775:
Capitol Reef Inn 360 W. Main St., P.O. Box 100. (435) 425-3271. 10 units. $53. Restaurant. Open Easter through October.
Sandstone Inn 955 E. Utah 24. (800) 458-0216 or (435) 425-3775. 50 units. $68-$95. AC, pool, restaurant.

For a more complete list of accommodations near the park, write or call park headquarters or visit the park website.

CAPITOL REEF

As the road heads north, it passes through the colorful badlands of the **Bentonite Hills** and follows a mesa called **The Hartnet** to the edge of a 400-foot escarpment overlooking **South Desert.** On the mesa's opposite side is a spectacular view into **upper Cathedral Valley.** In this vast open space, keep a lookout for soaring golden eagles.

Eroded spires and monoliths of Entrada sandstone jut 500 feet from the valley floor like enormous weathered teeth. The road loops to the south and drops among the formations, following the valley past such landmarks as the **Walls of Jericho,** the **Gypsum Sinkhole,** and the **Temples of the Sun** and **Moon.** The drive ends at Utah 24, near Caineville.

Isis Temple from Hopi Point on the West Rim

▶ GRAND CANYON

ARIZONA
ESTABLISHED FEBRUARY 26, 1919
1,217,403 acres

The road to the Grand Canyon from the south crosses a gently rising plateau that gives no hint of what is about to unfold. You wonder if you have made a wrong turn. All at once an immense gorge a mile deep and up to 18 miles wide opens up. The scale is so vast that even from the best vantage point only a fraction of the canyon's 277 miles can be seen.

Nearly five million people travel here each year; 90 percent first see the canyon from the South Rim with its dramatic views into the deep inner gorge of the Colorado River. So many feet have stepped cautiously to the edge of major overlooks that in places the rock has been polished smooth. But most of the park's 1,904 square miles are maintained as wilderness. You can avoid crowds by hiking the park's many trails or driving to the cool evergreen forests of the North Rim where people are fewer and viewing is more leisurely. The Grand Canyon boasts some of the nation's cleanest air, with visibility on clear days averaging 90 to 110 miles.

It's hard to look at the canyon and not be curious about geology. Rock that dates back 1.8 billion years lies at the bottom. Exactly how the river formed the canyon is still unclear, but geologists generally agree that most of the cutting occurred within the last five million years.

How to Get There

South Rim: From Flagstaff, Arizona (about 80 miles away), take US 180 skirting the San Francisco Peaks to South Rim entrance, or take US 89 to Cameron, then Ariz. 64 with views of the Little Colorado River Gorge to Desert View entrance.

North Rim: Take Ariz. 67 from Jacob Lake through the Kaibab National Forest to North Rim entrance. The two rims are 10 air miles apart but 215 miles by car, a 5-hour drive. Airports: Grand Canyon near South Rim; Flagstaff; Las Vegas; Phoenix.

When to Go

South Rim is open all year; North Rim facilities are closed from mid-October to mid-May. Ariz. 67 usually closes due to deep snows late November to mid-May. Hikers and mule riders to the inner canyon, where temperatures reach 118°F, prefer spring and fall; the prime river season is April through October.

How to Visit

On a 1-day visit to the South Rim take the **Hermit Road** west of the village for classic views of the main canyon. The drive is closed to automobiles March through November, but free buses take you to the overlooks. The best second-day activity is the **Desert View Drive** tour east of Mather Point for great views of the Colorado River and eastern canyon.

On a longer stay, take the North Rim's **Cape Royal Road** for broad panoramic vistas. You may also enjoy a hike on a backcountry trail; a mule ride down the **Bright Angel Trail;** a week-long raft trip through the canyon on the **Colorado River;** and a scenic flight for a bird's-eye view of the canyon. The mule and raft trips and backcountry hikes require reservations far in advance.

SOUTH RIM: HERMIT ROAD

7 miles; at least a half day; closed to vehicles March through November

Begin at the **Grand Canyon Visitor Center,** which is served by four new parking lots and a shuttle bus transit center. Stop in at the visitor center's new theater to watch the movie *Grand Canyon: A Journey of Wonder.* Then take a lovely 5-minute walk to **Mather Point** (a new wheelchair accessible ramp extends to the outlook) for a classic panoramic view into the heart of the Grand Canyon. Great solitary buttes rise from narrow ridges reaching out from the distant North Rim. Far below, a green cluster of Fremont cottonwood trees marks **Phantom Ranch,** a lodge and campground reached only by mule or foot. Take a shuttle bus to the museum at **Yavapai Point** to explore the canyon's geologic history. If bad weather threatens, duck into the glass-enclosed observation room and watch as storm clouds roll in.

Walk west from Yavapai Point on the paved rim trail to follow the **Trail of Time,** a geologic timeline on which each large step equals a million years. Touch rocks from each of the canyon layers as you follow the 1.3-mile trail to the **Verkamp's Visitor Center,** located in the 1905 Verkamp's Curios building at the west end of the historic Grand Canyon Village area.

Board the free Hermits Rest Route bus, which travels along Hermit Road between Hermits Rest Transfer and Hermits Rest Trailhead from March through November. Skirting the rim of the canyon for 7 miles, it offers superb views of the **Colorado River** and the labyrinth of

GRAND CANYON

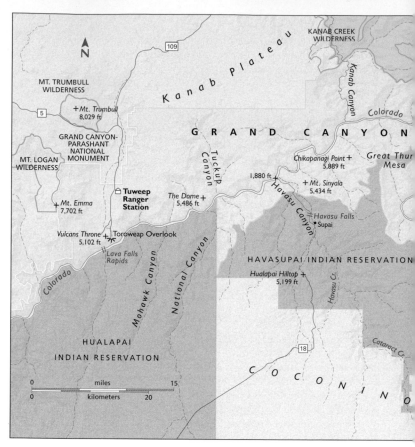

side canyons and broad platforms below the rim. The buses can be crowded at peak times of day.

The first stop is the **Trailview Overlook.** Here you get a hint of the canyon's size. To the south, the historic **El Tovar Hotel** and **Bright Angel Lodge** look small and insignificant perched on the brink of the great precipice. Mule strings and hikers file along the **Bright Angel Trail** as it zigzags 8 miles and 4,460 feet down to the river.

Don't miss **Hopi Point,** a promontory jutting deep into the gorge. Magnificent views 45 miles both eastward and westward make this an ideal spot for watching sunset or sunrise. To avoid crowds, leave the main overlook and walk along the **Rim Trail** (see p. 185) to find your own observation

point. Across the river rise the intricately carved walls of **Isis Temple** and tree-topped **Shiva Temple,** described as "the grandest of all buttes."

The bus route continues west, passing **Mohave Point** and skirting breathtakingly close to **The Abyss,** where a sheer cliff plunges 3,000 feet to a plateau below. From here the road follows the sweep of the rim out to **Pima Point,** where you see the Colorado River threading through the deep gorge. On a still day you can hear the distant rumble of **Granite Rapids** almost a mile below. What looks like a stream from above is a river 300 feet wide that, with its tributaries, drains 8 percent of the continental United States.

The road ends at **Hermits Rest,** a limestone building that looks as if Hobbits built it on the canyon's rim; it serves as a curio shop. Those with time and stamina can hike partway down the steep **Hermit Trail** to **Dripping Springs,** 7 miles and 6 to 9 hours round-trip. Here one of the earliest guides to the Grand Canyon, Louis Boucher, raised goldfish in a watering trough at the turn of the 20th century. It's a good place to see some of the canyon's 355 species of birds. Permits are not needed for day hikes, but first ask a park ranger for conditions and advisories. On the return, buses stop only at Pima, Mohave, and Powell Points.

For the adventurous, the **Rim Trail** hugs the canyon's edge for nearly 13 miles from Pipe Creek Vista to Hermits Rest, roughly paralleling Hermit Road. The walking path is paved to **Powell Point,** then turns into a dirt path as it winds to **Monument Creek Vista.** From here it is once again paved for both bicycle and foot traffic to Hermits Rest. The trail is generally level except for a steep stretch between the village and Trailview. Short hikes can be combined with rides by catching the shuttle bus at any of the main overlooks. You can also pick up the bus at the trail's end for an easy return.

SOUTH RIM: DESERT VIEW DRIVE

23 miles; a half to full day

Desert View Drive (Ariz. 64) begins just south of Mather Point. The drive skirts the rim eastward for 23 miles to **Desert View,** providing numerous pull-offs for long views of the main canyon. In summer, parking at the major overlooks can be a problem. Only the park shuttle is allowed on the Yaki Point/South Kaibab Trail-head road. (Board at the Canyon View Information Center.) Along the road are shaggy-barked Utah juniper and low clumps of Gambel oak.

On the way to **Yaki Point** you can leave the shuttle and hike the **South Kaibab Trail,** which switchbacks down the west side of Yaki Point. Allot a third of your time for going down and two-thirds for hiking back up. The trail eventually reaches the Colorado River at the bottom of the canyon, but a strenuous 3-mile, 2.5-hour round-trip takes you only partway down to **Cedar Ridge.** Even though you drop 1,140 vertical feet, none of the major landforms of the canyon look any closer. Fossil ferns lie exposed in the bedrock on the west side of Cedar Ridge.

Yaki Point provides a fine view of the darkly shining **Granite Gorge,** the innermost canyon. The imposing pyramid-shaped profile of **Vishnu Temple,** 7,500 feet high, dominates the eastern skyline. The practice of naming major park landforms after world deities began with Clarence Dutton, who published a classic report on the geology of the Grand Canyon in 1882.

Return to your car and follow the main road as it climbs into a tall ponderosa forest. Take the turnoff to **Grandview Point,** one of the finest vistas on the South Rim. From the overlook, **Grandview Trail** (occasionally closed due to rain) drops a rugged 3 miles to **Horseshoe Mesa,** where miners once worked copper ore from the Last Chance Mine. John Hance, a prospector known for his tall tales and quick wit, led the first sightseeing parties into the canyon near here in the 1880s. On one trip a woman with a knowledge of botany described to him how trees breathe. "You know," Hance said, "that explains something that has puzzled me a long time; I used to make camp under a big mesquite tree, and night after night that thing would keep me awake with its snoring."

Drive farther east to **Moran Point** for the best view of one of the Colorado's major rapids. Here you look directly down on **Hance Rapids;** its rocky 30-foot drop is considered by river guides to be among the most difficult to run. Continue on down the road, and if you need a change of pace, stop at the small **Tusayan Museum.** It displays well-designed exhibits of Indian cultures, and the nearby ruins offer a self-guided tour of an excavated ancestral Puebloan village from A.D. 1185.

Take your time when you reach **Lipan Point,** the finest view of the eastern canyon. Here the Colorado River makes a great bend to the west, where it has carved through the **Kaibab Plateau** to form the deepest portion of the Grand Canyon. Below, the river makes an S-curve around **Unkar Delta,** which prehistoric people extensively farmed.

Bypass **Navajo Point** and continue on to **Desert View,** where you might stop at the snack bar and curio shop. While here, climb the stairs to the top of the 70-foot **Watchtower,** built in 1932. On the tower's walls Indian artist Fred Kabotie painted murals depicting Hopi legends.

NORTH RIM: CAPE ROYAL ROAD
23 miles; a half to full day

Averaging a thousand feet higher than the South Rim, the North Rim's alpine vegetation and more varied vistas appeal to many travelers. Still, you won't find the South Rim crowds here. The focus is the historic **Grand Canyon Lodge,** built in the 1920s on the lip of the canyon and rebuilt after a disastrous fire in 1932. From its Sun Room you'll get an excellent view of **Bright Angel Canyon** incised 11 miles into the plateau and overshadowed by **Deva, Brahma,** and **Zoroaster Temples.**

Pick up a self-guiding pamphlet from the box by the log shelter near the parking lot. Follow one of the paved trails to **Bright Angel Point,** which divides a side canyon called **The Transept** from **Roaring Springs Canyon.** Listen for the sound of the springs cascading from a cave 3,000 feet below the rim. This is a fine spot for watching sunrise or sunset. Those needing to stretch their legs can take the **Transept Trail,** 1.5 miles along the nearly level canyon rim, or a short hike on the **North Kaibab Trail** (1 mile down takes you 650 feet beneath the rim—and that mile back up feels like 3).

From the lodge, drive north 3 miles to the **Cape Royal Road,** one of the most scenic drives in the park. It passes through forests of spruce, fir, locust, and ponderosa pine mixed with stands of quaking aspen and through lovely meadows of blue lupine and scarlet bugler. Long-eared mule deer often bound across the road, and you might glimpse the reclusive white-tailed Kaibab squirrel found only in the North Rim forests on the Kaibab Plateau.

Those looking for a dramatic sunrise perch can turn off onto the 3-mile road to **Point Imperial,** at 8,803 feet the highest viewpoint on either rim. Here amid tall evergreens you look across the canyon to the high plateau of the Navajo Indian Reservation. Evidence of a 2000 fire is visible in this vicinity

(you probably spotted more evidence along the first portion of Cape Royal Road). Return to the main road and continue on, passing through the forested **Walhalla Plateau.** Stop at **Vista Encantada** for superb views of the northeastern canyon and the carved pinnacles of **Brady** and **Tritle Peaks.**

The road ends at a parking lot on **Cape Royal.** A paved half-mile nature trail leads along a narrow peninsula past **Angels Window,** an opening eroded through the rock spur that frames the river below. Watch your children. From the overlook **Wotans Throne** and **Vishnu Temple** dominate the foreground. Across the canyon rise the **Palisades of the Desert.** The unusually broad vista here provides a fine vantage point to watch the sun set and to absorb what naturalist John Burroughs described as Grand Canyon's "strange new beauty."

MULE, RIVER, & AIR TRIPS

If the extremely challenging hike to the canyon floor (8 miles down

North Rim aspen in fall foliage

GRAND CANYON

Hikers on bridge along the North Kaibab Trail

the Bright Angel Trail and 6.5 miles on the steeper South Kaibab Trail) is not for you, consider going by muleback. (Though mule trips are not for everyone either—acrophobes especially!) Overnight mule trips do leave the South Rim to go to the bottom of the canyon at **Phantom Ranch,** which accommodates guests in rustic cabins and dormitories. The ranch lies in a deep gorge of the inner canyon near the confluence of Bright Angel Creek and the Colorado River. The creek's clear waters are known for their excellent trout fishing (license required). The lodge is the only place within the canyon where you can spend the night without camping, and it serves as a good base for hikes up Bright Angel Canyon. Advance reservations—as much as 6 months ahead for mule trips— are necessary.

Many regard a raft trip through the Grand Canyon as the experience of a lifetime. Long, quiet stretches through the scenic heart of the canyon are broken by more than 150 major rapids, three of which are consistently rated 10 on a scale of 10. Most trips stop for day hikes at waterfalls, Indian ruins, and interesting side canyons. A number of river companies offer the raft trips, which generally take 1 to 2 weeks; some companies offer partial trips. Write the park or check the park website for a list of the companies; reserve well in advance.

Companies giving helicopter and airplane tours are based at Grand Canyon Airport. Flights are no longer allowed below the rim, and because of safety and noise concerns, use of the canyon's airspace is being regulated.

CARVING THE GRAND CANYON

What looks timeless is constantly changing: The Grand Canyon's variegated layers encode 2 billion years of Earth's history.

Thousands of feet thick, the rock formed from sediments. About 1.8 billion years ago, cataclysmic geological forces crumpled and uplifted this rock to create a range of mountains probably 5 to 6 miles high. **(1)**

The tremendous heat and pressure recrystallized the rock to gneiss and schist; molten material from deep inside Earth oozed up, forcing itself into the rock and hardening into veins of pink granite. Over eons, wind and water gnawed the mountain range into a plain, and a primordial sea submerged it. Again, sediments wafted to the sea bottom, solidifying into rock; magma continued to well up from inside the Earth. **(2)**

About a billion years ago, Earth shuddered again, cracking its crust into giant fault blocks that tilted upward to form a second range of mountains. **(3)** The rains, frosts, and winds of millions of years wore away these mountains also.

Much of the Grand Canyon rock visible today (blue layers, **4**) accumulated over the gneiss and schist in the last 525 million years. During some ages the region sank beneath advancing seas and primitive shellfish fossilized in sea bottoms that hardened to shale. During other periods the restless region rose. Capping the Grand Canyon today— about 8,000 feet above sea level— is the youngest cream-colored limestone layer. This Kaibab limestone, approximately 300 feet thick, formed from the remains of countless corals, sponges, and other marine animals.

In recent geological time (about 6 million years ago) a young, southward-flowing river, today's Colorado, began to slice into the upper layers of the canyon. Gouging inch by inch over the centuries, the river eventually reached the basement rocks 4,000 feet below the rim. **(5)** Water still wears away at the massive gorge, ever widening and ever deepening the canyon's floor and walls.

GRAND CANYON

INFORMATION & ACTIVITIES

VISITOR & INFORMATION CENTERS
Grand Canyon Visitor Center near Grand Canyon Village open all year. Call (928) 638-7888. **North Rim Visitor Center** open mid-May to late October. Call (928) 638-7864.

SEASONS & ACCESSIBILITY
South Rim open all year. North Rim roads often close due to snow mid-November to mid-May. For weather and road information, call (928) 638-7888.

HEADQUARTERS
P.O. Box 129, Grand Canyon, AZ 86023. Phone (928) 638-7888. www.nps.gov/grca

ENTRANCE FEE
$25 per car for 7 days; $12 per person arriving on foot, bike, or motorcycle.

PETS
Allowed, leashed, on rim trails, but not below rim. Kennels available; call (928) 638-0534.

ACCESSIBLE SERVICES
Visitor centers and shuttle buses are wheelchair accessible. A permit allowing access to some areas closed to public traffic is available at the entrance gates of visitor centers and hotel lobbies. Free day-use wheelchairs are available at Grand Canyon Visitor Center.

THINGS TO DO
Free ranger-led activities: day and evening nature walks, slide shows, talks, cultural demonstrations, and campfire programs. Also, mule trips into canyon, hiking, bicycling, fishing, river rafting, air tours, cross-country skiing. For activities, call (928) 638-7888. Write headquarters for list of concessioners offering wide variety of tours. An Imax Theater featuring *Grand Canyon: The Hidden Secrets* is located a mile south of the South Rim Entrance, on Ariz. 64. (928) 638-2468.

SPECIAL ADVISORIES
• Be very careful near the rim; protective barriers are intermittent.
• Due to elevation, heat, and steep trails, carry water, eat salty snacks, avoid hiking at peak temperatures, and rest often.

OVERNIGHT BACKPACKING
Permits required; $10 fee plus $5 per person per night. Backcountry Information Center, P.O. Box 129, Grand Canyon, AZ 86023. (928) 638-7875.

CAMPGROUNDS
Four campgrounds, 7-day limit, 3 on South Rim, 1 on North Rim. **Mather** open all year; reservations recommended March to November; reserve through the National Parks Reservation Service (see p. 10); other times, first come, first served. **Desert View** (first come, first served) and **North Rim** (reservations recommended) mid-May to mid-Oct. **Trailer Village** open all year; reservations recommended; contact Xanterra Parks & Resorts (888) 297-2757. Fee $34 per night. Showers at North Rim and near Mather campground. Tent and RV sites at all campgrounds; hookups only at Trailer Village. Two group campgrounds; must reserve. Food services in park.

HOTELS, MOTELS, & INNS
(unless otherwise noted, rates are for 2 persons in a double room, high season). Reservations advised 6 to 9 months in advance.

INSIDE THE PARK (On South Rim):
The properties on the South Rim and at Phantom Ranch are operated by Xanterra Parks & Resorts, (888) 297-2757, www.xanterra.com.
Bright Angel Lodge & Cabins 89 units, some share baths. Cabins $133-$178. Rooms $81-$92. Restaurant.
El Tovar Hotel 78 units. $178-$426. AC, restaurant.
Kachina Lodge 49 units. $173-$184. AC.
Maswik Lodge 278 units. Cabins, $92 (June–Aug.); rooms, $92-$173. Restaurant.
Thunderbird Lodge 55 units. $173-$184.
Yavapai Lodge 358 rooms. $114-$163. Restaurant. Open March–Oct.
(In the canyon):
Phantom Ranch (reached by hiking, mule, or raft trips) Dorm $43 per night. Cabin $116 per night. Mule trip $500, incl. cabins and meals. AC, rest., shared showers. Reserve up to 13 months ahead.
(On North Rim):
Grand Canyon Lodge Forever Resorts, (877) 386-4383. www.foreverresorts.com. 209 units. $116-$187. Rest. Open mid-May–mid-Oct.

EXCURSIONS

LAKE MEAD
NATIONAL RECREATION AREA
BOULDER CITY, NEVADA

Lake Mead, water impounded from the Colorado River by Hoover Dam, is the center of this NRA, the nation's first. More than 2,000 bighorn sheep roam the desert canyons and plateaus surrounding the reservoir. 1,501,216 acres, part in Arizona. Hiking, biking, boating, fishing, naturalist programs, water sports. 1,021 campsites, 191 rooms, picnic areas, food services, handicapped access. Open all year. Adjoins Grand Canyon NP on west. Visitor center at US 93 and Lakeshore Dr., about 280 miles from Grand Canyon's South Rim entrance. (702) 293-8990.

WUPATKI
NATIONAL MONUMENT
FLAGSTAFF, ARIZONA

Nearly 900 years ago, people moved to the Wupatki area to farm the volcanic soil. Little more than a century later they left behind extensive accomplishments, including a 100-room pueblo, amphitheater, ball court, and pottery. 35,422 acres. Hiking, picnicking, scenic drives. Open all year. Off US 89, about 65 miles southeast of Grand Canyon NP. (928) 679-2365.

CANYON DE CHELLY
NATIONAL MONUMENT
CHINLE, ARIZONA

These spectacular red-rock canyons, spires, and mesas rival any natural site in the Southwest. The same is true of their cultural legacy: ancient Basketmaker pit houses, the remains of ancestral Puebloan dwellings on 1,000-foot cliffs, and many reminders of the Navajo past and present. Authorized Navajo guides offer tours into the canyons; only the White House ruin may be visited without a guide. 83,840 acres. Hiking, horseback riding, jeep tour, scenic drives. 93 campsites, food services, handicapped access. Open all year. Off US 191, about 230 miles east of Grand Canyon NP. (928) 674-5500.

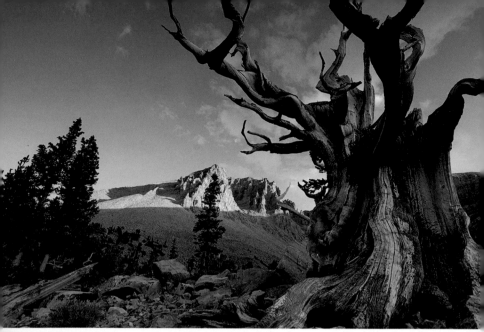

Bristlecone pines at tree line below Mount Wheeler

▶GREAT BASIN

NEVADA
ESTABLISHED OCTOBER 27, 1986
77,180 acres

An Ice Age landscape of glacier-carved peaks rises more than a mile from the desert floor. The park takes its name from the vast region that extends east from California's Sierra Nevada to Utah's Wasatch Range, and from southern Oregon to southern Nevada, encompassing most of Nevada and western Utah. Called Great Basin by explorer John C. Frémont in the mid-1800s, the region actually comprises not one but at least 90 basins, or valleys, and its rivers all flow inland—not to any ocean.

The park road winds up Wheeler Peak, the second highest mountain in Nevada. When the road ends at 10,000 feet, trails lead to the 13,063-foot summit and to the region's only glacier, near a stand of bristlecone pines. Great Basin is a young park compared to Yellowstone or Yosemite, yet within its confines are some of the world's oldest trees.

The bristlecones form the rear guard of a Pleistocene forest that once covered much of the region. Now surviving in scattered stands, some trees are 3,000 years old—meaning they were alive when Tutankhamun ruled Egypt.

In the flank of the mountain, at an altitude of 6,800 feet, lies Lehman Caves with 1.5 miles of underground passages. These formed when higher water tables during the Ice Age made pockets in the limestone. Park rangers guide visitors past flowstone, stalactites, and delicate white crystals that grow in darkness.

The number of visitors has reached more than 80,000 yearly since 1986, when the cave and neighboring mountains became a national park. But the park has 65 miles of trails, offering access to the hills and a chance to see glacial moraines, alpine lakes, and spectacular sweeping views of the surrounding Basin and Range Country.

How to Get There
From Las Vegas (about 300 miles away), take I-15 to US 93, then US 50 to Nev. 487. At Baker, take Nev. 488 to the park entrance. From Salt Lake City, Utah (about 250 miles away), take I-15 to US 50, then Nev. 487 to Baker and Nev. 488 to the park entrance. Airport: Ely (about 67 miles away).

When to Go
Great Basin is open year-round, but the upper 8 miles of Wheeler Peak Scenic Drive (beyond Upper Lehman Creek Campground) are closed November to May, or as long as heavy snows makes it impassable. In summer, the most popular time, temperatures are generally mild. September and October bring cool weather and smaller crowds. Hikers must beware of sudden thunderstorms that can catch them on exposed ridges at any time of year. The best time to view Wheeler Peak is in early morning. In winter, visitors enjoy excellent cross-country skiing.

How to Visit
On a 1-day visit, take the **Wheeler Peak Scenic Drive** for dramatic views

of high alpine landscapes. On your way back, stop at **Lehman Caves** for a chance to walk underground through intriguing passages.

Remember that the alpine world is fragile. At these elevations, plants grow slowly and their margin of survival is narrow. Stay on established roads and trails to avoid inadvertently damaging these areas.

WHEELER PEAK SCENIC DRIVE
12 miles; 1.5 hours to most of a day

This paved road climbs steeply from the visitor center to the Wheeler Peak Campground at 10,000 feet *(travel is closed to vehicles or trailers longer than 24 feet)*. Those not used to mountain driving may find both the view and the drive breathtaking. The road passes from the tough, drought-resistant pinyon-juniper woodland into the high-elevation forest of Engelmann spruce, limber pine, and aspen.

Begin the scenic drive near the visitor center. A short trail at the first pull-off takes you to the historic

Quaking aspens on Lehman Creek

GREAT BASIN

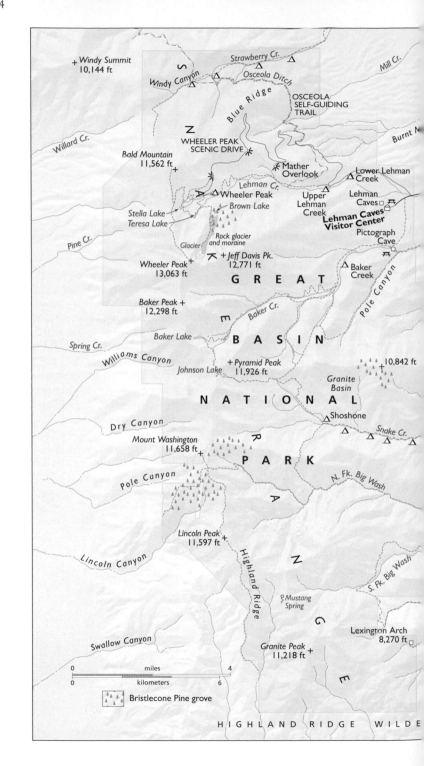

+ Windy Summit
10,144 ft

S

Windy Canyon

Strawberry Cr.

Osceola Ditch

Blue Ridge

OSCEOLA
SELF-GUIDING
TRAIL

Mill Cr.

Willard Cr.

N

WHEELER PEAK
SCENIC DRIVE

Burnt N

Bald Mountain
11,562 ft
+

Mather
Overlook

Lower Lehman
Creek

Lehman Cr.

Upper
Lehman
Creek

Lehman
Caves

Wheeler Peak

Brown Lake

Lehman Caves
Visitor Center

Stella Lake
Teresa Lake

Pine Cr.

Glacier

Rock glacier
and moraine

Pictograph
Cave

Wheeler Peak +
13,063 ft

+ Jeff Davis Pk.
12,771 ft

Baker
Creek

G R E A T

Pole Canyon

Baker Peak +
12,298 ft

Baker Cr.

B A S I N

Spring Cr.

Baker Lake

Williams Canyon

Johnson Lake

+ Pyramid Peak
11,926 ft

10,842 ft

Granite
Basin

N A T I O N A L

Dry Canyon

Shoshone

Snake Cr.

R

Mount Washington
11,658 ft
+

P A R K

N. Fk. Big Wash

Pole Canyon

A

Lincoln Peak
11,597 ft
+

N

Highland Ridge

S. Fk. Big Wash

Lincoln Canyon

Mustang
Spring

Lexington Arch
8,270 ft

G

Swallow Canyon

Granite Peak
11,218 ft
+

E

| 0 | miles | | | 4 |
| 0 | kilometers | | | 6 |

Bristlecone Pine grove

H I G H L A N D   R I D G E   W I L D E

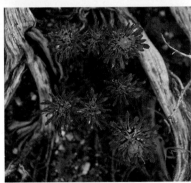

Cones on a young bristlecone pine *(top)*
Desert paintbrush *(bottom)*

Osceola Ditch, built in the late 1880s to carry water for hydraulic gold mining. Save this for your next trip, if pressed for time.

At the **Mather Overlook** take notice of the old stand of mountain mahogany. These usually grow as a shrub but here reach tree height. Pull off at **Peak Overlook** for spectacular views of **Wheeler Peak** on the right and **Jeff Davis Peak** on the left. The north face of Wheeler drops 1,800 feet to a glacier below. Snow often dusts the jagged walls of gray quartzite.

The road ends at Wheeler Peak Campground, where you have your choice of several fine walks. One of the most popular follows the 3-mile **Alpine Lakes Loop Trail** past **Stella** and **Teresa Lakes.** This leads you to a dramatic alpine setting with a barren, sawtooth ridge rising above the smooth surface of the lake.

If time and stamina allow, follow the **Wheeler Summit Trail** to the ridge above the lakes for an overview of the park and sweeping views of Great Basin's seemingly endless succession of mountain ranges. The trail leaves the Alpine Lakes Loop Trail near Stella Lake and climbs another 3,000 feet to the summit. Once above tree line, watch for sturdy alpine flowers like primrose and phlox. And be prepared for harsh weather. A terse entry in the summit register reads, "Wind took no prisoners."

Just as spectacular is the 4.5-mile **Bristlecone/Glacier Trail,** which takes you to **Wheeler Cirque,** a glacier-hollowed valley enclosed by sheer cliffs. At the far end lies the glacier, Great Basin's only permanent one and one of the southernmost in the country.

Before reaching the glacier be sure to take the **Bristlecone Forest Loop.** This self-guided trail passes ancient trees with twisted trunks that have been carved and polished by wind-driven snow and ice. Nearby a tree called Prometheus lived for almost 5,000 years until it was cut down in 1964, prior to the park's creation, as part of a climate study. Even after most of its trunk and branches die, a bristlecone pine can continue to survive, even if it is sustained by very little moisture. The tree holds onto its needles for 20 to 30 years, assuring stable photosynthesis regardless of environmental stress.

LEHMAN CAVES
0.6 mile; 1.5 hours

Lehman Caves—a single cavern despite its name—lays claim to beautiful formations. The ornate marble cave is decorated with stalagmites, helictites, flowstone, popcorn, and over 300 rare shield formations. Guided cave tours began in 1885 with Absalom Lehman, a miner turned rancher.

Today's tour tickets may be purchased up to 30 days in advance (either at the visitor center or by calling 775-234-7331). You have a choice of two tours: 90 minutes ($10) or 60 minutes ($8). (Visit www.nps.gov/grba/planyour visit/lehman-caves-yours.htm for more information.)

Inside Lehman Caves, the first room you visit is the **Gothic Palace.** The cave is so filled with columns, draperies, and stalactites that the first explorers used sledgehammers to break through them. Because of the cave's manageable scale, you get closeup views of bizarre helictites and delicate aragonite crystals.

The walkway takes you past fine examples of rare cave shields. These large disks grow from cracks in the ceiling, walls, and floors where seeping water deposits minerals in flat, circular forms. Continuing deeper, you reach two of the cave's most beautiful rooms. Rimstone pools and soda straws decorate the **Lake Room;** shields, massive columns, and bacon-rind draperies fill the **Grand Palace.**

A small variety of cave life makes its home here, including pack rats, cave crickets, and the rare pseudoscorpion—an arachnid with scorpion-like pincers. Bats, however, stay away, finding the cave's vertical entrance too hard to negotiate.

Stalactites and stalagmites in Lehman Caves *(top)*; new fallen snow along Wheeler Peak Scenic Drive *(center)*; death camas plant *(bottom left)*; Wheeler Peak reflected in a lake *(bottom right)*

INFORMATION & ACTIVITIES

VISITOR & INFORMATION CENTERS

Lehman Caves Visitor Center, located at Park Headquarters, is open all year. **Great Basin Visitor Center,** located in Baker, Nevada, is open in the summer. Phone park headquarters number for visitor information.

SEASONS & ACCESSIBILITY

Park open year-round. Snow may cover high-elevation trails until late June or July. Some park roads require four-wheel-drive vehicles. Call headquarters about current trail and road conditions.

HEADQUARTERS

100 Great Basin National Park, Baker, NV 89311. Phone (775) 234-7331. www .nps.gov/grba

ENTRANCE FEE

None for park. Fee for cave tours.

PETS

Permitted on leashes except in visitor center, caves, backcountry, and on trails.

ACCESSIBLE SERVICES

Visitor centers are wheelchair accessible, as are some campsites and picnic sites.

THINGS TO DO

Ranger-led activities: free nature talks, exhibits, movie, campfire programs. Also available, cave tours, Wheeler Peak Scenic Drive, hiking, fishing (license required), climbing, cross-country skiing.

SPECIAL ADVISORIES

• Park's high elevation can cause altitude sickness. People who have heart or respiratory problems should take it slowly.
• Don't expect to find water sources along the trails; always carry drinking water when hiking.
• Watch out for rattlesnakes along trails.
• Summer thunderstorms are common; check weather conditions with park before setting off on a hike.

OVERNIGHT BACKPACKING

Those heading out to the backcountry should stop at the park's visitor center and complete the free permit registration form. In addition to helping to ensure visitor safety, permits allow the park to monitor how its resources are being used.

CAMPGROUNDS

Four campgrounds, all with 14-day limit, all first come, first served. **Baker Creek** and **Upper Lehman Creek** open mid-May through October. **Wheeler Peak** open mid-June through September. **Lower Lehman Creek** open all year. Snowstorms may close campgrounds occasionally. No showers. Tent and RV sites; no hookups. Food services in the park in summer. Potable water available year-round at visitor center, and in summer at RV sanitary station, picnic areas, and developed campgrounds.

HOTELS, MOTELS, & INNS

(unless otherwise noted, rates are for 2 persons in a double room, high season)

In Baker, NV 89311:
The Border Inn (on US 50) P.O. Box 30. (775) 234-7300. 28 units. $42-$49. AC, restaurant, RV park.
Silver Jack Inn (on Main St.) P.O. Box 69. (775) 234-7323. 10 units. $49-$69. AC, restaurant.

In Ely, NV 89301:
Bristlecone Motel 700 Ave. I. (800) 497-7404 or (775) 289-8838. 31 units. $61-$95. AC.
Historic Hotel Nevada and Gambling Hall 501 Aultman St. (775) 289-6665. 62 units. $35-$125. AC, restaurant.
Jailhouse Motel and Casino 5th & High Sts. (800) 841-5430 or (775) 289-3033. 61 units. $58-$68. AC, restaurants.
Fireside Inn Motel 49 N. Mcgill Hwy. (2 miles north of Ely). (775) 289-3765. 14 units. $33-$61. AC.
Ramada Inn and Copper Queen Casino 805 Great Basin Blvd. (800) 851-9526 or (775) 289-4884. 65 units. $87-$119. AC, pool, restaurant.

For a complete list of accommodations, contact the White Pine Chamber of Commerce, (775) 289-8877, www.white pinechamber.com.

EXCURSIONS

HUMBOLDT-TOIYABE NATIONAL FORESTS
ELKO, NEVADA

This immense national forest is the largest in the continental United States. Contains glacier-carved Lamoille Canyon, historic mining towns, and Jarbridge Wilderness, in Nevada, one of the country's least used wilderness areas. About 6,300,000 acres. Hiking, boating, fishing, horseback riding, hunting, scenic drives, winter sports, water sports. 1,000 campsites, boat ramp, picnic areas, handicapped access. Open year-round; most campsites open late May through September. (775) 355-5301.

DESERT NATIONAL WILDLIFE REFUGE
LAS VEGAS, NEVADA

Wildlife is the focus of this Mojave Desert refuge, just a roll of the dice from Las Vegas. Bighorn sheep, mule deer, coyotes, and some 260 species of birds are found in the refuge, the largest in the lower 48. 1,600,000 acres. Primitive camping, hiking, hunting, scenic drives (high-clearance vehicle recommended). Open year-round. Interpretive kiosk at Corn Creek Field Station entrance, off US 95, about 250 miles from Great Basin NP. (702) 879-6110.

SPRING MOUNTAIN NATIONAL RECREATION AREA
LAS VEGAS, NEVADA

Many people are surprised to find a forest so close to Las Vegas: The Spring Mountains rise to almost 12,000 feet from the harsh desert of southern Nevada. The cool mountain forests are home to a wilderness of ponderosa pine, sheer limestone cliffs, and assorted wildlife. About 316,000 acres. Camping, scenic drives, hiking, wildlife viewing. Picnic areas. Take US 95 to the Kyle Canyon turnoff (Nev. 157). About 250 miles from Great Basin NP. (702) 515-5400.

GREAT BASIN

Cliff Palace, a 13th-century ancestral Puebloan site

▶ MESA VERDE COLORADO
ESTABLISHED JUNE 29, 1906
52,074 acres

At Mesa Verde, Spanish for "green table," multistoried dwellings fill the cliff-rock alcoves that rise 2,000 feet above Montezuma Valley. Remarkably preserved, the cliff dwellings cluster in canyons that slice the mesa into narrow tablelands. Here, and on the mesa top, archaeologists have located more than 4,800 archaeological sites (including 600 cliff dwellings) dating from about A.D. 550 to 1300.

The sites, from mesa-top pit houses and multistoried dwellings to cliffside villages, document the changes in the lives of a prehistoric people once dubbed the Anasazi. They are now more accurately called the ancestral Puebloans, and modern Pueblo tribes in the Southwest consider themselves descendants of these ancestral people. Some 40 pueblos and cliff dwellings are visible from park roads and overlooks; some of these are open to the public.

Beginning about A.D. 750, the ancestral Puebloans grouped their mesa-top dwellings in pueblos, or villages. About 1200 they moved into recesses in the cliffs. So sheltered, these later villages seem to stand outside of time, aloof to the present.

In 1888 two cowboys tracking stray cattle in a snowstorm stopped on the edge of a steep-walled canyon. Through the flakes they made out traces of walls and towers of a large cliff dwelling across the canyon. Novelist Willa Cather later described the scene: "The falling snowflakes sprinkling the piñons, gave it a special kind of solemnity. It was more like sculpture than anything else . . . preserved . . . like a fly in amber."

Climbing down a makeshift ladder, the excited cowboys explored the honeycombed network of rooms that they named Cliff Palace. Inside, they found stone tools, pottery, and other artifacts in rooms that had been uninhabited for some 600 years.

Why the Mesa Verde people eventually left their homes may never be known. Indeed, they lived in the cliff dwellings for only about the last 75 to 100 years of their occupation of Mesa Verde. Early archaeologists guessed warfare, and the evidence for this seems to concur. Archaeologists also think they may have been victims of their own success. Their productive dry farming allowed the Mesa Verde population to grow perhaps as high as 5,000. Gradually woodlands were cut, wild game hunted out, and soils depleted. Years of drought and poor crops may have been aggravated by village squabbles. By the end of the 13th century the ancestral Puebloans had left the plateau, never to return.

How to Get There
From Cortez, take US 160 east for 8 miles to the park entrance, then follow the winding park road 15 miles to Far View Visitor Center and 5.5 miles farther to the Chapin Mesa Archaeological Museum, and a cliff dwelling—Spruce Tree House. Trailers are not allowed past Morefield Village Campground. Airports: Cortez and Durango.

When to Go
Year-round. Wetherill Mesa, Far View Visitor Center, Cliff Palace Loop, Balcony House, and many services are closed in winter. Wildflowers bloom from April through September. In winter, cross-country skiing is allowed in Morefield and on the Cliff Palace Loop Road when conditions permit.

How to Visit
On a 1-day visit, begin early and stop first at the **Far View Visitor Center,** open mid-April to mid-October, to purchase tour tickets. Then go to the **Chapin Mesa Archaeological Museum** for an overview; and then visit nearby **Spruce Tree House** (no tickets required). From there drive the **Cliff Palace Loop Road.** In the afternoon, follow the **Mesa Top Loop Road.** Wear sturdy shoes and be prepared for some strenuous climbing if you plan to visit the cliff dwellings. Binoculars are useful for enhancing views across the canyon.

With extra time, visit less crowded **Wetherill Mesa.**

CHAPIN MESA MUSEUM & SPRUCE TREE HOUSE
2 hours to a half day

Before descending to the sites, go through the **Chapin Mesa Museum,** located in the park headquarters area. Here you can pick up self-guiding booklets to the major sites and view a 25-minute video.

Excellent dioramas bring to life the changing world of the Mesa Verde people. Also displayed are some of the Southwest's finest artifacts and Indian arts and crafts. Also view the collection of **Mesa Verde pottery.** Decorated with black geometric designs against a white background, the pots represent the highest artistic expression of the ancestral Puebloans.

The park naturally focuses on the dramatic cliff dwellings, but they represent only the final scene in a long story. The genius of the earlier culture was best expressed not in building but in basketmaking and

MESA VERDE

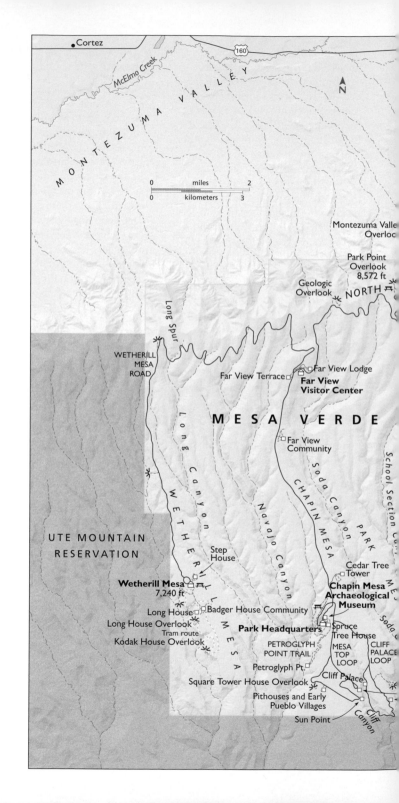

•Cortez

160

McElmo Creek

M O N T E Z U M A   V A L L E Y

miles 0 — 2

kilometers 0 — 3

N

Montezuma Valle
Overloc

Park Point
Overlook
8,572 ft

Geologic
Overlook

NORTH

Long Spur

WETHERILL
MESA
ROAD

Far View Terrace☐

☐Far View Lodge

**Far View
Visitor Center**

Long Canyon

M E S A   V E R D E

School Section Cur

☐Far View
Community

W E T H E R

Soda Canyon

CHAPIN MESA

PARK

Navajo Canyon

UTE MOUNTAIN
RESERVATION

Step
House

Cedar Tree
Tower

Wetherill Mesa
7,240 ft

☐

**Chapin Mesa
Archaeological
Museum**

Long House☐
Long House Overlook
Tram route
Kodak House Overlook

☐Badger House Community

L L

Park Headquarters

Spruce
Tree House

M E S A

PETROGLYPH
POINT TRAIL

MESA
TOP
LOOP

CLIFF
PALACE
LOOP

Soda

☐ Petroglyph Pt.

Square Tower House Overlook

Cliff Palace

Pithouses and Early
Pueblo Villages

Cliff
Canyon

Sun Point

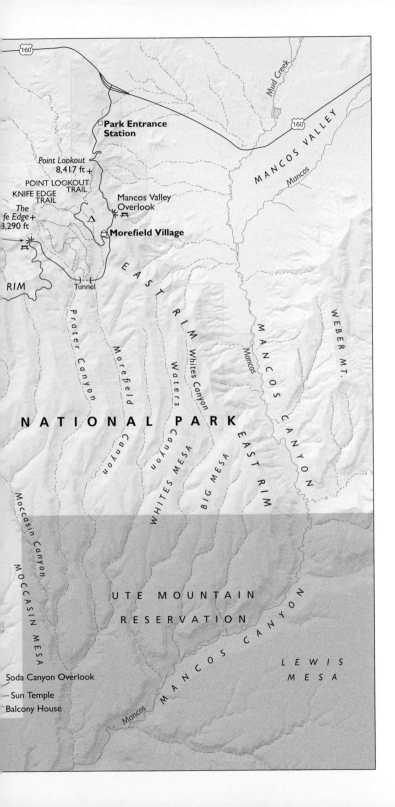

weaving. Look for outstanding examples throughout the museum.

Pick up a self-guiding booklet to Spruce Tree House and walk the paved quarter-mile trail to the park's best preserved site. Here you will see the skillful building techniques and stonework of the ancestral Puebloans; 90 percent of the stonework is original. Rangers will be on duty to answer questions. (The rangers lead guided tours from mid-November to early March.) The trail crosses the canyon bottom, thick with Gambel oak. The site got its name from a tall Douglas fir (formerly known as a spruce) that, it is said, early explorers climbed down to reach the site.

The cliff dwelling, in an alcove more than 200 feet wide, housed 60 to 100 people. Three of its eight kivas —underground ceremonial rooms— have reconstructed roofs. You may climb down a ladder into one of them through the smoke hole.

Either now or later—if time and stamina allow—take the 2.8-mile **Petroglyph Point Trail,** a self-guided nature walk that branches off the Spruce Tree House Trail. Register and pick up a guidebook at the trailhead. The trail offers a good place to stretch your legs, familiarize yourself with plants and their prehistoric uses, and see one of the park's largest petroglyphs, a panel 12 feet across.

CHAPIN MESA
12 miles; 1.5 hours

Two 6-mile one-way loops wind through Chapin Mesa's fire-scarred pinyon-juniper woodland. Begin by turning onto the **Cliff Palace Loop** and driving to the parking area at **Cliff Palace.** A short trail takes you to a striking view of the largest cliff dwelling in North America: The 150-room site once housed more than 100 people. A park ranger will meet you at the overlook and guide you down a quarter-mile trail to tour the dwelling 120 feet below (ticket required).

The ancestral Puebloans built their dwellings in natural shelters formed by water percolating down through the sandstone. Where it reaches the denser shale layer, it seeps horizontally through the canyon wall, forming springs. These weaken the overlying rock, eroding the cliff face into eye-shaped alcoves.

Continue driving to the **Balcony House** parking area. This 40-room dwelling is a highlight of the park. Rangers guide adventurous groups *(tickets required)* up a 32-foot ladder to an easily defended ledge site with a panoramic view of **Soda Canyon.** To leave Balcony House, you must crawl through a tunnel on your hands and knees. Balcony House is closed in winter; you can view it at a distance from a promontory at the end of the 0.75-mile **Soda Canyon Overlook Trail.**

Keep going along the road until the junction with the **Mesa Top Loop Road,** where you turn left. At the **Square Tower House** overlook, a 500-foot trail leads to a dramatic viewpoint above the park's tallest site, the four-story remnant of a more extensive, multitiered structure. The site itself is not open to the public.

Return to your car and continue a short distance to the **pit houses and early Pueblo villages** pull-off. The squarish, sunken pithouses, earliest of Mesa Verde's permanent dwellings, were forerunners of the kivas. Farther along the trail are the excavated remains of three villages built on the same site between A.D. 900 and 1075. They show the evolution in architectural style, from post-and-adobe construction to stone masonry.

Drive to **Sun Point Overlook,** saving **Sun Point Pueblo** for your next visit. Here at the junction of **Fewkes Canyon** and **Cliff Canyon** you see a dozen cliff dwellings—among them, distant views of Cliff Palace to the northeast; **Sunset House** perched on a high rock ledge to the east; and **Mummy House**—named for the naturally desiccated mummy of a child discovered there—directly across the canyon.

The road continues past **Oak Tree House** and **Fire Temple** pull-offs to **Sun Temple.** Built by skilled masons—the stones were molded and their surfaces "dimpled"—this long, D-shaped structure with doorless chambers presents an enigma to archaeologists. Never inhabited, it may have been a ceremonial center. The canyon edge next to the parking area offers a superb view of Cliff Palace.

WETHERILL MESA

12 miles; a half day or more

Accessible only in summer, the **Wetherill Mesa Road** starts on the west side of **Far View Visitor Center,** where you stop to purchase tickets for the 1.5-hour tour of Long House. The steep road takes you to several sites opened to the public in 1972 after an extensive archaeological study sponsored by the National Geographic Society and the National Park Service.

Drive to the kiosk area and park. Take the 1-mile, self-guided walk to **Step House,** named for its stairway. This site is noted for the pit houses that have been uncovered next to a multistoried pueblo put in the same alcove.

Return to the kiosk area and take the mini-tram to the head of **Long House Trail.** Rangers lead groups down the 0.75-mile trail to the park's second largest cliff dwelling—150 rooms with 21 kivas, an unusually high number. Gustaf Nordenskiöld, a Swedish scientist, excavated portions of **Long House** and other sites in 1891, publishing the first scientific report on Mesa Verde.

Extend your visit by taking the mini-tram to the half-mile, self-guided trail that threads through the pit houses and pueblos of **Badger House Community.** These show the contrast between life on the mesa top and in the canyon alcoves below. The mini-tram will return you to the kiosk area.

MESA VERDE

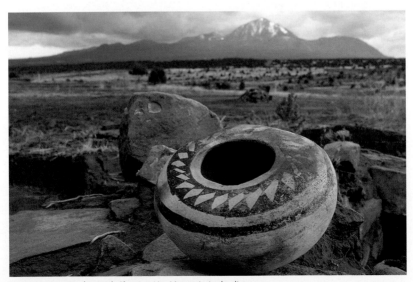

Ancient pottery seed jar with Sleeping Ute Mountain in the distance

INFORMATION & ACTIVITIES

VISITOR & INFORMATION CENTERS

Far View Visitor Center at northwest section of park open daily mid-April to mid-October. **Chapin Mesa Archaeological Museum** at southern end of park, located 20 miles from entrance, open daily year-round. Phone (970) 529-4465 for visitor information.

SEASONS & ACCESSIBILITY

Park open year-round, but most visitor facilities and services available mid-May to mid-October only. **Spruce Tree House** open all year; **Cliff Palace** open early April to early November; **Balcony House** open early May to mid-October; **Wetherill Mesa** open summer only. In winter, snow or ice may close Mesa Top Road. For weather and road conditions, call (970) 529-4461 or (970) 529-4465.

HEADQUARTERS

Mesa Verde National Park, CO 81330. Phone (970) 529-4465. www.nps.gov/meve

ENTRANCE FEE

$15 per car per week, Mem. Day–Labor Day; $10 other times. Additional tickets required for tours of Cliff Palace, Balcony House, and Long House; purchase for small fee at Far View Visitor Center.

PETS

Permitted on leashes. Not allowed in buildings, in sites, or on trails.

ACCESSIBLE SERVICES

Visitor center, museum, overlooks, and mesa-top sites, some campsites, and most restrooms are wheelchair accessible. Site tours are not accessible, but most major cliff dwellings can be viewed from the mesa-top roads and overlooks. Free brochure.

THINGS TO DO

Ranger-led activities: archaeological walks, tours of Cliff Palace and Balcony House (spring to fall), Spruce Tree House (winter), and Long House (summer only); evening programs. Also available, wayside exhibits, archaeological museum, self-guided tours; limited hiking (registration required for two trails), cross-country skiing, and snowshoeing.

SPECIAL ADVISORIES

• Visits to the cliff dwellings are strenuous. Wear sturdy shoes and use caution, especially if you have heart or respiratory problems.
• Hold on to your children on cliff trails and canyon rims.

OVERNIGHT BACKPACKING

Not permitted in park.

CAMPGROUNDS

One campground, **Morefield,** with a 14-day limit. Open mid-April to mid-October. First come, first served. Fees $20-$25 per night. Showers within 1 mile of campground. Tent and RV sites; 14 hookups. **Morefield Group Campsite** available first come, first served. Food services in park.

HOTELS, MOTELS, & INNS

(unless otherwise noted, rates are for 2 persons in a double room, high season)

INSIDE THE PARK:
Far View Lodge Mesa Verde Co., P.O. Box 277, Mancos, CO 81328. (800) 449-2288. 150 units. $120-$152. Restaurant. April–Oct.

OUTSIDE THE PARK:
In Cortez, CO 81321:
Cortez Mesa Verde Inn 640 S. Broadway. (888) 565-1027 or (970) 565-3773. 84 units. $88. AC, pool.
Best Western Turquoise Inn and Suites 535 E. Main St. (800) 547-3376 or (970) 565-3778. 77 units. $89-$164. AC, pool.
In Durango, CO 81301:
Strater Hotel 699 Main Ave. (800) 247-4431 or (970) 247-4431. 93 units. $169-$279. AC, restaurant.
In Mancos, CO 81328:
Mesa Verde Motel 191 Railroad Ave., P.O. Box 552. (800) 825-6372 or (970) 533-7741. 16 units. $85. AC.

For further suggestions, contact the Cortez Area Chamber of Commerce, (970) 565-3414, www.cortezchamber.com; or the Durango Chamber of Commerce, (888) 414-0835, www.durangobusiness.org.

EXCURSIONS

SAN JUAN NATIONAL FOREST
DURANGO, COLORADO

The vegetation ranges from high alpine forest to sage-and-pinyon desert in this rugged San Juan Mountains area. Contains lakes, rivers, wilderness areas, and many archaeological sites. Two million acres. Hiking, boating, climbing, bicycling, fishing, horseback riding, llama trekking, hunting, winter sports, water sports. 36 campgrounds, boat ramps, limited handicapped access. Open all year; most campsites open May through November. Information near Durango off US 160, about 50 miles east of Mesa Verde NP. (970) 247-4874.

AZTEC RUINS NATIONAL MONUMENT
AZTEC, NEW MEXICO

At Aztec, ancestral Puebloan people carefully planned and built over two centuries a large and complex settlement. Today it features the Southwest's only restored great kiva. 319 acres. Exhibits, trail, picnic areas. Open all year. Off N. Mex. 516, on Ruins Road, about 60 miles southeast of Mesa Verde NP. (505) 334-6174.

HOVENWEEP NATIONAL MONUMENT
CORTEZ, COLORADO

Hovenweep—a Ute term meaning "deserted valley"—consists of six ancestral Puebloan sites: two in Utah and four in Colorado. They feature stone pueblos and square, circular, and D-shaped towers. Square Tower Group—located in Utah midway between Cortez, Colorado, and Blanding, Utah—is best preserved and most accessible. 785 acres. Open all year. Interpretive exhibits, hiking. 30 campsites, picnic areas. Headquarters at Square Tower Group off Utah 262, about 55 miles from Mesa Verde NP. (970) 562-4282.

MESA VERDE

Fossilized logs, remnants of ancient conifers in Blue Mesa

▶PETRIFIED FOREST

ARIZONA
ESTABLISHED DECEMBER 9, 1962
135,000 acres

A sun-swept corner of the Painted Desert draws more than 600,000 visitors each year. While most come to see one of the world's largest concentrations of brilliantly colored petrified wood, many leave having glimpsed something more. The current 346 square miles of Petrified Forest open a window on an environment more than 200 million years old, one radically different from today's grassland.

Where you now see ravens soaring over a stark landscape, leathery-winged pterosaurs once glided over rivers teeming with armor-scaled fish and giant, spatula-headed amphibians. Nearby ran herds of some of the earliest dinosaurs. Scientists have identified several hundred species of fossil plants and animals in Petrified Forest.

The park consists of two main sections, and legislation in 2004 authorized increasing the size to 218,533 acres. Located in the south are the major concentrations of the famous colorful petrified wood; in the north rise the colorful banded badlands of the Painted Desert. Giant fossilized logs, many of them fractured into cordwood-size segments, lie scattered throughout, like headstones bearing a deceased's likeness.

Much of the quartz that replaced the wood tissue 200 million years ago is tinted in rainbow hues. Many visitors cannot resist taking rocks, despite strict regulations and stiff fines against removing any material. To see if the petrified wood was actually disappearing at an alarming rate, resource managers established survey plots with a specific number of pieces of wood; some were nearly barren in less than a week.

The problem is not new. Military survey parties passing through the region in the 1850s filled their saddlebags with the petrified wood. As word of these remarkable deposits spread, fossil logs were hauled off by the wagonload for tabletops, lamps, and mantels. In the 1890s gem collectors began dynamiting logs searching for amethyst and other quartz crystals. To prevent further destruction of its unique bounty, the area was designated a national monument in 1906 and a national park more than a half century later.

How to Get There
If you are traveling west on I-40, exit into park. When leaving the south end of the park, the road joins US 180. Follow US 180 for 19 miles to Holbrook and back to I-40. If you are traveling east on I-40, take the US 180 exit in Holbrook. The south entrance is 19 miles farther. After driving through the park, leave via I-40. Airport: Flagstaff. There is also a small airport in Holbrook.

When to Go
Year-round. Summer's dramatic thunderstorms enhance the beauty of the landscape. Fall, with its milder weather, also attracts many visitors. Winter on the Colorado Plateau can be cold with brief snowstorms, but moderate afternoon temperatures are not uncommon. The area blooms colorfully in spring; winds can be high.

How to Visit
You'll need to get out of the car to best experience this park. If you have only an hour, stop at the **Painted Desert Visitor Center,** drive **Blue Mesa Road** and stop at the overlooks, and visit **Kachina Point** and the **Rainbow Forest Museum.** If you have several hours, stop at the **Painted Desert Inn National Historic Landmark,** and walk the **Puerco Pueblo Trail** and **Giant Logs Trail.** With half a day, walk the trails at **Painted Desert Rim, Blue Mesa, Crystal Forest, Long Logs,** and **Agate House;** if you have a whole day, hike into the **Petrified Forest National Wilderness Area.**

THE PARK ROAD
28 miles; a half to full day

A scenic drive connecting the south and north entrances passes through high desert grasslands broken by unexpected escarpments and bare hills banded in pastels. Begin at the south entrance with a stop at the **Rainbow Forest Museum.** (Or, from the north, begin at the **Painted Desert Visitor Center** and reverse this tour.) Be sure to see the dioramas of the late Triassic landscape and the displays of fossils and early dinosaurs.

The museum sits in the **Rainbow Forest,** one of four major concentrations of petrified logs called "forests." Behind it winds the half-mile **Giant Logs Trail** (closes 15 minutes before park); the largest fossil log is **Old Faithful** with a 10-foot diameter.

From the museum, a half-mile trail (closes 30 minutes before park) takes you to the trailhead for the

PETRIFIED FOREST

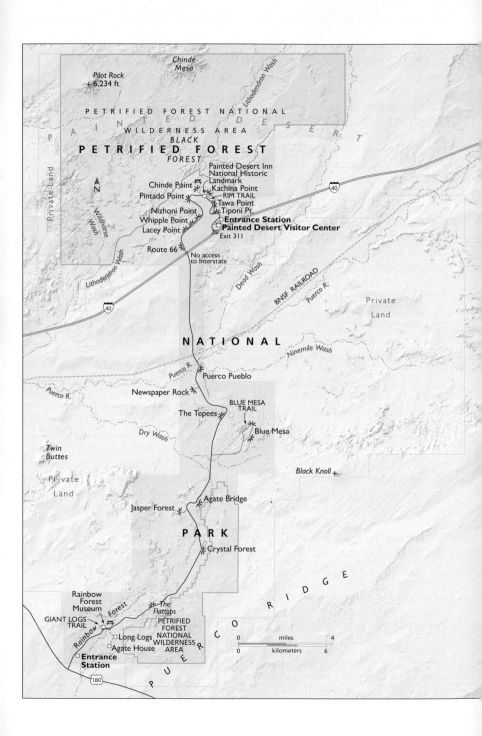

Chinde Mesa

Pilot Rock
+6,234 ft

Lithodendron Wash

PETRIFIED FOREST NATIONAL

WILDERNESS AREA

BLACK

PETRIFIED FOREST

FOREST

P A I N T E D   D E S E R T

P

Private Land

Wildhorse Wash

N

Painted Desert Inn
National Historic
Landmark
Chinde Point   Kachina Point
Pintado Point   RIM TRAIL
Nizhoni Point   Tawa Point
Whipple Point   Tiponi Pt.
Lacey Point   Entrance Station
                        Painted Desert Visitor Center
                        Exit 311

40

Lithodendron Wash

Route 66

No access
to Interstate

Dead Wash

Puerco R.

BNSF RAILROAD

Private Land

40

N A T I O N A L

Ninemile Wash

Puerco R.

Puerco R.

Puerco Pueblo

Newspaper Rock

The Tepees

BLUE MESA
TRAIL

Dry Wash

Blue Mesa

Twin Buttes

Black Knoll +

Private Land

P A R K

Agate Bridge

Jasper Forest

Crystal Forest

P U E R C O   R I D G E

Rainbow Forest Museum

Forest

The Flattops

GIANT LOGS TRAIL

Rainbow

Long Logs

PETRIFIED
FOREST
NATIONAL
WILDERNESS
AREA

Agate House

Entrance Station

180

0   miles   4
0   kilometers   6

0.6-mile Long Logs loop and the 1-mile round-trip Agate House trail.

At **Long Logs,** you will see the largest concentration of petrified wood in the park, with logs up to 120 feet long—many crisscrossed in logjams.

The majority of the park's petrified wood, including that found here, comes from tall conifers. These ancient trees grew more than 200 million years ago along waterways, where periodic flooding uprooted them. Tumbled and abraded, the fallen trees washed into logjams and were buried by sediment and volcanic ash. Silica-laden water percolated through the wood, replacing organic tissue with multicolored quartz.

Next, if you have time, strike out on the paved trail to **Agate House.** During the 1930s crews restored one of the rooms in this eight-room dwelling built by ancestral Puebloans more than 800 years ago. The prehistoric structure was of mortared, petrified wood and mud; the reconstruction uses concrete to stabilize the walls.

Continue your drive north, bypassing three turnoffs—**Crystal Forest, Jasper Forest,** and **Agate Bridge,** unless you have plenty of time. Take the 3-mile spur road that climbs **Blue Mesa.** You loop through strange badlands layered in blue, purple, and cream colors that change with weather and time of day.

Along the way, you'll spot the trailhead for the **Blue Mesa Trail,** which winds along a 1-mile, 45-minute route through the badlands. The trail is paved and nearly level except for one very steep section. Even if you can't take the full hike, park your car and walk 100 feet to where the trail begins to descend. Here are good views of the intricately eroded mesa.

Return to the main road and drive north through **The Tepees,** bare, conical hills whose reddish hues are produced by iron and other minerals.

The fabulous **Newspaper Rock,** two large boulders covered by more than 600 petroglyphs, can be viewed through scopes at the overlook. Continue driving a short distance to the **Puerco Pueblo,** one of the largest prehistoric sites in the park. Here you see the partially excavated remains of an ancestral Puebloan village left about 1380 as well as many fine petroglyphs of animals and geometric designs pecked into the outcropping rock.

Scientists believe a chiseled spiral here was used by the Indians as a solar calendar. The week preceding and following the summer solstice in mid-June, the sun interacts with this petroglyph. In the morning (8:30–9:30 a.m.) on the day of the summer solstice, rangers usually guide observers to the place where a shaft of sunlight pierces and fills the very center of the ancient symbol.

The road crosses the intermittent **Puerco River,** which divides the park in two. Only about 10 inches of precipitation fall each year, mostly in summer thunderstorms.

After crossing I-40, the drive reaches the edge of a volcanic escarpment overlooking a particularly colorful section of the **Painted Desert.**

Pull off at **Lacey Point,** the first of nine overlooks. Here the bare Chinle slopes are tinted in the earthy shades of a Navajo rug. The colors are especially vivid when the sun shines on sediment still wet from a thunderstorm.

Continue on to the sweeping panoramic vista at **Pintado Point**—the highest along the Painted Desert rim. Below lies **Lithodendron Wash,** and to the northeast is the **Black Forest,** an area of dark fossilized wood. In the distance stands the dark profile of **Pilot Rock,** at 6,234 feet the park's highest point.

PETRIFIED FOREST

INFORMATION & ACTIVITIES

VISITOR & INFORMATION CENTERS
Painted Desert Visitor Center at north entrance, just off I-40, and **Rainbow Forest Museum** near south entrance, just off US 180. **Painted Desert Inn National Historic Landmark,** 2 miles from the north entrance, also has historic information.

SEASONS & ACCESSIBILITY
Open all year; extended hours May through August. Snow or icy roads may close park temporarily in winter.

HEADQUARTERS
P.O. Box 2217, AZ 86028. Phone (928) 524-6228. www.nps.gov/pefo

ENTRANCE FEE
$10 per car, good for 7 days.

PETS & HORSES
Pets permitted on leashes except in public buildings. Horses permitted throughout park (except on marked trails; wilderness access permitted) in groups of four or less when accompanied by riders. Grazing prohibited. No water available.

ACCESSIBLE SERVICES
Visitor centers, museum, and restrooms are wheelchair accessible.

THINGS TO DO
Free ranger-led, year-round activities: nature talks, wildlife viewing, and bird-watching. Also available, a film, interpretive exhibits, self-guided auto tours, hiking, horseback riding (no rentals in area).

SPECIAL ADVISORIES
• Stay on trails to prevent damage to the fragile desert environment and personal injury from sharp edges of petrified logs.
• Take nothing from the park but memories, not even a tiny piece of petrified wood; pieces quickly add up to tons.
• Carry water when you hike; none is available outside developed areas.
• Do not approach any wildlife; as cute as they are, park animals may carry bubonic plague, Hantavirus, and rabies.

OVERNIGHT BACKPACKING
Allowed in wilderness area. Permit required; available free at visitor center or museum up to one hour before park closing.

CAMPGROUNDS
None in park, but food service available.

HOTELS, MOTELS, & INNS
(unless otherwise noted, rates are for 2 persons in a double room, high season)

In Holbrook, AZ 86025:
American Best Inn 2211 E. Navajo Blvd. (800) 551-1923 or (928) 524-2654. 40 units. $56. AC.
Best Western Adobe Inn 615 W. Hopi Dr. (877) 524-3948 or (928) 524-3948. 54 units. $98-$105. AC, pool.
Holbrook Comfort Inn 2602 E. Navajo Blvd. (800) 228-5150 or (928) 524-6131. 60 units. $85. AC, pool.

For additional accommodations, contact the Holbrook Chamber of Commerce, 100 E. Arizona St., Holbrook, AZ 86025. (928) 524-6558, www.holbrookchamberof commerce.com.

For a longer hike, walk through the rugged beauty of the **Petrified Forest National Wilderness Area.** The trail begins at **Kachina Point** behind the old **Painted Desert Inn,** originally built as a roadside inn, now open daily as a national historical landmark and museum. Once in the flats below the rim, the trail disappears, requiring you to do your own route-finding. Look for the Black Forest and **Onyx Bridge.** Finding the bridge can be an adventure since there are no landmarks to guide you.

The scenic drive ends at the **Painted Desert Visitor Center,** the park headquarters at the north entrance.

EXCURSIONS

EL MORRO
NATIONAL MONUMENT
RAMAH, NEW MEXICO

Here in 1605 Spaniard Juan de Oñate scratched his name at the base of a sandstone cliff. Others added inscriptions to the carvings of pre-Columbian Indians. Two ancestral Puebloan ruins sit on the cliff-top mesa. 1,279 acres. Hiking. 9 campsites (open May to mid-Oct.), picnic areas, handicapped access. Open year-round. On N. Mex. 53, off I-40, about 125 miles from Petrified Forest NP. (505) 783-4226.

EL MALPAIS NATIONAL
MONUMENT AND NATIONAL
CONSERVATION AREA
GRANTS, NEW MEXICO

El Malpais—"the badlands"—is located in the lava beds of western New Mexico. Featuring spatter cones, a 17-mile-long lava-tube system, and ice caves, the site also contains ancestral Puebloan ruins, a freestanding natural arch, and two wilderness areas. 376,000 acres. Primitive camping, hiking, bicycling, horseback riding, scenic drives. Open all year. Information center at N. Mex. 53 (23 miles south of Grants). About 140 miles east of Petrified Forest NP. (505) 783-4774.

WALNUT CANYON
NATIONAL MONUMENT
FLAGSTAFF, ARIZONA

More than 800 years ago, Indians now known as the Sinagua lived in caves in cliff dwellings here at the edge of Flagstaff. The Sinagua's name (Spanish for "without water") comes from the Spanish name for the nearby mountains. The cliff dwellings are accessible by trail. 3,579 acres. Visitor center, picnic areas. Open daily. Located off I-40, just east of Flagstaff. About 107 miles west of the I-40 exit at Petrified Forest NP. (928) 526-3367.

PETRIFIED FOREST

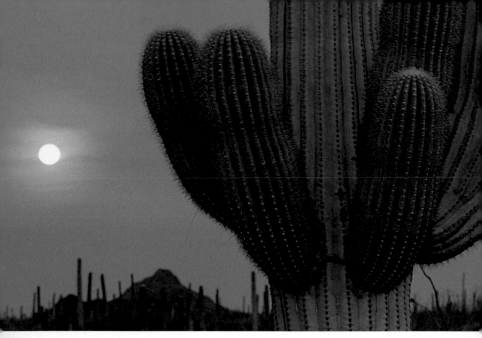

Saguaro cactuses, some reaching 30 feet in height, under moonlight

▶SAGUARO

ARIZONA
ESTABLISHED OCTOBER 14, 1994
91,445 acres

Symbol of the American Southwest and North America's largest cactus, the saguaro's imposing stature and uplifted arms give it a regal presence. Perhaps that's why this burly giant, whose only bits of exuberance are seasonal blossoms and figlike fruits at the tip of its limbs, has been dubbed the "desert monarch."

Carnegiea gigantea is the trademark of the Sonoran Desert, whose basins and ranges rumple 120,000 square miles of northwestern Mexico, southern Arizona, and southeastern California. Saguaro National Park is composed of two sections. The westerly Tucson Mountain District embraces about 24,000 acres of the hotter, drier, less-vegetated "low" Sonoran ecosystem, which occurs at an elevation around 3,000 feet. Thirty miles east, on the other side of Tucson's urban sprawl, is the 67,000-acre Rincon Mountain District, which occupies loftier

ground and has a cooler, slightly wetter "high desert" environment. Most of it is inaccessible except by foot or on horseback. Here the terrain inclines from saguaro forests into nearly pristine woodlands of oak and pine. Hikers pressing on to higher elevations find Douglas fir, ponderosa pine, and solitude.

The Sonoran Desert's extreme temperatures, perennial drought, frequent lightning, banshee winds, and voracious predators keep the saguaro forever at the limit of its endurance. Odds against survival rival a lottery: Though the cactus annually produces tens of thousands of pinhead-size seeds—some 40 million over a life that may last two centuries—few ever even sprout. Even fewer seedlings achieve the grandeur of towering 50 feet and weighing up to 16,000 pounds.

Though the saguaro may be the park's centerpiece, after wet winters the spring wildflower display can be breathtaking. The brilliant gold of the Mexican poppy is often the first-noticed bloom, while penstemons, lupines, desert marigolds, brittle-bushes, and globe mallows contribute their lively colors of red, lilac, blue, and yellow. Many trees, shrubs, and cactuses also bloom, including creosote bushes, paloverdes, ocotillos, chollas, and hedgehogs. Saguaros bloom in late spring.

How to Get There

Saguaro West: From Tucson take Speedway Boulevard west to Gates Pass Road, turning right on Kinney Road. *(Gates Pass not recommended for buses, RVs, and towed vehicles; instead take Ariz. 86 west from Tucson to Kinney.)*
Saguaro East: Take Broadway Boulevard east from central Tucson to Old Spanish Trail. Airport: Tucson.

When to Go

Year-round. From October through April, temperatures reach the upper 60s to mid-70s and can drop below freezing overnight. From May through September, highs routinely exceed 100°F. July through September is characterized by brief, fierce thunderstorms. Saguaros bloom nightly from late April into June.

How to Visit

On a 1-day visit, begin early and view the **Arizona-Sonora Desert Museum** before heading to **Saguaro West;** then pause at the **Red Hills Visitor Center** for an overview. Take the **Bajada Scenic Loop Drive,** stopping en route to walk the paved **Desert Discovery Nature Trail.** Return to Tucson, continuing east to Saguaro's **Rincon Mountain District.** Take the **Cactus Forest Drive** and walk the **Desert Ecology Trail.** For a scenic rest stop along the drive, visit **Mica View Picnic Area.**

SAGUARO WEST: TUCSON MOUNTAIN DISTRICT
about 25 miles; a half day

The drive west through **Tucson Mountain County Park** takes you past the excellent, zoolike **Arizona-Sonora Desert Museum** (2021 N. Kinney Rd., 520-883-1380; fee), whose 21 acres include every Sonoran Desert life zone and most of its animals and plants. It's worth a stop.

Continue on Kinney Road to the **Red Hills Visitor Center** with its decks and panoramic view. Here a unique slide show and desert life exhibits will enhance your understanding of what you'll encounter here and in Saguaro East. Walk the center's **Cactus Garden Trail,** a paved path through an unruly crowd of cactuses: hedgehog, barrel, fishhook, chainfruit cholla, and prickly pear to name but a few.

Saguaros thrive in the coarse, absorbent soil of *bajadas,* long desert mountain slopes of eroded rock, gravel, sand, and clay, where a mature plant's shallow, wide-ranging roots can absorb up to 200 gallons from one rainstorm, enough to last a year. The 9-mile **Bajada Loop Drive,** which begins 1.5 miles north of the visitor center, explores one of these life zones. En route, about 1 mile west, look left for the **Desert Discovery Nature Trail,** a half-mile path across a bajada at the base of the Tucson Mountains.

SAGUARO

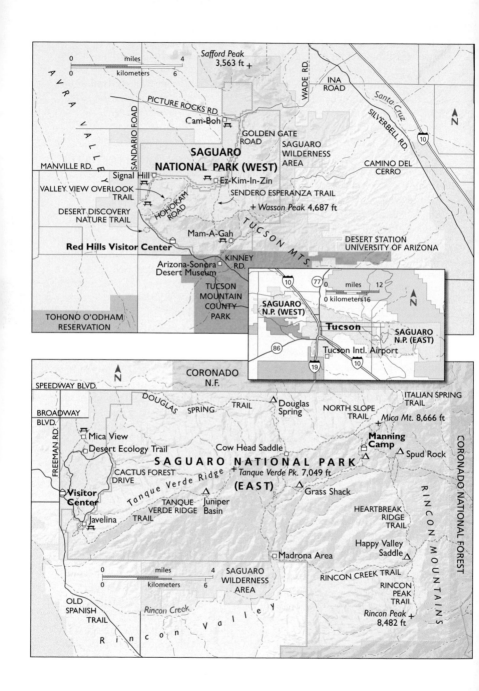

Safford Peak 3,563 ft

0 miles 4
0 kilometers 6

AVRA VALLEY

PICTURE ROCKS RD.
Cam-Boh

GOLDEN GATE ROAD

SANDARIO ROAD

INA ROAD

Santa Cruz

SILVERBELL RD.

SAGUARO NATIONAL PARK (WEST)

SAGUARO WILDERNESS AREA

MANVILLE RD.

Signal Hill

Ez-Kim-In-Zin

CAMINO DEL CERRO

VALLEY VIEW OVERLOOK TRAIL

SENDERO ESPERANZA TRAIL

+ Wasson Peak 4,687 ft

DESERT DISCOVERY NATURE TRAIL

HOHOKAM ROAD

Mam-A-Gah

TUCSON MTS.

Red Hills Visitor Center

DESERT STATION UNIVERSITY OF ARIZONA

KINNEY RD.

Arizona-Sonora Desert Museum

TUCSON MOUNTAIN COUNTY PARK

TOHONO O'ODHAM RESERVATION

10

77

0 miles 12
0 kilometers 16

N

SAGUARO N.P. (WEST)

Tucson

SAGUARO N.P. (EAST)

86

Tucson Intl. Airport

19

10

CORONADO N.F.

SPEEDWAY BLVD.

DOUGLAS SPRING TRAIL

Douglas Spring

NORTH SLOPE TRAIL

ITALIAN SPRING TRAIL

Mica Mt. 8,666 ft

BROADWAY BLVD.

FREEMAN RD.

Mica View

Desert Ecology Trail

Cow Head Saddle

Manning Camp

Spud Rock

S A G U A R O   N A T I O N A L   P A R K

CACTUS FOREST DRIVE

Tanque Verde Ridge

+ Tanque Verde Pk. 7,049 ft

(E A S T)

Grass Shack

Visitor Center

Javelina

TANQUE VERDE RIDGE TRAIL

Juniper Basin

HEARTBREAK RIDGE TRAIL

RINCON MOUNTAINS

CORONADO NATIONAL FOREST

Happy Valley Saddle

Madrona Area

0 miles 4
0 kilometers 6

SAGUARO WILDERNESS AREA

RINCON CREEK TRAIL

RINCON PEAK TRAIL

OLD SPANISH TRAIL

Rincon Creek

Rincon Valley

Rincon Peak + 8,482 ft

Hook right onto **Hohokam Road.**
(Part of the loop is one way; enter
here to drive it all in one direction.)
About 1.5 miles from the turnoff,
Valley View Overlook Trail winds up
about half a mile to panoramas of
rugged, cactus-studded landscapes.
Unpaved **Golden Gate Road** turns off
about a mile farther on and passes a
pleasant picnic area near the head of
Sendero Esperanza Trail, a moderately
strenuous, popular half-day hike into
the mountainous backcountry.

Backtrack on Golden Gate Road
past Hohokam Road to **Signal Hill
Picnic Area,** where rocks are etched
with centuries-old Hohokam petroglyphs. Archaeologists believe the
symbols, chipped through a brown
patina of iron-manganese oxide
called "desert varnish," signify ter-
ritorial claims, clan migrations,
personal accounts, visions, and pure
artistic whimsy.

Continuing through ironwood
and paloverde, the loop closes at
Sandario Road, an alternative route
back to Tucson via Picture Rocks,
Wade, and Ina Roads to I-10.

SAGUARO EAST: RINCON MOUNTAIN DISTRICT

about 25 miles; a half day

The higher elevations here create
Sonoran Desert environments different from Saguaro West's lowland
desert zone. A steady, east-trending
incline slants up into the roadless
Rincon Mountain wilderness area,
which is dotted with forests of oak,
pine, and fir accessible only by foot
or on horseback.

Make your first stop the **Rincon
Mountain Visitor Center.** If you plan to
hike into the backcountry, this is the
place to acquire trail guides, maps,

Hedgehog cactus in bloom *(top)*
Teddybear cholla cactus *(bottom)*

and permits. If time is limited, pick
up a guide to the **Cactus Forest Drive**
and take the 8-mile loop, where
many of the saguaros are over 150
years old.

About 2 miles along the route,
look left for a gravel road leading to
scenic overlooks at **Mica View Picnic
Area,** a pleasant place to stop. About
a mile farther, the quarter-mile

INFORMATION & ACTIVITIES

VISITOR & INFORMATION CENTERS
Red Hills Visitor Center (Saguaro West) on Kinney Road.
Rincon Mountain Visitor Center (Saguaro East) on Old Spanish Trail (park headquarters).

SEASONS & ACCESSIBILITY
Park open year-round.

HEADQUARTERS
3693 S. Old Spanish Trail, Tucson, AZ 85730. For information call (520) 733-5158 (Saguaro West) or (520) 733-5153 (Saguaro East). www.nps.gov/sagu

ENTRANCE FEE
$10 per vehicle.

PETS
Not permitted on trails, in backcountry, or in public buildings; elsewhere allowed on leashes.

ACCESSIBLE SERVICES
Visitor centers, nature trails, and roadside picnic areas wheelchair accessible.

THINGS TO DO
Ranger-led hikes and night walks, scenic drives, trail walks, bird- and wildlife-watching, picnicking, bicycling, backcountry hiking. Horseback riding is permitted on some trails.

SPECIAL ADVISORIES
• Avoid open and low-lying areas during thunderstorms, when lightning and flash floods pose a danger.
• Stay on trails. Abandoned mine shafts in Saguaro West make off-trail hiking and riding hazardous.
• Carry a flashlight at night to avoid encounters with rattlesnakes, scorpions, and Gila monsters.
• There is no water at picnic areas or along most trails. If hiking, carry at least one gallon of water per day.

OVERNIGHT BACKPACKING
Allowed only at designated backcountry sites. Use permits must be obtained at visitor centers in advance of trip.

CAMPGROUNDS
Six backcountry campsites in **Saguaro East,** accessible by foot, 6 miles from the nearest trailhead. $6 permit fee. Campground in **Tucson Mountain County Park,** next to Saguaro West.

HOTELS, MOTELS, & INNS
(unless otherwise noted, rates are for 2 persons in a double room, high season)

In Tucson, AZ:
Arizona Inn 2200 E. Elm St., 85719. (800) 933-1093 or (520) 325-1541. 95 units. $379-$419. AC, pool, restaurant.
Royal Sun Best Western 1015 N. Stone Ave., 85705. (800) 528-1234 or (520) 622-8871. 79 units. $79-$189. AC, pool, restaurant.
Hilton Tucson East 7600 E. Broadway, 85710. (800) 445-8667 or (520) 721-5600. 232 units. $159-$299. AC, pool, restaurant.

For more lodgings, contact the Tucson Metropolitan Chamber of Commerce, (520) 792-2250, www.tucsonchamber.org.

paved **Desert Ecology Trail** is designed to illustrate the crucial role of water in desert ecosystems. While highly informative, what you are more likely to remember from this 20-minute amble is the desert stillness.

Near the south end of the Cactus Forest loop road, consider walking part of the **Tanque Verde Ridge Trail,** which heads south and then east from the Javelina picnic area. In return for 3 miles or so of fairly vigorous uphill hiking, you'll experience cactus desert, the grassland above, and a bit of oak-juniper forest on the ridge. To the east is Rincon Peak, Tucson to the west. In the grassland zone, look for sotol, which was used by Native Americans to weave mats and other objects.

EXCURSIONS

SABINO CANYON
TUCSON, ARIZONA

Just minutes from Saguaro NP, in the eastern foothills of the Santa Catalina mountains, Sabino Canyon is a world away in terms of climate, vegetation, and wildlife. It beckons with towering cliffs, waterfalls, seasonal swimming holes, and a lush riparian zone. Free from vehicular congestion; a tram *(fee)* provides access to the upper canyon, picnic areas, and trails. Located on Sabino Canyon Rd. 15 miles northwest of Saguaro NP (East). (520) 749-2861 (tram information).

KARTCHNER CAVERNS STATE PARK
BENSON, ARIZONA

Discovered in 1974 but not opened to the public until 1999, Kartchner Caverns SP contains an extraordinary display of colorful speleotherms. Formations—some of the tiniest, most delicate growths, as well as the tallest column in Arizona—provide evidence of the role water plays in the creation of caves. Hiking, scenic drives, guided cave tours *(reservations reqd.)*, museum, amphitheater. 62 campsites, handicapped access. Visitor center off Ariz. 90, 45 miles southeast of Saguaro NP (East). (520) 586-2283.

ORGAN PIPE CACTUS NATIONAL MONUMENT
AJO, ARIZONA

Located on a road leading to the Mexican border, Organ Pipe NM was designated an international biosphere reserve by the United Nations in 1976. As a protected area, the Sonoran Desert, including its more than 20 species of cactuses, flourishes under nearly ideal wilderness conditions. Spring bloom is the most colorful time to visit. 330,689 acres. Hiking, scenic drives. 212 campsites. 150 miles southwest of Saguaro NP (West). (520) 387-6849.

SAGUARO

Court of the Patriarchs, sheer rock faces cut by gravity and water

▶ ZION

UTAH
ESTABLISHED NOVEMBER 19, 1919
148,733 acres

Rising in Utah's high plateau country, the Virgin River carves its way to the desert below through a gorge so deep and narrow that sunlight rarely penetrates to the bottom. As the canyon widens, the river runs a gantlet of great palisade walls rimmed with slickrock peaks and hanging valleys.

The scale is immense—sheer cliffs dropping 2,200 feet, massive buttresses, deep alcoves. Nineteenth-century Mormon pioneers saw these sculptured rocks as the "natural temples of God." They called the canyon Little Zion after the celestial city.

A million years of flowing water has cut through the red and white beds of Navajo sandstone that form the sheer walls of Zion. The geologic heart of the canyon began as a vast desert millions of years ago; almost incessant winds blew one dune on top of another until the

sands reached a depth of more than 2,000 feet. You can still see the track of these ancient winds in the graceful crossbedded strata of Zion's mighty cliffs.

Unlike the Grand Canyon where you stand on the rim and look out, Zion Canyon is usually viewed from the bottom looking up. The vertical topography confines most of Zion's 2.5 million yearly visitors between canyon walls.

Streamside on the canyon floor grow thick stands of Fremont cottonwood, box elder, willow, and, a short distance away, cactus and

Utah juniper. Vegetation changes rapidly as the terrain rises almost a mile in elevation. The high plateaus support Douglas fir and ponderosa pine.

Within the park's 232 square miles lies a landscape of remote terraces and narrow gorges. A number of these canyons are so hidden that early surveyors overlooked some that are 20 miles long. More than 100 miles of wilderness trails crisscross the backcountry, while 15 miles of paved trails encourage casual visits.

How to Get There

From Cedar City to the Kolob Canyons Entrance, take I-15 about 17 miles south. To Zion Canyon, take I-15 to Utah 17 then Utah 9 to the South Entrance (about 60 miles). From Kanab, take US 89 to Utah 9 (at Mt. Carmel Junction) to the East Entrance. From Las Vegas and St. George, take I-15 and Utah 9 to the South Entrance. Airports: Las Vegas, Nevada, and St. George, Utah.

When to Go

Open all year, but main season is March through October. Mild spring and fall temperatures are ideal for hiking. Summer rains can bring spectacular clouds and numerous waterfalls. Rock colors are heightened by contrast with winter snows, green summer foliage, deep blue fall skies.

How to Visit

On a 1-day visit, take the **Zion-Mt. Carmel Highway** and the **Zion Canyon Scenic Drive** (free shuttle *only* April through October) for the best overview of the park. For longer stays, begin with one of the classic walks in **Zion Canyon,** then take a road tour of the **Kolob Canyons** in late afternoon.

ZION-MT. CARMEL HIGHWAY & ZION CANYON

18 miles; a half to full day

The Zion-Mt. Carmel Highway (Utah 9) descends almost 2,000 feet from the high mesa country at the **East Entrance** to the **South Entrance** desert. Begin the drive on the east to see the park in the most dramatic possible way—from a tunnel on the wall of the canyon, 800 feet above the floor.

Shortly after passing through the East Entrance, stop at the **Checkerboard Mesa** pull-off. Here is a classic view of weathered sandstone beds crosshatched with vertical joints. Continue driving as the road winds along the normally dry creek bed. For the full impact of

Crossing the Virgin River on horseback

ZION

Virgin River Narrows

the approaching canyon, turn off at the **Canyon Overlook** parking area. If you are ready for a stop, this is a good place to stretch your legs along a 1-mile round-trip trail. You walk above the winding narrows of **Pine Creek** to an impressive view of **The West Temple** and the **Towers of the Virgin.**

The road disappears into the canyon wall at the narrow **Zion-Mt. Carmel Tunnel,** breaking into the blue sky again 1.1 miles farther. The tunnel was completed in 1930 at a cost of a half million dollars and the lives of two men. The road switchbacks down the side of **Pine Creek Canyon,** passing close to **The Great Arch,** which is 400 feet high. Geologists call it a blind arch because it is recessed into the cliff.

You next enter **Zion Canyon,** where Pine Creek meets the **North Fork Virgin River.** The canyon has an average width of half a mile, with walls 2,000 to 3,000 feet high. At Zion Canyon Visitor Center, catch a free shuttle for the 6.6-mile **Zion Canyon Scenic Drive** that follows the winding Virgin River. Get out at the **Court of the Patriarchs.** Here a short trail leads up the slope to a view of

ZION

Cottonwoods along canyon walls *(top left)*; the Subway *(top right)*; Virgin River Narrows *(center)*; milkvetch flowers *(bottom left)*; bighorn sheep *(bottom right)*

the **Three Patriarchs,** sheer faces carved by water and gravity from Navajo sandstone.

Back on the shuttle, the road continues past the **Emerald Pools** area. This is the trailhead for a popular stroll on a paved walkway to natural rock basins fed by small streams. The lowest pool on the climbing path is a tiny oasis tucked into the side of the cliff and sheltered by bigtooth maple trees.

After a sojourn at the pools, the shuttle continues past **Zion Lodge** to the Grotto picnic area, a good place to take a break. Here is the trailhead for **Angels Landing** and **West Rim Trail.**

A short distance farther, the shuttle reaches **Weeping Rock.** Here, the trailhead of a self-guided nature walk (half-mile round-trip) leads behind a curtain of water showering from the ceiling of an alcove. Water percolates through the sandstone until it hits shale and then seeps through to the surface of Weeping Rock—more than 1,000 years after falling as rain on the high plateau above. The strenuous **East Rim Trail** and a branch trail that climbs to **Hidden Canyon** start here.

Just past Weeping Rock, a stop offers superb views of **The Great White Throne** rising more than 2,300 feet above the river. The scenic drive ends where the canyon narrows at the **Temple of Sinawava,** named for the coyote-spirit of the Paiute Indians.

Here and elsewhere in the park, you should keep your eyes peeled for the tiny creatures that inhabit Sinawava—canyon tree frogs and plateau lizards. There are also more than 207 species of birds, including wild turkey, canyon wren, and the water-skimming American dipper.

KOLOB CANYONS ROAD

5.5 miles; 1 hour to a half day or more

One of the most spectacular and most accessible regions of the park is also one of the least visited. The **Hurricane Cliffs,** forming the western boundary of the plateau, screen the great towers of the Kolob from I-15. Follow the Kolob Canyons Road past the **Kolob Canyons Visitor Center** as it winds into **Taylor Creek Canyon.** Here you get a hint of what's to come when the jagged face of **Tucupit Point** appears.

Continue up the road, skirting the beautiful **South Fork** of **Taylor Creek.** Each vista becomes more striking than the last as you cross **Lee Pass,** the trailhead for routes into the hidden canyons of **La Verkin Creek.** If time and stamina allow, you can backpack (usually done as an overnight; permit required for overnight trips) the 14-mile round-trip to **Kolob Arch,** one of the world's largest freestanding natural arches, nearly 288 feet long.

Drive to the parking area at the end of the road for a dramatic view of the **Finger Canyons.** Sheer cliffs of pale red sandstone lift more than 2,000 feet into the blue sky. Narrow canyons work deep into the sides of **Timber Top Mountain,** connecting **Shuntavi Butte** with **Nagunt Mesa.**

OTHER HIKES

The full impact of Zion's great carved landscape is best experienced from a high vantage point above the river. The park's extensive trail system gives you a wide range of choices, from walks of half an hour to backpacking trips lasting for days.

The park's most popular trail is the **Riverside Walk,** an easy, 2-mile

ZION

round-trip amble. This paved path can be negotiated by strollers and assisted wheelchairs. Beginning where the Zion Canyon Scenic Drive ends at the Temple of Sinawava, the trail leads past hanging gardens of maidenhair fern and golden columbine and stands of shady cottonwood and ash. It ends where the North Fork rushes from a defile so narrow the only way to look is up. Flash floods here are a real danger; deeper in **The Narrows** the walls are 2,000 feet high but in places only 20–30 feet apart. In the 1960s, a sudden flood caught 26 hikers, drowning 5.

Perched midway between the river and the rim of the canyon, the high and open spire of rock called **Angels Landing** provides one of Zion's best overall views. The strenuous trail climbs 2.7 miles, at times cutting into a knife-edge ridge that joins the landing to the western wall. Sheer 1,200-foot drops surround the promontory on three sides and allow excellent cross-canyon views of the Great White Throne and down the deep cut of Zion Canyon. *Not recommended for those with a fear of heights.*

The **Observation Point Trail,** 8 miles round-trip, is not recommended for acrophobes either. One of the best routes to reach the very top of the canyon, the strenuous trail passes through a beautiful narrows and winds into the slickrock country. As it swings back to the main canyon, the trail cuts into the very edge of the cliff and opens to dramatic views. After a thunderstorm, clouds steaming up from the white sandstone of the western wall look as if the rock itself is evaporating.

Once on top, the route crosses a sandy mesa through stands of pinyon pine and juniper to **Observation Point,** with fine views of the main canyon. Stand here and listen to what Frederick Dellenbaugh called "the whisper of the wind that comes and goes, breathing with the sound of centuries."

Waterfalls in snow

INFORMATION & ACTIVITIES

VISITOR & INFORMATION CENTERS

Zion Canyon Visitor Center, near the South Entrance on Utah 9, and **Kolob Canyons Visitor Center,** in the park's northwest corner off I-15, are open daily.

SEASONS & ACCESSIBILITY

Park open year-round. Kolob Canyons Road and main roads in Zion Canyon are plowed in winter. Dirt roads are impassable when wet. Lava Point inaccessible in winter and early spring due to snow. Call headquarters for weather conditions. Shuttle service on Zion Canyon Scenic Drive. Pick up free shuttle in Springdale or at the Zion Canyon Visitor Center. Shuttle runs April through October.

HEADQUARTERS

State Rte. 9, Springdale, UT 84767. Phone (435) 772-3256. www.nps.gov/zion

ENTRANCE FEE

$25 per car per week. Also, $15 charge for escorting oversize vehicles through the mile-long tunnel on East Entrance road.

PETS

Not permitted in backcountry, on shuttles, in public buildings, or on most trails; elsewhere allowed on leashes.

ACCESSIBLE SERVICES

Visitor centers, museum, shuttles, some trails and restrooms are wheelchair accessible. Handicapped sites available in campgrounds.

THINGS TO DO

Free ranger-led activities: nature walks and talks, evening programs, children's programs. Zion Human History Museum. Also, hiking, horseback trail rides (inquire at Zion Lodge or call 435-679-8665) climbing, bicycling (bicyclists must transport their bikes through the long tunnel—check at entrance or visitor center), limited cross-country skiing.

SPECIAL ADVISORIES

• Summer temperatures in park can exceed 105°F. Always carry bottled or treated water when hiking—at least a gallon a day per person in summer.

OVERNIGHT BACKPACKING

Permits required, $10 (1-2 persons), $15 (3-7 persons), $20 (8-12 persons); available at visitor centers.

CAMPGROUNDS

Three campgrounds, 14-day limit. **Watchman** open all year; **South** open March–Nov.; **Lava Point** open May–Oct., depending on weather. Reservations for Watchman through the NRRS (see p. 10). Others, first come, first served. Fees $16 per night; $18 per night for sites with hookups at Watchman; $20 per night for river sites. Showers nearby but outside park. Tent and RV sites.

HOTELS, MOTELS, & INNS

(unless otherwise noted, rates are for 2 persons in a double room, high season)

INSIDE THE PARK:
Zion Lodge (off Utah 9) Xanterra Parks & Resorts, Springdale, UT 84767. (303) 297-2757. 122 rooms, with AC; 40 cabins. $163. Restaurant.
OUTSIDE THE PARK:
In Springdale, UT 84767:
Bumbleberry Inn 897 Zion Park Blvd. (800) 828-1534 or (435) 772-3224. 48 units. $98-$108. AC, pool, restaurant.
Canyon Ranch Motel 668 Zion Park Blvd. (435) 772-3357. 22 units, 4 with kitchenettes. $99-$139. AC, pool.
Cliffrose Lodge & Gardens 281 Zion Park Blvd. (800) 243-8824 or (435) 772-3234. 50 units. $159. AC, pool.
Driftwood Lodge 1515 Zion Park Blvd. (888) 801-8811 or (435) 772-3262. 43 units. $72-$169. AC, pool, restaurant.
Flanigan's Inn and Spa 428 Zion Park Blvd., P.O. Box 100. (800) 765-7787 or (435) 772-3244. 35 units. $129-$169. AC, restaurant.
Under the Eaves Inn 980 Zion Park Blvd. (435) 772-3457. 6 rooms. $95-$185. AC.
In Kanab, UT 84741:
Parry Lodge 89 E. Center St. (800) 748-4104 or (435) 644-2601. 89 units. $70. AC, pool, restaurant.
Shilo Inn 296 W. 100 North. (800) 222-2244 or (435) 644-2562. 115 units. $70-150. AC, pool.

For additional accommodations near Zion NP, contact Kane County Travel, 78 S. 100 East, Kanab, UT 84741. (800) 733-5263 or (435) 644-5033, www.kaneutah.com.

ZION

THE PACIFIC
SOUTHWEST

THE PACIFIC SOUTHWEST

Visitors to the national parks of the Pacific Southwest can bask on a tropical isle or climb a snow-clad peak. They can watch the vegetation change from tropical to subalpine in a single Hawai'i drive, observe plants and animals that make their home in only one place in the world, and see the Earth build itself.

The island parks, all of them on volcanoes except Channel Islands, are microcosms of evolution and laboratories of the effects of humans on the land. At Hawai'i Volcanoes and Haleakalā, preservation efforts seek to stem the damage done over centuries to the native plants, about 90 percent of which are endemic—found nowhere else. Some 2,600 miles southwest of Hawai'i, American Samoa National Park shelters fragments of tropical rain forest and coral reef as well as an endangered 3,000-year-old human culture. Off the coast of California, the Channel Islands safeguard numerous threatened seals, sea lions, and seabirds. They also harbor some 70 different species of endemic plants.

On the mainland, Sequoia & Kings Canyon and Yosemite National Parks provide haven for a multitude of plant and animal communities in what John Muir called "the range of light"—the Sierra Nevada. Chaparral and wild oats robe the foothills; cathedral-like groves of conifers embellish slopes; wildflowers overrun alpine meadows. Marmots and pikas scurry on the glacier-carved heights, some of which soar 12,000 feet.

To the south, Joshua Tree National Park preserves the unique high Mojave Desert habitat of the giant branching yucca, while the 120-mile-long, erosion-sculptured basin that is Death Valley National Park—the continent's hottest spot—shelters more than 900 plant varieties, as well as bobcats and desert bighorn sheep.

Yosemite and Sequoia & Kings Canyon lie about 4 hours apart by car. From Sequoia, 6 road hours will get you to Death Valley, with 3.5 more to Joshua Tree. A drive from there to the Channel Islands takes 3 hours, plus a 90-minute boat ride. To reach Hawai'i from California, count on at least a 5.5-hour flight, and to American Samoa, expect an 11-hour plane trip (see p. 233) plus a Honolulu layover.

Rugged ridges, Tutuila Island

▶AMERICAN SAMOA

AMERICAN SAMOA
ESTABLISHED OCTOBER 31,1988
13,500 acres—9,500 land,
4,000 marine

For some 3,000 years, the people of Polynesia's oldest culture have been keenly attuned to their island environment, holding it to be precious and managing it communally. The name they gave their land reflects their attitude: Samoa means "sacred earth."

Located roughly 2,600 miles southwest of Hawai'i, American Samoa, a United States territory, comprises five volcanic islands and two coral atolls. In 1988 Congress authorized the land for a national park. In 1993 Samoan chiefs agreed to sign a 50-year lease that enables the National Park Service to co-manage areas of rain forest, beach, and coral reef on three islands. Samoans help manage the park, and their villages offer a few guest facilities (ask the park about its unique homestay program).

The park protects hundreds of plant species in five distinct rain forest communities: lowland, montane, coast, ridge, and cloud. It is the only such rain forest on American soil. Among the fauna visitors can see are tropical birds and the flying fox—a fruit bat with the wingspan of a barn owl.

On **Tutuila,** American Samoa's largest island, lofty volcanic ridges overlook the deep blue waters of **Pago Pago Harbor.** Except for a few villages, and the scenic drive that skirts the harbor and the dramatic southern coastline, there is little level land. Atop this crumbled terrain and plunging steeply toward the sea on the island's northern side lies the park area—about 2,500 acres of land and some 1,200 acres of ocean.

Parkland on **Ta'u,** the eastern-most island, encompasses about 5,400 acres—including Lata Mountain, American Samoa's highest peak—and 1,000 acres offshore. Unforgettable is the panoramic view from the cloud forest toward the rugged cliffs of the southern coast. Small, remote **Ofu Island** includes what many call American Samoa's loveliest beach. Its main attraction is the 350-acre coral reef.

How to Get There

There are flights to Pago Pago from Honolulu twice a week that take 5.5 hours. Time from California is about 14 hours, including a 3- or 4-hour Honolulu layover. From the airport, taxi or rent a car to the Sadie's Hotel, Pago Airport Inn, Tessarea Vaitogi Inn, Tradewinds, or Motu-o-Fiafiaga Motel. From any of those accommodations you can reach the park visitor center in Pago Pago by bus or car, or by walking 25 minutes. There are also accommodations on Ta'u, Ofu, and Olosega. To get to Ta'u requires about a half-hour flight from Pago Pago. Travel to Ofu and Olosega is by boat only, for which you must hire a local fisherman. Ofu's park area begins at the edge of the airport; parkland on Ta'u is about a half-hour walk from the former airport.

When to Go

Any time. The islands are 14° south of the Equator, giving them a hot and rainy climate year-round. The heat and rain abate slightly from June through September.

How to Visit

Contact the park visitor center before you visit. For information, write National Park of American Samoa, Pago Pago, American Samoa 96799. Phone (684) 699-3982. www.nps .gov/npsa. Or drop in at the visitor center, located near the head of Pago Pago Harbor.

View of western Anacapa Island from Inspiration Point

▶CHANNEL ISLANDS

CALIFORNIA
ESTABLISHED MARCH 5, 1980
249,354 acres

Strung along a stretch of California coast are five separate pieces of land surrounded by 1,252 square nautical miles of sea. Channel Islands National Park and Channel Islands National Marine Sanctuary protect these islands, the sea around them, and a dazzling array of wildlife.

Two of the islands in this unusual park, Anacapa and Santa Barbara, were earlier designated a national monument, a refuge for nesting seabirds, seals, sea lions, and other long-threatened marine animals. When those islands and three others were joined in a national park, the mission of refuge continued.

Today the park manages a long-term ecological research program that may be the best in the park system. The marine sanctuary—established in 1980—extends for 6 nautical miles around each island. Among the resources it protects are giant kelp forests with nearly a thousand kinds of fish and marine plants. The park and sanctuary also guard the area from encroachment by another kind of island—the seagoing oil rigs of the Santa Barbara Channel.

About 70 different species of plants grow only on the islands, and some plants exist on but one of them. The islands shelter the only breeding colony of northern fur seals south of Alaska. To help native animals, park managers have gotten rid of such nonnative species as black rats, pigs, rabbits, and feral cats.

A permanent ranger resides on each island. Reservations are needed for camping. Fishing is strictly regulated. No private aircraft can land on the islands, and all airplanes must fly 1,000 feet above sea level.

Chumash Indians lived on the Channel Islands until the early 19th century. They traveled from island to island in plank canoes caulked with tar from oil seeps. The tar from such seeps still appears on beaches, reminding strollers of the reason for the oil rigs on the horizon.

How to Get There

Take US 101 to Ventura. Northbound, exit at Victoria Avenue; southbound, at Seaward Avenue. Follow park signs to the harbor and then to the visitor center on Spinnaker Drive. Get oriented here. Schedule your boat trip in advance as most boats depart early in the morning, then go to the nearby Island Packers office. Airports: Camarillo, Oxnard, Santa Barbara, and Los Angeles International.

When to Go

All-year park. Boat schedules peak in spring and summer, but you should be able to book a trip in any month. Best whale-watching time: late December through March, and July and August.

How to Visit

Your exploration of this unique park depends on your time and resources. Even a short stop at the mainland visitor center will give you an understanding and appreciation of the park. For a 1-day visit, see the closest islands, **Anacapa** or **Santa Cruz.** Take all necessities, especially food and water, and dress in layers for all types of weather. Trips to the other islands require substantial advance planning. (See Information & Activities p. 238.) The park cautions people from doing more than treading lightly on the islands, which are maintained for the well-being of the residents, both flora and fauna.

ANACAPA ISLAND
14 miles from Ventura; a full day

Before stepping aboard your Island Packers boat for the trip to Anacapa, take some time to explore the park's **visitor center** in Ventura. Among the attractions are an indoor marine life exhibit, a native plant garden, and Chumash artifacts. During the summer divers with cameras and microphones drop into the landing cove on East Anacapa Island to give people on the dock and in the center's auditorium a close-up of the underwater world.

Out on the water as your boat plies the **Santa Barbara Channel,** flyingfish skip through the waves and nearby pelicans skim over them. Oil rigs stand on dark stilts while gray whales may glide by during winter trips, and seals appear and disappear in the channel waters year-round.

Approaching the landing cove, the boat passes Anacapa's **Arch Rock** and sails close enough to the rocky coast for you to see resident California sea lions. At the end of the 60-minute voyage (which can be rough), you climb a ladder to the landing

CHANNEL ISLANDS

Western gulls on Anacapa Island

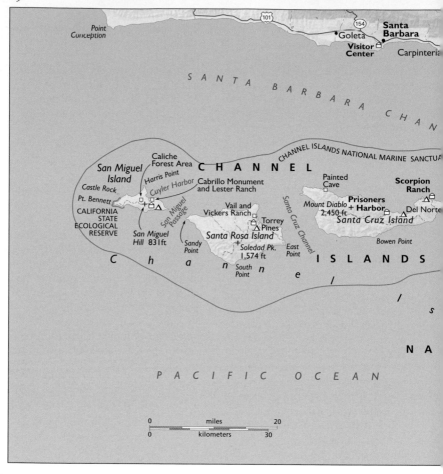

platform. Then you climb 154 steps up a metal-and-concrete stairway to the top of the cliff-girt island.

There you can walk the 1.5-mile nature trail on your own or behind a ranger who dispenses island lore: That plain brown plant (giant coreopsis) is a tree sunflower; in late winter and spring it bursts into glorious gold. The ground shells you walk on are remnants of a Chumash midden. The Indians hunted on the island and used it as a stopover on trips to the mainland. The trail skirts the edge of a cliff 150 feet above the sea. Stand well back from the unstable cliff edges. You are ominously warned: *Don't risk your life for a view.*

A building that looks like a Spanish mission church is not what it seems. The structure protects two large water tanks. According to local lore, vandals who once took potshots at the wooden tanks refrain from sniping at a "church." The few buildings date from days when the island lighthouse, now automated, had a crew. Your day ends with a descent to the boat, which picks up the passengers about 3 or 4 hours after arrival.

Anacapa consists of three islets. You visit only East Anacapa. Scuba divers, subject to strict conservation laws, plunge off Middle Anacapa to see the kelp forests or the remains of the S.S. *Winfield Scott,* which

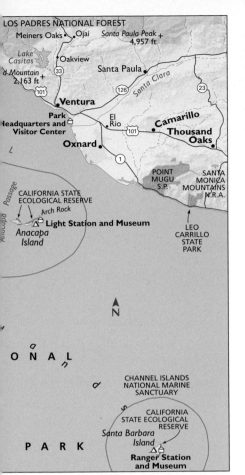

the island and private boat landings require a permit. The park owns the eastern end. Among its distinctive species are the island oak, the cat-size island fox, and the island scrub jay.

Santa Rosa (45 miles from Ventura; 53,000 acres) may have been inhabited by people as long as 13,000 years. Ranchers raised sheep then cattle on the island's grasslands from the middle of the 19th century until 1997. A freshwater marsh sustains waterfowl. There are more than 195 bird species on the island and 500 plant species.

San Miguel (55 miles from Ventura; 9,325 acres), the westernmost island, is home to five seal species. Over 30,000 haul out at a time on Point Bennett (16-mile round-trip hike). A bizarre caliche "forest" spikes a plateau. Caliche—a kind of limey sand—encrusted vegetation that died and decayed, leaving only the hollow, calcified sand castings.

Once used as a bombing range and missile test site, the island is owned by the United States Navy and administered by the National Park Service, which limits visitors to the beach, ranch, and campground unless accompanied by a park rangers.

Santa Barbara (52 miles from Ventura; 640 acres), once a sheep pasturage, has 5.5 miles of nature trails. In spring, crevices on the island's steep cliffs house the world's largest known breeding population of the remarkable Xantus's murrelet. When a chick is only 2 days old, it makes a bold foray into night, tumbling down to the sea where it joins its waiting parents. Except for the nesting season, the murrelet will spend the remainder of its life on the ocean. In spring and summer, you can usually see pelicans and sea lions, but don't expect to come across the rock-dwelling island night lizard. It is shy, secretive, and protected.

sank here in 1853 with no loss of life. Divers can take only photos. Consider a visit to the tide pools at **Frenchy's Cove.** The remainder of **West Anacapa** is closed to the public to protect the largest nesting brown pelican population on the U.S. Pacific coast.

THE OTHER ISLANDS

If you decide to go to the other islands, your visits will be controlled by weather, regulations, and boat and plane schedules.

Santa Cruz (21 miles from Ventura; 60,000 acres) is the largest of the Channel Islands. The Nature Conservancy runs the western portion of

INFORMATION & ACTIVITIES

VISITOR & INFORMATION CENTERS

Lagomarsino Visitor Center, 1901 Spinnaker Dr., Ventura; **Santa Barbara Visitor Center,** 113 Harbor Way, 4th Floor, (805) 884-1475; **East Anacapa Visitor Center.** Open all year.

HEADQUARTERS

1901 Spinnaker Dr., Ventura, CA 93001. Phone (805) 658-5730. www.nps.gov/chis

ACCESSIBILITY & BOAT INFORMATION

Park open all year. Access to islands subject to unpredictable weather conditions; the channel can be rough. Call headquarters for information.

To Anacapa, Santa Rosa, San Miguel, and Santa Barbara: Boat trips offered by Island Packers, the park's authorized concessioner (see below). Visitors using private boats must obey closed and restricted areas.

To Santa Cruz: Island Packers offers day trips to the eastern end. Landing permits for private boaters are required for Nature Conservancy property; call (805) 642-0345 ext. 510 or visit www.nature.org.

Boats from Ventura: Contact headquarters or Island Packers, 1691 Spinnaker Dr., Ste. 105B, Ventura, CA 93001. (805) 642-1393 for information and reservations or www.islandpackers.com. For weekend trips, reserve at least 3 to 5 days in advance.

Plane information: Channel Island Aviation (305 Durley Ave., Camarillo, CA 93010, 805-987-1301, www.flcia.com), the park concessioner, flies to Santa Rosa Island.

ENTRANCE FEE

None. For boat fares to islands, inquire at headquarters or Island Packers.

PETS

Not permitted in park headquarters or on islands.

ACCESSIBLE SERVICES

Visitor center at Ventura, restrooms, theater, exhibits, and observation tower accessible. Boats and islands are not.

THINGS TO DO

Santa Barbara Channel: Whale-watching late December through March and June through September.

Anacapa: Free naturalist-led walks; also, camping, bird-watching, wildlife-watching, tide pools, swimming and snorkeling, scuba and skin diving, fishing (license needed; certain areas closed).

Santa Barbara: Naturalist-led walks, camping, marine life observation, bird-watching, tide pools, camping.

Santa Rosa: Naturalist-led walks, camping, nature viewing, tide pools.

San Miguel: Free naturalist-led walk to caliche "forest"; camping, seal- and sea lion-watching, tide pools, camping.

Santa Cruz: New visitor center at Scorpion Valley, naturalist-led walks, camping, marine life observation, bird-watching.

SPECIAL ADVISORIES

• When hiking on islands, stay on trails and away from cliffs.
• All birds, animals, tide pools, shells, rocks, and plants are protected; do not take anything but photos.
• Avoid hantavirus, a potentially fatal virus carried by the deer mouse, by staying away from cabins and campsites where rodent droppings and burrows are evident.
• Fishing is prohibited.
• Sea kayaking from mainland to the islands (12 miles) is not for novices or for anyone not properly trained, conditioned, and equipped.

OVERNIGHT BACKPACKING

All five islands have campgrounds; 14-day limit. Reservations and permits required; contact the NRRS (see p. 10). $10 per night. Tent sites only. Drinking water at Scorpion on Santa Cruz and Bechers Bay on Santa Rosa. Group camping available. No food services.

HOTELS, MOTELS, & INNS

(unless otherwise noted, rates are for 2 persons in a double room, high season)

In Ventura, CA 93001:
Bella Maggiore Inn 67 S. California St. (800) 523-8479 or (805) 652-0277. 28 units. $75-$180. Restaurant.
Country Inn and Suites 298 S. Chestnut St. (800) 456-4000 or (805) 653-1434. 119 units. $169-$199. AC, pool.

Four Point Sheraton 1050 Schooner Dr. (800) 229-5732 or (805) 658-1212. 106 units. $129-$350. Pool, restaurant. **Inn on the Beach** 1175 S. Seaward Ave. (805) 652-2000. 24 units. $129-$195. **Pierpont Inn** 500 San Jon Rd. (800) 285-4667 or (805) 653-6144. 77 units. $159-$379. Spa, restaurant.

For additional lodgings, contact Ventura Visitor & Convention Bureau, (800) 463-6214 or (805) 648-2075, www.ventura-usa .com.

EXCURSIONS

SANTA MONICA MOUNTAINS NATIONAL RECREATION AREA
THOUSAND OAKS, CALIFORNIA

Here southern California's rare Mediterranean climate offers habitats ranging from chaparral to oak woodlands to rocky canyons to marshes and sandy beaches. Government and private efforts preserve the area's natural and cultural resources including Paramount Ranch (a working Hollywood set), spectacular Mulholland Drive, Zuma Beach, Cold Creek Canyon Preserve, and the Will Rogers State Historic Park. 154,095-acre boundary. Hiking, mountain biking, horseback riding. More than 300 campsites. Open all year, dawn to dusk (some parking areas 8 a.m. to sunset). Information at NRA headquarters in Thousand Oaks, about 30 miles west of Los Angeles. (805) 370-2301.

LOS PADRES NATIONAL FOREST
SANTA BARBARA, CALIFORNIA

This rugged forest preserves a vast area of central California coast and mountain ranges stretching over five counties. Chaparral and desert ecosystems are a short drive from Ventura. The Jacinto Reyes Scenic Byway (Calif. 33) threads through the forest north of Ojai. 1,700,000 acres. Camping, backpacking, hiking. Picnic areas. Open year-round. Information at Ojai Ranger Station, approximately 20 miles from Channel Islands NP. (805) 968-6640.

Early morning light falls on wind-rippled sand dunes near Zabriskie Point

▶DEATH VALLEY

CALIFORNIA & NEVADA
ESTABLISHED OCTOBER 31, 1994
About 3.4 million acres

The largest national park south of Alaska, Death Valley is known for extremes: It is North America's driest and hottest spot (with fewer than 2 inches of rainfall annually and a record high of 134°F), and has the lowest elevation on the continent—282 feet below sea level. Even with its extremes, the park still receives nearly a million visitors each year.

In 1849 emigrants bound for California's gold fields strayed into the 120-mile-long basin, enduring a two-month ordeal of "hunger and thirst and an awful silence." One of the last to leave looked down from a mountain at the narrow valley and said, "Good-bye, Death Valley."

The moniker belies the beauty in this vast graben, the geological term for a sunken fragment of the Earth's crust. Here are rocks sculptured by erosion, richly tinted mudstone hills and canyons, luminous sand dunes, lush oases, and a 200-square-mile salt pan surrounded by mountains, one of America's greatest vertical rises. In some years spring rains trigger wildflower blooms amid more than a thousand varieties of plants.

Native Americans, most recently the Timbisha Shoshone, found ways to adapt to the more recent and forbidding desert conditions that exist here now. Rock art and artifacts indicate a human presence dating back at least 9,000 years.

From 1883 to 1889, wagon teams hauled powdery white borax from mines since fallen to ruin, an enterprise that spread word of Death Valley's striking landscapes, deep solitude, and crystalline air.

As night falls, Death Valley's elusive populations of bobcats, kit foxes, and rodents venture out. Far above on steep mountain slopes, desert bighorn sheep forage among Joshua trees, scrubby junipers, and pines, while hawks soar on thermals rising into vivid blue, cloudless skies.

How to Get There

No public transit services serve the park. Most visitors arrive by automobile from Los Angeles or Las Vegas.

From Los Angeles, the most scenic route crosses the eastern Mojave Desert via I-15 through Barstow. At Baker it turns north onto Calif. 127 to Shoshone, where Calif. 178 runs west and north along the valley floor to Furnace Creek.

From Las Vegas, take Nev. 160 west 42 miles to Old Spanish Trail (Tecopa Rd.), continuing through Tecopa to Calif. 127, turning north to Shoshone and picking up Calif. 178 to Furnace Creek. You can also take Nev. 160 to Pahrump, turn west on Bell Vista Rd. to Death Valley Junction at Calif. 127, and turn left onto Calif. 190 to Furnace Creek. To include a visit to the early 20th-century Nevada gold-mining ghost town of Rhyolite, take US 95 to Beatty, picking up Nev. 374, which leads to Calif. 190.

When to Go

All-year park. Temperatures from November through February average between 43°F and 70°F in the main part of the park. From May through September, average highs range between 100°F and 116°F; overnight lows may top 100°F.

How to Visit

Death Valley's remote location and size make an automobile essential. An overnight stay allows time for the valley's vivid sunrises and sunsets, and a visit to the **Death Valley Museum** and **Furnace Creek Visitor Center.** Plan also to visit the **Harmony Borax Works** near the Furnace Creek Campground, to walk the 1-mile **Golden Canyon Interpretive Trail,** and to drive to **Zabriskie Point** for fine views of the valley.

A second day permits exploration of the valley's northern reaches and **Scottys Castle,** the retreat of an early 20th-century millionaire, and nearby **Ubehebe Crater,** blasted out during the region's volcanic past. If you are a seasoned hiker, consider the strenuous all-day hike from **Wildrose Canyon** to sweeping views atop 11,049-foot **Telescope Peak,** Death Valley's highest point.

ENTERING FROM THE EAST: SHOSHONE TO FURNACE CREEK

130 miles (including side trips);
1 to 2 days

From the mining town of Shoshone, head west on Calif. 178 through the **Amargosa Range,** whose colorful dusky palette reflects the high mineral content in its sediments. Crest 3,315-foot **Salsberry Pass,** and descend through the weathered **Black Mountains** to 1,290-foot **Jubilee Pass,** where wildflowers sometimes bloom in spring.

Approaching the ruins of gold-mining **Ashford Mill** and the **Death Valley Salt Pan**—the residue of a saline lake that existed over 10,000 years ago—you reach zero elevation. From here to Furnace Creek you travel *below* sea level, dipping to minus

DEATH VALLEY

242

282 feet at **Badwater Basin** 27 miles north, North America's lowest point. Park at Badwater, where sunrises ignite the ridgelines. Continue north 4 miles to the turnoff onto a rough road to **Natural Bridge,** an arch spanning a richly tinted conglomerate canyon. A quarter-mile trail to the bridge passes other striking formations.

About 1.5 miles north, look left for the half-mile spur road to **Devils Golf Course,** a meringue of rock salt pinnacles that forms as water evaporates up through the salty crust.

Another 5 miles north is the 9-mile one-way **Artists Drive** loop road through the **Artists Palette,** a rumpled terrain of volcanic ash whose yellows, reds, greens, and muted purples challenge plein-air painters. About 4 miles north, the moderate 1-mile-long **Golden Canyon Interpretive Trail** winds through a canyon that gleams as if dusted with gold at sunset.

Continue north to the Calif. 190 junction. If you want to rest or refuel, turn left to the **Furnace Creek Visitor Center.** If not, turn right onto Calif. 190 for the short drive to **Zabriskie Point,** a popular sunrise and sunset viewing spot, where rain and wind have shaped rock into dramatic contours. The promontory commands a broad view of mudstone badlands. To explore them, continue on for a mile to **Twenty Mule Team Canyon,** which is threaded by a 3-mile gravel loop road.

Return to the highway, turn right, and continue on the 13-mile spur road to 5,475-foot **Dantes View.** The mile-high panorama plunges to Badwater and sweeps across the salt pan to the forbidding **Panamint Range** and 11,049-foot **Telescope Peak.**

If you have not yet visited Furnace Creek, backtrack 24 miles to the **Furnace Creek Visitor Center.** Check for ranger-guided walks and evening programs (Oct.–March) and visit the **Death Valley Museum.**

Sand dunes near Stovepipe Wells

The springs at **Furnace Creek oasis** produce over a million gallons a day, watering exotic oleanders, palms, and tamarisk trees, and the incongruously verdant fairways of the golf course at the **Furnace Creek Ranch** *(private)*. Guests at the Furnace Creek Inn may explore the interior and gardens of this classic Spanish mission-style structure, constructed in 1927 of adobe and native stone.

FURNACE CREEK TO SCOTTYS CASTLE

90 miles (including excursions); a half day

One mile north of the Furnace Creek Visitor Center, leave your car and walk the quarter-mile paved **Harmony Borax Works Interpretive Trail** to the ruins of Death Valley's first successful borax mining venture. Original equipment includes a borax wagon with 6-foot-high rear wheels.

Continue north on Calif. 190 past the Beatty Cutoff to the 1-mile spur road to the **Salt Creek Interpretive Trail.** Spring-fed marshy pools here are home to Death Valley's unusual desert pupfish, descendant of creatures that flourished in the basin's ancient

lake at least 12,000 years ago. Like the oasis at Scottys Castle, this is a prime bird-watching area, frequented by many of the 350 species found in Death Valley, including peregrine falcons, hawks, and eagles.

As you continue along Calif. 190, the **Mesquite Flat** sand dunes ripple across 14 square miles. At sunrise and sunset the wind-sculptured waves of quartz-grain sand take on a rosy glow. Accessible via paved road before you arrive at Stovepipe Wells Village, these dunes have no established trails. There is a parking area from which you can begin your excursion.

Back in the car, backtrack to Scottys Castle Road, and continue about 30 miles to **Grapevine Canyon** and **Scottys Castle,** a Mediterranean-style architectural gem dating from 1922. Once the retreat of a Chicago couple, the ranch is named for frequent house guest Walter Scott. Daily on the hour, the Park Service conducts tours through the mansion, which holds original furnishings. (Reservations at www.recreation .gov; 877-444-6777.) Walk-ins are welcome, but in spring, be prepared to wait up to 2 hours for a tour. While waiting, consider a picnic outside, or an amble up **Windy Point Trail.**

INFORMATION & ACTIVITIES

VISITOR & INFORMATION CENTERS

Furnace Creek Visitor Center in Furnace Creek, off Calif. 190; **Scottys Castle Visitor Center and Museum,** off Nev. 267 on north end of the park; **Beatty Information Center,** US 95, Beatty, Nevada

SEASONS & ACCESSIBILITY

Open year-round.

HEADQUARTERS

Visitor Center, Calif. 190, P.O. Box 579, Death Valley, CA 92328. Phone (760) 786-3200. www.nps.gov/deva

ENTRANCE FEE

$20 per vehicle, good for one week.

PETS

Must be leashed at all times. Not allowed on trails or in backcountry.

ACCESSIBLE SERVICES

The Furnace Creek Visitor Center; Scottys Castle; and Furnace Creek, Texas Spring, and Sunset campgrounds are wheelchair accessible.

THINGS TO DO

Free ranger- and naturalist-led activities available mid-October to mid-April: nature walks and talks, evening programs, children's programs. Also, hiking, nature trails, living history tours, bicycling, bird-watching, horseback riding.

SPECIAL ADVISORIES

• Death Valley's heat can make any emergency situation life-threatening. For advice on hot weather travel, consult the *Death Valley Guide,* available at roadside kiosks, ranger stations, and the visitor center.
• Drink plenty of water; one gallon per person per day is recommended, two gallons if hiking. Emergency radiator water is available from barrels located along main park roads.
• Abandoned mineshafts and prospect holes pose dangers. Never enter an abandoned tunnel.
• Hat and sunglasses are essential.

• Desert rains, though brief, may cause flash floods. Never ford washouts, even in a 4-wheel-drive vehicle.

OVERNIGHT BACKPACKING

Backcountry camping permitted in areas at least 2 miles from main roads and a quarter mile from water sources. Free voluntary permits; hikers should register at visitor center and inquire about which areas prohibit camping.

CAMPGROUNDS

Nine campgrounds, 30-day limit. **Furnace Creek, Mesquite Spring, Emigrant, Wildrose** open all year; **Texas Spring** and **Sunset** open Oct. to April; **Thorndike, Stovepipe Wells,** and **Mahogany Flat** open March through Oct., depending on snow conditions. Reservations taken only for Furnace Creek (call NRRS; see p. 10); all others first come, first served. Fees: $12-$14 at Furnace Creek; $12 at Sunset, Stovepipe Wells, and Mesquite Spring; $14 at Texas Spring; free at Thorndike, Emigrant, Mahogany Flat, and Wildrose.

HOTELS, MOTELS, & INNS
(unless otherwise noted, rates are for 2 persons in a double room, high season)

INSIDE THE PARK:
Inn at Furnace Creek off Calif. 190. (800) 236-7916 or (720) 842-5271. 66 units. $335-$460. Open mid-Oct.–mid-May. Pool, restaurant.
Ranch at Furnace Creek off Calif. 190. P.O. Box 1, Death Valley 92328. (760) 786-2345. 224 units. $130-$213. Pool, restaurant.
Stovepipe Wells Village Motel Stovepipe Wells Village, P.O. Box 158, Death Valley 92328. (760) 786-2387. 83 units, $80-$155; 14 RV hookups, $31. AC, pool, restaurant.
Panamint Springs Resort Motel P.O. Box 395, Ridgecrest, CA 93536. (775) 482-7680. 14 units. $79-$149. Camping, RV sites, restaurant.

For additional lodgings, contact the Death Valley Chamber of Commerce, P.O. Box 15, Tecopa, CA 92384, (760) 852-4524, www .deathvalleychamber.com; or the Beatty Chamber of Commerce, 119 E. Main St., Beatty, NV 89003. (866) 736-3716 or (775) 553-2424, www.beattynevada.org.

DEATH VALLEY

Volcanic cinder slope

▶ HALEAKALĀ

HAWAI'I
ESTABLISHED AUGUST 1, 1916
34,294 acres

Haleakalā, a giant shield volcano, forms the eastern bulwark of the island of Maui. According to legend, it was here, in the awe-inspiring basin at the mountain's summit, that the demigod Maui snared the sun, releasing it only after it promised to move more slowly across the sky. Haleakalā means "house of the sun"; the park encompasses the basin and portions of the volcano's flanks.

A United Nations international biosphere reserve, the park comprises starkly contrasting worlds of mountain and coast. The road to the summit of Haleakalā rises from near sea level to 10,023 feet in 38 miles—possibly the steepest such gradient for autos in the world. Visitors ascend through several climate and vegetation zones, from humid subtropical lowlands to subalpine desert. Striking plants and animals such as the Haleakalā silversword and the nēnē may be seen in this mountain section.

The summit-area depression, misnamed Haleakalā Crater, formed as erosion ate away the mountain, joining two valleys. This 19-square-mile wilderness area, 2,720 feet deep, is the park's major draw.

From east of the crater's rim, the great rain forest valley of Kīpahulu drops thousands of feet down to the coast. The upper Kīpahulu Valley is a biological reserve *(no public access)*, home to a vast profusion of flora and fauna, including some of the world's rarest birds, plants, and invertebrates.

Some insects and plants evolved in the Kīpahulu Valley and live nowhere else.

Visitors reach the lower valley of Kīpahulu via the spectacular Hāna Highway with its 600-plus curves. Dominated by intense hues—azure sea, black rock, silver waterfalls, green forest and meadow—the coastal area was first farmed in early Polynesian times, more than 1,200 years ago. Mark Twain, who traveled to Hawai'i in 1866, may well have had this part of Kīpahulu in mind when he wrote: "For me its balmy airs are always blowing, its summer seas flashing in the sun; the pulsing of its surfbeat is in my ear; I can see its garlanded crags, its leaping cascades, its plumy palms drowsing by the shore."

How to Get There

Fly directly from the mainland, or from another Hawaiian island, to Kahului in central Maui. To reach the summit of Haleakalā, follow, sequentially, Hawaii 36, 37, 377, and 378. The 38-mile route is well marked, but note the last chance to buy food and gas is at Pukalani or Makawao. Continue on the switchback road through miles of lush mountain rangeland to the park's northwest entrance. Allow up to 2 hours.

For the 62-mile drive to Kīpahulu, allow up to 3.5 hours. Take Hawaii 36 from Kahului around the northeastern side of the island to the town of Hāna. The road to Hāna, which becomes Hawaii 360, is famous for its narrow, tortuous course along 1,000-foot sea cliffs, into deep gorges. This drive affords many views of waterfalls and cascade pools, but few places to access them. Proceed past Hāna on Hawaii 31 for about 12 miles. Follow signs to the park entrance and parking lot.

When to Go

All-year park. Most rain comes in winter, although temperatures remain fairly constant month to month. To avoid crowds, visit the summit after 3 p.m.; sunsets can be as spectacular as the famous sunrises. At Kīpahulu, avoid crowds by arriving early or camping overnight. Weather varies most at high elevations, and can change from very hot to rainy, cold, and windy in the same day. Temperatures can drop to freezing inside the wilderness area, although snow is rare. Coastal Kīpahulu stays warm but receives considerable rain all year.

How to Visit

It would be neither safe nor very enjoyable to try fitting both the **Haleakalā** summit and **Kīpahulu** coastal regions of the park into 1 day as the Hana Highway drive takes more than 6 hours alone both ways. To absorb more of the ambience of this unique sea-girt volcano, try to spend a day on the mountain, with a hike through the moonscape of the "crater," and a second day on the coast. Van and bus tours—some starting in predawn hours take in the magical summit sunrise—can be arranged from most island hotels—or visit at sunset and wait for the stars to appear. From May to September star programs are offered at Hosmer Grove.

Consider taking a guided walk from **Hosmer Grove** into the Nature Conservancy's **Waikamoi Preserve,** home of living treasures including various species of honeycreepers, the premier family of native Hawaiian birds. Reservations required; call ahead for the schedule (see Information & Activities p. 252).

Air tours that fly around Maui are available from Kahului, but regulations limit them to high altitude.

HALEAKALĀ

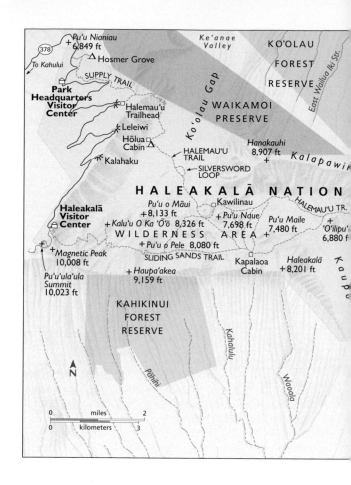

HOSMER GROVE TO HALEAKALĀ SUMMIT

11 miles; at least a half day

A short distance above the park entrance lies **Hosmer Grove,** a cool, shady spot to picnic and camp. You may recognize some of the trees, which include various pines and eucalyptus. About 1910, forester Ralph Hosmer planted trees from all over the world to test their potential for watershed protection and timber here. A half-mile loop trail will refresh you after your drive. Back on the road, you reach **Park**

Headquarters Visitor Center about a mile above the Hosmer turnoff. At this 7,000-foot elevation, you will see vegetation native to Hawai'i. In front of headquarters, plantings of Haleakalā geranium and silversword offer photo opportunities and biology lessons in adaptation and evolution. These two plants are endemic—found only on Haleakalā volcano.

After leaving headquarters, drive up the mountain through subalpine heath of soft earthy hues. In spring, māmane, a dominant shrub, brightens these slopes with sprays of yellow blossoms. You will find

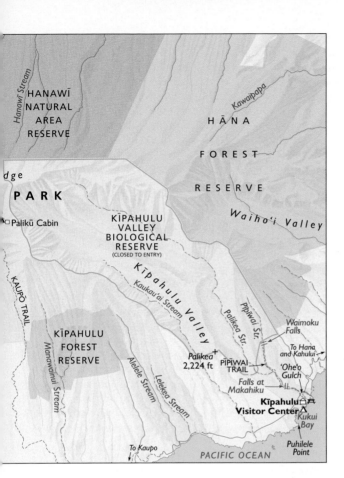

both native and invasive species in the area. With some luck you may see some of the famous honeycreepers—brightly feathered birds that may be descendants of the first land birds to reach Hawai'i. From their original ancestors, the honeycreepers have evolved at least 47 species, some of which are adapted to only one island, and some which have spread more widely. More than half of these species have become extinct. Driven from the lowlands by habitat change and disease, others, such as the critically endangered Nukupuu, are making their last stand high on the mountain.

Summit hikers often start at the **Halemau'u Trailhead**, 3.5 miles above the headquarters visitor center. This trail takes you through rolling country to the rim, then switchbacks as it steeply drops 1,000 feet down the spectacular northwest wall of the wilderness area to **Hōlua Cabin** and the campground (3.7 miles from the trailhead). The wall is broken here by **Ko'olau Gap,** a wide, wet canyon that descends to the sea. In this corner, vegetation thrives on moisture carried by waves of clouds that slowly ebb and flow in the gap, and you will find the leathery amau fern and other unusual plants.

Drive approximately 6 more miles to the **Haleakalā Visitor Center.** An exhibit shelter crowns the highest point—**Puʻu ʻUlaʻula,** or "red hill." At 10,023 feet, Puʻu ʻUlaʻula offers the ultimate view: Often you can see the giant volcanoes of the Big Island, as well as Maui's neighboring islands of **Lānaʻi** and **Molokaʻi** and sometimes, at night, far to the northwest, the lights of **Oʻahu.** Nearby, but outside the park, are the Haleakalā Observatories, a cluster of buildings that are closed to the public.

The best way to experience the wilderness area is on a multiday hike, spending the night at one of the three cabins or two campgrounds inside the crater. (Reserve well in advance for cabins—see Information & Activities p. 252.) One popular overnight trip involves hiking the **Sliding Sands Trail** to **Kapalaoa Cabin** (5.8 miles from the visitor center). This strenuous 7- to 10-hour hike loses and gains 3,000 feet on its descent and ascent through loose cinder. Many choose to exit via **Halemauʻu Trail,** an easier 8-mile hike from the cabin back to the road. You'll need to arrange a ride between the two trailheads.

KĪPAHULU: POOLS OF ʻOHEʻO

a full day

The Kīpahula Valley is located 12 miles beyond the town of Hana near the end of the famous Hana Highway. In this strip of parkland along the gorge of **Pīpīwai Stream,** visitors hike through lush rain forest and past breathtaking ocean overlooks *(Note: There is no safe approach to the ocean from this point).* Perhaps the area's greatest draw, however, is the cultural past of Hawaiʻi. Archaeological evidence shows that large numbers of Hawaiians once lived in Kīpahulu, from precontact inhabitants (before 1778) to those who worked as cattle ranchers at the turn of the 20th century and in the sugarcane industry from 1880 to 1925. Trails reveal traces of the past: stone-walled gardens, evidence of taro and sweet potato patches, and temple and shelter sites. Please respect this legacy by staying on the trails and reporting to park rangers anyone seen damaging cultural resources.

Camping is permitted on the oceanfront meadows south of the stream at the **Kīpahulu Campground.** Bring your own drinking water, or boil stream water or treat it with halozone. No permit is required, but there is a 3-night limit per 30 days.

If you have 2 or 3 hours (4 miles round-trip), take the **Pīpīwai Trail,** one of the most memorable short hikes in the islands. This walk is easy for anyone in good health, but it is usually slippery with mud in spots; wear sturdy footgear. Don't hike if the river is swollen.

Begin about 200 yards south of the ʻOheʻo bridge, near the Kīpahulu Visitor Center. Walk up through gently sloping pasture about half a mile to overlook the **Falls at Makahiku,** 184 feet high. After another half mile, the trail enters the woods and crosses two bridges near a lovely double falls. Continue about a mile more through lush forest, including a stand of dense, 50-foot-high invasive bamboo, which on a breezy day clacks and creaks with a mysterious percussive music. Aromatic ginger and ti form the understory. Your destination looms above the forest as you get close: **Waimoku Falls,**

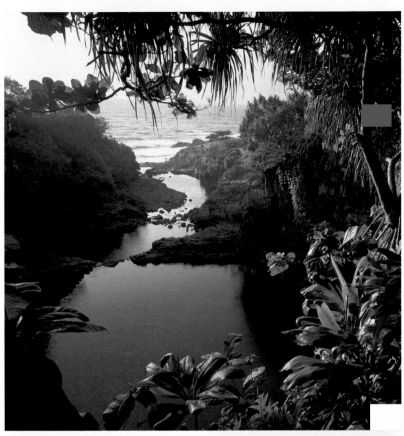

'Ohe'o Gulch

HALEAKALĀ

more than 400 feet high, fills its jungle clearing with cool mists. During much of the year, non-native mango, guava, and mountain apple provide refreshment.

Swimming is a pleasant pastime in this part of the park. Those who fancy a dip congregate around the big, cool pools and waterfalls below the Hawaii 31 highway bridge in **'Ohe'o Gulch,** but less crowded spots await upstream. Some pools are deep, but beware of slippery or hidden rocks. *Jumping from the rocks is not permitted!* Always check conditions at the visitor center as flash floods are dangerous and possible. There is no ocean access.

Silversword in bloom *(center)*
Iiwi, a tiny, rare honeycreeper *(bottom)*

INFORMATION & ACTIVITIES

VISITOR & INFORMATION CENTERS

Park Headquarters Visitor Center, 1 mile from summit area park entrance, (808) 572-4400. **Haleakalā Visitor Center,** near the summit, 11 miles from the park entrance, open daily all year. **Kīpahulu Visitor Center,** off Hana Highway, (808) 248-7375.

SEASONS & ACCESSIBILITY

All-year park. Call (866) 944-5025 for weather information from the National Weather Service.

HEADQUARTERS

P.O. Box 369, Makawao, Maui, HI 96768. Phone (808) 572-4400. www.nps.gov/hale

ENTRANCE FEE

$10 per car for a 3-day period; $25 for an annual pass (valid for all national parks in Hawaii).

PETS

Permitted on leashes in drive-in campgrounds only; not allowed on hiking trails.

ACCESSIBLE SERVICES

All visitor centers, park headquarters, and some campsites are wheelchair accessible. A free brochure about visiting Maui is available from Disability and Communication Access Board, 919 Ala Moana Blvd., Rm. 101, Honolulu, HI 96814. (808) 586-8121. www.hawaii.gov/health/dcab.

THINGS TO DO

Free naturalist-led activities: nature walks and hikes, interpretive talks, cultural demonstrations. Also available, hiking, horseback riding, swimming in pools of ʻOheʻo.

SPECIAL ADVISORIES

• Wilderness area hikes are at high altitudes, with lower oxygen levels; take it easy. Be prepared for unpredictable weather that can change quickly from heat to cold and rain.

• Water pools in ʻOheʻo Gulch often have strong currents and submerged rocks, and they are subject to flash flooding.

OVERNIGHT BACKPACKING

Tent camping allowed only at **Hōlua** and **Palikū** campsites; free permit required; issued first-come, first-served at park headquarters on the day of the hike; 2-night limit at each campground; limit of 3 nights total per 30 days. Three small, primitive cabins at **Hōlua, Kapalaoa,** and **Palikū** contain 12 bunks, minimum equipment; can be reached by trail only. Reservations made online at www.fhnp.org on a first-come, first-served basis (must be made within 90 days of visit); limited to 3 nights per 30 days (2 consecutive nights in one cabin); $75 per night; limit of 12 people. Call (808) 572-4400 for recorded information on cabins and campgrounds.

CAMPGROUNDS

Two drive-in campgrounds, both with 3-day limit. **Hosmer Grove** and **Kīpahulu** *(no water)* open all year, first-come, first-served. No fees. No showers. Tent sites; no hookups.

HOTELS, MOTELS, & INNS

(unless otherwise noted, rates are for 2 persons in a double room, high season)

In Hāna, HI 96713:
Aloha Cottages 83 Keawa Pl., P.O. Box 205. (808) 248-8420. 5 small cottages, 4 with kitchens, 1 with kitchenette, in residential areas of Hāna. $75-$100.
Hāna Kai Maui Resort Condominiums 4865 Uakea Rd., P.O. Box 38. (800) 346-2772 or (808) 248-7506. 18 units, kitchens. $195-$425.
Hotel Hāna Maui P.O. Box 9. (800) 321-4262 or (808) 248-8211. 71 units. $395. Restaurant.

In Kahului, HI 96732:
Maui Beach Hotel 170 Kaahumanu Ave. (888) 649-3222 or (808) 877-0051. 147 units. $110-$275. AC, pool, restaurant.
Maui Seaside Hotel 100 W. Kaahumanu Ave. (800) 367-7000 or (808) 877-3311. 186 units, 10 with kitchenettes. $145. AC, pool, restaurant.

In Kula, HI 96790:
Kula Lodge Rte. 377, 15200 Haleakalā Hwy. (800) 233-1535 or (808) 878-1535. 5 units. $125-$205. Restaurant.

For additional information, contact the Maui Visitors Bureau, 2270 Kalakaua Ave., Suite 801, Honolulu HI, 96815. (800) 464-2924, www.gohawaii.com/maui.

EXCURSIONS

WAIANAPANAPA STATE PARK
HĀNA, MAUI, HAWAI'I

Low volcanic cliffs and native hala (pandanus) forest line the coast in this remote, rugged park. Here, visitors can fish in the surf, explore a cave, observe an immense seabird colony, and hike the ancient coastal trail leading to Hāna. 122 acres. Hiking, fishing, swimming. Campground *(permits reqd.)*, 12 cabins, picnic areas. Open year-round. Off Hawaii 360 (Hāna Highway) about 80 miles from Haleakalā NP. (808) 587-0300.

IAO VALLEY STATE MONUMENT
WAILUKU, MAUI, HAWAI'I

Velvety moss-covered cliffs surround the verdant Iao Valley and its centerpiece, the Iao Needle, a 1,200-foot basalt spire sacred to the people of Maui. Swirling waters fashioned the spire from a natural altar in an ancient volcanic caldera. 6 acres. Observation pavilion, botanic gardens. Open year-round. End of Iao Valley Road, off Hawaii 32, about 40 miles from Haleakalā NP. (808) 587-0300.

HALEAKALĀ

Steam rising from volcano vent

▶ HAWAI'I VOLCANOES

HAWAI'I
ESTABLISHED AUGUST 1, 1916
333,000 acres

Hawai'i Volcanoes National Park, on the Big Island of Hawai'i, offers the visitor a look at two of the world's most active volcanoes: Kīlauea and Mauna Loa.

More than 4,000 feet high and still growing, Kīlauea abuts the southeastern slope of the older and much larger Mauna Loa, or "long mountain." Mauna Loa towers some 13,677 feet above the sea: Measured from its base 18,000 feet below sea level, it exceeds Mount Everest in height and mass. Mauna Loa's gently sloping bulk—some 19,000 cubic miles in volume—makes it the planet's most massive single mountain.

The park stretches from sea level to Mauna Loa's summit. Beyond the end of Mauna Loa Road lies Mauna Loa's wilderness area, where backpackers encounter freezing nights and rough lava trails amid volcanic wonders: barren lava twisted into bizarre shapes, cinder cones, gaping pits. Kīlauea, however, provides easy access to a greater variety of scenery and cultural sites.

On the slopes of Kīlauea, whose name means "spewing, much spreading," green rain forest borders recent lava flows. This landscape displays all stages of forest regeneration—from early regrowth of lichens and ferns to dense forest. The rain forest on the windward side of Kīlauea's summit gives way to the stark, windswept

Ka'ū Desert on the hot, dry south-western slope. At the shore, waves shape jagged cliffs; periodic eruptions send fresh lava flows to the sea.

Geological dynamism forms the park's primary natural theme, followed closely by evolutionary biology. Thousands of unique species have evolved on the isolated Hawaiian Islands. Cultural sites abound as well, reminders of the Polynesian pioneers who steered their great double-hulled canoes to Hawai'i beginning some 1,600 years ago, leading to the Hawaiian culture that defines the identity of these islands today.

The United Nations has named the park an international biosphere reserve and a World Heritage site. Many of the park's native plants and animals are in peril, threatened by non-native species like weedy invasive plants and feral pigs. The native species are carefully protected by the park, which has fenced the park's borders off from feral pigs and taken efforts to eradicate invasive weeds.

How to Get There

Fly to the island of Hawai'i, nick-named the Big Island. Airlines serve the Hilo and Kona airports from the mainland and from other Hawaiian Islands. From Hilo, Hawaii 11 rises 4,000 feet in 30 miles on your way past small towns, macadamia orchards, and rain forest to reach the park at Kīlauea's summit. From Kona, go south around the island on Hawaii 19 (which becomes Hawaii 11 in Kailua-Kona) past Kealakekua Bay, where Captain Cook met his death, and Ka Lae, or South Point, south-ernmost land in the 50 states. You'll reach the Kīlauea summit after a sce-nic 95-mile drive on a good road.

When to Go

Year-round. The weather is often driest in September and October.

The climate ranges from warm and breezy on the coast to cool and fre-quently wet at the summit of Kīlauea to nightly freezing with occasional snowstorms above about 10,000 feet on Mauna Loa. To avoid most tour bus crowds, plan to visit the major sights before 11 a.m. or after 3 p.m.

How to Visit

An intensive 1-day visit can cover highlights of the Kīlauea summit via **Crater Rim Drive** and the coastal region via **Chain of Craters Road.** Regular tours by bus and small van oper-ate daily from many Hilo and Kona hotels. Those with a botanical or ornithological bent will enjoy explor-ing **Mauna Loa Road** (accessible from Hawaii 11), which takes you through upland forest to the **Mauna Loa trail-head** at 6,662 feet: At **Kīpukapuaulu,** be sure to take the 1-mile loop trail winding through 100-acre kīpuka (an island of vegetation surrounded by a more recent lava flow) containing one of the richest concentrations of native plants and birdlife in Hawai'i.

Kīlauea eruption and lava flow

HAWAI'I VOLCANOES

Mauna Loa Weather Observatory
OBSERVATORY TRAIL
11,150 ft

MAUNA LOA FOREST RESERVE

Northeast Rift Zone

MAUNA LOA TRAIL

Pu'u 'Ula'ula (Red Hill) Cabin
10,035 ft

Steaming Cone 11,787 ft
Pōhaku Hanalei 12,423 ft

Mauna Loa Lookout 6,662 ft

North Pit
SUMMIT TRAIL
CABIN TRAIL
Moku'āweoweo Caldera

WILDERNESS AREA

Mauna Loa 13,679 ft
Mauna Loa Cabin

South Pit

'ĀINAPŌ TRAIL

Southwest Rift Zone

KAPĀPALA FOREST RESERVE

Area closed due to 2008 eruption

Ka'ōiki Pali

Ka'ū Desert Trailhead 3,040 ft

Mauna Iki 3,032 ft

KAU DESERT TRAIL

KA'Ū FOREST RESERVE

MAUNA ROAD

11

Southwest Rift Zone

Pepeiao Cabin

KA'AHA TRAIL

WILDERNESS AREA

Great Crack

Mauna Loa Observatory
Captain Cook
Mauna Loa 13,679 ft
Mountain View
11
Volcano
Hōnaunau
Kīlauea Caldera

HAWAI'I VOLCANOES NATIONAL PARK

Mīloli'i
11
Kahuku
Wai'ōhinu
Nā'ālehu
Nīnole
Pāhala
Punalu'u

PACIFIC OCEAN

0   miles   20
0   kilometers   30

N

Ka Lae (South Point)

KĪLAUEA SUMMIT: CRATER RIM DRIVE

11-mile loop; about a half day; check with park headquarters about any road closings. (Note: As of this writing, Crater Rim Drive is closed past Jaggar Museum because of high amounts of sulfur dioxide gas in the atmosphere from Halema'uma'u Crater, which became active again in 2008.)

Kīlauea's summit areas can be rainy and chilly at any time of the year, and visitors should be prepared. Dress in layers and be sure to wear sturdy shoes or boots if you plan to hike. Begin at the **Kīlauea Visitor Center,** and get the latest information on park roads and safety precautions. Several easy and scenic hiking trails and the **Volcano Art Center Gallery** are just a short stroll away. Walk to the left of the Volcano House (closed for renovations until late 2012) and take the trail to **Waldron Ledge,** which offers views of Mauna Loa and Kīlauea Caldera, a 3-mile-wide, 400-foot-deep depression that marks the volcanic summit. Native birds like bright red apapane can be spotted in this area.

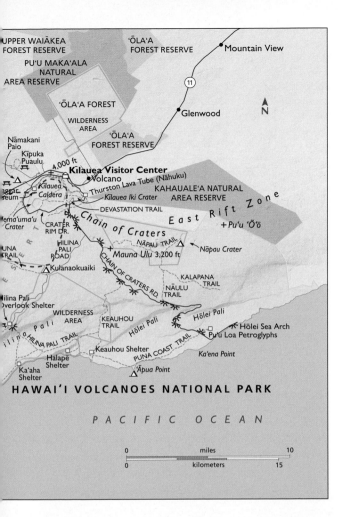

Then proceed clockwise on **Crater Rim Drive.** For a time, the road traverses rain forest featuring Hawaiian tree ferns that lend the roadsides a prehistoric look. Scenic turnouts begin with a huge crater, **Kīlauea Iki** ("little Kīlauea") just east of the main caldera. In 1959 Kīlauea Iki erupted in a lava fountain 1,900 feet high, a record for Hawaiian volcanism.

Visit **Nāhuku** (Thurston Lava Tube) by taking an easy 15-minute loop trail that starts in lush tropical rain forest. The lava tube formed when the surface of a lava stream cooled to a crust while the still molten interior lava flowed out.

From the parking area, trails lead down to the floor of **Kīlauea Iki Crater** and along its rim. You can take a loop hike or walk back to Volcano House in 2 to 3 miles. Either way, you'll pass dramatic vistas of the Kīlauea Caldera, vertical lava cliffs, and verdant rain forest.

Another option is the 4-mile **Kīlauea Iki Trail,** which winds around the rim and across the floor of a crater that last erupted in 1959. Taking about 2 hours to walk, the trail descends 400 feet, passing rain forest and hardened lava flows.

Continuing back along Crater Rim Drive, look for koaʻe kea, white-tailed tropic birds. They nest on cliffside ledges, often soaring above **Kīlauea** and visible from this overlook. With luck, you may spot a nēnē, an endemic Hawaiian goose probably descended from the Canada goose. The state bird of Hawaiʻi, the nēnē is a federally protected endangered species. Do not feed or approach any nēnē and take care to avoid hitting them when driving.

Devastation Trail is a memorable half-mile walk through the remains of a forest killed by falling cinders during the 1959 eruption. The forest is now beginning to recover.

As the road descends along the southwestern side of Kīlauea Caldera, you will notice the landscape becoming more arid. In the rain shadow of the summit, the **Kaʻū Desert** receives about half as much rain as the 100 inches which fall annually at the Kīlauea Visitor Center. It also bears the brunt of trade winds blowing sulfuric volcanic fumes and natural acid rain, which stunt some plants.

Halemaʻumaʻu Crater Overlook was damaged by the 2008 Halemaʻumaʻu summit eruption and is now closed. The crater is the home of Pele, goddess of the volcano, and many native Hawaiians still come to the park to revere her. You can get great views of the active crater and its plume of gas and ash from **Jagger Overlook**. After dusk, you can see the red glow of the lava reflected in the plume.

The **Hawaiian Volcano Observatory** of the U.S. Geological Survey (closed to public), and the small, excellent **Jaggar Museum** of volcano lore and research are next on your route. Nearing the visitor center once more, you'll pass fumaroles, or steam vents. Some have produced deposits of crystal-like sulphur and other colorful minerals, and a trek along the new boardwalk to the **Sulphur Banks** is recommended. From here it's a short hike back toward the visitor center.

CHAIN OF CRATERS ROAD

18 miles one way; about 3 hours

From the Kīlauea Visitor Center follow Crater Rim Drive clockwise to the well-marked turnoff for Chain

Lava aglow at night

of Craters Road. For about 4 miles as you head toward the coast, your route follows the upper part of the active **East Rift Zone** of Kīlauea volcano. Scenic turnouts and short walks bring you to the rims of several impressive craters. If you have time, hike the **Nāpau Trail** up **Puʻu Huluhulu** ("shaggy hill") to the overlook at the top, just over 1 mile. The overlook provides splendid views of the East Rift Zone and **Mauna Ulu,** the large, steaming domelike hill directly to the south. Look for steam from **Puʻu ʻŌʻō,** a major vent of Kīlauea's ongoing eruption, to the east, and from Halemaʻumaʻu to the northwest.

Back on Chain of Craters Road, you will drive over several miles of pāhoehoe lava flows produced when Mauna Ulu formed in the 1970s. At the turnouts, you stand on some of the newest ground on Earth. Pāhoehoe (PA-hoy-hoy) lava flows at more than 2,000°F. It begins fluid then chills to a smooth, ropy surface. This rock contrasts with āa (ah-ah)—thicker, slow-moving lava that has hardened into a chaotic jumble of rough jagged cinders.

The climate becomes drier, and patches of forest in various stages of recovery appear, as you descend toward the sea. Depending on weather conditions and wind direction, volcanic emissions can sweep down from active vents. Turnouts offer sweeping views of historic lava flows and white-capped waves pounding the black shoreline. About 21 miles off this coast, a huge undersea volcano is building a future Hawaiian island. Named Lōʻihi, the volcano could breach the ocean's surface in some 100,000 years.

A steep descent of about 800 feet marks **Hōlei Pali,** a cliff formed by vertical faulting; the huge coastal shelf is breaking away from the

Along the Devastation Trail *(top)*
Ripples of hardened pāhoehoe lava *(bottom)*

uplands and sinking into the sea, albeit slowly on a human time scale. Reaching the lowlands, look for the **Puʻu Loa Petroglyphs** turnout; a modest hike will bring you to fine examples of ancient Hawaiian carvings, some 24,000 images and figures pecked into the lava. Visitors are asked to stay on the boardwalk to help preserve these carvings. Your route along the coast takes you past several of their ancient Hawaiian settlements, though they are difficult to discern.

The road ends abruptly at a 2003 lava flow. Since 1986, an almost continuous flow of lava from Puʻu Ōʻō has buried several miles of the road, as well as the Kamoamoa picnic site and campground, and the Wahaʻula Visitor Center. Lava flow viewing and access are unpredictable; obey all off-limit signs and heed the instructions of any park rangers on duty here.

HAWAIʻI VOLCANOES

INFORMATION & ACTIVITIES

VISITOR & INFORMATION CENTERS

Kīlauea Visitor Center, located just off Hawai'i 11 on Crater Rim Drive, a quarter mile from park entrance gate, and the Thomas A. Jaggar Museum on Crater Rim Drive, 3 miles from park entrance gate, are both open all year.

SEASONS & ACCESSIBILITY

All-year park, open 24 hours a day. Chain of Craters Road is closed by lava flow at its eastern end. Crater Rim Drive is closed past Jagger Museum to the intersection at Chain of Craters Road due to the presence of volcanic gases. For eruption bulletins call (808) 985-6000.

HEADQUARTERS

P.O. Box 52, Hawai'i NP, HI 96718. Phone (808) 985-6000. www.nps.gov/havo

ENTRANCE FEE

$10 per car per week.

PETS

Not permitted on hiking trails or in backcountry; elsewhere must be leashed.

ACCESSIBLE SERVICES

Kīlauea Visitor Center, Jaggar Museum, Volcano House Hotel, Volcano Art Center Gallery all wheelchair accessible. Many paved trails and overlooks accessible with assistance. Kulanaokuaiki Campground fully wheelchair accessible. Free brochure available from Disability and Communication Access Board, 919 Ala Moana Blvd., Rm. 101, Honolulu, HI 96814. (808) 586-8121. www.hawaii.gov/health/dcab

THINGS TO DO

Free ranger-led activities: nature walks and talks, slide shows, films, museum exhibits on volcanism. Also, hiking, Hawaiian cultural demonstrations, art center, workshops, and seminars.

SPECIAL ADVISORIES

• Persons with heart or respiratory problems beware of sulfur dioxide fumes.
• Stay on marked trails; vegetation may conceal deep cracks.
• Coastline collapse can occur fast; do not go beyond barriers.
• Strong winds and unpredictable surf along the coast make swimming dangerous; it is prohibited in places.
• Do not enter any closed areas.

OVERNIGHT BACKPACKING

Registration at the visitor center is required. No fee.

CAMPGROUNDS

Two campgrounds, Kulanaokuaiki and Namakanipaio; 7-day limit. Open all year first come, first served. No fees. No showers. Tent sites only. Two patrol cabins on Mauna Loa Trail and one at Kīpuka Pepeiao may be used free, first come, first served. Must register at Kīlauea Visitor Center. Food services in Volcanic Village, outside the park.

HOTELS, MOTELS, & INNS

(unless otherwise noted, rates are for 2 persons in a double room, high season)

INSIDE THE PARK:
Check with park on status of Volcano House renovations.

OUTSIDE THE PARK:
In Hilo, HI 96720:
Country Club Hawaii Condo Hotel 121 Banyan Dr. (808) 935-7171. 148 units, 20 with kitchenettes. $79-$94. AC, restaurant.
Dolphin Bay Hotel 333 Iliahi St. (866) 935-1466 or (808) 935-1466. 18 units with kitchenettes. $99-$159.
Naniloa Volcanoes Resorts 93 Banyan Dr. (800) 367-5360 or (808) 969-3333. 325 units. $100-$140. AC, pool, restaurant.
In Kailua-Kona, HI 96740:
King Kamehameha's Kona Beach Hotel 75-5660 Palani Rd. (800) 367-2111 or (808) 329-2911. 440 units. $150-$250. AC, pool, restaurant.
In Pahala, HI 96777:
Colony One at Sea Mountain Punaluu (on Highway 11) P.O. Box 70. (800) 488-8301 or (808) 928-8301. 28 condos. $95-$170. Pool, tennis, golf.

For additional lodgings, contact the Chamber of Commerce of Hilo, 106 Kamehameha Ave., Hilo, HI 96720, (808) 935-7178; or the Big Island Visitor's Bureau, 250 Keawe St. Hilo, HI 96720, (808) 961-5797, www.gohawaii.com/big-island.

EXCURSIONS

MAUNA KEA OBSERVATORY
HILO, HAWAI'I

Mauna Kea, the world's highest mountain when measured from its base on the sea floor, is also the world's premier astronomical site. Clear, dry skies and a 13,796-foot elevation provide ideal viewing conditions; 11 countries have built state-of-the-art telescopes on the dormant volcano's summit. The Visitor Information Center of the Onizuka Center for International Astronomy is at 9,300 feet and has astronomical displays and evening stargazing from several telescopes, the largest being 16 inches. Stargazing programs are held every night. Saturday and Sunday tours to summit available for persons 16 and older who are not pregnant and have no heart or respiratory problems. Summit goers must provide their own vehicles equipped with four-wheel-drive. Seven-mile trail to summit from visitor center. Located off Hawaii 200 (Saddle Rd.), 34 miles from Hilo. (808) 961-2180.

'AKAKA FALLS STATE PARK
HONOMU, HAWAI'I

This park's ancient legend bears a decidedly modern ring: It says that the god 'Akaka, fleeing across the canyon after his wife returned home unexpectedly and discovered his infidelity, slipped and fell off 442-foot 'Akaka Falls. A self-guided paved path leads visitors through a lush jungle ablaze with colorful and fragrant blossoms to viewpoints over these falls and the 100-foot cascading Kahūnā Falls. 65 acres. No entrance fee for Hawai'i residents; others, $5 per car or $1 per person. No facilities other than the hiking trails, restrooms, scenic lookouts. Located at end of 'Akaka Falls Road, off Hawaii 220, 14 miles from Hilo. (808) 587-0311.

HAWAI'I VOLCANOES

Joshua trees etched against the sky at sunset

▶ JOSHUA TREE

CALIFORNIA
ESTABLISHED OCTOBER 31, 1994
794,000 acres

Two desert systems, the Mojave and the Colorado, abut within Joshua Tree, dividing California's southernmost national park into two arid ecosystems of profoundly contrasting appearance. The key to their differences is elevation.

The Colorado, the western reach of the vast Sonoran Desert, thrives below 3,000 feet on the park's gently declining eastern flank, where temperatures are usually higher. Considered "low desert," compared to the loftier, wetter, and more vegetated Mojave "high desert," the Colorado seems sparse and forbidding. It begins at the park's midsection, sweeping east across empty basins stubbled with creosote bushes. Occasionally decorated by "gardens" of flowering ocotillo and

cholla cactus, it runs across arid Pinto Basin into a parched wilderness of broken rock in the Eagle and Coxcomb Mountains.

Many newcomers among the 1.3 million visitors who pass through each year are surprised by the abrupt transition between the Colorado and Mojave ecosystems. Above 3,000 feet, the Mojave section claims the park's western half, where giant branching yuccas thrive on sandy plains studded by massive granite monoliths and rock piles. These are among the most intriguing and photogenic geological phenomena found in California's many desert regions.

Joshua Tree's human history commenced sometime after the last ice age with the arrival of the Pinto people, hunter-gatherers who may have been part of the Southwest's earliest cultures. They lived in Pinto Basin, which though inhospitably arid today, had a wet climate and was crossed by a sluggish river some 5,000 to 7,000 years ago. Nomadic groups of Indians seasonally inhabited the region when harvests of pinyon nuts, mesquite beans, acorns, and cactus fruit offered sustenance. Bedrock mortars—holes ground into solid rock and used to pulverize seeds during food preparation—are scattered throughout the Wonderland of Rocks area south of the Indian Cove camping site.

A flurry of late 19th-century gold-mining ventures left ruins; some are accessible by hiking trails, or unmaintained roads suited only to four-wheel-drive vehicles and mountain bikes.

How to Get There
The west and north park entrances are at the towns of Joshua Tree and Twentynine Palms. From Los Angeles, take I-10 east to Calif. 62 (Twentynine Palms Hwy.) to Twentynine Palms (about 140 miles total). The south entrance is located at Cottonwood Spring, approximately 25 miles east of Indio off I-10. Call (760) 367-5500 for recorded directions. Airports: Palm Springs, Los Angeles.

When to Go
All-year park. Temperatures are most comfortable in the spring and fall, with an average high and low of 85°F and 50°F. Winter brings cooler days, around 60°F, and freezing nights.

Summers are hot, with midday temperatures frequently above 100°F, and ground temperatures reaching 180°F. The Mojave Desert zone on the park's western half is on average 11 degrees cooler than the Colorado. In winter, snow may blanket the Mojave's higher elevations.

Spring blooming periods vary according to winter precipitation and spring temperatures, usually beginning in February at lower elevations and peaking park-wide in March and April, although cactuses may bloom into June. (Check with park headquarters.) For up-to-date wildflower information, visit www.nps.gov/jotr.

How to Visit
The park's premier attractions, forests of giant branching yuccas known as Joshua trees, massive rock formations, fan palm oases, and seasonal gardens of cholla and ocotillo, can be enjoyed on a leisurely half-day auto tour that includes both high and low desert zones—although most of your time will be spent in your car. Scenic paved roads lead to viewpoints, all campgrounds, and trailheads. Roadside interpretive exhibits have pull-outs and parking areas, and offer insights into the region's complex desert ecology, wildlife, and human history.

If you plan to explore the park by mountain bike, you would be wise to avoid the main paved roads, which are narrow and without shoulders. You'll find far greater solitude and safety cycling the park's backcountry dirt roads, many of which, like those in **Queen Valley,** date from the area's 19th-century homestead and gold-mining era. There are no mountain biking trails in the park. Be sure to acquire reliable information from headquarters about your route, as soft sand and occasional steep climbs can make for arduous pedaling.

JOSHUA TREE

For a half-day visit that starts from the park's northern boundary, take the **Park Boulevard loop** either from the town of Joshua Tree through the West Entrance Station, or from Twentynine Palms, by way of the North Entrance Station. If the air is clear (ask at the entrance about haze conditions), take the 20-minute side trip to 5,185-foot-high **Keys View,** which overlooks a vast panorama of arid desert basin and range stretching south into Mexico. If you are starting from Joshua Tree, return to Park Boulevard and continue east over **Sheep Pass** to **Jumbo Rocks,** turning right (south) onto Pinto Basin Road for the drive down into long vistas in the Colorado Desert zone. Be sure to stroll the self-guided nature trail through the **Cholla Cactus Garden.**

Backtrack to Twentynine Palms and the **Oasis Visitor Center,** which features a small cactus garden and superb desert ecology interpretive displays. It adjoins the historic **Oasis of Mara** (one of five spring-fed oases within the park's boundaries), where Indians once found water, shade, food, and game. If you are starting from Twentynine Palms and the Oasis Visitor Center, proceed south as far as the Ocotillo Patch, then backtrack to Park Boulevard and follow it westward to Joshua Tree.

PARK BOULEVARD

64 miles (including side trips);
a half to full day

A scenic drive connecting the north and west entrances skirts the sparse Colorado low desert ecosystem, then climbs into the Joshua tree forest and its surrounding plateau of mammoth rocks. Begin at the **Oasis Visitor Center** in Twentynine Palms,

or the **Joshua Tree Visitor Center** in the town of Joshua Tree, 5 miles from the West Entrance Station. (Or, if entering from the south, begin at the **Cottonwood Visitor Center** and follow Pinto Basin Road north and west past the Ocotillo Patch and the Cholla Cactus Garden to the Oasis Visitor Center.) All three visitor centers provide insights into how plants and animals survive the region's withering heat and aridity, and how its unusual geology was formed, though the Oasis Visitor Center's interpretive displays are more extensive.

The Oasis Visitor Center adjoins the **Oasis of Mara,** a cluster of fan palms (the only palms native to the Southwest desert), Fremont cottonwoods, arrow weeds, and mesquite shrubs watered by a seeping spring. Take the half-mile path to this scruffy bit of green, which once sustained Indian encampments and later slaked the thirst of prospectors and homesteaders. A minute's stroll leads to a shady respite amid the chatter of birds. (Bird-watchers may

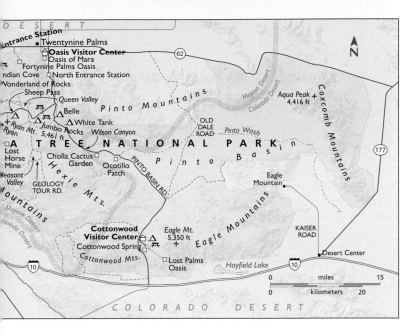

want to include a visit to **Cottonwood Springs,** an oasis sheltering many species and located about a mile from the Cottonwood Visitor Center at the south entrance.)

If your schedule allows, take time for short walks along nature trails that offer close-up looks at plant and animal life, or interesting terrain. (Park brochures describe trail highlights.) Consider starting early; sunlight playing across Joshua Tree's granite monoliths, peaks, and basins accentuates their contours and colors—especially at dawn and sunset—when rocks are aglow in warm pinks and yellows. Ask at a visitor center about ranger-led campfire talks, walks, and tours, or check campground bulletin boards.

Continue south from Twentynine Palms on Park Boulevard to the North Entrance Station. The road climbs, skirting the **Pinto Mountains** that rise to the east. Where the pavement forks (after about 5 miles), bear left onto Pinto Basin Road. You'll soon enter **Wilson Canyon** and the transition zone, where the

Mojave and Colorado Desert ecosystems join. The sweep of **Pinto Basin** trending east is in fact an ancient dry lakebed, and a typical Sonoran Desert landscape dominated by the pale creosote bush.

Stroll through the **Cholla Cactus Garden,** a picturesque cluster about 10 miles south of the fork and threaded by a short nature trail interestingly keyed to self-guided brochures provided there. Known as "jumping" cholla for the tendency of its spiny joints to break off and cling to hapless passersby, the crooked-arm cactus appears velvety but is actually covered by tiny, sharply piercing bristles.

Continue southeast about 2 miles to the **Ocotillo Patch,** where hundreds of the spindly Sonoran Desert plants seem to languish, their rigid gray spines wobbling skyward. After rains in March and April, their tips flame with dense bouquets of bloodred flowers, a lifesaver for hummingbirds migrating north from Mexico (and a highlight of the flowering calendar).

Diamond site pictographs

Backtrack northwest to the White Tank Campground and the **Arch Rock Nature Trail.** The easy 0.3-mile path to **Arch Rock** features interpretive information on how the surrounding geology and the natural arch were formed.

At the fork, turn left to rejoin Park Boulevard and enter the Mojave high desert. Westbound, you'll see mammoth granite formations rising from a sandy plateau. Some 800 million years in the making, worn by eons of weather into the contours of melting ice cream, the **Jumbo Rocks** are a product of this region's seismic restlessness— tectonic tumult evidenced by frequent small temblors that affect the flow of springs watering the park's oases.

Here visitors might likely see climbers scaling the monoliths, for Joshua Tree National Park contains one of America's most accessible, yet challenging, rock-climbing areas. Guidelines designed for safety and the protection of rock surfaces govern climbing within the park. Spectators gather in parking areas to watch the enthusiasts laden with equipment climb hand-over-hand up seemingly impossible routes.

Keep an eye out for aptly named **Skull Rock,** which flanks the road as you continue west toward **Hidden Valley,** a scenic garden of huge piled-up boulders resembling animals, human faces, and abstract forms. A popular picnic and camping area, this part of Joshua Tree is heavily populated by the park's trademark branching yucca. Named by early Mormon settlers who saw in its uplifted arms a symbol of the Biblical supplicant Joshua, *Yucca brevifolia* can reach 50 feet in height over a life span that may exceed 200 years. Some 25 bird species find protected nesting spots between its short, spiky leaves. The 1.25-mile **Hidden Valley Trail** follows a circuitous path through a stony maze to a "hidden" bowl where, according to local lore, rustlers once hid with their stolen cattle. The northern portion of this loop requires some boulder scrambling, so be sure to wear sturdy shoes.

If you're not yet ready for a picnic, take the 6-mile scenic side trip up to **Keys View.** Just short of a mile high (5,185 feet), the mountaintop is the park's premier vantage point for motorists. Smog and natural haze from the Los Angeles Basin sometimes obscure the horizon; however, clear days afford a splendid southerly panorama of Coachella Valley farmlands, the Salton Sea, and Sonoran Desert mountains in Mexico. Across the valley looms 10,804-foot Mount San Jacinto, towering above Palm Springs.

Park Boulevard continues northwest through the Joshua tree forest, and then descends to the West Entrance Station and the town of Joshua Tree.

INFORMATION & ACTIVITIES

VISITOR & INFORMATION CENTERS

Oasis Visitor Center, off Calif. 62 near Twentynine Palms and north entrance; **Joshua Tree Visitor Center** in the town of Joshua Tree, 5 miles from West Entrance Station; **Cottonwood Visitor Center,** off I-10 at south entrance.

SEASONS & ACCESSIBILITY
Open year-round.

HEADQUARTERS
74485 National Park Dr., Twentynine Palms, CA 92277. Phone (760) 367-5500. www.nps.gov/jotr

ENTRANCE FEE
$15 per vehicle, good for seven consecutive days; $30 for annual pass.

PETS
Permitted on leashes. Not allowed on trails or in backcountry (more than 100 yards from the road).

ACCESSIBLE SERVICES
The Oasis Visitor Center's interpretive displays, garden, and bookstore accessible, as are the 0.25- and 0.5-mile loop trails to Oasis of Mara. The Keys View wheelchair viewpoint is below the summit. The Cap Rock Nature Trail (0.5-mile loop from parking area) and the Bajada Nature Trail (0.25-mile loop) are accessible. No campsites are officially accessible, but Belle and White Tank camping areas have accessible restrooms.

THINGS TO DO
Free ranger-led activities and tours to Keys Ranch homestead (fee). Also, interpretive exhibits, self-guided cactus garden trails, auto touring, bicycling (on roads only), hiking, rock climbing, horseback riding on approved trails, bird-watching. ATVs and off-road motorized travel and biking prohibited.

SPECIAL ADVISORIES
• Always carry water, even on short hikes. No potable water in the park. Potable water available at the Oasis of Mara, at Black Rock and Cottonwood Camp-grounds, and at Indian Cove Ranger Station. Recommended: One gallon per person per day, two gallons if hiking.
• Campfires banned in backcountry. Bring own firewood for campgrounds.
• Rock climbers check regulations before undertaking climb.
• Use extreme caution around old mine workings—NEVER ENTER.
• Hikers should carry a compass, GPS, and topographic map. Established trails can be obscured.
• Archaeological sites should not be disturbed, including rock art. Climbing within 50 feet of rock art prohibited.

OVERNIGHT BACKPACKING
Registration required at backcountry boards. Check with rangers about current conditions. A permit is required for horses. Call (760) 367-5545.

CAMPGROUNDS
Nine campgrounds, all with 14-day limit from Sept. through May, and a 30-day limit rest of year. First-come, first-served basis. Fees $10-$15 per night. Group camping available at **Cottonwood, Indian Cove,** and **Sheep Pass** by reservation only. Call the NRRS (see p. 10). Fees $10-$15. Horses permitted at **Black Rock.**

HOTELS, MOTELS, & INNS
(unless otherwise noted, rates are for 2 persons in a double room, high season)

In Twentynine Palms, CA 92277:
Best Western Garden Inn & Suites 71487 Twentynine Palms Hwy. (800) 528-1234 or (760) 367-9141. 83 units, 12 with kitchenettes. $124. AC, pool.
Motel 6 72562 Twentynine Palms Hwy. (800) 466-8356 or (760) 367-2833. 123 units. $56. AC, pool.
In Indio, CA 92201:
America's Best Value Inn 43-505 Monroe St. (760) 347-4044. 60 units. $80-$150. AC, pool.
Indio Travelodge 80651 Hwy 111. (800) 578-7878 or (760) 342-0882. 52 units. $69-$95. AC, pool.
In Yucca Valley, CA 92284:
Travelodge Inn & Suites 54850 Twentynine Palms Hwy. (760) 365-3311. 64 units. $79. AC, pool.

For other information, contact Twentynine Palms Chamber of Commerce, (760) 367-3445, www.29chamber.org.

JOSHUA TREE

Moss creeping up red firs

▶ SEQUOIA & KINGS CANYON

CALIFORNIA
SEQUOIA
ESTABLISHED SEPTEMBER 25, 1890;
KINGS CANYON
ESTABLISHED MARCH 4, 1940
865,964 acres

Bigness—big trees and big canyons—inspired the separate found-ing of each of these parks. In 1943 Sequoia and Kings Canyon National Parks began to be jointly administered. The two contigu-ous parks are 66 miles long and 36 miles at their widest point.

Nearly 97 percent of these vast parks is wilderness. A backpacker can hike to a spot that is farther from a road than any other place in the lower 48 states. But visitors can easily reach Sequoia's famed attrac-tion, the Giant Forest of sequoias.

Relatively few visitors hike any of the parks' 800 miles of trails. Still, there are enough backpackers that officials protect the backcountry by regulating their numbers.

Mount Whitney, at 14,494 feet the highest peak in the United States south of Alaska, rises at the eastern border. Backpackers coming in from the east can get to Whitney in 1 or 2 days. From the park's western trailheads, they reach it by a nearly 70-mile, 8-day trek across the park's snowswept, glacier-dotted heights.

Some visitors are startled to learn that some of the smoke they see rises from "prescribed burning"—controlled fires deliberately set by employees to help the sequoias by removing undergrowth. In the past, when the park fought all fires, brush and dead-wood built up. (Seeds cannot germinate in duff, so they need fires to open groundcover.) The brush-fueled fires imperiled the sequoias—which resist flames at their bases but can die if fire attacks their crowns.

How to Get There

From Visalia (about 35 miles west), take Calif. 198 to Sequoia's Ash Mountain Entrance. From Fresno, take Calif. 180 to Kings Canyon's Big Stump Entrance. The road into Kings Canyon NP extends into Grant Cove (year round) and Cedar Grove (summer only). The Sequoia shuttle (877-287-4453; www.sequoiashuttle .com) costs $15 including entrance fee and may be accessed by reservation from Visalia, Exeter, or Three Rims. In addition, free in-park shuttles in the summer provide a relaxing option for visiting the most popular sections of the park. Airport: Fresno.

When to Go

Spring through fall is the best time for sequoia gazing. Generals Highway, which connects the parks, is open year-round except during heavy snows. From December until April, there is cross-country skiing and snowshoe-ing in sections of the park, including Giant Forest and Grant Grove.

How to Visit

The two immense parks challenge anyone planning a 1-day visit. To appreciate the rugged splendor, you must hike a trail. No east-west road crosses either park. But a drive-in visitor, in a day, can see sequoias in **Giant Forest,** along the **Generals Highway,** and in **Grant Grove,** weather permitting. A quiet walk in a grove of sequoias will give you more than a drive to named trees, which

may be surrounded by shutterbugs.

Stay long enough to explore both vast parks. Drive to Kings Canyon's beautiful valley, **Cedar Grove.** On another day visit **Crystal Cave** and climb **Moro Rock.** Hike in Sequoia's spectacular **Mineral King** area.

GIANT FOREST & GRANT GROVE

48 miles; a full day

From the **Ash Mountain Entrance,** on **Generals Highway,** drive 17 miles to **Giant Forest,** home of the **General Sherman Tree,** the world's largest tree. About 6 miles from the Ash Mountain Entrance, stop to see the Native American exhibit at **Hospital Rock.** Indians lived here from prehistoric times until the 1870s, when the white man's diseases killed many of them. The Western Mono made flour from acorns—the staple food of early residents. They crushed the acorns in small hollows worn into streamside bedrock; you can see several such rock mortars across the road.

The **Four Guardsmen,** a quartet of sequoias, stand as sentinels near the entrance to Giant Forest. Trails radiate from the star attraction, the General Sherman Tree, about 2,100 years old, 274.9 feet tall, and 102.6 feet in circumference, with a volume of 52,508 cubic feet. (In board feet, this is the equivalent of 119.3 miles of 1-by-12-inch planks.) A 13-story build-ing would fit beneath its first large branch. The tree was named by a pio-neer cattleman who had served under Gen. William Tecumseh Sherman.

The easy 2-mile **Congress Trail** (the name honors the institution that gave legal protection to the sequoias) takes 1 to 2 hours and begins near the champion tree. Along the way, you will see young sequoias (a mere 140 or so years old); sequoias scarred by

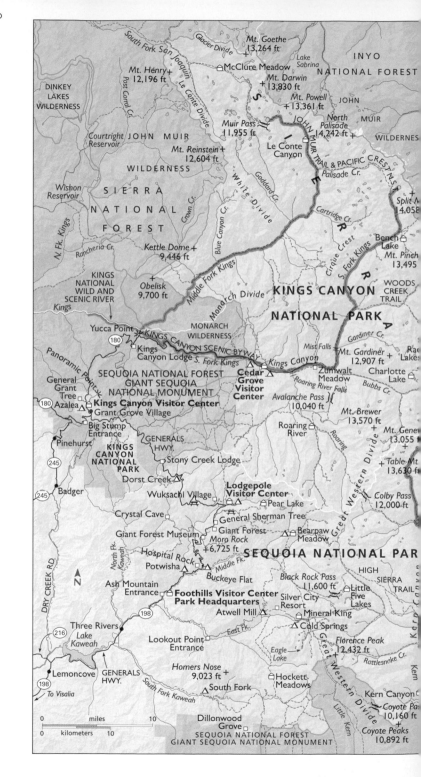

South Fork San Joaquin
Glacier Divide
Mt. Goethe
13,264 ft
Lake Sabrina
INYO
NATIONAL FOREST
McClure Meadow
Mt. Henry +
12,196 ft
Mt. Darwin
+ 13,830 ft
Mt. Powell
+ 13,361 ft
JOHN
MUIR
Post Corral Cr.
Le Conte Divide
S
Muir Pass
11,955 ft
North
Palisade
14,242 ft +
WILDERNESS
DINKEY
LAKES
WILDERNESS
Courtright
Reservoir
JOHN MUIR
Le Conte
Canyon
JOHN MUIR TRAIL & PACIFIC CREST NST
Palisade Cr.
Mt. Reinstein +
12,604 ft
WILDERNESS
E
Goddard Cr.
White Divide
Wishon
Reservoir
SIERRA
NATIONAL
FOREST
Crown Cr.
Blue Canyon Cr.
Cartridge Cr.
Split M
14,058
R
N. Fk. Kings
Rancheria Cr.
Kettle Dome +
9,446 ft
Middle Fork Kings
Cirque Crest
S. Fork Kings
Bench
Lake
Mt. Pinch
13,495
KINGS
NATIONAL
WILD AND
SCENIC RIVER
Kings
Obelisk
9,700 ft
Monarch Divide
KINGS CANYON
WOODS
CREEK
TRAIL
R
A
MONARCH
WILDERNESS
NATIONAL PARK
Yucca Point
180
KINGS CANYON SCENIC BYWAY
Kings
Canyon Lodge S. Fork Kings
Kings Canyon
Mist Falls
Gardiner Cr.
Mt. Gardiner
12,907 ft
Rae
Lake
Panoramic Point
SEQUOIA NATIONAL FOREST
GIANT SEQUOIA
NATIONAL MONUMENT
Cedar
Grove
Visitor
Center
Zumwalt
Meadow
Roaring River Falls
Charlotte
Lake
General
Grant
Tree
180
Azalea
Kings Canyon Visitor Center
Grant Grove Village
Avalanche Pass
10,040 ft
Bubbs Cr.
Mt. Brewer
13,570 ft
Mt. Gene
13,055
Big Stump
Entrance
Pinehurst
KINGS
CANYON
NATIONAL
PARK
GENERALS
HWY.
Stony Creek Lodge
Roaring
River
Roaring
Great Western Divide
+ Table Mt
13,630 ft
245
Badger
Dorst Creek
Wuksachi Village
Lodgepole
Visitor Center
Pear Lake
Colby Pass
12,000 ft
Crystal Cave
General Sherman Tree
N
DRY CREEK RD.
North Fk. Kaweah
Giant Forest Museum
Hospital Rock
Potwisha
Giant Forest
Moro Rock
+ 6,725 ft
Middle Fk.
Bearpaw
Meadow
SEQUOIA NATIONAL PAR
HIGH
SIERRA
TRAIL
Ash Mountain
Entrance
Buckeye Flat
Black Rock Pass
11,600 ft
Little
Five
Lakes
Foothills Visitor Center
Park Headquarters
Silver City
Resort
Atwell Mill
Mineral King
Cold Springs
Kern Canyon
Three Rivers
Lake
Kaweah
216
East Fk.
Eagle
Lake
Florence Peak
12,432 ft
Rattlesnake Cr.
198
Lookout Point
Entrance
Lemoncove
GENERALS
HWY.
Homers Nose
9,023 ft
South Fork
Hockett
Meadows
Great Western Divide
Little Kern
Kern Canyon
198
To Visalia
South Fork Kaweah
Coyote Pa
10,160 ft
+
Coyote Peaks
10,892 ft
0 miles 10
0 kilometers 10
Dillonwood
Grove
SEQUOIA NATIONAL FOREST
GIANT SEQUOIA NATIONAL MONUMENT
245
Pinehurst
198
Three Rivers

fire but standing tall because their bark, thick and lacking resin, protects them; and fallen sequoias—not rotting because they contain tannin, which helps them resist decay.

Return to Generals Highway and begin the 30-mile drive to **Grant Grove** in Kings Canyon NP by heading northwest to Calif. 180. Turn east on Calif. 180. Just beyond **Kings Canyon Visitor Center,** take the road on your left to the **General Grant Tree Trail,** a half-mile loop leading to the **General Grant Tree** (268.1 feet tall, 107.5 feet in circumference). The name of the tree recalls the 1890 name of the park, created to preserve General Grant Grove. To counter lumbering, champions of the sequoias bought more land to expand the 4-square-mile grove. (To understand the significance of the trees and their ecological management, visit the **Giant Forest Museum,** in the 1928 building designed by Gilbert Stanley Underwood.)

On the trail are many of the saved giants, along with a reminder of the years of casual havoc: **Centennial Stump,** a sequoia cut down for the 1875 Centennial in Philadelphia. Near the park entrance is **Big Stump Trail** (1-mile loop), where stumps, logs, and a pile of sawdust help you imagine the sequoia logging of the past.

Return to the visitor center and head east on the steep, narrow, 2.5-mile road to **Panoramic Point** (*no trailers or large vehicles allowed*). From the parking lot, take the 0.25-mile trail to the 7,520-foot ridge. Before you stretches the Sierra Nevada. You won't see Mount Whitney; the Great Western Divide blocks the view.

CEDAR GROVE
36 miles; a full day

Follow Calif. 180 for 30 miles north and east of Grant Grove, through

Sequoia National Forest. The road winds into the canyon of the **South Fork Kings River.** Stop at **Yucca Point** to gaze down on the wild river flanked by sheer canyon walls glistening in the sun. The road continues to **Cedar Grove,** a mile-deep valley. Scouring streams began the carving of the valley, which got its U-shape from subsequent glaciers that pushed into the canyon and widened the floor.

Incense cedar, ponderosa pine, black oak, live oak, white fir, and sugar pine grow in the valley's flats. In the 1870s the area attracted stockmen as well as gold and silver seekers. But John Muir, who explored here in 1873, would still recognize this beautiful high-country valley.

To best enjoy **Cedar Grove** Village park, get out and walk or bike, even for a short distance, to savor this hidden valley. The easy half-mile **River Trail** takes you from the South Fork Kings River to **Roaring River Falls.** From the parking lot you can hike along the curves of the river. Cross a suspension bridge and climb a slight rise for a view of the valley. Retrace your steps to the bridge and take the **Zumwalt Meadow Trail,** a 1-mile loop.

CRYSTAL CAVE

18 miles; cave tours mid-May–Oct.; a half day

The cave temperature is a constant 50°F, so take a jacket. Tickets must be purchased in advance at either the Lodgepole or Foothills Visitor Centers. Take the Generals Highway south from Lodgepole Visitor Center. Turn right down the rough, summer-only road *(no trailers or large vehicles)* to Crystal Cave. The twisting, dusty, 9-mile trip consumes about an hour. From the parking lot you walk a paved, steep path along a canyon wall, down to the entrance.

Don't expect multicolored lights or tales of goblins; the 1-hour tours introduce you to a cave that got its name from an unusual geological phenomenon. The cave is formed of marble—instead of limestone—that underground water slowly dissolved and then redeposited as dazzling stalactites, stalagmites, and columns.

MORO ROCK

4.6 miles round-trip; a half day

Although you can drive to Moro Rock (driving may be restricted in the summer), a huge granite monolith, via the 2-mile **Moro Rock-Crescent Meadow Road** from Giant Forest, you get a better perception of its setting by hiking. Either way, try for sunset when the view is spectacular. The 2-mile **Moro Rock Trail** begins near Giant Forest Museum. About 1.3 miles along the trail, a short path veers off to **Hanging Rock,** a high granite stage for viewing Sierra Nevada scenery.

Continuing on to the base of Moro Rock, you start climbing a stone stairway of nearly 400 steps (with spots for resting). Your 300-foot ascent takes you to 6,725 feet, about 4,000 feet above the canyon floor. You can look down on the tops of the giant sequoias. On clear days you can see the Coast Ranges, more than 100 miles west.

When you return from the summit, you can retrace your steps on the Moro Rock Trail or return to the Generals Highway via the 2.3-mile **Soldiers Trail,** named for the U.S. Cavalry troopers who patrolled the sequoias before the Park Service's rangers took over the task.

MINERAL KING

50 miles round-trip; at least a full day

Three miles north of the town of Three Rivers, near the Ash Mountain

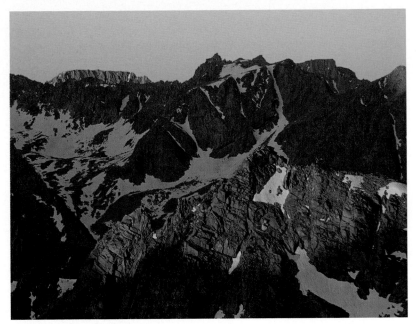

Evening in Kearsarge Pass, Kings Canyon

Entrance, is the sign for Mineral King, added in 1978. It was named in the 1870s by gold prospectors who gained little more than unfulfilled dreams from it. The 1960s dreams of a ski resort failed to come true because of public opposition.

Turn off Calif. 198 onto a narrow, twisting, 25-mile road. (One driver counted 29 turns in a single mile.) To avoid driving it twice in one grueling day, plan your schedule so that you'll be able to stay at least a night. But, if you must do it in a single day, start early. Mineral King is a hiker's paradise. And the road is the secret to the paradise's solitude. "The road is terrible," one grinning hiker said. "And we hope it stays that way."

During the summer, stop at the **Mineral King Ranger Station** and check to see whether a ranger-guided walk is scheduled that day. Or take a hike on your own. Get a map at the station, find a legal

parking place, and select a trail. Remember that all trails here begin at altitudes of at least 7,500 feet and climb steeply. If you are not acclimated to high elevations, you may suffer altitude sickness.

A good hike for beginners just getting their legs in shape is **Eagle Lake Trail,** which starts at the Eagle-Mosquito Parking Area. This trail starts gently, then begins to get steep near **Spring Creek,** which sprouts from the mountainside. Every switchback treats visitors to an overlook with a stunning view. Keep your eyes peeled for the sight of marmots (which sometimes eat car wires and tubes) standing up and watching back, and tiny pikas, which whistle and scurry around. After a 2-mile climb, you reach the **Eagle Sink Holes,** where water disappears just as suddenly as the creek appeared. Here you can turn around and start down or continue up another 1.5 miles to **Eagle Lake,** a tarn.

INFORMATION & ACTIVITIES

VISITOR & INFORMATION CENTERS

Sequoia: Lodgepole Visitor Center and **Giant Forest Museum,** Giant Forest area; **Foothills Visitor Center,** Ash Mountain, where Calif. 198 enters park; **Mineral King Ranger Station,** south of park. Foothills open daily all year; others open reduced hours in winter.
Kings Canyon Visitor Center open daily all year; **Cedar Grove Visitor Center,** on Calif. 180, open daily in summer. For visitor information call (559) 565-3341.

SEASONS & ACCESSIBILITY

Parks open all year. Roads to Mineral King and Moro Rock (Sequoia) and to Cedar Grove (Kings Canyon) closed winter; Generals Highway from Lodgepole to Grant Grove may close due to snow in winter. Call (559) 565-3341 for current weather and road information.

HEADQUARTERS

Ash Mountain, 47050 Generals Hwy., Three Rivers, CA 93271. Phone (559) 565-3341. www.nps.gov/seki

ENTRANCE FEE

$10 individual entry pass; $20 vehicle pass, valid 1-7 days. Annual pass, $30.

ACCESSIBLE SERVICES

Visitor centers are wheelchair accessible, as are some trails in Grant Grove and Giant Forest.

THINGS TO DO

Free naturalist-led activities (many offered in summer only): nature walks and talks, night sky watches, children's programs, evening programs, snowshoe walks. Also available, Crystal Cave tours (summer only, fee), nature center, fishing (license needed), horseback trail rides, pack trips, cross-country skiing.

OVERNIGHT BACKPACKING

Permits required. Reservations for specific trails and dates must be made by mail or fax (559) 565-4239. ($15 fee charged for reservations.) A few permits issued on departure day, first come, first served. Information (559) 565-3766.

CAMPGROUNDS

Sequoia: seven campgrounds, 14-day limit mid-June to mid-Sept. **Lodgepole, Potwisha,** and **South Fork** open all year. Others spring to fall, depending on weather. First come, first served, except Lodgepole and **Dorst Creek,** which require reservations through the NRRS (see p. 10) mid-May to mid-Oct. Fees $12-$20 per night. Showers near Lodgepole, closed in winter. RV sites at Dorst Creek, Lodgepole, and Potwisha; no hookups.
Kings Canyon: seven campgrounds, 14-day summer limit. **Azalea** open all year, others late April to mid-Sept. First come, first served. Fees $18 per night, more for group camps. Showers nearby. Tent and RV sites; no hookups. Reservations required for group campsites; write Sunset/Canyon View Group Sites, P.O. Box 926, Kings Canyon National Park, CA 93633 or call (559) 565-4335.

HOTELS, MOTELS, & INNS
(unless otherwise noted, rates are for 2 persons in a double room, high season)

INSIDE THE PARKS:
For the following lodges in Sequoia NP, call (888) 252-5757, www.visitsequoia.com:
Bearpaw High Sierra Camp Six group tent cabins, central showers. $350, incl. meals. Mid-June–mid-Sept.
Wuksachi Lodge 102 units. $200-$300. Restaurant.

For the following lodges in Kings Canyon NP/Sequoia NF, call (559) 335-5500, www .kingscanyon.com:
Cedar Grove Lodge 21 units. $119-$135. AC, restaurant. May through Oct.
John Muir Lodge 36 lodge rooms, $172-$186; 9 bath cabins, $129-$140; 27 Meadow Camp cabins, $77-$92; 15 tent cabins, $62-$77. Restaurant.
Stoney Creek Lodge 11 units. $149-$189. Restaurant. Mid-May–mid-Oct.

OUTSIDE THE PARKS:
In Three Rivers, CA 93271:
Western Holiday Lodge 40105 Sierra Dr. (559) 561-4119. 54 units. $129-$189.
Lazy J Ranch Motel 39625 Sierra Dr. (888) 315-2378 or (559) 561-4449. 18 units, 6 with kitchenettes. $115-$155. AC, pool.
The River Inn and Cabins 45176 Sierra Dr. (800) 793-7309 or (559) 561-4367. 16 units. $99-$399. AC.

EXCURSIONS

SEQUOIA NATIONAL FOREST
PORTERVILLE, CALIFORNIA

Thirty-eight groves of sequoias are only part of the attractions. Four stretches of wild and scenic rivers and six wilderness areas provide recreational challenges; part of the site has been declared a national monument. 1,136,095 acres. Hiking, boating, white-water rafting, climbing, cycling, fishing, horseback riding, scenic drives, winter sports. 2,000-plus campsites, picnic areas, handicapped access. All year. Adjoins Sequoia and Kings Canyon NP on south, west, north. (559) 784-1500.

PINNACLES NATIONAL MONUMENT
PAICINES, CALIFORNIA

Rising abruptly from gentle hill country, the spires and crags of the Pinnacles formation are the remains of a volcanic mountain formed 200 miles south. Pulled north and west by the San Andreas Rift, the Pinnacles are still migrating. Hiking trails, ranging from easy to strenuous, take visitors from chaparral-covered slopes, through caves, to the high peaks. 26,000 acres. Climbing, picnic areas, handicapped access. Visitor center off Calif. 25, about 130 miles west of Sequoia and Kings Canyon NP. (831) 389-4485.

INYO NATIONAL FOREST
BISHOP, CALIFORNIA

Inyo is home to many natural wonders, including Mount Whitney, Mono Lake, Mammoth Lakes Basin, and the ancient bristlecone pine forest. It also contains parts of nine wilderness areas, notably the John Muir and Ansel Adams. 2,000,000 acres. Hiking, boating, climbing, cycling, fishing, horseback riding, hunting, scenic drives, winter sports, water sports. 73 campgrounds, boat ramp, picnic areas. Most campsites open May through October. Visitor center at Mammoth Lakes on Calif. 203. (760) 873-2400.

SEQUOIA & KINGS CANYON

Yosemite Valley's El Capitan in early morning light

▶ YOSEMITE

CALIFORNIA
ESTABLISHED OCTOBER 1, 1890
747,956 acres

In a high-country meadow two hikers crouch near the edge of a mirroring lake and watch a pika as it harvests blades of grass for a nest deep within a huge rock pile. When they resume walking, there is no other person in sight for as far as they can see. And on this sparkling summer's day, the view seems endless.

In the valley's crowded mall, families stroll by, eating ice cream, dodging bicycles. People pile in and out of buses. Shoppers hunt for souvenirs. Kids hang around a pizza place. Rock climbers, coils of rope slung over their shoulders, swap stories over beer on a patio. On a summer's day about 14,000 people are in Yosemite Village.

Both the solitude of the alpine ridge and the throngs of the valley are part of the experience when you visit Yosemite National Park. "No temple made with human hands can compare with Yosemite," wrote John Muir, whose crusading led to the creation of the park. To this temple come 4 million visitors annually. And about 90 percent of them go to the valley, a mile-wide, 7-mile-long canyon cut by a river, then widened and deepened by glacial action. Walled by massive domes and soaring pinnacles, it covers about one percent of the park. In summer, the concentration of autos brings traffic jams and air pollution.

Beyond the valley, some 800 miles of marked trails offer hikers easy jaunts or grueling tests of endurance in the High Sierra wilderness. Even the casual visitor can explore this solitude without getting outfitted for a backpack expedition.

This park, roughly the size of Rhode Island, is a United Nations World Heritage site. Here, in five of the seven continental life zones, live the mule deer and chipmunks of the valley and the marmots and pikas of the heights; the brush rabbit and chaparral of the near desert; the dogwood and warblers of mid-elevation forests; the red fir and Jeffrey pine of mile-high forests; the dwarf willow and matted flowers of Yosemite's majestic mountains.

How to Get There

From Merced (about 70 miles away): Follow Calif. 140 to the Arch Rock Entrance. Merced is one of the gateway communities for the Yosemite regional bus service (www.yarts.com or 877-989-2787). Also from the west: Take Calif. 120 to the Big Oak Flat Entrance.

From the south, via Fresno: Calif. 41 takes you to the South Entrance.

From the northeast, via Lee Vining: Follow Calif. 120 to the Tioga Pass Entrance (closed mid-November to late May, depending on weather).

Trains stop at Merced; check with Amtrak about buses to Yosemite. Airports: Fresno and Merced.

When to Go

All-year park. Avoid holiday weekends. Expect filled campgrounds from June through August and some crowding in late spring and early fall. Be sure you have reserved accommodations before attempting an overnight visit. You will find skiing and other winter activities in the Badger Pass Ski Area from about Thanksgiving to mid-April.

How to Visit

When a visitor asked a Yosemite ranger what he would do if he had only a day to visit the park, the ranger answered, "I'd weep." If you must zip through this huge park in a day, begin with **Yosemite Valley.**

But even a dawn-to-dusk, 1-day visit hardly allows enough time for more than a tour of the valley plus a look at one or two of the park's other major areas, such as the vistas from **Glacier Point** (road closed in winter beyond the ski area) and the sequoias of the **Mariposa Grove.**

As an alternative take the High Sierra **Tioga Road** (closed in winter) to explore the park's alpine country. Better still, stay long enough to get beyond the crowds and discover the sense of seclusion this great park can give you along one of its trails.

YOSEMITE VALLEY

12 miles; at least a half to full day

Don't add to the traffic congestion by driving the heavily used one-way valley roads. Park at one of the lots along the shuttle bus route and take one of the free buses, which loops through the east end of the valley or elsewhere in the park. (See inset map on pp. 280-281.) You can also explore the valley on a rented bike or on foot. Or, buy a ticket for a 2-hour guided tram tour. (The open-air trams also venture out on moonlit nights and glide through the ghostly light that bathes the valley.)

If you're traveling by shuttle bus, get off at the **Valley Visitor Center** in **Yosemite Village,** where an award-winning film introduces Yosemite's history, grandeur, and geology. For an easy stroll in an oasis of quiet, look for **Cook's Meadow** just south of the visitor center. The trail begins at the west end of the mall; pick up a self-guiding brochure. Deer and humans sometimes encounter each other here. Keep your distance.

YOSEMITE

STANISLAUS NATIONAL FOREST

EMIGRANT WILDERNESS

HUMBOLDT-TOIYAB

HOOVER WILDERNESS

Emigrant Lake

Bond Pass 9,700 ft

Dorothy Lake

Mary Lake

Buckeye Pass 9,572 ft

Peeler L

W. Fork Cherry Cr.

Styx Pass 7,660 ft

Haystack Peak 10,003 ft

Tilden Lake

Rock Is. P. 10,160 ft

Cherry Cr.

Richardson Peak 9,877 ft

Kibbie Luke

Kendrick Cr.

Frog Cr.

Jack Main Canyon

Kerrick Canyon

Piute Mountain 10,541 ft

Piute Cr.

Benson Po 10,100 f

Cherry Lake

Lake LaurEleanor Lake

Lake Vernon

Tiltill Mt. 8,988 ft

Rancheria Cr.

Benson Lake

Pleasant Valley

Volunteer P 10,481 ft

Falls Cr.

PACIFIC CREST

Tiltill Cr.

Wapama Falls

Tiltill Valley

Rancheria Falls

Pettit Peak 10,788 ft

Virginia Lake

Waterwhe Falls

O'Shaughnessy Dam

Miguel Meadow

Hetch Hetchy

Smith Peak 7,751 ft

Hetch-Hetchy Reservoir

Rancheria Mt.

Grand Canyon of the Tuolumne River

NATIONAL

Tuolumne

Poopenaut Valley

YOSEMITE

Tuolumne

Hetch Hetchy Entrance

TOULUMNE NATIONAL WILD & SCENIC RIVER

Morrison Cr.

Mather

Bald Mountain 7,261 ft

White Wolf

Tuolumne Peak 10,845 ft

Aspen Valley

TIOGA RD.

Lukens Lake

Yosemite Cr.

Mt. Hoffmann 10,850 ft

May Lake

120

Big Oak Flat Entrance Information Station

120

S. Fk. Tuolumne

Yosemite Creek

Porcupine Flat

Olmsted Pt.

120

Tenaya Lake

Hodgdon Meadow

NATIONAL

Sunrise

BIG OAK FLAT ROAD

Tuolumne Grove

Cascade Cr.

Tamarack Cr.

Clouds Rest 9,926 ft

Merced Grove

Crane Flat

El Capitan 7,569 ft

Yosemite Falls

Yosemite Village

Half Dome 8,842 ft

Merced

Tamarack Flat

Tunnel View

Little Yosemite Valley

STANISLAUS NATIONAL FOREST

Moss Cr.

Arch Rock Entrance

Bridveil Falls

Yosemite Valley

Glacier Point 7,214 ft

PARK

Mt. Starr King 9,092 ft

Mount Clo 11,522

EL PORTAL RD.

Grouse Cr.

GLACIER POINT ROAD

Merced

140

El Portal

Summit Meadow

Mono Meadow

Yosemite West

Badger Pass Ski Area

Bridalveil Creek

Illilouette Cr.

WAWONA RD.

MERCED NATIONAL WILD & SCENIC RIVER

Westfall Meadows

Ostrander Lake

Ostrander Ski Hut

Horse Ridge

Merced Pass 9,300 ft

South Fork Merced

Alder Cr.

Chilnualna Cr.

Buena Vista Crest

Buena Vista Pk. 9,709 ft

Moraine Mountain 9,776 ft

SIERRA NATIONAL FOREST

Turner Ridge

Crescent Lake

Wawona Dome 6,897 ft

Chiquito Pass 8,060 ft

140

Pioneer Yosemite History Center

Wawona

Wawona Information Station

0 miles 10
0 kilometers 15

41

South Entrance

Mariposa Grove

Walk around the nearby Indian Village, where exhibits and bark houses evoke the life of the valley's earlier dwellers. Visit the **Indian Cultural Museum** to see the baskets and other works of art produced by Yosemite area tribes.

At the bustling village shops you can find just about what you would find in any resort-town mall. But if you want to see the park, don't tarry here.

Get back on the bus and travel to the **Yosemite Falls** shuttle bus stop. The upper, middle, and lower falls form the highest waterfall in North America (2,425 feet) and the fifth tallest in the world. A 1-mile wheelchair accessible walk takes you to the base of **Lower Yosemite Fall.** If you have the stamina and another full day, take the strenuous 3.6-mile hike to **Upper Yosemite Fall,** where you will be rewarded with spectacular valley views away from the crowds. (Look for the trailhead across from shuttle stop 7.)

Reboard the bus, and crane your neck for other scenic wonders. Get off when you want to absorb them; you will not have to wait long for another bus. Alight at the stop near the **Happy Isles Nature Center.** After a walk around these two bridge-linked river islands, consider hiking the moderately strenuous 1.5-mile trail to the top of 317-foot **Vernal Fall.** From higher up this trail, you can see **Nevada Fall** with its 594-foot cascade.

A gentle hike from the next shuttle bus stop takes you to lovely **Mirror Lake** a mile away; there a 5-mile trail loops around it and above it *(Note: As of this printing, the loop trail is closed following a rockfall; visitors can walk 2 miles of the trail and then return.)* In spring and early summer, the lake's serene surface reflects stunning mountain scenery; during the summer, most of its contents

YOSEMITE

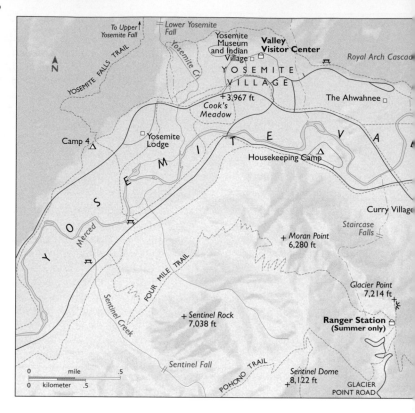

evaporate. Massive **Half Dome,** a cracked block of gray granite gnawed by a glacier, soars 4,788 feet above the valley floor, its sheer face dominating this part of the valley.

As the shuttle turns back toward Yosemite Village, you'll pass the **Royal Arches,** glacier-carved granite shells. You will see the full spectrum of Yosemite accommodations along the shuttle bus route: from tents, RV sites, and clusters of concrete shelters to comfortable lodges, cabins, and a 1927 luxury hotel—the Ahwahnee.

GLACIER POINT & MARIPOSA GROVE

52 miles one way; a half to full day

Leave the valley by taking Calif. 41 (the Wawona Road) to the **Wawona**

Tunnel. Park at the turnout at the tunnel's eastern end and walk over to the **Tunnel View** to see what has been called the most photographed vista on Earth. Opening out before you is a granite panorama which encompasses El Capitan, Half Dome, Sentinel Rock, **Cathedral Rocks,** and 620-foot **Bridalveil Fall,** in the late afternoon a scrim of shimmering rainbows.

On the 3,593-foot vertical wall of **El Capitan** you may spot tiny figures of climbers. During their ascent, which may take days, they sleep in slings hanging from the cliff.

About 7 miles beyond the tunnel, turn left on **Glacier Point Road.** This 16-mile road, flanked by fir-and-pine forests, terminates in a small parking lot. Walk about 300 yards to the first of several overlooks on Glacier Point, which thrusts 3,214 feet above

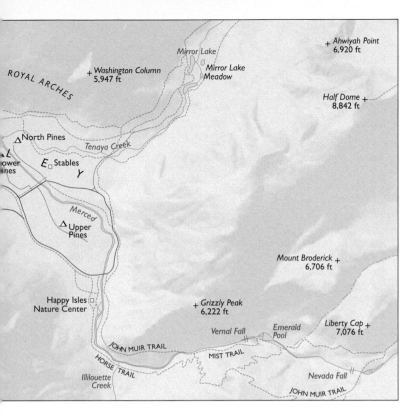

the valley, providing an enormous stage for a spectacular scene of lights and shadows. Mirror Lake lies below; Half Dome looms across; Vernal Fall and Nevada Fall hang like white tassels in the distance. An arduous hike up **Four Mile Trail** takes you in 3 or 4 hours to Glacier Point's breathtaking vistas; the El Capitan bus drops visitors at the Four Mile Trailhead.

Return to the intersection of Calif. 41 and drive south 13 miles to **Wawona,** site of a hotel, golf course, and other facilities. Stop at the **Pioneer Yosemite History Center,** where, in summer, visitors can enter restored buildings and chat about the past with costumed interpreters who portray such real people as a cavalry trooper, a 19th-century homesteader, and a mountaineer. From conversations with

these players you'll learn Yosemite Valley's recent history, which, according to legend, began in 1851 when members of the Mariposa Battalion were tracking down Indians accused of raiding nearby trading posts.

Word of the radiantly beautiful valley spread quickly, and the

Gaylor Lakes area of the park

first tourists arrived in 1855. They were soon followed by homesteaders and hotelkeepers. Next came the nation's early conservationists, who campaigned to protect not only the valley but also a grove of giant sequoias.

On June 30, 1864, President Lincoln took time out from the Civil War to sign a bill granting both the valley and this grove to the state of California. It was a momentous occasion: never before had a nation set aside land as a wilderness preserve. Yosemite became a national park in 1890, although not until 1906 did California formally give the original grants back to the federal government. More land was added in 1913, the year automobiles were again allowed to enter the park after a ban.

Return to Calif. 41 and continue south. Near the **South Entrance** continue straight to Yosemite's other long-cherished feature, the **Mariposa Grove** (shuttle bus recommended from Wawona). From early May to late October you can take a guided tram tour of the grove's giant sequoias *($11 adult, $5.50 child)*. Or, you can walk among them at any time of year.

The best known of the grove's more than 200 giant sequoias is the **Grizzly Giant,** whose estimated age, around 1,500 years, makes it one of the oldest living sequoias. A trail takes you past the **Fallen Monarch;** its shallow roots help explain why winds sometimes topple these giants.

Another fallen star, the **Wawona Tunnel Tree,** recalls another era. The living sequoia, gutted in 1881 to make a drive-through tree for horse-drawn wagons, became a photogenic attraction for generations of automobile travelers. The tree toppled in 1969. The decision not to cut a hole in another tree symbolized the dawning of an ecologically enlightened age.

TIOGA ROAD & TUOLUMNE MEADOWS

124 miles round-trip; at least a full day

Take the **Big Oak Flat Road,** a modern version of an old mining town road, west out of the valley for 9 miles to 6,200-foot **Crane Flat** (a local term for "meadow"). Turn right onto **Tioga Road,** which climbs into an alpine world of snowy peaks, crystal lakes, wind-tousled meadows, and relatively few people. The road (closed in winter) crosses the park. Even in July you may see snow alongside the road. Stop at the frequent turnouts for magnificent views and interpretive signs that explain the geology behind the splendor.

Gauge your time and gasoline. Beyond Crane Flat, the nearest gas station on this winding, climbing mountain road is 1 mile east of the **Tuolumne Meadows Visitor Center,** 55 miles from **Yosemite Valley.**

Millions of years ago the Tuolumne Meadows were under a sea of ice more than 2,000 feet deep. Wildflowers—among them Jeffrey shooting stars, Indian paintbrushes, monkeyflowers, and marsh marigolds—carpet this High Sierra realm in spring and summer. Trails of varying difficulty branch out here and elsewhere along the road. Some trails link five commercially run High Sierra camps with showers and dining halls. (Reservations required. See Information & Activities p. 284.) The camps are spaced 8 to 10 miles apart to accommodate the modest hiker.

One of the paths here is a segment of the **Pacific Crest National Scenic Trail** north of the meadows. It goes down toward the steep Grand Canyon of the Tuolumne River.

Back on Tioga Road, you'll climb to 9,945-foot **Tioga Pass,** the highest automobile pass in California. At a trailhead here you can take a half-day alpine hike that rewards you with glimpses of both beauty and history.

The 2.5-mile trail climbs sharply from 9,945 feet to about 10,500, then descends to **Middle Gaylor Lake,** a gem set in a broad meadow prowled by marmots and Belding ground squirrels. The trail again winds upward, first to **Upper Gaylor Lake,** then to a surprise: the ruins of a stone cabin, rusting bits of machinery, and half-filled shafts—relics of a failed 19th-century silver mine.

YOSEMITE

California poppy *(top left)*; California spotted owl *(top right)*; Yosemite Valley spring flowers *(bottom)*

INFORMATION & ACTIVITIES

VISITOR & INFORMATION CENTERS

Valley Visitor Center open all year. **Tuolumne Meadows Visitor Center** near Tioga Pass Entrance open summer only. Information also available at **Happy Isles Nature Center,** in valley, and **Big Oak Flat Entrance** on Calif. 120 at western edge of park, both open spring through fall; and **Wawona Information Station,** open summer through fall.

SEASONS & ACCESSIBILITY

Open all year. Tioga (Calif. 120 east) and Glacier Point Roads closed from about mid-Nov. to late May. Call (209) 372-0200 for recorded conditions. In winter, call (209) 372-1000 for Badger Pass ski information. Free shuttle buses operate in the valley year-round and at Wawona and Tuolumne Meadows in summer.

HEADQUARTERS

P.O. Box 577, Yosemite National Park, CA 95389. Phone (209) 372-0200. www.nps.gov/yose

ENTRANCE FEE

$20 per vehicle for one week.

PETS

Not permitted in buildings, backcountry, trails, except paved trails. Kennel available.

ACCESSIBLE SERVICES

Visitor centers, the nature and art centers, and some trails are wheelchair accessible. Free brochure.

THINGS TO DO

Free naturalist-led activities: day and evening walks, talks, hikes, children's programs, living history; cultural interpretation. Auto tours, bus and tram tours, concerts, art and photography classes, museums, horseback riding—call (209) 372-8348. Climbing, fishing, swimming, ice skating, skiing.

OVERNIGHT BACKPACKING

Free permit required; issued first come, first served; apply up to 24 hours in advance of trip to a park wilderness permit station. Advance reservations available by mail ($5 service fee); write wilderness office at park address. Call (209) 372-0200 for more information. Overnight backpacking permits can be requested online at www.nps.gov/yose.

CAMPGROUNDS

Thirteen campgrounds; in summer, 7-day to 14-day limits; other times vary limits. Seasons vary, check for specific sites. Reservations through the NRRS (see p. 10) required year-round for all in the valley, except Camp 4; for **Hodgdon Meadow** spring through fall; and for **Crane Flat** and half of **Tuolumne Meadows** in summer. Fees $10-$20 per night. Most have RV sites, without hookups. Four group campgrounds. Reservations can be made at www.recreation.gov or by calling (877) 444-6777.

HOTELS, MOTELS, & INNS

(unless otherwise noted, rates are for 2 persons in a double room, high season)

INSIDE THE PARK:
DNC Parks & Resorts at Yosemite, Inc., 6671 N. Palm Ave., Fresno, CA 93704, operates the following accommodations. Reservations: (801) 559-4949 or online at www.yosemitepark.com.
The Ahwahnee (Yosemite Valley) 123 units. $339-$1,106. AC, pool, restaurant.
Curry Village (Yosemite Valley) 71 cabins, 414 tent-cabins, 18 stoneman rooms. $39-$168. Pool, restaurant.
High Sierra Camps 6 camps with a total of 204 tent-cabins. Accessible by hiking trail only. Guided trips available. $151 per person incl. breakfast, dinner. Late June to Labor Day (opening dates may vary). Reserve online Sept. through Nov.
Tuolumne Meadows Lodge (8,775 feet, at Tuolumne Meadows) 69 tent-cabins, central showers. $107. Rest. Open mid-June–mid-Sept. (opening dates may vary).
Wawona Hotel (Calif. 41, 41 miles south of Yosemite valley) (209) 375-6556. 104 rooms, 50 private baths. $99-$217. Restaurant.
White Wolf Inn (Tioga Rd.) (801) 559-4884) 14 cabins, private baths; 24 tent-cabins, central bath. $99-$115. Restaurant. Open summer.
Yosemite Lodge at the Falls (Yosemite Valley) 245 rooms. $99-$208. Pool, restaurant.

EXCURSIONS

STANISLAUS NATIONAL FOREST
SONORA, CALIFORNIA

This High Sierra forest offers an array of activities—from white-water rafting on the Tuolumne River to trout fishing on Alpine Lake. Contains parts of three wilderness areas. 898,322 acres. Hiking, boating, horseback riding, off-road-vehicle routes, scenic drives, winter sports. 1,450 campsites, boat ramp. Open all year; backcountry generally open June–Oct. Most campsites open May–Oct. Adjoins Yosemite NP on north and west. Information office, 19777 Greenley Rd. (off Calif. 108), Sonora. (209) 532-3671.

DEVILS POSTPILE NATIONAL MONUMENT
MAMMOTH LAKES, CALIFORNIA

2011 marked the 100th anniversary of Devils Postpile NM—Pres. William H. Taft signed it into existence on July 6, 1911. Surrounded by the Inyo National Forest, this monument boasts a spectacular formation of 60-foot-high basalt columns born of volcanic fire and carved by the ice of overriding glaciers. At Rainbow Falls, water plunges 101 feet over a rhyodacite cliff. 798 acres. Hiking, fishing, shuttle bus. 21 campsites. Open mid-June–mid-Oct. Off Calif. 203 about 40 miles from Yosemite NP. (760) 934-2289.

SIERRA NATIONAL FOREST
MARIPOSA, CALIFORNIA

Sierra offers both rugged backcountry and developed recreational facilities. Contains parts of five wilderness areas, Kings River white water, groves of sequoias, and 11 major reservoirs. 1,303,037 acres. Hiking, boating, bicycling, fishing, horseback riding, picnic areas, winter sports. 1,500 campsites, boat ramps, handicapped access. Open all year; some areas closed in winter. Most campsites open May–Oct. Adjoins Yosemite NP. Office at 1600 Toll House Rd., Clovis. (559) 297-0706.

YOSEMITE

THE ROCKY MOUNTAINS

THE ROCKY MOUNTAINS

Craggy peaks capped by glimmering glaciers, fields run riot with wildflowers, lakes as smooth and blue as a summer sky—these images from the Rocky Mountains epitomize for many just what a national park should look like.

Yet this region offers more than mountains, since the forces that created the peaks contoured neighboring landscapes as well. The Black Hills of South Dakota uplifted along with the Rocky Mountains some 70 million years ago, cracking as they buckled upward. Enlarged by acidic ground-water, the cracks eventually produced the numerous underground passageways of Wind Cave. Streams flowing from the young Rockies also laid down the colorful mud that rivers would later carve into the buttes and gorges of the Dakota badlands, showcased in Badlands and Theodore Roosevelt National Parks. To the south the wind eroded the peaks and created the dunes in Great Sand Dunes National Park and Preserve, and water continues to carve the gorge in Black Canyon of the Gunnison National Park.

The Rockies' parks preserve the spirit of America's frontier in their rugged scenery and abundance of wildlife. Yellowstone and Waterton-Glacier—together with surrounding public lands—remain a stronghold of the grizzly bear. In some of the parks visitors can watch elk, bighorn sheep, mule deer, and remnants of the great bison herds that once thundered across the plains.

Rockies parks provide case studies in how wilderness manages itself. In Yellowstone, for instance, the visitor can get excellent glimpses of natural recovery in the wake of forest fires. Less encouraging are the real estate development and plans for industry on the fringes of some parks. Such activities can shrink the habitats of wide-roaming animals, endangering their future.

The Rocky Mountain region invites the visitor to experience peaks along the Continental Divide, plus geysers, prairies, caverns, badlands, sand dunes—and lots of driving. Count on a drive of 520 miles from Rocky Mountain National Park to Grand Teton and nearly 400 miles from Yellowstone to Waterton-Glacier.

THE ROCKY MOUNTAINS

Tortuous landforms of Badlands National Park

▶ BADLANDS

SOUTH DAKOTA
ESTABLISHED NOVEMBER 10, 1978
244,300 acres

They call it The Wall. It extends for a hundred miles through the dry plains of South Dakota—a huge natural barrier ridging the landscape, sculptured into fantastic pinnacles and tortuous gullies by the forces of water. Those who pass through the upper prairie a few miles north might not even know it exists. Those who traverse the lower prairie to the south, however, can't miss it; it rises above them like a city skyline in ruins, petrified.

The Badlands Wall, much of which is preserved within the boundaries of Badlands National Park, may not conform to everyone's idea of beauty, but nobody can deny its theatricality. It's been compared to an enormous stage set—colorful, dramatic, and not quite real. Water, the main player on this stage, has been carving away at the cliffs for the past half million years or so, and it carves away an entire inch or more in some places each year. But

there have been other players, too. Beasts with names like titanothere and archaeotherium once roamed here; their fossilized bones can be found by the hundreds. And today the Badlands Wall serves as a back-drop for bison, pronghorn, and big-horn sheep, as well as the million human visitors who pass through the park every year.

A national monument since 1939, Badlands acquired the South (Stronghold) Unit in 1976, adding yet another dimension to the drama. This large stretch of land belongs to the Oglala, and one of their most sacred places is now preserved within it. It was here, on Stronghold Table, that the final Ghost Dance took place in 1890, just a few weeks before more than 150 Lakota were massacred at Wounded Knee, 25 miles south.

How to Get There
The park is about 3 miles south of I-90 at S. Dak. 240, 75 miles east of Rapid City and 27 miles west of Kadoka. Airport: Rapid City.

When to Go
All-year park. Summer is the most popular season, though daytime temperatures may top 100°F. Spring and fall are usually pleasant, with moderate temperatures and fewer crowds. Winters can be bitterly cold, but snow accumulations are rarely a problem in this arid climate.

How to Visit
The 30-mile **Badlands Loop** provides a rich eyeful of classic badlands for a 1-day **North Unit** visit (a shorter loop can be devised as described below). Make sure to take advantage of the informative nature trails. For those with a second day and a pioneering spirit, a trip to the park's undeveloped **South Unit** can be rewarding; don't fail to check with rangers about road conditions before going.

BADLANDS LOOP ROAD—NORTH UNIT
32 or 89 miles; a half or full day

Enter the park at the **Northeast Entrance** off S. Dak. 240 and stop at the **Big Badlands Overlook** for your first view of **The Wall** from above. Before you are the characteristic tiered cliffs of the badlands, drop-ping sharply to the lower prairie, where the **White River** meanders between a fringe of cottonwoods.

Stop next at the **Windows Overlook** the trailhead for three short nature walks—each of which is highlighted by exhibits and/or wayfinding markers. While these trails may sound like the components of an architectural tour, they are actually brief forays into the Badlands Wall. The **Door Trail** (0.4 mile round-trip, boardwalk) passes through a narrow opening in The Wall into a jumble of barren, eroded hills reminiscent of the lunar surface. The **Window Trail** (0.1 mile round-trip, paved) leads to a natural window overlooking a deeply cut canyon. And the rough **Notch Trail** (1.5 miles round-trip) leads up a ladder and along the side of a gully to a break in The Wall, where you can look out over prairie and badlands, the White River, and the Pine Ridge Reservation on the plain below.

Back in the car, a short drive brings you to the head of the **Cliff Shelf Nature Trail.** This half-mile, steep loop takes you through a fascinating microenvironment in the badlands. For many years, a giant block of stone has been slipping from the surrounding cliffs, creating this relatively flat shelf. This dynamic process has compacted the stone, making it less porous and allowing water to collect here. The resulting vegetation makes this place a delightful oasis in the otherwise barren wall. You can see mule deer browsing at dawn or dusk, and flamboyant magpies careering across the sky anytime.

Stop next at the **Ben Reifel Visitor Center,** where a video and various exhibits provide a good introduction to the park's history and geology. From this point, the road descends to the lower prairie for a brief stretch and then begins a

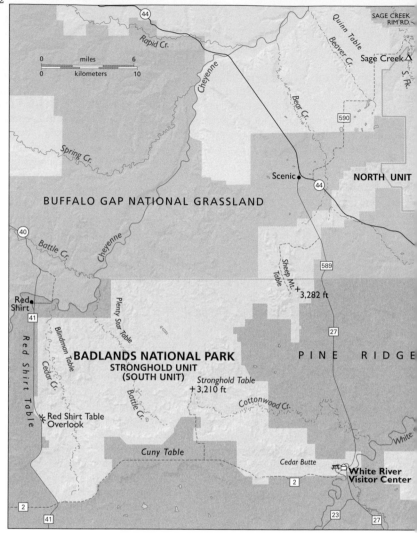

gradual, stunning climb back up the Badlands Wall. The **Fossil Exhibit Trail** takes you on a quarter-mile paved trail through an area dense with fossils. Casts of some are displayed at trailside.

At mile marker 17 the accessible **Prairie Winds Trail** (150 feet, boardwalk) features a restoration of native prairie plants. The road then continues level punctuated by a dozen or so pullouts each offering a slightly different perspective on the knife-sharp ridges, twisted canyons,

and multicolored hills that characterize this broken terrain. Spectacular among these are the **Yellow Mounds** and **Pinnacles Overlooks.** The later with its views into the Badlands Wilderness Area and bighorn sheep viewing (accessible by steep stairs).

If you're short of time, exit the park at this point and rejoin the interstate at the town of Wall. Otherwise make a left turn onto Sage Creek Rim Road and continue along the **Sage Creek Unit** of the **Badlands Wilderness.** This is excellent wildlife

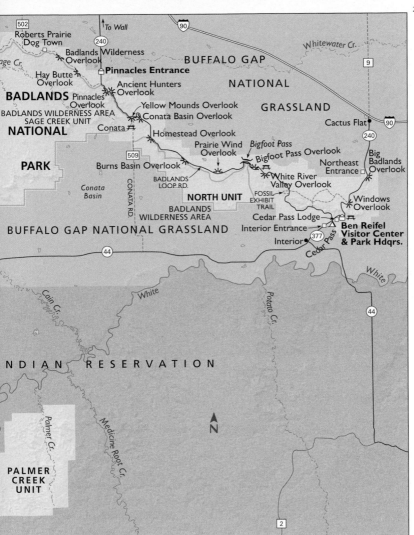

country; bison and pronghorn are numerous, and the road passes a town of those always entertaining prairie dogs. Longer hikes into the wilderness area start at the primitive campground about a mile off the road near the park's western boundary.

Beyond the campground turnoff, the road leaves the park. To complete the loop, continue along unpaved County Road 590 and make a left (south) onto S. Dak. 44. If you're heading toward Rapid City, turn

right; this stretch takes you through beautiful **Cheyenne River Valley** prairie and gives you views of the Black Hills. The highway goes through Scenic, the turnoff for the **South Unit,** if you want to continue directly there.

SOUTH UNIT DRIVE
about 45 miles; at least a half day

The South Unit is almost entirely undeveloped, so exploring it by car

Buffalo grazing on prairie grasses

will involve backtracking, driving on rough dirt roads, and putting a lot of wear and tear on your vehicle. For your safety, be sure to check with a ranger before setting out.

Begin in the town of **Scenic,** with its automobile graveyard and shanty-like saloon, and go south on County Road 589 for 4 miles. The turnoff for **Sheep Mountain Table** is marked. Follow the road across the flats and up a seemingly impregnable cliff to a grass-topped table dotted with yuccas. If you go to the juniper grove at the road's end, you can stand on a finger of high land and be almost surrounded by a stunning assort-ment of rock spires and pinnacles—perhaps the park's best view.

Return to the paved road and con-tinue south for 16 miles until you arrive at the **White River Visitor Center** (open summer). It is operated by the Oglala Tribe and offers exhibits on Indian culture and a video. Here you

can also get detailed directions to the many other sites worth visiting in the South Unit.

A visit to the **Stronghold Table** will either be a disappointment or the emotional culmination of your visit, depending on your perspective and imagination. Getting there involves driving some extremely rutted tracks through lonely grasslands, where you will probably get lost (bring along a topographical map). It also involves opening and closing many gates. The reward for this effort? An unspectacu-lar view, but the chance to stand in the place where, in December 1890, a group of Sioux danced the Ghost Dance for the last time. In this impas-sioned ritual, dancers fell into hypnotic trances, "died," and envisioned the paradise soon to come, sweeping the white man from the land and repopu-lating it with bison, elk, and prong-horn. If you go there, keep in mind that for Indians this is a sacred place.

INFORMATION & ACTIVITIES

VISITOR & INFORMATION CENTERS
Ben Reifel Visitor Center, in the North Unit, open daily all year.
White River Visitor Center, in the South Unit, open only in summer.

SEASONS & ACCESSIBILITY
Park open year-round. Snowstorms may block roads temporarily in winter. Call park headquarters to check on current road and weather conditions and accessibility to the undeveloped South Unit.

HEADQUARTERS
Interior, SD 57750. Phone (605) 433-5361. www.nps.gov/badl

ENTRANCE FEE
$15 per car.

PETS
Permitted on leashes in developed areas like roads, campgrounds, and parking lots, except in the Sage Creek Unit of Badlands Wilderness. Not permitted on trails.

ACCESSIBLE SERVICES
Visitor centers and some trails are wheelchair accessible. Free brochure available.

THINGS TO DO
Free naturalist-led activities during summer: nature walks and hikes, evening programs, night walks, fossil demonstrations. Also, interpretive exhibits and audiovisual programs, hiking, wildlife-watching.

SPECIAL ADVISORIES
• Prairie rattlesnakes and cactuses live here: Watch where you step when walking.
• Bison are unpredictable and can be dangerous: Keep your distance.
• Be prepared for sudden changes in weather and severe thunderstorms in summer. Check weather conditions by contacting headquarters or a visitor center before you hike.

OVERNIGHT BACKPACKING
No permit required; ask a ranger for advisories. Registries available at several locations and the visitor center.

CAMPGROUNDS
Two campgrounds, both with a 14-day limit. **Sage Creek** rarely fills up and is open all year, first come, first served; no fee. **Cedar Pass** is run by Forever Resorts (605) 433-5460; fee is $15 per night; $28 per night for sites with electrical hook-ups. (Heavy snows may close campsites in winter.)

HOTELS, MOTELS, & INNS
(unless otherwise noted, rates are for 2 persons in a double room, high season)

INSIDE THE PARK:
Cedar Pass Lodge 20681 S. Dak. 240 (near visitor center), Interior, SD 57750. (605) 433-5460. 22 cabins. $85-$115. AC, restaurant. Mid-April–mid-Oct.

OUTSIDE THE PARK:
In Interior, SD 57750:
Badlands Inn (half mile from park entrance) P.O. Box 103. (605) 433-5401. 25 units. $95. AC. Mid-May–Labor Day.

In Wall, SD 57790:
Best Western Plains Motel (1.5 blocks off I-90) 712 Glenn St., P.O. Box 393. (800) 528-1234 or (605) 279-2145. 74 units. $95-$125. AC, pool. March through Nov.
Motel 6 Tenth Ave., P.O. Box 76. (605) 279-2133. 41 units. $66. AC, pool.
Sunshine Inn 608 Main St. (800) 782-2613 or (605) 279-2179. 26 units. $71. AC.
Walls Econolodge 804 Glenn St., P.O. Box 426. (605) 279-2121. 49 units. $100. AC, pool. May through Oct.

For additional accommodations, contact the Wall Chamber of Commerce, P.O. Box 527, Wall, SD 57790. (888) 852-9255 or (605) 279-2665, www.wall-badlands.com.

BADLANDS

Sheer canyon walls of the South Rim of Black Canyon

▶ BLACK CANYON OF THE GUNNISON

COLORADO
ESTABLISHED OCTOBER 21, 1999
30,750 acres

Sheer walls of dark gray stone rise more than 2,700 feet above the swift and turbulent Gunnison River to create one of the most dramatic canyons in the country. Deeper than it is wide in some places, this great slit in the Earth is so narrow that sunlight penetrates to the bottom only at midday. The park protects the deepest, most thrilling 14 miles of the gorge, about 75 miles upstream of the Gunnison's junction with the Colorado River.

Imagine chiseling two parallel walls of hard gneiss and schist running the length of Manhattan and standing higher than two Empire State Buildings stacked atop one another, with water as your only tool. At the inconceivable rate of 1 inch per century, it would take all of human history just to cut through 5 feet of rock. What you see from the rim is the product of two million years of patient work.

The metamorphic rocks exposed at the bottom of the canyon are nearly two billion years old, dating from the Precambrian or oldest era of the Earth. Here and there swirling pink veins of igneous pegmatite shoot through the walls, livening up the canyon's somber appearance.

Indians and white explorers generally avoided the formidable canyon up through the 19th century. In 1900, five men attempted to run the river in wooden boats to survey it as a possible source of irrigation for the Uncompahgre Valley. After a month, with their boats in splinters and their supplies gone, they gave up. But the next year two men ran it in ten days on rubber air mattresses. A water diversion tunnel was soon in the works; the four-year project, dedicated in 1909, resulted in a 6-mile-long tunnel through rock, clay, and sand. The labor was so grueling and dangerous that the average period of employment was only two weeks. Today, three dams upstream have further tamed the Gunnison, but the canyon and its section of river remain wild.

Rim drives and hikes offer plenty of opportunities for peering into the magnificent canyon and marveling at its cliffs and towers of stone. Ravens, golden eagles, and peregrine falcons soar the great gulf of air out in front. On top grows a thick forest of Gambel oak and serviceberry, which provide cover for mule deer and black bears, while farther down the canyon Douglas firs thrive in the shade, and cottonwoods and box elders find footholds along the river.

How to Get There

The South Rim is located 15 miles northeast of Montrose, via US 50 and Colo. 347. The North Rim is 80 miles by car from the South Rim, via US 50W and Colo. 92. Turn south off Colo. 92 onto the 15-mile park road, the first half of which is paved. Airports: Montrose and Gunnison.

When to Go

Summer is the most popular time to visit. But be prepared to perspire if you hike at midday on exposed trails, and bring lots of water. Crisp days in late spring and early fall make for excellent walks. Winter affords opportunities for backcountry camping, cross-country skiing, and snowshoeing. With the rim at 8,000 feet above sea level, winter can set in as early as November and last until April. Snow closes vehicle access to the North Rim; the South Rim road stays open as far as the second overlook year-round.

How to Visit

You can spend most of the day driving the 7-mile (one-way) **South Rim** and exploring its 5 or so miles of trails. The very hardy may want to walk down to the canyon floor. If you have more time, visit the **North Rim** and its 5-mile unpaved drive.

SOUTH RIM

Rim Drive, 7 miles one way; 2 to 3 hours

With a dozen scenic overlooks and several short trails, this dramatic drive offers plenty of topside angles on the canyon and river. The first overlook, **Tomichi Point,** allows access to the **Rim Rock Trail,** which

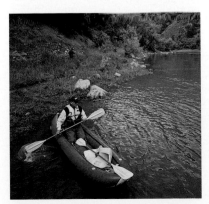
Fly fisherman in inflatable kayak on the Gunnison

runs north-south for about a mile
between the campground and the
visitor center. This trail gives you
fine views of the vertiginous walls
of the eastern part of the canyon
and the glinting ribbon of water
sluicing down its middle. You walk
through a scrubby forest of Gambel
oak and sagebrush, studded with
pinyon pine and juniper. The latter
has dark purple berries and a cedary
look and smell. Breathe in the
refreshing air; look for tracks
of elk, bobcat, mountain lion, and
other rim dwellers; and listen for
the scold of Steller's jays.

Make a 2-mile loop by following
the **Uplands Trail** across the road.
Continue up through scrub oak forest before walking past the visitor
center and rejoining the Rim Rock
Trail. At the **visitor center,** exhibits
on the park's geology, history, flora,
and fauna will help get you started.

Just outside the visitor center you
can take the invigorating **Oak Flat
Trail,** which makes a loop of about
2 miles and gets you a little way
below the rim. Head west, then turn
right at the River Access sign and
dip into a grove of aspens. At the
next junction, turn left and wind
through a thicket of scrub oak to
an outcrop with a good view. Circle
back through a forest of aspen and
Douglas fir.

One of the shortest ways to the
canyon floor is the **Gunnison Route,**
off the Oak Flat Trail. It's a mere
mile to the river, but it's a tough
one—even for those in good shape,
the walk down takes at least an
hour. Since most of the canyon
is a designated wilderness, hikers
end up following drainage gullies,
which plunge 1,800 vertical feet over
scree slopes littered with big rocks.
To avoid ankle injuries in some
places, crouch and slide; a mounted

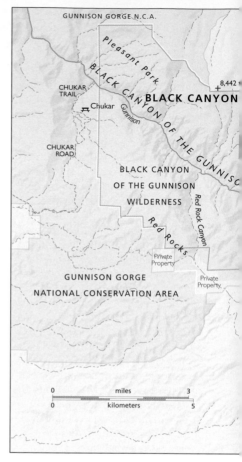

80-foot-long chain helps out on
one stretch, but the rest is a wild
free-for-all. At the bottom, rest
and massage your legs, staring up
at the spectacular stonework all
around. The walk back up—at times
a hand-over-hand pull—is harder
than the downhill.

Back on the road, continue driving northwest. The aptly named
Pulpit Rock offers a terrific long view
of the river knifing its way through
the canyon. A walk out to **Chasm
View** takes you to within about
1,100 feet of the North Rim, on
the opposite side of the canyon.
At this point, the canyon's 1,800-
foot depth exceeds its width, and
it looks extremely narrow. But the

narrowness is a result of the river's precipitous angle and its high volume. You're left with a sense of something newly created, which in geological terms is true.

The road now bends southwest. Several pull-offs provide views of the magnificent **Painted Wall,** a 2,250-foot sheer cliff decorated with stripes and flourishes of pink and white crystalline pegmatite, an extrusion of magma that seeped into cracks and hardened. Take the **Cedar Point Nature Trail,** an easy 0.6-mile out-and-back, to views of the wall, the river, and islands of stone rising from the canyon depths.

Drive on to **High Point,** the end of the road and, at 8,289 feet, one

of the highest places on the rim. From here it is a dizzying 2,689-foot drop to the river. You can take a 1.5-mile round-trip walk out to **Warner Point** for exquisite canyon views to the north. When you turn to the south you can see the verdant farmlands of the Uncompahgre Valley irrigated by water diverted from the canyon's own Gunnison River. Beyond rise the San Juan Mountains. The trail meanders among pinyon pine, juniper, mountain mahogany, and white-flowering serviceberry. Other plants scattered about include Fendler bush, mule's ear, lupine, and scarlet gilia, the last bearing lovely tubular flowers.

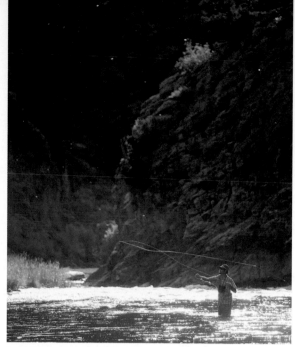

Trout fisherman casting his line in the Gunnison River

NORTH RIM

Rim Drive (unpaved), 5 miles one way; 2 to 3 hours

While it is only 1,100 feet from one side of the canyon to the other, you must endure an 80-mile drive to reach the North Rim from the South Rim—the last several miles of it unpaved along Black Canyon Road. You can also reach the North Rim from the east side—a 90-mile drive on US 50 and Colo. 92 through the Curecanti National Recreation Area. On the North Rim, you'll find yourself in a remote and awesome wilderness where the canyon walls plunge nearly vertically.

Whichever way you come, leave Colo. 92 at Black Canyon Road and follow it to the end. Turn right and drive to the ranger station, where one of the finest hikes in the park begins. The **North Vista Trail** wanders in and out of scrub forest along the rim for 1.5 miles. Detour at **Exclamation Point** for a jaw-dropping look into the canyon's depths. Turn around, or continue 2 more miles to trail's end on Green Mountain. This difficult section climbs from 7,702 feet to 8,563 feet. Here stirring panoramas surround—starting to the west with the Uncompahgre Plateau; turning north, the Grand Mesa; continuing east, the West Elk Mountains; and finally to the south, the San Juan Mountains.

Once back at the ranger station, drive about a mile south and get out for the short **Chasm View Nature Trail,** which meanders through a pinyon-juniper forest and comes out at two stunning overlooks. White-throated swifts and violet-green swallows dart from cliffside nests. The southern 4 miles of the drive zigzag along the canyon's rim. At **Balanced Rock View** and **Kneeling Camel View,** near the end of the drive, steep unmarked routes wind down side canyons to the river.

INFORMATION & ACTIVITIES

VISITOR & INFORMATION CENTERS

Visitor center open daily except holidays in winter. **North Rim Ranger Station** open in summer only.

SEASONS & ACCESSIBILITY

South Rim open daily, limited access in winter; North Rim Road and Ranger Station closed in winter. Contact park for current information.

HEADQUARTERS

102 Elk Creek, Gunnison, CO 81230. Phone (970) 641-2337. www.nps.gov/blca

ENTRANCE FEE

$15 per vehicle per week; yearly fee $30.

PETS

Pets allowed in park on leash; not allowed on trails or in backcountry.

ACCESSIBLE SERVICES

South Rim: visitor center, comfort stations, 2 camping sites; and Tomichi Point, Chasm View, and Sunset View overlooks. **North Rim:** Balanced Rock overlook accessible.

THINGS TO DO

Free naturalist-led activities. Exhibits, scenic drives, hiking, fishing, kayaking, rock climbing, winter activities.

SPECIAL ADVISORY

• Permits required for all inner canyon routes; available at visitor center and North Rim Ranger Station.

OVERNIGHT BACKPACKING

Backcountry permits required. Wood fires prohibited; use camp stoves only.

CAMPGROUNDS

South Rim: 88 sites; **North Rim:** 13 sites. Auto campgrounds $12-$18 per night. All sites first come, first served, usually available. Vault toilets, limited water, no hookups.

For accommodations, contact the Montrose Visitors & Convention Bureau, (800) 923-5515 or (970) 249-5000; and the Gunnison Country Chamber of Commerce, (970) 641-1501, www .visitmontrose.net.

View of the Painted Wall in Black Canyon

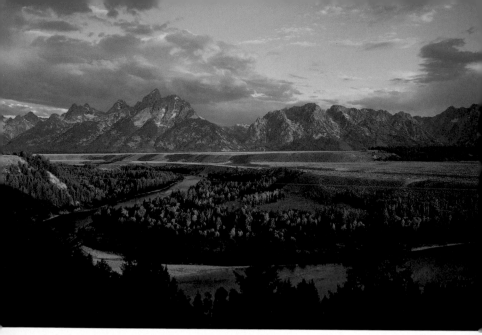

Snake River meandering through Jackson Hole toward the Tetons

▶ GRAND TETON

WYOMING
ESTABLISHED FEBRUARY 26, 1929
309,994 acres

The peaks of the Teton Range, regal and imposing as they stand nearly 7,000 feet above the valley floor, make one of the boldest geologic statements in the Rockies. Unencumbered by foothills, they rise through steep coniferous forest into alpine meadows strewn with wildflowers, past blue and white glaciers to naked granite pinnacles. The Grand, Middle, and South Tetons form the heart of the range. But their neighbors, especially Mount Owen, Teewinot Mountain, and Mount Moran, are no less spectacular.

A string of jewel-like lakes, fed by mountain streams, are set tightly against the steep foot of the mountains. Beyond them extends the broad valley called Jackson Hole, covered with sagebrush and punctuated by occasional forested buttes and groves of aspen trees— excellent habitats for pronghorn, deer, elk, and other animals. The Snake River, having begun its journey in southern Yellowstone National Park near the Teton Wilderness, winds leisurely past the Tetons on its way to Idaho. The braided sections of the river create wetlands that support moose, elk, deer, beaver, trumpeter swans, sandhill cranes, Canada geese, and all sorts of ducks.

The Tetons are normal fault-block mountains. About 13 million years ago, two blocks of Earth's crust began to shift along a fault line, one tilting down while the other lifted up. So far, movement has measured some 30,000 vertical feet, most of it from the subsidence of Jackson Hole.

Before Europeans arrived, the Teton area was an important plant-gathering and hunting ground for Indians of various tribes. In the early 1800s, mountain men spent time here; it was they who called this flat valley ringed by mountains Jackson's Hole after the trapper Davey Jackson. (In recent times the name has lost its apostrophe and s.) The first settlers were ranchers and farmers. Some of their buildings are historic sites today, although ranching is still practiced in the vicinity. When the park was established, it included only the mountains and the glacial lakes at their feet. Portions of the valley were added in 1950.

Today the park's 485 square miles encompass both the Teton Range and much of Jackson Hole. Park roads, all in the valley, offer an ever changing panorama of the Tetons. Most visitors never go far from the road. But the Tetons are popular with hikers; backcountry trails climb high into the mountains—and behind them. Easy trails in the valley lead around lakes and alongside wetlands where visitors may see moose, elk, deer, and all kinds of birds.

How to Get There

From Jackson, take US 26/89/191 north past the National Elk Refuge; the entrance station and Moose Visitor Center are at Moose. From Dubois, follow US 26/287 to Moran Junction and turn north to the Moran Entrance Station.

From Yellowstone NP's South Entrance, the John D. Rockefeller, Jr., Memorial Parkway leads directly into the park. Airport: The Jackson Hole Airport is inside the park.

When to Go

Any time of year is a joy in the Tetons. Most people visit during July and August, when it's sunny and warm, after the snow has melted in the high country. In September and October, the days are pleasant, nights are brisk, the park is less crowded, and the animals are still active. You have a better chance of seeing elk in the fall than in summer.

Winter, although spectacular, can be very demanding; snowshoeing, skate-skiing, walking, and cross-country skiing are popular. The main park road, US 26/89/191, remains open all year, but snow closes Teton Park Road (the "inner road") north of Cottonwood Creek to vehicles from November through April. The Moose-Wilson Road is also closed. At Teton Village, just south of the park, you'll find excellent downhill skiing.

How to Visit

On a 1-day visit in the summer take the **Teton Park Road** from **Moose Junction** to **Jenny Lake** for excellent views of the **Tetons** and short walks or longer hikes. On the second day, go farther north to **Signal Mountain** and **Jackson Lake.** For a longer stay, consider floating the **Snake River,** hiking, canoeing, climbing, or attending a ranger-guided activity.

TETON PARK ROAD & JENNY LAKE LOOP

17 miles; at least a half day

From **Moose Junction,** cross the **Snake River** to the **Craig Thomas Discovery and Visitor Center,** which

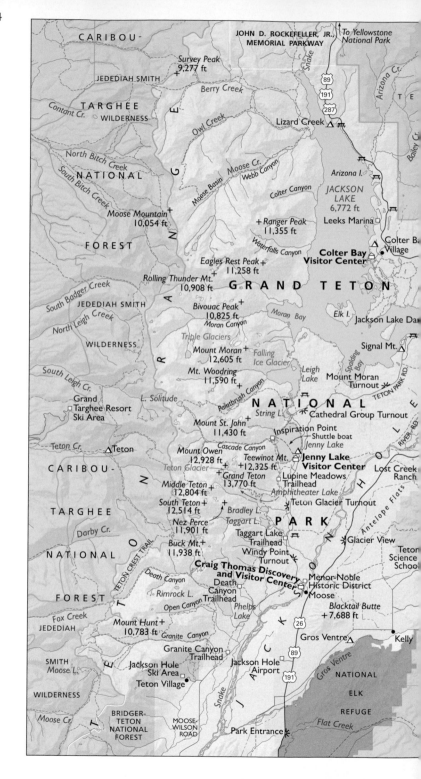

CARIBOU-

JOHN D. ROCKEFELLER, JR. MEMORIAL PARKWAY

To Yellowstone National Park

Survey Peak 9,277 ft

JEDEDIAH SMITH

Berry Creek

Snake

TARGHEE WILDERNESS

Contant Cr.

Owl Creek

Lizard Creek

89 191 287

North Bitch Creek

South Bitch Creek

NATIONAL

Moose Basin

Moose Cr.

Webb Canyon

Colter Canyon

Arizona I.

JACKSON LAKE 6,772 ft

Bailey Cr.

Moose Mountain 10,054 ft

FOREST

Ranger Peak 11,355 ft

Leeks Marina

Colter B.

Colter B. Village

Waterfalls Canyon

Eagles Rest Peak 11,258 ft

Colter Bay Visitor Center

Rolling Thunder Mt. 10,908 ft

GRAND TETON

South Badger Creek

JEDEDIAH SMITH

North Leigh Creek

Bivouac Peak 10,825 ft

Moran Canyon

Moran Bay

Elk I.

Jackson Lake Dam

WILDERNESS

Triple Glaciers

Mount Moran 12,605 ft

Falling Ice Glacier

Signal Mt.

South Leigh Cr.

Mt. Woodring 11,590 ft

Leigh Lake

Mount Moran Turnout

Spalding Bay

TETON PARK RD.

L. Solitude

Grand Targhee Resort Ski Area

Paintbrush Canyon

String L.

NATIONAL

Cathedral Group Turnout

SNAKE RIVER RD.

Teton Cr.

Teton

Mount St. John 11,430 ft

Inspiration Point

Shuttle boat

Jenny Lake

CARIBOU-

Mount Owen 12,928 ft

Cascade Canyon

Teton Glacier

Teewinot Mt. 12,325 ft

Grand Teton 13,770 ft

Jenny Lake Visitor Center

Lost Creek Ranch

TARGHEE

Middle Teton 12,804 ft

South Teton 12,514 ft

Lupine Meadows Trailhead

Amphitheater Lake

Teton Glacier Turnout

Antelope Flats

Darby Cr.

Nez Perce 11,901 ft

Bradley L.

Taggart L.

PARK

NATIONAL

Buck Mt. 11,938 ft

Taggart Lake Trailhead

Windy Point Turnout

Glacier View

Teton Science School

TETON CREST TRAIL

Craig Thomas Discovery and Visitor Center

Menor-Noble Historic District

Moose

FOREST

Death Canyon

Rimrock L.

Open Canyon

Death Canyon Trailhead

Phelps Lake

Blacktail Butte 7,688 ft

JEDEDIAH

Fox Creek

Mount Hunt 10,783 ft

Granite Canyon

26

Gros Ventre

Kelly

SMITH

Moose L.

Granite Canyon Trailhead

Jackson Hole Ski Area

Teton Village

Jackson Hole Airport

89

191

NATIONAL

WILDERNESS

Moose Cr.

BRIDGER-TETON NATIONAL FOREST

MOOSE-WILSON ROAD

Snake

Park Entrance

Flat Creek

ELK

REFUGE

Gros Ventre

includes a large exhibit area, a theater, and a bookstore. The first right turn after the entrance station leads to **Menor-Noble Historic District,** a pioneer homestead. Save that for another day; there are mountains ahead. The **Teton Park Road** climbs up from the river onto a sage-covered flat with the whole Teton panorama in view. You will see the mountains clearly throughout this drive from various changing angles; each viewpoint reveals striking perspectives different from the last.

If you look toward the mountains at Taggart Lake Trailhead, you can see the results of a 1985 forest fire. An easy trail offers a close-up view of forest regeneration—an especially interesting and encouraging sight if you plan to visit Yellowstone, where fires burned extensively in the summer of 1988.

Stop at Teton Glacier Turnout for a close-in view of the three Tetons. The Grand Teton, at 13,770 feet, is the highest point in the range. A major route used by climbers follows the left-hand, southern skyline; just as it appears, there is no easy way to the top. Looking to the left of the Grand, you see the **Middle** and **South Tetons.** The sharp pinnacle jutting up over the shoulder of the South Teton (actually in front of it), is the peak called **Nez Perce.** To the right of the Grand are the sharp

The craggy Tetons rise beyond a rustic barn.

Looking over a field of wildflowers into Targhee National Forest

peak of **Mount Owen** and, in the foreground, the craggy battlements of **Teewinot Mountain.**

Notice the steep, glacier-carved gulch coming straight down from the Grand Teton. At the head of the gulch, beneath the mountain's near-vertical northeast face, lies **Teton Glacier.** During an ancient ice age, glaciers covered Jackson Hole to a depth of 3,000 feet and carved the canyons in the Teton Range. The glaciers that exist now only at high elevations established themselves more recently.

If you can take your eyes off the mountains, scan the sage flats on both sides of the road for pronghorn, elk, deer, and coyotes, especially in the fall. Across Jackson Hole to the southeast is the **Gros Ventre Range,** where herds of elk and mule deer roam the deeply forested gorges and bighorn sheep the highest peaks.

Heading north, the **Lupine Meadows** spur road leads to a major trailhead. From here you can take a very rewarding but strenuous hike, which climbs 3,000 feet to **Amphitheater Lake** near tree line. Lupine Meadows itself is a good place to look for wildlife in the evening.

Back on the main road, the **South Jenny Lake** area is next, but unless you're planning to hike around the lake, or to take the boat across to **Cascade Canyon** at this point in your tour, you should drive past it for now.

Four miles ahead is the junction for **Jenny Lake Scenic Drive,** where a narrow 1-mile loop road provides the best approach to the area, which many consider to be the scenic heart of the Tetons. The road angles back to the southwest, offering stunning views of the central peaks. Stop at **Cathedral Group Turnout** to take it all in. The north face of the Grand is visible from here, flanked by Teewinot on the left and Owen on the right. North of them, in order, are precipitous **Cascade Canyon** (one of the park's best hikes), **Mount Saint John, Mount Woodring,** and then the massive, flat-topped **Mount Moran.** Moran's **Falling Ice Glacier** is prominent. Notice also the obvious line of black rock rising above the glacier. Called a black dike, it was caused when molten rock intruded into a crack in the older metamorphic rock called gneiss, before the Tetons rose. The dike, now exposed by erosion of the gneiss, actually stands out from the mountain face near the summit. Similar dikes are on the Middle Teton (not visible from here) and Grand Teton.

Just ahead, a short road forks off the scenic drive and leads to tiny **String Lake,** the most popular place for swimming. An easy trail leaves from the end of the road to follow the shoreline through open forest to sparkling **Leigh Lake,** named after a 19th-century mountain man, Richard "Beaver Dick" Leigh, who, it was said, could "trap beaver where there warn't any." The lake has superb views of soaring Mount Moran, and, in summer, the water is sometimes warm enough for swimming.

Continuing on, the scenic drive reaches **Jenny Lake** and becomes one way. For understandable reasons, this place is highly popular; the road in summer is crowded with vehicles. Even so, if you desire solitude amid the grandeur, you can generally find it. Leave your car in a parking area and walk down to the shore. Instantly you are isolated from the world of automobiles. If you have more time, catch the boat that usually leaves three times an hour from the southeast end of the lake. Near the parking area you will find the **Jenny Lake Visitor Center,**

restrooms, ranger station, a store, and a campground for tents only.

The passenger boat crosses Jenny Lake to join **Cascade Canyon Trail.** It is a half-mile walk to **Hidden Falls,** one of the park's beauties. A half-mile farther, aptly named **Inspiration Point** overlooks the lake. If you still have the energy, the trail is not steep after Inspiration Point, and the views keep getting better. You might consider walking back to the visitor center along the south shore; the easy trail is nearly 3 miles long.

JACKSON LAKE

about 30 miles; at least a half day

Start at North Jenny Lake Junction on the Teton Park Road. Drive north 2.5 miles through sage land and lodgepole pine to the **Mount Moran Turnout.** Mount Moran, at 12,605 feet, is more than 1,000 feet lower than the Grand Teton, but you wouldn't know that looking up. On its summit a patch of sandstone corresponds to a sandstone layer an estimated 24,000 feet below where you stand; 13 million years of movement on the Teton fault has separated the layers by some 30,000 feet.

North of Mount Moran, **Bivouac Peak, Rolling Thunder Mountain,** and **Eagles Rest Peak** dominate the most remote section of the park, cut off from roads and easy trail access by **Jackson Lake,** just ahead. The natural lake was enlarged by a dam built before the park was established.

Before you get to the lake, take the right-hand turn to **Signal Mountain.** The road, on which trailers and RVs are not allowed, winds to the summit of a low mountain which, because it stands alone in Jackson Hole, provides a panoramic view of the region. There's no better place than here to appreciate the unusual geology of the Teton area:

GRAND TETON

Jackson Lake *(top)*; Mount Moran and its reflection *(center left)*; bull moose in rut *(center right)*;
climbing Blacktail Butte, just east of Moose *(bottom left)*; thundering downhill stream *(bottom right)*

the abrupt meeting of valley floor and the Teton Range; the meandering course of the Snake River through deposits of gravel and clay brought down by Ice Age glaciers; and the ranges to the east. From Signal Mountain, it is easy to see why the early trappers thought of mountain-ringed valleys like this one as holes.

Back on the Teton Park Road, you pass Signal Mountain Campground and cross the Snake River over the rebuilt dam. A mile farther, the road joins US 89/191/287. If you're headed north toward Yellowstone, it's worthwhile to turn right and take a short side trip (about a mile) to **Oxbow Bend,** for a classic view of the Tetons dominated by Mount Moran. Wildlife frequents this area.

Going north once again, stop at **Willow Flats Overlook.** The willows are a likely place to see moose. Failing that, scan the meadows below the bridge just to the north as you cross **Pilgrim Creek.**

A few minutes north, **Colter Bay Visitor Center** has an excellent **Indian Arts Museum.** Consider stretching your legs on the easy 3-mile **Colter Bay Nature Trail;** self-guiding booklets can be had at the trailhead or at the visitor center.

North of **Colter Bay,** the main road stays close to the lake. Just before Lizard Creek Campground, you catch one last glimpse of the Tetons and Jackson Lake, before entering dense lodgepole forest. Ten miles farther, along the John D. Rockefeller, Jr., Memorial Parkway, is the South Entrance to Yellowstone NP.

OTHER HIKES & ACTIVITIES

Grand Teton has more than 200 miles of maintained trails; many lead up canyons separating the major peaks. All trails have something to offer, but they vary in difficulty, and some are more scenic than others. Keep in mind that most trails begin at about 6,800 feet, so shortness of breath can come quickly.

Cascade Canyon is most popular. Begin at Jenny Lake and either walk along the lakeshore or take the boat across to Hidden Falls and Inspiration Point. It is a long hike to **Lake Solitude**—7 miles if you take the boat, 9.5 miles if you walk the lakeshore—but it's worthwhile to go at least partway up the canyon. (Ask when the last boat returns to the parking lot; those extra 2.5 miles around the lake can seem a lifetime after a long hike.)

From Lupine Meadows parking area, the **Amphitheater Lake Trail** climbs to 9,700 feet and rewards those who make the strenuous 10-mile round-trip with a breathtaking view of Jackson Hole. The lake nestles beneath craggy peaks; allow 8 hours minimum.

Death Canyon Trailhead, off the Moose-Wilson Road, leads to a nice view of **Phelps Lake;** from there, the trail climbs to join the **Teton Crest Trail,** a magnificent route that traverses the range and ends at **Paintbrush Canyon** near String Lake, a trip of about 40 miles and 3 days (backcountry permit required).

Consider taking a raft trip on the **Snake River** for fine Teton views and a chance to see beaver, otters, moose, eagles, ospreys, and waterfowl. Ask about outfitters at a visitor center or check the park newspaper, *Grand Teton Guide.*

You can also sign up for a mountain climbing lesson; rent a canoe and paddle on a lake; or take a summer course that is taught by the **Teton Science School.** The school offers 1- to 5-day seminars on ecology and the region's natural history for ages 8 and up.

GRAND TETON

INFORMATION & ACTIVITIES

VISITOR & INFORMATION CENTERS

Craig Thomas Discovery & Visitor Center, at park's south end, open daily all year. **Colter Bay Visitor Center,** on Jackson Lake, open mid-May through September. **Jenny Lake Visitor Center** open June through Labor Day. Call (307) 739-3399.

SEASONS & ACCESSIBILITY

Main road into park (US 26/89/191) open year-round. Snow closes side roads from about November to May. Call headquarters for winter road conditions.

HEADQUARTERS

P.O. Drawer 170, Moose, WY 83012. Phone (307) 739-3300. www.nps.gov/grte

ENTRANCE FEE

$25 per car, good for one week at both Grand Teton and Yellowstone. $50 annually for both parks.

PETS

Permitted on leashes except on trails, at ranger-led activities, in backcountry, visitor centers; not permitted on boats on Snake River or lakes except Jackson Lake.

ACCESSIBLE SERVICES

Visitor centers, Indian Arts Museum, some restrooms, some ranger-led activities are accessible. Also, some trails and Menor-Noble Historic District.

THINGS TO DO

Free ranger-led activities: wildlife walks, watches, and talks, day and twilight hikes, bicycle tours, campfire programs, children's and skill development programs, snowshoe walks. Also, boat cruise, natural history seminars, boating (permit required), river rafting, climbing, bicycling, horseback riding (stables in park), fishing (license required), snowshoeing, cross-country skiing, dogsledding, snowmobiling. Ask for list of concessioners offering rental and guide services.

OVERNIGHT BACKPACKING

Permits required, free; from visitor centers and Jenny Lake Ranger Station. A third of permits can be reserved for a $25 fee; the rest are first come, first served. Reserve between January and mid-May at www.nps.gov/grte, by fax at (307) 739-3438, or by mail to Grand Teton National Park, Backcountry Permits, P.O. Box 170, Moose, WY 83012.

CAMPGROUNDS

Seven campgrounds. **Jenny Lake** has 7-day limit, others 14-day. Generally late May to Oct., except **Lizard Creek,** mid-June to early Sept. Five are first come, first served. $17 per night. Showers at **Colter Bay.** Only tent sites at Jenny Lake; all others have tent and trailer sites, two with hookups. Group campsites at **Gros Ventre** and **Colter Bay**; reservations (307) 543-2811. RV sites only at **Colter Bay RV Park,** $22 per night. Reservations required; contact Grand Teton Lodge Co. (see below). Food services in park.

HOTELS, MOTELS, & INNS

(unless otherwise noted, rates are for 2 persons in a double room, high season)

INSIDE THE PARK:
The following 3 lodges and cabins are operated by Grand Teton Lodge Co., P.O. Box 250, Moran, WY 83013. (800) 628-9988 or (307) 543-2811.
Colter Bay Village and Marina 166 cabins. $89-$179. Rest. Late May–late Sept.
Jackson Lake Lodge (5 miles north of Moran Jct.) 385 units. $199-$650. Restaurant, pool. Late May–early Oct.
Jenny Lake Lodge 31 cabins. $620-$885, all incl. Restaurant. Late May–early Oct.
Signal Mountain Lodge P.O. Box 50, Moran, WY 83013. (800) 672-6012 or (307) 543-2831. 79 units. $130-$300. Restaurants. Early May–mid-Oct.
Triangle X Ranch Moose, WY 83012. (307) 733-2183. 22 cabins. $1,500-$1,850 per person, per week, all incl. Late May–Oct.
OUTSIDE THE PARK:
Lost Creek Ranch (8 miles north of Moose) P.O. Box 95, Moose, WY 83012. (307) 733-3435. 13 cabins. $6,500-$15,000 per week, all incl. June–Sept.

Contact the Jackson Hole Chamber of Commerce for a full list of accommodations: P.O. Box 550, Jackson Hole, WY 83001. (307) 733-3316, www.jacksonhole chamber.com.

EXCURSIONS

NATIONAL ELK REFUGE
JACKSON, WYOMING

In winter, visitors can ride a horse-drawn sleigh into the protected winter range for a herd of 5,000 elk. The refuge offers supplemental feeding to the animals, many of which migrate south from Yellowstone, and Grand Teton NP. 24,700 acres. Fishing (Aug. through Oct.), scenic drives, visitor center. Open year-round, dawn to dusk. Adjoins Grand Teton NP on south. (307) 733-9212, www.fws.gov/nationalelkrefuge.

BRIDGER-TETON NATIONAL FOREST
JACKSON, WYOMING

This immense forest encompasses wildlife-rich Jackson Hole; the glaciers and lakes of the Wind River Range; and Two Ocean Creek along the Continental Divide. Contains three wilderness areas. 3.4 million acres. Hiking, boating, fishing, horseback riding, hunting, water sports, winter sports. 30 campgrounds, boat ramps. Open all year; campgrounds open spring to fall. Adjoins Grand Teton NP on east. (307) 739-5500, www.fs.fed.us.

CARIBOU-TARGHEE NATIONAL FOREST
IDAHO FALLS, IDAHO

Here, on the Tetons' western flank, lies a forest of lodgepole pine and fir with many rivers, streams, and lakes. Contains two wilderness areas. 1,810,000 acres, part in Wyoming. Hiking, boating, fishing, horseback riding, hunting, picnic areas, winter sports, water sports. 32 campgrounds, boat ramp. Open all year; campsites open late May through September. Adjoins Grand Teton and Yellowstone NP. (208) 524-7500, www.fs.fed.us.

GRAND TETON

Wave-like contours of dunes at the foot of the Sangre de Cristo Mountains

▶ GREAT SAND DUNES

COLORADO
ESTABLISHED SEPTEMBER 13, 2004
149,137 acres

Visitors to the Great Sand Dunes experience an undeniable sense of wonder, just as happens in so many of our most spectacular national parks. In contrast to the sudden shock of walking to the rim of the Grand Canyon, though, or topping a rise to view Crater Lake, the emotions evoked by this otherworldly landscape arrive in slow motion.

The dunes appear in the distance as you approach, but at first seem dwarfed by their backdrop, the 13,000-foot peaks of the Sangre de Cristo Mountains. Not until you're nearly at their border does their vast scale become apparent: dunes up to 750 feet tall, extending for mile after mile—an ocean of sand hills of breathtaking magnitude. That's just how the explorer Zebulon Pike described them in 1807: "Their appearance was exactly that of a sea in a storm (except as to color), not the least sign of vegetation existing thereon."

The dunes sprawl across part of southern Colorado's San Luis Valley, a broad, arid plain between the San Juan Mountains on the west and the Sangre de Cristos on the east. Streams and creeks flowing out of the San Juan Mountains over millennia carried gravel and sand into shallow lakes in the San Luis Valley. During drought periods, these lakes dried, releasing the sand particles to the action of the wind. Strong prevailing southwesterly winds carry the tiny grains toward the Sangre de Cristos, piling them up against the foothills. The resulting dunes are the tallest in North America, covering more than 30 square miles. Adults hike across them and marvel at their beauty; children run and slide down their steep faces, enjoying a playground of fairy-tale proportions.

Winds that can top 40 miles an hour reshape the crests of the tall dunes, and smaller dunes may "migrate" several feet in a week. The dunes show a remarkable permanence of form, though, which geologists attribute to opposing winds. Prevailing southwesterly winds blow the dune mass northeasterly toward the mountains, and occasional but powerful northeasterlies blow the dunes back toward the southwest. This back-and-forth action of the winds piles the dunes vertically, and contributes to the stability of the dunefield.

The need to protect the water that protects the dunes has led to a number of changes at Great Sand Dunes. Through a cooperative effort among government agencies and private conservation groups, the purchase of private lands, identified as important to the protection of park resources, was completed on September 13, 2004. The new entity comprises the original national monument, lands west of the monument known as the Baca Ranch, and mountains east of the monument previously managed by the U.S. Forest Service. This latter realm was established as a preserve in 2000 to safeguard the streams flowing into the area. The official designation is Great Sand Dunes National Park and Preserve.

All this means that visitors have access to a great diversity of habitats, beginning in wetlands, and continuing up through grasslands, dunes, montane woodlands, and arriving even higher at the spruce-fir forests and tundra of the summits of the Sangre de Cristos, with seven peaks over 13,000 feet. The region's geology and biology make it a fascinating place, unique among our national parks. It's well worth the drive across southern Colorado, even if all you do is gaze in awe at this extraordinary and lovely terrain.

How to Get There

From the east or north, take US 160 west from Walsenburg 59 miles to Colo. 150 and drive north 16 miles. From the south or west, take US 285 to Alamosa and drive 14 miles east to Colo. 150, continuing north to the park and preserve. Airport: Colorado Springs.

When to Go

Year-round. Moderate temperatures make spring and fall best. The sand surface can get very hot in summer, although they can be traversed comfortably early and late in the day; summer is also the park's most crowded season. Winter snow curtails trips into the high mountains, though the dunes can still be visited.

How to Visit

Stop at the **visitor center** for interactive exhibits about the Great Sand Dunes environment, and to learn the schedule of ranger-led walks and programs (summer only). From there, proceed to the dunes parking lot. Then walk out into the dunes, going as far and climbing as high as time and energy permit; the **High Dune** is a popular, moderately strenuous destination.

Kids and adults alike enjoy splashing along **Medano Creek,** which meanders along the base of the dunes (when there is enough water from the spring snowmelt from the Sangre de Cristo peaks). The **Montville Nature Trail** and the **Mosca Pass Trail** offer additional options for exploration, from short walks to mountain hikes.

If you have a high-clearance four-wheel-drive vehicle, and are very careful, you can drive the **Medano Pass Primitive Road,** which leads 11 miles up into the Sangre de Cristo Mountains in the national preserve, exploring different habitats along the way, from foothills to coniferous forest at the 9,982-foot pass.

THE DUNES & MEDANO CREEK

short hikes; a half day

A 20-minute video at the **visitor center** offers a good introduction to the geology and history of the park. Rangers in summer present programs here, as well as at other sites and trails. Depending on when you visit, guided events might include nature walks, children's activities, or presentations on wildlife, plants, hiking, geology, or the archaeology of the dunes.

Begin your exploration at the **Dunes** parking lot. The imposing dunes, like buff-brown miniatures of the surrounding Sangre de Cristo crests, rise invitingly to the west. But first take time to discover **Medano Creek.** This widely variable stream flows along the edge of the dunes; the moisture it carries is a vital part of the dune system environment. Kids may want to build sand castles, or just enjoy a shoes-off walk along the squishy streambed. The wet sand is a good place to look for the tracks

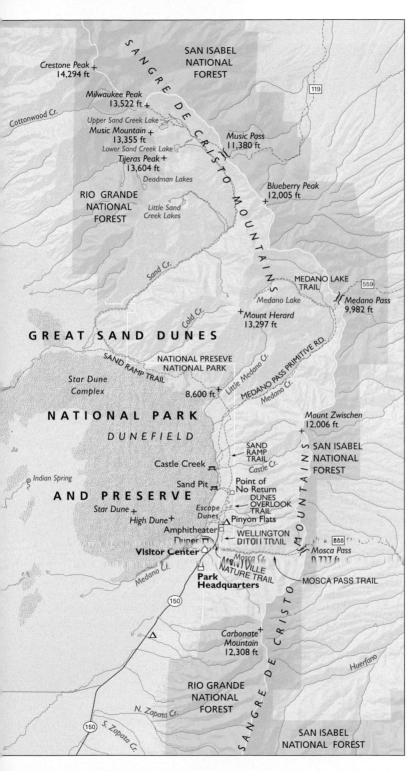

SAN ISABEL
NATIONAL
FOREST

Crestone Peak +
14,294 ft

119

Milwaukee Peak +
13,522 ft

Cottonwood Cr.

Upper Sand Creek Lake
Music Mountain +
13,355 ft
Lower Sand Creek Lake

Music Pass
11,380 ft

Tijeras Peak +
13,604 ft

Deadman Lakes

Blueberry Peak +
12,005 ft

RIO GRANDE
NATIONAL
FOREST

Little Sand
Creek Lakes

Sand Cr.

MEDANO LAKE
TRAIL

559

Cold Cr.

Medano Lake

Medano Pass
9,982 ft

GREAT SAND DUNES

+ Mount Herard
13,297 ft

NATIONAL PRESERVE
NATIONAL PARK

SAND RAMP TRAIL

MEDANO PASS PRIMITIVE RD.

Little Medano Cr.

Star Dune
Complex

8,600 ft +

Medano Cr.

Mount Zwischen
12,006 ft +

NATIONAL PARK

DUNEFIELD

SAND
RAMP
TRAIL

SAN ISABEL
NATIONAL
FOREST

Castle Cr.

Castle Creek

Indian Spring

Sand Pit

Point of
No Return

AND PRESERVE

DUNES
OVERLOOK
TRAIL

Star Dune +

Escape
Dunes

Pinyon Flats

High Dune +

WELLINGTON
DITCH TRAIL

888

Amphitheater
Dunes

Mosca Pass
9,737 ft

Visitor Center

Mosca Cr.

MONTVILLE
NATURE TRAIL

Park
Headquarters

MOSCA PASS TRAIL

Medano Cr.

150

Carbonate +
Mountain
12,308 ft

Huerfano

150

N. Zapata Cr.

RIO GRANDE
NATIONAL
FOREST

S. Zapata Cr.

SAN ISABEL
NATIONAL FOREST

SANGRE DE CRISTO MOUNTAINS

GREAT SAND DUNES

Flowers of the narrowleaf yucca *(top)*
View from the summit of High Dune *(bottom)*

of coyotes, kangaroo rats, mule deer, or bobcats.

Medano Creek usually flows only in spring, carrying snowmelt down from the mountaintops. When it contains adequate water, watch for a phenomenon called "surge flow," which occurs when a small, temporary dam of sand upstream collapses, sending down a wave of water that can be up to a foot high.

Next, hike out into the dunes, where you'll quickly learn that walking in the soft sand is more strenuous than you might think. Take your time, and angle up the ridgelines of the dunes, rather than climbing straight up. While it might seem like fun to go barefoot, remember that in summer the sand surface can reach blistering temperatures. Wear protective shoes, as well as a hat, and apply sunscreen. Carry plenty of water if you plan on walking far. One thing you don't need to be concerned about is poisonous animals: There are no snakes or scorpions in the dunes.

You can strike out in any direction, but be sure to keep track of your location. While most can easily orient themselves by noting the peaks of the Sangre de Cristos, a compass or GPS unit isn't a bad idea for extended hikes. Many make the 1-mile (one-way) trip to the aptly named **High Dune,** which towers 650 feet above the floor of the San Luis Valley. You'll find a great panorama at the top, taking in mountains, dunes, and valley. Another mile to the west rises the **Star Dune,** with an equally fine view. "Star" dunes are so named because they have three or more "arms," rather than the single axis of most dunes.

Photography in the dunes is best early and late in the day, when the low angle of the sun creates shadows that accentuate their contours and crests.

Visitors survey their surroundings from the top of High Dune.

GREAT SAND DUNES

A night walk into the dunes can be a little eerie, but thrilling in its sense of solitude and peace. When the moon is out, the dimly lit landscape seems even more haunting.

EAST OF THE DUNES

a full day or more

Although the dunes are fascinating and beautiful, there is a certain uniformity about them, and very few plants and animals make their homes there. The same is certainly not true for the foothills and high peaks of the Sangre de Cristo range, a large part of which is now encompassed in **Great Sand Dunes National Preserve.** (The preserve is administered similarly to the adjoining park, although hunting is allowed.) Here, you can hike or, with the proper vehicle, drive from the scrubby habitat of junipers and pinyon pines, along creeks lined with aspens and cottonwoods, up into forests of ponderosa pine and, even higher, spruce and fir. Alpine tundra tops the tallest summits above tree line, where only grasses, compact shrubs, low wildflowers, and other ground-hugging plants can survive.

East of the main road, just north of the visitor center, you'll find a parking area for three varied trails. The easy, half-mile **Montville Nature Trail** loops into the foothills, where you might spot mule deer, a least chipmunk, a desert cottontail, or a coyote. Black-billed magpies, long-tailed and conspicuous, have learned to beg for food (don't feed them or other wildlife), and friendly mountain chickadees flit from tree to tree. The **Wellington Ditch Trail** splits off the Montville trail partway around the loop, following an old irrigation ditch 1 mile north to the NPS campground.

Also beginning at the Montville trailhead, the **Mosca Pass Trail** follows an old toll road up Mosca Creek, a tributary of Medano, across the national park boundary and into the preserve. You'll walk past cottonwoods and aspens, ascending into a forest of Engelmann spruce and subalpine fir, reaching 9,737-foot Mosca Pass after 3.5 miles; the elevation gain is just under 1,500 feet. For a moderate amount of effort, you'll get a fine overview of the way habitats change with altitude in the Rockies.

Visitors with a four-wheel-drive, high-clearance vehicle can take the **Medano Pass Primitive Road,** which follows the park's eastern border before heading into the national preserve, climbing to reach 9,982-foot Medano Pass 11 miles from the road entrance. This trip offers a nonstrenuous way to explore the high Sangre de Cristos, although certain hazards must be taken into account. The road traverses soft sand for several miles and is not recommended for smaller SUVs lacking wide tires and high ground clearance. Even large vehicles may need to lower tire pressure to make it through the sand without bogging down. (Air to reinflate tires is available near the park amphitheater.) The road crosses creeks several times, which can be problematic during spring high water, and it's closed in winter.

Like the Mosca Pass Trail, the Medano Pass road provides a virtual natural history lesson along with excellent scenery. Ascending from the foothills into lush montane forest is, in effect, like traveling from the southwestern desert to Canada. Ecologists call the different habitats encountered along mountain slopes life zones—each an altitudinal band boasting its own related set of plants and animals. Pinyon jays and mule deer, for instance, dwell among the arid-looking habitat of scattered junipers and pinyon pines, while gray jays and bighorn sheep live high on the mountain slopes.

One of the preserve's most popular hikes begins along the Medano Pass road, a half-mile west of the pass. The **Medano Lake Trail** climbs 1,900 feet in 4 miles to reach the lake, strikingly situated in a cirque under 13,297-foot Mount Herard. The trail passes through aspen groves that turn brilliant yellow in fall. The last mile of the trail is rugged, and to have a view westward over the sand dunes you must expend even more effort, climbing to the summit of Mount Herard above the lake. Your reward is a visit to an alpine world of flowery meadows, dense spruce-fir woodland, and wind-stunted trees at timberline, where bighorn sheep roam and Clark's nutcrackers give their raucous calls. Listen for the sharp squeaks of pikas, mammals that live among rockpiles, looking like small rabbits without the long ears.

A rainbow formed from mist rolling off the Sangre de Cristo Mountains

INFORMATION & ACTIVITIES

VISITOR & INFORMATION CENTER

The **visitor center** on Colo. 150 is open year-round with exhibits and viewing area. (719) 378-6399.

SEASONS & ACCESSIBILITY

The park is open year-round. Sand temperatures can spike to 140°F during the summer, but air temperatures in the 80s are normal.

HEADQUARTERS

11500 Hwy. 150, Mosca, CO 81146. Phone (719) 378-6300. www.nps.gov/grsa

ENTRANCE FEE

$3 per person per week; $15 annual pass

PETS

Permitted on leashes except in wilderness areas and at backcountry campsites. Be aware that mountain lions, coyotes, and bears hunt within the park. Horses are not allowed in the main dunes use area.

ACCESSIBLE SERVICES

Access to the dunes is difficult for persons with traditional wheeled chairs. Check with the visitor center about borrowing a "sand wheelchair." Accessible camping sites available at Pinyon Flats campground as well as at the Sawmill Canyon Backcountry Campsite along Medano Pass Primitive Road. Check with park staff to answer other questions.

THINGS TO DO

Dunes hiking, photography, wildlife viewing, snowshoeing, nature walks, climbing, cross-country skiing, birdwatching. Summer events include a Junior Ranger Day.

OVERNIGHT BACKPACKING

Free backcountry permits required for overnight camping. Primitive camping permitted without fires. Backcountry camping is allowed with horses and pack animals in most of the park and preserve. Groups are limited to six people and animals within the park borders and 15 in the preserve. Check with park officials on specific limitations.

CAMPGROUNDS

Pinyon Flats Campground has 88 campsites. **Loop 1** campsites are open year-round on a first-come, first-served basis. $14 per night. **Loop 2** campsites may be reserved (visit www.recreation.gov). Individual sites are $20 per night. Outside the park, **San Luis Lakes State Park** (15 miles west on County Road 6) has 51 campsites with views of the Sangre de Cristo Mountains and the Great Sand Dunes. (719) 378-2020. $18 per night and $6 daily entrance fee. Also **Oasis Campground,** 7900 Hwy. 150 N. Mosca, CO. (719) 378-2222 (campground reservations for RV and cabins). 130 tent sites, $18 first come, first served; 20 RV sites, $28. Also available, 4 camping cabins ($40).

SPECIAL ADVISORIES

• Shoes are necessary for walking on the dunes as midday sand can burn bare feet.
• Carry plenty of water—more than you normally would—for hikes of any length.
• Wear plenty of sunscreen and a protective head covering.

HOTELS, MOTELS, & INNS

(unless otherwise noted, rates are for 2 persons in a double room, high season)

OUTSIDE THE PARK:

Great Sand Dunes Lodge 7900 Hwy. 150 N. Mosca, CO 81146. (719) 378-2900. 12 rooms. $95-$125. Pool.

For other local accommodations, contact the park or visit www.nps.gov/grsa/planyourvisit/lodging.htm; the Alamosa Chamber of Commerce, (719) 589-3681, www.alamosa.org, for information on locations near the main entrance; or the Custer Chamber of Commerce, (719) 783-9163, www.custercountyco.com/westcliffe .htm, for information on the lodging near Westcliffe and the preserve entrance.

GREAT SAND DUNES

Hallet Peak at dawn, shrouded by blowing snow

▶ROCKY MOUNTAIN

COLORADO
ESTABLISHED JANUARY 26, 1915
265,873 acres

Nowhere else in the United States can a visitor see so much alpine country with such ease. A mere 2-hour drive from Denver, Trail Ridge Road takes visitors into the heart of Rocky Mountain National Park, traversing a ridge above 11,000 feet for 10 miles. Along the way, tiny tundra flowers and other wild blooms contrast with sweeping vistas of towering summits; 78 of them exceed 12,000 feet. Alpine lakes reflect the grandeur.

The summits form at least the third generation of mountains to rise in this region. The first probably protruded as islands above a shallow sea more than 135 million years ago, when dinosaurs reigned. Another range grew out of a later sea some 75 million years ago. Over the eons these summits eroded to rolling hills, which rose once again, although unevenly: Some portions sank along fault lines, helping create the striking texture of the current scenery.

Rock as old as that at the bottom of the Grand Canyon—nearly 2 billion years—caps the Rockies' summits. Within the last million years, glaciers, grinding boulders beneath them, carved deep canyons into the landscape. Erosion later scoured the more jagged summits into their present profiles.

Rocky Mountain, though only about an eighth the size of Yellowstone, accommodates as many visitors—3 million or so a year. Overcrowding worries park officials and conservationists, who cite distressed animals, trodden plants, and eroded trails. Condominium development is crowding the park's borders also, shrinking the habitats of elk and other wildlife and threatening to turn the park into an island of nature.

How to Get There

Take I-25 north from Denver (about 77 miles away) to Colo. 66, west through the town of Lyons, up US 36 to Estes Park; or south from Cheyenne, Wyoming (about 90 miles away), then US 34 west at Loveland. From the west, pick up US 34 at Granby. Airport: Denver.

When to Go

The park is busiest early July to mid-August, when the park receives about half its yearly visitors. Trail Ridge Road stays open from roughly late May to mid-October, weather permitting; most trails thaw out by around July 4. In May, subalpine wildflowers start to bloom; in early July, the tundra flowers start. September is a prime time to visit: Elk move to lower elevations, so you can easily hear their mating bugles and the aspens turn golden. In winter there is cross-country skiing and snowshoeing.

How to Visit

On a 1-day blitz from the east entrance, drive spectacular **Trail Ridge Road** as far as **Farview Curve** for the classic overview of the park's mountains, valleys, and tundra. If you wish, make a loop by driving one-way, unpaved **Old Fall River Road** west, then Trail Ridge Road east. Old Fall River Road gives you an intimate look at a wooded mountainside, but it's usually closed by snow until early July. *(Neither Old Fall River Road or Trail Ridge Road have guardrails or shoulders, and are very winding.)*

With more time, you can drive all the way to **Grand Lake** on the west side the first day, and take a trip to **Bear Lake** the second day. Spend extra time on the excellent nature trails and day hikes.

If you go in summer, plan to hike early in the day as you do not want to be caught above tree line between about 12 and 4 p.m., when lightning storms might occur.

TRAIL RIDGE ROAD TO GRAND LAKE, VIA FARVIEW CURVE

50 miles; at least a full day

Trail Ridge Road (US 34) roughly follows a 10,000-year-old trail; prehistoric people once hunted where you'll drive. The road climbs to a land like the vast arctic expanses of Siberia, Alaska, and northern Canada. Take a jacket, hat, gloves, and sunscreen. From Estes Park, enter the park on US 36 and stop by the visitor center to pick up information—including a useful booklet ($1) about Trail Ridge Road—and a weather report. (If coming from the west on US 34, stop at the visitor center near Grand Lake and reverse this tour.) Continue straight on US 36 after the entrance station. The road skirts the base of **Deer Mountain** through open ponderosa woodland.

At **Deer Ridge Junction,** either continue straight on Trail Ridge Road or, if it's summer, detour to the right, circling through **Horseshoe Park** and past **Sheep Lakes** to look for bighorn sheep, which sometimes

ROCKY MOUNTAIN

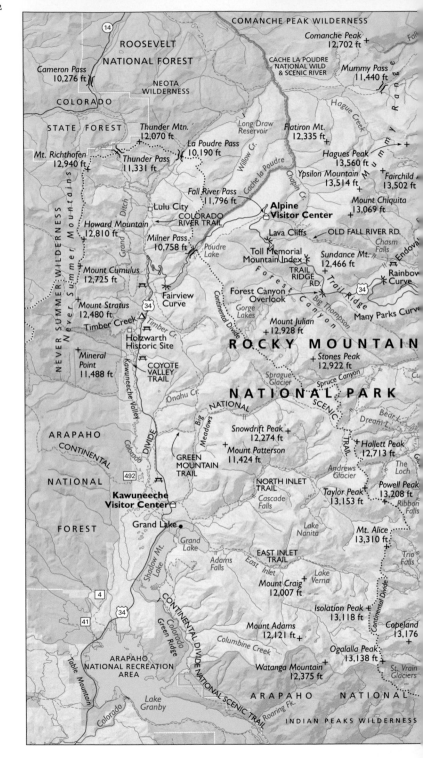

COMANCHE PEAK WILDERNESS

14

ROOSEVELT
NATIONAL FOREST

Comanche Peak
12,702 ft +

CACHE LA POUDRE
NATIONAL WILD
& SCENIC RIVER

Mummy Pass
11,440 ft +

Cameron Pass
10,276 ft

NEOTA
WILDERNESS

COLORADO

Hague Creek

STATE FOREST

Long Draw
Reservoir

Thunder Mtn.
12,070 ft

Flatiron Mt.
12,335 ft +

Willow Cr.

Thunder Pass
11,331 ft

La Poudre Pass
10,190 ft

Cache la Poudre

Hagues Peak
13,560 ft +

Mt. Richthofen
12,940 ft +

Chapin Cr.

Ypsilon Mountain
13,514 ft +

Fairchild
13,502 ft +

Fall River Pass
11,796 ft

Mount Chiquita
13,069 ft +

Howard Mountain
12,810 ft +

Lulu City
COLORADO
RIVER TRAIL

Alpine
Visitor Center

Milner Pass
10,758 ft +

Lava Cliffs

OLD FALL RIVER RD.

Chasm
Falls

Endova

Poudre
Lake

Toll Memorial
Mountain Index

Sundance Mt.
12,466 ft +

Mount Cumulus
12,725 ft +

TRAIL
RIDGE
RD.

Big Thompson

34

Rainbow
Curve +

Fairview
Curve

34

Forest Canyon
Overlook

Forest Canyon

Trail Ridge

Many Parks Curve

Mount Stratus
12,480 ft +

Gorge
Lakes

Mount Julian
+ 12,928 ft

Continental Divide

Timber Creek

Timber Cr.

ROCKY MOUNTAIN

Holzwarth
Historic Site

Stones Peak
12,922 ft +

Mineral
Point
11,488 ft +

COYOTE
VALLEY
TRAIL

NATIONAL PARK

Sprague
Glacier

Spruce Canyon

NATIONAL

Onahu Cr.

Bear

Kawuneeche Valley

Big Meadows

Snowdrift Peak
12,274 ft +

SCENIC

Dream L.

ARAPAHO
CONTINENTAL

Colorado

DIVIDE

GREEN
MOUNTAIN
TRAIL

Mount Patterson
11,424 ft +

Andrews
Glacier

TRAIL

Hallett Peak
12,713 ft +

The
Loch

NATIONAL

492

NORTH INLET
TRAIL

Taylor Peak
13,153 ft +

Powell Peak
13,208 ft +

Ribbon
Falls

Kawuneeche
Visitor Center

Cascade
Falls

FOREST

Grand Lake •

Lake
Nanita

Mt. Alice
13,310 ft +

4

Grand
Lake

Adams
Falls

EAST INLET
TRAIL

East Inlet

Lake
Verna

Trio
Falls

Shadow Mt. Lake

34

Mount Craig
12,007 ft +

Isolation Peak
13,118 ft +

Continental Divide

41

CONTINENTAL DIVIDE NATIONAL SCENIC TRAIL

Mount Adams
12,121 ft +

Copeland
13,176 +

Colorado

Green Ridge

Columbine Creek

Ogalalla Peak
13,138 ft +

St. Vrain
Glaciers

Table Mountain

ARAPAHO
NATIONAL RECREATION
AREA

Watanga Mountain
12,375 ft +

ARAPAHO

NATIONAL

Colorado

Lake
Granby

Roaring Fk.

INDIAN PEAKS WILDERNESS

NEVER SUMMER WILDERNESS

Never Summer Mountains

Grand Ditch

A North American elk

visit the natural mineral lick there. In fall, schedule in some time to see Horseshoe Park at dawn or dusk to view elk; bugling mating calls start soon after sunset. In summer and early fall, take Old Fall River Road to Fall River Pass (see next tour), or return to Deer Ridge Junction and turn west onto US 34, Trail Ridge Road.

Continue along Trail Ridge Road, which soon enters the sub-alpine zone which is dominated by forests of Engelmann spruce and subalpine fir. Stop again at the parking area on the right just past **Many Parks Curve,** and walk back to the overlook. The "parks" in the Rockies are mountain meadows: When the glaciers of the last ice age melted, they often left lakes, dammed in by debris the glaciers had pushed along their edges. The lakes eventually silted up and drained, becoming flat meadows. In another 5.8 miles, the road crosses tree line, where subzero winter temperatures and 100-mph winds blast trees into twisted shrubs. Higher still, the road enters alpine tundra. Don't miss the 5-minute stroll to the overlooks of **Forest Canyon,** a glacier-carved, U-shaped valley 2,500 feet below. *Do stay on* *the trail*—damaged tundra plants take decades to recover.

Back in your car, drive on 2 miles, crossing smooth mountaintops that are part of a plain formed when an ancestral mountain range eroded. The plain was uplifted largely intact and remained above the Ice Age glaciers. Stop at Rock Cut (12,110 feet) and hike the 1-mile round-trip, paved nature trail. High altitude can cause dizziness and nausea, *so walk slowly, drink water, and don't overdo.* (If you feel ill, descend to a lower elevation.) The trail leads from a parking lot to the Toll Memorial Mountain Index, a peak-finder atop a rock pile. The 360-degree views of mountain, tundra, and weird rocks are splendid.

About 4 miles farther along the road, exhibits on alpine life—and a chance to quench your thirst—await you at the Alpine Visitor Center and the Trail Ridge store and snack shop at Fall River Pass.

To continue the tour, exit the visitor center parking lot and turn right. Trail Ridge Road crosses the Continental Divide after about 4 miles, at **Milner Pass,** named for the surveyor of a never built railway route through the Rockies. Water flowing east of the divide will eventually find its way to the Atlantic, and water wending west will flow to the Pacific. The overlook at **Farview Curve,** about 2 miles farther, provides a riveting view of the **Never Summer Mountains** and glacier-carved **Kawuneeche Valley.** Through this valley winds the infant **Colorado River,** whose headwaters lie just 5 miles north. About halfway up on the western part of the Never Summer range, you can see a horizontal scar. It is the 14-mile-long **Grand Ditch,** built between 1895 and 1937 to divert

water from the wetter western side of the Continental Divide to the drier Great Plains to the east.

If short of time, turn back now. Otherwise continue the 14 miles remaining on Trail Ridge Road, descending to the beaver ponds, willows, and conifer forests of the valley floor. You might spot moose, reintroduced in 1978 after settlers eliminated them in this area. Hunters also killed off wolves, grizzly bears, and bison in the region.

In the late 19th century, smatterings of silver and gold lured miners by the hundreds to the valley. Resulting boomtowns vanished as quickly as they arose when mining claims proved unprofitable. From the **Colorado River Trailhead,** about 4 miles past Farview Curve, an easy 2-mile hike brings you to the decaying 1870s cabins of miner Joe Shipler. About 1.7 miles farther up the trail lies the site of **Lulu City,** once a bustling mining camp. Whether or not you hike, pick up an engaging leaflet on the human and natural history of this area at the visitor center.

Stop again 2 miles down the road to stroll the easy half-mile through the rippling grasses, and over the Colorado River, to **Holzwarth Historic Site,** a dude ranch dating from the 1920s. By that time it had become clear that the real gold was in tourists' pockets. Return to your car; the road exits the park near Grand Lake.

OLD FALL RIVER ROAD TO FALL RIVER PASS
9.4 miles; a scant half day

Old Fall River Road provides an unpaved (15 mph) drive up the original historic road through conifer forest and tundra. This narrow road

Bierstadt Lake

has tight switchbacks and no guard-rails, so drive cautiously. There is a self-guided auto tour for the drive, and booklets are for sale at the visitor center just before the **Fall River Entrance Station** *(no RVS or vehicles over 25 feet long)*. En route, you'll see traces of ancient glaciers and of recent rockslides and avalanches.

You can enter the park at the entrance station on US 34 or turn north off US 36 at Deer Ridge Junction. (See **Trail Ridge Road** pp. 321-324 for information on Sheep Lakes and Horseshoe Park.) Turn onto the **Endovalley** road. The huge assembly of boulders the road crosses at the Alluvial Fan is a reminder of the 1982 Lawn Lake flood. A dam, built prior to the creation of the park, burst one July morning, releasing a flood that turned the **Roaring River** into a tree-ripping torrent and deposited boulders, mud, and debris as far as the main street of Estes Park.

Pull over at the Alluvial Fan trailhead and take a few minutes to stroll the short paved pathway through the debris—up to 44 feet thick—and observe how nature recovers: Young aspens and conifers and dozens of species of willows and grasses are claiming the area,

as are a wide variety of birds and other animals. Walk back to your car along the trail, not the road.

As you drive on, note the scars on the aspens: Elk and other animals gnaw the bark, which then becomes infected with the black fungus you see; given enough damage, the aspens eventually die. Research has shown that the elk herd in the park and the Estes Valley was larger, less migratory, and more concentrated than it would have been under natural conditions. This lack of mobility has resulted in the decline of habitat for a wide variety of plants and animals. At Endovalley, continue on to the one-way Old Fall River Road with your self-guiding booklet. Join Trail Ridge Road at Fall River Pass.

BEAR LAKE ROAD
10 miles; at least a half day

Popular especially for its trails, wildflowers, views, and fall foliage, Bear Lake Road starts off US 36 just past the **Beaver Meadows Entrance Station.** Make your first stop the **Moraine Park Visitor Center.** Buy a booklet for the nature trail, an easy stroll that starts in front of the building. Along the

Squirrel scavenging near Bear Lake

trail, be sure to smell the ponderosa pine bark; its vanilla scent is luscious.

The paved road is kept open to **Bear Lake** year-round. Parking lots at Bear Lake and Glacier Gorge fill quickly. You may want to take advantage of the free shuttle bus, which is available at the Park & Ride daily during summer. The bus comes frequently; its schedule is in the park newspaper.

The road tunnels through stands of lodgepole pine and aspen—dazzling in fall. At **Sprague Lake** you'll find one of the park's wheelchair-accessible trails; as you stroll along, the forest thins out a bit to offer distant views of Flattop and Hallett peaks.

At **Bear Lake,** buy a booklet and stroll the half-mile **Bear Lake Nature Walk,** enjoying this dramatic, frequently photographed scenery as you learn about forest ecology. The park's most popular hike climbs a mile from Bear to **Dream Lake,** over which tower the distinctive profiles of **Hallett Peak** and **Flattop Mountain.**

For a more challenging hike to another spectacular lake, start from the **Glacier Gorge Trailhead,** about three-quarters of a mile back down the road. The **Loch Trail** passes **Alberta Falls** in a mile, and reaches the rocky shoreline of **The Loch** in a moderately steep 2.9 miles.

OTHER HIKES

The park's excellent network of more than 350 miles of trails presents you with endless possibilities, just a few of which are listed below. See a ranger for details and ideas on less crowded walks.

Sprague Lake: Located off Bear Lake Road, Sprague Lake is a fishing pond created by Abner Sprague. Here's an easy, half-mile walk, a loop dominated by views of Continental Divide peaks.

Wild Basin: This corner of the park—14 miles south of Estes Park off Colo. 7—offers fine day hikes, including those to **Calypso Cascades** (1.8 miles) and **Ouzel Falls** (2.7 miles) through mixed conifer forests along **North Saint Vrain Creek** and its tributaries.

Longs Peak, Chasm Lake: More than 800 people were counted climbing Longs on a summer's day. The predawn climb (7.5 miles one way) to the park's tallest peak requires planning—check with a ranger, especially about lightning and technical climbing. The trail to Chasm Lake (4.2 miles one way) is also a challenging one. Both routes begin at Longs Peak Ranger Station, 1 mile off Colo. 7, 10 miles south of Estes Park. *Note parking is limited.*

Cub Lake: The **Cub Lake Trail** (an easy 4.6-mile round-trip) is one of the first to melt out in the spring. It is known for birding and wildflowers, including the yellow water lilies afloat on Cub Lake in summer. The trail begins from a spur road off Bear Lake Road at **Moraine Park.**

Green Mountain Trail to **Big Meadows:** This easy trail (3.6 miles round-trip) passes through a variety of habitats. It starts from Trail Ridge Road, about 3 miles north of the Grand Lake Entrance.

INFORMATION & ACTIVITIES

VISITOR & INFORMATION CENTERS

Beaver Meadows Visitor Center, on US 36 at east entrance to park, and **Kawuneeche Visitor Center,** on US 34, open daily all year. **Alpine Visitor Center,** late May to mid-Oct. (weather permitting). **Fall River Visitor Center,** on US 34 west of Estes. Park at Fall River entrance, open daily May through Oct. and weekends in winter. **Moraine Park Visitor Center,** May to mid-Oct. Call (970) 586-1206 for information.

SEASONS & ACCESSIBILITY

Park open year-round. Trail Ridge Road closes mid-October to late May, depending on snow. Old Fall River Road closes October to early July. In summer, free shuttle bus service on Bear Lake Road.

HEADQUARTERS

1000 Hwy. 36, Estes Park, CO 80517. Phone (970) 586-1206. www.nps.gov/romo

ENTRANCE FEE

$20 per car; $40 annual.

PETS

Allowed in parking lots, campgrounds, and picnic areas. Not permitted on trails or in backcountry. Must be on leash and must not make noise that disrupts visitors or wildlife. May not be left alone in vehicles.

ACCESSIBLE SERVICES

Visitor centers are wheelchair accessible, as are some amphitheaters in campgrounds, but not all restrooms. Also accessible, the Lily Lake, Bear Lake, and Sprague Lake nature walks and the Coyote Valley Trail. Handicamp, at Sprague Lake, accommodates wheelchair backcountry campers; call (970) 586-1242.

THINGS TO DO

Free ranger-led activities (most in summer only): nature and history walks, hikes, talks, slide shows, arts programs, snowshoe walks. Also, hiking, horseback trail rides, bicycling, fishing, ice fishing, rock climbing, mountain climbing, cross-country skiing, snowshoeing.

OVERNIGHT BACKPACKING

Permits required, obtainable by mail or in person from headquarters or the Kawuneeche Visitor Center. Call (970) 586-1242. Fees charged for backcountry permits in summer.

CAMPGROUNDS

Five campgrounds. 7-day limit June through September. Additional 14 days permitted other times of year. Reservations are recommended at **Aspenglen, Glacier Basin,** and **Moraine Park** campgrounds. Reserve through www.recreation.gov or (877) 444-6777. **Longs Peak, Timber Creek,** and some sites at Moraine Park are open year-round. $20 per site per night in summer; $14 per site per night in winter, when water is not available. No showers. RV sites at all except Longs Peak; no hook-ups. Reservations for **Glacier Basin** group sites in summer (www.recreation.gov). Café in Trail Ridge Store (summer only).

HOTELS, MOTELS, & INNS

(unless otherwise noted, rates are for 2 persons in a double room, high season)

In Estes Park, CO 80517:
Aspen Lodge Ranch Resort 6120 Hwy. 7. (970) 586-8133. 56 units. $589 per person, all inclusive, for 3-day minimum. April–Dec. Pool.
Romantic RiverSong Bed & Breakfast Inn P.O. Box 1910. (970) 586-4666. 10 units. $165-$350, includes breakfast.
The Stanley Hotel 333 Wonderview Ave. (888) 827-1973 or (970) 586-3371. 140 units. $179-$850. Pool, restaurant.
Wind River Ranch 5770 Hwy. 7. (800) 523-4212 or (970) 586-4212. 28 units. $1,750-$1,875 per person per week. June–Sept.
In Grand Lake, CO 80447:
America's Best Value Inn Bighorn Lodge 613 Grand Ave. (970) 627-8101. 20 units. $75-$160.
Black Bear Lodge 12255 Hwy. 34. (970) 627-3654. 17 units, 9 with kitchenettes. $88-$135. Pool.
Western Riviera Motel 419 Garfield. (970) 627-3580. 16 rooms, 23 cabins. $115-$275.

For additional accommodations, contact the Estes Park Visitor Center, (800) 473-7837, www.estesparkcvb.com; or the Grand Lake Chamber of Commerce, (800) 531-1019, www.grandlakechamber.com.

ROCKY MOUNTAIN

EXCURSIONS

ROOSEVELT NATIONAL FOREST
FORT COLLINS, COLORADO

This high mountain forest in the Front Range offers craggy peaks with canyons and passes and clear alpine lakes. Contains six wilderness areas. 650,022 acres. Hiking, boating, fishing, horseback riding, scenic drives, bicycling, winter sports. More than 800 campsites, boat ramp, picnic areas. Three campgrounds open all year; others May through Sept. Backcountry accessible July through Oct. Jointly administered with Arapaho NF. Adjoins Rocky Mountain NP on east. Information at Fort Collins off I-25, 45 miles from Rocky Mountain NP. (970) 295-6600.

ROUTT NATIONAL FOREST
STEAMBOAT SPRINGS, COLORADO

High grasslands, forests, and jagged peaks along the Continental Divide. Alpine lakes brim with trout. Also contains waterfalls and parts of three wilderness areas. 1,124,774 acres. Hiking, boating, fishing, horseback riding, winter sports, water sports. 450 campsites, boat ramp, picnic areas, handicapped access. Most campsites open June through Sept. Information at Steamboat Springs, off US 40, about 75 miles from Rocky Mountain NP. (307) 745-2300.

ARAPAHO NATIONAL WILDLIFE REFUGE
WALDEN, COLORADO

Ringed by mountains, Arapaho's carefully maintained irrigated meadows provide essential nesting habitat for waterfowl such as gadwall, lesser scaup, mallard, and wigeon. Black-crowned night herons breed on the property and sage grouse winter in upland hills. Features 6-mile-long auto tour (closed in winter). 24,804 acres. Fishing, hunting, scenic drives, nature trails. Open year-round, dawn to dusk. Headquarters on Colo. 125 south of Walden, about 60 miles from Rocky Mountain NP. (970) 723-8202.

329

ARAPAHO NATIONAL FOREST
FORT COLLINS, COLORADO

The nation's highest paved highway traverses the steep mountains of this ski-country forest. Five wilderness areas, virgin timber, alpine lakes, and streams. 770,604 acres. Hiking, boating, climbing, bicycling, fishing, horseback riding, hunting, scenic drives, winter sports, water sports. 633 campsites, boat ramp, picnic areas. Open year-round, most campsites open June through September. Visitor center at Idaho Springs on I-70, about 50 miles south of Rocky Mountain NP. (970) 295-6600.

FLORISSANT FOSSIL BEDS NATIONAL MONUMENT
FLORISSANT, COLORADO

Some 34 million years ago a nearby volcanic field erupted, trapping wildlife in the ash that fell on ancient Lake Florissant. Up to 1,700 species of fossil deposits including insects, plants, and numerous fish, bird, and small mammal species have been excavated. 5,998 acres. Hiking, horseback riding. Picnic areas, handicapped access. Open all year, 9 a.m. to 5 p.m. Visitor center on Teller County Road 1, off US 24, about 150 miles south of Rocky Mountain NP. (719) 748-3253, www.nps.gov/fifo.

DINOSAUR NATIONAL MONUMENT
DINOSAUR, COLORADO

Apatosaurus, Diplodocus, Stegosaurus—these Jurassic period giants once roamed here. White-water rafting on Green and Yampa Rivers and Fremont pictographs and petroglyphs are also featured. 210,278 acres, part in Utah. Hiking, rafting, fishing. 125 campsites, picnic areas, handicapped access. Open all year; most campsites open May through September. Dinosaur Quarry on Utah 149, off US 40, about 220 miles west of Rocky Mountain NP. (435) 781-7700, www.nps.gov/dino.

ROCKY MOUNTAIN

Bison wading in park stream

▶THEODORE ROOSEVELT

NORTH DAKOTA
ESTABLISHED NOVEMBER 10, 1978
70,447 acres

Theodore Roosevelt is unique among the scenic parks in that it preserves not only an extraordinary landscape but also the memory of an extraordinary man. It honors the president who probably did more for the National Park System than anyone before or since.

Theodore Roosevelt, who would later establish five national parks and help found the U.S. Forest Service, first came to Dakota Territory as a young man in 1883 to "bag a buffalo." He tried cattle ranching with no luck, but returned many times over the next 13 years, developing into a confirmed conservationist. It was the rugged badlands that taught him a healthy respect for nature while toughening him physically and mentally. "I would not have been President," he would later say, "had it not been for

my experience in North Dakota."

The history of the North Dakota badlands, however, goes back long before Roosevelt—65 million years, to be exact. It was then that streams flowing from the newly risen Rockies began depositing sediments here, while wind and streams simultaneously deposited volcanic ash from volcanoes erupting in the west. This landscape would later be carved by the Little Missouri River and its tributaries. The results of this ongoing process of deposition and erosion are spectacular: wildly corrugated cliffs; steep, convoluted gullies; and dome-shaped hills, their layers of rock and sediment forming multicolored horizontal stripes that run for miles.

This austere landscape is home to a surprisingly dense population of wildlife. Bison, pronghorn, elk, white-tailed and mule deer, wild horses, and bighorn sheep inhabit the park, as do numerous smaller mammals, amphibians, and reptiles. After a rainy spring, a wealth of wildflowers colors the river bottomlands and prairie flats. And perhaps best of all is the shortage of one particular mammal—human beings. This relatively isolated park is hardly ever crowded, so you can experience the gorgeous loneliness of the badlands much the way Roosevelt did more than a hundred years ago.

How to Get There
South Unit: From Bismarck, 130 miles east, take I-94 west across the prairie to the entrance near Medora. From points south, use US 85 north to Belfield, then I-94 west 17 miles to Medora. **North Unit:** US 85 north from Belfield will bring you to the North Unit entrance. Airports: Dickinson and Bismarck, North Dakota, and Billings, Montana (280 miles).

When to Go
Although this is an all-year park, portions of the park road may close in winter, and services are quite limited from October to May. Summer is the most popular time to visit; the days are very long. Late spring and early autumn are best for wildflower enthusiasts.

How to Visit
If you have only 1 day, take the **Scenic Loop Drive** in the **South Unit,** allowing yourself time for nature trails and longer hikes. A second day can be devoted to the **Scenic**

Drive in the **North Unit,** 70 miles away. A visit to the undeveloped site of Roosevelt's **Elkhorn Ranch** or guided horseback trip from the **Peaceful Valley Ranch** in the South Unit can fill out a longer stay.

SOUTH UNIT: SCENIC LOOP DRIVE
36 miles; a half to full day

Start at the **visitor center** in Medora, where you can visit the relocated **Maltese Cross Cabin.** The rustic headquarters of Roosevelt's first ranch, it contains period furnishings, ranching equipment, and some of Roosevelt's personal belongings. Then follow the road up the side of the eroded cliff to the **Medora Overlook.** Here you get a good view of the rough little town that epitomized the Wild West back in Roosevelt's day.

Continue on, making sure to stop at the roadside prairie dog town (they bark warnings to each other as you approach). A little farther along is the **Skyline Vista.** Here you are on

Interior of Roosevelt's Maltese Cross Cabin

THEODORE ROOSEVELT

a high plateau, looking over the broken badlands. Actually, you are not so much "up" as the badlands are "down." The plateau is just a remnant of the original prairie before erosion took its toll, scooping out the bewildering landscape below.

The road descends again to the **River Woodland Overlook.** Beyond the row of cottonwood trees on the left lies an agent of the visual feast around you—the **Little Missouri River.** Notice how, in this arid environment, the vegetation is rigidly stratified according to the availability of water. There are tall cottonwoods near the river, and dark green junipers on the relatively moist northern hillsides and in places where water-bearing layers are exposed. On the dry southern slopes, where sun quickly evaporates rainwater, little grows except grasses.

Continue right past East River Road to begin the **Scenic Loop Drive.** When you reach **Scoria Point,** you are deep into classic badlands territory. The bricklike material around you, which provides the brightest color in the badlands palette, was formed when a layer of black coal ignited. It baked the gray clay above, turning it into the reddish material known locally—but inaccurately—as scoria (the correct name is clinker).

Along the next 6 miles of road, you will encounter two self-guided nature trails that are well worth taking. The **Ridgeline Nature Trail,** while only 0.6 mile long, involves some strenuous climbing; a pamphlet at the trailhead introduces the complex interaction of wind, fire, water, and vegetation in this harsh environment. The **Coal Vein Trail,** at the end of the short unpaved road branching off at mile 15.6 (there's a sign), is a full mile but less difficult; look for the manifold effects of a lignite bed that burned here from 1951 until early 1977. Between these two

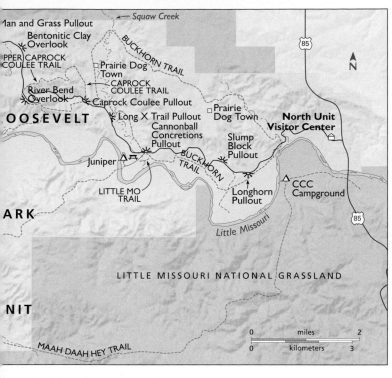

Man and Grass Pullout
— Squaw Creek
Bentonitic Clay
Overlook
BUCKHORN TRAIL
PPER CAPROCK
COULEE TRAIL
Prairie Dog Town
CAPROCK COULEE TRAIL
River Bend Overlook
Caprock Coulee Pullout
OOSEVELT
Long X Trail Pullout
Cannonball Concretions Pullout
Prairie Dog Town
North Unit Visitor Center
Slump Block Pullout
85
Juniper
BUCKHORN TRAIL
LITTLE MO TRAIL
Longhorn Pullout
CCC Campground
ARK
NIT
Little Missouri
85
LITTLE MISSOURI NATIONAL GRASSLAND
N
0 miles 2
0 kilometers 3
MAAH DAAH HEY TRAIL

To Elkhorn Ranch
Government Creek
Round Horse Camp (restricted access)
Prairie Dog Town
WIND CANYON TRAIL
SCENIC LOOP DRIVE
Jules Cr.
LITTLE MISSOURI NATIONAL GRASSLAND
le Missouri
ig
OOSEVELT
JONES CREEK TRAIL
Prairie Dog Town
Jones Creek
lateau
Peaceful Valley Ranch
Halliday Well Site
NATIONAL PARK
TALKINGTON TRAIL
Prairie Dog Town
PADDOCK CREEK TRAIL
rairie Dog Town
Scoria Point Overlook
SOUTH UNIT
Buck Hill 2,855 ft
Prairie Dog Town
RIDGELINE TRAIL
North Dakota Badlands Overlook
COAL VEIN TRAIL
TALKINGTON TRAIL
Prairie Dog Town
94
Painted Canyon Visitor Center
N
0 miles 2
0 kilometers 3
LITTLE MISSOURI NATIONAL GRASSLAND

Weird rock formations by moonlight *(top)*; prairie dog eyeing a rattler *(center)*; calf from the South Unit's bison herd *(bottom)*

trails, pull off at the **North Dakota Badlands Overlook** for an exceptional view of the surroundings.

One and a half miles past the turnoff for Coal Vein is the short road to **Buck Hill.** Take the 100-yard path to the summit for a 360-degree panorama of the eastern end of the park and beyond. Those oil wells on the horizon remind you that,

although the badlands stretch for hundreds of miles, the park does not.

Return to the main road and turn right. The backstretch of the loop, running from Buck Hill to **Wind Canyon,** offers several possibilities for longer hikes. The **Talkington Trail** can be followed to the east or to the west, but even better is the **Jones Creek Trail** at mile 21. This trail follows a deeply eroded creek bed for about 3.5 miles, bisecting the loop road and offering good opportunities to see wildlife. Since this trail is not a loop, you'll want to turn back at the half-way point or arrange to be picked up at the other end.

Back in the car, continue to the **Wind Canyon Trail.** This short but steep path offers a double treat: Not only do you get a magnificent vista of a long oxbow curve in the Little Missouri River, you also get a glimpse of how wind plays a part in shaping this unique landscape. The prevailing winds pick up sand from the riverbed and elsewhere and blow it into the northwest-facing canyon to your left, sandblasting the rock into smooth, bizarre shapes.

Back on the road, you pass another prairie dog town and then the **Peaceful Valley Ranch** on your right. These historic buildings have had a number of incarnations over the years, from working cattle ranch to park headquarters. These days the ranch is the headquarters for the park's saddle horse conces-sion, so you can stop for a ride (late May to early Sept.) before rejoining the entrance road back to the visitor center.

NORTH UNIT: SCENIC DRIVE

28 miles round-trip; a half to full day

Many people regard the North Unit as the more attractive of the two major portions of the park. Certainly the canyons seem steeper here, the river bottomlands lusher, and the blue, black, red, and beige stripes on every butte more pronounced. Located about 52 miles north of I-94, the North Unit is also more isolated, and consequently less visited. According to one ranger, there are times off-season when visitors can be almost alone in the North Unit.

Starting at the visitor center, take the **Scenic Drive** west into the park. Stop at the **Longhorn Pullout** to try and catch a glimpse of the park's demonstration herd of longhorn steers, kept here to commemorate the historic Long-X Trail, the major conduit for longhorns traveling from Texas to the Long-X Ranch just north of the park. If you hike the 11-mile **Buckhorn Trail Loop,** you'll travel along a part of this Old West "highway."

Stop at the **Slump Block Pullout** to see badlands erosion in action. The small hill to your right was once part of the higher cliff beyond—until unstable underlying sediments caused this piece to slump away. Try matching the diagonal layers of the slump block to the horizontal layers on the cliff to see how the block once fit in.

Pull off at the **Cannonball Concretions Pullout** to see how weathering agents have eroded out sandstone spheres formed by groundwater minerals cementing. Opposite the pullout, look for the **Little Mo Nature Trail.** This easy half-mile loop takes you through typical river woodlands, and a guide leaflet (available at the trailhead) allows you to identify many native plants the Plains Indians used for medicine, food, and raw materials. Be on the lookout for beaver and white-tailed deer.

Returning to the car, follow the road to the **Caprock Coulee Pullout,** where you can pick up the nature trail of the same name. Take this easy trail 0.75 mile up a dry canyon (a "coulee") to a grove of pedestal rocks ("caprocks"). The harder caprocks protect the sediments below while the surrounding sediments erode away, leaving the mushroom-shaped formations (called hoodoos) around you. At the end of the nature trail, you can either turn back or make a 5-mile loop by continuing to the **Upper Caprock Coulee Trail,** a choice which involves some steeper climbing but lots of opportunities to view wildlife.

Beyond the Caprock Coulee parking lot, the road climbs steeply to the level of the original prairie. At the top, the **River Bend Overlook** offers an absolutely stunning vista of the deep Little Missouri River Valley and the extensive badlands on either side. The **Bentonitic Clay Overlook** a little farther on offers a less dramatic but perhaps more instructive view. The blue-colored bentonite layer visible for miles is composed of an extremely absorbent volcanic ash that flows when wet. The plasticity of this layer accounts for much of the dynamism of the badlands landscape.

The road now traces the edge of a grassy plateau. This is prime bison territory; you may even have to wait while a herd crosses the road in front of you. At the **Man and Grass Pullout** you can get some idea of the extensive grasslands that made this part of Dakota worth the trip up the Long-X Trail. Finally, the road ends—spectacularly—at the **Oxbow Overlook.** After enjoying the visual banquet of badlands, return along the same road to the visitor center.

THEODORE ROOSEVELT

INFORMATION & ACTIVITIES

VISITOR & INFORMATION CENTERS

Medora Visitor Center and the **Maltese Cross Cabin,** at the entrance to the South Unit, open daily all year. **Painted Canyon Visitor Center,** in the southeastern part of the South Unit off I-94, open from mid-April to mid-November. **North Unit Visitor Center,** open daily April through September, and weekends in winter. Call headquarters for visitor information.

SEASONS & ACCESSIBILITY

Park open all year, but access may be limited in winter due to snow. The South Unit road from Medora Visitor Center through Wind Canyon to the north boundary is kept plowed, but not the Scenic Loop Drive. The North Unit road is plowed from the entrance to the Caprock Coulee Trailhead. Call headquarters for weather and road information.

HEADQUARTERS

P.O. Box 7, Medora, ND 58645. Phone (701) 623-4466. www.nps.gov/thro

ENTRANCE FEE

$5 per person, maximum of $10 per vehicle per week; $20 annually.

PETS & HORSES

Pets are permitted on leashes except on trails and in buildings. Horses are prohibited in campgrounds, picnic areas, and on self-guided trails.

ACCESSIBLE SERVICES

Visitor centers, restrooms, campground sites, and some trails are wheelchair accessible. Check at the visitor centers for a list of accessible facilities.

THINGS TO DO

Free ranger-led activities: nature walks and talks, tours of Roosevelt's Maltese Cross Cabin (mid-June to mid-Sept.), evening campfire programs. Also hiking, horseback riding (contact the Peaceful Valley Ranch in South Unit, 701-623-4568), interpretive exhibits, auto tours, limited canoeing and float trips, fishing (license required).

SPECIAL ADVISORIES

• View bison from a distance; they are known to attack if provoked.
• Rattlesnakes and black widow spiders often live in prairie dog burrows; be alert for them when hiking.
• Ticks are abundant in early summer.
• Do not feed the prairie dogs; they bite and may carry disease.
• Be prepared for extremes of temperatures and sudden violent thunderstorms.

OVERNIGHT BACKPACKING

Permits required. They are free and can be obtained at visitor centers.

CAMPGROUNDS

Two campgrounds, both with a 15-day consecutive limit (30 days per year). **Cottonwood** and **Juniper** open all year, first come, first served. Fees $10 per night. No showers. Tent and RV sites; no hookups. No water available October to April. Three group campgrounds, **Cottonwood, Juniper,** and **Roundup** (horses); reservations required; contact park headquarters.

HOTELS, MOTELS, & INNS

(unless otherwise noted, rates are for 2 persons in a double room, high season)

In Dickinson, ND 58601:
Comfort Inn 493 Elk Dr. (701) 264-7300. 116 units. $130. AC, pool.
Oasis Inn 1000 W. Villerd St. (701) 225-6703. 35 units, 6 with kitchenettes. $80. AC.
Ramada Inn 532 15th St. W. (800) 272-6232 or (701) 227-1853. 192 units. $159. AC, pool, restaurant.

In Medora, ND 58645:
Badlands Motel 501 Pacific Ave. (800) 633-6721 or (701) 623-4444. 115 units. $125-$135. AC, pool.
The Bunkhouse 400 E. River Rd. (800) 633-6721 or (701) 623-4444. 135 units. $79-$89. AC, pool. Late May–Oct.
Rough Riders Hotel 301 3rd Ave. (800) 633-6721 or (701) 623-4444. 76 units. $175-$199. AC, restaurant.

In Watford City, ND 58854:
Roosevelt Inn 600 2nd Ave. S.W., P.O. Box 1003. (800) 887-9170 or (701) 842-3686. 44 units. $95. AC, pool.

EXCURSIONS

LITTLE MISSOURI NATIONAL GRASSLAND
DICKINSON & WATFORD CITY, NORTH DAKOTA

Bighorn sheep, elk, pronghorn, eagles, hawks, and grouse live in the prairie and badlands around Theodore Roosevelt NP. 1,259,000 acres. Hiking, horseback riding, hunting. 5 campgrounds. Open all year; campgrounds late May to Labor Day. Information in Dickinson, off I-94. (701) 250-4443, www.fs.fed.us.

LAKE ILO NATIONAL WILDLIFE REFUGE
DUNN CENTER, NORTH DAKOTA

Waterfowl nest in the grasslands surrounding 1,240-acre Lake Ilo, offering recreation not found on all refuges. 4,000 acres. Boating, fishing, picnic areas, nature trail, archaeological exhibits, scenic drives. Open year-round. Located on N. Dak. 200, about 50 miles east of Theodore Roosevelt NP's North Unit. (701) 548-8110, www.fws.gov/refuges.

LOSTWOOD NATIONAL WILDLIFE REFUGE
KENMARE, NORTH DAKOTA

Ducks, marsh birds, grouse, hawks, Baird's sparrows, and Sprague's pipits inhabit this globally important bird area with shallow glacial lakes, attracting bird-watchers from near and far. 26,904 acres. Hiking, hunting, scenic drives. Auto tour is possible May through September, dawn to dusk. Located off N. Dak. 8, about 135 miles northeast of Theodore Roosevelt NP's North Unit. (701) 848-2722, www.fws.gov/refuges.

Prince of Wales Hotel on Waterton Lakes

▶ WATERTON-GLACIER

ALBERTA, CANADA, & MONTANA
ESTABLISHED JUNE 18, 1932
Waterton Lakes, 129,700 acres
Glacier, 1,013,572 acres

Waterton-Glacier International Peace Park World Heritage site contains 1,800 square miles of what naturalist John Muir called "the
best care-killing scenery on the continent." Multihued summits—
whittled by ancient glaciers into walls and horns—rise abruptly
from gently rolling plains. Some 762 lakes, dozens of glaciers, and
innumerable waterfalls glisten in forested valleys. A scenic highway crosses the park, making much of its beauty accessible to the
casual visitor. More than 700 miles of trails await hikers and horseback riders.

In 1932 Canada and the United
States declared Waterton Lakes
National Park (founded in 1895) and
neighboring Glacier National Park
(founded in 1910) the world's first
International Peace Park. While
administered separately, the park's
two sections cooperate in wildlife

management, scientific research,
and some visitor services.

The tremendous range of topography in Waterton-Glacier supports
a rich variety of plants and wildlife.
Almost 2,000 plant species provide
food and haven for more than 60
native species of mammals and

260 species of birds. In the 1980s the gray wolf settled into Glacier for the first time since the 1950s.

But now oil, gas, and logging projects proposed or under way near the park's respective borders endanger the habitats of both water and land animals, including elk, bighorn sheep, and the threatened grizzly. Park officials and conservation groups are working with the U.S. Forest Service, the state of Montana, the Canadian government, the Blackfeet Tribe, and private companies to try to protect critical habitats, even those that extend beyond park boundaries. Recent agreements between the state of Montana and the province of British Columbia have taken measures to eliminate coal, oil, and gas development in the Canadian Flathead.

Sheltered valleys and bountiful food have lured people here for nearly 10,000 years. Ancient cultures tracked bison across the plains, fished the lakes, and traversed the mountain passes. The Blackfeet controlled this land during the 18th and much of the 19th centuries.

How to Get There

Approach West Glacier (from Kalispell, Montana, about 35 miles) and East Glacier Park from US 2. US 89 leads to Many Glacier and St. Mary in the east, US 89 and Mont. 17 (Chief Mountain International Hwy.) form the shortest connection between Glacier and Waterton Lakes. Coming from Canada, follow Alberta 2, 5, or 6. Amtrak trains from Chicago and Seattle stop year-round just outside the park at West Glacier (Belton), Essex, Browning, and East Glacier Park; by prior arrangement, buses take travelers into the park. Nearest airports: Kalispell and Great Falls, Montana; and Lethbridge, Alberta.

When to Go

Summer. Road rehabilitation occurs on portions of the Going-to-the-Sun Road before and after the core summer season with possible closures. (Mid-June–mid-Sept. delays are limited to a maximum of 30-40 minutes during a one-way trip across Logan Pass.) All of Going-to-the-Sun Road is open generally from mid-June to mid-September; Chief Mountain International Highway, mid-May to late September. Trails at lower elevations are usually clear of snow by mid-June; higher trails can remain snowed-in until mid-July. Cross-country skiing is popular from December to April in areas of the park.

How to Visit

Spend your first day on and around the **Going-to-the-Sun Road,** considered by many one of the world's most spectacular highways. On a second day, travel the **Chief Mountain International Highway** north to Waterton Lakes, enjoying the contrast of peak and prairie. Drive Waterton's **Akamina Parkway** and **Red Rock Parkway.** Stay at least another day to visit Glacier's **Many Glacier.** For a longer visit, drive to **Two Medicine** for a boat ride and walk to an exquisite lake, then continue on to the Walton **Goat Lick Overlook,** both also in Glacier. If you have the stamina and overnight reservations, hike or ride horseback to one of the two remaining chalets built in Glacier early in the 20th century by the Great Northern Railway.

GOING-TO-THE-SUN ROAD

50 miles; a full day. Note: Vehicles longer than 21 feet and wider than 8 feet prohibited on this road.

Begin early at **Apgar** on Glacier's west side. At the visitor center

WATERTON-GLACIER

ALBERTA
B.C.

Sage Creek

Waterton

WATERTON

Red Rock
Canyon
RED ROCK
PKWY.

Bison Paddock

Park Entrance
Lower Waterton L.

South Kootenay
Pass

Mt. Blackiston
9,581 ft

LAKES

Crandell
Mt.

Visitor Reception Centre

Golf Course

NATIONAL

BLOOD

Upper Rowe Lake

AKAMINA
PKWY.

Waterton Park

INDIAN

AKAMINA-KISHINENA
PROVINCIAL PARK

*Cameron
Lake*

PARK

RESERVE
Belly
River

BRITISH COLUMBIA

Upper

Customs

MONTANA

*Waterton
Lake*

Belly

*Kintla
Lake*

Kintla Peak
10,101 ft

*Agassiz
Glacier*

Goat Haunt

Kintla Lake

Mount Cleveland
10,466 ft

GABLE Mt.
9,262 ft

*Bowman
Lake*

*Quartz
Lake*

LIVINGSTON

*Continental
Divide*

Many Glacier

*Swiftcurrent
Lake*

Bowman
Lake

Iceberg L.

Granite
Park
Chalet

Josephine L.

486

GLACIER

*Logging
Lake*

RANGE

Garden Wall

Grinn
Glacie

FLATHEAD

Polebridge

Longfellow Pk.
8,904 ft

NATIONAL

Goin
to-th
Sun M

Polebridge

INSIDE
NORTH FORK
ROAD

Logan Pass
Visitor Center
6,646 ft

9,642

NATIONAL

Quartz
Creek

GOING-TO-THE-SUN
ROAD

FOREST

OUTSIDE
NORTH FORK
ROAD

Avalanche Creek

Hidden L.

Avalanche L.

Jackson
Glacier

Logging Creek

PAR

Camas
Creek
Entrance

McDonald Falls

*Sperry
Glacier*

Jacks
Glaci

miles   10

Lake McDonald

Big Creek
Outdoor
Education Center

Big Creek

Sprague Creek

Sperry Chalet

Mt. Jackson
10,052 ft

kilometers   15

Apgar Mts.

Fish Creek

*Lake
McDonald*

Whitefish Range

Apgar Visitor Center

West Entrance
Park Headquarters

Loneman
Mountain
7,181 ft

*Whitefish
Lake*

West Glacier

486

FLATHEAD

WHITEFISH
LAKE
STATE PARK

FLATHEAD NATIONAL
WILD & SCENIC RIVER

2

NATIONAL

Middle Fork Flathead

Whitefish

*Teakettle Mt.
5,936 ft*

Coram

FOREST

Flathead Range

93

Columbia
Falls

Hungry Horse

40

*S. Fk.
Flathead*

93

2

206

Great Northern
Mountain
8,705 ft

Glacier Park
International
Airport

Flathead

Swan Range

GREAT
BEAR
WILDERNES
AREA

*Hungry
Horse
Reservoir*

35

pick up details about trails and, since this is grizzly and black bear country, cautionary advice on avoiding bear encounters. Take time to admire **Lake McDonald** from the vantage point a little farther down the road. The park's largest lake, McDonald is 10 miles long and 472 feet deep; a 2,000-foot-thick glacier gouged out its basin. Kootenai Indians, who performed lakeshore ceremonies, called the waters Sacred Dancing Lake.

Continue driving along the Apgar loop and turn left at Going-to-the-Sun Road. Then pull over at **McDonald Falls,** on your left after about 10 miles. Stroll down to the viewpoint and note the layered rock. Waterton-Glacier's mountains are built mainly of sedimentary rock formed from mud and sand at the bottom of a sea that existed here for nearly a billion years. Over the eons, pressures in the Earth uplifted, thrusted, and folded the seabed into mountains. The rock exposed at McDonald Falls is among the oldest in the park.

Pull over near the campground at **Avalanche Creek** and start the self-guided **Trail of the Cedars** on the right side of the road. This wheelchair-accessible trail is on a boardwalk. The easy, quite popular, a 0.75-mile nature stroll acquaints you with the cedar-hemlock forest through which you've been driving. Along the trail, Avalanche Creek tumbles through contoured walls of surprisingly red stone, formed during a period when the sea here retreated. In contact with oxygen, iron-bearing minerals in the mud formed the bright red mineral hematite that colors the rock. Extend your walk, if you wish, by taking the **Avalanche Lake Trail** from near the gorge up to glacier-fed **Avalanche Lake.** The gently

WATERTON-GLACIER

Massive Grinnell Glacier

climbing trail, about 4 miles round-trip, offers fine views of creek, lake, and waterfalls.

Return to your car. Ahead, in about 2 miles, you'll see the **Garden Wall,** part of the Continental Divide. West of the divide, waters flow to the Pacific; east of it, to the Arctic or Atlantic. Two glaciers ground down opposite sides of a ridge to form the knife-edged Garden Wall. At the **Bird Woman Falls** viewpoint (some 10 miles from the campground at Avalanche Creek), an exhibit illustrates how glaciers also carved this spectacular U-shaped valley. Glacier National Park takes its name from the huge rivers of ice that sculptured the landscape during ice ages of the last two million years.

At **Logan Pass,** atop the Continental Divide, the peaks crowd around as if close enough to touch. Park and walk up the hill past the visitor center to take the **Hidden Lake Overlook Nature Trail.** Be sure to buy or borrow a self-guiding pamphlet at the trailhead. The 3-mile round-trip begins on the boardwalk and offers vast displays of wildflowers framed by dramatic peaks. A breathtaking vista of **Hidden Lake** awaits you at the overlook. Watch for mountain goats grazing, marmots sunning, and golden eagles scanning for rodents. *Always stay on the trail:* Alpine plants, growing for short seasons in thin soil, are extremely fragile.

Return to your car and turn right onto the main road. Soon you'll be approaching **Going-to-the-Sun Mountain**—at 9,642 feet, the highest in this area of the park. The name comes, depending on which story you believe, from a Blackfeet legend or an early explorer. The legend says that Napi, the creator, came to help the Blackfeet, then climbed this mountain to return to the sun.

Pull over again to view **Jackson Glacier,** one of the few glaciers visible from the road, about 4.5 miles east of Logan Pass. The turnoff for **Sun Point** leads to picnic tables, fine vistas of **St. Mary Lake,** and a nature trail that introduces the ecology of the drier eastern portion of the park. Next, stop at the **Wild Goose**

Island Overlook, 1.5 miles down the road, and again at the display about Triple Divide Peak, less than 3 miles beyond. Crossing grasslands punctuated by groves of aspen and conifers, the Going-to-the-Sun Road ends at Divide Creek, the border of the Blackfeet Reservation.

CHIEF MOUNTAIN HIGHWAY TO WATERTON LAKES

75 miles; at least a full day

Chief Mountain International Highway begins north of Babb off US 89. Chief Mountain (9,080 feet) dominates the horizon to your left, a solitary peak that commands awe. Blackfeet seeking spiritual guidance still tie a traditional offering of colored cloth to trees at its base.

Chief Mountain also represents the easternmost extension of the Lewis Overthrust, a major geological feature. About 10 miles after the U.S.-Canada customs station, pull over for a superb view of Waterton Valley and a display that identifies the summits.

Follow the signs for Waterton Lakes National Park. The park's main information center will be on your right, about 4 miles beyond the park entrance, just before Waterton Park townsite. On your left stands the Prince of Wales Hotel, which commands a first-rate view of Upper Waterton Lake from its lobby. For a loftier panorama, climb the steep but gratifying Bear's Hump Trail, 2 miles round-trip. The path starts from the visitor center.

At road's end awaits Waterton Park townsite, a village of about a hundred year-round residents. It blossoms in summer with eateries and gift shops. Wildlife is often on hand: Bighorn sheep and deer may be hiding in the shadows or out in the open; you'll less likely spot the rare mountain lion or bear. On the lakeshore, near the marina, is the Peace Park Pavilion Exhibit. Back in your car, turn onto Akamina Parkway, which traces Cameron Valley 10 miles to Cameron Lake. At the lake, which lies in a large glacier-carved basin, rent a boat, fish for trout, or stroll the 2-mile round-trip Cameron Lakeshore Trail through the forest of Englemann spruce and subalpine fir. *Do not continue past the end of the trail—grizzlies are often sighted there.*

Back in your car, return to Alberta 5; turn left, then left again onto 10-mile-long Red Rock Parkway. The prairie here brims with flowers in May, June, and early July. In about 3 miles, near Crandell Mountain Campground, stop at the exhibit on ancient Indian life. Drive on to the road's end at Red Rock Canyon, where archaeologists found a camp dating from 8,400 years ago. Don't miss the half-mile Red Rock Canyon Loop Trail.

MANY GLACIER & SWIFTCURRENT VALLEY

13 miles from Babb; at least a half day

Many Glacier, named for the glaciers on surrounding mountains, is a hiker's Eden and a good place to see bighorn sheep and other wildlife. A dam a few miles outside the park created Lake Sherburne, on your left as you enter the park. The lake submerged much of Altyn, a boomtown built during the mining frenzy that started and fizzled out here at the turn of the 20th century.

Just beyond the lake, to your left, is the Many Glacier Hotel. The Great Northern Railway built it in 1915 to help promote tourism along its tracks. The company also built more than a dozen backcountry tent camps and chalets in Waterton-Glacier. Park at the hotel and, for an easy walk and fine introduction to the area's plants, animals, peaks, and glaciers, take the **Swiftcurrent Nature Trail.** This 2.5-mile loop around the lake starts at the shore south of the hotel. The trail traverses both 400-year-old spruce-fir and 60-year-old lodgepole pine forests, planted in the aftermath of a great fire in 1936.

For an easy 2.5-mile stroll through old-growth forest, go on the **Swiftcurrent and Josephine Lakes** boat tour and hike. With more time and plenty of stamina, join a naturalist-led hike (8 miles) and boat ride (fee) to the edge of **Grinnell Glacier,** one of the largest in the park. Check departure times in the park newspaper.

OTHER SIGHTS & TRAILS

Before hiking, be sure to stop by a visitor center or ranger station to pick up maps and schedules—and check for trail closings due to bears.

Drive to **Two Medicine,** inside the park's southeastern border off Mont. 49, and take the boat across **Two Medicine Lake.** Then walk past **Twin Falls** through huckleberry meadows to **Upper Two Medicine Lake,** which is surrounded by brightly colored cliffs (4.4 miles round-trip). Back in your car, head south on Mont. 49 and west on US 2 to the **Goat Lick Overlook.** A natural salt lick attracts mountain goats from miles around, usually in spring and early summer.

From Logan Pass, the **Highline Trail** offers splendid panoramic views as it crosses Glacier's high country to Waterton townsite (43.6 miles). The trail follows in part the slopes of the Garden Wall, a razor-backed arête, between McDonald Valley and the

Many Glacier area. Consider a stop along the way at **Granite Park Chalet** (7.6 miles one way), one of the Great Northern's two remaining chalets. (The other chalet, **Sperry,** was recently restored. Sperry can be reached by horse or on foot from **Jackson Glacier Overlook** or Lake McDonald.) Part of the trail is cut into the cliff face, so it is not for the fainthearted.

From Many Glacier, **Iceberg Lake Trail** leads you among wide panoramas to an iceberg-studded turquoise lake, a 10-mile round-trip. **Cracker Lake Trail,** 12.2 miles round-trip, parallels boulder-strewn **Canyon Creek** part way to this glacier-fed lake. Nearby lie remains of **Cracker Mine.**

From Akamina Parkway, **Rowe Meadow** (a moderately strenuous, 6.5-mile round-trip) offers a rainbow of wildflowers in early summer. Climb another 0.7-mile to **Upper Rowe Lake** through an alpine larch forest. The **International Peace Park Hike,** held on Wednesday and Saturday mornings (reservations required), leads 8.4 miles from Waterton Park to **Goat Haunt** in the United States. Return by boat.

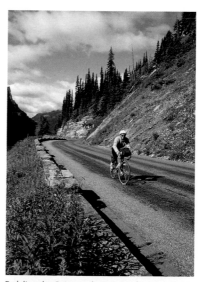

Pedaling the Going-to-the-Sun Road

INFORMATION & ACTIVITIES

VISITOR & INFORMATION CENTERS

Waterton: Waterton Visitor Centre in Waterton Park; (403) 859-5133. Usually open mid-May through Sept. call ahead. **Glacier: Apgar Visitor Center,** West Entrance, open May–mid-Oct., weekends rest of the year. **Logan Pass Visitor Center,** open mid-June to late Sept. **St. Mary Visitor Center** at East Entrance open mid-May to mid-Oct.

SEASONS & ACCESSIBILITY

Parks open year-round; winter snows limit access and services.

HEADQUARTERS

Waterton: Box 200, Waterton Park, AB ToK 2Mo, Canada. Phone (403) 859-2224. **Glacier:** P.O. Box 128, West Glacier, MT 59936. Phone (406) 888-7800. www.nps .gov/glac

ENTRANCE FEES

Waterton: Canadian $8 per adult/$4 per child (under 6 free). **Glacier:** $25 per car valid for 7 days; $35 one-year pass.

ACCESSIBLE SERVICES

Waterton: Park Pavilion, Heritage Centre, Cameron Lake exhibit building wheelchair accessible. Several camping facilities, Lake Linnet Trail, drive through the Bison Paddock, and most restrooms. **Glacier:** Most visitor center facilities accessible; also Trail of the Cedars, Running Eagle Falls Trail, Oberlin Bend Trail, Goat Lick Overlook, Apgar Bike Path.

THINGS TO DO

Waterton: Free interpreter-led activities: theater programs, guided walks, hikes. Also, swimming, fishing (license needed), boating, nature courses, horseback rides, cross-country skiing, and cycling. **Glacier:** Free naturalist-led activities: walks and hikes, slide talks, campfire programs, Going-to-the Sun shuttle (July & Aug.). Hiking, horseback rides, boating, fishing (no license), biking, launch tours, nature courses, cross-country skiing.

OVERNIGHT BACKPACKING

Permits required. Call in advance about reservations and fees. Waterton backcountry: (403) 859-5133; Glacier backcountry: (406) 888-7800.

CAMPGROUNDS

Waterton: Three campgrounds, 14-day limit. Open mid-May–early Sept., **Townsite** open to mid-Oct. Townsite reservable, others first come, first served. Fees Can. $16-$33. Must reserve at **Belly River Group Campgrounds;** contact park. **Glacier:** 13 campgrounds, limit 14 days July–Labor Day, otherwise 30 days. **Apgar** and **St. Mary** open all year, others late spring–mid-fall. Reservations for **Fish Creek, St. Mary,** and half of **Apgar** group sites through the NRRS (see p. 10). Others first come, first served. Fees $10-$23 per night.

BACKCOUNTRY CHALETS

Granite Park Chalet ($85 plus $10 for optional linen; $73 for additional person in same room) and **Sperry Chalet** ($180 per room plus $130 per additional person, incl. meals) offers full-service backcountry lodging. (888) 345-2649.

HOTELS, MOTELS, & INNS

(unless otherwise noted, rates are for 2 persons in a double room, high season)

INSIDE WATERTON, Alberta TOK 2MO:
Aspen Village Inn (403) 859-2255. 50 units. Can. $135-$250.
Bayshore Inn 111 Waterton Ave. (403) 859-2211 or (403) 238-4847. 70 units. Can. $199. Restaurant. April to Oct.
Crandell Mt. Lodge Mt. View Rd. (403) 859-2288. 17 units. Can. $140-$220.
Prince of Wales Hotel (near Waterton Townsite) Reservations: Glacier Park, Inc. (see below). (406) 892-2525. 86 units. Can. $256-$800. Rest.

INSIDE GLACIER:
The following open from June to mid-Sept. Contact Glacier Park, Inc., P.O. Box 2025, Columbia Falls, MT 59912. (406) 892-2525, www.glacierparkinc.com. All have restaurants.
Glacier Park Lodge 161 units. $145-$450.
Lake McDonald Lodge, Cabins & Motor Inn 100 units. $122-$173.
Many Glacier Hotel 214 units. $145-$225.
Rising Sun Motor Inn 72 units. $118-$134.
Swiftcurrent Motor Inn & Cabins 88 units. $70-$134.
The Village Inn at Apgar 36 units. $130-$225.

EXCURSIONS

FLATHEAD NATIONAL FOREST
KALISPELL, MONTANA

Recreation opportunities abound here amid mountains, lakes, wild and scenic rivers, and more than 2,000 miles of trails. Contains parts of three wilderness areas, notably the Bob Marshall. 2.4 million acres. Hiking, boating, climbing, fishing, horseback riding, scenic drives, winter sports, water sports. 400 campsites, boat ramp, picnic areas. Open all year; campsites open June to mid-Sept. Visitor center off US 2 at Hungry Horse Dam, about 7 miles from Waterton-Glacier NP. (406) 758-5208, www.fs.fed.us.

LEWIS & CLARK NATIONAL FOREST
GREAT FALLS, MONTANA

This forest has two sections separated by plains: The Rocky Mountain front section boasts steep terrain with parts of two wilderness areas; the Jefferson section contains gentler peaks and broad plateaus. Large bighorn herd. 1.8 million acres. Hiking, boating, climbing, fishing, horseback riding, winter sports, water sports. 24 campsites (open late spring to fall), 5 winter cabins (reservations required), boat ramp, handicapped access. Adjoins Waterton-Glacier NP on south. (406) 791-7700, www.fs.fed.us.

KOOTENAI NATIONAL FOREST
LIBBY, MONTANA

With a climate closer to that of the Pacific coast than to Montana, Kootenai features virgin stands of western red cedar. Lake Koocanusa, 90 miles long, and many other streams and reservoirs offer abundant recreation. Contains Cabinet Mountains Wilderness. 2.2 million acres. Hiking, boating, climbing, bicycling, fishing, scenic drives, winter sports. 509 campsites, most open late spring to fall. Information at Libby on US 2. 120 miles from Waterton-Glacier NP. (406) 293-6211, www.fs.usda.gov/kootenai.

PINE BUTTE SWAMP PRESERVE
CHOTEAU, MONTANA

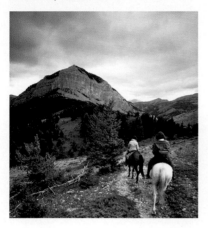

Pine Butte, a 500-foot promontory, overlooks this Nature Conservancy refuge dedicated to maintaining the essential habitat of the grizzly. Also contains many other wildlife species, including lynx, mountain lion, sandhill crane, golden eagle, mink, and bighorn sheep. Features the Egg Mountain duckbill dinosaur nesting site; daily paleontological tours during summer. Permission required to explore. 18,000 acres, along the Teton River. Hiking. The Pine Butte Guest Ranch offers horseback riding, natural history tours (open June through Sept.). Preserve open all year. Off US 89, about 60 miles southeast of Waterton-Glacier NP. (406) 466-5526.

BENTON LAKE
NATIONAL WILDLIFE REFUGE
GREAT FALLS, MONTANA

More than 200 species of birds find food, protection, and carefully maintained nesting areas on this prairie marsh in the midst of wheat fields and grasslands. Northern pintail, gadwall, Canada goose, and white-faced ibis are among the species that nest in the ancient glacial lake bed that holds the marsh. 12,383 acres. Hunting, bird-watching, self-guided auto tour. Open when accessible (snow drifts often cover road Nov. to March), dawn to dusk. Headquarters off US 87, 100 miles from Waterton-Glacier NP. (406) 727-7400, www.fws.gov/refuges.

WATERTON-GLACIER

The Great Plains of the Black Hills

▶ WIND CAVE

SOUTH DAKOTA
ESTABLISHED JANUARY 9, 1903
28,295 acres

Too many visitors leave Wind Cave National Park knowing only half of its charms. Ironically, the half they know is the half that's not visible from the surface.

Above the spectacular underground labyrinth for which the park is named lies an unusual ecosystem with elements from both the mixed-grass prairie of the western Great Plains, and the ponderosa pine forests of the Black Hills. Thus, the park plays host to plant and animal species from several distinct geographical areas—prairie falcons and meadowlarks from the grasslands coexist here with nuthatches and wild turkeys from the forests.

Wildlife could be the major draw here. Because of the park's small size and relatively large bison population, the chances of seeing bison —the so-called American buffalo—

are probably better at this park than at almost any other; indeed it's often difficult to avoid the great beasts. The park's bison are descendants of 14 bison reintroduced to the park in 1913 from the New York Zoological Society.

Pronghorn, mule deer, and prairie dogs are present in large numbers—and highly visible since more than 60 percent of the park is open grassland. Elk live in the forest fringes; you probably won't see many, but if you have the good luck to come in the autumn you'll hear their eerie bugling.

Belowground lies Wind Cave. The first recorded discovery of the cave occurred in 1881, when two brothers named Bingham heard a loud whistling noise coming from the cave's only natural entrance.

Today, more than 130 miles of explored passages make Wind Cave one of the world's longest caves. Because the cave is relatively dry, it contains few of the stalactites and stalagmites that you find in other caves. But it has many unusual mineral formations, including perhaps the world's best collection of boxwork, a calcite formation resembling irregular honeycombs. Perhaps it's most distinctive feature may be the strong winds that alternately rush in and out of its mouth, equalizing air pressure between the passages inside and the atmosphere outside, and causing the noise the Binghams heard.

How to Get There

For the scenic route from Rapid City (74 miles away), take US 16 to US 16A south, detouring for a glimpse of Mount Rushmore, to S. Dak. 87 south. This route—*not open to RVs and trailers*—takes you along the Needles Highway and through Custer State Park to Wind Cave's north entrance.

The faster route is to follow S. Dak. 79 south from Rapid City to Hot Springs and then turn north onto US 385 to the south entrance. From the west, take US 16 east to Custer and US 385 south from there. Airport: Rapid City.

When to Go

All-year park. Although the cave and visitor center are open every day except Thanksgiving and Christmas and New Year's Day, the park offers far fewer cave tours off-season (late September to May). Late spring to midsummer is best for viewing wildflowers. Saturdays and Sundays

in summer are the days least likely to be crowded. The campground is rarely, if ever, full.

How to Visit

A good plan of action for a single-day visit would be to spend the morning in **Wind Cave** on one of the shorter introductory tours and the afternoon exploring the park's prairies and forests on the **Scenic Drive.** A second day would be the time for one of the longer **Candlelight** or **Cave Tours.**

People with physical limitations will want to stick to the shorter, less strenuous tours, although even the shortest involves climbing up and down about 150 steps. (If claustrophobia is a problem for you, you might think twice about entering the cave at all.)

Wear good walking shoes, and, since the cave temperature is a constant 53°F, take a jacket even on hot summer days. Reservations for Candlelight and Wild Cave Tours are recommended. You must be 8 years old for the Candlelight Tour and 16 years old for the Wild Cave Tour.

WIND CAVE: GUIDED TOURS
1 hour to a half day

All tours begin at the historic 1936 **visitor center,** where exhibits provide important background information. A video explains the connection between the park's subsurface world and the aboveground prairie. The same forces that lifted the nearby Black Hills created cracks in the limestone layers beneath the present-day park. Water seeped into these cracks and, over millions of years, gradually dissolved the rock, creating the maze of passages and tunnels we see today.

WIND CAVE

The cave's famous boxwork, a calcite formation

Most first-timers will choose to take either the **Natural Entrance Tour,** which lasts about an hour and 15 minutes, or the **Fairgrounds Tour,** which is 15 minutes longer. These tours introduce you to the underground world, and stress basic information about caves and cave formations; they take you through such colorfully named places as the **Post Office** (named for the extensive boxwork on the walls), the **Devil's Lookout,** and the **Bachelor's Quarters.**

The **Garden of Eden Tour** is an easy loop around from the elevator to the **Garden of Eden** and lasts about one hour; it is the best choice for people who are short on time or have physical limitations.

CUSTER STATE PARK

Rankin Ridge
5,013 ft

WIND CAVE NATIONAL PARK

BLACK HILLS NATIONAL FOREST

Visitor Center

Bachelor's Quarters

Three-way Stair

N

0 miles 4
0 km 6

Elks Room
3,911 ft

Elevator Building
4,055 ft

Assembly Room
3,863 ft

Rome

Garden of Eden

Muddle Room

Omnibus Hall

Hot Springs

If you are a history buff, by all means take the **Candlelight Tour** (summer only). Conducted by the light of candle lanterns, this 2-hour tour harks back to the 1890s, when Wind Cave was managed by the Wonderful Wind Cave Improvement Company and tours were measured by the number of candles needed to complete them. The tour goes past the **Blue Grotto** to the **Pearly Gates** and beyond; it stresses the cave's ambience and exploration. The tour involves some stooping and stair-climbing.

For those in good condition with a keen interest in caves, the park offers the 4-hour **Wild Cave Tour**, designed to simulate a cave

exploration trip. Park staff lead participants into the ghostly far reaches of the cave. You crawl through narrow openings, squeeze into tight passages, and make a glorious mess of yourself (take a change of clothes). The guide's commentary focuses on recreational caving and its impact on cave ecology.

SCENIC DRIVE

13 miles; at least a half day

Begin on US 385 at the southern boundary of the park, about 11 miles north of Hot Springs. At **Where the Wind Blows Pullout** you get the first of many excellent views of the prairie, much as it existed before the plows of the white man drastically changed it. You may see bison and pronghorn grazing side by side on the grassy hillsides. The **Bringing Back the Bison Pullout** a little farther on overlooks a site where bison lick salt from the soil.

From the visitor center, drive out to the campground for the self-guided **Elk Mountain Nature Trail.** This easy 1-mile hike takes you through a transitional prairie-and-pine-forest environment, where you'll see the grasses and trees encroaching on each other's domain. An accompanying trail guide points out some of the plant life around you, including prickly pear cactus and yucca.

Back on the road, continue to the junction with S. Dak. 87 and turn right, stopping at the **Life in the Prairie Dog Town Pullout** just after the turn. This is a good place to observe these once abundant rodents, who survive the predation of many natural enemies by their system of scanning territory and warning their fellows of imminent danger.

WIND CAVE

INFORMATION & ACTIVITIES

VISITOR & INFORMATION CENTER
Visitor center located 11 miles from Hot Springs on US 385; both it and the cave open all year. A variety of tours offered daily Memorial Day to Labor Day.

SEASONS & ACCESSIBILITY
Open year-round.

HEADQUARTERS
Hot Springs, SD 57747. Phone (605) 745-4600. www.nps.gov/wica

ENTRANCE FEES
None. Fees for cave tours: **Garden of Eden** $7, **Natural Entrance Cave** $9, **Fairgrounds Cave** $9, **Historic Candlelight Cave** $9, **Wild Cave Tour** $23; children ages 6 to 16 fees range from $3.50-$4.50.

ACCESSIBLE SERVICES
The visitor center and a cave tour are wheelchair accessible.

THINGS TO DO
Ranger-led activities: a variety of cave tours, nature walks, campfire talks. Also, interpretive exhibits, scenic drive, nature trails, hiking, bicycling, wildlife-watching.

OVERNIGHT BACKPACKING
Permits required; free at visitor center.

CAMPGROUNDS
One campground; 14-day limit. Fees $12 per night mid-May to mid-September; $6 per night rest of year, with reduced services. First come, first served. Tent and RV sites; no hookups or showers.

HOTELS, MOTELS, & INNS
(unless otherwise noted, rates are for 2 persons in a double room, high season)

In Custer, SD 57730:
Bavarian Inn Motel P.O. Box 152. (800) 657-4312 or (605) 673-2802. 64 units, 1 condo. $99. AC, pool, restaurant.
Dakota Cowboy Inn 208 W. Mt. Rushmore Rd. (605) 673-4659. 48 units. $105. AC, pool. April–early Oct.

In Hot Springs, SD 57747:
America's Best Value Inn by the River 602 NW River St. (888) 605-4292 or (605) 745-4292. 31 rooms, $90; 3 cabins, $90. AC, pool.

Also, contact adjacent Custer State Park for information about its lodges: HC 83 Box 70, Custer, SD 57730. (800) 710-2267 or (605) 255-4515, www.custerstatepark.info.

Your approach will probably set off a cacophony of barks. If you stay in the car, you'll have more to watch; cars don't spook the prairie dogs but people do. At dawn or dusk, watch the outskirts of the prairie dog town for patrolling coyotes.

The road now climbs from the prairie into the higher ponderosa pine forests that cover much of the Black Hills. Stop at the **Exposing the Past Pullout** to learn about the granite core of the Black Hills. Other pullouts show how various kinds of plants and animals coexist in this dynamic prairie-forest border area.

Turn right at the **Rankin Ridge Pullout** and follow the half-mile road to the trailhead. The Rankin Ridge Trail, a 1-mile loop, climbs up among the pines to a fire tower.

Back in the car, return to the main road and continue to the north entrance of the park to complete the tour. Those with high-clearance vehicles may wish to make a loop by turning right on unpaved Park Road 5. This road connects with Park Road 6 and then 7-11 Road (County Rd. 101); it takes you through pronghorn and bison territory. Turn right on 7-11 Road to return to US 385 south of the park.

EXCURSIONS

BUFFALO GAP
NATIONAL GRASSLAND
WALL, SOUTH DAKOTA

These mixed grasslands and badlands dotted with prairie dog towns offer superb rock hunting. 591,727 acres. Hiking, birding, horseback riding, hunting, mountain biking, camping. Open year-round. National Grassland Visitor Center at Wall, off I-90, about 130 miles from Wind Cave NP. Surrounds Badlands NP. (605) 279-2125.

MOUNT RUSHMORE
NATIONAL MEMORIAL
KEYSTONE, SOUTH DAKOTA

Colossal visages of Washington, Jefferson, Theodore Roosevelt, and Lincoln gaze out over the Black Hills NF. From June through September the sculptor's studio is open; an evening program ends in the dramatic lighting of the memorial (mid-May through early October). 1,278 acres. Food services, handicapped access. Located on S. Dak. 244, about 40 miles north of Wind Cave NP. (605) 574-3171.

JEWEL CAVE
NATIONAL MONUMENT
CUSTER, SOUTH DAKOTA

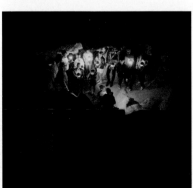

Sparkling crystals of calcite are the "jewels" of this 142-mile-long cave. 12,776 acres. Cave tours, hiking, picnic areas, visitor center. Open all year (some tours year-round). In Black Hills NF on US 16, about 35 miles northwest of Wind Cave NP. (605) 673-8300.

WIND CAVE

Morning Glory Pool hot spring

▶YELLOWSTONE

WYOMING, IDAHO, & MONTANA
ESTABLISHED MARCH 1, 1872
2,221,766 acres

Yellowstone is a geological smoking gun that illustrates how violent the Earth can be. One event overshadows all others: Some 640,000 years ago, an area many miles square at what is now the center of the park suddenly exploded. In minutes the landscape was devastated. Fast-moving ash flows covered thousands of square miles. At the center only a smoldering caldera remained, a collapsed crater 45 by 30 miles. At least two other cataclysmic events preceded this one. Boiling hot springs, fumaroles, mud spots, and geysers serve as reminders that another could occur.

Yellowstone, however, is much more than hot ground and gushing steam. Located astride the Continental Divide, most of the park occupies a high plateau surrounded by mountains and drained by several rivers. Park boundaries enclose craggy peaks, alpine lakes, deep canyons, and vast forests. In 1872,

Yellowstone became the world's first national park, the result of great foresight on the part of many people about our eventual need for the solace and beauty of wild places.

In early years, what made Yellowstone stand out was the extravaganza of geysers and hot springs. The wild landscape and the bison, elk, and bears were nice but, after all, America was still a pioneer country filled with scenic beauty and animals.

As the West was settled, however, Yellowstone's importance as a wildlife sanctuary grew. The list of park animals is a compendium of Rocky Mountain fauna: elk, bison, mule deer, bighorn sheep, grizzly bears, black bears, wolves, moose, pronghorn, coyotes, mountain lions, beaver, trumpeter swans, eagles, ospreys, white pelicans, and more.

During the summer of 1988, fire touched many sections of the park, in some areas dramatically changing the appearance of the landscape. Yet not one major feature was destroyed. The geysers, waterfalls, and herds of wildlife are still here. Many places show no impact at all, while those that are regenerating benefit both vegetation and animal life. Side by side, burned areas and nonburned areas provide an intriguing study in the causes and effects of fire in wild places. Yellowstone has witnessed bigger natural events than this and may well again.

Of far greater concern to environmentalists than the fires are the impact of the increasing numbers of visitors, the threatened grizzly bear population, and, on nearby lands, the planned development of natural resource projects. Cooperative management between the park and the six forests that make up the greater Yellowstone ecosystem is essential if wildlife and thermal features are to survive.

How to Get There

There are five entrances: from the west, West Yellowstone (Montana); from the north and northeast, Gardiner and Cooke City (Montana); from the east, on US 14/16/20 from Cody (Wyoming); and from the south, at Flagg Ranch (Wyoming), which is north of Grand Teton National Park and Jackson (64 miles away). Airports: West Yellowstone (summer only), Bozeman, and Billings in Montana; Cody and Jackson in Wyoming.

When to Go

More than half of the 3 million annual visitors come in July and August. In September and early October, the weather is good, the visitors few, and the wildlife abundant. In May and June, you can see newborn animals, but the weather may be cold, wet, and even snowy. Between about November through April most park roads are closed to vehicles.

During the winter season, mid-December to mid-March, Yellowstone becomes a fantasy of steam and ice; facilities are limited but sufficient. Only the road between the North and Northeast Entrances stays open to cars, but guided snowmobiling is permitted on

Bull moose wading in the Yellowstone River

YELLOWSTONE

355

ATIONAL FOREST
BSAROKA-BEARTOOTH

CUSTER
NATIONAL
FOREST

WILDERNESS

GALLATIN N.F.

Buffalo Cr.

Slough Creek

Cooke
City

Silver
Gate

MONTANA
WYOMING

Northeast Entrance

212

McBride Lake

Barronette Peak +
10,442 ft

+ Abiathar Peak
10,928 ft

Hellroaring Cr.

Petrified
Tree

△ Slough Creek

Yellowstone
Institute

△ Pebble Creek

Tower-Roosevelt
Ranger Station

Soda Butte Cr.

Cache Cr.

NORTH

+ Cache Mountain
9,601 ft

ABSAROKA

Tower
Camp

Tower Fall

Specimen Ridge

Lamar Valley

+
Mount
Norris
9,985 ft

Mt. Washburn
10,243 ft
+

Mirror Plateau

LAMAR RIVER TR.

WILDERNESS

Canyon Village
Visitor Center

Lamar

Miller Creek

Parker Peak
10,190 ft +

and Canyon of
the Yellowstone

Saddle Mountain +
10,670 ft

Pollux Peak
+ 11,063 ft

NATIONAL PARK

Castor Pk. +
10,866 ft

Yellowstone River

lley

Sulphur Caldron

White
Lake

+ Pelican Cone
9,643 ft

SHOSHONE

Mud
Volcano

LeHardys
Rapids

Pelican Valley

Pyramid Peak +
10,508 ft

N. Fork Shoshone

ke Village

Fishing Bridge
Visitor Center

idge
Bay

Gull Point

Turbid Lake

Lake Butte
8,731 ft

NATIONAL

Stevenson I.

Avalanche Peak
10,568 ft

East Entrance

Dot I.

Yellowstone
Lake
7,733 ft

Sylvan
Lake

Sylvan Pass
8,537 ft

20 14
16

Frank
Island

Mount Doane
10,656 ft +

FOREST

+
Mount
Stevenson
10,352 ft

+ Mount Langford
10,778 ft

WASHAKIE

Mount Schurz
+ 11,163 ft

WILDERNESS

The Promontory

Southeast Arm

South Arm

Continental
Divide

Colter Peak
10,683 ft
+

+ Eagle Peak
11,367 ft

Heart
Lake

Chipmunk Cr.

Trail
Lake

THOROFARE TRAIL

+ Turret Mountain
11,006 ft

verlook Mt.
9,370 ft +

Grouse Cr.

Two Ocean Plateau

Yellowstone

Mountain Cr.

TETON

CONTINENTAL DIVIDE
NATIONAL SCENIC TRAIL

Snake

The Trident

N

lt. Hancock
10,214 ft

Thorofare
Ranger Station

Thorofare Creek

Bridger
Lake

WILDERNESS

BRIDGER-TETON NATIONAL FOREST

Two Ocean Pass
8,140 ft

0   miles   10
0   kilometers   15

YELLOWSTONE

some groomed roads. Heated snow coaches offer tours and give cross-country skiers access to about 50 miles of groomed trails.

How to Visit

The 142-mile **Grand Loop Road** forms a figure eight, with connecting spurs to the five entrances. In early years, visitors took a week going around the loop—still a good idea. On any visit, start with the geyser basins and **Mammoth Hot Springs** to see wildlife and thermal features *(caution: both can be hazardous if approached too closely)*. On the second day, travel to the **Grand Canyon of the Yellowstone, Hayden Valley,** and **Yellowstone Lake.**

On a longer stay, visit the **northern range,** or consider a boating or fishing trip on Yellowstone Lake; a backcountry excursion on foot or horse; or any of the numerous easy nature trails throughout the park.

Your best chance of seeing wildlife is in early morning or evening.

Mud pot near the Grand Canyon

GEYSER BASINS: OLD FAITHFUL TO MAMMOTH

51 miles; a full day

Begin by leaving your car in the parking lot at **Old Faithful.** Check at the visitor center for predicted eruption times of the major geysers. While there, pick up an **Upper Geyser Basin** map (also available from area dispensers). Wait on benches near the visitor center for the eruption of Old Faithful (named and celebrated for its steadiness rather than a predictable schedule of eruptions) or walk the path that circles it. Almost any point along the path offers a good view of the eruption, so don't worry if you're not at the benches when it happens. You can see from here that Old Faithful is not alone. The mile-long Upper Geyser Basin contains the world's greatest concentration of hot springs and geysers.

Try to allow a minimum of two hours to see more of it. This must be done on foot, but trails are easy and diversions many. The best choice is to start from the back side of Old Faithful, on the trail that crosses the **Firehole River** to **Geyser Hill,** and follow the map (or your nose; you can't get lost here). You can cross the river at several points and return on the other side, making the walk as long or short as you like. You'll pass dozens of colorful boiling springs and delicate formations of geyserite, a silicate mineral deposited by hot

Morning Glory Pool, named for the flower

water. Chances are good to see one or more geysers erupt at short range. Keep an eye out for elk and bison. **Morning Glory Pool,** named for its resemblance to the flower, marks the far end of the basin.

Back in your car, drive north. **Black Sand Basin** is worth a quick stop, but bypass **Biscuit Basin.** The road follows the Firehole River several miles to **Midway Geyser Basin,** where a 20-minute stroll on the boardwalk takes you past the enormous crater of **Excelsior Geyser.** It erupted for two days in 1985. A huge boiling vat, it produces about 4,000 gallons of scalding water each minute. The boardwalk continues across the delicate terraces of **Grand Prismatic Spring,** 370 feet wide, the largest and most beautiful hot spring in the park. The bright colors are caused by algae and bacteria and archaea, different types of which thrive in different water temperatures.

Two miles farther, turn right on the one-way **Firehole Lake Drive** to **Great Fountain Geyser.** Check the prediction board for the estimated time of eruption. Great Fountain goes off every 11 hours or so. If you have the time, wait. This eruption is one of the best. A bit farther along is **White Dome Geyser.** Its cone may be massive, but its eruption is a thin spray. Perhaps centuries ago it had more power. Yellowstone is always changing.

Rejoin the main road at **Fountain Paint Pot,** a cauldron of hot reddish-pinkish mud, blooping and spitting—always entertaining. Any hot spring could become a mud pot with the right balance of acidity, moisture, and clay; however, a constant flow of water keeps most springs clear.

For the next few miles, rest your eyes on meadows and forest. Look for bison on **Fountain Flat;** also for purple-colored western fringed gentian, the park flower. **Fountain Flat Drive** is closed to vehicles 1 mile from the main road. But it's open to visitors walking to **Goose Lake,** a peaceful picnic site. The

Firehole River, warmed by hot water from springs and geysers along its course, flows through the meadows and along the main road before dropping into a canyon with nice waterfalls; to see them, turn left on **Firehole Canyon Drive** just before **Madison Junction.**

At Madison Junction, a left turn follows the Madison River to the West Entrance, but stay on the road to Norris. In this area, the fires of 1988 burned extensively. Their effects—the jagged sweeps of charred lodgepole pine forest—will be visible for a long time. However, millions of new lodge-pole pines have since grown back (the fires' heat released seedlings from cones on the forest floor). And, because the fires moved erratically, the burned areas are not far from unburned areas, another source of seeds for regrowth.

The road climbs beside the **Gibbon River** to **Gibbon Falls** and continues through the **Gibbon Canyon** and large meadows, where elk are commonly seen, to Norris.

Norris Geyser Basin contains the hottest ground in the park, as well as the world's tallest geyser, **Steamboat.** The geyser's eruptions are infrequent and unpredictable; it may stay quiet for years at a time. Steamboat last erupted on May 23, 2005, the third time since October 2, 1991. Contrast its sleepy behavior with that of **Echinus,** which may go off a few times a day.

Highlights of the drive north include the steamy fumaroles of **Roaring Mountain** that snore rather than roar and **Obsidian Cliff,** an outcrop containing black volcanic glass that was valued for arrow points by Indians throughout the area. The road crosses **Gardners Hole,** with nice views of the **Gallatin Range** to the west, and drops toward Mammoth through **Golden Gate,** cliffs gilded with the bright yellow lichen that grows on them.

At **Mammoth Hot Springs** you can drive or walk around the dozens of colorful steaming terraces. They are made of travertine—calcium

Minerva Terrace at Mammoth Hot Springs

carbonate—which the hot water brings to the surface from beds of limestone. The formations look quite different from the silica-based geyserite deposits seen elsewhere in the park. The park's newest and largest visitor centers are at Canyon and Old Faithful. The **North Entrance** is located 5 miles down the **Gardner River Canyon.**

Storm Creek fire 1988 *(top)*
Fumaroles in Norris Geyser Basin *(bottom)*

YELLOWSTONE LAKE & RIVER: CANYON TO WEST THUMB

37 miles; at least a half day

From the **Canyon Village Visitor Center,** follow the one-way **Canyon Rim Drive** to lookout points for great views of the canyon and the **Yellowstone River's** 308-foot **Lower Falls,** nearly twice as high as Niagara. The bright yellow, orange, and red of the canyon walls are caused by heat and chemical action on gray or brown rhyolite rock.

Walk the rim trail from **Inspiration Point** to **Grandview Point** for the best look at the canyon's natural grandeur. Also consider the paved but strenuous **Brink of the Lower Falls Trail,** which descends several hundred feet through steep forest. Standing beside the green river where it suddenly drops into space is one of the most exciting experiences in the park.

Continue south on the main road. The **Upper Falls** are, at 109 feet high, almost as impressive as the Lower Falls and easier to reach. A short trail leads to **Upper Falls View.** Half

a mile farther south, a side road crosses the river to **Artist Point,** the best overall view of the canyon.

Upriver, the Yellowstone flows gently through the sage-covered hills of **Hayden Valley.** Go slowly and stop often in the roadside parking areas; this is prime wildlife country. American white pelicans and trumpeter swans share the river with Canada geese, gulls, and ducks. Bison are visible most of the year. *Keep your distance.* Use binoculars to check meadows across the river for grizzlies digging for roots or rodents. Grizzlies are often seen in the open; black bears, their smaller, shier relations, rarely. But be careful not to surprise one; both are dangerous.

Well-named **Mud Volcano** and **Black Dragon's Caldron** are not pretty to look at, but they are impressive. Springs in this area have been known to hurl football-size blobs of mud tens of feet. From here to the lake, the **Yellowstone River** provides excellent catch-and-release fishing for cutthroat trout. At **Le Hardys Rapids** in June you can watch cutthroat jumping on their way to spawning grounds (no fishing).

Look for trout also at **Fishing Bridge** (no fishing allowed) where the river flows out of the lake. Two miles farther east is **Pelican Valley,** a lush lakeside meadow where you might find moose or white pelicans.

Return to the loop road, following the shore of **Yellowstone Lake** most of the next 21 miles. This is the largest lake in North America above 7,000 feet. The **Absaroka Range,** visible across the blue waters, was named for the Absaroka, or Crow Indians. The volcanic peaks define the park's eastern boundary.

Bison frequent the meadows near **Bridge Bay,** while moose favor ponds along the **Gull Point Road. Gull Point** is a good picnic site.

West Thumb, almost a separate lake, is a water-filled caldera created by an eruption about 168,000–175,000 years ago, a smaller version of the great Yellowstone caldera. A boardwalk leads around the **West Thumb Geyser Basin,** a modest group of thermal features made charming by its location beside the lake.

NORTHERN RANGE

Between Mammoth Hot Springs and Cooke City, Yellowstone is warmer and drier than the interior. Called the Northern Range for its importance as wintering ground for large animals, this area is characterized by sagebrush and grassy valleys. Open all year, the road from Mammoth stays high above the Yellowstone River, crosses it near **Tower-Roosevelt,** and follows the **Lamar River** and **Soda Butte Creek** to the **Northeast Entrance,** a magnificent little-used gateway. A few miles past Tower, **Specimen Ridge** contains the world's largest concentration of petrified trees. More than a hundred plant species, including redwoods, are found in layers of volcanic ash from repeated eruptions 50 million years ago.

HIKING, FISHING, & BOATING

More than a thousand miles of trails lead to wilderness valleys, mountaintops, lakes, and thermal basins. Take horses and a guide for a week-long trip, or go on foot for an hour or two. Even a short walk can put you in a wilderness setting beyond roads and crowds. Ask for recommended hikes at any visitor center.

Yellowstone offers fine trout fishing, especially for the fly fisherman. Required permit is, available at visitor centers and ranger stations. Regulations are complicated, and often different for sections of any given stream, so read them carefully. Guide are available at fishing shops in surrounding communities.

Motorboating is permitted on most of **Yellowstone Lake** and **Lewis Lake;** passenger boats operate from **Bridge Bay Marina** for sightseeing and fishing (permits required for all watercraft including float tubes). Other lakes are limited to hand-propelled craft. Rivers and streams are closed to all boating to avoid disturbing wildlife; an exception is the channel between Lewis and **Shoshone Lakes,** where paddlers are permitted.

Bison grazing near Firehole River *(top)*; landing a cutthroat trout on Slough Creek *(center)*; male elk during mating season *(bottom left)*; rust-colored cones that release seeds after fire *(bottom right)*

INFORMATION & ACTIVITIES

VISITOR & INFORMATION CENTERS

Mammoth Hot Springs/Albright Visitor Center open all year. **Old Faithful Visitor Center** open May through October and mid-December to mid-March, depending on weather. **Canyon Village Visitor Center,** near center of park, and **Fishing Bridge and Grant Village Visitor Centers,** on Yellowstone Lake, open May through September (reduced hours in Sept.).

SEASONS & ACCESSIBILITY

Park open year-round. Road from North Entrance to Northeast Entrance open all year; other roads closed to cars Nov. through mid-April. Call headquarters for latest weather and road conditions.

HEADQUARTERS

P.O. Box 168, WY 82190. Phone (307) 344-7381. www.nps.gov/yell

ENTRANCE FEES

$25 per vehicle, good for one week at both Yellowstone and Grand Teton. $50 annual pass.

ACCESSIBLE SERVICES

Visitor centers; exhibits; Madison; Bridge Bay; Grant, Mammoth, Madison, and Canyon Campgrounds; most restrooms; amphitheaters; and many ranger-led activities and walks are wheelchair accessible. Brochure available.

THINGS TO DO

Free naturalist-led activities: nature walks, evening programs. Also hiking, boating (boat required), fishing (permit required), horseback riding (stables at Roosevelt, Canyon, and Mammoth), bicycling, stagecoach rides, natural history and photography courses, art exhibits, children's activities, bus and boat tours, snow-coach tours, and winter activities.

OVERNIGHT BACKPACKING

Permits required. They are free and available at visitor centers and ranger stations; apply in person not more than 48 hours in advance of use. Advance reservations $20.

CAMPGROUNDS

Twelve campgrounds, all with 14-day limit (except Fishing Bridge RV Park) from May through October; other times 30-day limit. **Mammoth** open all year, others open late spring to mid-fall. Reservations accepted for **Fishing Bridge RV Park, Madison, Grant Village, Canyon Village,** and **Bridge Bay;** contact Xanterra Parks & Resorts, P.O. Box 165, Yellowstone NP, WY 82190. (866) 439-7375 or (307) 344-7311. All others first come, first served. Fees $12-$20 per night; Fishing Bridge RV Park $28-$37. Pay showers near several campgrounds. Both tent and RV sites at most campgrounds; at Fishing Bridge RV Park hard-sided units only. Hookups at Fishing Bridge RV Park only. For group campgrounds, reserve through Xanterra Parks & Resorts. Food services in park.

HOTELS, MOTELS, & INNS

(unless otherwise noted, rates are for 2 persons in a double room, high season)

INSIDE THE PARK:
The following are operated by Xanterra Parks & Resorts, Yellowstone NP, P.O. Box 165, WY 82190. For reservations call (866) 439-7375 or (307) 344-7311.
Canyon Lodge 527 cabins, $96-$179. 81 rooms, $170. Restaurant.
Grant Village 300 units. $152. Restaurant. May through Sept.
Lake Lodge Cabins 186 units. $69-$179. Restaurant. June-late Sept.
Lake Yellowstone Hotel & Cabins 194 rooms, 102 cabins. $130-$223. Restaurant. Mid-May-early Oct.
Mammoth Hot Springs Hotel & Cabins 97 rooms, 116 cabins. $81-$217. Restaurant. May-Oct. and late Dec.-early March.
Old Faithful Inn 327 units. $96-$236. Rest. Early May-late Oct.
Old Faithful Lodge Cabins 97 cabins. $67-$110. Mid-May-late Sept.
Old Faithful Snow Lodge & Cabins 100 rooms, 34 cabins. $96-$206. Restaurant. Mid-May-late Oct. and mid-Dec.-mid-March.
Roosevelt Lodge Cabins 80 cabins. $65-$110. Restaurant. Mid-June-early Sept.

See also Grand Teton NP listings p. 310.

EXCURSIONS

SHOSHONE NATIONAL FOREST
CODY, WYOMING

Theodore Roosevelt dubbed this forest's North Fork the "most scenic 52 miles in the United States." Elk (wapiti) find a year-round home here in the lee of the Absaroka and Beartooth Ranges, as do bighorn sheep, grizzlies, moose, and deer. Contains parts or all of five wilderness areas. 2,433,000 acres. Hiking, white-water rafting, fishing, horseback riding, hunting, winter sports. 374 campsites, food services, picnic areas. Campsites open June through September. Adjoins Yellowstone NP on the east. (307) 527-6241.

RED ROCK LAKES NATIONAL WILDLIFE REFUGE
LAKEVIEW, MONTANA

In this Centennial Valley refuge, trumpeter swans and nesting sandhill cranes find shelter among grasslands, lakes, and marshes. Large mammals include moose, mule deer, pronghorn, and coyotes. 45,000 acres. 10 campsites, hiking, canoeing, fishing, hunting, scenic drives. Snow closes roads in winter. Off US 20/191, about 45 miles from Yellowstone NP. (406) 276-3536.

BIGHORN CANYON NATIONAL RECREATION AREA
FORT SMITH, MONTANA

Water-based recreation is the focus of this 71-mile-long reservoir impounded from the Bighorn River by the Yellowtail Dam. Fossils exposed in steep canyon walls, wildlife from six life zones, and historic and archaeological sites also featured. Surrounded by Crow Reservation. 120,284 acres. Hiking, boating, bicycling, fishing (and ice fishing), hunting, scenic drives, water sports. 125 campsites, boat ramps, picnic areas, handicapped access. Visitor center at Lovell on US 14A, about 100 miles east of Yellowstone NP. (307) 548-5406.

THE PACIFIC
NORTHWEST

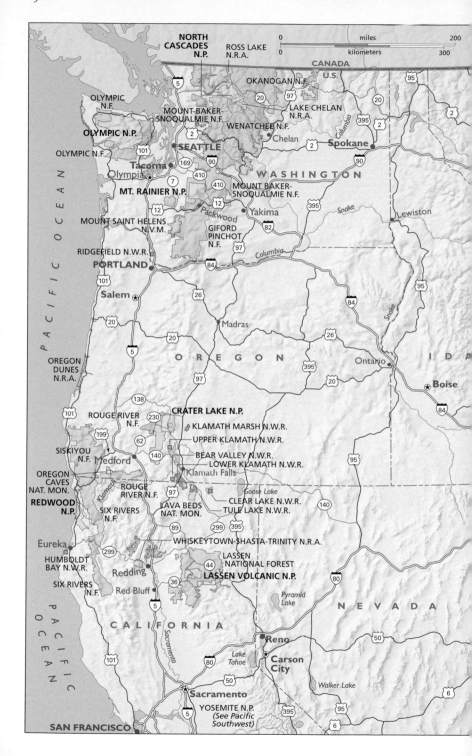

NORTH
CASCADES
N.P.

ROSS LAKE
N.R.A.

0   miles   200
0   kilometers   300

CANADA
U.S.

OKANOGAN N.F.

OLYMPIC
N.F.

MOUNT BAKER-
SNOQUALMIE N.F.

LAKE CHELAN
N.R.A.

OLYMPIC N.P.

WENATCHEE N.F.

Chelan

OLYMPIC N.F.

SEATTLE

W A S H I N G T O N

Spokane

Tacoma

Olympia

MT. RAINIER N.P.

MOUNT BAKER-
SNOQUALMIE N.F.

Yakima

Snake

Lewiston

MOUNT SAINT HELENS
N.V.M.

Packwood

GIFORD
PINCHOT
N.F.

RIDGEFIELD N.W.R.

Columbia

PORTLAND

Salem

Madras

O R E G O N

Ontario

I D A

Boise

OREGON
DUNES
N.R.A.

Snake

ROUGE RIVER
N.F.

CRATER LAKE N.P.

KLAMATH MARSH N.W.R.

UPPER KLAMATH N.W.R.

SISKIYOU
N.F.

Medford

BEAR VALLEY N.W.R.

LOWER KLAMATH N.W.R.

OREGON
CAVES
NAT. MON.

ROUGE
RIVER N.F.

Klamath Falls

REDWOOD
N.P.

SIX RIVERS
N.F.

ROUGE
RIVER N.F.

Goose Lake

LAVA BEDS
NAT. MON.

CLEAR LAKE N.W.R.

TULE LAKE N.W.R.

Eureka

WHISKEYTOWN-SHASTA-TRINITY N.R.A.

HUMBOLDT
BAY N.W.R.

LASSEN
NATIONAL FOREST

SIX RIVERS
N.F.

Redding

LASSEN VOLCANIC N.P.

Red Bluff

Pyramid
Lake

N E V A D A

C A L I F O R N I A

Sacramento

Reno

Lake
Tahoe

Carson
City

Walker Lake

Sacramento

YOSEMITE N.P.
(See Pacific
Southwest)

SAN FRANCISCO

Columbia

P A C I F I C   O C E A N

P A C I F I C   O C E A N

THE PACIFIC NORTHWEST

In the late 19th and early 20th centuries, East Coast loggers pushed west, downing mile after mile of the continent's primeval forests. Today, almost all of the large ancient forests left in the lower 48 states grow in the Pacific Northwest, most of them in national forests and parks.

Visitors to Mount Rainier, Olympic, and North Cascades can hike cathedral-like glades of Douglas fir, western red cedar, and other conifers. The redwoods in the park named for them include trees in their second millennium, some of the tallest on Earth. In Olympic, temperate rain forests soar near some of the nation's wildest coastline; in the United States, only there and at Mount Rainier do such forests still exist. All these ancient forests knit together the lives of hundreds of species of plants, animals, and microbes in a web we don't fully understand. Yet that web is increasingly threatened as trees in private, state, and national forests are cut down.

The Northwest is also known for its volcanoes, many of which, including Mount Rainier and Mount St. Helens, lie in the Pacific Ring of Fire, the great belt of crustal instability responsible for three-quarters of the world's active volcanoes. Visitors to Lassen Volcanic National Park can see evidence of the planet's violence in broken mountains and boiling mud pots. At Crater Lake, they can imagine the titanic forces that collapsed a mountaintop, turning it into a lake 6 miles wide and the deepest in the nation. They can marvel at the majesty of cloud-swathed Mount Rainier, which grew on a foundation of lava flows from extinct volcanoes, and now shoulders breathtaking wildflowers and more glaciers than any other U.S. peak south of Alaska.

Each of the region's northernmost national parks is less than half a day's drive from Seattle. This group merits at least a week of touring, more if you want to visit other natural areas nearby. The more southern peaks can each be seen in a day, but allow plenty of time for travel between them. Beautiful but winding Calif. 299 that connects the Lassen Volcanic and Redwood areas can wash out in spring, so check conditions if that's when you plan to go.

THE PACIFIC NORTHWEST

Wizard Island just before the sun rises over Crater Lake

▶ CRATER LAKE

OREGON
ESTABLISHED MAY 22, 1902
183,224 acres

Few forget their first glimpse of Crater Lake on a clear summer's day—21 square miles of water so intensely blue it looks like ink, ringed by cliffs towering up to 2,000 feet above. The mountain bluebird, Indian legend says, was gray before dipping into the waters.

The tranquil Gem of the Cascades is set in a dormant volcano called Mount Mazama, one in the chain of volcanoes that includes Mount St. Helens. Mount Mazama's eruption about 5700 B.C. catapulted volcanic ash miles into the sky and expelled so much pumice and ash that the summit soon collapsed, creating a huge, smoldering caldera.

Eventually, rain and snowmelt accumulated in the caldera, forming a lake more than 1,900 feet deep, the deepest lake in the United States. Wildflowers, along with hemlock, fir, and pine, recolonized surroundings. Black bears and bobcats, deer and marmots, eagles and hawks returned.

Scientists have yet to understand completely Crater Lake's ecology. In 1988 and 1989, using a manned submarine, they discovered evidence that proves hydrothermal venting exists on the lake's bottom and may play a role in the lake's character.

Crater Lake forms a superb setting for day hikes. Thanks to some of the cleanest air in the nation, you can see more than 100 miles from points along many of the park's 90 miles of trails. Forests of mountain hemlock and Shasta red fir predominate near the caldera rim. At the rim twisted whitebark pine testify to the harshness of the long winter. Ponderosa pine, the park's largest tree, and lodgepole pine are common farther down from the rim.

How to Get There
Enter the park from the west (Medford, about 85 miles away) or the south (Klamath Falls, about 65 miles away) on Oreg. 62, or in summer from the north on Oreg. 138. Airports: Medford and Klamath Falls.

When to Go
Go in the summer to see the lake at its best. Oreg. 62 and the access road leading to Rim Village remain open in winter, and both snowshoeing and cross-country skiing are popular. The drive around the lake usually closes in October because of snow; some years, the drive may not reopen completely until mid-July. Peak wildflower viewing is late July/early August.

How to Visit
Spend at least a half day touring the 33-mile **Rim Drive,** enjoying its many overlooks and several hiking trails. On a second day, consider a hike down to the shore for the two hour narrated boat tour of the lake. Some tours stop at **Wizard Island;** if time and weather permit, climb to the top of it and catch a later boat back.

RIM DRIVE & GODFREY GLEN TRAIL
33 to 38 miles; a half to full day

Rim Drive circles Crater Lake, providing more than 25 scenic overlooks and some good picnic areas. *(Trailers and other oversize vehicles not recommended on east Rim Drive.)* Begin by parking in **Rim Village** and strolling

to the **Sinnott Memorial Overlook,** a prime vantage point over the lake. Crater Lake's vivid color is a sign of purity and depth. The lake contains few minerals and impurities. Its only fish—rainbow trout and kokanee salmon—were introduced. As sunlight penetrates the deep, pure lake, water molecules absorb the colors of the spectrum except for blue, which is scattered back to the surface. Scientists have found green moss growing at a record 460 feet below the surface, indicating that sunlight may penetrate deeper here than in any other body of water in the world.

To begin your lake tour, set your car's trip odometer at zero as you leave Rim Village parking lot. Head west or clockwise around the lake, and be careful: The road is narrow and has sharp curves. Watch out for bikers, pedestrians, and wildlife on the roadway. Turn right at 0.1 mile for Rim Drive. The first stop (mile 1.3) brings you near **Discovery Point,** where, on June 12, 1853, a group of gold prospectors happened upon the lake, which they named Deep Blue Lake. Indians, believing the lake sacred, had told no outsiders about it. **Hillman Peak,** to the far left on the rim, is named for one of the prospectors. The peak is a 70,000-year-old volcano—one of the compact cluster of overlapping volcanic cones that formed Mount Mazama. It was cleaved in half when the summit collapsed. At 1,978 feet above the water, it forms the highest point on the rim.

The overlook at mile 4 offers a good view of **Wizard Island,** named for its resemblance to a sorcerer's hat. Rising 764 feet above the surface of the lake, Wizard Island is a classic cinder cone—built of red-hot cinders ejected from the caldera floor sometime after Mount Mazama collapsed. An Indian legend portrays the island as the head of Llao, Chief

To Medford

UMPQUA N.F. 138

Cascade Mountai Pass 5,925 ft

Rogue 230

North Entrance Station

Boundary Springs

Desert Ridge

+ Gaywas Peak 6,781 ft

N

miles 4
0
kilometers 6
0

Crescent Ridge

+ Bald Crater 6,478 ft

PUMICE DESERT

Timber Crater 7,424 ft

Desert Cone 6,672 ft

ROGUE RIVER NATIONAL FOREST

+ Oasis Butte

PACIFIC CREST N.S.T.

CRATER LAKE NATIONA

+ Grouse Hill 7,412 ft

Crater Creek

Sphagnum Bog

Red Cone Spring

CLEETWOOD TRAIL

RIM DRIVE

Llao Rock 8,049 ft

Steel Bay

Palisade Point

North Junction

Merriam Point +

Llao Bay

Hillman Peak 8,151 ft

Devils Backbone

Crater Lake

Bybee Creek

The Watchman 8,013 ft

Wizard Island

Average surface elevation 6,173 ft

Lightning Spring

RIM DRIVE

Discovery Point

Phantom Ship Overlook

Castle Creek

To Medford

62

Rim Village Visitor Center (summer only)

Cafeteria and Gift Shop

Sinnott Overlook

Kerr Notch

Sun Notch +

Dutton Ridge

Thousand Springs

+ Castle Point 6,276 ft

Steel Information Center Park Headquarters

CASTLE CREST WILDFLOWER TRAIL

Vidae Falls

Union Creek

Annie Spring

GODFREY GLEN TRAIL

Annie Spring Entrance Station

Duwee Falls

Sun Cr.

Mazama Village

ANNIE CREEK CANYON TRAIL

Arant Point 6,800 ft

+ Crater Pk. 7,263 ft

ROGUE RIVER NATIONAL FOREST

Union Peak + 7,709 ft

62

Baldtop 6,200 ft +

PUMICE FLAT

Scoria Cone 6,648 ft

Annie Creek

Red Blanket Creek

Stuart Falls

PACIFIC CREST N.S.T.

Goose Nest 7,249 ft +

WINEMA NATIONAL FOREST

SKY LAKES WILDERNESS

Jerry Mountain +

+ Goose Egg 7,124 ft

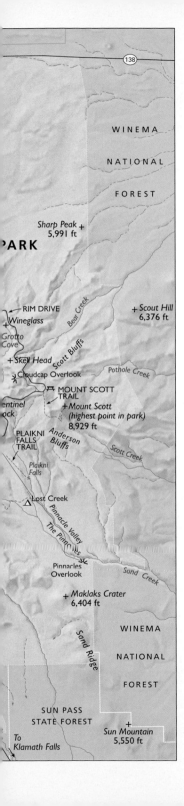

of the Below World. Skell, Chief of the Above World, killed and dismembered Llao in the final, literally earth-shattering battle waged on the mountain. Time and weather permitting, you'll enjoy superb views in every direction if you take the moderately steep, 0.8-mile trail that leads to the historic fire tower on **The Watchman** peak (8,013 feet) that begins south of the overlook.

Back in the car, turn away from the lake at the **Mount Thielsen Overlook** on the left. A plaque identifies the major cascade landmarks including the **3 Sisters Wilderness.** When the road forks at North Junction (mile 6.1), bear right to stay on Rim Drive. (Straight leads to the **North Entrance.**)

Steel Bay (mile 8.8) commemorates William Gladstone Steel, who dedicated his fortune and career to making Crater Lake a national park. Steel became fascinated by the lake when he read about it in a newspaper used to wrap his lunch. Seventeen years of lobbying, culminating in a personal appeal to President Theodore Roosevelt, succeeded in making it the country's sixth national park in 1902. Steel led the efforts to build Rim Drive and the Crater Lake Lodge.

Six miles farther on, pull off the road at **Skell Head** for another excellent view of the entire lake. **Mount Scott,** highest point in the park, looms ahead as you drive on toward Cloudcap. Mount Mazama's oldest lava flows—dated at 400,000 years old—are found here. Phantom Ship, an island to the southwest, consists of erosion-resistant lava from the long extinct Phantom cone. Dwarfed by the surrounding cliffs, it nevertheless stands 160 feet above the water.

Circle back to Rim Drive and turn right. For a closer look at Phantom Ship, (in some light it seems to vanish and reappear), stop at **Kerr Notch** (mile 23.2), one of the U-shaped

CRATER LAKE

valleys carved by a glacier before Mount Mazama erupted. A road leads to **The Pinnacles,** a valley of spires of hardened volcanic ash. After Kerr Notch, bear right to stay on Rim Drive.

At mile 31.2 you can stretch your legs on the **Castle Crest Wildflower Trail.** This fragrant half-mile loop begins in a forest of mountain hemlock and red fir, then enters a meadow run riot with flowers. Watch your step—the wet rocks can be slippery.

From here you can either head back to Rim Village or, if time permits, turn left toward Oreg. 62 and, after 2.3 miles, park on the left for a final stroll on the **Godfrey Glen Trail,** an easy, 1-mile-loop nature trail. The path leads through forest that developed on a flow of pumice and ash 250 feet thick. The fluted pinnacles on the walls of the gorges began as the same material, but hot gases seeped up from within the Earth and hardened these areas. They defied erosion as the creeks formed canyons.

BOAT TOUR & HIKES

The mile-long **Cleetwood Trail,** which begins on the north side of the lake, leads down to the water and the landing for the boat tour *(fee).* The hike back up is strenuous (and there's no

Ghostly conifers cling to the rim of Crater Lake.

other way); only attempt the trail if you are in good physical condition. Wear sturdy shoes and bring water, a snack, a hat, and a jacket.

The boat tour shows you the lake from a different perspective. You will see waterfalls and geological features invisible from the rim, and a ranger discusses the geology and natural history of Crater Lake. Tours leave at 10 a.m., 11 a.m., 12 p.m., 2 p.m., 3 p.m., and 4 p.m. Fee is $29 for adults, and $19 for children ages 3–17. *(July–mid-Sept., weather permitting).*

To explore the island on your own, take the relatively steep **Wizard Island Summit Trail** (0.9 mile one way) that begins at the island's dock and winds through mountain hemlock, Shasta red fir, and wildflowers to the crater at the top. There are superb views of bleached, contorted whitebark pines against the blue water, and a wonderful panorama of the inside of the 90-foot-deep crater.

Another good park hike is the **Annie Creek Canyon Trail,** a 1.7-mile self-guided loop that winds through beds of wildflowers to the bottom of a deep, stream-cut canyon and back. It begins behind the amphitheater at the Mazama Campground.

The **Mount Scott Trail** starts on the left side of Rim Drive and climbs to the highest point in the park. This 2.5-mile strenuous hike offers panoramic views of both Crater Lake and the Klamath Basin. On this trail you might see falcons, hawks, and eagles, particularly in fall.

The **Plaikni Falls Trail,** which was completed in 2010, opens annually in July. Drive 8.5 miles from park headquarters and turn right on the Pinnacles Road. Travel 1 mile and park in the pullout to the left. Klamath tribes chose the name which translates "from the high country." Allow an hour to visit the spring-fed **Sand Creek Falls** beneath Anderson Bluffs.

INFORMATION & ACTIVITIES

VISITOR & INFORMATION CENTERS
Rim Village Visitor Center, on rim overlooking the lake, 7 miles off Oreg. 62, open daily from early June to mid-Oct. Closed rest of year.
Steel Center, located at park headquarters, open daily all year.

SEASONS & ACCESSIBILITY
South Entrance open year-round. North Entrance open mid-June to mid-October, weather permitting. East side of Rim Drive, from Cleetwood Cove to park headquarters, may remain closed by snow until mid-July. Call (541) 594-3000 for weather information.

HEADQUARTERS
P.O. Box 7, Crater Lake, OR 97604. Phone (541) 594-3000. www.nps.gov/crla

ENTRANCE FEE
$10 per car per week; $20 annual; includes Oregon Caves National Monument and Lava Beds National Monument.

PETS
Permitted within 50 feet of roads, and in established parking areas, developed campgrounds, and picnic areas. Not permitted in buildings or on trails.

ACCESSIBLE SERVICES
Most viewpoints accessible to wheelchairs, as are visitor centers, Mazama Campground, the café and gift shop at Rim Village, Crater Lake Lodge, 1-mile Godfrey Glen Trail, Plaikni Falls Trail.

THINGS TO DO
Free naturalist-led activities: nature walks, children's Junior Ranger programs, campfire programs. Fees for the ranger-narrated boat tours (adults $25, seniors $22, children $15). Also: hiking, bicycling, fishing, snowshoeing, and cross-country skiing.

SPECIAL ADVISORY
• Hiking inside the caldera rim prohibited. Access to lake at Cleetwood Trail only. Volcanic rock and soil are unstable and dangerous to climb on.

OVERNIGHT BACKPACKING
Free permits required. Can be obtained at Steel Information Center, Ranger station at Park headquarters and Rim Village Visitor Center during the summer.

CAMPGROUNDS
Two campgrounds, both with 14-day limit. **Lost Creek,** tent only, open mid-July to late September; $10 per night. **Mazama,** tent and RV sites, open late-June to mid-October; $21-$27 per night. Some hookups. Reservations available for about half the sites at Mazama; otherwise both first come, first served. Showers and food at Mazama Village. Food services at Rim Village and Annie Creek Restaurant.

HOTELS, MOTELS, & INNS
(unless otherwise noted, rates are for 2 persons in a double room, high season)

INSIDE THE PARK:
Rim Village/Crater Lake Lodge 1211 Ave. C, White City, OR 97503. (888) 774-2728. 71 units. $149-$275. Late May to late Sept. **The Cabins at Mazama Village** (888) 774-2728. 40 units. $124. Late May to late Sept.

OUTSIDE THE PARK:
In Chiloquin, OR 97624:
Melita's Motel 39500 Hwy. 97. (541) 783-2401. 14 units. $55-$60. 17 RV hookups. $27. AC, rest.
Williamson River Resort 31900 Modoc Pt. Rd. (541) 783-2071. 7 cabins, $100; 12 RV sites, $21.
Rapids Motel 33551 Hwy. 97 N. (541) 783-2271. 10 units. $45-$52.
In Diamond Lake, OR 97731:
Diamond Lake Resort 350 Resort Dr. (541) 793-3333 or (800) 733-7593, www .diamondlake.net. 90 rooms, cabins, studios units. $99-$489.
In Prospect, OR 97536:
Union Creek Resort 56484 Hwy. 62. (866) 560-3565. 21 cabins, 13 with kitchenettes; 9 rooms with shared baths. Cabins $80-$225; rooms $53-$58.

Ask the park for a complete list of accommodations within a 1-hour drive, or contact Travel Klamath, 205 Riverside Dr. Suite B, Klamath Falls, OR 97601. (800) 445-6728 or (541) 882-1501, www.discoverklamath .com.

CRATER LAKE

EXCURSIONS

ROGUE RIVER NATIONAL FOREST
MEDFORD, OREGON

Sugar pines and Douglas firs cloak the western Cascades where the Rogue River emerges from underground lava tubes. The forest contains six wilderness areas, numerous lakes, and a stretch of the Pacific Crest Trail. 1.8 million acres, part in California. Hiking, boating, fishing, horseback riding, hunting, scenic drives, winter and water sports. 815 campsites, food services, boat ramp, picnic areas. Open all year; most campsites open May through September. In two sections; one adjoins Crater Lake NP on west and south, with entrance at Prospect on Oreg. 62. Reach other section by following I-5 south of Ashland, about 85 miles from Crater Lake NP. (541) 858-2200.

OREGON CAVES NATIONAL MONUMENT
CAVE JUNCTION, OREGON

Guided tours take visitors through the "Marble Halls of Oregon," chambers and corridors formed by groundwater dissolving marble bedrock. 480 acres. Hiking. National Historic Landmark The Chateau at the Oregon Caves (23 rooms, May–Oct.), food services, picnic areas. Cave tours open mid-March through mid-October. East on Oreg. 46 about 20 miles from Cave Junction, about 150 miles from Crater Lake NP. (541) 592-2100, www.nps.gov/ovca.

LAVA BEDS NATIONAL MONUMENT
TULELAKE, CALIFORNIA

Myriad lava-tube caves and cinder cones mark this rugged terrain where prehistoric Indians left glyphs on the soft rock. Excellent spring and fall bird-watching. 46,560 acres. Hiking, summer tours, battle sites. 41 campsites, picnic areas. Open year-round. Headquarters 30 miles south of Tulelake (26 miles off Calif. 139), about 120 miles south of Crater Lake NP. (530) 667-8100.

OREGON DUNES
NATIONAL RECREATION AREA
REEDSPORT, OREGON

Forty-seven miles of towering dunes—some as high as 400 feet—stretch along the Pacific coast, inviting visitors to explore. Half of area open to off-road vehicles. The 426 wildlife species include black bear, black-tailed deer, and tundra swan. 32,000 acres. 13 hiking trails, boating, fishing, horseback riding, swimming. 13 campgrounds, picnic areas, handicapped access. Open all year. Headquarters at Reedsport on US 101, about 200 miles west of Crater Lake NP. (541) 271-3611.

KLAMATH BASIN NATIONAL
WILDLIFE REFUGES
TULELAKE, CALIFORNIA

These six refuges protect diverse habitats—marsh, open water, meadows, croplands, coniferous forest, sagebrush and juniper uplands, rocky slopes—and numerous waterfowl. The basin also provides a home for the largest wintering bald eagle population in the lower 48 states. Hiking, boating, fishing, hunting. Open all year, dawn to dusk, except Bear Valley and Clear Lake. In Oregon: Klamath Marsh, 40,885 acres; Upper Klamath, 14,966 acres; Bear Valley, 4,120 acres; Lower Klamath, 50,912 acres (part in Calif.). In California: Tule Lake, 39,116 acres; Clear Lake, 24,123 acres. Visitor Center near Tule Lake off Calif. 139, about 100 miles from Crater Lake NP. (530) 667-2231, www.fws.gov/klamathbasinrefuges/.

CRATER LAKE

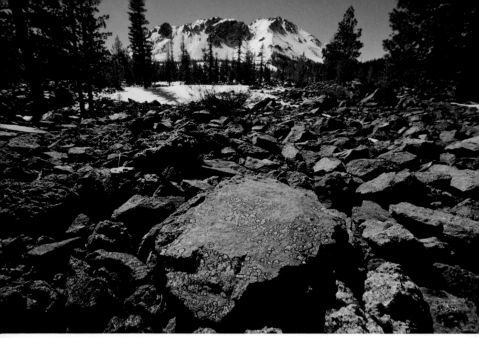

Mount Lassen looms over a landscape of conifers and lichen-speckled rocks.

▶ LASSEN VOLCANIC

CALIFORNIA
ESTABLISHED AUGUST 9, 1916
106,372 acres

On June 14, 1914, three men climbed Lassen Peak to see why a seemingly dormant volcano had started rumbling 16 days before. Now, peering into a newborn crater, they felt the ground tremble. As they turned and ran down the steep slope, the mountain erupted. Rocks hurtled through the ash-filled air. One struck a man, knocking him out. Ashes rained down on the men. They seemed doomed. But the eruption stopped as suddenly as it had begun, and the three men survived.

From 1914 to early 1915, Lassen spewed steam and ashes in more than 150 eruptions. Finally, on May 19, 1915, the mountaintop exploded. Lava crashed through the 1914 crater. A 20-foot-high wall of mud, ash, and melted snow roared down the mountain, snapping tree trunks. Three days later, a huge mass of ashes and gases shot out of the volcano, devastating a swath a mile wide and 3 miles long. Above the havoc a cloud of volcanic steam and ash rose 30,000 feet.

Eruptions of steam, ash, and tephra continued until June 1917, when the volcano resumed its quiet profile, with minor steam clouds occasionally reported. Since 1921

Lassen Peak has remained quiet. But it is still considered an active volcano, the centerpiece of a vast panorama, where volcanism displays its spectaculars—wrecked mountains, devastated land, bubbling cauldrons of mud. Until Mount St. Helens blew in 1980, Lassen's eruption was the most recent volcanic explosion in the lower 48 states. Ecologists now study Lassen's landscape to see what the future may bring to the terrain around St. Helens.

How to Get There
From Redding (about 45 miles away), take Calif. 44 east to Calif. 89 junction and continue to Manzanita Lake park entrance; from Red Bluff, follow Calif. 36 east to Mineral, turn north on Calif. 89 to southwest entrance. The three other entrances —at Warner Valley, Butte Lake, and Juniper Lake—are reached via unpaved roads. Airports: Redding and Chico, California; Reno, Nevada.

When to Go
The volcanic areas are best visited in summer and fall. Heavy snows close most of the park highway in winter. But visitors still enjoy snowshoe hikes and cross-country skiing at the southern and northern entrances.

How to Visit
On a 1-day visit, drive the **main park road,** linking Calif. 89. The road, snaking across the western side of the park between the southwest and Manzanita Lake entrances, takes you near the major volcanic features. Explore **Bumpass Hell** and other sites along the way. If you can stay longer, climb **Cinder Cone,** an outstanding example of the results of volcanism, and, if you have the stamina for a more demanding trek, try **Lassen Peak.**

PARK ROAD & BUMPASS HELL TRAIL
30 miles; a half to full day

If you start at the southwest entrance, your first stop on this twisting, climbing road will be the **Sulphur Works.** You walk by sulfur fumes and see hissing fumaroles, sputtering mud, and gurgling clay tinted in pastels by minerals. Here was the heart of ancestral Brokeoff volcano. The peaks around you once formed part of the rim, created by lava oozing from the inner Earth 600,000 to 200,000 years ago. Layer by layer, the lava built a mountain 11,500 feet high and 11 miles across.

Brokeoff's repeated eruptions, hydrothermal activity, and weather weakened the structure of the volcano, which collapsed, leaving behind a bowl-like caldera. Glaciers later scoured the caldera, wiping out the last remains of this massive volcano. **Lassen Peak,** born at least 27,000 years ago, emerged at the base of the old Brokeoff volcano.

At **Bumpass Hell,** the road's next major stop, note a large balanced rock at the edge of the parking lot; it's a glacial erratic—a polished, glacier-borne boulder. The fairly easy 3-mile **Bumpass Hell Trail** takes about 2 hours. Go on it if you have time. The place is named after K. V. Bumpass, a local guide and promoter who, in the 1860s, plunged a leg through the thin crust covering a seething mud pot. Though badly burned, he wisecracked about his easy descent into hell.

As you walk along, you'll note (and smell) sulfurous vapors drifting over parts of the trail, which leads down to a boardwalk that winds past roiling mud pots, rumbling fumaroles, and hissing boiling

LASSEN VOLCANIC

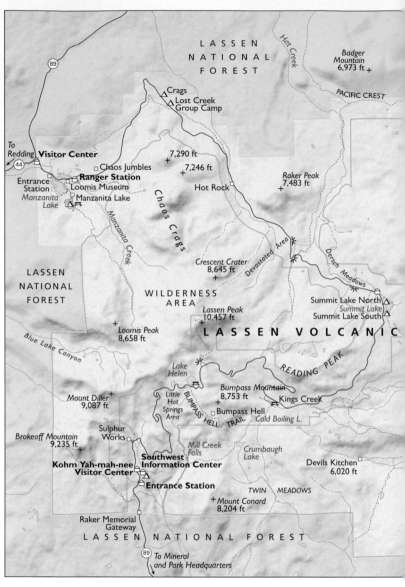

springs. At the springs' steamy
pools look for floating golden flakes.
They are crystals of iron pyrite—
fool's gold—carried along in the
superheated steam.

Resume driving on the road,
which curves around Lassen Peak.
Continue to the **Devastated Area,**
wrecked by the massive May 1915
eruption. Amid the scarred and
fallen trees notice the signs of

renewal: Young trees and stubborn
grasses are growing in a slow, natural comeback unaided by human
hand. The road offers many turnoffs
for viewing the crags and canyons
that are Lassen's volcanic heritage.

You'll pass churned-up landscape
dubbed **Chaos Crags** and **Chaos
Jumbles;** if space along the road
permits, stop and walk around it.
Here, about 300 years ago, a nearby

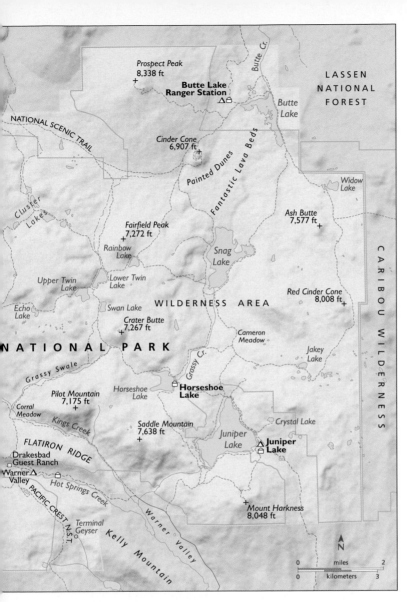

volcanic dome suddenly collapsed, perhaps because of an earth tremor. Millions of tons of rock, riding a cushion of trapped air, sped across 2 miles of flat land. The horizontal avalanche smashed into a mountain and veered into a creek, damming it and forming **Manzanita Lake.**

Just beyond, the road ends its course through the park and enters Lassen National Forest.

CINDER CONE NATURE TRAIL

32-mile drive, 5-mile hike; a full day

The trail begins near Butte Lake Campground, reached via Calif. 44 and a marked gravel road. **Cinder Cone,** a nearly symmetrical, 755-foot-high mound of lava surrounded by multicolored cinders—light lava that

INFORMATION & ACTIVITIES

VISITOR & INFORMATION CENTERS

Loomis Museum at **Manzanita Lake** is open daily from mid-June through Labor Day. The new **Kohm Yah-mah-nee Visitor Center** at the southwest entrance opened Fall 2008. Contact the park headquarters for current hours.

SEASONS & ACCESSIBILITY

Park and both its entrances open year-round. The main park highway can be closed by snow from late October to late June. For road conditions in the park, phone (530) 595-4480 or check the park website.

HEADQUARTERS

P.O. Box 100, Mineral, CA 96063. Phone (530) 595-4480. www.nps.gov/lavo

ENTRANCE FEE

$10 per car; good for 7 days. Those entering on foot or by bicycle pay $5 for 7 days.

ACCESSIBLE SERVICES

Park headquarters, Kohm Yah-mah-nee Visitor Center, Loomis Museum, some restrooms, the Devastated Area Interpretive Trail, the Sulphur Works, and some picnic areas are wheelchair accessible.

THINGS TO DO

Among the free ranger-led activities are nature walks and hikes, talks, nature and geology demonstrations, children's programs, evening programs, and snow-shoe walks. Other activities include hiking, swimming, fishing, boating (no motors), and cross-country skiing.

OVERNIGHT BACKPACKING

Wilderness permits required. They are free and can be obtained at headquarters, visitor centers, Summit Lake Ranger Station, and Butte Lake, Warner Valley, and Juniper Lake trailheads. No wood fires permitted.

CAMPGROUNDS

Eight campgrounds, **Summit Lake-North** and **Summit Lake-South** have a 7-day limit; all others have a 14-day limit. Most sites open late June through Sept., weather permitting. First come, first served. Fees $10-$18 per night. Showers are available at **Manzanita Lake.** Roads to Warner Valley and Juniper Lake not recommended for RVs. Three group campgrounds; for reservations contact NRRS (see p. 10). Food services in park.

HOTELS, MOTELS, & INNS

(unless otherwise noted, rates are for 2 persons in a double room, high season)

shattered in the air and fell back down—stands black and solitary above a pine forest. Don't expect to hurry on the trail, a round-trip of about 5 miles. Walking on loose cinders is like walking through sand: Your feet sink with every step. At the top (6,907 feet), you will see the craters of recent eruptions; the last was in the mid-1600s.

LASSEN PEAK TRAIL

5 miles round-trip; a half to full day

This steep, zigzagging trail begins at 8,463 feet, near the park road, and takes you to the 10,457-foot summit. The going can get tough for people used to sea level. Before you climb, acclimatize to the park's high elevations. Carry water, wear a hat, and take a jacket. Turn back if a storm threatens; the peak is a lightning attractor. Lassen has scant vegetation. But you can almost always spot a ground squirrel. And sometimes thousands of tortoiseshell butterflies suddenly flit by, their shadows cascading along the grayish volcanic rocks. At the summit, you can see the hardened vestige of the 1915 lava flow. And visible on a clear day, 75 miles away, is Mount Shasta.

INSIDE THE PARK:
Drakesbad Guest Ranch (47 miles southeast of headquarters) Chester, CA 96020. Call (530) 529-1512, ext 120; 6 lodge rooms, 4 cabins, 6 bungalows. $176-$201 per person. Meals included. Pool. June–early Oct.
OUTSIDE THE PARK:
In Mineral, CA 96063:
Lassen Mineral Lodge (on Calif. 36E, 9 miles from park gate) P.O. Box 160. (530) 595-4422. 20 units, $75-$95. Rest.
In Redding, CA 96002:
Best Western Plus Hilltop Inn 2300 Hilltop Dr. (800) 336-4880 or (530)

221-6100. 114 units. $159-$169. AC, pool, restaurant.
Red Lion Hotel 1830 Hilltop Dr. (800) 547-8010 or (530) 221-8700. 192 units. $134-$164. AC, pool, restaurant.
Quality Inn 2059 Hilltop Dr. (530) 221-6530. 90 units. $106. AC, pool.
Vagabond Inn 536 E. Cypress Ave. (530) 223-1600. 71 units. $75. AC, pool, rest.

For more information on places to stay, contact the park or the Greater Redding Chamber of Commerce, 747 Auditorium Dr., Redding, CA 96001. (530) 225-4433, www.reddingchamber.com.

EXCURSIONS

LASSEN NATIONAL FOREST
SUSANVILLE, CALIFORNIA

Volcanic features dot this mountain forest surrounding Lassen Volcanic National Park. Also contains many lakes and streams. One million acres. Hiking, boating, fishing, horseback riding, hunting, winter sports, water sports. More than 40 campgrounds, boat ramp, picnic areas, handicapped access. Open year-round; most campsites open from mid-May to mid-October. Information at Chester on Calif. 36, about 40 miles from Lassen Volcanic NP. (530) 595-4444.

WHISKEYTOWN-SHASTA-TRINITY NATIONAL RECREATION AREA
WHISKEYTOWN, CALIFORNIA

Here in Gold Rush country, three impounded lakes provide unlimited opportunities for recreation on, in, and around water. Backcountry hiking and recreational gold panning also featured. 217,823 acres. Hiking, boating, fishing, horseback riding, mountain biking, scenic drives, water sports. 693 campsites, cabins, boat ramp, food services, handicapped access. Open year-round. Whiskeytown headquarters on Calif. 299, off I-5, about 60 miles west of Lassen Volcanic NP. (530) 242-3400. For Shasta and Trinity units call (530) 226-2500.

LASSEN VOLCANIC

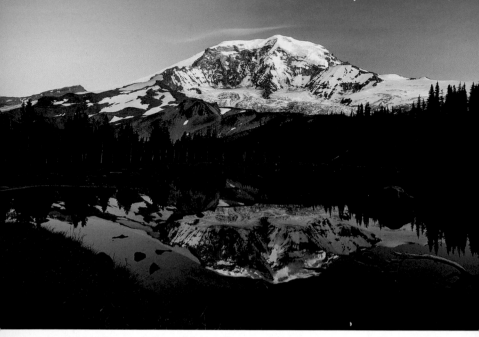

Mount Rainier, known to Indians as Tahoma—"the great mountain"

▶MOUNT RAINIER

WASHINGTON
ESTABLISHED MARCH 2, 1899
235,625 acres

One of the world's most massive volcanoes, Mount Rainier can dominate the skyline for 100 miles before you reach the park named after it. At nearly 3 miles in height, Mount Rainier is the tallest peak in the Cascade Range; it dwarfs 6,000-foot surrounding summits, appearing to float alone among the clouds.

Mount Rainier may be the centerpiece of the national park, but it is hardly the only attraction. Here, less than 3 hours' drive from Seattle, you can stroll through seemingly endless fields of wildflowers, listen for cracking glacier debris, wander among trees more than a thousand years old. The park's convenient location, however, also leads to weekend traffic jams, both summer and winter, and guarantees you company on popular trails.

Mount Rainier is the offspring of fire and ice. Still active, it was probably born more than a half million years ago, on a base of lava spewed out by previous volcanoes. Lava and ash surged out of the young volcano's vent thousands of times, filling the neighboring canyons and building up a summit cone, layer by layer, to a height of some 16,000 feet.

Even while Mount Rainier was growing, glaciers carved valleys on and around the mountain. The 25 major glaciers here form the largest collection of permanent ice on a single U.S. peak south of Alaska.

Volcanic action and glacial erosion have repeatedly altered Mount Rainier's edifice, which currently stands at 14,410 feet high. The mountain last erupted about a century ago.

How to Get There

From Seattle (95 miles) or Tacoma (70 miles) to the Nisqually Entrance (open year-round), take I-5 to Wash. 7, then follow Wash. 706. From Yakima, take Wash. 12 west to Wash. 123 or Wash. 410, and enter from the park's east side (Stevens Canyon or White River Entrances closed in winter). For the northwest entrances (Carbon River and Mowich Lake), take Wash. 410 to Wash. 169 to Wash. 165, then follow the signs. Carbon River Road washed out in a Nov. 2006 flood *(check with the park for closure information)*. Airports: Seattle, Washington, and Portland, Oregon.

When to Go

Year-round. Wildflowers are at their best in July and August. High trails may remain snow covered until mid-July. Cross-country skiing and snowshoeing are popular in winter. Summer and winter, to miss the crowds, time your visit to midweek.

How to Visit (Summer)

If you have only a day, drive from the **Nisqually Entrance** in the southwest to the flowered fields of **Paradise,** then on to **Sunrise,** the highest point accessible by car, open early July to early October.

If you have 2 days, take the same route but do it more leisurely: Plan to explore as far as Paradise the first day, then tour **Stevens Canyon Road** and the route to Sunrise the next; arrive before 10 a.m. to catch the early light and wend your way back.

For a longer stay, drive out and re-enter the less known northwest corner *(check for road closures)* at **Carbon River** for a look at a rain forest and a hike to a dark, shiny glacier. Because Mount Rainier creates its own clouds and can hide for days or weeks at a time, come prepared to focus on delights close at hand: waterfalls, woods, and wildflowers.

NISQUALLY TO PARADISE

19 miles; a half to full day

The pilgrimage to Paradise has been a classic for over a century. The first miles of your tour wind through a forest of giant Douglas fir, western red cedar, and western hemlock. As you cross **Kautz Creek,** about 3 miles from the Nisqually Entrance, look for flood debris and dead trees amid the recovering forest. In 1947 the **Kautz Glacier** disgorged a flash flood of meltwater. The flood raged down the creek valley, carrying volcanic debris, trees, and boulders, and burying the road under 50 feet of mud. Similar, though mostly smaller, mudflows occur at least every few years at Mount Rainier.

Park at **Longmire Museum,** 7 miles from the entrance. Pioneer James Longmire discovered mineral springs here in 1883 and built Mount Rainier's first hotel; his ads for miraculous water cures helped generate early tourism and a constituency for the creation of the park. Take time for the easy half-mile **Trail of the Shadows** that starts on the opposite side of the main road. While in Longmire, also visit the **Wilderness Information Center,**

MOUNT RAINIER

Carbon River Entrance
CARBON RIVER ROAD

To (165)

MOUNT BAKER-SNOQUALMIE

June Cr.

Falls Cr.

Rust Ridge

Ipsut Creek

Chenuis Mountain

Chenuis Cr.

W. Fk. White

Tirzah Peak
5,208 ft

Wallace Peak

Carbon

Arthur Peak
5,483 ft

North Park

Florence Peak
5,508 ft
5,939 ft Tolmie Peak

Ipsut

Castle Peak
6,110 ft

Mother Mountain

Crescent Mt.

Mosquito Flat
Natural Bridge

Sluiskin Mountain

Ipsut Pass

(165)

Mowich Lake

Meadow Cr.

N. Mowich

Hessong Rock
6,385 ft

Mount Pleasant
6,454 ft

Spray Park

Goat Island Rocks

Observation Rock
8,364 ft

Vernal Park

Old Desolate

Skyscraper Mountain
7,078 ft

Granite Cr.

Ptarmigan Ridge

S. Mowich

Giant Falls

North Mowich Glacier

Carbon

Carbon Glacier

Winthrop Glacier

Burroughs M

MOUNT RAINIER

Golden Lakes

Sunset Park

Glacier

NATIONAL PARK

Glacier Basin

Liberty Cap
14,122 ft

Emmons Glaci

WONDERLAND TRAIL

N. Puyallup

Klapatche Ridge

Klapatche Park

Puyallup Glacier

Columbia Crest
14,411 ft

MOUNT

RAINIER

Little Tahoma Pk.
11,138 ft

Tokaloo Rock
7,684 ft

St. Andrews Park

Tahoma Glacier

Point Success
14,153 ft

Gibraltar Rock
12,660 ft

Ingraham Glacier

Cowlitz Glacier

Round Pass
3,900 ft

S. Puyallup

Emerald Ridge

Glacier Island

Pyramid Park

Pyramid Pk.
6,937 ft

Kautz Glacier

Nisqually Glacier

Panorama Point
6,800 ft

Gobblers Knob
5,485 ft

Lake George

Mount Ararat
6,010 ft

Iron Mt.
6,283 ft

NISQUALLY VISTA TRAIL

Paradise

Mazama Ridge

Mount Wow

Satulik Mountain
5,577 ft

Cougar Rock

Henry M. Jackson Memorial Visitor Center

Narada Falls

Reflection Lakes

Louise L.

To Tacoma

Tenas Cr.

(706)

Kautz Cr.

Paradise

Ricksecker Point

Bench L.

Snow L.

Tatoosh Range

Plummer Pk.
6,370 ft

Tumtum Pk.
4,678 ft

TRAIL OF THE SHADOWS
Longmire Museum

Longmire Wilderness Information Center

Wahpenayo Pk.
6,231 ft

Unicorn Pk.
6,917 f

Nisqually Entrance
Sunshine Point

Nisqually

(52)

Butter Creek

TATOOS

N

0   miles   4

0   kilometers   6

GIFFORD PINCHOT

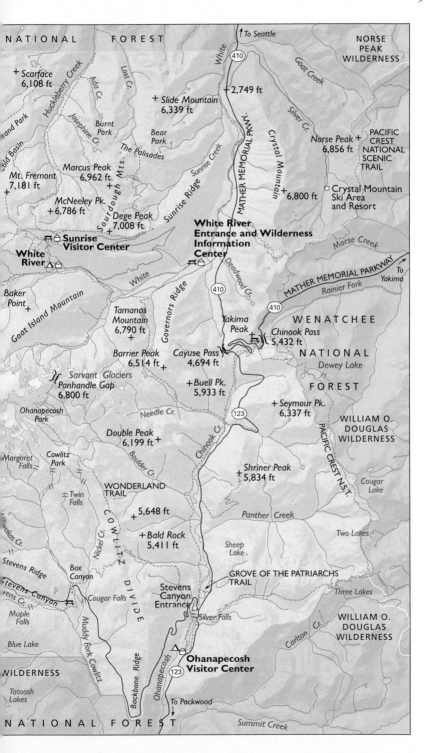

NATIONAL   FOREST

↑ To Seattle

NORSE PEAK WILDERNESS

+ Scarface 6,108 ft

Huckleberry Creek

Ada Cr.

Lost Cr.

+ 2,749 ft

Goat Creek

Silver Cr.

PACIFIC CREST NATIONAL SCENIC TRAIL

+ Slide Mountain 6,339 ft

Josephine Cr.

Burnt Park

Bear Park

The Palisades

Sunrise Creek

MATHER MEMORIAL PKWY.

Crystal Mountain

Norse Peak + 6,856 ft

rand Park

old Basin

Marcus Peak 6,962 ft

Mt. Fremont 7,181 ft

McNeeley Pk. + 6,786 ft

Sourdough Mts.

+ Dege Peak 7,008 ft

Sunrise Ridge

+ 6,800 ft

□ Crystal Mountain Ski Area and Resort

Sunrise Visitor Center

White River

White River Entrance and Wilderness Information Center

Morse Creek

White

Deadwood Cr.

MATHER MEMORIAL PARKWAY

To Yakima

Baker Point +

Goat Island Mountain

Governors Ridge

410

Rainier Fork

410

Tamanos Mountain 6,790 ft +

Yakima Peak

WENATCHEE

Chinook Pass 5,432 ft

Barrier Peak 6,514 ft +

Cayuse Pass 4,694 ft

NATIONAL

Dewey Lake

Sarvant Glaciers Panhandle Gap 6,800 ft

+ Buell Pk. 5,933 ft

FOREST

Ohanapecosh Park

Needle Cr.

+ Seymour Pk. 6,337 ft

WILLIAM O. DOUGLAS WILDERNESS

Double Peak 6,199 ft +

Chinook Cr.

123

Margaret Falls

Cowlitz Park

Boulder Cr.

Shriner Peak + 5,834 ft

Cougar Lake

Twin Falls

WONDERLAND TRAIL

PACIFIC CREST N.S.T.

+ 5,648 ft

Panther Creek

Two Lakes

llivolcas Cr.

COWLITZ

+ Bald Rock 5,411 ft

Sheep Lake

Stevens Ridge

Box Canyon

Nickel Cr.

GROVE OF THE PATRIARCHS TRAIL

Three Lakes

tevens Canyon

vens Cr.

Cougar Falls

DIVIDE

Stevens Canyon Entrance

Maple Falls

Muddy Fork Cowlitz

Silver Falls

Carlton Cr.

WILLIAM O. DOUGLAS WILDERNESS

Blue Lake

Backbone Ridge

Ohanapecosh

Ohanapecosh Visitor Center

123

WILDERNESS

Tatoosh Lakes

→ To Packwood

NATIONAL   FOREST

Summit Creek

MOUNT RAINIER

388

Camping on 4-mile-long Nisqually Glacier

closed between October and May, for trail and weather information and backcountry permits.

Back in your car, continue east for about 6.5 miles, then take the spur road to the right to **Ricksecker Point.** To the south loom the saw-toothed peaks of the **Tatoosh Range,** dramatic remains of former molten flows that predate Mount Rainier by some 14 to 16 million years. Glaciers that developed and receded during the last million years carved the sharp pinnacles and the steep-sided mountainside hollows called cirques. Below meanders the **Nisqually River,** which originates at the snout of the **Nisqually Glacier,** which faces you on Mount Rainier. This glacier is about 4 miles long and flows downhill 6 to 12 inches every summer's day.

Rejoin the highway. Another 1.5 miles brings you to the **Narada Falls** parking area. The shimmering, 168-foot plunge of the **Paradise River** is well worth the steep but short walk down to the viewing area below the bridge. Climb back up to your car and proceed; in less than 3 miles you'll reach the most popular part of the park.

"It looks just like paradise!" exclaimed Martha Longmire in 1885 on first sighting the rolling hills swathed in wildflowers and framed by Mount Rainier's white dome. An average of 140 inches of precipitation falls here each year; as many as 40 species of flowers bloom on the thin, volcanic soil during July and August. Park near the **Henry M. Jackson Memorial Visitor Center,** or the **Paradise Inn,** built in 1916.

Begin your exploration of Paradise meadows on the **Nisqually Vista Trail** (1.2 miles), especially if time is short. This easy nature walk starts at the staircase adjacent to the lower Paradise parking lot, and winds through subalpine meadows on the way to superb views of **Nisqually**

Glacier. Its booklet acquaints you with the geology and meadow life of Mount Rainier.

Make sure you stay on the path, no matter how tempting a meadow stroll. Trampling by just a few people can kill these fragile plants. The park is still at work replanting old trails and other damaged areas. Only recently have the meadows recovered from the Camp of the Clouds, a tent city in operation here from 1898 to 1915.

If you're up to tackling some steep hills, try the 5-mile **Skyline Trail.** Start at the west end of the lower parking lot. The trail will take you to **Panorama Point** for some spectacular views.

PARADISE TO SUNRISE

45 miles; a half to full day

Leaving Paradise, turn left at the sign for **Sunrise** and Yakima. You'll soon pass the glacier-carved **Reflection Lakes** on your left; on a calm morning, the reflection looks as solid as the mountain. Continue a mile past the lakes' pullover and park on the right for a 2.5-mile, hilly, round-trip walk to **Snow** and **Bench Lakes,** gems surrounded by the steep headwalls of the Tatoosh Range.

Drive on and stop after about 3 miles at an overlook of **Stevens Canyon.** Huge glaciers grating through this river gorge deepened and widened it into a classic U-shaped valley. Tributaries of **Stevens Creek** spill from the canyon's rim as waterfalls. Drive on another 3 miles, to **Box Canyon** (just past the picnic area). Park and cross the street for the nearly level half-mile **Canyon Stroll** and you'll see a 100-foot-deep gorge whose straight walls were carved by the **Muddy Fork** of the **Cowlitz River.**

Continue another 9.5 miles, then park to walk the **Grove of the Patriarchs** nature trail. This easy 1.3-mile loop leads to an island in the **Ohanapecosh River** dominated by grand Douglas firs, western red cedars, and western hemlocks, many of them 500 to 1,000 years old. After rejoining the road, turn left on Wash. 123 for Sunrise. If time allows, take a short detour south on Wash. 123 to visit the **Ohanapecosh Visitor Center.**

At **Cayuse Pass,** continue north on Wash. 410, then make a sharp left toward the **White River Entrance.** The road ends at **Sunrise.** Subalpine fir and whitebark pine grow here. Near tree line, harsh temperatures and winds stunt the trees into twisted shrubs called krummholz, or elfin timber; trees only inches in diameter may be 250 years old. Fragile wildflowers bloom among

MOUNT RAINIER

Marmot dining on lupine *(top)*
Northern saw-whet owl *(bottom)*

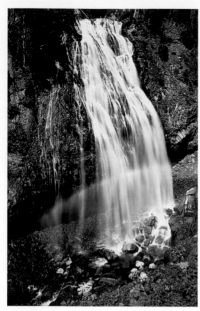

Narada Falls in summer

hill and follow the signs. The trail soon enters tundra. Compact little plants sport exquisite lilliputian blossoms and leaves that are a dull gray from the tiny hairs that protect them against drying winds. *It is most important that you stay on the trail:* If trod on, these delicate plants can take decades to heal.

At Second Burroughs it feels as if you can almost touch Mount Rainier's imposing peak. Return to your car via the **Sunrise Rim Trail.**

THE NORTHWEST CORNER: CARBON RIVER & MOWICH LAKE
16 miles; a half day or more

Note: The Carbon River Road is closed to vehicles just inside the park boundary following major flooding in 2006. The road is now open only to hiking and bicycling. Bicycles are permitted on the road to Ipsut Creek Campground but not on trails beyond that point. Pets are prohibited beyond the park entrance.

To get a feel for a rare inland temperate rain forest, take the **Carbon River Road** (it forks left off Wash. 165 about 6 miles past Wilkeson). Stop at the entrance to take the quarter-mile self-guided **Carbon River Rain Forest Trail** loop among colossal Sitka spruces, Douglas firs, and western red cedars. Return to Wash. 165, turning sharply uphill (left) at the fork. The rough, unpaved road climbs 16 miles to **Mowich Lake** (open July to Oct.). At the road's end, a primitive campground and picnic area sit next to the lake. Backcountry trails lead north to excellent views at **Tolmie Peak** lookout (5.6 miles round-trip) and south to 300-foot **Spray Falls** (4 miles round-trip). Note that potable water is not available at Mowich Lake, so be sure to bring enough of your own.

grass and sedge in terrain inhospitable to trees.

At the visitor center, ask about snow conditions on the higher trails. If time is short, take the self-guided **Sourdough Ridge Nature Trail** for 1.5 miles, then the **Emmons Vista Trail** for half a mile. The Sourdough Ridge trail, which starts with a climb, introduces you to the plants and animals of the subalpine region. The former flourish in this fertile but fragile volcanic soil. The Emmons Vista Trail offers an easy way to view **Emmons Glacier,** Mount Rainier's largest, covering more than 4 square miles.

If you have more time and energy, and the snow has melted *(snow on the slopes can be dangerous if you're not equipped with an ice ax and trained to use it)*, take the **Burroughs Mountain Trail** (5 miles to **First Burroughs,** or 6 miles to **Second Burroughs).** Begin as you did for the Sourdough Ridge Nature Trail, but turn left about half way up the

Clockwise from top: Giant red paintbrush and daisies along Tatoosh Range; western pasqueflowers; pink mountain heather; fireweed; phlox; shooting stars; glacier lilies

INFORMATION & ACTIVITIES

VISITOR & INFORMATION CENTERS

Longmire Wilderness Information Center open daily late May to early Oct.
Longmire Museum open all year.
Henry M. Jackson Memorial Visitor Center, at Paradise, open daily from early May to mid-Oct., weekends and holidays in winter.
Ohanapecosh Visitor Center, at park's southeast entrance, open daily Memorial Day to mid-Oct.
Sunrise Visitor Center open daily, early July to mid-Sept., weather dependent.

SEASONS & ACCESSIBILITY
Park open year-round. Many roads closed by snow from late November through May or June. Call (360) 569-2211 for recorded weather, road, and trail information, or in the Nisqually area tune in to 1610 AM.

HEADQUARTERS
55210 238th Ave. East, Ashford, WA 98304. Phone (360) 569-2211. www.nps.gov/mora

ENTRANCE FEE
$15 per car per week; $30 annual.

PETS
Permitted leashed on roads. Pets not allowed on trails or in the backcountry.

ACCESSIBLE SERVICES
Most public buildings and some restrooms are wheelchair accessible. Portions of some trails may be accessible (assistance may be needed). Inquire at park for details.

THINGS TO DO
Free naturalist-led activities: nature and history walks, hikes, campfire and children's programs, talks, films, illustrated programs. Also available, hiking, mountain climbing, fishing (Washington state license required), cross-country skiing, snowshoeing.

SPECIAL ADVISORIES
• Mount Rainier is an active volcano. While eruptions are usually preceded by an increase in earthquake activity, other hazards, such as mudflows, glacial outburst floods, or rockfalls can occur without warning.
• Watch out for falling rocks, debris, and avalanches. Look up!
• Some areas may be subject to flash floods, especially in late summer and fall. Inquire about current conditions before hiking.
• Stop by a visitor center for additional safety information.

OVERNIGHT BACKPACKING
Permit required; available from visitor centers, ranger stations, and wilderness centers, where you can also get help with your trip planning. For reservation information, contact the Wilderness Information Center at (360) 569-4453.

CAMPGROUNDS
Four campgrounds, all with 14-day limit. Open late spring to early fall. Fees $12-$15 per night. Showers available in the visitor center at Paradise. Both tent and RV sites; no hookups. Advance reservations required at **Cougar Rock** and **Ohanapecosh** from late June to Labor Day. Call NRRS (see p. 10). All others, first come, first served. Food services in park.

HOTELS, MOTELS, & INNS
(unless otherwise noted, rates are for 2 persons in a double room, high season)

INSIDE THE PARK:
The following are operated by Mt. Rainier Guest Services, P.O. Box 108, Ashford, WA 98304. (360) 569-2275, www.mtrainier guestservices.com.
National Park Inn (at 2,700-foot level of Mount Rainier) 25 units, 18 with private baths. $112-$148. Restaurant. Open year-round.
Paradise Inn (at 5,400-foot level of Mount Rainier) 118 units, 86 with private baths. $109-$159. Restaurant. Late May– early Oct.

For more information on area accommodations, contact the park's Guest Services (see above) or refer to the website.

EXCURSIONS

GIFFORD PINCHOT NATIONAL FOREST
VANCOUVER, WASHINGTON

Dense coniferous forest offers superb views of Mount St. Helens. Contains glaciers and seven wilderness areas. 1.3 million acres. Hiking, boating, climbing, fishing, horseback riding, hunting, winter sports, water sports. 65 campgrounds (30 primitive), 3 group campgrounds, picnic areas, handicapped access. Open all year; most campsites open mid-May through mid-September. Adjoins Mount Rainier NP on the south. Information at Randle on Wash. 12, about 10 miles from the park. (360) 891-5001.

MOUNT ST. HELENS NATIONAL VOLCANIC MONUMENT
AMBOY, WASHINGTON

This monument owes its existence to Mount St. Helens's eruption laying waste the surrounding forest. Witness the rebirth of a forest through interpretive programs and tours. 110,000 acres. Hiking, bicycling, climbing (reservations required), fishing, scenic drives, winter sports. Picnic areas, handicapped access. Open year-round, but winter snows close many roads. Within Gifford Pinchot NF. Four visitor centers east of Castle Rock on Wash. 504. Many viewpoints and trails accessed from the north via Wash. 12 at Randle and from the south via Wash. 503 at Woodland. (360) 449-7800.

MOUNT RAINIER

RIDGEFIELD NATIONAL WILDLIFE REFUGE
RIDGEFIELD, WASHINGTON

Established to protect the winter habitat of the dusky Canada goose, this site on the floodplain of the Columbia River provides a winter haven for many waterfowl species. It also serves as a year-round home for great blue herons and a resting spot for migrating sandhill cranes. 5,150 acres. Hiking, hunting, scenic drives. Open all year, dawn to dusk (winter best time). Off I-5, about 90 miles from Mount Rainier NP. (360) 887-4106.

Glacier-carved peaks of the North Cascades

▶ NORTH CASCADES

WASHINGTON
ESTABLISHED OCTOBER 2, 1968
*684,000 acres, includes two
recreation areas*

With glacier-clad peaks rising almost vertically from thickly forested valleys, the North Cascades are often called the American Alps. The national park forms one unit of the North Cascades National Park Service Complex. The two other units—Ross Lake National Recreation Area and Lake Chelan National Recreation Area—contain most visitor facilities.

The park complex preserves virgin forests, fragile subalpine meadows, and hundreds of glaciers. Mule deer and black-tailed deer graze the high meadows, where black bears gorge on berries and hoary marmots sunbathe. Mountain goats clamber on rock faces. Mountain lions and bobcats, seldom seen, help keep other wildlife populations in balance.

The wildness and ruggedness of the park especially lure hikers, backpackers, and mountaineers. "A more difficult route to travel never fell to man's lot," complained trapper Alexander Ross, who came here in 1814. But today the main road (through Ross Lake NRA) and easy access into the park—on some of its nearly 400 miles of trails— also allow more casual visitors to experience the peaceful forests and the drama of the mountains.

The region forms part of the Cascade Range, named for its innumerable waterfalls. The range extends from British Columbia to northern California. A geological theory proposes that the mountains began as a microcontinent several hundred miles out in the Pacific Ocean. Over the eons a series of islands floated on their plate toward North America. About a hundred million years ago, the plate smashed into the North American continent, folding and crumpling into a mountain range as it lodged against the landmass. Those mountains eroded; the Cascades you see today rose only five or six million years ago.

The western part of the park differs markedly from the east. Moisture blows in from Puget Sound and the Strait of Juan de Fuca. It hits the western slopes and rises, condensing to rain and snow. Western red cedars, hemlocks, and Douglas firs luxuriate on slopes that receive 110 inches of precipitation a year. When the winds reach the east, they are mostly wrung dry: Only 35 inches of precipitation fall in Stehekin at the head of Lake Chelan. Arid-dwelling sagebrush and ponderosa pine grow in the peaks' rain shadow.

How to Get There
From Seattle (about 115 miles from the park), take I-5 to Wash. 20, also called the North Cascades Highway. From the east, get on Wash. 20 at Winthrop. To reach Stehekin Valley, either hike over Cascade Pass from the Cascade River Road (2-day hike) or take a ferry, or a chartered floatplane from Chelan, at the southern tip of Lake Chelan. Chelan is on US 97. Airports: Seattle and Bellingham and Wenatchee.

When to Go
Summer gives the best access, though snow can block high trails into July. The North Cascades Highway, from Ross Dam to beyond Washington Pass at Silver Star Creek, closes in winter. Stehekin, a year-round community, offers winter cross-country skiing.

How to Visit
On a day trip, take the **North Cascades Highway** through the **Ross Lake National Recreation Area** for an overview of the recreation area's lakes and dams, the park's mountains, and the glacier-fed **Skagit River**. If you have 2 days, drive up the 23-mile **Cascade River Road** (only the first 10 miles are paved) and picnic and hike among the park's peaks and alpine meadows. On a longer stay, drive south to **Chelan,** and take the ferry or fly to **Stehekin** to overnight in a serene, isolated community or in the backcountry.

CASCADES HIGHWAY: MARBLEMOUNT TO WASHINGTON PASS
60 miles; a half to full day

The ease of driving the North Cascades Highway belies the terrain's ruggedness, although names supplied by explorers and climbers attest to it: Mount Terror, Mount Despair, Damnation Peak, Mount Fury, Mount Challenger. This trans-mountain road was completed only in 1972.

Enter the **Ross Lake National Recreation Area** after crossing **Bacon Creek,** 6.5 miles beyond the Wilderness Information Center at Marblemount. Parallel to the road, the **Skagit River** appears emerald in summer—evidence of the park's many glaciers. As they move, glaciers

NORTH CASCADES

MOUNT BAKER
WILDERNESS

(542)

Nooksack

Silver Fir
Goat Mt.
6,890 ft

Mt. Hermann
6,286 ft

Mount Baker
Ski Area

Heather
Meadows
Visitor Center

MOUNT BAKER
WILDERNESS

+Mt. Shuksan
9,131 ft

Chilliwack Lake

CHILLIWACK LAKE
PROVINCIAL PARK

BRITISH COLUMBIA
WASHINGTON

To Hope, B.C.
SKAGIT
VALLEY
PROVINCIAL
PARK

Hozomee

Copper Mt.
7,142 ft

Silver Cr.

Chilliwack

Mt. Redoubt
8,969 ft

Perry Cr.

Whatcom Pass
5,206 ft

LITTLE BEAVER TRAIL

Little Beaver Cr.

ROSS

Arctic Cr.

LAKE

Whatcom Pk.
7,574 ft

NORTH CASCADES

+ Mt. Challenger
8,207 ft

Mt. Prophet
7,640 ft

NATIONAL

Baker

Mt. Fury +
8,291 ft

Picket Ra.

Big Beaver Cr.

BIG BEAVER TRAIL

Ross

RECREATION

Ross Lake

Park Creek
Baker
Lake
Resort

Shannon Creek

NATIONAL PARK

Mt. Despair
7,292 ft

AREA

Baker
Lake

Noisy Cr.

Sourdough Mt.
6,120 ft

Ross Lake
Resort

Horseshoe
Cove

Upper
Baker Dam

Thunder Cr.

NOISY-
DIOBSUD
WILDERNESS

Bacon Pk.
7,061 ft

Bacon Cr.

Mt. Triumph
7,271 ft

NORTH UNIT

Gorge Creek
Falls

Ross Dam.

Diablo

HAPPY
CREE
FORE
WAL

Goodell Creek

Gorge
Lake

Diablo
Lake

Lake
Shannon

Skagit

Newhalem

North Cascades
Visitor Center

Colonial Creek
Colonial Pk.
7,771 ft

Ruby Mt.
7,408 ft

Baker Dam
Concrete

MOUNT BAKER

The Portage

Snowfield Pk.
8,347 ft

Neve
Glacier

THUNDER
CREEK
TRAIL

Sauk Mt.
5,541 ft

(20)

Skagit

ROCKPORT S.P.

Wilderness
Information
Center

Marblemount

Rockport

Illabot Cr.

Lookout Mt.
5,699 ft

NORTH CASCADES

Marble
Creek

Cascade

McAllister
Glacier

Inspiration
Glacier

Eldorado Pk.
8,868 ft

NATIONAL

Sauk

SNOQUALMIE

(530)

+Suiattle Mt.
5,040 ft

Suiattle

Forbidden Peak
8,815 ft

Mt. Loga
9,087 f

CASCADE RIVER ROAD

Boston Pk.+
8,894 ft

Boston C

SOUTH

Mineral Park

Johannesburg Mt.
8,200 ft

Cascade Pas
5,392 ft

CASCADE PASS TRAIL

Cottonwood

Stehek

Mt. Chaval
7,127 ft

Mt. Formidable
8,325 ft

Glory Mt.
7,228 ft

Stillaguamish

Hurricane Pk.
6,414 ft

South
Cascade
Glacier

Flat Cr.

LeConte
Glacier

W. Fk. Agnes Cr.

Sentinel Pk.
8,261 ft

(530)

Darrington

NATIONAL

Prairie Mt.
5,678 ft

Buck Cr.

FOREST

Green Mt.+
6,500 ft

Downey Cr.

Dome
Glacier

Chickamin
Glacier

Dome Pk.
8,920 ft

PACIFIC
CREST
NATIONAL
SCENIC
TRAIL

South Fk.

MOUNTAIN LOOP HWY

White Chuck+
Mountain
6,989 ft

Downey
Creek

Sulphur Cr.

Sulphur Creek

Lime Mt.+
6,772 ft

SUIATTLE TRAIL

Miners Ridge

N

GLACIER PEAK
WILDERNESS

Dusty
Glacier

0   miles   10

0   kilometers   15

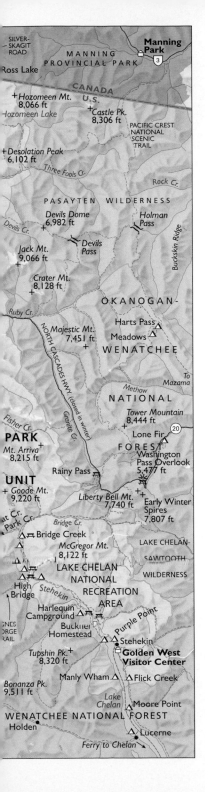

grind bedrock into a fine "flour." Water carrying a high concentration of glacial flour reflects the green and blue part of the light spectrum. In winter bald eagles feast on salmon running the Skagit.

At **Goodell Creek Bridge** (milepost 119), look left to catch a rare glimpse of the high, sawtoothed peaks of the **Picket Range.** Discover the natural and human history of these mountains along trails or at the **North Cascades Visitor Center.** The visitor center features slide and film programs about the North Cascades Wilderness. Nearby is **Sterling Munro Viewpoint,** an accessible viewpoint trail.

Farther east on Wash. 20, turn right onto Main Street in **Newhalem,** (milepost 121) to visit **Skagit Tours Information Center** to learn about Seattle City Light and its dams on the Skagit River. The company's dams—Gorge, Diablo, and Ross—generate about a quarter of Seattle's peak-time electricity. They created **Diablo, Ross,** and **Gorge Lakes.** To haul men and materials for construction, the company built a railway from Rockport to Diablo in the 1920s.

Drive on to **Diablo,** another City Light settlement, by turning left at milepost 126. Near here in 1901, pioneer Lucinda Davis and her three children cleared land and put up a roadhouse to feed and house the miners who still trudged the mountains in the wake of two abortive gold rushes. The Davis family built the first hydroelectric project on the Skagit—a waterwheel that generated enough electricity to power three lightbulbs. A reproduction of the waterwheel stands next to the modern Diablo powerhouse.

Contact the Skagit Tours Information Center (206-684-3030 or www.seattle.gov/light/tours/skagit) to see if there is room on City Light's 2-hour tour of Diablo Lake.

NORTH CASCADES

Lake Chelan, ringed by the snowcapped Chelan Mountains

If you are without a boat, this is the only way to actually get on the water. (Or board a City Light ferry traveling between **Diablo** and **Ross.** This enjoyable 1-hour round-trip begins across Diablo Dam Road at the parking for the Ross Lake Resort.)

Drive back to the highway and, if you are looking for an invigorating climb, turn right after about 4 miles just past milepost 130 at Colonial Creek Campground. Behind the amphitheater the **Thunder Woods Nature Trail** begins. This moderately steep 1-mile loop rises among giant, fragrant cedar trees, some of them more than three centuries old. The red cedar—characterized by ropy, cinnamon-colored bark and flat, fernlike foliage—provided Indians with wood for canoes and houses and fiber for mats, clothing, and baskets. To extend your walk, continue along the 19-mile **Thunder Creek Trail** for a while; the views are good and the hiking relatively easy at first. (Eventually it ascends to Park Creek Pass at 6,100 feet.)

When you're back in the car, don't miss the **Diablo Lake Overlook** (1,600 feet), milepost 132. Amid the splendid scenery are exhibits that honor Senator Henry M. Jackson, who helped create the park and to whom Congress dedicated it in 1987. The highest mountain visible here is **Colonial Peak** (7,771 feet) to the southwest; note the glacial cirque, or bowl-shaped depression, carved out of its side. North is **Sourdough Mountain,** site of a fire lookout.

Near milepost 134 you'll find an informative 0.3-mile boardwalk nature trail, the **Happy Creek Forest Walk.** A few miles farther on, the highway leaves the park complex and enters the **Okanogan National Forest** (milepost 139). For a superb view of Cascade peaks, follow the road about 20 miles to **Washington Pass Overlook** (5,477 feet), the highest point on the North Cascades Highway. Exit to the left at milepost 162, and walk to the overlook. Directly to the south is massive **Liberty Bell Mountain** (7,740 feet), south of that the **Early Winter Spires** (7,807 feet). With binoculars you might spot climbers and mountain goats on the solid granite faces.

CASCADE RIVER ROAD
45 miles round-trip; a half day

The Cascade River Road, only one of two roads that enter the national park—and the only one accessible from the state highway system—passes through national forest for most of its length. The road starts in front of the Buffalo Run Inn in Marblemount. Before departing, pick up maps and check road conditions at Marblemount's **Wilderness Information Center.** The 23-mile road becomes progressively narrower, steeper, and bumpier, though high-clearance cars can travel it in an hour without difficulty *(trailers should not attempt the last few miles).* The drive ends at a parking lot and picnic area (3,660 feet) between the glacier-studded summits of **Johannesburg Mountain** (8,200 feet) to the west and **Boston Peak** (8,894 feet) to the east.

Hikers will enjoy the 3.75-mile trail to **Cascade Pass** (5,392 feet). The Skagit and Chelan Indians used the pass to and from **Lake Chelan** for hunting and trading. The trail leaves the lowland forest to enter woods of silver fir, mountain hemlock, and Alaska yellow cedar, then flower-strewn subalpine meadows. Stay on the path; previous visitors have damaged the fragile meadow flora.

Park employees grow native plants in a greenhouse in Marblemount, then backpack them in for planting in summer to revegetate the pass. Contact the volunteer coordinator about volunteer opportunities with the park's revegetation project.

STEHEKIN VALLEY

1 or 2 nights

Stehekin has been a tourist hideaway since hotels first opened here at the turn of the 20th century and miners spread tales of magical scenery. On the northern shores of glacier-carved Lake Chelan and inaccessible by road, Stehekin is a community of hardy contemporary homesteaders, complete with a one-room schoolhouse in use from 1921 to 1988.

The valley offers many lodging alternatives as well as backcountry camping without backpacking: Simply fill out a backcountry permit after you get there, take a shuttle bus and stake your claim.

Even if you don't plan to camp, head for the **Golden West Visitor Center** when you arrive at Stehekin Landing to pick up hiking maps and schedules of tours and buses. Be sure to ask about trail conditions; high trails can be closed by snow or flood damage. In addition, a 2003 flood damaged the park road so access is limited.

After lunch, tour the **Buckner Homestead.** Home of the William Buckner family from 1911 to 1970, it offers a look at the challenges of frontier life.

Next morning follow the nature trails near the landing. The informative 0.75-mile **Imus Creek Nature Trail** starts near the visitor center, and the **McKellar Cabin Historical Trail** begins just past the post office. Or catch the early shuttle bus *(fee)* upvalley; it currently can access a number of trailheads. Ask a ranger for the latest bus schedule.

For an easy hike try the **Agnes Gorge Trail,** 5 miles round-trip and level. Get off the Stehekin shuttle at **High Bridge** near the intersection with the Pacific Crest Trail and walk across the bridge, past the sign for **Agnes Creek,** to the trailhead for **Agnes Gorge.** The trail provides excellent views of the 210-foot gorge and **Agnes Mountain** (8,115 feet). Be sure to keep a bus schedule with you at all times to avoid being stranded.

If you like to hike and backcountry camp, a good bet is the **Horseshoe Basin Trail** (off the **Cascade Pass Trail**), a moderately steep 3.9-mile trail that passes more than 15 waterfalls among spectacular glacier and mountain views. Though the trail itself is short, the 14.4 miles to the trailhead are no longer accessible by bus and take several days to hike.

INFORMATION & ACTIVITIES

VISITOR & INFORMATION CENTERS

North Cascades Visitor Center (near Newhalem) open daily May through Oct. Call (206) 386-4495.
Information center on Wash. 20 (North Cascades Hwy.), Sedro Woolley, open daily late May through early Oct., weekdays rest of year.
Wilderness Information Center in Marblemount (just west of park boundary off North Cascades Hwy.), open daily summer only.
Lake Chelan NRA: Golden West Visitor Center (Stehekin), access by ferry, floatplane, or foot, open seasonally. Limited hours in winter; call headquarters for info.

SEASONS & ACCESSIBILITY

Park open year-round; snow prevents access to much of it from mid-October to April.

HEADQUARTERS

810 State Rte. 20, Sedro-Woolley, WA 98284. Phone (360) 854-7200. www.nps .gov/noca

ENTRANCE FEE

No entrance fee, but $5 for docking fee on Lake Chelan. $30 for annual pass.

PETS

Prohibited in national park except on Pacific Crest Trail, if leashed. Permitted on leashes in NRA.

ACCESSIBLE SERVICES

Information facilities and numerous short trails near North Cascades Highway are wheelchair accessible.

THINGS TO DO

Free naturalist-led activities: **Ross Lake NRA:** guided nature walks, evening campfire programs. **Lake Chelan NRA:** nature and Buckner Orchard walks, evening programs. Also available, hiking, boating, fishing, hunting (NRA only, in season), horseback riding, rafting on Skagit River, cross-country skiing. In summer, tours of Diablo Lake. Reserve at least a month in advance through Seattle City Light's Skagit Tour Desk, (206) 684-3030, www.seattle.gov/light/tours/skagit.

OVERNIGHT BACKPACKING

Permits required; available free at Wilderness Information Center in Marblemount and Golden West Visitor Center or obtain a permit at the closest ranger station.

CAMPGROUNDS

Ross Lake NRA: Three campgrounds, 14-day limit. **Colonial Creek** open midspring to mid-fall. **Newhalem Creek** open mid-May to early Oct. **Goodell Creek** open all year. All first come, first served. Fees: None to $12 per night. No showers. Tent and RV sites; no hookups. Goodell Creek and Newhalem Creek Group Campground, reservations required; call (877) 444-6777 or go to www.recreation.gov.
Lake Chelan NRA: Three campgrounds, **Harlequin, Bullion,** and **Purple Point,** 14-day limit. Open mid-spring to mid-fall. First come, first served. No fees. Backcountry permit required. Public showers are located near Purple Point. Tent sites only. Reservations required at **Harlequin Group Campground** (contact Golden West Visitor Center in Stehekin, 360-854-7365). Limited food service is available in Lake Chelan NRA.

HOTELS, MOTELS, & INNS
(unless otherwise noted, rates are for 2 persons in a double room, high season)

In Ross Lake NRA:
Ross Lake Resort (Access by boat or foot) 503 Diablo St., Rockport, WA 98283. (206) 386-4437. 15 units floating on lake, kitchens. $122-$261. Mid-June–late Oct.
In Lake Chelan NRA:
Stehekin Landing Resort P.O. Box 3, Stehekin, WA 98852. (509) 682-4494 or (800) 536-0745. 28 units. $123-$159. Restaurant.
Silver Bay Inn P.O. Box 85, Stehekin, WA 98852. (800) 555-7781. 4 cabins, $135-$375. May–Oct.
Stehekin Valley Ranch P.O. Box 36, Stehekin, WA 98852. (509) 682-4677 or (800) 536-0745. 14 cabins, some with showers. $85-$95 per person, meals. June–early Oct.
In Birdsview-Concrete, WA 98237:
Cascade Mountain Inn 40418 Pioneer Ln. (360) 826-4333. 6 units. $155-$195, incl. breakfast.

For accommodations in Chelan, contact Lake Chelan Chamber of Commerce, 102 East Johnson Ave., Chelan, WA 98816. (800) 424-3526 or (509) 682-3503, www .lakechelan.com.

EXCURSIONS

MT. BAKER-SNOQUALMIE NATIONAL FOREST
EVERETT, WASHINGTON

The Cascades' evergreen-covered western slopes feature active and dormant volcanoes, glaciers, lakes, streams, and waterfalls. Eight wilderness areas. Long winter sports season. Over 1.7 million acres. Hiking, boating, swimming, climbing, fishing, horseback riding, scenic drives, winter sports. More than 700 campsites, boat ramp, picnic areas. Open all year; campsites open May through Sept. Roads often impassable in winter. Located between North Cascades NP to the north and Mount Rainier NP to the south. (800) 627-0062 or (425) 783-6000.

SKAGIT RIVER BALD EAGLE NATURAL AREA
ROCKPORT, WASHINGTON

This wildlife area is the favored wintering ground of several hundred bald eagles that feed on chum salmon carcasses along the upper Skagit River. Population peaks in mid-Jan. 10,000 acres. Marked viewing vistas with handicapped access located off Wash. 20 about 10 miles from North Cascades NP. Skagit River Interpretive Center is located in Rockport at Howard Miller Steelhead Park. (360) 853-7626.

OKANOGAN AND WENATCHEE NATIONAL FOREST
OKANOGAN, WASHINGTON

In a remote, rugged mountain area, this national forest features high peaks, mountain lakes, meadows, evergreens, and open woodlands. Contains the Pasayten and Lake Chelan-Sawtooth Wildernesses. 1,790,633 acres. Hiking, boating, climbing, fishing, horseback riding, hunting, scenic drives, winter sports. 38 campgrounds, boat ramp, picnic areas. Open year-round; most campsites open May through October. Adjoins North Cascades NP on east. (509) 826-3275.

NORTH CASCADES

Club moss on vine maple and bigleaf maple in the Hoh Rain Forest

▶OLYMPIC

WASHINGTON
ESTABLISHED JUNE 29, 1938
922,000 acres

Encompassing 1,441 square miles of the Olympic Peninsula, Olympic National Park invites visitors to explore three distinct ecosystems: subalpine forest and wildflower meadow; temperate forest; and the rugged Pacific shore. Because of the park's relatively unspoiled condition and outstanding scenery, the United Nations has declared Olympic both an international biosphere reserve and a World Heritage site.

Inside the park, the Olympic mountain range is nearly circular, contoured by 13 rivers that radiate out like the spokes of a wheel. No road traverses the park, but a dozen spur roads lead into it from US 101, making it easily accessible from outside the park.

Residents of the Olympic Peninsula refer to it as a gift from the sea, and its features were indeed shaped by water and ice. The rock of the Olympics developed under the ocean—marine fossils are embedded in the mountain summits. Another component, basalt, originated from undersea lava vents. About 30 million years ago, the plate carrying the Pacific Ocean floor collided with the plate supporting the North American continent. As the heavy oceanic plate slid beneath the lighter continental plate, the upper layers of seabed jammed against the coastline, crumpling into what would become the Olympic Mountains. Glaciers and streams sculptured the mountains into their current profiles.

Glaciers nearly 1-mile thick also gouged out Puget Sound and Hood Canal to the east, and the Strait of Juan de Fuca to the north, isolating the peninsula from the mainland.

Ice Age isolation led to the 15 animals and 8 plants that evolved nowhere else on Earth, including the Olympic mountain milkvetch, Olympic marmot, Olympic Mazama pocket gopher, Olympic mud minnow, Beardslee, and crescent trout.

There are also the 11 mammals common in the nearby Cascades and Rockies that either died out in the Olympics or never found their way into the peninsula. The missing include the grizzly bear, lynx, and mountain sheep.

The mountain goats found here are non-native. They were introduced in the 1920s before the park was established. The goat population eventually boomed to over 1,000 and so damaged Olympic's alpine meadows in 1981 the park staff began efforts to manage their numbers within the park.

Moist winds from the Pacific condense in the cool air of the Olympics and drop rain or snow, bestowing on the mountains' western slopes the wettest climate in the lower 48 states. Mount Olympus, which crowns the park at 7,980 feet, receives 200 inches of precipitation a year.

How to Get There

Approach the park from US 101, which skirts three sides of the Olympic Peninsula. The main visitor center and entrance are in Port Angeles. From Seattle, take the Washington State Ferry to Bainbridge Island, then drive north to Wash. 104 to join US 101 west to Port Angeles, a drive of about 60 miles. Airports: Port Angeles, Seattle, Sequim, and Olympia.

When to Go

All-year park. Summer is the "dry" season, but be prepared for cool temperatures, fog, and rain at any time. Hurricane Ridge opens for skiing on winter weekends and holidays, weather permitting.

How to Visit

Plan to spend at least 2 days. On the first day, stroll subalpine meadows at **Hurricane Ridge** while admiring the peaks and glaciers in the distance. Savor the **Lake Crescent** area and, if you're feeling energetic, wind up with a dip at **Sol Duc Hot Springs.**

On the second day, drive to the **Hoh Rain Forest** and sample its nature trails before heading west for the Pacific Ocean beaches and tide pools. If you have more time, consider a trip to **Ozette** along the coast, or visit less known **Quinault.**

DRIVE TO HURRICANE RIDGE, LAKE CRESCENT, & SOL DUC

76 miles; a very full day

Plan to spend the night in the area to get an early start. At the **visitor center** in Port Angeles, inquire about the weather on Hurricane Ridge and pick up a tide table for the next day.

On a clear day, the ridge offers spectacular views of the **Olympic Mountains** and northward as far

OLYMPIC

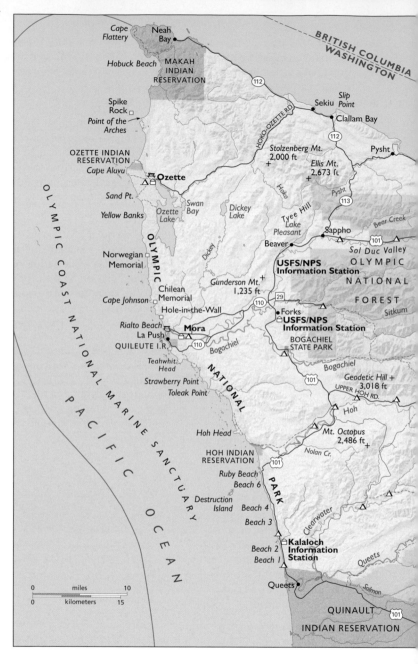

as the Strait of Juan de Fuca and Canada's Vancouver Island. The 17-mile drive to Hurricane Ridge—so named for the force of its winter winds—takes you from lowland forest to tree line, nearly a mile above sea level, and reveals some of the remarkable geology of the peninsula.

After the tunnels, 9 miles in, stop at a pullover and look at the rock faces above the road. The bubbles of rock, called pillow basalt,

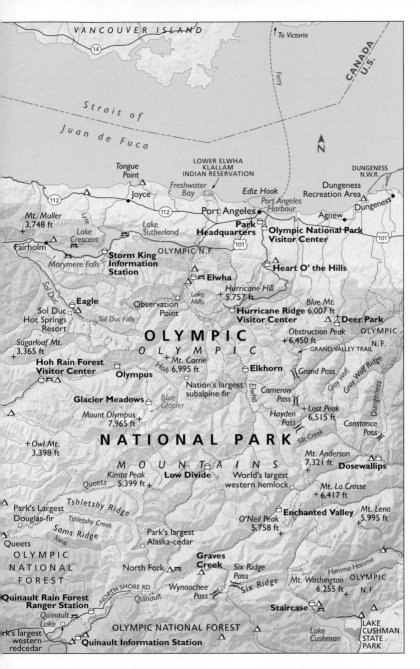

are a clue that these mountains began under the ocean; when hot lava oozes into seawater, its surface cools and hardens quickly, often forming the globules you see here.

Drive on toward **Hurricane Ridge Visitor Center.** Plaques identify the peaks and glaciers of the inner Olympics. **Mount Olympus** carries 7 of Olympic's 60 named glaciers. Its **Blue Glacier** can receive up to

100 feet of snow a year and flows downhill as much as 5 inches a day.

You will probably see black-tailed deer here, and possibly Olympic marmots that whistle when approached. Most of the trees are subalpine fir. Their distinctive steeple shape helps shed snow. Near tree line, a 3-foot-tall tree may be 100 years old; summer wildflowers thrive where no tree can take hold.

Fine picnic sites lie near the road's end, about a mile beyond Hurricane Ridge. Try the partly paved **Hurricane Hill Trail,** starting where the road ends, for 3 miles (round-trip; 700 foot elevation change) of wildflowers and stunning mountain views. Layers of sedimentary rock along the trail stand folded and tilted on end from the continental collision.

If you prefer to continue driving—some of it is tricky—take the 8-mile, unpaved road to **Obstruction Peak,** from the east end of the Hurricane Ridge parking lot, for the park's best windshield view of Mount Olympus and some of Olympic's most diverse wildflower displays. (The road generally opens by July 4.) **Grand Valley Trail** (3.5 miles one way) starts at the parking lot at road's end. Take at least a short stroll on it for grand ridgetop views.

Back in your car double back to Port Angeles and pick up US 101 west. Here, the highway passes **Lake Sutherland** before tracing the southern shore of **Lake Crescent.** Carved by a glacier, the two lakes began as one, but a great landslide created the dam that now divides them. Indian legend says that Mount Storm King, angered at the fighting between the Quileute and Clallam Indians, threw down a boulder, killing the combatants and splitting the lake in two. Lake Crescent, 600 feet deep, is known for its azure waters and trout.

Turn off at the **Storm King Information Station** to walk the

Marymere Falls Trail, a 1.75-mile round-trip through lowland forest to a graceful, 90-foot waterfall. Fifty cents buys a booklet that identifies the trees—mostly Douglas fir and western hemlock, with a few western red cedar. Back in the car, time permitting, turn left 1.5 miles west of Fairholm to take the 14-mile road to **Sol Duc.** Indians may have used the hot springs for medicinal treatments. Travelers have soothed tired muscles in pools here since a resort was first established in 1912. In case you want to stroll before you soak, the **Sol Duc Falls Trail,** starting at the end of the road, leads through three-quarters of a mile of dense forest to a waterfall.

HOH RAIN FOREST TO THE PACIFIC BEACHES

45 miles; a full day

The Hoh Rain Forest is located 2.5 hours from Port Angeles. To see it and the coast, continue skirting the park as you drive west and south on US 101. Check the schedule of guided tide-pool walks in your park newspaper and then decide whether to go first to the rain forest or to the beaches.

For the rain forest, take the **Upper Hoh Road** inland 19 miles to the visitor center. You'll pass large recently reforested areas on private, state, and national forest lands, once entirely clear-cut. Logging is prohibited in the park, yet environmentalists cite evidence of damage done to park wildlife—some of whose living area extends outside the park—by shrinking habitat.

Glacier-carved Lake Crescent

Two nature trails start behind the visitor center and are well worth taking: the **Hall of Mosses Trail** (0.75 mile) and the **Spruce Nature Trail** (1.25 miles). This is an enchanted land. Sitka spruce, western hemlock, and western red cedar, measuring up to 25 feet in circumference, tower 300 feet in the air. Club moss and licorice ferns drape the conifers and bigleaf maples, suffusing the air with green. Seedlings, unable to compete on the crowded forest floor, sprout luxuriantly on fallen trees, called nurse logs. Aged giants, lined up in colonnades, stand on huge roots called stilts where their nurse log rotted away. You may see or hear the eerie bugle of the Roosevelt elk, named for Theodore Roosevelt. (He so loved them, the park was almost named Elk Park.) The elk are members of the largest unmanaged herd in the nation.

To see how the forest develops, take the Spruce Nature Trail. Where the **Hoh River** has shifted course in the last few decades, the first trees to move in needed full sunlight to grow—red alder, willow, and Douglas fir. Later, shade-tolerant spruce and hemlock will succeed these pioneers to dominate the forest. As you stroll, note how the downed trees provide nutrients for the emerging seedlings.

After your forest sojourn, rejoin US 101 south, stopping at **Ruby Beach.** Walk the trail down to the sand—and keep track of where you came out of the woods. It might be hard to find the trail again, and the tough, oval-leaved shrubs off the trail are virtually impenetrable.

Olympic preserves over 60 miles of coastal wilderness: To the north, the beaches tend to have more pebbles and rocks; to the south, the beaches are broader and sandier. Rock outcroppings called sea stacks, isolated from the shoreline by erosion, have caused many a shipwreck.

The driftwood you might have to climb over once grew where you just were: upriver in the forest. Toppled by a winter storm or undercut by a flooding creek, trees tumbled downstream to the sea. *Beware: Picturesque at low tide, drift logs can suddenly roll with lethal force at high tide.*

You may see harbor seals, the most common marine mammal

on this coast, swimming or loung-
ing on the rocks. In the spring and
fall, California gray whales dive and
spout near land on their migration
between Alaska and Baja California.
Gulls and crows drop clams from
50 feet in the air to crack them open
on the rocks. Bald eagles soar from
their forest perches to nab fish.

Continue south on US 101 and
turn left at the sign for the big
cedar tree, one of the world's largest. Standing at the end of a short
spur road, the tree looks like a thing
conjured up from the land of Oz.
Monstrous, its girth exceeds 66 feet.

The stretch of road from here to
the park's southwest border is dotted with overlooks and short access
trails to the beaches. If it's low
tide—and you missed the guided
tide-pool walk—try the trail at
Beach 4, just north of milepost 160.
A short, steep hike brings you to the
shoreline and the rocky tide pools.
Alternately battered by waves and
dried out by the sun, tide pools nevertheless teem with life. An area 1
foot square may support 4,000 individual creatures belonging to more
than 20 species. Look closely to spot
gooseneck and acorn barnacles, peri-
winkle snails, and rocks with holes
drilled by piddock clams. Brightly
colored sea stars, or starfish, prowl
the rocky pools, preying on the mus-
sels and other mollusks. Green sea
anemones stun their tiny prey with
stinging cells on their tentacles.
Purple sea urchins dine on bits of
kelp and other algae.

To view a third mood of Olympic
beach, park near **Beach 1,** a stroller's
delight, at milepost 155. Follow the
sign to the **Spruce Burl Trail** for a
brief detour before descending to the
sand. Near the ocean, Sitka spruce
commonly develop large, nobby
growths that may be triggered by

a virus, a bacterium, or some sub-
stance carried in the ocean spray.

For a remote and peaceful visit
to the rain forest, drive south to
Quinault (32 miles from Kalaloch)
and take the North Shore spur road.
Walk the half-mile **Maple Glades
Nature Trail** from near the **Quinault
Rain Forest Ranger Station** or the
2.2-mile round-trip **Irely Lake Trail,**
which begins a quarter mile before
the North Fork Campground.
Look for beaver dams, herons, and
ospreys, which often nest at the lake.

OZETTE
a full day

Remote Ozette, a town near the
northernmost realm of the park,
offers a good departure point for
supreme coastal hiking. To get
there, take US 101 to Sappho, then
head north to Wash. 112; follow this
into Sekiu. From here, head southwest to the town.

For a level 9.3-mile loop, take
the triangular route shaped by the
**Ozette Lake-Cape Alava-Sand Point
Trail.** The jaunt begins at the ranger
station on the north end of **Ozette
Lake** (*where you must register*), off
Hoko-Ozette Road. The 3-mile trail
goes southwest to Sand Point, tun-
neling through coastal forest, taking
you over marshes and bogs on
wooden walkways.

You emerge at the Pacific at
Sand Point. Here head north along
the rocky beach to **Capa Alava,** the
westernmost point of the contigu-
ous United States. Along the way,
you are treated to stunning seacoast
scenery, tide pools filled with sea
critters, and rock etchings left by
Indians who lived by whaling and
fishing. Watch for rhinoceros auk-
lets, tufted puffins, oyster catchers,
and perhaps even a black bear.

INFORMATION & ACTIVITIES

VISITOR & INFORMATION CENTERS
In Port Angeles, the **Olympic National Park Visitor Center,** 3002 Mt. Angeles Road; call (360) 565-3132.
The **Hoh Rain Forest Visitor Center** off US 101 at western edge of park, (360) 374-6925.
Hurricane Ridge Visitor Center open all year, weather permitting.
In summer, information stations open at **Storm King** on Lake Crescent, **Kalaloch,** and other locations.

SEASONS & ACCESSIBILITY
Park open year-round. Some roads closed in winter. For weather and road information, call (360) 565-3131. For park information, tune in to 530 AM in the Port Angeles and Lake Crescent areas.

HEADQUARTERS
600 E. Park Ave., Port Angeles, WA 98362. Phone (360) 565-3000. www.nps.gov/olym

ENTRANCE FEE
$15 per vehicle for 7-day pass, $30 for an annual pass.

ACCESSIBLE SERVICES
Visitor centers and some campsites are accessible to wheelchairs. Also accessible are Hurricane Ridge's paved trails; a short loop trail into the Hoh Rain Forest; the Madison Falls Trail in the Elwha Valley, and the Moments in Time Trail at Lake Crescent.

THINGS TO DO
Free naturalist-led activities: meadow, forest, beach, and tide-pool walks; campfire programs. Also available, hiking, boating, fishing (no license needed), climbing, swimming, wind-surfing, waterskiing, river rafting, cross-country and alpine skiing, snowshoeing.

SPECIAL ADVISORIES
• Be careful when hiking along the coast; rocks and logs can be slippery and unstable.
• Be aware of incoming tides (current tables posted at trailheads).
• Surf logs can roll and kill.

OVERNIGHT BACKPACKING
Call ahead for reservations. Permits required; obtain at Wilderness Information Center (at the Olympic National Park Visitor Center, 360-565-3131), visitor centers, ranger stations, or trailheads.

CAMPGROUNDS
Fifteen campgrounds, all with a 14-day limit. **Deer Park, North Fork,** and **Queets** campgrounds do not allow RVs. All first come, first served except for **Kalaloch,** which accepts reservations in summer—contact NRRS (see p. 10). Fees: $10-$18. No showers. Three group campgrounds; reservations required; contact headquarters. Food services in park.

HOTELS, MOTELS, & INNS
(unless otherwise noted, rates are for 2 persons in a double room, high season)

INSIDE THE PARK:
Kalaloch Lodge (on US 101, 36 miles south of Forks) 157151 Hwy. 101, Forks, WA 98331. (360) 962-2271 or (866) 525-2562. 20 rooms; 44 cabins, 38 with kitchenettes. $107-$245. Restaurant.
Lake Crescent Lodge (on US 101) 416 Lake Crescent Rd., Port Angeles, WA 98363. (360) 928-3211 or (888) 723-7127. 45 units, 40 with private bath. $68-$231. Restaurant. Mid-May–mid-Oct.
Log Cabin Resort (on Lake Crescent) 3183 E. Beach Rd., Port Angeles, WA 98363. (360) 928-3325. 28 units, 3 with kitchenettes; $55-$165. 3 tent sites, $25; 35 RV hookups, $40. Restaurant. May through Sept.
Sol Duc Hot Springs Resort (12 miles off US 101) 12076 Sol Duc Hot Springs Rd., Port Angeles, WA 98363. (360) 327-3583 or (866) 476-5382. 33 cabins, 11 kitchens. $141-$172. Pool, restaurant. Late March–mid-Oct.

For other lodgings, contact Port Angeles Regional Chamber of Commerce, 121 E. Railroad, Port Angeles, WA 98362. (360) 452-2363, www.portangeles.org.

OLYMPIC

Coast redwoods, a grove of giants

▶ REDWOOD

CALIFORNIA
ESTABLISHED OCTOBER 2, 1968
131,983 acres, including 3 state parks

Sometimes, when the morning fog caresses the great trees, you can imagine the past flowing through the long, misty shadows . . . Vast redwood forests flourishing across a lush and humid North America . . . After the final ice age, a last stand here in the sustaining climate along the Pacific coast . . . Tree after tree falling to the loggers. Then, in a windswept moment, the past vanishes and you stand beside other visitors, gazing up at the Earth's tallest living things. That is the essence of Redwood National and State Parks.

The park, near the northern limit of the coast redwoods' narrow range, preserves the remnants of a forest that once covered two million acres and, at the turn of the 20th century, was badly threatened by logging. The state of California and the Save the Redwoods League came to the rescue by acquiring hundreds of groves and protecting them within 26 state parks. Three redwood state parks—**Jedediah**

Smith, Del Norte Coast, and **Prairie Creek**—were encompassed by the national park when it was created in 1968.

Logging on surrounding private land, however, threatened the parks' protected redwoods. Soil and sediments from the logged-over tracts washed into the rivers and creeks, settling to the bottom downstream. Silt deposits can smother redwoods —for the giants are amazingly vulnerable. And the waterlogged soil weakens the trees' resistance to wind. Their roots are shallow, often under 10 feet deep.

In 1978 Congress added 48,000 acres to the national park's 58,000 acres, including about 33,000 that had been logged. The raw, clear-cut land, a park official wrote, had "the look of an active war zone." Today, in an epic earthmoving project—a redwood renaissance—crews are reclaiming vast stretches of logged-over lands. Hillsides, carved away for logging roads, are being restored. Most of the 400 miles of roads have been erased. It will take at least 50 years for the scars of logging to disappear and another 250 or so years for the resprouted redwood seedlings to grow to modest size.

The renaissance has added a new dimension to the traditional rite of staring up at redwoods. Today's visitor can look at hillsides shorn of giants and know that generations from now the young trees growing there will be giants once again.

How to Get There

Tree-lined US 101, the Redwood Highway, runs the length of the park. From the south, take US 101 to the Thomas H. Kuchel Visitor Center near Orick, about 40 miles north of Eureka. From the north, enter through Crescent City, also an information center site. From the east, take US 199, another redwood-flanked highway, to Hiouchi. Airports: Arcata and Crescent City.

When to Go

Year-round. Summer draws highway-clogging crowds, so think about a visit in spring or fall. In both seasons, bird migrations enhance the redwood groves. Rhododendrons burst forth in late spring; deciduous trees add color in fall. Rains, welcome to the redwoods but not to visitors, drench the park in winter.

How to Visit

US 101, with its many redwood sentinels, gives you a windshield-framed panorama of the trees. But to appreciate the redwoods, you must walk among them. If you have only a day to visit this 50-mile-long park, stop and see the **Lady Bird Johnson Grove** and **Big Tree.** Hike or just stretch your legs (depending on your time) along the **Coastal Trail** and savor the Pacific prospect of the park. For a longer stay, visit the **Tall Trees Grove,** drive **Howland Hill Road,** and end your visit with a splash in **Smith River** or a jouncy drive to **Fern Canyon** and **Gold Bluffs Beach.** If you are driving an RV or towing a trailer, some stretches of road may be closed to you; check at information centers.

LADY BIRD JOHNSON GROVE & BIG TREE

13 miles; 2 hours

Just before Orick, stop at the **Kuchel Visitor Center** (once the site of a redwood lumber mill) to see the exhibits, and then continue north on US 101 to the Bald Hills Road sign. Turn right and drive 2 miles to **Lady Bird Johnson Grove,** a jewel that gives you an understanding of the entire park treasure. On the grove's 1.5-mile round-trip trail you feel the cool, moist air that redwoods need. You see a hollowed-out tree that still lives. Such redwoods—"goose-pen" trees—once sheltered settlers' fowl and livestock. You smell and touch the many plants that share the redwoods' domain. Most of all, you feel the peace; visitors speak quietly in this pillared place.

Return to US 101 and continue north about 4 miles. Exit US 101

REDWOOD

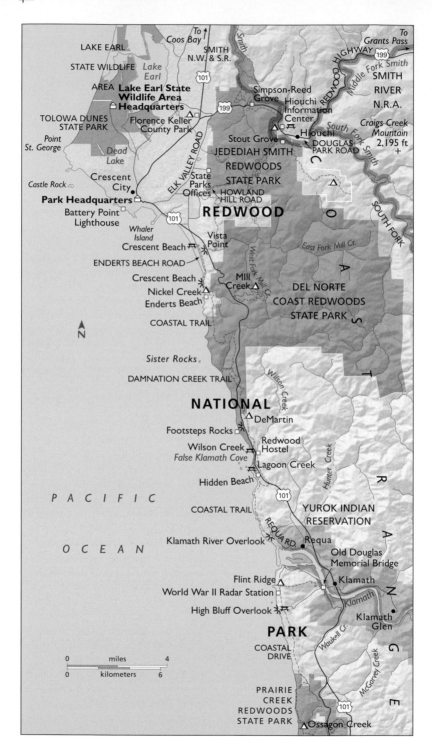

To Coos Bay

To Grants Pass

LAKE EARL

STATE WILDLIFE

Lake Earl

SMITH
N.W. & S.R.

Smith

REDWOOD HIGHWAY

199

Middle Fork Smith

SMITH
RIVER
N.R.A.

AREA **Lake Earl State**
Wildlife Area
Headquarters

TOLOWA DUNES
STATE PARK

101

199

Simpson-Reed
Grove

Hiouchi
Information
Center

Hiouchi

South Fork Smith

Craigs Creek
Mountain
2,195 ft

Point
St. George

Florence Keller
County Park

Stout Grove

JEDEDIAH SMITH

DOUGLAS
PARK ROAD

Dead
Lake

REDWOODS
STATE PARK

Castle Rock

Crescent
City

State
Parks
Offices

HOWLAND
HILL ROAD

Park Headquarters

REDWOOD

SOUTH FORK

ELK VALLEY ROAD

Battery Point
Lighthouse

101

Whaler
Island

Vista
Point

West Fork Mill Cr.

East Fork Mill Cr.

Crescent Beach

ENDERTS BEACH ROAD

Crescent Beach

Mill
Creek

DEL NORTE

Nickel Creek
Enderts Beach

COAST REDWOODS

COASTAL TRAIL

STATE PARK

N

Sister Rocks

DAMNATION CREEK TRAIL

Wilson Creek

NATIONAL

DeMartin

Footsteps Rocks

Redwood
Hostel

Wilson Creek

Hunter Creek

False Klamath Cove

Lagoon Creek

Hidden Beach

101

COASTAL TRAIL

YUROK INDIAN
RESERVATION

P A C I F I C

REQUA RD.

Klamath River Overlook

Requa

Old Douglas
Memorial Bridge

O C E A N

Flint Ridge

Klamath

World War II Radar Station

Klamath

High Bluff Overlook

R A N G E

Klamath
Glen

PARK

COASTAL
DRIVE

Waukell Cr.

McGarvey Creek

miles   4

kilometers   6

PRAIRIE
CREEK
REDWOODS
STATE PARK

Ossagon Creek

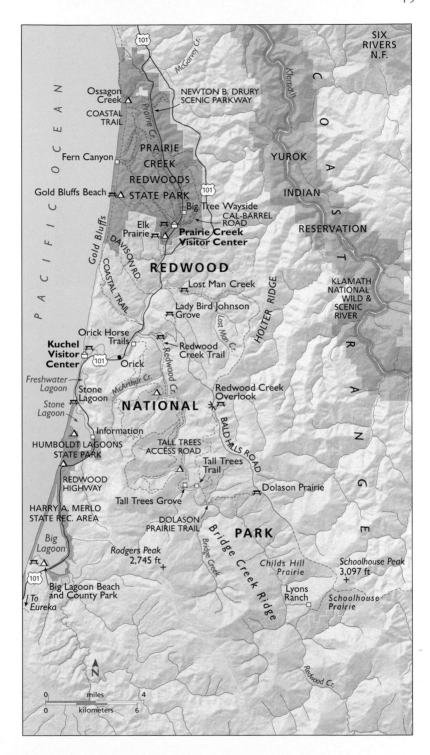

SIX RIVERS N.F.

McGarvey Cr.

101

Klamath

OSSAGON Creek △

COASTAL TRAIL

NEWTON B. DRURY SCENIC PARKWAY

Prairie Cr.

YUROK

Fern Canyon □

PRAIRIE CREEK REDWOODS STATE PARK

INDIAN

Gold Bluffs Beach ⊨△

101

Big Tree Wayside
CAL-BARREL ROAD

Elk Prairie ⊨△

Prairie Creek Visitor Center

RESERVATION

Gold Bluffs

DAVISON RD.

REDWOOD

Lost Man Creek ⊨

HOLTER RIDGE

KLAMATH NATIONAL WILD & SCENIC RIVER

COASTAL TRAIL

Lady Bird Johnson Grove ⊨

Lost Man Cr.

Orick Horse Trails □

Kuchel Visitor Center ⊨

Redwood Creek Trail

Redwood Cr.

C O A S T

101

● Orick

McArthur Cr.

Redwood Creek Overlook

Freshwater Lagoon

Stone Lagoon △

NATIONAL

BALD HILLS ROAD

R A N G E

Stone Lagoon ⊨

△ Information

TALL TREES ACCESS ROAD

Tall Trees Trail

HUMBOLDT LAGOONS STATE PARK △

△

Tall Trees Grove

Dolason Prairie ⊨

REDWOOD HIGHWAY

HARRY A. MERLO STATE REC. AREA

DOLASON PRAIRIE TRAIL

PARK

Big Lagoon

⊨△

Rodgers Peak 2,745 ft +

Bridge Creek

Bridge Creek Ridge

Childs Hill Prairie

Schoolhouse Peak 3,097 ft +

101

Big Lagoon Beach and County Park

Lyons Ranch □

Schoolhouse Prairie

↓ To Eureka

Redwood Cr.

N

PACIFIC OCEAN

0 — miles — 4
0 — kilometers — 6

REDWOOD

The Pacific shoreline

for the Newton B. Drury Scenic Parkway. Near the entrance to **Prairie Creek Redwoods State Park,** pull into the turnout to watch the free-roaming Roosevelt elk that live in the park. A mile ahead on the right is a wayside sign for **Big Tree.** A short trail from the parking lot leads to the aptly named tree. It's 304 feet tall, 23.7 feet in diameter, 66 feet in circumference, and at least about 1,500 years old. Here the experience is singular: you and one great tree.

COASTAL TRAIL
4 miles one way; at least 2 hours

From Orick, drive north 20 miles on US 101, passing Klamath, and turn left onto Requa Road. Park and picnic at **Klamath River Overlook,** a high hill. On a clear day you can see 65 miles down the bluff-guarded coast. **The Klamath Section** of the Coastal Trail begins here, heads west, and then veers north along the wild, driftwood-decorated shore. Yurok Indians walk these shores,

as did Jedediah Smith, the first white man to reach California's northern coast by land.

The trail, often bowered by branches of spruce and alder, sometimes seals you from the sight—though not the sounds—of the ocean. But there are many spots where you can sit and gaze out to sea. In spring and fall you may see migrating gray whales. Almost any time you will see gulls, cormorants, and ospreys.

A short side path leads down to **Hidden Beach.** Even on a day when the park is crowded yours may be the only footprints on the sand. Look at the ocean but don't swim: The undertow is dangerous all along the park's coast. The beach walk ends at a wall of gnarled black rocks. Follow your footprints back to the path and return to the trail, which heads north along the wild shore, then veers inland.

The north trailhead is at **Lagoon Creek,** where fresh water and forest meet ocean and high bluff. If you don't want to trudge the 4 miles back, have someone drive up to meet you at the parking lot.

TALL TREES GROVE

3.7 miles; a half day

Obtain a permit to drive your vehicle to the Tall Trees Grove parking area, off Bald Hills Road. (Permits can be obtained at the Crescent City, Prairie Creek, and Kuchel Visitor Centers.) From the parking area, the trail is a very steep 3.7-miles round-trip. The hike down to the grove, replete with ferns and rhododendrons, takes at least 30 minutes. Plan on another 30 to 45 minutes in the grove among the giant coast redwoods. The star is the **Tall Tree,** which measures over 362 feet. These are some of the world's tallest known trees. They are estimated to be between 600 and 1,500 years old.

HOWLAND HILL ROAD

8 miles; about 2 hours

Just south of Crescent City, take Elk Valley Road northeast. Keep a sharp watch on your right for the turnoff to Howland Hill Road, once a miners' supply road partially redwood-planked for oxcarts and horse-drawn wagons. The 6-mile road winds between redwoods that loom much closer than the ones along the highways. Mostly unpaved and often one lane, motor homes and trailers are not recommended. Stop at **Stout Grove,** where you can see one of many groves set aside, this one donated by the wife of a logging company owner. Take time to enjoy the 5-mile trail among the redwoods. (In summer you can also reach the grove from the **Hiouchi Information Center** via a footbridge across the crystal-clear **Smith River.)**

Continue past the grove to Douglas Park Road, which ends at South Fork Road. Turn left to US 199 and drive west about 2.5 miles to the Hiouchi Information Center. Park here and sign up for an interpretive walk with a ranger. Or, continue west on US 199 to **Walker Road,** where you'll find several short pleasant self-guided trails.

GOLD BLUFFS BEACH & FERN CANYON

20 miles; a half day

From the Kuchel Visitor Center, head north for 4.5 miles to Davison Road, on your left. Elk are often spotted along the first few hundred yards on this road. Its rough dirt surface bounces you for about 4 miles down to **Gold Bluffs,** named for the gold found here. The road continues for 4 miles along the beach, ending near **Fern Canyon,** where a 0.75-mile loop trail climbs to a prairie—site of a vanished mining camp. Back down the canyon, walk through elk-roamed grass to a beautiful, desolate beach sprinkled with driftwood and often shrouded in fog.

Return the way you came, pausing to admire the fern-covered, 50-foot-high walls. The more adventurous can make a longer 7.6-mile hike by climbing the **Friendship Ridge Trail** and connecting with **West Ridge Trail** to Butler Creek before heading back toward the ocean. Return to the parking area at Fern Canyon via the windswept southern stretch of the **Coastal Trail.** Be on the lookout for a variety of birds, including pelicans, terns, gulls, and wading birds. In the fall or spring scan the horizon for the telltale spouts of migrating gray whales, en route to or from their winter retreat in Baja California.

REDWOOD

INFORMATION & ACTIVITIES

VISITOR & INFORMATION CENTERS

Crescent City Park Headquarters Newton B. Drury Visitor Center, at north end of park, open daily all year.
Kuchel Visitor Center, at south end of park near Orick, also open all year.
Hiouchi Information Center, at north end of park, open spring through summer.

SEASONS & ACCESSIBILITY
Open year-round.

HEADQUARTERS
1111 2nd St., Crescent City, CA 95531. Phone (707) 464-7335. www.nps .gov/redw

ENTRANCE FEE
No admission fee. $8 day-use fee for Jedediah Smith, Del Norte Coast, and Prairie Creek State Parks.

PETS
Permitted on leashes except on trails and in backcountry.

ACCESSIBLE SERVICES
Visitor centers, Crescent Beach, Lagoon Creek picnic area, Klamath Overlook, and some trails are accessible to wheelchairs.

THINGS TO DO
Free naturalist-led activities: tide-pool and seashore walks, evening programs. Also hiking, canoeing, guided kayak trips, horseback riding, freshwater and ocean fishing (need license), swimming (inland only), whale-watching.

SPECIAL ADVISORIES
• Be aware that ticks may transmit Lyme disease.
• Ocean swimming is not advised due to extremely cold water and treacherous undertow.

OVERNIGHT BACKPACKING
Permit required; can be obtained free at the national park information centers and state park visitor centers. The national park lands offer three backcountry campsites—**DeMartin, Flint Ridge,** and **Nickel Creek;** 14-day limit. Open all year, first come, first served. No fees. Tent sites only. No showers.
Ossagon Creek campsite in Prairie Creek State Park is available to bikers and hikers only ($5 per night). Reserve at Prairie Creek Visitor Center.

CAMPGROUNDS
There are four state-run campgrounds inside the park—**Gold Bluffs Beach, Jedediah Smith, Mill Creek,** and **Elk Prairie;** 15-day limit. Mill Creek open April to October; others open all year; Gold Bluffs Beach may close in bad weather. Showers available nearby. Tent and RV sites; no hookups; large RVs not recommended and trailers prohibited at Gold Bluffs Beach. Fees $35 per night. Reservations recommended from mid-May through August and available at www.reserveamerica.com. (Gold Bluffs Beach available on a first-come, first-served basis only.) The reservations number for these state-run campgrounds is (800) 444-7275. No food services inside park.

HOTELS, MOTELS, & INNS
(unless otherwise noted, rates are for 2 persons in a double room, high season)

In Crescent City, CA 95531:
Best Value Inn 440 Hwy. 101N. (707) 464-4141. 61 units. $98.
Curly Redwood Lodge 701 Hwy. 101S. (707) 464-2137. 36 units. $69-$77.
Econo Lodge Crescent City 725 Hwy. 101N. (707) 464-6106. 52 units. $69-$80.
Front Street Inn 102 L St. (707) 464-4113. 30 units. $60-$80.

In Eureka, CA 95501:
Carter House Inns 301 L St. (800) 404-1390 or (707) 444-8062. 31 units. $155-$595, incl. breakfast. Restaurant.

In Klamath, CA 95548:
Historic Requa Inn 451 Requa Rd. (866) 800-8777 or (707) 482-1425. 10 units. $99-$169, incl. breakfast (evening meal available).
Motel Trees 15495 Hwy. 101. (800) 848-2982 or (707) 482-3152. 23 units. $61. Restaurant.

EXCURSIONS

HUMBOLDT BAY
NATIONAL WILDLIFE REFUGE
LOLETA, CALIFORNIA

The islands and wetlands of Humboldt Bay provide critical habitat for the brant, a small, stocky sea goose. From late winter to early spring, thousands of brants use the refuge as a staging area en route to northern nesting grounds. Other waterfowl and peregrine falcons are also present. 3,500 acres. Excellent bird-watching from the Hookton Slough Trail and Salmon Creek. Off US 101, about 40 miles south of Redwood NP. (707) 733-5406.

SIX RIVERS NATIONAL FOREST
EUREKA, CALIFORNIA

Six major rivers cross this mountain forest of pine, fir, spruce, and cedar, providing nearly 10 percent of the state's runoff. Recreational opportunities include white-water rafting, kayaking, and excellent steelhead and salmon fishing. Contains parts of four wilderness areas. 957,590 acres. Hiking, boating, fishing, horseback riding, hunting, scenic drives, winter sports, water sports. 355 campsites, boat ramp, picnic areas, handicapped access. Open all year, though most off-highway routes close in winter. Most campsites open May through November, weather permitting. Composed of four ranger districts. For information contact the superintendent's office in Eureka on US 101, about 30 miles from Redwood NP. (707) 442-1721.

REDWOOD

ALASKA

ALASKA

In 1867 Secretary of State William Seward bought Alaska from Russia for two cents an acre—and the public labeled the vast empty land Seward's Folly. Today, more than 14 billion barrels of oil have gushed through the Prudhoe Bay pipeline, and Alaska's wilderness and wildlife attract visitors by the thousands.

Eight national parks protect 42.1 million acres of these natural treasures. Katmai and Lake Clark lie along the Pacific Ring of Fire—a region of active volcanoes, earthquakes, giant brown bears, and salmon. Whales, sea lions, and flocks of seabirds seek out the cold, food-laden waters of Glacier Bay and Kenai Fjords. Wrangell-St. Elias is a jumble of mountains and glaciers so rugged that many remain unnamed and untrodden by humans. Above the Arctic Circle, Gates of the Arctic and Kobuk Valley protect the tundra and migrant herds of caribou. By comparison, Denali seems civilized with its nearby railroad and hotels; yet here the wildlife is so abundant and visible, the park is called a "subarctic Serengeti."

Alaska parks include national preserves that allow hunting, vast wilderness areas that prohibit buildings and roads, and native-owned lands still used for subsistence in a tradition thousands of years old.

In 1989 the *Exxon Valdez* ran aground in Prince William Sound, spilling nearly 11 million gallons of oil, the largest such spill in U.S. history. The slick spread into the Gulf of Alaska and onto the beaches of Katmai and Kenai Fjords. It killed more than 3,500 sea otters and 350,000 seabirds, as well as unknown numbers of scavenging mammals. Although the long-term consequences for the habitat are still unknown, years of winter storms and massive environmental cleanup efforts have made the effects of the oil spill invisible to the naked eye.

Most of Alaska's national parks are accessible only by plane or boat, but you can drive to Denali and Wrangell-St. Elias and to the edges of Kenai Fjords and Gates of the Arctic. The loop connecting Anchorage to Denali to Fairbanks to Wrangell-St. Elias, with a side trip to Kenai Fjords, is 1,100 miles. It's a 600-mile round-trip from Fairbanks to Gates of the Arctic on the unpaved Dalton Highway. Alaska parks are rugged, yet fragile; tread lightly.

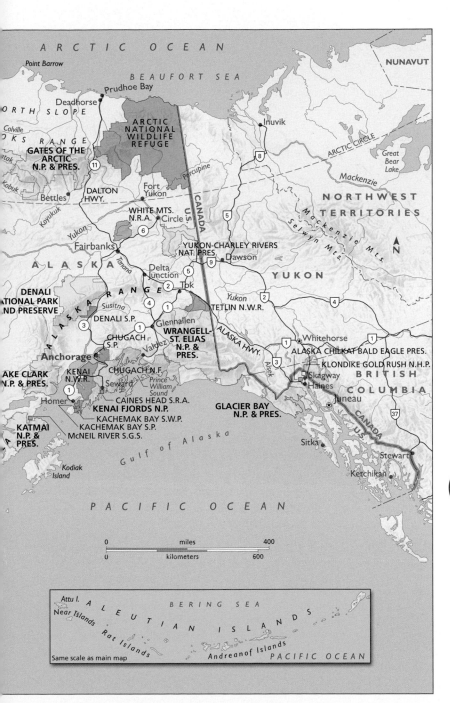

ARCTIC   OCEAN

Point Barrow

BEAUFORT   SEA

NUNAVUT

Prudhoe Bay

Deadhorse

ARCTIC NATIONAL WILDLIFE REFUGE

Inuvik

ARCTIC CIRCLE

Great Bear Lake

ORTH SLOPE

Colville

OKS RANGE

GATES OF THE ARCTIC N.P. & PRES.

⑪

DALTON HWY.

Bettles

Koyukuk

Kobuk

tok

Yukon

Fort Yukon

Percupine

CANADA

Mackenzie

NORTHWEST TERRITORIES

Selwyn Mts.

Mackenzie Mts.

WHITE MTS. N.R.A.

Circle

⑥

Fairbanks

Tanana

ALASKA

DENALI NATIONAL PARK ND PRESERVE

ALASKA   RANGE

Susitna

DENALI S.P.

③

④

Delta Junction

YUKON-CHARLEY RIVERS NAT. PRES.

⑤

⑨

②

Tok

⑤

Dawson

YUKON

Yukon

②

④

①

CHUGACH S.P.

①

Glennallen

WRANGELL-ST. ELIAS N.P. & PRES.

TETLIN N.W.R.

Valdez

ALASKA HWY.

Alsek

Whitehorse

①

①

ALASKA CHILKAT BALD EAGLE PRES.

KLONDIKE GOLD RUSH N.H.P.

Anchorage

CHUGACH N.F.

Prince William Sound

Seward

③

Skagway

Haines

BRITISH

AKE CLARK N.P. & PRES.

KENAI N.W.R.

①

CAINES HEAD S.R.A.

Juneau

COLUMBIA

Homer

KENAI FJORDS N.P.

KACHEMAK BAY S.W.P.

KACHEMAK BAY S.P.

McNEIL RIVER S.G.S.

GLACIER BAY N.P. & PRES.

CANADA

U.S.

㉟

KATMAI N.P. & PRES.

Kodiak Island

Gulf   of   Alaska

Sitka

Stewart

Ketchikan

PACIFIC   OCEAN

0   miles   400

0   kilometers   600

ALASKA

Attu I.

Near Islands

ALEUTIAN

Rat Islands

BERING   SEA

ISLANDS

Andreanof Islands

PACIFIC OCEAN

Same scale as main map

N

Sable Pass in the summer

▶ DENALI

ALASKA
ESTABLISHED FEBRUARY 26, 1917
6,075,029 acres

On any summer day in Denali, Alaska's most well-known national park, hundreds of people see sights that will stay with them the rest of their lives. Perhaps a golden eagle will soar off the cliffs at Polychrome Pass, or 20 Dall sheep will rest on a green shoulder of Primrose Ridge, or a grizzly will ramble over the tundra at Sable Pass. Maybe a caribou will pause on a ridgetop, silhouetted by the warm light of day's end, or a loon will call across Wonder Lake, or clouds will part to reveal the great massif of Mount McKinley, 20,320 feet high, the roof of North America.

The drama is always there. To see it, all you need to do is travel the 92-mile park road. The farther you go, the more you'll see, for the sub-arctic landscape will open up as big as the sky and the animals will move through it with wild, ancient poetry.

Other North American parks have their wildlife, but none has animals so visible or diverse as Denali. And other parks have their mountains,

but none with a stature so stunning, a summit so towering as McKinley.

Denali's visitors have increased almost 200 percent in 30 years. Accommodating them without eroding the park's wilderness has been a struggle. A bus system that permits maximum wildlife viewing while holding down traffic has been designed. Campgrounds are modest and unobtrusive. And the

wilderness areas have strict overnight camping ceilings to prevent
overcrowding and damage to
the flora and fauna. Unless you
plan ahead by using the park's
easy-to-use reservation system,
you may have to wait a day or two
to get your preferred campsite or
bus reservation.

How to Get There
From Anchorage, take Alas. 1
(Glenn Hwy.) 35 miles north to
Alas. 3 (George Parks Hwy.). Go
north 205 miles. From Fairbanks,
take Alas. 3 west and south 120
miles. In summer, the Alaska Rail-
road runs between Anchorage and
Fairbanks and stops daily at the
Denali railroad station. In winter,
the train runs on weekends only.
Air service available in summer to
nearby airstrips from Anchorage,
Fairbanks, and Talkeetna.

When to Go
In summer, there are up to 21 hours
of daylight. Buses carry visitors into
the park late May to mid-September.
June is usually less crowded than
July and August. In late August or
early September, the tundra turns
rich tones of red, orange, and yellow. In winter, visitors can take the
road 3 miles to park headquarters
and cross-country ski, snowshoe, or
dogsled from there.
 May and early June are the best
times to climb Mount McKinley;
after June, avalanches and crevasses
threaten. Most mountaineers fly
from Talkeetna and land at 7,200
feet on the Kahiltna Glacier to begin
a climb that will take 15 to 30 days.

How to Visit
The more time the better, but plan
on at least 2 days. The park is under-
going significant changes to handle
the increased visitors; check ahead
for road and trail changes.

Any private vehicle can travel the
park road for 15 miles to **Savage River
Check Station;** after that only those
with camping permits for Teklanika
River Campground may continue.
For everyone else, shuttle buses and
tour buses operate on the road by
day and into evening, late May to
mid-September; schedules vary.
 The 85-mile shuttle bus trip along
the park road to **Wonder Lake** takes
11 hours round-trip but stops at des-
tinations along the way. Visitors can
take other buses as far as Kantishna,
the end of the road, a 13-hour round-
trip. Take a jacket, binoculars, and
lunch (available near the **Denali
Visitor Center** or outside the park; no
food along the way). In the park, consider getting off the bus for a hike;
buses will stop almost anywhere. To
get on another bus, just wave one
down. In busy times, you may have
to wait a while for one with space.
 Park campgrounds and buses fill
quickly, so plan for the possibility
of staying a night or two in a hotel
or private campground if you must
wait for a campsite or bus ticket.
 Mount McKinley is often covered
with clouds; you may be more likely
to get a clear view of it early or late
in the long day.

PARK ROAD BY BUS
92 miles one way; 13 hours round-trip

Although the complete trip takes a
full day, shorter bus rides into the
park can provide an equally enjoyable visit. Your bus journey begins
at the **Wilderness Access Center** (mile
0.6), surrounded by the spruce
forest and taiga.
 Within minutes you'll see the
railroad station used by the Alaska
Railroad, and the new **Denali Visitor
Center** campus. After a mile you'll
pass park headquarters, where sled

DENALI

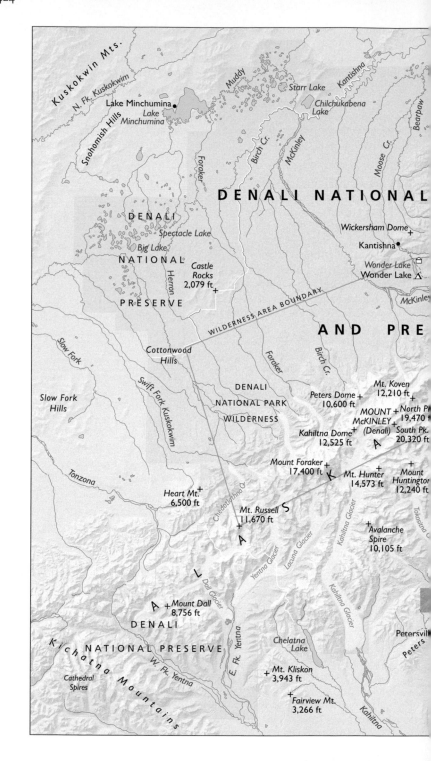

Kuskokwin Mts.

N. Fk. Kuskokwim

Lake Minchumina
Lake
Minchumina

Snohomish Hills

Muddy

Birch Cr.

Starr Lake

McKinley

Chilchukabena
Lake

Kantishna

Moose Cr.

Bearpaw

DENALI NATIONAL

DENALI

Spectacle Lake

Big Lake

Castle
Rocks
2,079 ft

Wickersham Dome
Kantishna

Wonder Lake
Wonder Lake

McKinley

NATIONAL

Herron

PRESERVE

WILDERNESS AREA BOUNDARY

AND PRE

Foraker

Slow Fork

Cottonwood
Hills

Foraker

Birch Cr.

Slow Fork
Hills

Swift Fork Kuskokwim

DENALI

NATIONAL PARK

WILDERNESS

Peters Dome +
10,600 ft

Mt. Koven
12,210 ft

MOUNT + North Pk.
McKINLEY 19,470
(Denali) South Pk.
20,320 ft

Kahiltna Dome
12,525 ft

Tonzona

Mount Foraker +
17,400 ft

Mt. Hunter +
14,573 ft

Mount
Huntington
12,240 ft

Heart Mt. +
6,500 ft

Chedotlothna G.

Mt. Russell
11,670 ft

Avalanche
Spire
10,105 ft

Yentna Glacier

Lacuna Glacier

Kahiltna Glacier

Kahiltna Glacier

Tokositna

Dall Glacier

Mount Dall
8,756 ft

DENALI

Kichatna Mountains

NATIONAL PRESERVE

Cathedral
Spires

W. Fk. Yentna

E. Fk. Yentna

Chelatna
Lake

Mt. Kliskon
3,943 ft

Fairview Mt.
3,266 ft

Petersvil

Peters

Kahiltna

Mount McKinley out of the clouds

dogs are kept for winter patrols and summer demonstrations.

Soon the road begins climbing out of the taiga and into the treeless expanse of the tundra. Magnificent vistas open up; on clear days **Mount McKinley** can be seen 70 miles to the southwest. As the bus crosses the **Savage River Bridge** (mile 14.8), note how the gentle, glacier-sculptured topography to the south meets the rugged river-cut canyon to the north; this spot marks the farthest advance of a glacier that flowed north out of the **Alaska Range** and across the valley thousands of years ago.

The road winds below **Primrose Ridge** before dropping into a marshy flat where spruce trees lean haphazardly. This "drunken forest" forms as permafrost thaws and the land slumps gradually downhill, tilting the trees. Watch for moose here and in other spruce forests, especially in areas with willow.

Just beyond Teklanika River Campground (mile 29) is the **Teklanika River Bridge.** Like other rivers in Denali, the Teklanika is braided by channels. Its Athabaskan name means "middle water." The road passes Igloo Creek Campground and cuts between **Igloo** and **Cathedral Mountains,** favorite haunts of Dall sheep, the world's only species of wild white sheep. Watch for them on the upper slopes.

If you want to see grizzly bears, a good place is up the road at **Sable Pass** (3,895 feet). Grizzlies feed primarily on roots, berries, and other plant materials, and occasionally on arctic ground squirrels, moose calves, injured caribou, and carrion. To protect the bears' habitat, this area is closed to off-road foot traffic.

About 5 miles farther, the road climbs a steep slope to **Polychrome Pass** and a spectacular view of the Alaska Range to the south. Below see the **Plains of Murie,** where fast running water has created alluvial terraces. At mile 53.1 the **Toklat River** has special significance, for it was here (5 miles north of where the bridge crosses the river today) that naturalist Charles Sheldon built a cabin and wintered in 1907–08. The area so inspired him that he moved back East and spent 9 years lobbying for legislation to create Alaska's first national park. Originally called Mount McKinley, the park in 1980 was renamed Denali—an Athabaskan name for the mountain meaning "the great one."

The road reaches its highest elevation at **Highway Pass** (3,980 feet) before descending to cross **Stony Creek** and climbing again to the **Stony Hill Overlook,** where, weather permitting, Mount McKinley looms into view 40 miles away. Watch for caribou as they funnel through the Stony Hill area. Although the total Denali herd numbers about 2,000, caribou usually move in small groups. They can appear almost any time of day anywhere in the lowlands between the park road and the Alaska Range.

The newly redesigned **Eielson Visitor Center** (mile 66) is a surprise, blending perfectly into its hillside surroundings while providing commanding views of Mount McKinley and the Alaska Range.

Continuing west beyond the center, the road cuts along a steep cliff, then enters gentler terrain as it comes within a mile of the dark, gravel-covered snout of the **Muldrow Glacier** to the south. Beginning just below the summit of Mount McKinley, the Muldrow flows 35 miles through a granite gorge and across the tundra to its terminus. Twice in the last hundred years (and for reasons not fully understood) the Muldrow has surged forward, most recently in the winter of 1956–57, when it advanced 5 miles.

The road passes several ponds where chances improve for sighting beaver, moose, and waterfowl and finally arrives at Wonder Lake Campground. Here the shuttle bus will either turn around for the 5.5-hour trip back or continue on to **Kantishna.**

Twenty-seven miles to the south looms Mount McKinley, its north face—the **Wickersham Wall**—rising more than 14,000 feet in a single precipice, one of the greatest mountain walls in the world. And just north of the campground lies **Wonder Lake,** 2.6 miles long, 280 feet deep, and home to lake trout, burbot, and moose that occasionally wade in belly deep to feed on aquatic vegetation near the shore. Loons, grebes, and mergansers also visit.

HIKES

In a park larger than New Hampshire, the hiking opportunities are endless. Most of the maintained trails are near the Denali Visitor Center. Maps are available at the nearby Denali bookstore or other locations near the park entrance.

The **Horseshoe Lake Trail** winds gently through a handsome forest of aspen and spruce 1.25 miles to **Horseshoe Lake,** an old oxbow of the **Nenana River.** It takes about 1.5 hours round-trip. Branching off this trail is a more strenuous one, the **Mount Healy Overlook Trail.** Climbing 1,700 feet in less than 3 miles (one way), it breaks above timberline and arrives at the overlook among wildflowers, rock outcrops, arctic ground squirrels, and pikas. And, if the weather is clear, Mount McKinley is visible more than 80 miles to the southwest. A new accessible quarter-mile trail begins at the Savage Cabin

DENALI

Arctic ground squirrel surveying the action *(top left)*; red fox *(top right)*; Dall sheep rams on a ridge, the Alaska Range stretching away beyond them *(bottom)*

Campground and leads to **Savage Cabin,** where summer living history demonstrations are held.

For those seeking a moderate hike, the 3-mile **Triple Lakes Trail** is a good choice with its excellent views of **Mount Fellows, Pyramid Mountain,** and other peaks in the Alaska Range at its beginning.

In the backcountry, hiking is a matter of taking whatever route you wish—down a drainage, up a ridge, across a valley. The object is to spread out and tread lightly, and leave no evidence of your visit.

Popular backcountry hiking areas (without trails) include Primrose Ridge, Mount Wright, Igloo Mountain, Cathedral Mountain, Calico Creek, Tattler Creek, Polychrome Cliffs, Stony Dome and Stony Hill, Stony Creek, Sunrise Glacier, Sunset Glacier, Thoroughfare Ridge, and around Wonder Lake. Some of these hikes take an hour or more, some take several days.

Since a backcountry management unit might be closed or full, those wishing to camp are required to check at the Backcountry Information Center before choosing an overnight hike. Some areas may be restricted in order to protect critical wildlife habitats, and animal activity may temporarily close backcountry sections.

INFORMATION & ACTIVITIES

VISITOR & INFORMATION CENTERS

Denali Visitor Center (mile 1.6) open mid-May to mid-Sept.
Murie Science and Learning Center (mile 1.7) serves as winter visitor center.
Talkeetna Ranger Station open daily mid-April to Labor Day; weekdays rest of year.

SEASONS & ACCESSIBILITY

Park open all year. Park road open, weather permitting, late-May to mid-Sept. to buses. Car travel to Savage River, 15 miles into the park, permitted. Those with camping reservations are permitted to drive to the Teklanika River Campground (mile 29). If the road is passable, private vehicles are allowed to drive the first 30 miles when the buses are not running. During snow season, park road is not plowed beyond headquarters (mile 3.1), which limits access to skiers, snowshoers, and dogsledders.

HEADQUARTERS

P.O. Box 9, Denali, AK 99755. Phone (907) 683-2294. www.nps.gov/dena

ENTRANCE FEE

$10 fee per person per week; $20 per vehicle; $40 annual.

SHUTTLE BUSES

From the Wilderness Access Center, buses depart regularly from 5 a.m. to 3 p.m., late May–mid-Sept. Reserve in advance. Fees range from $23 to $44 for adults, depending on destination. For reservations, call (800) 622-7275 or (907) 272-7275. Trips not narrated, but buses stop for wildlife-watching. Daily campers' buses. Also, Tundra Wilderness tour ($107), Natural History tour ($64), and Kantishna Experience tour ($159). (800) 622-7275 or (907) 272-7275 for required reservations; www.reservedenali.com.

ACCESSIBLE SERVICES

Most buildings accessible to wheelchairs, as are some tour and shuttle buses. Please advise staff of need when making reservations.

THINGS TO DO

Free ranger-led activities: nature walks and hikes, children's programs, sled-dog demonstrations, talks, slide shows, and films. Also, narrated bus tours, hiking, limited fishing, mountain climbing, rafting, horseback riding, cross-country skiing, dogsledding.

OVERNIGHT BACKPACKING

Backcountry divided into units with limits (2-12) on the number of campers. Permits required; available free at Backcountry Information Center, first come, first served. Must carry bear-proof containers. Backpacker shuttle fee $29.25.

CAMPGROUNDS

Five campgrounds (294 sites), 14-day limit from mid-May to mid-Sept.; other times, 30-day limit. Riley Creek open all year. Others open late spring to early fall. In summer, reservations strongly recommended (800) 622-7275 or (907) 272-7275 or www.reservedenali.com. Fees $9-$28 per night. RV sites except at Sanctuary and Wonder Lake and Igloo Creek; no hookups. Buses transport campers to Teklanika River, Sanctuary, Igloo Creek, Wonder Lake, and farther. Must reserve for Savage River Group Campground (phone/website above).

HOTELS, MOTELS, & INNS

(unless otherwise noted, rates are for 2 persons in a double room, high season)

INSIDE THE PARK:
Camp Denali and North Face Lodge P.O. Box 67, Denali NP, 99755. (907) 683-2290. Camp Denali: 18 cabins, central showers. North Face Lodge: 15 rooms. $1,545 for a 3-night package; $2,060 for 4-night package, all inclusive. Early June–mid-Sept.
Denali Backcountry Lodge Denali NP, 99755. (866) 875-8456. 42 units. $355-$515 per person per night, all inclusive. June–Sept.
Kantishna Roadhouse Denali NP, 99755. (800) 942-7420. $435 per person, all inclusive, 2-day min. June–mid-Sept.
OUTSIDE THE PARK:
Denali Cabins P.O. Box 229, Denali NP, 99755. (907) 683-2643. 45 units. $126-$208. June–mid-Sept.
Denali Princess Wilderness Lodge 2385 Parks Hwy., Denali NP, 99755. (800) 426-0442 or (907) 683-2282. 656 units. $299. Restaurant. Mid-May–mid-Sept.

DENALI

ALASKA EXCURSIONS

DENALI STATE PARK
TALKEETNA, ALASKA

Wedged between the Talkeetna Mountains and the Alaska Range, 325,240-acre Denali State Park abuts the larger national park. The state park contains terrain and animals similar to its neighbor, but provides additional accessibility and camping when the neighboring national park is full. There are 4 developed campgrounds with more than 120 campsites and 2 year-round cabins (reservations required). Located on Parks Hwy. Mileposts 131.7–169.2. (907) 745-3975.

CHUGACH NATIONAL FOREST
ANCHORAGE, ALASKA

The Chugach includes 3,550 miles of coastline, more than 200 bird species, and numerous glaciers, including one, the Portage, that is easily accessible from Anchorage. 5,400,000 acres. 400 campsites, 36 cabins. Activities: hiking, boating, climbing, bicycling, fishing, horseback riding, hunting, picnic areas, scenic drives, winter sports, water sports. Handicapped access. Open all year; most campsites open late May to early September. Visitor center at Portage on Seward-Anchorage Hwy., about 45 miles southeast of Anchorage. (907) 743-9500.

KENAI NATIONAL WILDLIFE REFUGE
SOLDOTNA, ALASKA

Large numbers of moose share this refuge with bears, mountain goats, Dall sheep, loons, eagles, and salmon, rainbow trout, and arctic char. Nearly 2,000,000 acres including two large glacier-carved lakes—Skilak and Tustumena. Activities: camping, hiking, boating, fishing, hunting, picnicking, scenic drives, water sports. Handicapped access. Adjacent to Kenai Fjords NP. Visitor center at Soldotna on Sterling Hwy., about 110 miles southwest of Anchorage. (907) 262-7021, www.kenai.fws.gov.

TETLIN NATIONAL WILDLIFE REFUGE
TOK, ALASKA

Bounded by the Alaska Highway on the north and Wrangell-St. Elias NP on the south, Tetlin's 930,000 acres offer a wilderness experience among marshes, lakes, ponds, rivers, forests, and hills abundant with waterfowl and fish. Facilities include 23 campsites, picnic areas, boat ramp. Activities include hiking, boating, fishing, and hunting. Open all year. Visitor center on Alaska Hwy. (milepost 1229) about 300 miles southeast of Fairbanks. (907) 883-5312, www .tetlin.fws.gov.

YUKON-CHARLEY RIVERS NATIONAL PRESERVE
EAGLE, ALASKA

For millennia, the Yukon corridor has seen passing boats and sleds and migrating herds of caribou, but humans have made little imprint. Breeding ground for a large population of peregrine falcons. With its tributary, the Yukon offers superb boating and floating. 2,527,000 acres. Activities include primitive camping, climbing, fishing, hunting. Open all year. Gateway towns of Circle and Eagle reached by Steese and Taylor Hwys. respectively. Access by boat or air charter. Information at Eagle headquarters. (907) 547-2233.

DENALI

WHITE MOUNTAINS NATIONAL RECREATION AREA
FAIRBANKS, ALASKA

The jagged White Mountains preside over wild Beaver Creek and an extensive winter cabin/trail system, inviting a close-up look by skiers, dog mushers, and snowmobile riders. Summer hiking trail traverses spruce forests and alpine ridges for 22 miles to reach the creek. 1,000,000 acres. Activities include primitive camping, 12 cabins (reservations required), boating, climbing, fishing, horseback riding. Open all year. Trailheads located off Steese and Elliot Hwys. 30 to 70 miles north of Fairbanks. (800) 437-7021 or (907) 474-2251.

The Alatna River, looping through a pass in the Brooks Range

▶GATES OF THE ARCTIC

ALASKA
ESTABLISHED DECEMBER 2, 1980
8,500,000 acres

"The view from the top gave us an excellent idea of the jagged country toward which we were heading. The main Brooks Range divide
was entirely covered with snow. Close at hand, only about ten miles
to the north, was a precipitous pair of mountains, one on each
side of the North Fork. I bestowed the name Gates of the Arctic
on them."

It was the early 1930s, and Robert
Marshall had found his wilderness
home, a remote, uncluttered source
of inspiration that would make him
one of America's greatest conservationists. Gates of the Arctic was the
ultimate North American wilderness. Congress created the park to
keep it that way.

Climb practically any ridge in
the heart of the park and you'll see
a dozen glacial cirques side by

side; serrated mountains that
scythe the sky; and storms that
snap out of dark, brooding clouds.
Six national wild rivers—Alatna,
John, Kobuk, Noatak, North Fork
Koyukuk, and Tinayguk—tumble
out of high alpine valleys into
forested lowlands. The park lies
entirely above the Arctic Circle,
straddling the Brooks Range,
one of the world's northernmost
mountain chains.

Along with Kobuk Valley National Park and Noatak National Preserve, Gates of the Arctic protects much of the habitat of the western arctic caribou herd. Grizzlies, wolves, wolverines, and foxes also roam over the severe land in search of food. Ptarmigan nibble on willow, and gyrfalcons dive for ptarmigan.

Shafts of cinnabar sunlight pour through the mountains at 2 a.m. in June, setting the wild land ablaze. In this mammoth mountain kingdom—the northernmost reach of the Rockies—the summer sun does not set for 30 straight days.

"No sight or sound or smell or feeling even remotely hinted of men or their creations," wrote Marshall. "It seemed as if time had dropped away a million years and we were back in a primordial world."

How to Get There

Bush pilots say that where the road ends, the real Alaska begins. And so it is in Gates of the Arctic. You can fly or walk in; most people fly. From Fairbanks (about 250 miles away), scheduled flights serve Anaktuvuk Pass, an Eskimo village within the park borders; Bettles/Evansville; and Ambler, to the west. From Bettles/ Evansville, Ambler, Fairbanks, or Coldfoot, you can air taxi into the park. Allow time for bad weather and delayed flights. From Anaktuvuk Pass, you can hike into the park.

Or, you can drive up from Fairbanks on the unpaved Dalton Highway (a pipeline haul road that's also open to the public) and hike to the park from several points along the road. But it's a long, hard walk into the interior.

When to Go

Summer. It is short, but days are very long and for a while temperatures may be relatively mild. Weather is highly unpredictable. Expect snow or rain in any month. August can be very wet, with freezing temperatures by mid-month. Mosquitoes and gnats are bad in late June and July. Fall colors peak in mid-August at high elevations, late August to early September at low elevations.

How to Visit

Allow enough time to savor the subtle beauty of this vast wilderness. A combination river-hiking trip offers the best of both. Air taxis are equipped to land on lakes and gravel bars for drop-offs and pickups.

Plan carefully and bring everything you need; there are no visitor facilities in the park. Some of the lichens you'll see as you hike have taken 150 years to reach full growth. Plants in the northwest can withstand extreme changes in temperature and sunlight, but they are also fragile and easily damaged—when hiking in groups, spread out over the tundra to avoid forming trails.

Write or call Bettles Ranger Station before planning a trip. There are no trails in the park, but you can ask for suggestions about areas to visit, along with names of air taxis, guides, and outfitters who operate in the park.

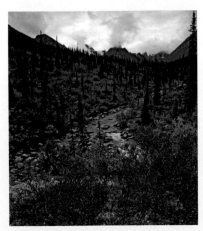

Arrigetch Creek

GATES OF THE ARCTIC

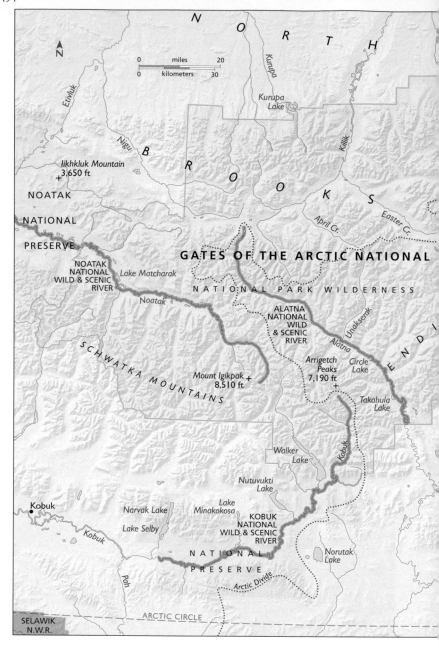

RIVER TRIPS

Rivers are the main travel routes through the park. Alaska natives and caribou have followed them for centuries. Near some are lakes on which aircraft can land. Camping is good on the gravel bars, but be aware that summer rainstorms can quickly raise water levels. Most rivers are at their highest in May and June. Hiking is difficult but

NATIONAL
PARK S +
Castle Mt. 3,409 ft
WILDERNESS

S L O P E

Chandler

Anaktuvuk

Nanushuk

Itkillik

Itkillik
Lake

ARCTIC
NATIONAL
WILDLIFE
REFUGE

Shainin
Lake

NATIONAL PRESERVE

Atigun

Chandler
Lake

Arctic Divide

Anaktuvuk Pass
Ranger
Station

R A N G E

M O U N T A I N S

Summit Lake

Atigun
Pass
4,752 ft

Agiak

JOHN
NATIONAL
WILD & SCENIC
RIVER

John

N. Fk.

+ Mount Doonerak
7,457 ft

Gates of the Arctic
+

DALTON
HIGHWAY

'ARK AND PRESERVE

Frigid Crags +
5,501 ft

+ Boreal Mountain
6,654 ft

Hunt
Fork
Lake

John

TINAYGUK
NATIONAL
WILD & SCENIC
RIVER

Tinayguk

Redstar Creek
Lakes

O T T

NATIONAL PARK
WILDERNESS

Wild
Lake

N. Fk. Koyukuk

Wiseman

iakuk Lake

John

Wild

NORTH FORK
KOYUKUK
NATIONAL
WILD & SCENIC
RIVER

Mt. Fk. Koyukuk

Coldfoot

Arctic Interagency
Visitor Center &
Ranger Station

Ranger
Station

11

A l a t n a   H i l l s

Evansville
Bettles

Koyukuk

S. Fk. Koyukuk

ICE ROAD
(winter use
only)

Prospect Creek

YUKON FLATS
NATIONAL
WILDLIFE
REFUGE

Alatna

KANUTI

NATIONAL WILDLIFE

REFUGE

Allakaket

ARCTIC CIRCLE

rewarding; the easiest places to travel are often the alpine areas. The following rivers are a sampling of what the park has to offer:

Below Takahula Lake the **Alatna River** is ideal for a first wilderness float trip. It takes 4 to 7 days, running gently down from the treeless Arctic Divide through beautiful tundra to the forested **Koyukuk River** lowlands. There are put-ins at **Takahula Lake, Circle Lake,** or the unnamed

Bleached caribou antlers on the tundra *(top)*; purple saxifrage *(bottom)*

lakes upstream. Most boaters take out at the village of Allakaket (75 and 85 miles from Takahula and Circle Lakes, respectively), where the Alatna meets the Koyukuk River.

John River is a mere stream at its headwaters, Anaktuvuk Pass (the permanent settlement of the inland Nunamiut Eskimo), but it gains power and momentum as it flows through the heart of the park. **Hunt Fork Lake** is the best put-in; water levels above this point are usually too low. The John River drops into lowland forest and joins the Koyukuk River just downstream of Bettles, a journey of a hundred miles.

Kobuk River begins at **Walker Lake** (with a portage) and runs south and west through mountains, canyons, foothills, and lowlands. Kobuk village, 140 river miles from Walker Lake, serves as a takeout location. Or you can continue downriver to Ambler and on through Kobuk Valley NP to Kiana.

North Fork Koyukuk begins at **Summit Lake** and cuts between **Boreal Mountain** and **Frigid Crags**—the **Gates of the Arctic**—then flows past **Redstar Creek Lakes** and continues south 100 miles to Bettles.

Creating one of the largest wilderness river basins on the continent, the **Noatak** flows 450 miles from Gates of the Arctic through Noatak preserve into the Chukchi Sea. The trip from a put-in at **Lake Matcharak** to Noatak village is 350 miles. The river, a major thoroughfare in a trackless realm, demands minimal boating skills but maximal planning. Allow a month for the trip.

The seldom visited **Tinayguk** flows through a broad glacier-cut valley and joins the Koyukuk below Boreal Mountain and Frigid Crags. Put in along the Tinayguk 35 miles north of where it joins the Koyukuk. (Consult local maps and outfitters for the exact location.) Float down to the Koyukuk, then continue on for another 80 miles to Bettles.

INFORMATION & ACTIVITIES

VISITOR & INFORMATION CENTERS

There are no visitor centers or facilities of any kind within the park. **Bettles Ranger Station** is open year-round in Bettles. During the summer, a ranger station is open in Anaktuvuk Pass. An **interagency visitor center** is staffed in Coldfoot.

SEASONS & ACCESSIBILITY

Park open year-round. Access by air or foot; there are no roads to the park (except Dalton Highway, an unpaved pipeline haul road that's parallel to park's east boundary). There are no roads in the park. Contact park headquarters before planning a visit.

HEADQUARTERS

Bettles Ranger Station, P.O. Box 30, Bettles, AK 99726. Phone (907) 692-5494. www.nps.gov/gaar

PETS

Only pack dogs allowed.

ACCESSIBLE SERVICES

Bettles and Anaktuvuk Pass Ranger Stations and Coldfoot Visitor Center.

THINGS TO DO

Hiking (no established trails), backpacking, canoeing, kayaking and rafting, fishing (license required), hunting (in preserve only, with license), rock and mountain climbing. Winter: cross-country skiing, snowshoeing, dogmushing, skiing. Ask park for list of licensed guides, outfitters (www.nps.gov/gaar/planyourvisit/cuaholders.htm).

SPECIAL ADVISORIES

• Bring all supplies with you—Fairbanks has a full selection, few available in communities of Bettles and Anaktuvuk Pass.
• Gas stations are on the Dalton Highway at milepost 56 and at Coldfoot, milepost 173.6. There are no other facilities along the Dalton Highway.
• Visitors should be skilled in outdoors; firearms may be carried for protection.
• Grizzly and black bears are unpredictable and dangerous. Visit ranger station in Bettles or Coldfoot for advice on preventing an encounter. Bear-resistant food containers are required for all food carried into the park.
• Eskimos and other native Alaskans use the park for subsistence fishing and hunting; respect them and their property.
• Mid-June through July, prepare for mosquitoes and gnats; bring insect repellent, a head net, and insect-proof tent.
• Swift currents, freezing water can make river crossings hazardous. Hypothermia is possible in 24-hour sunlight.

OVERNIGHT BACKPACKING

No permit required, but get up-to-date bear information from ranger station. Orientation available at ranger stations. Food, stoves, and all equipment must be carried. Camp on gravel bars to avoid damaging fragile tundra. Required bear barrels are loaned free of charge.

CAMPGROUNDS

None; backcountry camping only. The BLM's Marion Creek Campground is located at mile 180 on Dalton Highway.

HOTELS, MOTELS, & INNS

(unless otherwise noted, rates are for 2 persons in a double room, high season)

INSIDE THE PARK:

Arrigetch Park Wilderness Cabin (on Alatna River) P.O. Box 80424, Fairbanks, AK 99708. (877) 479-6354 or (907) 479-6354, www.gofarnorth.com. 1 cabin, sleeps 4. $2,995 per person (min. 2 people) for 3-night all-inclusive package, including round-trip air travel from Fairbanks and guide. Mid-June–early Sept.
Gates of the Arctic Caribou Cabin (on headwaters of the Alatna River) see contact info above. 1 cabin, 6 beds, 3-night $3,595 per person (min. 2 people). All-inclusive package includes round-trip air travel from Fairbanks and guide. July–early Sept.

OUTSIDE THE PARK:

Coldfoot Camp Mile 175, Dalton Hwy., Coldfoot, AK 99701. (907) 474-3500. 80 units. $199. Restaurant.
Iniakuk Lake Wilderness Lodge see contact info for Arrigetch cabin above. 5 rooms, shared bath. $1,495 per person per day (min. 2 people). All-inclusive package includes airfare from Fairbanks and guides. Mid-June–mid-Sept; mid-March–mid-April.

GATES OF THE ARCTIC

Sunset view of Adams Inlet, from Muir Inlet

▶GLACIER BAY

ALASKA
ESTABLISHED DECEMBER 2, 1980
3,280,198 acres

When Capt. George Vancouver sailed the Alaska coast in 1794, Glacier Bay did not exist. It lay beneath a sheet of glacial ice several miles wide and thousands of feet thick. Since then, in one of the fastest glacial retreats on record, the ice has shrunk back 65 miles to unveil new land and a new bay, now returning to life after a long winter's sleep.

Scientists call Glacier Bay a living laboratory for the grand processes of glacial retreat, plant succession, and animal dynamics. It is an open book on the last ice age. At the southern end, where the ice departed 200 years ago, a spruce-hemlock rain forest has taken root. Farther north, the more recently deglaciated land remains rugged and has become thinly vegetated.

The bay branches into two major arms, the west arm and Muir Inlet, which themselves branch into smaller inlets. There, on slopes deglaciated 30 years ago, alder and willow grow, while mosses, mountain avens, and dwarf fireweed pioneer the exposed areas.

The new vegetation creates habitats for wolves, moose, mountain goats, black bears, brown bears, ptarmigan, and other wildlife, and the sea supports a food chain that includes salmon, bald eagles, harbor seals, harbor porpoises, humpback whales, and killer whales—all in an environment less than 200 years old.

Glacier Bay is home to seven tidewater glaciers that calve, including McBride, Margere, and Johns Hopkins Glaciers. In part because of variations in snow accumulations, most glaciers in the eastern and southwestern areas of the bay are receding, while several on its west side are advancing.

The glaciers calve icebergs that hit the water with a sound like cannon shot. "White thunder," the Tlingit called it, the awesome voice of glacial ice. An iceberg's color often reveals its makeup; compacted bergs are blue, while those filled with trapped air bubbles are white.

How to Get There

By boat or plane only. From Juneau, take a scheduled flight 53 miles to Gustavus. Catch the bus to Glacier Bay Lodge and Bartlett Cove Campground, 10 miles away at the park's southern end. Charter flights also service Gustavus from Juneau, Skagway, Haines, and Hoonah. Contact the Alaska Marine Highway (for systems reservations call 907-456-3941 or 800-642-0066, or visit www .dot.state.ak.us/amhs) about ferries from Juneau to Gustavus. Private boats can enter the bay with permits (required June to August) obtained by phone, by mail from headquarters at Bartlett Cove, or online (www.nps.gov/glba).

When to Go

Late May to mid-September. Summer days are long and temperatures cool. May and June have the most sunshine. September is often rainy and windy.

How to Visit

Glacier Bay is a marine highway. Most visitors experience the park from the deck of a cruise ship, or a tour boat, or from waterline in a sea kayak. Many of the large cruise ships that travel southeast Alaska's Inside Passage go into Glacier Bay. Other tours offer accommodations at **Glacier Bay Lodge** (the park's center of activity) and a 1-day trip to the glaciers and back. Campers and kayakers can take the boat and be dropped off at one of two sites up the bay, either to be picked up at a later date or to paddle back to Bartlett Cove.

THE LOWER BAY

The lower bay reaches from **Bartlett Cove** north to **Tlingit Point,** where it separates into its two arms and continues north. Bartlett Cove has the only three maintained trails in the park. Beginning at the **Glacier Bay Lodge,** the **Forest Loop Trail** is a 1-mile, 1-hour round-trip through the young spruce-hemlock rain forest. A wheelchair-accessible boardwalk covers the first part of the trail out to **Blackwater Pond.**

For a half-day more rugged trip, the **Bartlett River Trail** begins at the roadside, a half mile from the lodge, and winds another 1.5 miles through the rain forest to the **Bartlett River,** ending in a quiet meadow. It's not unusual to see red squirrels, blue grouse, and black bears along either of these trails.

If you want to kayak, the **Beardslee Islands** just north of Bartlett Cove offer a maze of shorelines and waterways—a quiet counterpoint to the cars and boats coming and going at the cove. In addition, these islands provide a good locale for spotting whales.

Sitakaday Narrows reaches across the lower bay and creates strong and dangerous whirlpools and currents as the tides (rising and falling an average of 15 feet in 6 hours) rush

GLACIER BAY

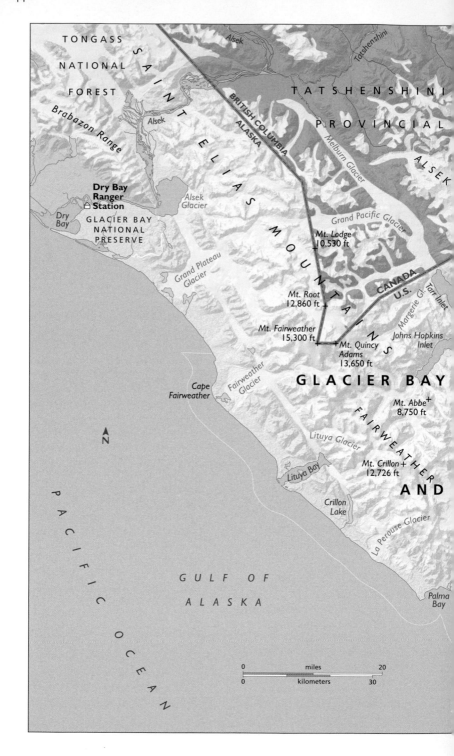

TONGASS

NATIONAL

FOREST

Brabazon Range

SAINT ELIAS

Alsek

Alsek

Dry Bay
Ranger
Station

Dry
Bay

GLACIER BAY
NATIONAL
PRESERVE

Alsek
Glacier

Grand Plateau
Glacier

BRITISH COLUMBIA
ALASKA

TATSHENSHINI

PROVINCIAL

Tatshenshini

ALSEK

Melburn Glacier

ALSEK

Grand Pacific Glacier

Mt. Lodge
10,530 ft

MOUNTAINS

CANADA
U.S.

Mt. Root
12,860 ft

Margerie Gl. Tarr Inlet

Mt. Fairweather
15,300 ft

Mt. Quincy
Adams
13,650 ft

Johns Hopkins
Inlet

Cape
Fairweather

Fairweather
Glacier

GLACIER BAY

Mt. Abbe
8,750 ft

FAIRWEATHER

Lituya Glacier

Mt. Crillon
12,726 ft

Lituya Bay

Crillon
Lake

AND

La Pérouse Glacier

N

PACIFIC

GULF OF

ALASKA

Palma
Bay

OCEAN

0	miles	20
0	kilometers	30

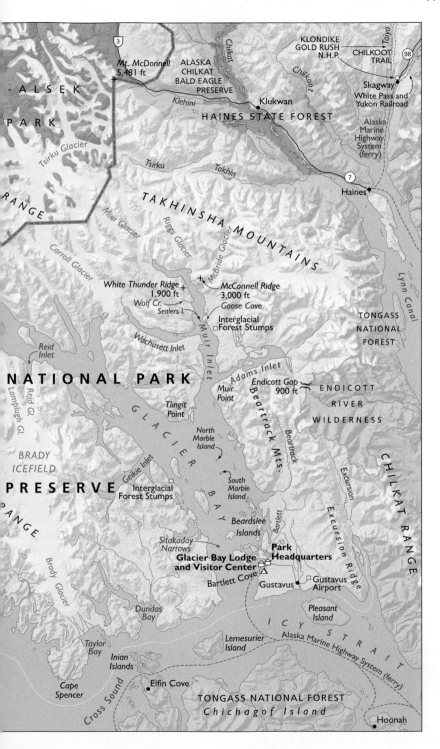

③

Mt. McDonnell
5,481 ft

ALASKA
CHILKAT
BALD EAGLE
PRESERVE

KLONDIKE
GOLD RUSH
N.H.P.

CHILKOOT
TRAIL

98

Chilkat

Chilkoot

Skagway
White Pass and
Yukon Railroad

Klehini

Klukwan

HAINES STATE FOREST

Alaska
Marine
Highway
System
(ferry)

- ALSEK

PARK

Tsirku Glacier

Tsirku

Takhin

7

Haines

R A N G E

T A K H I N S H A   M O U N T A I N S

Muir Glacier

Riggs Glacier

McBride Glacier

Carroll Glacier

White Thunder Ridge
1,900 ft

Wolf Cr.

Sealers I.

McConnell Ridge
3,000 ft

Goose Cove

Interglacial
Forest Stumps

Lynn Canal

TONGASS

NATIONAL

FOREST

Reid
Inlet

Wachusett Inlet

Muir Inlet

Muir
Point

Adams Inlet

Endicott Gap
900 ft

ENDICOTT

RIVER

WILDERNESS

N A T I O N A L   P A R K

Reid Gl.
Lamplugh Gl.

BRADY
ICEFIELD

P R E S E R V E

G L A C I E R

Tlingit
Point

North
Marble
Island

Beartrack Mts.

Beartrack

CHILKAT   RANGE

Geikie Inlet

Interglacial
Forest Stumps

South
Marble
Island

B A Y

Beardslee
Islands

Excursion

Excursion Ridge

R A N G E

Brady Glacier

Sitakaday
Narrows

Glacier Bay Lodge
and Visitor Center

Bartlett Cove

Park
Headquarters

Bartlett

Gustavus

Gustavus
Airport

GLACIER BAY

Dundas
Bay

Pleasant
Island

I C Y   S T R A I T

Taylor
Bay

Inian
Islands

Lemesurier
Island

Alaska Marine Highway System (ferry)

Cape
Spencer

Cross Sound

Elfin Cove

TONGASS NATIONAL FOREST
Chichagof Island

Hoonah

over it. *Check the tide before venturing out.* Watch for phalaropes, gulls, terns, and other birds feeding as the swirling water flushes small fish to the surface. To the north, the **Marble Islands** rise out of the middle of the bay. The deglaciated islands support colonies of gulls, cormorants, puffins, and murres *(off-limits to visitors during the summer)*. Keep your eyes peeled for Steller sea lions on **South Marble Island.**

THE WEST ARM

The bay's west arm contains the park's highest mountains and most active tidewater glaciers. Clear days afford visitors stunning views of the **Fairweather Range** (of the St. Elias Mountains) which is crowned by **Mount Fairweather** at 15,300 feet; cloudy days lend a moody, rich blue cast to the tidewater faces of the **Margerie, Grand Pacific, Lamplugh,** and **Reid Glaciers.**

In the wildest inlet—**Johns Hopkins**—glaciers tumble down 8,000-foot mountain peaks. Each June thousands of harbor seals give

Steller sea lions

birth to their pups on icebergs in Johns Hopkins Inlet (to protect the seals, the inlet is closed seasonally).

Blue Mouse Cove and the northwest corner of **Reid Inlet** are protected anchorages. Good camping can be found almost anywhere (except in Johns Hopkins Inlet because of its steep terrain). Hiking is just a matter of going where the spirit and the topography take you. Brown bears are common. This is their home, and you are the visitor. Please exercise caution.

MUIR INLET

Reaching 25 miles into the park's northeast corner, **Muir Inlet** is a mecca for kayakers. Tour boats seldom come here. Check for closures at park headquarters. The camping is good, and so is the hiking, if you avoid thickets of alder.

Adams Inlet branches east off lower Muir Inlet and is a favorite among kayakers. You can time your entry and exit by the strong tides that flow in and out through the narrow opening. To the north, **Sealers Island** was once a breeding site for arctic terns and black oystercatchers.

Nearby is **Goose Cove.** In contrast to the tidewater glaciers that are advancing in the west arm, most in Muir Inlet are in retreat. The **McBride** and **Riggs Glaciers** separated from the retreating **Muir Glacier** in 1941 and 1960 respectively; since then, all three continue to retreat.

A journey up **White Thunder Ridge** or **McConnell Ridge** rewards hikers with spectacular views of upper Muir Inlet. Both hikes are strenuous. Be prepared to struggle through alder. Each hike takes a full day and climbs about 1,500 feet.

INFORMATION & ACTIVITIES

VISITOR & INFORMATION CENTERS
Information centers are located on the dock at **Bartlett Cove** and at **Glacier Bay Lodge.** Call (907) 697-2627 for visitor information.

SEASONS & ACCESSIBILITY
Park open year-round, but late May to mid-September is visitor season; transportation and facilities limited rest of year. Call the park before going in the off-season. There are no roads to the park; access by airplane, boat, or ferry only. Allen Marine Tours (888-289-0081) offers ferry service between Auke Bay (north of Juneau) and Bartlett Cove. The Alaska Marine Highway System (800-642-0066) offers limited ferry service from Juneau to Bartlett Cove. Visitors with private boats need a permit from June through August; phone (907) 697-2627.

HEADQUARTERS
P.O. Box 140, Gustavus, AK 99826. Phone (907) 697-2230. www.nps.gov/glba

ENTRANCE FEE
None.

PETS
Permitted on leashes on Bartlett Cove roads only. Prohibited in backcountry; boaters must keep pets aboard vessels.

ACCESSIBLE SERVICES
Glacier Bay Lodge is accessible to wheelchairs. One trail, with a stretch of boardwalk, is also accessible.

THINGS TO DO
Free ranger-led activities (from Glacier Bay Lodge): nature walks, films, and evening programs. Also available, kayaking, fishing (license required), scheduled boat tours, glacier viewing, whale- and bird-watching, hiking, berry picking, mountain and glacier climbing (for the experienced only), aerial sightseeing, cross-country skiing. For information and reservations for ranger-guided boat tours from Bartlett Cove, contact Glacier Bay Lodge, Inc., (888) 299-8687. Ask the park for a list of other concessioners offering a variety of rental and guide services. Or visit www.visitglacierbay.com.

SPECIAL ADVISORIES
• Do not get close to icebergs when boating, and do not climb on the glaciers.
• Insect repellent may be useful.
• Be aware of bears. Obtain safety guidelines from information centers or rangers.

OVERNIGHT BACKPACKING
Permit required. Backcountry users must receive orientation from rangers before setting out. Use of Park Service food storage canisters required.

CAMPGROUNDS
One campground only; Bartlett Cove has 14-day limit. Open all year; first come, first served. No fees. Showers at lodge (within a mile) available only seasonally. Warming hut provided. Tent sites only. Bartlett Cove Group Campground; open all year; first come, first served.

HOTELS, MOTELS, & INNS
(unless otherwise noted, rates are for 2 persons in a double room, high season)

INSIDE THE PARK:
Glacier Bay Lodge P.O. Box 179, Gustavus, AK 99826. (888) 229-8687 or (907) 697-4000. 55 units. $175-$202. Packages that include airfare available. Restaurant. Mid-May–early Sept.

OUTSIDE THE PARK:
In Gustavus, AK 99826
Annie Mae Lodge P.O. Box 55. (800) 478-2346 or (907) 697-2346. 11 units. $176-$200, includes continental breakfast and ground transportation.
Glacier Bay Country Inn P.O. Box 5. (800) 628-0912 or (907) 697-2288. 10 units. $198-$235 per person, includes meals. Mid-May–mid-Sept.
Gustavus Inn P.O. Box 60. (907) 697-2254. 13 units, 11 with private baths. $205 per person, includes meals and some activities. May–early Sept.

Alaska brown bears fishing for salmon at Brooks Falls

▶ KATMAI

ALASKA
ESTABLISHED DECEMBER 2, 1980
4,021,327 acres

Volcanoes and bears—powerful, unpredictable, and awe inspiring—embody the wild heart of Katmai. Within the borders of the national park and preserve are 15 volcanoes, some of them still steaming, and North America's largest population of protected brown bears—about 2,000 of them.

You can hike, kayak, and canoe here. You can fish waist-deep in rivers as clear as glass. And you can watch the best fish catcher of all, the great Alaska brown bear, sometimes diving completely under the water for its prey, sometimes catching fish in midair. At the end of the day you can relax in a rustic yet sumptuous lodge on the shore of a sapphire lake and recount the day's enchantments.

In 1912 a volcano here erupted with a force ten times that of Mount St. Helens in 1980. Suddenly news of Katmai, a place hardly anyone had heard of, was on front pages around the world. Ash filled the air, global temperatures cooled, acid rain burned clothing off lines in Vancouver, British Columbia, and on Kodiak Island, just across Shelikof Strait from Katmai, day became night.

Leading a 1916 expedition sponsored by the National Geographic Society, botanist Robert Griggs ascended Katmai Pass from Shelikof Strait. "The whole valley as far as the eye could reach was full of hundreds, no thousands—literally, tens of thousands—of smokes curling up from its fissured floor," he wrote. The smokes were fumaroles steaming 500 to 1,000 feet into the air. Griggs, who named the Valley of Ten Thousand Smokes, spearheaded the campaign to include Katmai in the National Park System.

Today, the smokes are gone from the valley. But steam vents still appear elsewhere in the park.

How to Get There

From Anchorage, scheduled jets fly the 290 miles to King Salmon, park headquarters; from there, June to mid-September, daily floatplanes fly the last 33 miles to Brooks Camp, site of a summer visitor center and the center of activity. Air charters can be arranged into other areas. You can drive the 9 miles from King Salmon to Lake Camp, at the western end of the park on the Naknek River, then go by boat to Brooks Camp, the Bay of Islands, and other areas of Naknek Lake.

When to Go

June to early September. Only then, with transportation from between Brooks Camp and the Valley of Ten Thousand Smokes, are the lodges, cabins, and Brooks Camp Campground open. Bear-watching, an increasingly popular pastime, is best in July when the sockeye salmon spawn (bear-watching suffers a brief lull in June and again in August). Fishing and hiking are good throughout summer, but come prepared for rain. Heavy snowpack may remain in the upper elevations into July. Summer daytime temperatures range from the mid-50s to mid-60s; the average low is 44°F.

How to Visit

If your time is short, get to **Brooks Camp.** People, fish, bears, boats, and planes concentrate here. Compared to the rest of the park, it's crowded.

But the lodge and campground are comfortable (reservations required) and the bear viewing unforgettable. You'll find good hiking and fishing.

If at all possible, take the bus or van tour 23 miles out from Brooks Camp to the **Valley of Ten Thousand Smokes.** Return the same day or hike into the valley and camp. You can extend your stay by boating or flying to the many other lakes, streams, rivers, and lodges in the park. Pick your area, make a safe plan, and go.

BROOKS CAMP & VALLEY OF TEN THOUSAND SMOKES

Some very pleasant hikes begin near Brooks Camp. The trail you'll first want to take goes to the bear-viewing platform. The 1-mile trail starts at Brooks Camp and winds gently through the forest to **Brooks Falls,** ending at the viewing platform. Wooden steps ascend a balcony overlooking the fascinating spectacle of jumping fish and feeding bears. Averaging a thousand pounds and measuring up to ten feet long, these Alaska brown bears are the largest land carnivores on the continent of North America.

The hike up **Dumpling Mountain** is a good day trip. The trail begins at the campground and climbs to an 800-foot overlook in 1.5 miles. From there you can continue another 2 miles over alpine tundra to the summit, elevation 2,440 feet. Both the overlook and summit afford tremendous views of **Naknek Lake** and the surrounding mountains.

The most popular and spectacular hiking in the park is in the **Valley of Ten Thousand Smokes.** There's no other landscape like it in the world. Daily tours connect Brooks Camp with the **Three Forks Overlook** and

KATMAI

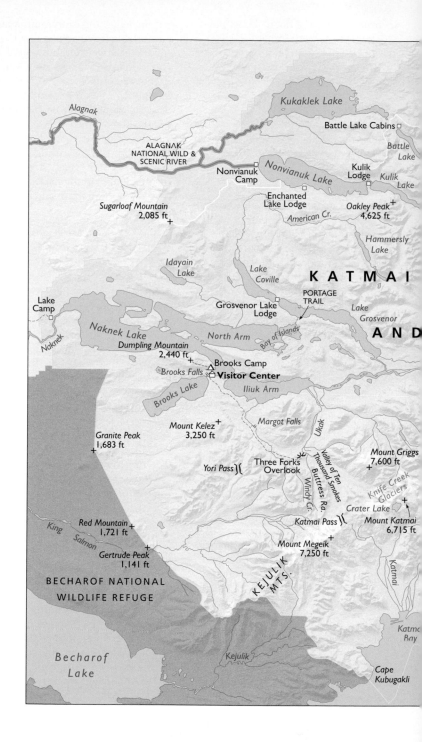

Alagnak

ALAGNAK
NATIONAL WILD &
SCENIC RIVER

Nonvianuk
Camp

Kukaklek Lake

Battle Lake Cabins □

Battle
Lake

Nonvianuk Lake

Kulik
Lodge

Kulik
Lake

Enchanted
Lake Lodge

Oakley Peak +
4,625 ft

Sugarloaf Mountain
2,085 ft +

American Cr.

Hammersly
Lake

Idayain
Lake

Lake
Coville

K A T M A I

Lake
Camp

Naknek Lake

Grosvenor Lake
Lodge

PORTAGE
TRAIL

Lake
Grosvenor

A N D

North Arm

Bay of Islands

Naknek

Dumpling Mountain
2,440 ft +

Brooks Camp
Visitor Center

Brooks Falls

Iliuk Arm

Brooks Lake

Margot Falls

Ukak

Mount Kelez +
3,250 ft

Mount Griggs
7,600 ft

Granite Peak
1,683 ft
+

Yori Pass)(

Three Forks
Overlook

Valley of Ten
Thousand Smokes

Buttress Ra.

Windy Cr.

Knife Creek
Glaciers

Crater Lake

Mount Katmai
6,715 ft

Katmai Pass)(

King

Salmon

Red Mountain +
1,721 ft

Gertrude Peak +
1,141 ft

Mount Megeik +
7,250 ft

Katmai

BECHAROF NATIONAL

WILDLIFE REFUGE

KEJULIK
MTS.

Katma
Bay

Becharof
Lake

Kejulik

Cape
Kubugakli

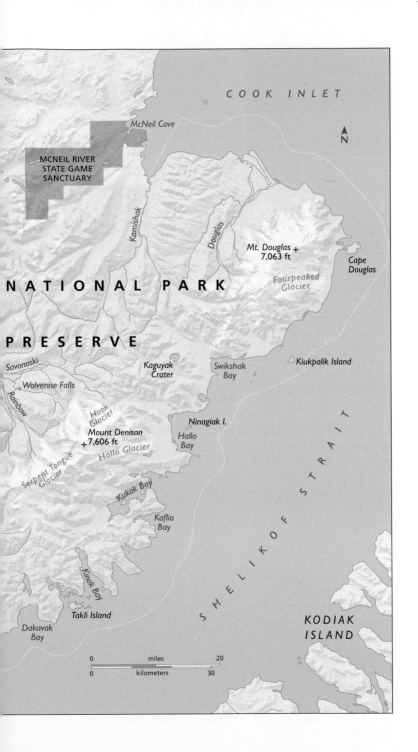

COOK INLET

N

McNeil Cove

MCNEIL RIVER
STATE GAME
SANCTUARY

Kamishak

Douglas

Mt. Douglas +
7,063 ft

Cape
Douglas

Fourpeaked
Glacier

N A T I O N A L   P A R K

P R E S E R V E

Savonoski

Wolverine Falls

Rainbow

Kaguyak
Crater

Swikshak
Bay

Kiukpalik Island

Hook
Glacier

Mount Denison
+7,606 ft

Hallo Glacier

Ninagiak I.

Hallo
Bay

Serpent Tongue
Glacier

Kukak Bay

Kaflia
Bay

S H E L I K O F   S T R A I T

Kinak Bay

Takli Island

KODIAK
ISLAND

Dakavak
Bay

KATMAI

miles		
0		20
0	kilometers	30

Valley of Ten Thousand Smokes

a cabin at the north end of the valley, where you can camp or picnic. A short trail descends 200 feet to where the **Ukak River** roars through a bedrock canyon crowned by cliffs of volcanic ash.

To hike into the valley, take the trail that begins a half mile back from the end of the road and plan to camp overnight. The trail crosses **Windy Creek,** passes the north end of the **Buttress Range,** crosses the **River Lethe,** and finally climbs 1,000 feet to the Baked Mountain Cabin, a shelter available for overnights. The challenging 12-mile trip takes a full day; *drinking water is scarce.* The river crossing can be extremely dangerous; be sure to be briefed at the visitor center before you hike.

Due south 5.5 miles from the cabin is **Katmai Pass,** where Robert Griggs first beheld the valley in 1916. Strong winds often funnel through here.

A fascinating side trip between **Baked Mountain** and Katmai Pass is to **Novarupta,** a 200-foot-high dome of volcanic rock that was the extrusion plug of the great eruption. Scientists believe most of the 1912 lava and ash spewed out through a fissure here, drawing magma from nearby **Mount Katmai** and causing its summit to collapse into a caldera.

To reach the caldera (a strenuous 1- to 2-day trip), head east from Novarupta or Baked Mountain to the stagnant, ash-covered **Knife Creek Glaciers,** then climb 3,800 feet up ash and ice to the caldera rim, where, if you peer over the edge, you'll see what Robert Griggs saw: "a wonderful lake, of a weird vitriolic robin's-egg blue."

WATER & AIR TRIPS

Boaters, kayakers, and canoeists find no shortage of places to explore in Katmai. Guides and equipment are available for hire through Brooks Lodge or one of the other, smaller lodges catering mostly to fishermen. An especially popular and picturesque spot is the **Bay of Islands** in the **North Arm** of Naknek Lake, 22 miles from Brooks Camp.

For serious paddlers looking for the wild side of Katmai, the **Savonoski Loop** is an 85-mile round-trip from Brooks Camp that takes 4 to 8 days, depending on weather. You paddle through the Bay of Islands, portage to **Lake Grosvenor,** and float the **Grosvenor** and **Savonoski Rivers** into the **Iliuk Arm** of Naknek Lake for the return to Brooks Camp. (Follow the shorelines, for wind can suddenly transform lakes from tranquil to tempestuous.)

If you'd like to take a river trip, inquire about the **Alagnak River,** a designated wild and scenic river, and the **Ukak River,** which, with class V rapids, is an excursion for the very experienced only.

Like Alaska's other national parks, Katmai is spectacular from the air. Flight-seeing trips can be arranged in **King Salmon** or Brooks Camp. Swing over the Valley of Ten Thousand Smokes, through Katmai Pass, up the coast from **Katmai Bay** to **Swikshak Bay,** over **Kaguyak Crater,** and down the Savonoski River back to Brooks Camp. Take plenty of camera batteries and a calm stomach.

INFORMATION & ACTIVITIES

VISITOR & INFORMATION CENTERS

Brooks Camp Visitor Center and the concessions are open from June to mid-Sept. All visitors to Brooks Camp are required to attend the 20-minute orientation on bear etiquette. For visitor information contact park or Katmailand, Inc., the park's concessioner, at 4125 Aircraft Dr., Anchorage, AK 99502; or call (800) 544-0551 or (907) 243-5448. **King Salmon Interagency Visitor Center** is open year-round (907-246-4250).

SEASONS & ACCESSIBILITY

Park open year-round. Scheduled flights from Anchorage to King Salmon with connecting seaplane flights to Brooks Camp in the park available June to mid-Sept only. Reserve well in advance. Accessible by private or charter plane all year; the park has a list of licensed air charter companies.

HEADQUARTERS

P.O. Box 7, King Salmon, AK 99613. Phone (907) 246-3305. www.nps.gov/katm

ENTRANCE FEE

None.

ACCESSIBLE SERVICES

Brooks Lodge is accessible, but with assistance.

THINGS TO DO

Free ranger-led activities. Daily interpretive programs, evening programs, nature walks. Also, bus trips to the Valley of Ten Thousand Smokes, bear-watching, hiking, kayaking, canoeing, boating, mountain climbing, aerial sightseeing, fishing (license required; available in park), float trips. Katmailand, Inc., has guides, boating, and fishing equipment available at Brooks Lodge. Reserve ahead. Ask the park for a list of other approved outfitters and guides within its borders.

SPECIAL ADVISORIES

• Alaskan brown bears are unpredictable and dangerous; stay far away from them unless at the bear-viewing platforms.
• Be very careful when crossing glacial streams.
• When hiking into the valley to Baked Mountain Cabin, be sure to carry sufficient water.
• Take a guide when kayaking unless extremely experienced; check with visitor center before leaving on skills needed and weather conditions.

OVERNIGHT BACKPACKING

Camping allowed anywhere in park without reservations, except at Brooks Camp (see below). Bear-resistant food canisters required for overnight stays, available free at Brooks Camp or King Salmon visitor centers.

CAMPGROUNDS

One designated campground, Brooks Camp (with 7-day limit in July). Open June to mid-Sept.; reservations required. Call the NRRS (see p. 10) for reservations. Campground fee $8 per night per person. Showers at Brooks Lodge. Tent sites only. Three-sided shelters for cooking. Limited food services in park.

HOTELS, MOTELS, & INNS

(unless otherwise noted, rates are for 2 persons, double room, high season)

INSIDE THE PARK:

Katmailand, Inc., offers multiday package tours from Anchorage that can include airfare; lodging at Brooks Lodge, Grosvenor Lake Lodge, or Kulik Lodge; meals; guides; fishing tackle; rafts; licenses; and boats or planes to fishing spots. For information, write Katmailand, Inc., 4125 Aircraft Dr., Anchorage, AK 99502; or call (800) 544-0551 or (907) 243-5448; www.katmailand.com.
Brooks Lodge 16 cabins. Packages starting from $949 per person. June–mid-Sept.
Grosvenor Lake Lodge 3 cabins. Packages starting from $2,700 per person. June–Oct.
Kulik Lodge 12 cabins. Packages starting from $2,800 per person. Mid-June–late Sept.

KATMAI

Northwestern Glacier in the summer, as seen from Northwestern Fjord

▶ KENAI FJORDS

ALASKA
ESTABLISHED DECEMBER 2, 1980
607,000 acres

Distill the essence of coastal Alaska into one place—wild, dynamic, and scenic, rich with the signatures of glaciers, light with the marks of people, unforgiving in stormy seas, unforgettable in warm sunshine—and you have Kenai Fjords, the smallest national park in Alaska. Here the south-central part of the state tumbles into the Gulf of Alaska; here the land challenges the sea with talonlike peninsulas and rocky headlands, while the sea itself reaches inland with long fjords and hundreds of quiet bays and coves.

The Harding Icefield is the park's crown jewel, 714 square miles of ice up to a mile thick. It feeds over three dozen glaciers flowing out of the mountains, 6 of them to tidewater. The Harding Icefield is a vestige of the massive ice sheet that covered much of Alaska in the Pleistocene era.

The ancient ice gouged out Kenai's fjords, creating habitats for throngs of sea animals. About 20 species of seabirds nest along the rocky coastline; the most charismatic of the birds are clown-faced puffins. Bald eagles swoop along the towering cliffs, and peregrine falcons hunt over the outer islands. Seabirds by the tens of thousands migrate or congregate here.

Approximately 27 land mammals, and 10 marine mammals including harbor seals, Steller sea lions, and sea otters, live here and are regularly seen along the coast. Moose, black bears, wolverines, and coyotes roam narrow bands of forest between the coast and icefield. And just above them, on the treeless slopes, climb sure-footed mountain goats.

How to Get There

Seward is the gateway to Kenai Fjords. To get to Seward, take the Seward Highway (Alas. 9) south from Anchorage. The 130-mile drive is spectacular. Buses and small charter planes also connect Anchorage and Seward.

You can also charter a flight from Seward or Homer directly to the park. In summer, the Alaska Railroad serves Seward from Anchorage (with connections to Fairbanks and Whittier).

When to Go

Usually summer. The days lengthen; the seas calm down. The road to Exit Glacier generally opens in May and closes with the first snowfall, usually in October. Many winter visitors ski the road into Exit Glacier, or snowmobile in. Flight-seeing trips can be arranged in Seward any time of the year, subject to weather.

How to Visit

For recommendations on getting around the park, visit the **Kenai Fjords National Park Information Center** near the small boat harbor. The most popular and accessible area in the park is Exit Glacier, 13 miles northwest of Seward. You can drive to it or take a tour bus. Trails offer half-hour hikes to the glacier and a full-day round-trip hike to the Harding Icefield.

Otherwise, hiking is a matter of exploring wilderness shores and ridges accessible only by boat

and plane. From mid-May to late September, daily tour boats from Seward offer round-trip half-day and full-day excursions to the fjords and outlying islands. Charter boats take kayakers and campers to any fjord they wish (most often Aialik Bay) and pick them up the same day or days later. Kayaking, fishing, and backpacking guides are available. Ask the park for a list.

From Seward or Homer you can book a breathtaking 1-hour flight over the Harding Icefield and Kenai coast. For extended adventures, ski-planes drop off and pick up skiers on the icefield, and floatplanes do the same for kayakers in the fjords, weather permitting.

EXIT GLACIER & HARDING ICEFIELD

Exit Glacier is one of many rivers of ice that flow off the Harding Icefield. From Seward, follow the highway north to mile 3.7, where a paved road will lead you 9 miles to a parking lot.

Short trails lead to views of Exit Glacier, which formed this landscape. A 1-mile accessible loop leads to a panoramic view of the **Exit Glacier Valley**—you can see the glacier spilling down from Harding Icefield to its terminus in the outwash plain. A moderately strenuous hike over newly deglaciated bedrock leads you to the edge of **Exit Glacier.** There is no trail to the toe of the glacier, but if water levels are low and you're not afraid to get your feet wet, you can make your way across the outwash plain toward the glacier.

The **Harding Icefield Trail** branches off the main paved trail and climbs 3,000 feet in 4.1 miles, ending at the edge of **Harding Icefield,** a vast expanse of ice

KENAI FJORDS

KENAI

NATIONAL

WILDLIFE

REFUGE

Tustumena Lake

Skilak Glacier

Killey Glacier

Indian Glacier

Tustumena Glacier

Fox

FJORDS

HARDING ICEFIELD

Truuli Peak
6,612 ft

Chernof Glacier

NATIONAL

Sheep Creek

Fox

M O U N T A I N S

PARK
+6,450 ft

Northwestern Glacier

Holgate Glac

Striation
Island

HARD

Northwestern
Lagoon

Bradley
Lake

Kachemak
Bay

Dinglestadt Glacier

McCarty Gl.

Kachemak Gl.

K E N A I

Nuka
Glacier

Nuka

Kvasnikoff Falls

+Iceworm Peak
5,800 ft

+Storm Mountain
3,793 ft

North Arm

□Cabin

North Arm

+Palisade Pk.
3,442 ft

McCarty Fjord

Two Arm
Bay

+Cloudy Mountain
1,810 ft

Thunder Bay

Ha

Beauty
Bay

Yalik Glacier

West Arm

Shelter
Cove

GULF

Petrof Glacier

Yalik
Point

Ragged
Island

Nuka
Bay

ALASKA MARITIME
NATIONAL
WILDLIFE REFUGE

KACHEMAK
BAY
STATE
WILDERNESS
PARK

KACHEMAK BAY
STATE PARK

Nuka
Passage

NUKA
ISLAND

PYE
ISLANDS

stretching as far as the eye can see. The upper section of the trail is usually snow covered; the lower portion can be slippery and muddy after rain. Ask a ranger about current conditions and sign in at the trail register. On the slopes you may see mountain goats and black bears.

THE FJORDS

Daily tour boats travel down **Resurrection Bay,** pass picturesque **Caines Head** and **Callisto Head,** then round rugged **Aialik Cape** and enter **Aialik Bay,** the most visited fjord in the park. The **Holgate** and **Aialik Glaciers** flow into this fjord. Tour boats usually visit the Holgate, then return to Seward via the **Chiswell Islands** (part of the Alaska Maritime NWR), an excellent place to see Steller sea lions resting on rocks and nesting seabirds.

Endless exploring awaits boaters and hikers on the shores of Kenai Fjords. If you are without a guide, be sure to inquire at the information center about weather, landing sites, tides, and hazards. The farther down the coast to the southwest, the fewer the people. Narrow **Granite Passage** is an exciting entrance into **Harris Bay.** From 1910 to 2000, **Northwestern Glacier** retreated more than 9 miles and opened up **Northwestern Lagoon** at the head of Harris Bay. The lagoon should be entered on calm water and at high tide only. Once you are inside and on the shore, you will find excellent hiking, especially to **Northeastern, Southwestern,** and **Sunlight Glaciers.**

Down the coast, **Thunder Bay** is a welcome anchorage during bad weather. A narrow waterway cuts between the mainland and the **Pye Islands.** From here, **McCarty Fjord** slices 23 miles into the coast, its steep walls rising 4,000 feet over either

KENAI FJORDS

side of **McCarty Glacier.** The **West** and **North Arms** of **Nuka Bay** offers a variety of terrain and wildlife. Watch for the craggy profile of **Palisade Peak,** a 900-foot waterfall, with historic gold mines. Look for black bears, moose, and river otters near the **Nuka River,** for shorebirds along the mudflats at **Shelter Cove,** and for black-sand beaches around **Yalik Point,** at the park's southern end.

Horned puffins *(top)*; sea otter *(center left)*; Steller sea lions *(center right)*; humpback whale in Aialik Bay *(bottom)*

INFORMATION & ACTIVITIES

VISITOR & INFORMATION CENTERS
Kenai Fjords National Park Information Center in Seward, in small boat harbor on 4th Ave., open daily from Memorial Day to Labor Day; shorter hours fall and spring.
Nature Center at Exit Glacier open summer only. Phone (907) 422-0573 for automated visitor information.

SEASONS & ACCESSIBILITY
Park open year-round, but, from about mid-Oct. to May, snow may close the road to Exit Glacier. Access then is by ski, snowmobile, dog team, or snowshoe only. Call headquarters for information about weather and road conditions.

HEADQUARTERS
P.O. Box 1727, Seward, AK 99664. Phone (907) 422-0500. www.nps.gov/kefj

ENTRANCE FEE
None.

PETS
Permitted leashed on the road to Exit Glacier and in parking areas. Prohibited on all trails.

ACCESSIBLE SERVICES
Exit Glacier is the most accessible area. A 1-mile accessible loop leads to impressive views of Exit Glacier valley. The information center is also wheelchair accessible.

THINGS TO DO
Free ranger-led activities: In summer (from the Nature Center at Exit Glacier), walks to the glacier's base, and all-day hikes to the icefield. Guided hikes along Harding Icefield are offered Saturdays in July and August. Also, advanced mountain climbing, sailing, fishing (license required), wildlife-watching, cross-country skiing, dogsledding, snowshoeing. Authorized commercial guides offer camping, fishing, kayaking, flight-seeing, and boat trips for exploring the fjords and watching seabirds, whales, porpoises, and other wildlife. Call park headquarters or visit the park's website for a list of companies that do business in the park.

SPECIAL ADVISORIES
• If planning a backcountry trip without a guide, first check conditions with park staff.
• Hypothermia is a danger on the icefield, even in summer.
• Do not venture out in a boat unless well experienced in rough water.
• Remember glaciers are moving bodies of ice, they can pose a danger when portions break off; crevasses should not be crossed by the inexperienced.
• Beware of brown bears and moose. Contact the Information Center.

OVERNIGHT BACKPACKING
Permits, free at the Information or Nature Center, are voluntary; voluntary registration is requested for Harding Icefield.

CAMPGROUNDS
One walk-in campground at Exit Glacier. Two cabins in the fjords available May through Sept. for overnight use by permit. Access by boat or plane only. In winter, a public-use cabin is available at Exit Glacier. Contact the Alaska Public Lands Information Center at (866) 869-6887.

HOTELS, MOTELS, & INNS
(unless otherwise noted, rates are for 2 persons in a double room, high season)

In Seward, AK 99664:
Breeze Inn 303 N. Harbor St., P.O. Box 2147. (907) 224-5237. 100 units. $139-$269. Restaurant.
Hotel Seward (on 5th Ave.) P.O. Box 2288. (800) 440-2444 or (907) 224-8001. 38 units. $229-$259.
Marina Motel (on Alas. 9) P.O. Box 1134. (907) 224-5518. 26 units, 1 with a kitchenette, 1 handicapped room. $125-$140.
Murphy's Alaskan Inn 911 4th Ave., P.O. Box 736. (907) 224-8090. 24 units. $129-$169.
Van Gilder Hotel 308 Adams St., P.O. Box 609. (907) 224-3525. 24 units. 3 with shared baths, $119; 21 with private baths, $159-$199.

KENAI FJORDS

Winds ripple the surface of the Great Kobuk Sand Dunes.

▶ KOBUK VALLEY

ALASKA
ESTABLISHED DECEMBER 2, 1980
1,750,000 acres

"Now we were alone between fringes of spruce by a clear stream where tundra went up the sides of mountains," wrote John McPhee in *Coming into the Country*. The Kobuk Valley, said McPhee, "was, in all likelihood, the most isolated wilderness I would ever see." Located entirely above the Arctic Circle, Kobuk Valley has fewer tourist visits than any other national park. Float a river here in late August and the only other humans you're likely to encounter are Inupiat hunting the caribou that migrate through each year.

Thirteen thousand years ago, when continental glaciers covered much of North America and a land bridge connected Alaska and Asia, Kobuk Valley was an ice-free refuge with grassy tundra similar to that found in Siberia today. Bison, mastodons, and mammoths roamed the valley, along with the humans who hunted them. Since then, the climate has shifted, and sea level has risen to flood the land bridge; many of the early mammals have disappeared. But today's shrubby flora harbors relics of the preglacial steppe, and in the cold, hard ground lie the legacies of ancient animals and peoples.

Here the Kobuk Valley, cordoned off by the Baird and Waring

Mountains, protects the midsection of the Kobuk River, the drainage of the wild and scenic Salmon River, and an array of wildlife. This is where the boreal forest reaches its northern limit, and the North American and Asiatic flyways cross. Pockets of tundra blend into birch and spruce, dwarfed by blasts of freezing air. And along the Kobuk River stretch 25 square miles of active sand dunes, where summer temperatures can climb to 100°F.

Kobuk Valley National Park's management plan encourages traditional native subsistence practices over tourism, so no facilities or trails lie within the park.

How to Get There

Commercial planes fly daily from Anchorage to Kotzebue, where the park's information center is located. Planes can be chartered in Kotzebue and boats are available in neighboring villages.

When to Go

Summer is the best time to visit. Days are long (from about June 3 to July 9 the sun doesn't set), and temperatures in many places can reach into the 80s or higher. Ice breaks up on the Kobuk River in May and begins to reform by mid-October. Mid-June to late July is best for wildflowers. August can bring rain and September snow. In late August, the aspens begin to turn yellow and the tundra red, and the caribou migration begins.

How to Visit

Take a combination river-hiking trip that alternates between days out on the open water with days exploring the surrounding land. That way you can paddle to different landing points, leave your gear in the canoe, and hike unencumbered. Bring everything you need;

no visitor facilities exist within the park. The **Kobuk River,** wide and placid, is a pleasant river to travel by canoe, kayak, or motorboat. Most people put in at Ambler and take out at Kiana, both outside the park. You can also float or paddle the **Salmon,** a wild and scenic river, but it has rougher water and is harder to reach. Hiking in higher elevations is excellent, but the park maintains no trails or river crossings. So be sure to plan your trip carefully.

While in the park, be respectful of private lands, most of which are along the Kobuk River.

KOBUK RIVER

Beginning in the central Brooks Range, the Kobuk River flows west 200 miles, winds slowly through the park for 61 miles, dropping only 2 to 3 inches per mile, and then continues west to drain into **Hotham Inlet,** off **Kotzebue Sound.** At times its placid aspect makes it seem more like a lake than a river, with a current that's hardly detectable.

Although steep bluffs sometimes rise above the riverbanks, there are limitless hiking opportunities from the Kobuk. Both shores have forest, lakes, and tundra; the south shore has sand dunes also. When you hike, stay on high ground to avoid swamps. In late August and early September you can sit on a bluff and watch caribou in striking autumn pelage as they swim across the river. Huge antlers and white ruffs mark the bulls.

A river trip through the park from Ambler to Kiana, with plenty of time for hiking, takes about a week. Or, if you want a more ambitious trip (2 to 3 weeks, depending on weather and river conditions), begin 5 miles below **Walker Lake,** in

KOBUK VALLEY

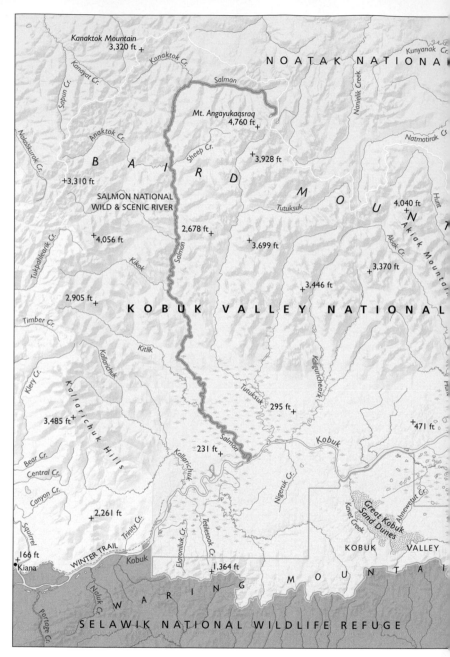

Gates of the Arctic National Park (see p. 432), and paddle or motor all the way to Kiana.

On either trip you'll pass **Onion Portage,** a river bend, where for thousands of years migrating caribou have crossed the Kobuk. Here, in 1961, archaeologist J. Louis Giddings dug into the earth and could hardly believe his eyes. He artifact-bearing layers, reflecting seven cultural traditions of flint-working technology, the oldest dating back about 9,000 years.

Today, the archaeological site is inactive and overgrown. But in late summer and fall, Inuit hunt caribou here as they've done for millennia. Hiking is good at Onion Portage. The name comes from the wild chives growing here.

GREAT KOBUK SAND DUNES

Farther downstream sprawl the Great Kobuk Sand Dunes, a 25-square-mile mini-Sahara. Visitors arrive by the river and leave their boats on shore in order to take the arduous, 4-hour, round-trip hike to the dunes to experience the adventure of scaling them. An Ice Age relic, the dunes formed from the windblown outwash of melting glaciers. A special combination of topography and eastern and northern winds keeps the dunes moving and inhospitable to vegetation. Some dunes measure 200 feet high. Older, thinly vegetated dunes surround this ever changing landscape located 35 miles above the Arctic Circle.

KOBUK VALLEY

had discovered what a Smithsonian Institution ethnologist would later call "the most important archaeological site ever found in the Arctic." Giddings' 2-acre plot yielded 30

Brown bear

Caribou migrating across the Kobuk River *(top)*
Easily stowed inflatable craft for river runners *(center)*
Cranberries, club moss, and sphagnum in the tundra *(bottom)*

INFORMATION & ACTIVITIES

INFORMATION CENTER
Located 80 miles from the park, the **Northwest Arctic Heritage Center** in Kotzebue is open daily, call for hours.

SEASONS & ACCESSIBILITY
Open year-round but access—by charter aircraft from Kotzebue—generally June through Sept. (The Kobuk River usually thaws by June 1 and freezes by mid-Oct.) There are no roads to or in the park. Contact park headquarters before visiting. If you plan to fly in, ask the park for a list of licensed companies.

HEADQUARTERS
P.O. Box 1029, Kotzebue, AK 99752. Phone (907) 442-3890. www.nps.gov/kova

ENTRANCE FEE
None.

PETS
Permitted, but please check with rangers.

ACCESSIBLE SERVICES
Northwest Arctic Heritage Center accessible to wheelchairs; otherwise none.

THINGS TO DO
Films and summer programs available at the Northwest Arctic Heritage Center. Rafting, kayaking, canoeing, hiking, sportfishing (license required), and aerial sightseeing are available in park. Commercial outfitters offer private guide services for floating, fishing, trekking trips. Contact headquarters for a list of those licensed to work in the park.

SPECIAL ADVISORIES
• Take a guide along unless you are well experienced in the wilderness.
• Mosquitoes and gnats can be brutal; bring plenty of repellent, a head net, and an insect-proof tent.
• Inuit own much of the land along the river and engage in subsistence hunting and fishing. Respect their activities and property.
• Be prepared for severe arctic weather at any time.

OVERNIGHT BACKPACKING
No permit required, but call park for current information on weather, river conditions, bears, and resident subsistence activities before venturing out.

CAMPGROUNDS
None; backcountry camping only.

HOTELS, MOTELS, & INNS
(unless otherwise noted, rates are for 2 persons in a double room, high season)

In Kotzebue, AK 99752:
Bayside Inn 303 Shore Ave., P.O. Box 336. (907) 442-3600. 12 units. $150. Restaurant.
Bibber's Bed & Breakfast 398 Lagoon St. (907) 442-2693.
Nullagvik Hotel 308 Shore Ave. (907) 422-3331.

KOBUK VALLEY

EXCURSION

CAPE KRUSENSTERN NATIONAL MONUMENT
KOTZEBUE, ALASKA

For 5,000 years, the Inupiat people have forged a living on this stretch of gravel projecting into the Chukchi Sea; its 114 beach ridges, rich in artifacts, reveal their archaeological benchmarks. Today, the large land and sea mammals are crucial to local subsistence. 678,840 acres. Primitive camping, boating, fishing. Access by plane from Kotzebue. (907) 442-3890.

Turquoise Lake, tinted by glacial silt

▶ LAKE CLARK

ALASKA
ESTABLISHED DECEMBER 2, 1980
4,045,000 acres

"Think of all the splendors that bespeak Alaska," conservationist John Kauffmann has written. "Glaciers, volcanoes, alpine spires, wild rivers, lakes with grayling on the rise. Picture coasts feathered with countless seabirds. Imagine dense forests and far-sweeping tundra, herds of caribou, great roving bears. Now concentrate all these and more into less than one percent of the state—and behold the Lake Clark region, Alaska's epitome."

Diversity is Lake Clark's hallmark. The Turquoise-Telaquana Plateau has tundra similar to Alaska's North Slope, while the coast has forests similar to the southeast panhandle. Black bears and Dall sheep approach their southern limits here, and Sitka spruce, Alaska's state tree, reaches its northern limit. Three rivers— the Mulchatna, Chilikadrotna, and Tlikakila—have been officially designated part of the Wild and Scenic system.

The Chigmit Mountains, spine of the park, are as rugged as mountains get. They lie on the edge of the North American plate where the oceanic plate slides under it, and their jumbled contours reflect centuries of geological violence. Two volcanoes here, Iliamna and Redoubt, are still active and vent gases regularly. Redoubt erupted in 1966, spewing clouds of ash 40,000 feet into the air—and it erupted dramatically again in late 1989 and March 2009. The area averages one to two earthquakes per year that register at least a 5 on the Richter scale.

Archaeological finds show that humans, most recently Dena'ina Indians, have lived in the area for centuries. The abundant salmon and game made their settled existence possible.

How to Get There

Take a plane into the heart of the park, or travel by boat or plane to the coast. Bush pilots in Anchorage say, "Lake Clark is just out the back door"—a 1-hour flight. From Anchorage you can charter a plane to Port Alsworth, a small community on the southeast shore of Lake Clark. The flight through Lake Clark Pass takes you over immense blue glaciers, winding rivers, and snowcapped mountains. Planes also land on the coast for salmon fishing.

Another alternative is to take a scheduled flight from Anchorage to Iliamna, 30 miles outside the park, and an air taxi from there into the park. Air taxis fly in from Homer and Kenai, too. To reach the park by boat, you must travel down Cook Inlet from Anchorage or across the inlet from the Kenai Peninsula.

When to Go

Summer. Wildflowers are best in late June. Autumn colors peak in early September at upper elevations, in mid-September lower down. June through August, daytime temperatures usually hover in the 50s and low 60s in the eastern part of the park and are somewhat higher in the western part and the interior.

How to Visit

Most visitors fly into the interior lake region of the park. Air taxis can make drop-offs and pickups at prearranged places—depending on weather conditions. The smaller lakes offer excellent kayaking, and several rivers give kayakers and rafters great white-water experiences.

Hiking is good around the lakes and from lake to lake. Fishing is usually first class. Contact park headquarters in Anchorage for information on approved guide services and lodges. Remember to make your reservations early. If you don't plan to be completely self-sufficient, be sure to make thorough arrangements before going and plan for the possibility of delays due to weather changes.

ON THE LAKES & RIVERS

Fishing is superb on the lakes and rivers of this fly-in park. Rainbow trout, arctic grayling, northern pike, and five kinds of salmon—king, chum, coho, humpback, and sockeye —lure anglers, many of whom take off from Port Alsworth, site of the park's field headquarters.

As in many Alaska parks, a kayak in Lake Clark is an invitation to freedom. You can explore large areas, carry a lot of gear, and take intermittent hikes as the mood strikes you. Keep in mind that sudden winds can stir up large waves in a matter of minutes. Good lakes for paddling are **Telaquana, Turquoise, Twin, Lake Clark, Kontrashibuna,** and **Tazimina.**

Another way to see the country is to let a river take you through it. Your options are long trips (averaging 3 to 4 days) on the wild and scenic **Mulchatna, Chilikadrotna,** and **Tlikakila,** or short trips (generally 1 to 2 days) on the **Tanalian** and the **Tazimina.** Hire a guide or check with rangers on water conditions, places to put in and take out, and what to look out for along the way.

LAKE CLARK

Snowcap
Mountain

Merrill
Pass

Merril

A L A S K A

The
Tusk

Neacola

Two
Lakes

Necons

**Ranger
Station**

Telaquana Lake

WILDERNESS AREA

Telaquana
Pass

Whitefish Lake

Telaquana

LAKE CLARK NATIONAL PRESERVE

Stony

Stony

MULCHATNA
NATIONAL WILD
& SCENIC
RIVER

Mulchatna

Turquoise
Lake

+ Telaquana Mountain
8,020 ft

L A K E   C L A R K

N A T I O N A L   P A R K

Bonanza Hills

CHILIKADROTNA
N.W.&S.R.

**Ranger
Station**

Twin
Lakes

Chilikadrotna

Snipe
Lake

TLIKAKILA
NATIONAL WILD
& SCENIC RIVER

Chigmit Mountains

A N D   P R E S E R V E

Fishtrap
Lake

Lachbuna
Lake

Portage
Lake

Tlikakila

Caribou
Lakes

LAKE CLARK
NATIONAL PRESERVE

Kijik

Little
Lake Clark

Crescent
Lake

Portage
Cr.

Koksetna

Kijik
Lake

LAKE CLARK

Tuxedni

Tuxedni Glacier

Tanalian Mt.
3,960 ft

WILDERNESS
AREA

Port Alsworth
**National Park
Field Headquarters**

+
Kontrashibuna
Lake

R A N G E

Tanalian R.

Upper Tazimina
Lake

Iliamna
Volcano +
10,016 ft

Sixmile
Lake

Nondalton

Pickeral
Lakes

Lower
Tazimina
Lake

Tazimina

A L E U T I A N

Hickerson
Lake

**Ranger
Station**

Newhalen

+
Roadhouse
Mountain

Pedro
Bay

Pile Bay
Village

Chinitna Bay

Iliamna

Newhalen

ILIAMNA
LAKE

Pile

Pile Bay

Iniskin
Peninsula

Autumn rainbow over Stony River

HIKING

When in a park with no trail system and only one maintained hiking trail, planning and route selection are critical. So is being prepared: wind and rain gear for swift changes in the weather and repellent for mosquitoes. If you intend to hike without a guide, consult with a park ranger before starting out and take a good map with you. Some general rules for hikers: Stay as long as possible on dry tundra where footing is good, avoid heavy brush, and choose your river crossings carefully. Hiking is generally best above 2,000 feet in the interior (where the dry tundra begins), or along the coast on the numerous gravel river bars. Below tree line the vegetation can be thick and nearly impenetrable, especially the alder.

The 2.5-mile **Tanalian Falls Trail** is the only developed trail in the park. Beginning in Port Alsworth, this easy hike takes you through a forest of black spruce and birch, past bogs and ponds, up along the tumbling

LAKE CLARK

Tanalian Mountain rising from Lake Clark shores *(top)*; alpine bearberry and lichens *(bottom left)*; arctic ground squirrel nibbling a fireweed flower *(bottom right)*

Tanalian River to the falls, then on to **Kontrashibuna Lake,** a half mile beyond. Watch for moose in the ponds, arctic grayling in the river, Dall sheep on **Tanalian Mountain,** and bears everywhere.

Another hike from Port Alsworth is the strenuous 3,600-foot climb up **Tanalian Mountain.** You can begin the climb off the Tanalian Falls Trail, or by hiking the shore of Lake Clark and heading up a ridge where

the walking is easier, a round-trip of about 7 miles.

North of Lake Clark, several lakes offer excellent hiking. You can take an air taxi to one and hike to another, or stay at one lake—a world in itself—and go on day hikes along the shore and up the ridges. If a lake-to-lake trek appeals to you, try the 16 miles from **Telaquana Lake** south to **Turquoise Lake,** or from Turquoise Lake 13 miles south to

INFORMATION & ACTIVITIES

VISITOR & INFORMATION CENTERS
Field headquarters and a **visitor center** are located in Port Alsworth, on the south shore of Lake Clark (907-781-2218); Homer (2181 Kachemak Dr., 907-235-7903). Call Anchorage headquarters at (907) 644-3626, for visitor information.

SEASONS & ACCESSIBILITY
Park open and accessible by small aircraft from Anchorage, Kenai, Homer, and Iliamna year-round. There are no roads to or in the park. Weather changes rapidly. Call Port Alsworth at (907) 781-2218 for up-to-date conditions.

HEADQUARTERS
240 W. 5th St., Suite 236, Anchorage, AK 99501. Phone (907) 644-3626. www.nps .gov/lacl

ENTRANCE FEE
None.

PETS
Park recommends that you leave your pets at home because they can attract bears.

ACCESSIBLE SERVICES
Most park buildings and lodges are accessible.

THINGS TO DO
Minimal interpretive programs (June through Sept.). Also, hiking, backpacking, climbing, rafting, kayaking, fishing (license required), boating, bird-watching and wildlife-watching, aerial sightseeing, hunting (in preserve). Call or write headquarters for a list of concessioners offering a variety of guide services in the park, or visit the website at www.nps .gov/lacl/visiting_the_park.htm

SPECIAL ADVISORIES
• You must possess good wilderness skills if you intend to hike, camp, or fish without a guide.
• Do not trespass on or in any way disturb the property of local residents.
• Be sure to bring insect repellent. A head net and insect-proof tent are also desirable.

OVERNIGHT BACKPACKING
No permit required, but campers are encouraged to contact field station before setting out. (907) 781-2218.

CAMPGROUNDS
None. Backcountry camping only. No showers or other visitor amenities except in lodges. Restrooms at the field headquarters at Port Alsworth.

HOTELS, MOTELS, & INNS
(unless otherwise noted, rates are for 2 persons in a double room, high season)

OUTSIDE THE PARK:
Newhalen Lodge (On Six Mile Lake near Nondalton). (907) 294-2233 (lodge) or (907) 522-3355 (all year). 9 rooms. Sportfishing packages. $7,900 per person, per week all inclusive. June–Oct.

Contact park headquarters for additional lodgings in and near the park.

LAKE CLARK

Twin Lakes. From Twin Lakes you can hike 17 miles to **Portage Lake,** a beautiful tarn in an alpine valley, and from there 11 miles to **Lachbuna Lake,** over a ridge and down the arduous **Portage Creek** drainage to Lake Clark.

For a longer, wilder, and more demanding hike through truly spectacular country, try taking the 50-mile trek from **Telaquana Lake** east over **Telaquana Pass,** along the **Neacola River** to **Kenibuna Lake.** From there, continue your hike to the huge rock spire called **The Tusk.**

Flowing Kennicott Glacier, with Mount Blackburn at left

▶WRANGELL-ST. ELIAS

ALASKA
ESTABLISHED DECEMBER 2, 1980
13,188,000 acres

Even in a state famous for its size, Wrangell-St. Elias stands out. It is by far the largest of our national parks—almost six times the size of Yellowstone. You fly over it and see mountains beyond mountains, glaciers after glaciers, rivers upon rivers. You float a river and watch the moods and mountains change by the minute. As you walk the tundra, you find Dall sheep and mountain goats grazing.

Four major mountain ranges converge here: the volcanic Wrangells, the Alaska, the Chugach, and the St. Elias—tallest coastal mountains in the world. Together they contain 9 of the 16 highest peaks in the United States, 4 of them above 16,000 feet. There are more than 150 glaciers; one, the Malaspina, is larger than Rhode Island. In 1980 Wrangell-St. Elias and adjoining Kluane National Park Reserve in Canada, along with Glacier Bay National Park and Tatshenshini in British Columbia, were designated a United Nations World Heritage site.

Vast and rugged as it is, the park is not a fortress. Two roads lead into small communities, remnants of the gold- and copper-mining towns that thrived in the early days of the 20th century. Today not mining but the nearly limitless hiking, rafting, kayaking, and climbing opportunities beckon.

How to Get There

Drive, take a bus, or charter a plane. By car from Anchorage, take Alas. 1 (Glenn Hwy.) 189 miles northeast to Glennallen. Continue northeast 74 miles along the Copper River and the park's northern boundary to Slana, where an unpaved road branches 42 miles into the park, ending at Nabesna mine.

Or, head toward McCarthy on the Richardson Hwy. from Glennallen 32 miles southeast to the Edgerton cutoff (Alas. 10), then turning left and continuing 33 miles to Chitina. There the pavement ends but a road follows an old railroad bed about 60 miles into the park. Buses run regularly in summer from Anchorage to Tok with stops in Glennallen.

Air charters into the park operate out of Anchorage, Fairbanks, Yakutat, Cordova, Glennallen, Gulkana, Tok, Chitina, McCarthy, Nabesna, and Northway. Commercial jets service Yakutat and Cordova. In summer, the Alaska State Ferry serves Valdez and Cordova.

When to Go

Summer. Lodges and guide services operate in the park from mid-May to mid-September. June is best for wildflowers; July has the warmest days; berries ripen in August. Be prepared for cloudy skies, but September can be beautiful with clear skies, autumn colors, no mosquitoes, and a dusting of new snow on the mountain peaks. March and April offer excellent cross-country skiing for those of strong will.

How to Visit

Take one of the two unpaved roads into the park. The **McCarthy Road** is maintained and usually passable in summer, though a four-wheel drive may be needed in other seasons. Stop at park headquarters in Copper Center for latest road conditions. The **Slana-Nabesna Road** is also maintained, including some stream crossings, but can require four-wheel drive in high water. Both roads end at trailheads for many backcountry hikes.

Or, charter a plane into a remote part of the park and hike or run a river. Several commercial companies offer guided rafting or kayaking trips on the rivers and in the spectacular coastal bays. You can get a full listing of them from the park.

McCARTHY ROAD TO KENNECOTT

60 miles one way; a half day

From the town of Chitina and the confluence of the **Chitina** and **Copper Rivers,** the road follows the abandoned Copper River and Northwest Railroad bed. At mile 17 the road crosses the **Kuskulana River Bridge.** It spans 525 feet, crossing 238 feet above the river. Another abandoned railroad trestle spans the **Gilahina River** at mile 28.5. Near the end of the road are parking spots and the **Kennicott River.** To reach the old mining town of **McCarthy** on the other side of the river, walk across a footbridge and catch a shuttle bus. Today it's tiny, but McCarthy had a population near 2,000 in mining days.

From McCarthy, a dirt road climbs 500 feet in 5 miles to the former town and millsite of **Kennecott.** You can take a bus or rent a bike in McCarthy if you prefer not to walk. Kennecott was once the site of the world's richest copper mine. From 1906 to its closing in 1938, it yielded 591,000 tons of copper and 900,000 ounces of silver. Today, the silent 14-story mill and other Kennecott buildings are still dressed in mineral oxide red with white trim. Currently being renovated, they form one of

WRANGELL-ST. ELIAS

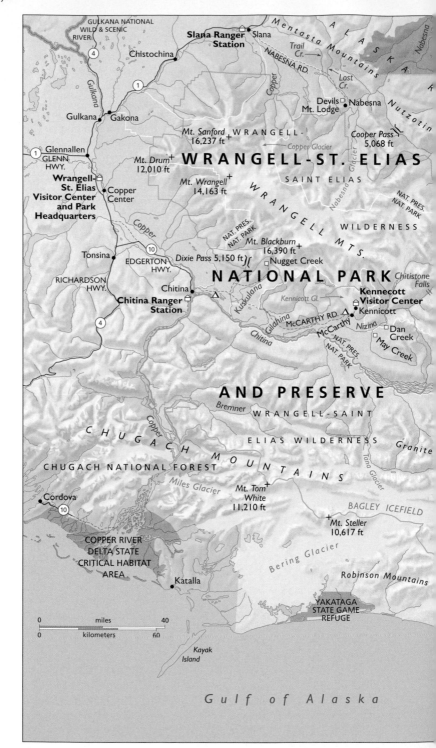

GULKANA NATIONAL
WILD & SCENIC
RIVER

**Slana Ranger
Station** □ Slana

Mentasta Mountains

A L A S K A

Nabesna

4

Chistochina

Trail
Cr.

NABESNA RD.

Lost
Cr.

Nutzotin

Copper

1

Devils □ Nabesna
Mt. Lodge

Cooper Pass
5,068 ft

Gulkana ● ● Gakona

Mt. Sanford + W R A N G E L L -
16,237 ft

Copper Glacier

WRANGELL-ST. ELIAS

Nabesna Glacier

SAINT ELIAS

1 Glennallen
GLENN
HWY.

Mt. Drum +
12,010 ft

**Wrangell-
St. Elias
Visitor Center
and Park
Headquarters**

● Copper
Center

Mt. Wrangell +
14,163 ft

WRANGELL MTS.

W I L D E R N E S S

NAT. PRES.
NAT. PARK

Copper

NAT. PRES.
NAT. PARK

Mt. Blackburn +
16,390 ft

Tonsina ●

Dixie Pass 5,150 ft)(

□ Nugget Creek

Chitistone
Falls

10

EDGERTON
HWY.

NATIONAL PARK

Kennecott Gl.

**Kennecott
Visitor Center**
● Kennicott

RICHARDSON
HWY.

Chitina

Kuskulana

Kennecott Gl.

Δ

□ Dan
Creek

4

**Chitina Ranger
Station**

Gilahina

McCARTHY RD.

McCarthy

Nizina

May Creek

Chitina

NAT. PRES.
NAT. PARK

AND PRESERVE

Bremner

WRANGELL-SAINT

Granite

C H U G A C H

ELIAS WILDERNESS

Tana Glacier

Copper

M O U N T A I N S

CHUGACH NATIONAL FOREST

Miles Glacier

Mt. Tom +
White
11,210 ft

BAGLEY ICEFIELD

● Cordova

10

Mt. Steller +
10,617 ft

COPPER RIVER
DELTA STATE
CRITICAL HABITAT
AREA

Bering Glacier

Robinson Mountains

● Katalla

YAKATAGA
STATE GAME
REFUGE

0	miles	40
0	kilometers	60

Kayak
Island

G u l f   o f   A l a s k a

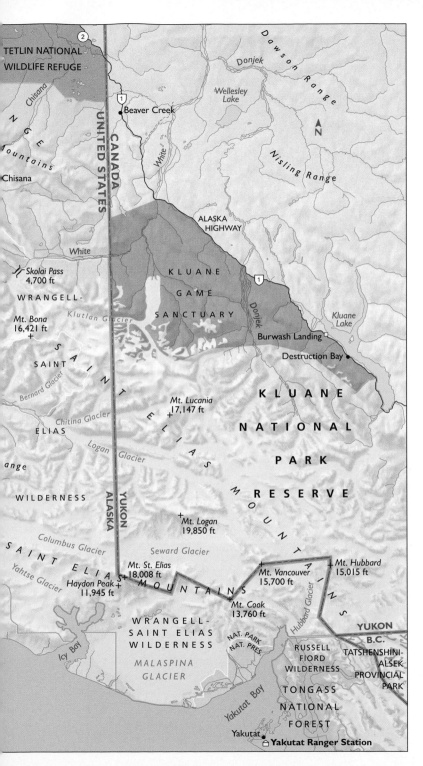

TETLIN NATIONAL
WILDLIFE REFUGE

Chisana

Dawson Range

Donjek

Wellesley Lake

②

① Beaver Creek

CANADA
UNITED STATES

White

N G E
ountains

Chisana

ALASKA HIGHWAY

Nisling Range

White

// Skolai Pass
4,700 ft

KLUANE

WRANGELL-

GAME

Mt. Bona
16,421 ft
+

Klutlan Glacier

SANCTUARY

S
A
I
N
T

Donjek

①

Kluane Lake

Burwash Landing ⊡

SAINT

Bernard Glacier

E
L
I
A
S

Destruction Bay ●

Mt. Lucania
17,147 ft
+

K L U A N E

Chitina Glacier

ELIAS

Logan   Glacier

ange

WILDERNESS

YUKON
ALASKA

N A T I O N A L

P A R K

R E S E R V E

M
O
U
N
T
A
I
N
S

+ Mt. Logan
19,850 ft

Columbus Glacier

Seward Glacier

S
A
I
N
T   E
L
I
A
S

Yahtse Glacier

Mt. St. Elias
+ 18,008 ft

Haydon Peak +
11,945 ft

M O U N T A I N S

Mt. Vancouver
15,700 ft
+

+ Mt. Hubbard
15,015 ft

Icy Bay

WRANGELL-
SAINT ELIAS
WILDERNESS

*MALASPINA
GLACIER*

NAT. PARK
NAT. PRES.

+ Mt. Cook
13,760 ft

Hubbard Glacier

YUKON

B.C.

RUSSELL
FIORD
WILDERNESS

TATSHENSHINI-
ALSEK
PROVINCIAL
PARK

TONGASS

NATIONAL

Yakutat Bay

FOREST

Yakutat ●

⌂ Yakutat Ranger Station

WRANGELL-ST. ELIAS

Alaska's most photogenic collections of historic structures and are on the National Register of Historic Places. After exploring the town of Kennecott, you can hike the trail north of town for spectacular views of the Kennicott and Root Glaciers.

NABESNA ROAD

42 miles one way; a half day

Since parts of this road into the **Wrangell Mountains** are subject to washouts, check conditions with the park before you set out. Beginning in **Slana,** the road passes homesteads and fishing camps on privately owned land and then climbs over the watershed divide (mile 25) between the **Copper River,** which drains into the Gulf of Alaska, and the **Nabesna River**, which drains into the **Tanana,** the Yukon, and finally the Bering Sea. There are excellent views of **Mount Sanford** and the **Copper Glacier** to the southwest. The final 4 miles, from **Devil's Mountain Lodge** to **Nabesna,** are the most rugged.

OTHER HIKES & WATER TRIPS

At mile 14.5 on the McCarthy Road, the **Nugget Creek-Kotsina Road** branches northeast 2.5 miles to the **Nugget Creek Trail.** A thousand feet higher and 15 miles later, the trail arrives at a public-use cabin beneath Mount Blackburn, where you can picnic and camp. (Reservations required in summer.) A dozen day hikes can be taken from here. Watch for Dall sheep. A little more than a mile past the Nugget Creek trailhead begins the **Dixie Pass Trail.** Climbing 3,600 feet in 10 miles, it's a strenuous hike, but worth it if the weather is clear.

Off the Nabesna Road, **Trail Creek** at mile 30 and **Lost Creek** at mile 30.8 offer good hiking routes. Little of the route's trails are defined; simply follow the creekbeds northward as far as you like. Though the hiking is not generally difficult, you will run into rocky patches and may have to hop or wade the creeks. But you will be rewarded with excellent views of the upper Copper River basin. Talk to a ranger and fill out a backcountry itinerary before any overnight stays.

Commercial outfitters offer rafting trips down the **Nabesna, Copper, Kennicott, Chitina,** and **Nizina Rivers**. Short trips last 3 hours; extended ones 2 weeks. There are all classes of water, and it's a fun way to see Wrangell-St. Elias. Contact the park for a full listing of the outfitters that operate there.

Kennecott Mine, silent since 1938

INFORMATION & ACTIVITIES

VISITOR & INFORMATION CENTERS
Park headquarters at mile 106.8 on Richardson Highway at western edge of park. Open daily Memorial Day through Labor Day, weekdays the rest of year. Information also available at **Yakutat, Slana,** and **Chitina Ranger Stations,** all outside park boundaries. Chitina and Slana closed October through April.

HEADQUARTERS
P.O. Box 439, Copper Center, AK 99573. Phone (907) 822-5234. www.nps.gov/wrst

SEASONS & ACCESSIBILITY
Park open year-round, but best time is mid-May through September. Snow limits winter access. Call headquarters for road conditions before attempting to drive to the park.

ENTRANCE FEE
None.

PETS
Permitted on leashes except in public buildings.

ACCESSIBLE SERVICES
None.

THINGS TO DO
No park-organized activities, but the following are available: hiking, horseback riding (rentals in McCarthy), pack trips, river running, kayaking, jet-boat rentals, lake fishing, mountain climbing, air tours, cross-country skiing. Ask park for list of companies that offer guide and outfitting services, or visit the park website at www.nps.gov/wrst/wrstcommercialservices.htm.

SPECIAL ADVISORIES
• This is a wilderness park; hikers and backpackers must be wholly self-sufficient; do not attempt the backcountry without a guide unless you're experienced and equipped.

• Choose your river crossings carefully; many rivers are impassable.
• Be respectful of native camps, fishnets, and other private property.
• Mosquitoes can be brutal in June, July, and August; bring repellent, a head net, and an insect-proof tent.

OVERNIGHT BACKPACKING
Permit not required, but best to register before going into backcountry.

CAMPGROUNDS & CABINS
Two private campgrounds within park: Tram Station Campground and Glacier View Campground at end of McCarthy Road. Camping also available at several roadside pull-outs along Nabesna Road. First come, first served. No fee. The park also maintains 14 public-use cabins; some require reservations in summer. Contact headquarters for information.

HOTELS, MOTELS, & INNS
(unless otherwise noted, rates are for 2 persons in a double room, high season)

INSIDE THE PARK:
Kennicott Glacier Lodge (in Kennecott) P.O. Box 103940, Anchorage, AK 99510. (800) 582-5128 or (907) 258-2350. 25 rooms shared baths, $195; 10 rooms private baths, $255.

OUTSIDE THE PARK:
Copper Center Lodge (mile 101.5 on Old Richardson Hwy.) Drawer J, Copper Center, AK 99573. (907) 822-3245. 21 rooms, 11 with private baths. $120-$165. Restaurant.
Gakona Lodge (on Alas. 1, north of Glennallen) P.O. Box 285, Gakona, AK 99586. (907) 822-3482. 9 rooms, shared baths $95. May through Sept. Restaurant.

Contact headquarters for additional accommodations in and near the park.

WRANGELL-ST. ELIAS

ACKNOWLEDGMENTS

We are indebted to the many individuals and the federal, state, and private agencies that helped prepare this guide, especially to the National Park Service and the superintendents and chiefs of interpretation and their staffs at each park.

ILLUSTRATIONS CREDITS

Abbreviations for terms appearing below: (t)-top; (b)-bottom; (l)-left; (r)-right; (c)-center; BSP-Biological Photo Service; NGS-National Geographic Society Image Collection; NPS-National Park Service; PR-Photo Researchers, Inc.

Cover, Phil Schermeister; 2-3, Julie Lubick/Shutterstock; 4, kavram/Shutterstock; 6-7, William Britten/iStockphoto.com; 8, Mauricio Handler/NGS.

The East

12 (t), Tom Jones; (c), Stephen J. Krasemann/Peter Arnold, Inc.; (b), David Muench; 13, QT Luong/TGP; 18, Adam Jones/Getty Images; 20, Angelo Lomeo; 24, Raymond Gehman/CORBIS; 25, Alan Nyiri; 27 (t), Bill Silliker, Jr.; (c), Joel Sartore/www.joelsartore.com; (b), Jeff Lepore/PR; 28, NPS; 29, Ian Shive/Getty Images; 31, geoff aiken/Bigstock.com; 32, Brian Skerry/NGS; 33 (t), Peter Leahy/Shutterstock; (cl), Charles V. Angelo/PR; (cr) & (bl) & (br), Stephen Frink; 35 (t), James Valentine; (c), C.C. Lockwood; (b), Caulion Singletary; 36, Raymond Gehman; 37, Raymond Gehman; 40, luiz rocha/Bigstock.com; 41, Michael S. Quinton/NGS; 43 (t), Arthur Morris/ CORBIS; (b), David Muench/CORBIS; 44, Tom Jones; 47, Tom Jones; 48, Tom Jones; 50, Matt Bradley; 52, Matt Bradley; 54, James P. Blair; 58, Phil Schermeister; 59, Phil Schermeister; 61 (tl) & (tr) & (cl) & (cr), Phil Schermeister; (b), Todd Winner/iStockphoto.com; 63 (t), James Valentine; (c), Farrell Grehan; (b), Palms/Dreamstime.com; 64, Marc Muench/CORBIS; 68, Dennis Flaherty; 69 (t), NPS; (b), Raymond Gehman/CORBIS; 70, Raymond Gehman; 72 (t), Larry Ulrich; (c), David Muench/CORBIS; (b), Dick Durrance II; 73 (t), James Randklev/CORBIS; (c), David Muench/CORBIS; (b), James Valentine; 74, Mark E. Gibson/CORBIS; 75, Matt Bradley; 78, Matt Bradley; 79 (t), Richard Hamilton Smith/CORBIS; (c) & (b), Matt Bradley; 80, Tom Bean/CORBIS; 83, John & Ann Mahan; 84, Jim Brandenburg/Minden Pictures; 86 (t), John & Ann Mahan; (c), Richard Hamilton Smith/CORBIS; (b), John & Ann Mahan; 87 (t), John & Ann Mahan; (c), Carl R. Sams; (b), Rod Planck/PR; 88, Marc Muench/Alamy; 90-91, Richard Schlecht; 91 (l) & (r), Chip Clark; 92, Laurence Parent; 92-93, Richard Schlecht; 95 (t), Dan J. Dry; (b), David Muench/CORBIS; 96, NPS; 100, NPS; 101, Jeff Nagy/iStockphoto.com; 103 (t), Carr Clifton; (c), David Muench/CORBIS; (b), Jeff Lepore/PR; 104, M. Dillon/CORBIS; 108, Jodi Cobb/NGS; 111, Stephen Frink; 112, Phil Schermeister; 113, Per Breiehagen/Getty Images; 116, Phil Schermeister; 117 (t) & (b), Phil Schermeister; 119 (t), John & Ann Mahan; (c), Jim Zipp/PR; (b), Richard Hamilton Smith/CORBIS.

The Southwest

120 (t), Larry Ulrich; (c), George F. Mobley/NGS; (b), David Muench; 121, Tom2898/Dreamstime.com; 124, Phil Schermeister; 125, Phil Schermeister; 128, Phil Schermeister; 129, Medford Taylor/NGS; 130, Eric Foltz/iStockphoto.com; 132, Dave Hughes/iStockphoto.com; 133, David Muench/ CORBIS; 134, Phil Schermeister; 138, Michael Nichols/NGS; 139, Phil Schermeister; 141 (t), Wendy Shattil/Bob Rozinski; (c), Lewis Kemper; (b), Wendy Shattil/Bob Rozinski; 142, Phil Schermeister.

The Colorado Plateau

148 (t), Farrell Grehan; (c) & (b), Larry Ulrich; 149, Tom & Pat Leeson; 152, RIRF Stock/iStockphoto.com; 153, Phil Schermeister; 156, Phil Schermeister; 157, Phil Schermeister; 159 (t), Farrell Grehan; (b), Larry Ulrich; 160, Phil Schermeister; 161, Phil Schermeister; 163, Phil Schermeister; 165 (t), Fred Hirschmann; (c), Raymond Gehman/CORBIS; (b), Pat O'Hara; 166, Mikhail Choumiatsky/iStockphoto.com; 167, Phil Schermeister; 169, Phil Schermeister; 170, Phil Schermeister; 171, Phil Schermeister; 172 (t), Phil Schermeister; (b), Paul Lemke/iStockphoto.com; 174 (t), Tom Till Photography; (c), Farrell Grehan; (b), Donna Ikenberry/Animals Animals; 175 (t), Larry Ulrich; (b), Neil Rabinowitz/CORBIS; 176, Phil Schermeister; 177, Phil Schermeister; 178, Phil Schermeister; 180 (l) & (r), Phil Schermeister; 182, Larry Ulrich; 187, Jack Dykinga; 188, George H. H. Huey; 189, Ned Seidler/NGS; 191 (t), Jeff Gnass; (c), Larry Ulrich; (b), Jeff Gnass; 192, Bill Hatcher/NGS; 193, Phil Schermeister; 195 (t) & (b), Phil Schermeister; 197 (t), Fred Hirschmann/Getty Images; (c) & (bl), Phil Schermeister; (br), Fernley/Dreamstime.com; 199 (t), Jack Olson; (c), Joe McDonald/CORBIS; (b), Jan Nachlinger; 200, Phil Schermeister; 205, Ira Block/NGS; 207 (t), Larry Ulrich; 207 (c) & (b), Tom Till Photography; 208, Phil Schermeister; 213 (t) & (c), Fred Hirschmann; (b), George H. H. Huey; 214, Phil Schermeister; 217 (t), Chee-Onn Leong/Shutterstock; (b), Phil Schermeister; 219 (t), David Muench/CORBIS; (c), AP/Wide World Photos; (b), Joe Raedle/Getty Images; 220, TexPhoto/iStockphoto.com; 221, Phil Schermeister; 222, Tyson Sugihara/iStockphoto.com; 224 (tl), Phil Schermeister; (tr), Harry Thomas/iStockphoto.com; (c), Steven Castro/Shutterstock; (bl) & (br), Phil Schermeister; 226, Oleksandr Buzko/iStockphoto.com.

The Pacific Southwest

228 (t), Steve Raymer/NGS; (c), Harald Sund; (b), Shutterstock; 229, Jeff Gnass; 232, Kip Evans/Alamy; 234, Phil Schermeister; 235, Phil Schermeister; 239 (t), Caroline Sheen; (b), David Muench; 240, Phil Schermeister; 244, Phil Schermeister; 246, Larry Dale Gordon/CORBIS; 251 (t), David Muench; (c), NPS; (b), Robert J. Western/NPS; 253 (t), Jeff Gnass; (b), Douglas Peebles/CORBIS; 254, CORBIS; 255, Douglas Peebles/CORBIS; 258, Paul A. Souders/CORBIS; 259 (t), Darodents/PacificStock; (b), Jeff Gnass; 261 (t), Roger Ressmeyer/Starlight Collection/CORBIS; (b), Chad Ehlers/Alamy; 262, Phil Schermeister; 266, Phil Schermeister; 268, Jon Mullen/iStockphoto.com; 273, Phil Schermeister; 275 (t) & (b), Pat O'Hara; (c), NPS; 276, Phil Schermeister; 281, Phil Schermeister; 283 (tl) & (tr), Phil Schermeister; (b), Sasha Buzko/Shutterstock; 285 (t), Pat O'Hara; (c), Lewis Kemper; (b), QT Luong/TGP.

INDEX

Index Abbreviations
Bureau of Land Management = BLM
National Forest = NF
National Historic Park = NHP
National Marine Sanctuary = NMS
National Monument = NM
National Park = NP
National Recreation Area = NRA
National Recreation Trail = NRT
National Wildlife Refuge = NWR
State Park = SP

MAP KEY and ABBREVIATIONS

National Park .... N.P.
National Park and Preserve .... N.P. & Pres.
National Preserve .... Nat. Pres.
National Conservation Area .... N.C.A.
National Historical Park .... N.H.P.
National Memorial .... Nat. Mem.
National Monument .... Nat. Mon.
National Natural Landmark .... N.N.L.
National Recreation Area .... N.R.A.

National Forest .... N.F., Nat. For.
National Recreation Area .... N.R.A.
National Volcanic Monument .... N.V.M.
State Forest .... S.F.

National Wildlife Refuge .... N.W.R.
National Wildlife Range
State Game Refuge
State Game Sanctuary .... S.G.S.
State Wildlife Area
Habitat Area

National Grassland

Bureau of Land Management .... B.L.M.
National Monument (B.L.M.) .... Nat. Mon.
National Recreation Area (B.L.M.) .... N.R.A.

State Park .... S.P.
State Historic Site........................... S.H.S.
State Primitive Park
State Recreation Area .... S.R.A.
State Wilderness Park...................... S.W.P.
Provincial Park .... P.P.
County Park

Indian Reservation .... I.R.
Reserve (Canada)

Built-up Area

U.S. Interstate	U.S. Federal, State or Provincial Highway	Other Road
5	50 33 1	J59

Unpaved Road	Trail	Ferry

Railroad / Tram	Continental Divide	Fault Line

Wilderness Area	National Marine Sanctuary	National Wild & Scenic River

Military Reservation	National boundary	State boundary

⊛   State capital   Intermittent
      Provincial capital   river

⌂   Ranger Station   Intermittent
      Visitor Center   lake
      Park Headquarters

                       Dry lake

□   Point of interest

△   Campground   Sand dunes

⊼   Picnic area   Falls

⇛   Overlook   Spring
      Viewpoint   o   Geyser

+   Elevation   Glacier

≍   Pass   Swamp

)-(Tunnel   Reef

⟶   Dam   Shipwreck

POPULATION

●	**DENVER**	above 500,000
●	**Sacramento**	50,000 to 500,000
●	Helena	10,000 to 50,000
•	Morton	under 10,000

OTHER ABBREVIATIONS

Admin.	Administrative	Pk.	Peak
AVE.	Avenue	PKWY.	Parkway
Cr.	Creek	P.P.	Provincial Park
DR.	Drive	PRES.	Preserve
E.	East	Pt.	Point
Fk.	Fork	R.	River
ft.	feet	Ra.	Range
Gl.	Glacier	RD.	Road
Hdqrs.	Headquarters	Rec.	Recreation
HWY.	Highway	Res.	Reservoir
I.-s.	Island-s	S.	South
L.	Lake	ST.	Street
M.	Middle	TERR.	Territory
Mt.-s.	Mount-ain-s	TR.	Trail
N.	North	U.S.F.S.	United States Forest Service
NAT.	National	W.	West
N.M.S.	National Marine Sanctuary	WILD.	Wilderness
N.S.T.	National Scenic Trail		

National Geographic Guide to National Parks of the United States, 7th ed.

Thomas B. Allen, John L. Culliney, Carole Douglis, Kim Heacox, Catherine Herbert Howell, Gary Krist, Mark Miller, Jeremy Schmidt, Gene S. Stuart, John M. Thompson, Scott Thybony, Mel White, *Writers*

Published by the National Geographic Society

John M. Fahey, Jr., *Chairman of the Board and Chief Executive Officer*

Timothy T. Kelly, *President*

Declan Moore, *Executive Vice President; President, Publishing*

Melina Gerosa Bellows, *Executive Vice President; Chief Creative Officer, Books, Kids, and Family*

Prepared by the Book Division

Barbara Brownell Grogan, *Vice President and Editor in Chief*

Jonathan Halling, *Design Director, Books and Children's Publishing*

Marianne R. Koszorus, *Design Director, Books*

Barbara Noe, *Senior Editor*

Carl Mehler, *Director of Maps*

R. Gary Colbert, *Production Director*

Jennifer A. Thornton, *Managing Editor*

Meredith C. Wilcox, *Administrative Director, Illustrations*

Travel Publications

Keith Bellows, *Vice President, Editor in Chief*

Staff for 2011 Edition

Caroline Hickey, *Project Manager*

Olivia Garnett, *Text Editor*

Sanaa Akkach, *Art Director*

Matthew Propert, *Illustrations Editor*

Linda Makarov, *Designer*

Patricia McNally, *Researcher*

Michael McNey, *Map Production*

Judith Klein, *Production Editor*

Robert Waymouth, *Illustrations Specialist*

Samantha Basham, Craig Kisylia, Jane Sunderland, *Contributors*

Manufacturing and Quality Management

Christopher A. Liedel, *Chief Financial Officer*

Phillip L. Schlosser, *Senior Vice President*

Chris Brown, *Technical Director*

Nicole Elliott, *Manager*

Rachel Faulise, *Manager*

Robert L. Barr, *Manager*

The National Geographic Society is one of the world's largest nonprofit scientific and educational organizations. Founded in 1888 to "increase and diffuse geographic knowledge," the Society works to inspire people to care about the planet. National Geographic reflects the world through its magazines, television programs, films, music and radio, books, DVDs, maps, exhibitions, live events, school publishing programs, interactive media and merchandise. *National Geographic* magazine, the Society's official journal, published in English and 33 local-language editions, is read by more than 40 million people each month. The National Geographic Channel reaches 370 million households in 34 languages in 168 countries. National Geographic Digital Media receives more than 15 million visitors a month. National Geographic has funded more than 9,600 scientific research, conservation and exploration projects and supports an education program promoting geography literacy. For more information, visit www.nationalgeographic.com.

For more information, please call 1-800-NGS LINE (647-5463) or write to the following address:

National Geographic Society
1145 17th Street N.W.
Washington, D.C. 20036-4688 U.S.A.

For information about special discounts for bulk purchases, please contact National Geographic Books Special Sales: ngspecsales@ngs.org

For rights or permissions inquiries, please contact National Geographic Books Subsidiary Rights: ngbookrights@ngs.org

Seventh Edition:
ISBN: 978-1-4262-0869-0

Printed in China
11/RRDS/1